# GAME OF MY LIFE

## GREEN BAY

# PACKERS

# GAME OF MY LIFE

## GREEN BAY

## PACKERS

MEMORABLE STORIES OF PACKERS FOOTBALL

## CHUCK CARLSON
### FOREWORD BY BOB HARLAN

Sports Publishing books may be purchased in bulk at special discounts for sales promotion, corporate gifts, fund-raising, or educational purposes. Special editions can also be created to specifications. For details, contact the Special Sales Department, Sports Publishing, 307 West 36th Street, 11th Floor, New York, NY 10018 or sportspubbooks@skyhorsepublishing.com.

Sports Publishing® is a registered trademark of Skyhorse Publishing, Inc.®, a Delaware corporation.

Visit our website at www.sportspubbooks.com

10 9 8 7 6 5 4 3 2 1

Library of Congress Cataloging-in-Publication Data is available on file.

ISBN: 978-1-61321-204-2

Printed in the United States of America

*For Theresa: You're still the one.*

*Thanks for the advice.*

# Contents

# Acknowledgments

Many thanks are in order for a number of people who made this book possible and, hopefully, enjoyable. First there's my old friend Bob Snodgrass, who always seems to call with another project just when I'm ready to start peeling paint off the walls in boredom. And, of course, there are the good people at Sports Publishing, who have never been anything but thoroughly professional and extremely accommodating.

I'd also like to thank the public relations staff for the Green Bay Packers, featuring the ubiquitous Lee Remmel, who was recently named the team historian, as well as director of public relations Jeff Blumb and assistant director Aaron Popkey. As always, they bent over backwards to help out whenever they could.

Thanks are in order, too, to Dan Kohn, sports editor at *The Northwestern*, for diving in on short notice to copyedit and offer suggestions on a very raw, very long project. It was a big help. I'd also like to thank my wife, Theresa, and my boys, Brian, Patrick and Michael, for showing remarkable patience as I pounded away on this project and forgot they existed. I owe them a night out.

Finally, a big thank you to the Packers players who took the time out to share their stories with me. In most cases, they didn't know me from a hole in the wall, but they opened up and spoke candidly and passionately about a subject, and a time, that still matters to them. And for that I will always be appreciative.

# Foreword

There have been so many great games played in the history of the Green Bay Packers that I thought it might be an impossible task to single out just one. When you've been with an organization as long as I have (I started out as an assistant general manager in 1971, and it seems like just yesterday) you can recall so many great games and unforgettable moments.

As it turns out, it wasn't that difficult a decision after all.

For me it was January 12, 1997, the day the Packers beat the Carolina Panthers to win the NFC championship and earn a trip to Super Bowl XXXI in New Orleans. That was a special game in many ways for me. It was a chance to watch as this franchise, which so many people had given up on just a few years earlier, came back in such a remarkable way. It was knowing that the job so many people had done to make the Packers a contender again had been more successful than we could have dared hope.

But this was the game of my life because it was played at Lambeau Field in front of what I believe are the best fans in all of football. When I think of special games, I always come back to the fact that it should never happen in a little place like Green Bay. The thought sometimes is that special games have passed us by. But they haven't, and that game against the Panthers, played in the kind of brutally cold weather that made it even more perfect, made that point clearly.

Of course the Super Bowl victory over New England two weeks later was special as was winning the NFC championship game the following year in San Francisco. I can think of so many incredible games over the years, and they all make me smile and realize how lucky I am to be involved with a franchise like this.

But that one game on that one day summed up everything the Green Bay Packers were, are, and always will be, and I will never forget anything about it.

In *Game of My Life: Green Bay Packers* you'll read about games that mattered the most, spoken in the words of the players who were there. It is a journey back in time to the games that still hold special places in the hearts and heads of Packers players who understood even then that they were part of a very special time and place. And it's a journey every Packers fan should make.

—Bob Harlan, former President and CEO, Green Bay Packers

# Introduction

Some memories came quickly and some memories came slowly. In some cases, they had to be coaxed out of hibernation and pried loose from places many of them hadn't visited in years. In other cases they came in torrents, almost to the point where they didn't know where to stop.

But in every case, the memories were there and ready to see daylight again. All they needed was a reason to come out again. After all, every one of them remembered the games of their lives.

"How much time do you want?" asked one ex-player when approached about the idea of reliving the greatest he ever played.

When told 20 minutes would do just fine, he laughed.

"Twenty minutes?" he said. "I don't have that kind of time."

One hour later, our interview ended.

"Thanks," he said at the conclusion. "That was fun."

Brother, was it ever.

When this journey began, the task of finding Green Bay Packers and having them recount the games of their lives seemed daunting, though not especially difficult.

After all, what player from the golden era of Vince Lombardi wouldn't automatically recount the epic "Ice Bowl" of 1967 when the Packers and Dallas Cowboys waged a war of simple survival that, at times, bore very little resemblance to a football game and was more about the best ways to avoid frostbite?

It was the game when Bart Starr snuck in for the winning touchdown that secured the Packers' second straight trip to the Super Bowl but more importantly became a part of NFL lore and legend that everyone involved in will never forget.

Or what player from the 1970s wouldn't immediately remember the Packers' 1972 NFC Central Division title, the only one the Packers won that decade?

Who from the 1980s could forget the 1983 Monday night shootout with the powerful Washington Redskins, a game that with each passing year gets a new layer of myth added to it?

And how about the 1990s when the Packers rose from the dead, won a Super Bowl and became the NFL gold standard for how to run an organization and how to treat players?

The replay game in 1989? Brett Favre's first touchdown pass in 1992? Chester Marcol's 1980 touchdown scamper against the Chicago Bears in 1979? The first Super Bowl? The second Super Bowl? Maybe the third Super Bowl?

Though this is a franchise overstuffed with great and memorable history, truly great games could be counted rather quickly, couldn't they?

The 1997 NFC title game? Lombardi's first win as Packers coach in 1959? The Monday night win over Minnesota in 2000 when Antonio Freeman caught a touchdown pass flat on his back?

How tough could it be? They think that because, for some reason, everyone figures they know the Packers better than the Packers know themselves.

Maybe it's because it's a franchise that has always made itself accessible to anyone willing to look. Maybe it's because this is a franchise that has thrived on the small-town, blue-collar ethic that makes it attractive to everyone who likes underdogs and long shots.

For whatever reason, the Packers' history has always been a book thrown open for public consumption and constant scrutiny. It also leads to the belief that everyone knows everything about this team.

But a funny thing happened. What we (OK, me) thought we knew, we did not know. What we assumed as fact was more like speculation. And what we (OK, me again) thought was the most precious of memories for Packers players wasn't close to what the conventional wisdom might have been.

It was wonderful, refreshing and surprising. And it proved one more time that we can take nothing for granted when it comes to a franchise we think we know as well as our family.

Willie Davis, the Hall of Fame defensive end, laughed when asked why he didn't mention the "Ice Bowl" as the game of his life.

"Because it really wasn't a very good game," he said simply.

When former quarterback Don Majkowski was asked why he didn't immediately jump on the "Replay Game" in 1989 as his best game, he was equally blunt.

"Because it wasn't," he said.

And isn't that the way it's supposed to be? Memories are very special and very individual and have no patent on them. What is special to one person may not even register in the brain cells of the person who was involved. And what may not have seemed particularly significant to longtime, rabid fans may never have left the minds of the players who took part.

The game of their lives is open to wonderful interpretation. There are no guidelines and no right answers. It is about the game that matters the most to the player who played the game, and that's as it should be. It isn't always about wins or losses or great performances as opposed to poor ones. It's the game that stands out above all others for its knee-buckling significance or for its ability to, in some cases, make a player still shiver in remembrance.

Great games are great games, and they will always hold their shelf lives, no matter how many years go by. Those games will take care of themselves. This book was a voyage of discovery that plumbed the depths of memories long asleep and sometimes forgotten.

Indeed, Hall of Fame guard Jerry Kramer has reveled proudly in his years with the Packers and has lost count of how many times he's talked about Vince Lombardi and the Ice Bowl. But when asked to recount the game of his life, he was taken aback.

"Nobody's ever asked me that before," he said.

Memories are a funny thing. They are personal and public; they can be full of detail or maddeningly obscure. The memories of days past can belong only to the person who lived through it, and everyone else can only watch from a distance, whether they want to or not.

In the end, *Game of My Life: Green Bay Packers* is a journey back in time and, in some ways, a look forward. It is a chance to look inside the head of the player who was there and, perhaps, understand a little bit better what happened and why it happened.

To be a Green Bay Packer has always been to live under the microscope of public examination. Most of the players have understood that and dealt with it, and others have even flourished in it. But it has always been part of the game.

In the following pages, Packers from the distant past, the not-so-distant past and the present talk about the games that mattered most to them. Some will be a surprise; some will not. Hopefully they will all be entertaining.

But this much seems certain. The stories come from places most of us have never been allowed to see before, and that alone makes them special.

# CHAPTER 1

# JIM
# TAYLOR

*"It was colder than any other game I played in."*

**Name:** James Charles Taylor
**Birthdate:** September 20, 1935
**Hometown:** Baton Rouge, Louisiana
**Current residence:** Baton Rouge, Louisiana
**Position:** Fullback
**Height:** 6-foot-0
**Playing weight:** 215
**Years:** 1958-66
**College:** Louisiana State University
**Accomplishments:** Was an All-America running back at LSU in 1957 and was the Packers' second-round draft pick...Rushed for more than 1,000 yards for five straight years from 1960-64...Inducted into the Pro Football Hall of Fame in 1976...Rushed for 8,207 yards, which is still the Packers' all-time leading mark...Held the record for single-season rushing record with 1,474 yards in 1962 until it was broken in 2003 by Ahman

Green…His 81 rushing touchdowns also remains a club record…NFL MVP in 1962…Named to five Pro Bowls…Was inducted into the Packers Hall of Fame in 1975.

**The game:** The New York Giants, December 30, 1962, at Yankee Stadium

# THE LIFE OF JIM TAYLOR

The letter from the young Jim Taylor to Green Bay Packers personnel and scouting director Jim Vainisi dated November 19, 1957 was heartfelt and, perhaps, just a little desperate.

*Dear Mr. Vainisi,*

*Reference to your letter dated November 11, 1957. I am very much interested in playing professional football. Football is a great sport and I enjoy playing it. Yes, I would be interested in playing with the Green Bay Packers. My military status is 1A Category 4. Yes, I will be able to play pro ball before entering the service. I prefer either the United States or Canada. Fullback is a position I feel I can play better.*

*Sincerely,*
*Jim Taylor*
*Baton Rouge, Louisiana*

It was a different time and a different place and a different attitude back then. Though it was evolving quickly, football was still what you did when you were waiting to do something else with the rest of your life. Most players had off-season jobs to supplement their income because playing football did not pay all the bills. And, of course, there was always the military obligation that often forced players to leave for weeks on end to satisfy commitments to something larger than the NFL.

And Jim Taylor, the crew cut battering ram who looked like he was born with a broken nose, came out of Louisiana and was certainly no different.

**Jim Taylor.** *Vernon J. Biever photo*

He was already a star when he went to really the only college any self-respecting kid out of the bayou could go to—Louisiana State University, just down the road from where he grew up.

At LSU, he developed the attributes that would make him a Hall of Famer with the Packers. In today's NFL, the fullback is all but a forgotten position, manned by guys who do little more than block for the tailback and pick up blitzing linemen.

"We ran mostly between the tackles," he recalled. "You didn't run outside much then."

But back in the 1950s and '60s, all the great backs were full-backs, and they did everything from blocking to catching passes to running the ball.

Taylor joined a Packers team in 1958 that already featured Heisman Trophy winner Paul Hornung at halfback. And in those days, there were no guarantees for a second-round draft choice like Taylor.

Back then there were no high-profile and high-priced agents who negotiated staggering signing bonuses and long-term deals. More often than not, the player hammered out his own deal with the team, and it wasn't necessarily an easy process. And in the Packers' case, the player had to negotiate with a towering, intimi-dating figure like coach and general manager Vince Lombardi, who took over in 1959.

"Lombardi was tough to deal with," Taylor said. "He was very, very tough to deal with. In my first deal with him I signed for $9,500 and a $1,000 bonus, and you had to earn your position. Back then there were 34 guys on the team and I hung on and made it, but I had to do a lot of things. There's a lot more specialization now."

But by his third season, Taylor was ready to explode. He ran for 1,101 yards, scored 11 touchdowns, and became the first Packer since Tony Canadeo in 1949 to rush for more than 1,000 yards. That began a streak of five straight years in which Taylor rushed for more than 1,000 yards.

But the pinnacle came in that 1962 season when Taylor ran for a league-best 1,474 yards and scored 19 touchdowns. By that stage, he was the focal point of the infamous "Packers Sweep" that was little more than a pitch to Taylor and his ability to follow the blocks of his offensive line and gain huge chunks of yardage.

"It was nothing fancy," said Taylor, who ripped off his longest run from scrimmage (83 yards) from that sweep. "We were going to make you respect it, and we defied you to stop it."

# THE SETTING

It was no secret that the Packers and New York Giants hated each other in ways most people could not understand. There was jealousy, sure, that always played a role, especially since the Giants had been an established power for years while the Packers were clearly the new rising force in the NFL.

This was the Packers' third straight trip to the NFL championship game, having lost two years earlier to the Philadelphia Eagles before embarrassing the Giants 37-0 the next year in Green Bay.

"We knew they wanted revenge, but there was no jawing back and forth," Taylor said. "The AFL [the newly established American Football League] had some of that, but this was the class of the NFL and you just lined up and played the game."

The Giants went into the game with a 12-2 record, while the Packers were 13-1.

There was also plenty of gamesmanship going on, as two days before the game, coach Vince Lombardi insisted that halfback and kicker Paul Hornung was "perfect" for the game even though everyone in the Packers organization knew Hornung had no chance of playing with his knee injury.

# THE GAME OF MY LIFE
### By Jim Taylor

In 1961, we played the [NFL championship] in Green Bay and faced the New York Giants. We had had a pretty outstanding year and were riding high when we faced them in '61. We had beaten them that year 37-0, I think, and we went into 1962 and had another outstanding year, going 12-2 or 13-1 (it was 13-1). We were going to play the Giants again for the championship, but this time in New York.

This was the year Paul Hornung was out [with a knee injury], so we went with Tom Moore and Elijah Pitts at halfback. Jerry Kramer was doing the kicking.

I remember there were blizzard conditions at Yankee Stadium. The wind was swirling and it was 25 below zero. It was colder than any other game I ever played in. It was probably as cold as the "Ice Bowl," but you had to blank all that out and play. You poured it all out, knowing it was your last game.

It was a packed house, and they wanted revenge. They had the field covered, so it wasn't quite frozen over, but by the end of the first quarter it was. I remember we were trying on different kinds of shoes to get traction and we wondered if we should run in tennis shoes. It was tough getting anything going. I had six stitches in my elbow and I was bleeding from my mouth after being knocked out of bounds. I wasn't making a lot of yardage. It was a real hard-fought game.

They kept giving me the ball, and [Giants middle linebacker] Sam Huff kept busting my butt. There was no footing, and I kept running out of bounds. I tried to count the cheap shots Sam Huff put on me out of bounds.

In the fourth quarter, we were finally threatening to score. Bart Starr handed it off to me and I went off left tackle. Huff tackled me and said, "Taylor, you stink." Then we ran the exact same play, and I ran about seven yards. I skated into the end zone. I held up the ball and said, "Hey Sam, how do I smell from here?"

We won the game 16-7. I was brutally beat up. After that season, I came down with hepatitis and I missed the Pro Bowl. I was just run down from the end of the season, and sometimes you need rest and rejuvenation. I checked into a hospital for two weeks.

**Despite a gashed elbow, Jim Taylor rushed for a rugged 85 yards and a huge touchdown in the 1962 NFL title game against the New York Giants.** *Vernon J. Biever photo*

# GAME RESULT

Taylor was simply spectacular in the game. Despite the gash on his elbow, which required seven stitches to close, and a lacerated tongue, compliments of Giants linebacker Sam Huff, Taylor rushed for 85 yards against the Giants in some of the worst field conditions imaginable.

The Packers led 10-0 at halftime on Taylor's touchdown run and a Jerry Kramer field goal, but the Giants got back into it in the third quarter when Jim Collier recovered a blocked punt in the end zone. But that was all the Packers defense allowed that day.

And when Kramer added his third field goal late in the fourth quarter, the Packers sewed up the game.

Neither team really did a whole lot offensively, as the Packers managed 244 total yards and the Giants 291 yards.

# WHAT BECAME OF JIM TAYLOR?

After nine seasons with the Packers in which he rolled up a club-record 8,207 yards rushing, Taylor went home—back to the fledgling New Orleans Saints for the 1967 season.

It wasn't an easy decision, and it was made even more difficult by a contract battle with Vince Lombardi that Taylor knew he wasn't going to win.

It was more ceremonial than anything, as Taylor, the Louisiana kid who had made it big in the frozen north for the powerful Packers, went to a franchise just starting out.

"I was a big draw for the Saints because it was their first year," Taylor said. "It was a big deal."

Taylor's numbers weren't especially noteworthy, as he rushed for just 390 yards on 130 carries, caught 38 passes and scored two touchdowns. But that was hardly the point. Taylor was a fixture in Louisiana, and his presence made all the difference.

But he also knew that after that season, it was time to give it up. He retired and remained with the Saints as a radio color commentator and then as a traveling scout. He was named to the Pro

Football Hall of Fame in 1976 and is now all but retired, though he did make a trip to Green Bay during the 2003 season when Ahman Green broke the single-season team rushing record of 1,474 yards that Taylor had established in 1962.

"I'm not envious or jealous," Taylor said of Green's accomplishment. "Any back who works that hard, you encourage them to excel. You're proud for them."

# CHAPTER 2

# CHESTER MARCOL

*"Everything was new to me."*

**Name:** Czeslaw Boleslaw Marcol
**Birthdate:** October 24, 1949
**Hometown:** Opole, Poland
**Current residence:** Dollar Bay, Michigan
**Position:** Kicker
**Height:** 6-foot-0
**Playing weight:** 190
**Years:** 1972-80
**College:** Hillsdale College
**Accomplishments:** Inducted into the Packers Hall of Fame in 1986...NFC Rookie of the Year in 1972...All-Pro in 1972 and 1974...Pro Bowl in 1972 and 1974.
**The game:** Minnesota Vikings, December 10, 1972, at Metropolitan Stadium

# THE LIFE OF CHESTER MARCOL

Simply, there has never been a player for the Packers like Chester Marcol. He was not the best player the Packers had ever seen, and he certainly wasn't the most athletic. But there was something about the bespectacled kicker with the thunderous right leg that made him a fan favorite then and carries on his popularity even today.

A native of Poland who spoke no English, he came to America in 1965 at age 15 with his mother and his three siblings after his father, a member of Poland's Communist Party, committed suicide at age 39.

The family settled in little Imlay City, Michigan, where his grandparents and relatives lived, and he was forced to start a new life. After all, he left a life he loved in Poland for a country in which he didn't understand the customs or the language.

But he did understand sports and more specifically, soccer. That fall, he was asked to try out for the football team and to kick a strangely shaped ball through two upright posts. It wasn't soccer, but for a kid in a new country and a new environment, it was at least something he could make sense of.

"I said no at first," Marcol said.

But he changed his mind, and his ability to routinely kick footballs through the uprights made him a local legend. Even then, Marcol, who had been a goalkeeper on the Polish junior national team before leaving the country, didn't know what the big deal was. Kicking was second nature to him.

He took that ability down the road to Hillsdale College, where he eventually became a four-time NAIA All-American and caught the eye of the Green Bay Packers, who were desperately looking for a consistent kicker. In fact, from 1968 to 1971, the Packers went through nine kickers, who among them made 45 percent of their field goals.

That's when coach Dan Devine made the stunning decision not only to draft a placekicker in the second round of the 1972 NFL Draft, but to take a placekicker no one had really heard of from a school few could find with a magnifying glass and a map. But Marcol was thrilled when the Packers selected him.

"I think it was the perfect place for me," he said. "But the Packers were the last team I thought of playing for. I could have guaranteed you that I was going to be drafted by the Dallas Cowboys. They even called me that morning and told me I was going to be drafted by them. I really wanted to play for the Cowboys because I was a sprinter and [Cowboys star wide receiver] Bob Hayes was a sprinter. The first game I ever saw was Dallas against Detroit, and I remember watching Bob Hayes."

But the Packers made the call, and it proved golden for Marcol and the Packers.

His rookie season, Marcol hit 33 of 48 field goals and led the NFL in scoring with 128 points as the Packers won their first division title since 1967. He was an All-Pro, Rookie of the Year, and an NFC All-Star, and he became a favorite of Packers fans everywhere. He was every man; he was one of them. He was no product of a football factory university, and he was wonderfully lacking in ego.

# THE SETTING

These were uncharted waters for the current crop of Packers. There were still some holdovers from the glory years, the fading gasp of a dynasty that grew too old too quickly. But for the most part, these were new players who knew only about the history and wanted to write their own.

Since their last burst of glory in 1967 when they won their second straight Super Bowl by plowing over the Oakland Raiders, the Packers had fallen on relatively hard times. Vince Lombardi stepped down after nine years as head coach and moved uncomfortably and unwillingly into the sole role of general manager. Taking his place in 1968 was longtime lieutenant Phil Bengtson, who could not have been more different from Lombardi. Soft-spoken and professorial, Bengtson struck a far different pose from the volcanic and impassioned Lombardi.

The players certainly noticed, as did Lombardi, who stayed up in the press box during games and quietly stewed. The result was a 6-7-1 season, the first losing campaign since the distasteful final days of Ray McLean in 1958 when the Packers were considered the dregs of the NFL.

Many of the same players who had been a part of the dismantling of the Raiders only months earlier in Miami—Bart Starr, Elijah Pitts, Ray Nitschke, Willie Wood, Boyd Dowler, and Dave Robinson—were still on hand this season, but it was all starting to change, and watching from high above, Lombardi could see and feel it, too.

Lombardi left the following season to become coach and general manager of the Washington Redskins and, truly, the soul of the Packers organization went with him.

Bengtson had no better luck in 1969 or 1970, so the day after a demoralizing 20-0 season-ending loss to the Lions, Bengtson resigned, and three weeks later Dan Devine, the head coach at the University of Missouri, was brought in.

Devine was intellectual and rather unapproachable, and players grew to either love him or despise him. But if 1971 was any indication, he was certainly no better than Bengtson. Devine's first Packers team managed a pitiful 4-8-2 record, its worst since 1958, and there seemed no reason to think anything would change in 1972. But it did.

That was Marcol's first season, and his ability to give the Packers almost automatic points from anywhere on the field took the pressure off marginal NFL quarterback Scott Hunter to have to make plays.

The offense belonged to the running back tandem of MacArthur Lane and John Brockington and a superb defense that was slowly but surely being overhauled.

The Packers got a huge dose of confidence in the season's third week when they beat the defending Super Bowl champion Dallas Cowboys 16-13 in Milwaukee and followed it up with a 20-17 win over the hated Chicago Bears thanks to Marcol's 37-yard field goal with 30 seconds to play.

The Packers closed that season strongly, routing Detroit and then clinching the division title the following week at Minnesota.

The Packers finished that season 10-4 and earned a first-round playoff game in Washington against another rejuvenated franchise. Employing an eight-man front, the Packers couldn't run anywhere, and Hunter certainly couldn't pass the Packers to victory. Though Marcol's 17-yard field goal in the second quarter gave Green Bay a 3-0 lead, the rest of the day belonged to the Redskins, as they won 16-3.

The Packers wouldn't see the postseason again until 1982 and wouldn't enjoy another division title until 1995.

# THE GAME OF MY LIFE
*By Chester Marcol*

I don't even have to think about it. The fondest memory was in 1972 when we beat the Minnesota Vikings and won the Central Division. It was the coldest game I ever played in. I have never in my life been so cold. The field was tough, and they had a tarp on it and the heater going. The field looked like icing on a cake. That was the only time I remember wearing a ski mask under the helmet, and back then everything was so bulky that wearing that ski mask hurt my head. I remember I had difficulty taking a deep breath, it was so cold. We didn't even practice the Saturday before the game because it was so cold, and that was the only time I remember not practicing before a game.

The Vikings weren't as good as they had been, but they were still the Vikings. [Quarterback] Fran Tarkenton was still Fran Tarkenton and they had beaten us earlier in the season in Green Bay [27-13].

But I did real well. I kicked three field goals, and John Brockington ran for over 100 yards. MacArthur Lane had around 90, and we beat the heck out of them, 23-7.

That was my rookie year, and that game was huge for me because every stadium I went into was a novelty. Everything was new to me. You have to remember I came from Poland and I went

Chester Marcol was the NFL Rookie of the Year in 1972 and capped a great season with three field goals in the NFC Central Division-clinching win over the Vikings. *Vernon J. Biever photo*

to Hillsdale College, so we're talking about going from something very small to something huge. It's hard to believe that was a profession. I was in awe.

There was so much excitement on the sidelines in that game. [The Met] was a stadium where you were so far away and both teams were on the same sideline like it was at County Stadium [in Milwaukee].

I hated kicking in stadiums like that, and I give a lot of credit to the people who played before me. It was very hard to figure out the wind in stadiums like that. I remember one of the field goals I kicked in that game and I thought, "Oh no, that's five yards to the right," and when it was done it was right down the middle. On the other side of the field, it was impossible to get it there from 31 yards. And I could kick a long way.

I remember after the game we flew over [Lambeau Field] and the stadium was lit up. There were thousands of people at the airport and it took me three hours to get out of there.

We were really excited because we'd made it back to the playoffs and there was the possibility of a Super Bowl. As time goes on and with the nucleus we had, we thought we could add on to the roster and get better, but I don't know what the heck happened. We never made it back.

# GAME RESULT

Since the Packers relinquished control of the NFC Central Division in 1967, the Minnesota Vikings were more than happy to fill the vacuum. Led by a solid offense and a dominating defense, the Vikings won the division from 1968 through 1971 and, after the Packers' brief interruption in 1972, took control again from 1973 to 1978.

But in 1972, it just didn't quite come together for Minnesota as it stumbled to a 7-7 record, which proved to be its worst since it was 3-8-3 in 1967.

None of that mattered to the Packers, however, who gladly took control of the division after the Vikings stumbled early out of the gate in a Monday night loss to Washington.

And this was still a dangerous and talented team, as evidenced by the fact that two months earlier the Vikings had spanked the Packers, 27-13, in Lambeau Field as Minnesota intercepted four Hunter passes. Paul Krause and Wally Hilgenberg each brought one back for a touchdown, and the Vikings' defense held the Packers' vaunted ground game to 102 yards.

Perhaps that's what made the win in Minneapolis so much sweeter. And indeed that game was far different from the one played in Green Bay.

Brockington rushed for 114 yards and Lane added 99 yards and a touchdown as the Packers took command almost from the beginning. Marcol kicked field goals of 36, 42, and 10 yards, Hunter played his typical ball-control game by completing just seven of 14 passes for 74 yards, and the defense rode two interceptions from rookie Willie Buchanon to the win. The Packers gained 270 yards in the game, and the Vikings were shut down to just 144.

# WHAT BECAME OF CHESTER MARCOL?

Marcol played nine seasons for the Packers and led the league in scoring twice. His 120 career field goals were a team record until Chris Jacke first shattered it 16 years later followed by Ryan Longwell after that.

He remained a popular figure his entire tenure in Green Bay and was the center of one of the most memorable games in Packers history.

It came on September 7, 1980, the season opener in what proved to be his final go-round with the team. Facing the Bears at Lambeau Field, Marcol had already kicked field goals of 41 and 46 yards, and the teams were tied at 6-6, forcing overtime. The

Packers drove into scoring position, and Marcol faced a routine 34-yard field goal that would win the game.

But Marcol's kick was blocked by Bears lineman Alan Page and the ball bounced back toward Marcol, who grabbed it out of midair and scampered, mostly out of sheer terror, into the end zone for the incredible 12-6 win.

Marcol was presented with the game ball, but few knew then the demons he was wrestling with. He had started using cocaine in training camp, and that, along with an alcohol abuse problem he had battled for years, proved a deadly combination. Overwhelmed by his addictions, his play started to suffer, and on October 8 of that season, he was released.

Out of football, he tried numerous times to clean himself up but failed. In 1986, he reached rock bottom when he drank battery acid in an attempt to kill himself. He survived and has fought his way back ever since.

He's sober now and living with his second wife, Carole, and their two kids, Mariah, 10, and Michael, seven. But life is still a struggle. He contracted hepatitis C from a blood transfusion and he has heart problems.

He helped out a local high school as a football coach for several years but now spends most of his time "collecting retirement" and fishing. He still loves Green Bay and relishes his days with the Packers.

"It's a unique environment," he said. "I have people stop by when I'm ice fishing and ask me about signing this and signing that. It was a great time."

# CHAPTER 3

# JESSE WHITTENTON

*"I made Howard Cosell apologize."*

**Name:** Urshell "Jesse" Whittenton
**Birthdate:** May 9, 1934
**Hometown:** Big Springs, Texas
**Current residence:** Santa Teresa, New Mexico
**Position:** Cornerback
**Height:** 6-foot-0
**Playing weight:** 195
**Years:** 1958-64
**College:** Texas Western
**Accomplishments:** All-Pro 1961-62...Pro Bowl in 1961 and 1963...Inducted into Packer Hall of Fame in 1976.
**The game:** New York Giants, December 3, 1961, at Milwaukee County Stadium

# THE LIFE OF JESSE WHITTENTON

Even before joining the Green Bay Packers in 1958 after two relatively undistinguished seasons with the Los Angeles Rams, Jesse Whittenton was no stranger to success.

A local kid from El Paso's Ysleta High School, he passed on offers from Texas and Arizona to stay close to home and play for Texas Western University, which would become Texas-El Paso. As a two-way star he helped lead the Miners to two Sun Bowl titles—whacking Southern Mississippi, 37-14, in 1954, and crushing Florida State, 47-20, in 1955.

Against Southern Miss, he caught a 29-yard touchdown pass. But against the Seminoles the following year, Whittenton had a huge game at quarterback. He threw for three touchdowns, ran for two more and kicked five extra points to account for 35 of Texas Western's 47 points. He also played defensive back.

"We were 14-point underdogs and they were pretty cocky," Whittenton said of a Florida State team that featured a halfback named Buddy Reynolds, who would one day be known as Burt Reynolds.

# THE SETTING

In 1961, the Green Bay Packers were almost all the way back. It had been one of the proud, old NFL franchises that had dominated the league in the 1930s and '40s under Curly Lambeau. But after winning their sixth league championship in 1944, the Packers went through a frightful tailspin.

In the 15 years that followed, the Packers didn't get even a sniff of a championship and during a particularly black period from 1948 through 1958, the Packers never even saw the sunny side of the .500 mark. Rock bottom was reached in 1958, Whittenton's first season in Green Bay, when the Packers went 1-10-1 under Ray McLean. "We were just awful," Whittenton said.

But, as has been documented so often by so many, everything started to change in 1959 when the Packers hired a former New York Giants assistant coach by the name of Vince Lombardi.

**Jesse Whittenton.** *Vernon J. Biever photo*

"He worked our butts off," Whittenton said. "His philosophy was always that we'll try it his way first, and if it doesn't work maybe we'll try it your way. I loved playing for him."

The results were almost immediate as the Packers went 7-5, including a season-ending four-game winning streak. In 1960, the improvement continued as Green Bay posted an 8-4 record and won its first conference title in 16 years.

In the NFL championship game December 26 at Philadelphia's Franklin Field, the Packers couldn't hold a 6-0 lead and eventually fell to the Eagles, 17-13—the only playoff loss Lombardi ever suffered. "He told us then that we hadn't been beaten; we had just run out of time," Whittenton said. "We took that to heart."

Perhaps that's what helped the Packers in Milwaukee the next year against the Giants when they needed a huge play, somewhere, to stop New York.

That game was the first of three epic victories the Packers had over the Giants in a one-year span. Four weeks after the comeback win in Milwaukee, the Packers pounded the Giants 37-0 for their first NFL title since 1944, and the following year, the Packers beat New York again for the league title.

# THE GAME OF MY LIFE
### *By Jesse Whittenton*

The most significant game I was involved in was when we played the New York Giants in Milwaukee. We had to win that game to win the Western Conference championship.

The Giants were winning, and they were down on around our 20-yard line late in the game. [Giants running back] Alex Webster got the ball on a handoff, and he came right into the line and had enough yardage to get the first down. They could have run out the clock and won the game. But he had the ball hanging loose in his arms, and it was just like he was handing it to me. He fumbled at around the 18-yard line, and I recovered and we went right back up the field and scored to win the game.

Then in the NFL title game [on December 31] I remember I was going to be covering [Giants wide receiver] Del Shofner for most of the game. Howard Cosell said at the time that Jesse Whittenton couldn't cover [Giants star receiver] Del Shofner with a blanket. Dale caught one curl-in pass the entire game, and we beat them 37-0.

Cosell came up to me a few weeks later and said, "I'm never wrong, but I was wrong about you. You could cover Del Shofner with a blanket, and I want to apologize." I made Howard Cosell apologize.

# GAME RESULT

Whittenton's remarkable play became known as the "steal," and Whittenton was nicknamed Jesse "James" Whittenton for the theft that left the Giants dazed and a little confused.

After all, the Giants were in command and needed only another first down or two to put the game away. But when Whittenton saw Webster come right at him after gaining a first down, he had only one thought.

"I went after the ball instead of the man," he said at the time, breaking one of the cardinal rules of defensive football. "It was just lucky. If I had missed it, he might have run for 10 or 15 minutes."

But he didn't miss, and the Packers took over on the Giants' 30. Five plays later, Jim Taylor stormed into the end zone from three yards out, and the Packers had the improbable victory. Afterward, Webster still didn't know what had really happened.

Taylor was magnificent again as he usually was in big games. He ran for 186 yards and two touchdowns, and Paul Hornung, who received a weekend pass from his military service in Fort Riley, Kansas, kicked two field goals and ran for another 54 yards.

Military service was mandatory those days and rarely could players get a pass like that, but when Vince Lombardi contacted President John Kennedy and told him how much the Packers needed Hornung, the pass magically appeared. However, star linebacker Ray Nitschke, who was serving at Fort Lewis, Washington, couldn't get a pass and missed the game.

# WHAT BECAME
# OF JESSE WHITTENTON?

As much as Jesse Whittenton loved football, he loved golf more.

"I was a member of the Oneida Country Club [in Green Bay] and I was playing in a celebrity golf tournament back then, and I drew Vince Lombardi as my partner," Whittenton said. "I shot a 66 and he said to me, 'You're in the wrong profession.'"

He began to think that maybe Lombardi had a point, so after the 1964 season, at the still young age of 30 and with the Packers at the height of their power, he retired.

Whittenton already owned a supper club in Green Bay and made his cousin, Don Whittington, a partner. Whittenton, though a native of dusty West Texas, had grown to love Wisconsin and planned to stick around. His cousin went back to Texas and told Whittenton of an opportunity to buy a golf course near El Paso.

He asked Lombardi what he thought of the deal that called for no money down, nothing to pay monthly and free water for eight years.

"Lombardi said, 'You're not old enough to retire, but you'd be a damned fool not to take advantage of it,'" Whittenton said.

Never one to argue with his coach, he did.

Whittenton sold everything he had and bought the course in 1965 for $887,000. Whittenton and his cousin sold the course in 1969, and he's been in the golf business ever since.

In those days, he had hooked up with a young, cocky golfer named Lee Trevino, and he convinced Trevino to buy into the golf course. Those two have been friends ever since.

In the late 1980s he took a stab at joining the PGA Seniors Tour and was second alternate out of the qualifying school. "I made just enough money to pay expenses, but I sure had a lot of fun," he said.

He has rebuilt golf courses all throughout West Texas and only recently opened a driving range in El Paso that he plans to sell soon. "I think I'll completely retire this time," he said. Whittenton died May 22, 2012 in Las Cruces, New Mexico. He was 78.

# CHAPTER 4

# WILLIE BUCHANON

*"We turned everything loose."*

**Name:** Willie James Buchanon
**Birthdate:** November 4, 1950
**Hometown:** Oceanside, California
**Current residence:** Oceanside, California
**Position:** Cornerback
**Height:** 6-foot-0
**Playing weight:** 190
**Years:** 1972-78
**College:** San Diego State
**Accomplishments:** NCAA All-American in 1971...Associated Press NFL Rookie of the Year in 1972...NFC Defensive Rookie of the Year in 1972...Inducted into Packer Hall of Fame in 1993.
**The game:** San Diego Chargers, September 24, 1978, at San Diego Stadium

# THE LIFE OF WILLIE BUCHANON

He was one of the best athletes Oceanside, California, ever produced.

A great football player and track athlete, Willie Buchanon was one of those gifted athletes that, once you saw him, you never forgot. He was an integral and popular part of the community, and anybody who knew him knew that, one day, Willie would make it big.

And they were all right.

Buchanon took his considerable football skills first to nearby MiraCosta College before going to San Diego State, where he earned All-America honors as a senior and Most Valuable Player accolades in the 1971 East-West Shrine Game.

And by then, of course, he was high on the draft board of every NFL team in the league. The Green Bay Packers were no exception. They were convinced Buchanon was a player who could make a difference immediately and dramatically. God knows they could use all the help they could get.

Green Bay was mired in a run of mediocrity it had not known since the 1950s, and Devine, who was coming off a 4-8-2 record in his first season as Packers coach, knew the heat would come down hard and quickly if improvement wasn't soon.

In fact, in the four years since they had won Super Bowl II, the Packers had not retuned to the playoffs and had only one winning season. And while four substandard seasons may not have been reason for panic and angst in some NFL cities, it was not acceptable in Green Bay. Those performances had already cost Phil Bengtson his job, and Devine didn't want to join him any time soon.

So the 1972 draft was huge for the Packers as they tried to put the pieces back together. And Buchanon figured to be a major part of that reconstruction project. The Packers actually had two first-round draft picks that season, and they knew they had hit it big on both of them.

Buchanon was the seventh player taken overall, the guy they hoped would be the "shutdown cornerback" before such a phrase really existed. Quick and smart and rangy, he would provide the cornerstone for a defense that was already close to being excellent but just needed another element.

The second first-rounder, and the 11th player taken overall, was Nebraska quarterback Jerry Tagge, a Green Bay native who had a superb college career but was also a product of an exceptional system. He was going to replace finally and completely the icon Bart Starr as well as the functional Scott Hunter.

To put it charitably, the Packers batted .500 on their first-round picks that year. Buchanon became everything the Packers had hoped, while Tagge...did not.

Buchanon slipped into the secondary as a rookie and played there like he'd been there forever. He finished with four interceptions and led a secondary that allowed barely 140 yards a game.

It was the season Devine, the players, and Packers fans had hoped for as they went 10-4 and won the NFC Central Division by a game and a half over the Detroit Lions. That set up the Packers' first playoff game since 1968—in Washington against the Redskins.

No one really knew it at the time, but the Packers' 16-3 loss to the Redskins would start a perplexing 10-year playoff drought that none of the players involved ever could quite figure out.

"We had the talent," Buchanon said with a sigh.

After his rookie season, Buchanon wouldn't see a winning season in Green Bay again until 1978, his final year, when they went 8-7-1 but missed out on the playoffs with two devastating losses to end the season.

Buchanon also suffered through his share of personal adversity, breaking his leg in 1973 and missing eight games and losing out on 12 more games in 1975 with another leg injury.

But those were the exceptions. On the field, he became part of a secondary that grew closer than brothers and he learned more about football and life than he ever thought he could.

**Willie Buchanon.** *Vernon J. Biever photo*

"I learned a lot in 1972," he said. "[Packers fullback] MacArthur Lane pulled me aside and mentored me about the NFL. He told me about coaches, agents, playing, attitude, everything. He just told me everything there was to know about the mental aspect of the game. He's still my idol and he's still probably one of the best athletes that ever played."

Ironically one of Lane's most important messages to the young cornerback was the need to look after himself.

"He told me, 'There will come a time when you're going to be just another person,'" said Buchanon, who had faith enough in his abilities to negotiate his last two pro contracts, something that's unheard of these days.

He also developed an airtight bond with his mates in the secondary—Johnnie Gray, Steve Luke, and Mike McCoy.

"We called ourselves 'The Gray Zone,' because we were the guys who didn't win any [championship] rings," he said.

In his last year in Green Bay, Buchanon found he wasn't too old to learn something new. The Packers' first-round draft choice that season, an elegant wide receiver from Stanford named James Lofton, showed him just how to approach the game the way it needed to be approached.

"I never saw a wide receiver work as hard as he did," Buchanon said, marveling at it even today. "He kept me on my toes. I had to use all my knowledge to beat him."

# THE SETTING

He had waited six years to play in his hometown, and when Willie Buchanon saw the Packers' schedule for 1978, he smiled. It had finally happened and he couldn't wait.

Most of Oceanside, a community 30 miles down the coast from San Diego, had followed Buchanon through his entire career. But with him playing in Wisconsin, it might as well have been Neptune, as difficult as it would have been to see him in person.

It was one of those days when everything fell into perfect alignment. The Chargers were 11-point favorites against the

Packers, even though star quarterback Dan Fouts wasn't expected to play because of a thumb injury.

But it quickly became obvious that the Packers, even in 107-degree heat, were taking this game a lot more seriously than the hosts. The Packers' offense was nothing special, and the defense knew that it might have to dominate if the Packers were going to win.

It was also a special day for Buchanon because this was a continuation of his self-styled marketing tour that would show the rest of the league that, while he was embroiled in contract woes with the Packers, he could still play the game.

And while there were no such things as free agents at that time, he was doing all he could to show all that he was one.

Buchanon also played the season for an old friend, "Chilly" Willie Walker, who had died that year.

"I dedicated that season to him," Buchanon said.

# THE GAME OF MY LIFE
### By Willie Buchanon

It would have to be September 24, 1978, in San Diego. That was my last year with the Green Bay Packers. I was playing out my option, and this was the first time in my career I'd returned to San Diego since I had played at San Diego State. I was hyper for the game and I was ready to play football.

I wanted to let the rest of the league know that Willlie Buchanon could still play. I was marketing myself. I wanted to stay in Green Bay, but I also wanted to let the rest of the league know I could still play. The Packers had rejected my offer, so I was playing my option without any injury protection.

I remember that date so plainly because I ended up getting four interceptions and returned one for a touchdown, and we beat the Chargers 24-3. It was 107 degrees on the football field, and the Santa Ana winds were really blowing. Fans were falling over from heat exhaustion.

I remember that the day before the game I took a picture that's still on my wall. It was of the secondary. We took it in the stadium, and it was Mike McCoy, Steve Luke, and Johnnie Gray, and we said that this was my hometown and we were going to show the fans that we could play football in Green Bay. The players were playing for me and with me.

We went out there with reckless abandon and turned everything loose. I was really ready to play, and I was like that the whole season.

I grew up 35 miles down the road and I had over 300 tickets I bought for the game. All of Oceanside was there because they hadn't seen me play in that part of the country before. It was a fun event. I was looking forward to that game ever since I saw it on the schedule. We beat them really badly, and after the game [Chargers coach] Tommy Prothro was fired and Don Coryell was hired. And Don Coryell had been my college coach.

I ended up playing out the season in Green Bay and then signing with San Diego. I didn't want to leave Green Bay, and the difference was only about $25,000.

# GAME RESULT

Buchanon did indeed play the game of his life at the best possible time. Those four interceptions, one of which was taken back 77 yards for the touchdown that accounted for the final margin, remains a Packers record until this day. Perhaps even more important, though, is that two of those interceptions came in the end zone to squelch Chargers drives.

For whatever reason, the Chargers had no clue that day against the Packers. Starting quarterback James Harris threw two interceptions, forcing Prothro to insert the ailing Fouts, who fired two more interceptions of his own. Even the No. 3 quarterback, some guy by the name of Cliff Olander, got into the charity by throwing the fifth interception of the game. That last one went to Buchanon, who took it back 77 yards for the score with 2:16 to play.

Buchanon of course was the star, with the four interceptions that tied an NFL record and which remains a Packers record he shares with Bobby Dillon. But Buchanon also added nine unassisted tackles in the game.

The Chargers completely disintegrated in the game, not only flinging five interceptions but losing six fumbles and managing just 245 total yards.

"It was a disaster," Prothro wailed afterward.

Packers coach Bart Starr wasn't all that thrilled with his team's offensive performance, either. Quarterback David Whitehurst completed just seven of 14 passes for 92 yards. Amazingly, the Packers won easily, despite gaining only 127 yards on offense.

# WHAT BECAME OF WILLIE BUCHANON?

The great Willie Buchanon marketing tour of 1978 worked superbly. He finished with nine interceptions that season and, when contract talks continued to go nowhere, the Packers traded him to the Chargers following the season for a first- and seventh-round draft pick. He was reunited with his old college coach, Don Coryell.

Buchanon found himself hip-deep in one of the NFL's most prolific and entertaining teams—especially on offense. It was a team that featured quarterback Dan Fouts, tight end Kellen Winslow and a jailbreak offense called affectionately (and otherwise) "Air Coryell."

But for all the pyrotechnics of that offense and for all the games those Chargers won, they never made it to the Super Bowl. Buchanon played four seasons for the Chargers before retiring.

He stayed in the San Diego area and became a successful real estate broker. With his partner, Mark Stone, Buchanon recently started another real estate company, Stonemark Properties.

But there is so much more to the post-football Willie Buchanon. He went back and has taught history and geography in every school—from elementary to college—he ever attended. He also helps coach track at his high school alma mater, Oceanside High School; he is the music minister at his church, and he is involved in numerous charities around the country.

He also takes a father's pride in his son, William, who is a wide receiver at the University of Southern California and whom Willie has tutored more than a little.

And he still thinks often about Green Bay and the team he never really wanted to leave in the first place.

"I would have taken $150,000 from the Packers, and they told me they couldn't pay me that because I'd be the second highest player on the team behind Lynn Dickey," he said with bemusement. "I wanted to stay there with my defense, but I have no regrets."

And to this day, he has nothing but good feelings about his Green Bay years.

"It was truly the best football-playing town in America," he said. "The fans and the stadium—it was all about playing football. Green Bay really gave you an opportunity to concentrate on playing football."

Then he laughed again.

"There was nothing else to do."

# CHAPTER 5

# JERRY KRAMER

*"It was a hell of a football game."*

**Name:** Gerald Louis Kramer
**Birthdate:** January 23, 1936
**Hometown:** Jordan, Montana
**Current residence:** Parma, Idaho
**Position:** Offensive guard
**Height:** 6-foot-3
**Playing weight:** 245
**Years:** 1958-68
**College:** University of Idaho
**Accomplishments:** All-Pro in 1960-63 and 1967-68...Named to Pro Bowl in 1962, 1963 and 1967...Named to Packers All-Time Modern Era team, All-Century team and 50th Anniversary Team...Inducted into Packer Hall of Fame in 1975...Author of five books, including the bestselling *Instant Replay* in 1968.
**The game:** New York Giants, December 30, 1962, at Yankee Stadium

# THE LIFE OF JERRY KRAMER

Jerry Kramer was always something a little more than a football player. Urbane and witty, he came from the mountains of Idaho with a view of the world and of life that made him one of the great spokesmen for the Lombardi-era Packers.

He was, of course, the superb right guard known more for the block that sprung Bart Starr on that epic quarterback sneak in the "Ice Bowl." But he was always a whole lot more than that. A three-time All-Pro and a five-time Pro Bowler, he was the athletic prototype of the 1960s offensive lineman, and there are few to this day who understand why he isn't in the Pro Football Hall of Fame though he has been on the ballot for decades.

More than that, he survived more than his share of injuries that would have kept most careers from starting. For example, at age 15 he was accidentally shot in the right arm with a shotgun and required four operations and skin grafts. Two years later, a nearly eight-inch-long piece of wood penetrated his groin and lodged near his spine while he was chasing a calf in a pasture.

In football, he chipped a vertebra in his neck, suffered a concussion and a detached retina, battled through torn ligaments in his ankle and, in 1964, missed the entire season when he underwent surgery on a tumor in his liver as well as surgery to have pieces of wood removed from his abdomen.

So this—in case there was any doubt—was one tough guy.

At the University of Idaho, Kramer had already established himself as a quality offensive lineman and, in those days when every player did what it took to help the cause, as a field goal kicker as well.

"I was second in the nation in field goals in 1957," Kramer said with a laugh. "With three."

Ironically it would be his ability to kick with that ungainly square-toed right shoe that would be the key to the most memorable game of his career.

"I remember my last game at the University of Idaho, and it was a nasty day," he said. "It started Friday night, and it was rain

**Jerry Kramer.** *Vernon J. Biever photo*

before it turned to snow. And there were about 18 inches of snow on the ground before it turned back to rain. And we could only plow the field once, so it was just a swamp. And I know there were a few students at the game, but the paid attendance was one."

It was a far cry from what he would run into a few years later at Yankee Stadium.

Kramer recalled his rookie season with the Packers when he was called on to try a field goal in an exhibition game in Boston when it was no certainty at the time he would even make the team.

"I look up in the stands and there are like 45,000 people there, and I'm just pissing in my pants, I'm so nervous," he said. "My right leg is shaking so bad that it's jumping up and down and I beat on it to try to stop it from shaking. So I kick the ball and it hits one of the offensive linemen right in the ass. The PA announcer says, 'The kick is blocked,' and I say, 'Thank you.'"

But Kramer found his spot with the Packers and soon became one of the irreplaceable figures on an offensive line that was almost as famous as the guys who ran and threw and caught the ball.

# THE SETTING

The Giants were mad. The Giants were embarrassed. And the Giants wanted revenge after the 37-0 whipping the Packers had put on them the year before in Green Bay.

That day, the changing of the guard had officially begun in the NFL. The old-school dominance of the New York Giants was ending, and the Packers were emerging as the long dormant power now ready to rise again.

Now it was time for the sweet rematch and merciful redemption. But this time it was in Yankee Stadium, in front of their own fans, and the Giants knew—as veteran teams usually do—that this might be the surge of greatness for this team.

Nonetheless, the Packers went in as seven-point favorites and the weather report suggested it might snow and then turn to rain. There was nothing said of the biting, swirling wind that would sweep into the stadium and make it almost impossible to play.

The Giants were led by the aerial acrobatics of Y.A. Tittle, who had set a league record that year with 33 touchdown passes. And Lombardi, again playing the mind games he was so proficient at, extolled the wonders of the Giants and insisted this team was much better than the one the Packers had crushed the year before.

"They have a better offensive line," Lombardi said at the time, and Giants coach Allie Sherman insisted his team was better because Tittle had a second year in the offense to learn his teammates and the plays better.

The Packers, of course, were the Packers. They would do what they always did, and that meant a healthy dose of fullback Jim Taylor, just enough of Bart Starr's passing and the great defense that always seemed to come through when it had to.

The question, though, was the kicking game. Paul Hornung, despite Lombardi's claims to the contrary, stood no chance of playing due to a knee injury. That meant Kramer would do the field goal kicking and defensive back Willie Wood would handle the kickoffs.

And in a game between evenly matched opponents like this, the kicking game likely would make the difference. It's something Jerry Kramer knew all too well.

Back then, kicking was still just a job and not a specialty as it is today. Soccer-style kickers? They played soccer and stayed away from football. At that time, the kicking chores were often handled by someone from the offense who kicked straight on and wore one of those square-toed shoes that looked like something from the Spanish Inquisition.

But Kramer enjoyed it, and when the opportunity came, he was no longer the skittery rookie he'd been in that preseason game in Boston. He was a now a seasoned NFL player who knew what his job entailed.

And the Packers would need him more than they ever thought.

# THE GAME OF MY LIFE

*By Jerry Kramer*

I had a little burden on me that day because I was doing the kicking. Paul Hornung had been injured and wasn't able to play, and I was the backup field goal kicker. It was a bitter day, bitter cold, and I think with the wind it was very comparable to the cold of the Ice Bowl.

The wind was so ferocious in Yankee Stadium that I remember they had those old wooden benches on the sidelines that looked like something from a high school locker room. They were really small and quite ancient. The wind was blowing so hard that it actually blew the benches over at halftime and blew them onto the field, maybe 10 yards from the sidelines and onto the playing field. It was obviously a hell of a day to be trying to kick field goals.

Now walking into Yankee Stadium is a hell of a thrill. Walking in it with all those ghosts is another elevation of that. To be on the field and playing is an incredible experience. It was just awesome to be there.

We were going to try a field goal fairly early on. And there's Ed Katcavage and Andy Robustelli and Rosie Grier and Sam Huff is breathing heavily, and I'm saying to myself, "What in the world are you doing being on the same field with these greats?" I must have taken a wrong turn somewhere.

But I was not only awed by the moment and the stadium, but I was awed to be on the field with those great players. By then I had more experience, so I was able to keep my wits about me.

I ended up kicking three field goals and we won the game. We had beaten the Giants quite soundly the previous year for the championship, so it was a different story in their back yard. It was a hell of a football game. They blocked a punt somewhere in the first half, and we scored and kicked a couple of field goals along the way. So with two and a half minutes left to go, they hadn't scored again and if we could make a field goal, it looked like we could win the game. I knew if I made the last field goal, then we would win the game.

**Jerry Kramer's three field goals in the swirling winds of Yankee Stadium were the key to the Packers' 1962 NFL title over the New York Giants.** *Vernon J. Biever photo*

The wind was howling and carrying on, and I was kicking the ball outside the left upright and the wind carried it through the middle. It was a wonderful moment. It was a moment that running backs and quarterbacks have when you actually win a football game. I didn't feel that way in the Ice Bowl. That was supposed to be what you were out there for. I knew I had to make that block in the Ice Bowl and there was pressure. But it just didn't seem as much pressure as that Giants game.

It was a sensational moment and the team voted me the game ball. The funny thing is that the sportswriters voted [linebacker Ray] Nitschke the game Corvette, and I got the game ball. Things always stay the same on the offensive line.

# GAME RESULT

More than any game he ever played with the Packers, that one stood out for Jerry Kramer. He was the focal point of one of the most famous plays in football history, Bart Starr's quarterback sneak in the "Ice Bowl" in 1967. After all, he threw the key block that sprung Starr and put that game in the hall of the immortals.

"I think that whole final drive in the Ice Bowl was such a magnificent event that I really think of that game in terms of that [final] drive than in terms of the quarterback sneak," Kramer said. "I felt better in the Giants game because of the pressure of the moment."

Indeed, Kramer's three field goals from 26, 29, and 30 yards were all huge, but none was more important than the final 30-yarder with just two minutes to play. That's because if Kramer nailed it, it would give the Packers a nine-point lead and all but ensure, especially in those weather conditions, that New York could not make some miracle comeback.

All season Kramer's teammates had made fun of his rather unorthodox kicking style.

"I had a tendency to follow through very short," he said. "I was quite stiff in the joints because I was just a grunt in the middle of the pile. But my follow-through was a bit short, and the guys would really get on me in the locker room. They'd say, 'Sports quiz! Who is this?' and then they'd do a follow-through of about eight inches. They'd jack me around pretty good."

But on this frigid day and with everything on the line, there was no joking around. And that became clear when Kramer stepped into the huddle prior to the kick.

Several teammates looked at him somberly and said, "This is the ballgame, Jerry." Fellow guard Fuzzy Thurston said simply, "Keep your head down, buddy."

He did just that and, short follow-through and all, he drilled it through the uprights for the field goal that sealed the win.

"You didn't really think about it at the time," he said, though he remembers vividly being mobbed by his teammates as well as the heartfelt, solid handshake from Lombardi. "The biggest was it would have been nice to come off the field and catch your breath. I had to do a lot of running."

# WHAT BECAME OF JERRY KRAMER?

Unlike many players who leave the game with no idea of what to do once the game didn't need them anymore, Kramer was lucky. Sort of.

In June of 1967, he began a daily diary of life in the NFL that became the book *Instant Replay*. Written with New York sports writer Dick Schaap, who became a lifelong friend after that, the book looked into the NFL the way no book had ever done before, and it was an instant success when it was published in 1968.

That was also the same year he retired from football, a shimmering part of five world championship teams including the first two games of what would be known as the Super Bowl. A year later, he wrote *Farewell to Football*, his ode to the game that had treated him so well.

He was the editor of a third book, *Lombardi: Winning is the Only Thing* in 1970 and in 1984, after a reunion of the Packers who won the first Super Bowl, he wrote *Distant Replay*, again with Schaap's help.

"I thought there might be something to say there, and there was," he said. "I visited with several of the guys, and it was a huge emotional experience."

What proved to be so emotional was the hold their old coach still had on many, if not all, of the players who had sweated and bled and worked for him. It was nearly 15 years after Lombardi's death, and the man and his influence still hung over them like a shadow.

"I knew it had been a powerful influence on my life and the other guys, but I didn't realize how strong it was until [that reunion]," Kramer said. "Just about every guy from Super Bowl I was at a crossroads in his life. For example, Lee Roy Caffey [a linebacker from 1964-69] had a bank charter down in Texas that he tried to get four or five different times. But they'd turned him down every time. Lee Roy's partners were getting discouraged and wanted to quit and he said to them, 'You can quit, but I can't. If Lombardi found out he'd kill me.'" When I saw the depth of that impact, it made me feel like there was still something to say. That's what really got me. I didn't expect that."

He has dabbled in writing on and off since, even working on a screenplay about Lombardi that first caught the attention of the late actor George C. Scott, who reveled in the thought of playing the old coach.

But it never came together back in the 1970s, though Kramer hasn't given up hope of one day getting a movie made about his coach. Asked if he thought a film about a coach dead nearly 35 years could still be relevant today, he said with a laugh, "What do you think?"

And who would he pick to play Lombardi these days? Without hesitation he said Jack Nicholson.

Kramer was also involved in a nutrition business that went bankrupt.

"I'm trying to figure out what to do now," he said.

Mostly, though, he's made a nice career out of being a former Packer from the glory years, and he has been a popular speaker nationally who will go anywhere to talk about the team he loves.

"I have tried to retire several times," he said. "And I don't seem to be very good at it."

# CHAPTER 6

# LYNN
# DICKEY

*"We could do anything we wanted."*

**Name:** Clifford Lynn Dickey
**Birthdate:** October 19, 1949
**Hometown:** Paola, Kansas
**Current residence:** Leawood, Kansas
**Position:** Quarterback
**Height:** 6-foot-4
**Playing weight:** 220
**Years:** 1976-85
**College:** Kansas State
**Accomplishments:** Two-time All Big-Eight quarterback...Led NFL in passing in 1983...Led Packers in passing for eight seasons...Third in team history in passes attempted (2,831), completed (1,592), and touchdown passes (133)...Leads team in most yards passing in a season (4,458 in 1983)...Inducted into Packer Hall of Fame in 1992.
**The game:** Washington Redskins, October 17, 1983, at Lambeau Field

# THE LIFE OF LYNN DICKEY

Lynn Dickey is still the biggest thing to come out of Osawatomie High School. He was one of those once-in-a-lifetime high school hotshots who automatically made everybody better the minute he stepped on the field. And at Osawatomie, located 35 miles south of Kansas City in tiny Paola, Kansas, Clifford Lynn Dickey was about as good as anyone was going to see.

He proved it in 1966 when he led his high school to an unbeaten season and a state championship, and he gladdened the hearts of many Kansas residents when he decided to stay close to home and play football at Kansas State.

And it was more of the same in Manhattan, where in his career, Dickey passed for 6,208 yards and 29 touchdowns in three seasons. He still owns many of the significant passing records at K-State and finished his career by throwing for more than 380 yards four times, including a 439-yard strafing of Colorado in 1969. But the game that stays in the hearts of many longtime Kansas State fans also came in 1969, when he threw for 390 yards in a 59-21 pounding of Oklahoma in what remains the Sooners' worst loss ever.

Dickey was a two-time All-Big Eight Conference selection and was named Most Valuable Player of the East-West Shrine Game after his senior season. So impressive was his collegiate career that the Associated Press named him the greatest quarterback in Big Eight history and his No. 11 was the first retired by the university.

For Lynn Dickey, the road always seemed to be lined with success at every turn. And when he was taken by the Houston Oilers in the third round of the 1971 NFL draft, there seemed no reason to think anything would change. But the NFL, as too many college stars have found over the years, is a different animal from what they had experienced before.

The players are better, the game is faster, the expectations are constant and virtually unattainable, and the time you have to prove yourself is practically nonexistent. Dickey found that out in

**Lynn Dickey.** *Vernon J. Biever photo*

four rugged seasons with the Oilers. Injury and inconsistency dogged him all the time, and in four seasons he completed just 155 of 294 passes for 1,953 yards, eight touchdowns, and a staggering 28 interceptions.

In today's NFL, those kinds of numbers would have sent a player into another line of work. But back then, there was at least a little more patience with players with the kind of intrinsic ability Dickey had.

And there was a team in desperate need of a quarterback that was ready to try to pull that potential out of Dickey, no matter what it took. The Green Bay Packers had struggled horrendously at quarterback ever since the immortal Bart Starr had retired after the 1971 season. And in April 1976, the Packers were ready to take a chance on another quarterback who might at least be able to reside in the same ballpark as Starr.

# THE SETTING

It will go down, with little argument, as the worst trade in Packers history.

In 1974, the Packers inexplicably sent their first-, second- and third-round picks of the 1975 draft and their first and third selections in 1976 to the Los Angeles Rams for John Hadl, a quarterback who was already on the down slope of a career that hadn't been anything spectacular in the first place. But that's how desperate the Packers were for a quarterback.

Since Starr's retirement (and his subsequent assumption of the role as the team's offensive coordinator in 1972), the Packers were simply lost at the quarterback position. In 1972, Scott Hunter and Jerry Tagge combined to complete fewer than half of their passes with six touchdowns and nine interceptions. In 1973, Tagge, Hunter and Jim Del Gaizo again could not get to the 50-percent completion mark and managed to combine for six touchdown passes and 17 interceptions. In 1974, Hadl, Tagge, and the ancient Jack Concannon threw for five touchdowns and 21 interceptions, and in 1975, Hadl was horrific, throwing for 2,095 yards but with just six touchdowns and a mind-bending 21 interceptions.

After what the sainted Starr had done in his 16-year Hall of Fame career, it was practically sacrilege what those guys under center had done for the Packers. On top of that, by 1975 Starr had replaced Dan Devine as head coach, making the situation even more depressing.

So, barely a week before the NFL draft in 1976, the Packers decided to cut their losses and try to look toward the future. That's when they dealt Hadl, defensive back Ken Ellis, a fourth-round pick that year, and a third-rounder in 1977 to the Oilers for Lynn Dickey.

It seemed to be a trade that would work for everyone involved. Dickey, who had struggled with a hip injury the previous season, hadn't worked out in Houston and needed a change of scenery, and the Packers still needed a quarterback and wanted to put as much distance between themselves and John Hadl as possible.

There was no doubt this was another gamble with such a valuable position, but the Packers had almost no choice. And for a while, Dickey seemed to be the guy they needed that season. He played well enough, throwing for 1,465 yards and seven touchdowns (but also heaving up 14 interceptions) before suffering a separated shoulder against the Chicago Bears in the 10th week of the season and missing the rest of the year.

It got even worse in 1977 when Dickey continued to struggle, throwing 14 interceptions to just five touchdowns. Then in the ninth game of the season, Dickey severely broke his leg on the final play of the game against the Rams. The injury was so bad it forced him to miss the entire 1978 season. Still the Packers stuck with him.

In 1979, Dickey sat back as Whitehurst, who had started every game the previous season with decidedly mixed results (2,093 yards, 17 interceptions, and 10 touchdowns in an 8-7-1 campaign that barely saw the Packers miss the playoffs) stayed in control. But by week 14, Starr had seen enough of mediocre quarterbacking.

He inserted Dickey for the final three weeks, and he completed 50 percent of his passes with five touchdowns and four interceptions, the first time since Starr himself in 1968 that a Green Bay quarterback had more touchdowns than picks. Then again, the Packers also lost two of those three games. But at least Starr believed he had a direction to go.

Things changed in the next two seasons, though, as Dickey became the clear leader on the offense; however, little changed on the scoreboard. In the next two years, Dickey threw for more than 6,000 yards and 32 touchdowns. But he also missed three more games due to injury in 1981, threw 40 interceptions, and the Packers went 13-18-1 on the field.

Bart Starr, who had shown so much faith and patience in Dickey, lost his duties as general manager after the 1980 season, but in 1981, he was rewarded with a two-year contract extension as head coach after Green Bay went 8-8 but still missed the playoffs.

Then in 1982, all the pain and suffering and heartache that accompanied this franchise seemed to finally be worth it. It was a season shortened to eight regular-season games by a vitriolic players strike. It shut the league down for 57 days and ended up pitting player against player, coach against player and fan against player. It was one of those classic no-win situations that, not surprisingly, no one really won.

The NFL resumed play on November 21, and the Packers, who had been 2-0 when the strike began, finished with a solid 5-3-1 record that was good enough to get them into the postseason "tournament." Dickey certainly did his part to help, throwing for nearly 1,800 yards and 12 touchdowns.

The important thing was that the Packers, for the first time since 1972, were in the playoffs and, even more remarkable, they hosted a playoff game for the first time since the legendary "Ice Bowl" 15 years earlier.

In his postseason activity, Dickey was superb. In the opening-round game against the St. Louis Cardinals, he completed 17 of 23 passes for 260 yards and threw two touchdown passes to John Jefferson and one each to James Lofton and Eddie Lee Ivery in a thunderous 41-16 win.

In a second-round game at Texas Stadium against the Dallas Cowboys, he rang up 332 yards and a touchdown to Lofton, but he was also intercepted three times as Dallas advanced 37-26.

But these were the numbers the Packers had longed to see from a quarterback. Besides, the NFL was going through a less than subtle change on offense. Rules were opening up the game, and coaches—like San Diego's Don Coryell and San Francisco's Bill Walsh—were starting to use the passing game as more of a down-the-field weapon than anyone else before. Offense was becoming the name of the game, and Dickey and his Packers were becoming an integral part of it.

# THE GAME OF MY LIFE
### *By Lynn Dickey*

That Washington Redskins game was the most memorable only because the Redskins were coming off a season as defending

Super Bowl champions. No one gave us much of a chance, and it was a Monday night game, so that was special, too.

In warmups for that game, it seemed the ball was just spinning. I can't explain it. Some days you can just tell in warmups that it's going to be a good day. And during the game I couldn't throw a wobbly pass if I tried. I was getting great protection and they were getting no rush on me whatsoever. It was like shooting fish in a barrel in the first half. Of course, we were having trouble stopping them too.

But I remember going back to Wednesday morning of that week—I forget who we played the week before—but the Redskins had seen the last three or four weeks' tape of the games we'd played. I think it was Redskins tight end Don Warren, though I wouldn't swear to it, who made a comment that made it back to our bulletin board in a hurry. He said that this game was going to be a rout. [Coach] Bart [Starr] got hold of that, and he didn't let things get under his skin often, but that did.

He put it up on the overhead projector that Wednesday and alluded to it every day after that. On the night of the game we went out for warmups and came back in, and before we were ready to come back out he put that quote back up on the overhead projector. He said, "This is what these guys think of you." He also said, "It's going to be a rout," but he added, "He didn't say which way," which we thought was kind of cool. It was a little extra pump for us.

It was just a fun game. You knew you were on Monday night television, and I think that game was the first one after the World Series had ended, so a lot of people were watching. Pretty much we could do whatever we wanted to do that night.

I don't remember the score at the half, but right toward the end of the third quarter, it was 35-34 or something and (offensive coordinator) Bob Schnelker looked at me on the sidelines and elbowed me and said, "Keep plugging away. They can't stop us." He said we may have to score 40 points to win this game, and, looking back, we probably should have lost the game.

Lynn Dickey played on some horrible Packers teams and never got the credit he deserved for being one of the NFL's most dangerous passers.
*Vernon J. Biever photo*

I remember Leotis Harris was hurt. He was the normal right guard, and Greg Koch was our normal right tackle. We just signed a new guy, Charlie Getty, and he played right guard. Koch and I were always arguing about something, and in the huddle during the game I saw Koch had his head down. His nickname was "Bubba," and I said, "Bubba, what's wrong?" And he said, "Man, I've got a headache." It turns out [Redskins mammoth defensive tackle] Dave Butz was head-butting him on every play, and Koch had this terrible headache.

I told him, "He's only got a one-yard jump on you, and he's getting a 10-yard jump on me. Just play your game." He said, "I'll do my job and you do yours." We argued like that in the huddle all the time. But Dave Butz didn't get to me the whole game.

I remember [left tackle] Karl Swanke got tangled up with [Washington star defensive end] Dexter Manley and he got into a scrap with Manley early in the game. He didn't get to me either. For the most part I had excellent protection.

There were a lot of ironies in the game, too. In Houston, I was the holder for Mark Moseley, and he kicked four field goals that night. He was a great kicker. He had lead in that right toe of his.

I remember at the end of the game after we kicked the field goal [to take a 48-47 lead], [Redskins quarterback] Joe Theismann did a wonderful job of leading them right back down the field and I'm thinking, "Oh my God, we scored 48 points and we're going to lose this thing." Joe had a great game, and we had a pretty good duel that night.

After the game, [Redskins fullback] John Riggins comes over to me and the first thing out of his mouth is, "Some rout, huh?" It was just a crazy night. When you go to Lambeau Field you go there to have fun, and I think everybody had fun that night.

And it seems like every other year, it might be snowy outside and you can't get out of Kansas City, somebody will ask about the game and, since I have it on tape, I'll pop it in and look at it. I guess there will be a game like that again at some point. But at that time, when we weren't expected to do anything, it was a special night. Sometimes, when you least expect it, it will become a wild and crazy night.

# GAME RESULT

Where to start? Early in that season, it was already obvious that the Packers were a phenomenal offensive machine. In the six games Green Bay had played prior to the Monday night orgy, it had already piled up 41 points against Houston, 27 against the Los Angeles Rams and 55 in a humiliation of the Tampa Bay Buccaneers.

Unfortunately for the offense, which could score from nearly anywhere on the field at any time, the Packers' defense had the same reputation. Anyone could score on that unit from anywhere at any time.

During those same six games, in fact, the defense surrendered 38 points to those same Oilers, 27 to the Giants, and 38 in an embarrassing loss to the Lions the week before. For the season, the Packers averaged 386 yards per game. The defense allowed an average of 400.

So it was no surprise to anyone that when the 5-1 Redskins steamed into Lambeau Field behind their formidable offense of Joe Theismann, John Riggins, Joe Washington, Charlie Brown, Art Monk, and an offensive wizard like coach Joe Gibbs, no one gave the Packers much of a chance. The Redskins, coming off their first Super Bowl title, would go on to set an NFL record for most points in a season, but like the Packers, the defense had a tendency not to show up on occasion.

But the Packers, 3-3 and lucky to be that, figured they had very little to lose.

"We knew no one could really stop us on offense," center Larry McCarren recalled.

Ironically, it was the defense that set the tone in the game and provided the first points when linebacker Mike Douglass forced a Joe Washington fumble and returned it 22 yards for the touchdown barely a minute into the game. That was only the beginning.

Over the next 59 minutes, the two teams would wage the kind of war never before seen by Monday night football fans. Dickey completed 22 of 30 passes for 387 yards and three touchdowns and Theismann completed 27 of 39 passes for 398 yards and two scores.

The two teams combined for 95 points and 770 total yards, and by the time it was over, it took a shanked Mark Moseley field goal from 39 yards out to preserve Green Bay's 48-47 victory.

It was a game that remains the highest scoring in Monday night history and it remains a game that is as much a topic of conversation now as it was then.

# WHAT BECAME OF LYNN DICKEY?

In 1983, Lynn Dickey enjoyed the kind of season most quarterbacks can barely even dream about it. That year, he set a club record by throwing for an astounding 4,458 yards as four receivers—Lofton, Jefferson, tight end Paul Coffman, and running back Gerry Ellis—all caught at least 50 passes. Dickey also threw 32 touchdown passes but, as became part of the equation with him, 29 interceptions came along with them.

But he triggered one of the most fearsome offenses in the league, ringing up 6,172 total yards, second best in the entire NFL, and the 429 points were a team record until 1996. Unfortunately, the defense got no better and, in fact, was the NFL's worst, surrendering a ghastly 439 points, still a team record. Yet somehow, the Packers managed an 8-8 record.

But it was nowhere near good enough, and after nine seasons, one trip to playoffs, and a record of 53-77-3, Starr was fired as head coach and replaced by another legend from the golden era, former right tackle Forrest Gregg.

For Dickey the end was already in sight. Though he threw for 3,195 yards and 25 touchdowns in 1984, he became part of a three-quarterback merry-go-round in 1985 that also included Randy Wright and former Seattle Seahawk Jim Zorn. Dickey started 10 games and threw for just over 2,200 yards and 17 touchdowns as Green Bay went 8-8 for the second straight year.

His last start, though, was a memorable one. In a December 1 blizzard at Lambeau Field, he led the Packers' offense to 512 total yards in a 21-0 win over Tampa Bay. Later that week, though, while working out, Dickey injured his neck and never played again.

Once he left the game, Dickey toyed with the idea of coaching.

"But the main reason I didn't get into coaching was the commitment and the time," he said. "It was never really my type of commitment. If it was a nine-to-five job I'd do it, but it's not nine to five and it never will be."

Today he works in the automobile extended warranty business as a salesman and he gets up to Wisconsin frequently.

And even now, he remembers back to the incredible October night more than 20 years ago when everything fell into place.

"It's amazing," he said. "I could almost tell you everything that was going to happen in that game. I can still hear the audibles. It was really something."

# Chapter 7

# WILLIE DAVIS

*"I'm not going to be denied."*

**Name:** William Delford Davis
**Birthdate:** July 24, 1934
**Hometown:** Lisbon, Louisiana
**Current residence:** Inglewood, California
**Position:** Defensive end
**Height:** 6-foot-3
**Playing weight:** 240
**Years:** 1960-69
**College:** Grambling State
**Accomplishments:** Inducted into Pro Football Hall of Fame in 1981...Five-time Pro Bowler and five-time All-Pro...Never missed a game in a 12-year career spanning 162 games...Holds all-time team record for recovered fumbles with 21...Inducted into Packer Hall of Fame in 1975.
**The game:** New York Giants, December 31, 1961, at City Stadium

# THE LIFE OF WILLIE DAVIS

It's a story as old as football itself. Find a kid who loves football and chances are his mother won't want him to play. It's a maternal thing that runs deeper than the ocean—no mother wants to see her little baby get hurt, and football was the surest way to get a mom worrying.

Willie Davis' mom, Nodie, who raised Willie and his two siblings by herself, was the perfect example. The problem was, Willie Davis loved football and was a star at Booker T. Washington High School in Texarkana, Arkansas.

He recalls a story about how he never told his mother he was playing high school football.

But the story fell apart the third week of the season when the team had to play a road game and Willie knew she'd find out because he'd be out so late.

Mom acquiesced and Willie flourished. He earned a football scholarship at Grambling University and was a two-year team captain and an NAIA All-American.

Though he harbored thoughts of playing professionally, he wasn't sure what chance he'd have playing for a small school like Grambling. He got his answer thanks to a 19-tackle performance in a late-season upset win over Florida A&M that a number of pro scouts were watching.

He went on to become a 17th-round draft pick of the Cleveland Browns in 1956, though his career was put on hold due to army service in 1956-57.

He came out of the service and back to the Browns, but the team had trouble finding a position for him. First on the offensive line and then to the defensive line and back again, coach Paul Brown was uncertain what to do with him. And the frustration on both sides was growing.

That's when the fateful decision was made that would alter the future of Willie Davis and the Green Bay Packers.

**Willie Davis.** *Vernon J. Biever photo*

# THE SETTING

Even today Davis wonders what might have happened if he hadn't ended up with the Packers. He runs it through his mind and wonders what would have happened if the Browns had showed infinite patience and kept him. Or worse, what if they had thrown up their hands and released him? What would have happened to him then?

"Coming to Green Bay was the best thing that ever happened to me," he said.

But that's hardly how he felt at the time when, prior to the 1960 season, frustrated at his inability to find a real position for Davis, Brown dealt him to the Packers for end A.D. Williams. No one is quite sure what happened to A.D. Williams, who had played the 1959 season in Green Bay and caught one pass for 11 yards. Few have to ask whatever happened to Willie Davis.

At the time, though, Davis was shocked by the thunderbolt out of nowhere and briefly considered quitting football altogether rather than play in the NFL hinterland like Green Bay.

But he would get the chance to *play* in Green Bay, something that was never a sure thing in Cleveland. Coach Vince Lombardi loved Davis' size and quickness and saw him as the prototypical defensive end.

"I consider speed, agility, and size to be the three most important attributes for a defensive lineman," Lombardi told Davis at the time. "Give me a man who has any two of those dimensions and he'll do OK. But give him all three and he'll be great. We think you have all three."

That's all Davis needed to hear. He settled in at left end and for the next decade never left.

After coming up short in the NFL title game in 1960 against the Eagles, the Packers were back in 1961, looking for their first title since 1944.

# THE GAME OF MY LIFE
*By Willie Davis*

Championship games will always highlight your memory more than anything, even though they may not have been your best game in terms of individual performances. I remember the championships as if they were yesterday and remember the plays even as they occurred. The 1961 championship game in Green Bay against the Giants was one of the best total performances I'd ever seen. We beat them 37-0.

I think it was so memorable because of what it meant for us that we had not been able to achieve the year before against the Eagles [a 17-13 championship loss in Philadelphia]. Much of what emanated from that Eagles game was what Vince Lombardi told us. He said after that game that we would never lose another championship game as long as he was coaching. That was pretty strong talk. That's why I think we went out and decimated the Giants. The offense, the defense, everybody played at a level that, in my mind, was one of our best performances.

Add to that the fact that it was played in Green Bay and it was the first championship in a long, long time. It had all the things that would cause you to remember it for a long, long time. When we won the second championship [in 1962], it was important, but it was played in New York and it was just about the coldest game I ever played in.

But the 1961 game, I remember it was a cold Wisconsin day. It was nothing like the "Ice Bowl," but it was cold. It was the kind of day that Lombardi would often characterize as "our kind of day." And it was. It was cold, but you could play comfortably. It was a good day.

I was talking to Forrest Gregg just a few weeks ago and he was saying he had been able to get a complete copy of the 1961 game. I told him I needed to get one too, and he said, "I can see why, because they called your name a lot [on the public address]." It was one of my better games. I was playing [Giants] right tackle Jack Stroud, and I just remember every time they threw the ball we got pressure on the ball. It was strictly attitude. I said, "I'm not going to be denied today." It was a game built around confidence.

And as we dominated the game, the fans really got into it. I would say it was a love affair that day. It was something I don't think happened in any other game, because I remember them yelling out "Go get 'em, Willie." They were having a ball.

It was the greatest memory I had in football and it had to compare to my being traded from Cleveland to Green Bay and believing for a minute that Green Bay was the worst place in the NFL. [Browns coach] Paul Brown used to describe Green Bay as the Siberia of football. But it was the greatest 10 years of my life.

# GAME RESULT

It was difficult for some Packers fans to remember, but playing for the championship used to be commonplace in Green Bay. From 1929 through 1944, the Packers won six championships and became perhaps the first truly great franchise in a league still searching for its place in America.

On December 17, 1944, the Packers beat the New York Giants 14-7 for another title, and there seemed no end in sight to what the Packers could do.

But it did end—thunderously and quickly. In 1945, the Packers went 6-4, and by 1948 there was a losing season, and eight more would follow over the next decade. That's what made 1961 so special.

And when the Packers took the field against the Giants on that cold day, it was the first playoff game played in Green Bay since that championship game in 1944.

The Packers made it one to remember, too. After a scoreless first quarter, the Packers buried the Giants under 24 second-quarter points, led by Paul Hornung, who was playing on leave from the army. He scored on a six-yard run to start the scoring, and after Ray Nitschke and Hank Gremminger interceptions, Bart Starr threw touchdown passes to Boyd Dowler and Ron

Kramer. Hornung ended that barrage with a 17-yard field goal and a 24-0 lead.

It was already over.

The Packers' defense, led by Davis and Nitschke, held the Giants to six first downs and 240 total yards, including just 31 rushing. The Packers also forced five turnovers, four interceptions and a fumble, and the defense chalked up the first NFL title game shutout in 12 years. Offensively, the Packers finished with 345 yards, and Hornung was the star. Rushing for 89 yards, with his 19-yard field goal in the quarter, he set an NFL championship scoring mark of 19 points.

"This is the greatest team in the history of the National Football League," Lombardi proclaimed at the time.

He hadn't seen anything yet.

And Willie Davis was a massive part of it. For most of the 1960s, Davis was the preeminent defensive end in the NFL and all he knew, it seemed, were championships. From 1960 to 1967, he played in seven NFL championship games and was on the winning side six times—including in the first two of those games they would come to call the Super Bowl.

He would become a part of myth and lore and legend along with his Packers teammates and, collectively, their names would be uttered with a kind of reverence unknown to pro sports up to that point.

But these were not marble men. They were not statues who needed only to spend their days adjusting themselves on their pedestals. They were flesh and blood humans who bled and cried and were wracked by the doubts that haunted everyone else. And Willie Davis was no different.

He remembers only too well the first NFL-AFL championship game in January, 1967. In past years, these Packers at least knew what to expect. They knew what stood in front of them and they could deal with it, because familiarity, if it didn't breed confidence, at least led to an understanding of what the job was.

But on this day, the Packers were facing the Kansas City Chiefs. The Kansas City Chiefs? These were not the Dallas

Cowboys or the Cleveland Browns or New York Giants—real teams from the only league that the Packers figured mattered.

But the football world was changing. The established NFL and the upstart AFL were merging into one league and the necessary result was that the best of the NFL had to play the AFL's champ, and that meant that the Packers were at center stage.

And the Packers knew, as did coach Vince Lombardi, that this was a no-win situation for the NFL. Win the game and it was what was expected. Lose? Oh my God, the thought was too awful to contemplate. Willie Davis understood that along with every other Packer.

"I'm lying in bed the night before the game and I'm wide awake," Davis said. "I'm asking myself what concerns me most personally and what concerns me about the team. I answered my concerns about me. There was a lot of confidence, but I had to be careful not to make the big mistake. I didn't want to make the mistake that would cost us the game. Our whole philosophy at Green Bay was that on defense we had to make a team earn every touchdown. And we had to do it by making the other team travel the length of the field. And if you made a team run that many plays, there was always something that seemed to happen to upset that continuity. We wanted to make sure that happened again."

Lombardi also stressed to his team not to take the Chiefs lightly.

"He'd say, 'Look at their roster, it's full of the top college players from the last five years. You've got to know these guys have an excellent chance to be a good football team against you.'"

He never said, however, that the Chiefs had a chance to beat the Packers. Lombardi would never say something like that. And there was more a sense of relief than true joy after the Packers' 35-10 win. It was much the same the next year when the Packers pounded the Oakland Raiders.

And while the Packers had put their names among the NFL's best of all time, even they knew it could not last.

# WHAT BECAME OF WILLIE DAVIS?

By 1969, Willie Davis knew the end had come not only for himself but the golden years of the Green Bay Packers. The players who had made up the backbone of those incredible teams were either retiring or being traded.

Lombardi left the sidelines for one uncomfortable season as general manager in 1968. Max McGee, Fuzzy Thurston, and Don Chandler retired while Jerry Kramer, Ray Nitschke, Henry Jordan, Forrest Gregg, Willie Wood, and Davis were all heading in that direction. The dynasty was ending. Davis played through the 1969 season and decided his time had come as well.

It is a common and sad story about how players leave pro sports and are ill equipped to handle the real world that follows. But Willie Davis didn't fall into that trap.

Actually, he learned a valuable lesson from his experience in Cleveland, realizing that one day you can be on a pro team and the next you could be history. He told himself even then that he was not going to be caught flat-footed when his football career ended.

He majored in industrial arts at Grambling, and late in his career in Green Bay, he went after his master's degree in business from the University of Chicago. Once he retired, job offers came from the private sector as well as from football, where NFL teams thought he'd make a good assistant coach and several colleges thought he'd be a terrific head coach.

But Davis had his sights set on other things. He went into the Schlitz Brewing Company management program in 1967 and then in 1970 took over the Schlitz distributorship in Los Angeles. Since then he has become one of Southern California's most successful businessmen.

He serves on 10 corporate boards of directors including megapowers like Dow Chemical and Sara Lee Corp. He still maintains his ties in Wisconsin as well, serving on the boards of Johnson Controls Inc. and Wisconsin Energy Corp. He is president of All Pro Broadcasting, a radio chain with stations in Milwaukee and Los Angeles, which generates about seven million dollars in revenues.

These were plans that Davis set out to accomplish long ago. Driven first by his love of football, then by Lombardi and finally by his desire to be a success after football, Davis achieved nearly everything he set out to do. He says now he will scale back on his board of director duties and try to enjoy life a little more.

But he remains passionate about the Green Bay Packers. He never misses an opportunity to return for games and he will always be on hand for alumni functions. He was an early and strident backer of the Packers' original and controversial plan to renovate Lambeau Field to the tune of $295 million. And when the plans were first unveiled, Davis was there to offer full support.

He knows how fortunate he was to land in what, for him, was the perfect situation. And he made the most of it.

"I look at it and I realize I ended up playing for one of the greatest coaches ever and absolutely the greatest fans ever," he said. "And that's an enjoyment that still endures."

# CHAPTER 8

# KEN RUETTGERS

*"It was as electric as it had ever been."*

**Name:** Kenneth Francis Ruettgers
**Birthdate:** August 20, 1962
**Hometown:** Bakersfield, California
**Current residence:** Sisters, Oregon
**Position:** Left tackle
**Height:** 6-foot-5
**Playing weight:** 285
**Years:** 1985-95
**College:** University of Southern California
**Accomplishments:** First-round draft choice of the Packers in 1985.
**The game:** Pittsburgh Steelers, December 24, 1995, at Lambeau Field

# THE LIFE OF KEN RUETTGERS

To understand a complicated guy like Ken Ruettgers is to try to understand the impossible. And in many ways that's exactly the way he wanted it.

This was not some mastodon-like offensive lineman who understood words of only two syllables or less. He was bright, well read, and opinionated, and would just as soon talk about the politics of abortion or the role of the United Nations as he would about his blocking assignment that Sunday.

As well, this was an offensive lineman who was also a quality athlete. At Garces High School in Bakersfield, he was certainly a star in football as both an offensive tackle and defensive end. But he also played basketball, threw the shot and discus, and even lettered in golf.

He was good enough to earn a scholarship at Southern Cal and, after two years as a backup guard, he was moved to tackle, where he thrived. Unfortunately, he was also getting an early taste of the injury bug that would plague him most of his NFL career and that would lead to one of the great disappointments in his football career. He missed all of his 1980 season with a broken hand and knee injury.

But by the time he was through playing at USC and earning his B.S. in business administration, he had developed a reputation as a solid, steady left tackle. And the Packers noticed.

The left tackle position remains the most vital on the offensive line, because that's where the most damage can be done by a defense. Using the theory that most quarterbacks are right-handed, when they drop back to throw, their blind side is to the left. Consequently that's where most defenses put their best pass rusher, because a great rush at a quarterback who can't see him coming is usually the recipe for mayhem. So the offensive line is made and broken by how well the left tackle plays.

The Packers liked Ruettgers so much coming out of college that on draft day in 1985, they gave up the 14th pick overall to the

**Ken Ruettgers.** *Tom G. Lynn/Time Life Pictures/Getty Images*

Buffalo Bills for the Bills' seventh pick and a second-round selection just so they could move up to get Ruettgers.

It proved to be an inspired move as Ruettgers would play in all 16 games as a rookie and start twice. By the next season, he had moved in as the starting left tackle, and for the next decade he rarely budged for anything except injury.

# THE SETTING

This was new territory for Ken Ruettgers, who in 10 years of toiling in virtual anonymity on the Packers' offensive line had been a part of exactly four winning seasons and had yet to see anything resembling a playoff game.

He had played for former Packers legends like Forrest Gregg in the early years, and then Lindy Infante took over in 1988 and seemed to have the team poised to do great things, especially after a 10-6 performance in 1989 that left the Packers just short of the playoffs.

But they fell back again the next two years, and Mike Holmgren, Ruettgers' third head coach, took over. He too seemed like he had the Packers going where they needed to go with 9-7 records three straight years and playoff appearances in 1993 and 1994. But it was time for the next step, wasn't it?

The Packers had proven they could reach the playoffs, but both times it had been as a wild card, and life as an NFL wild card is rarely a pleasant experience. They needed a division title and the chance to prove that they had truly arrived. And 1995 looked to be the season when that would happen.

All the pieces were in place. There was a young, charismatic quarterback named Brett Favre who could throw footballs where no one else even dreamed of throwing them. He threw to an up-and-coming wider receiver named Robert Brooks and a burly tight end named Mark Chmura, and Edgar Bennett was a young talented back.

On defense, Reggie White had put the Packers on the map, veteran Sean Jones provided a fearsome bookend to White, and

Leroy Butler was developing into one of the NFL's best safeties. So it was all there for the taking.

But by midseason, the Packers were still nothing more than an average team. After a disastrous loss to the Minnesota Vikings in the Metrodome in which Favre and backup quarterback Ty Detmer were both knocked out of the game with injuries, Green Bay stood at a pedestrian 5-4.

Then came the turning point of the season. Favre had badly sprained his ankle against the Vikings, and few figured he'd play the following Sunday in a huge matchup with the Chicago Bears. Detmer had already been ruled out of the game with a thumb injury, and the Packers were so desperate for a healthy quarterback that Holmgren lured a friend and protégé from the San Francisco 49ers, Bob Gagliano, out of retirement to take snaps just in case.

But Favre knew what no one else did. Around-the-clock treatments on the ankle and a plan to tape it so tightly that it would essentially be a cast would allow him to play. And he knew it.

Favre then produced a game that Packers fans still remember with awe. Hobbling around on the ankle, he completed 25 of 33 passes for 336 yards, five touchdowns, and no interceptions as the Packers beat the Bears.

From there, the Packers took off, winning five of six, including a 34-23 win in New Orleans on December 16 that secured another playoff spot. But another playoff spot isn't all the Packers were looking for. With a win over Pittsburgh the following week, Green Bay could wrap up its first NFC Central Division title since 1972.

It was there for the taking.

# THE GAME OF MY LIFE
## *By Ken Ruettgers*

It was the last game of the season and it was right around Christmas. We needed a win to win the division and to get home-field advantage in the playoffs. And it was one of those typical slugfests. The Packers were a very physical team at Lambeau Field and Pittsburgh, of course, was a very physical team. It was just one of those games that went back and forth for the whole game. It was really something.

Both teams really went back and forth, and right at the end, the Steelers drove down and [wide receiver] Yancey Thigpen was wide open in the end zone for the winning touchdown. I'm on the sideline and I remember thinking, "This is it, this is the whole season." [Quarterback] Neil O'Donnell went on play action and Thigpen was all alone and I went, "Oh man." Even from the sidelines watching it, it looked like it was in slow motion. And then he dropped the ball. I couldn't believe it.

The crowd and the atmosphere and the lights were on, and it was just an unbelievable scene. We took over [for the final few snaps] and there's Brett in the huddle and Robert Brooks is smiling. I remember a Beatles song came on the PA and Brooks started doing an air guitar. It was as electric as it had ever been in Lambeau since I'd been there in 11 years. I remember going into the locker room after the game, and I'm not a very expressive celebratory person, but it was a sweet moment. [Team president] Bob Harlan and I had invited Rush Limbaugh to the game, and we all celebrated with a cigar.

I remember we had hats made that said "NFC Central Division Champs." I'm glad we didn't have to burn them. It was a big step.

There were other great games like the Bears and Packers, but this one was the march toward the Super Bowl that had to be made. This started it all.

# GAME RESULT

Even today, no one really understands how Yancey Thigpen dropped a pass that could not have been placed in his arms any better. But it happened, and all the sheepish Thigpen, a Pro Bowl wide receiver, could say was "Merry Christmas, Green Bay."

The Packers could have won the division the easy way by getting some help from Tampa Bay in its season finale against Detroit.

In perhaps the ultimate irony, after 11 years with the Packers, Ken Ruettgers retired in the middle of the 1996 season, two months before the Packers won the Super Bowl. *Vernon J. Biever photo*

But the Buccaneers couldn't come through, losing to the Lions 37-10. That meant the Packers would have to take the division by force.

Green Bay led 14-10 at halftime and built its advantage to 21-13 after three quarters to set up the final dramatics.

Early in the fourth quarter, the Packers were driving for another score when Favre was clobbered by unblocked Steelers linebacker Kevin Greene. Favre, who had been smacked around all day by the swarming Steelers defense, was truly shaken up after this one. He stood up, then went to a knee and began spitting up blood. According to Ruettgers, the blood came from Favre biting his tongue during the hit, but it looked far more sinister than that. Whatever it was, it forced him out for the rest of the series, and the Packers had to settle for a Chris Jacke field goal and 24-13 lead.

Pittsburgh roared back and scored a touchdown, though it missed the crucial two-point conversion that could have made all the difference.

When the Packers couldn't move on their next possession, Pittsburgh quarterback Neil O'Donnell methodically drove the Steelers toward another score, a Steelers win and more heartache for the Packers.

But deep in Packers territory, the drive stalled, and on fourth down with 11 seconds to play, O'Donnell rolled and looked for Thigpen, who was wide open in the left corner of the end zone after he beat Packers cornerback Lenny McGill.

O'Donnell lofted the ball so gently and so effortlessly that the air came out of the stadium. It was over. And then Thigpen simply dropped the ball, setting off a huge celebration on the Packers' sideline.

The Packers won 24-19, though Pittsburgh, which would end up losing to Dallas in Super Bowl XXX, dominated much of the game. The Steelers had 398 total yards to Green Bay's 359 and held the edge in time of possession and first downs. Favre threw for 301 yards, and Robert Brooks had a huge game with 11 receptions for 137 yards.

# WHAT BECAME
# OF KEN RUETTGERS?

Players never know when the end is staring them in the face. Then again, maybe they do and they just don't want to acknowledge its existence. Whatever it was for Ken Ruettgers, that game would end up being the highlight of his career. And probably somewhere deep down, Ruettgers knew it.

The Packers went on to host a first-round playoff game and beat the Atlanta Falcons. Then they went to San Francisco and defied the odds one more time by shocking the powerful 49ers in Candlestick Park. That set up the NFC championship game in Dallas against a Cowboys team the Packers had lost to five straight times, including the last two years in the postseason.

And though the Packers led the Cowboys heading into the fourth quarter, two Dallas touchdowns sent the Packers home disappointed one more time.

The next step had been taken, but it still wasn't far enough.

But this was the end of the line for Ruettgers. Plagued for several years by a chronic knee problem, he told the Packers that he might not be able to play in 1996.

The Packers pleaded with him to rehab the knee in the off-season and try to play. But in the meantime, they drafted another USC left tackle, John Michels, with their first pick in the draft—just in case. They also signed a free agent, Bruce Wilkerson, who would pay massive dividends down the road.

The plan was for Ruettgers to play one more season and tutor the young Michels; then Ruettgers could slip away into pain-free retirement in 1997. But the plan never came together. Despite off-season surgery, a degenerative knee problem kept Ruettgers out of training camp and Michels was thrown into action immediately, even though he was far from ready.

Ruettgers started the season on the physically unable to perform list, and by the time he was ready to come off at midseason, he knew he was through. On November 20, he announced his retirement and could only watch longingly as the Packers rolled to the

Super Bowl title he had spent 11 long years striving for. Michels couldn't hold the job, and by the playoffs, Wilkerson had taken over.

As for Ruettgers, he swears there are no regrets.

"When you get off the plane and you can barely walk down the stairs, it just wasn't worth it," he said. "If it was doable, there might have been regrets. But I just couldn't do it."

Ruettgers segued seamlessly into life after football. He stayed in Green Bay with his wife, Sheryl, and three kids for the next year or so, coaching some football and figuring out what he wanted to do with the rest of his life. He went to work for a publishing company in Sisters, Oregon, and then formed a nonprofit company called "Games Over" to help former players transition to life after sports. He's also working toward his doctorate in philosophy.

"The Packers were such a big part of our lives," he said.

# CHAPTER 9

# MIKE DOUGLASS

*"Everything fell together."*

**Name:** Michael Reese Douglass
**Birthdate:** March 15, 1955
**Hometown:** Los Angeles, California
**Current residence:** Alpine, California
**Position:** Linebacker
**Height:** 6-foot-0
**Playing weight:** 210
**Years:** 1978-85
**College:** San Diego State
**Accomplishments:** Packers fifth-round draft pick in 1985 ...Played eight seasons in Green Bay and never missed a game...Named All-Pro in 1982 and 1983...Inducted into Packer Hall of Fame in 2003.
**The game:** Tampa Bay Buccaneers, October 2, 1983, at Lambeau Field

# THE LIFE OF MIKE DOUGLASS

He isn't sure where the nickname came from or even who gave it to him, but it fit perfectly: Mad Dog. He was a linebacker's linebacker, with the mentality and physical gifts that made him one of the most consistent players around.

At San Diego State, he was a terror, posting a stunning 193 tackles and a staggering 32 quarterback sacks in his final two seasons for the Aztecs. His size was an issue, however, because even in the late 1970s, 200-pound linebackers weren't exactly what NFL teams were looking for.

Nonetheless, the Packers made Douglass one of their fifth-round draft picks in 1978, a draft that also produced James Lofton and John Anderson. And almost immediately, Douglass proved that size is only an issue if you don't have the heart.

He saw considerable playing time as a rookie, then moved in as the starting right linebacker in 1979 and did not leave for the next eight seasons.

In 1981, he finished with a career-high 146 tackles, the second most in club history, and he was tabbed by the state media as the Packers' Defensive Player of the Year.

# THE SETTING

The Packers of 1983 were a study in schizophrenia that would have left any psychiatrist seeking treatment. They were fearsome on offense with weapons like Lofton, John Jefferson, Paul Coffman, Gerry Ellis, and quarterback Lynn Dickey.

These Packers rang up 6,172 total yards, the second best total in the NFL behind the San Diego Chargers, and they scored 429 points, a franchise record that stood for 13 years.

But the defense was simply horrendous. Whether it was the scheme or the execution or just the personnel, for every point the offense scored, the defense seemed to give back two. Eight times opponents gained more than 400 yards on the Packers' defense, and only twice all season did the defense hold teams under 20

**Mike Douglass.** *Vernon J. Biever photo*

points. For the season, the defense gave up a not-quite-believable 400 yards per game, the worst in the NFL and the most given up by any team in the league except for the 1981 Colts.

It was a team of wild fluctuations from game to game, from quarter to quarter and sometimes from play to play. Indeed, after that nearly perfect 55-14 win over Tampa Bay, the Packers went to Detroit the following week and were lathered by the Lions 38-14. The next week was the infamous and epic Monday night win over Washington followed by an overtime loss to Minnesota.

So it's not hard to understand how the Packers, who had an offense that was good enough to make the playoffs, staggered in with an 8-8 record and cost Bart Starr his job as head coach.

But even that season, with a defense that seemed practically helpless at time, Douglass did his fair share. He was named All-Pro that season after posting 127 tackles, forcing four fumbles, recovering four others, and returning two of them for touchdowns. He also had five and a half quarterback sacks.

# THE GAME OF MY LIFE
*By Mike Douglass*

It was against Tampa Bay in 1983 at home. I think it was the fact that it was during the time that Tampa was starting to get more recognition as a solid team and I remember they had beaten us badly in Tampa the year before [actually it was 1981 and Tampa won 37-3. Because of the strike in 1982, the two teams didn't play each other]. But this was the perfect day for football and the whole idea was to take them apart. I think we beat them 55-14, and it was a big win for us.

Defensively we were unstoppable. In that game I had a sack that turned into a fumble, and I ran it in for a 35-yard touchdown. Phillip Epps had an 80-yard punt return. The special teams did well, our defense was good, and the offense was dynamite. I think all the wide receivers caught at least four balls for us. It was just one of those days when everything fell together.

I remember that it had never been so loud in that stadium. I think the fans really kept up the juice and the excitement. They didn't give us a chance to come down. The crowd stayed in the game from the first whistle to the end. I remember walking through the parking lot before the game and it was crazy out there. I used to spend a lot of time in the parking lot after the game and after that one I knew that was the way football was supposed to be played. Our 12th man [the crowd] was definitely there.

Sometimes you think Packers fans are totally geared toward the game, but they were in tune. They were waiting for us to turn a corner. And those teams were always a lot of fun. We were just a man short here or there.

I watched almost every one of our offensive plays. I always wanted to see what was going on. James Lofton was my roommate,

**Mike Douglass (53), celebrating with cornerback Mark Lee, never missed a game in eight seasons with the Packers.** *Vernon J. Biever photo*

and John Jefferson I've known since San Diego State. These were guys you knew would be superstars, and you didn't want to miss a play.

# GAME RESULTS

The Buccaneers never had a chance in this one. It was the Packers' offense operating at peak efficiency and the Packers playing the way they would not play the rest of the season. The combination was devastating.

And it began the very first time the Packers touched the ball when Phillip Epps returned a Bucs punt 90 yards for the game's first score. It continued on Green Bay's next possession when Dickey connected with Jessie Clark on a 75-yard touchdown pass.

Then it really got interesting.

In a record-setting second-quarter barrage, the Packers scored 35 points on a Harlan Huckaby touchdown run followed by another Dickey touchdown toss to tight end Paul Coffman.

Then Douglass got in on the fun, sacking Tampa Bay quarterback Jack Thompson and forcing a fumble. He gathered up the loose ball and ran 35 yards for the touchdown. Then fellow linebacker John Anderson joined the festivities by hauling back an interception 27 yards for a score. The onslaught ended when Dickey found James Lofton for a 57-yard scoring strike. The dust had settled and the Packers led 49-7—and even this defense wasn't going to let a lead like that slip away.

The 49 first-half points set an NFL record first established by the Packers in 1967 and showcased just about every weapon this remarkable offense had to offer.

For the game the Packers rolled up 519 yards, including 355 through the air and 164 rushing. Meanwhile the defense—which would suffer its share of indignities as the season continued—shimmered, holding the Buccaneers to 293 total yards and forcing three turnovers.

It was a humiliating performance by the winless Bucs, who just three years earlier had been a game away from going to the

Super Bowl. And afterward, a seething coach John McKay was in no mood to face anyone, especially the media.

When a reporter had barely gotten a word out of his mouth to ask the first question, McKay erupted, saying "Get the hell away from me before I punch you in the mouth."

With that he wheeled and walked out. After all, there really was nothing to say.

# WHAT BECAME
# OF MIKE DOUGLASS?

In eight seasons, Mike Douglass never missed a game for the Green Bay Packers. Not once. Despite playing a jaw-rattling position like linebacker, and playing it at only 205 pounds, Douglass was the epitome of consistency, dedication and, perhaps, just a little good luck.

In those years, he led the Packers in tackles three times and even managed 11 interceptions. The capper came in his final season with the Packers in 1985 when he picked off a pass against Detroit and returned it 80 yards for a touchdown in a 26-23 win. But in his years, the Packers were always just a step behind no matter how much of an effort he put in. Still, he rarely showed any frustration.

To his credit, Douglass had always taken care of his body and knew that to handle the rigors of the NFL, he had to keep his body in top condition. He followed that creed from his earliest days in Green Bay and he still does it today.

He played for the Packers until 1985 and then played one season for the San Diego Chargers before deciding to give it up. From there, the next step was a logical one.

With his devotion to nutrition and keeping his body in perfect shape, he became a professional body builder and won dozens of competitions around the nation. But unlike many body builders who use steroids and other growth hormones to build mass, Douglass competed only in drug-free competitions.

Even today, nearly 20 years after leaving the game, he remains a physical specimen. He has opened a string of personal training and nutritional stores around California. His classes stress proper nutrition, and to that end most of his clubs have kitchens that hold cooking classes.

"I found the fountain of youth and I take it to the hilt," he said. "I don't even have any scars [from football] that make me remember playing. I definitely attribute that to how I live my life. It enabled me to recover after every game."

He remains close with many former teammates and he still has his fond memories of playing for the Packers, though he's one of the players who never enjoyed playing in the cold weather.

"I never adjusted to it," he said. "Forrest always felt that if you were going to play outside you should practice outside. Football is a mental state of mind and you adapt to the cold. And it was an advantage for us. You knew it could always get colder, and the other team starts thinking that it can get colder, too. So it did help us."

But in the long run, it didn't help all that much. In Douglass' eight seasons in Green Bay he saw two winning seasons and another four 8-8 seasons. He played in one playoff game, during the strike-shortened 1982 season.

Still, that didn't diminish his love of playing in Green Bay.

"I remember one day at practice this kid comes up to me for an autograph and I was baffled," he said. "We weren't doing that good, but he still wanted my autograph. I asked him why, and he said, 'Dude, you guys are the Green Bay Packers.' That put it in my mind that this was a unique organization. It was nice to be part of that whole development."

# CHAPTER 10

# RON KRAMER

*"It was a complete pleasure to beat the Bears."*

**Name:** Ronald John Kramer
**Birthdate:** June 24, 1935
**Hometown:** Girard, Kansas
**Current residence:** Fenton, Michigan
**Position:** Tight end
**Height:** 6-foot-3
**Playing weight:** 230
**Years:** 1957-64
**College:** University of Michigan
**Accomplishments:** Named All-Pro in 1962 and 1963...Named to Pro Bowl in 1962...Inducted into Packers Hall of Fame in 1975...All-America tight end at Michigan.
**The game:** Chicago Bears, September 29, 1957, at City Stadium

# THE LIFE OF RON KRAMER

There was almost nothing Ron Kramer couldn't do when it came to athletics. Born in Kansas, he moved to Detroit and eventually the University of Michigan, where he earned nine letters—three each in football, basketball, and track.

In basketball, he set Michigan's all-time scoring record with 1,124 points, a mark that stood until 1961. On the track team, he was a gifted high jumper. But it was in football where Kramer really flourished.

He was a superb receiver and a good punter and placekicker, and when the occasion called for it, he could run the ball as well. In three seasons with the Wolverines, Kramer caught 53 passes for 880 yards and nine scores, and he averaged 41 yards on his punts.

The Green Bay Packers, who were in the midst of a 12-year funk, knew they could use all the help they could get, so after taking Hornung, the Heisman Trophy winner from Notre Dame, with their bonus pick, they selected Kramer with the fourth pick in the 1957 draft. Kramer and Hornung would become infamous buddies and closer than brothers in many respects.

"I'd always get into his tree about being the MVP [of the college All-Star game]," Kramer said. "We still talk two or three times a week."

Kramer made an immediate impact on a Packers team desperate for any kind of playmakers, and he ended up catching 28 passes his rookie season before wrecking his knee in the final game of the season.

# THE SETTING

There was City Stadium and then there was City Stadium. The first park by that name was built behind the new East High School and served as the Packers' home from 1925 to 1956. By the end of that tenure, though, the old stadium was more pre-Colombian art than anything resembling a modern stadium of the day.

**Ron Kramer (88).** *Vernon J. Biever photo*

Knowing a new stadium was needed if the Packers wanted to stay viable, the residents of Green Bay passed a referendum in April of 1956, and the new City Stadium was built for the princely sum of $960,000. It seated 32,500 and featured the same bowl shape that it still has today despite a $295 million renovation.

In 1957, however, while the Packers remained wildly popular, their efforts on the field left much to be desired. The team hadn't won a championship since 1944, and three coaches—the legendary Curly Lambeau, Gene Ronzani and now Blackbourn— hadn't been able to re-create the magic. Indeed, in that period, Green Bay enjoyed just three winning seasons, and it would get worse before it got better.

Still, on a gorgeous fall afternoon, the Packers opened their new stadium. It was a day of pageantry and spectacle, featuring a parade as well as the appearances of vice president Richard Nixon, Miss America Marilyn Van Derbur, NFL commissioner Bert Bell, and biggest of all, actor James Arness, who played Marshall Matt Dillon in the popular TV show *Gunsmoke*.

And there was no better opponent for the Packers to face in the first game of their new digs than the hated Bears, who had clobbered the Packers twice the year before and whom the Packers had beaten just once in the previous four years.

# THE GAME OF MY LIFE
### *By Ron Kramer*

Everybody wants to put it in their minds that the most important games were championship games. I was drafted into Green Bay, into this little town, and they played in this stadium that seated 22,000 people. I went to the University of Michigan where we had 100,000 seats, so when I got here I said, "What's going on?" It sort of boggled my mind. I didn't know if I wanted to come up here. But they drafted me and they said you can make $20,000, and I said that's a hell of a deal to do what I wanted to do.

I went to Michigan because I wanted to be in business, and I decided through [Michigan coach] Fritz Crisler that I was going to try to do what Crisler told me. That's when I met Paul Hornung and we played in an All-Star game together and drove up to Green Bay in his 1948 or '49 Ford from Chicago.

So we get up here and we go through training camp with [coach] Lisle Blackbourn and the veterans suddenly decide they like us. Then it's our first game and it's the Chicago Bears, and everybody hated the Bears.

But there were 32,500 people there, and you would have thought we were playing for the world championship. I remember Richard Nixon was there and he was very gracious. He was everywhere, and it was like one of those times in my life where it was more important than a championship. It's what everybody dreams about. We beat the Bears, and that's what made that game important.

I remember everybody who played had a great game. It was just one of those days. It was opening day and it was a new stadium. We went on to win just two more games that season, but we beat the Bears. It was sort of neat.

It was such an absolute and complete pleasure to beat the Bears in the first game I ever played in. And you know what? I still don't care for them.

## GAME RESULT

It was as true then as it is now when it comes to the Packers-Bears rivalry. The Packers could lose every game in a season, but if they beat only the Bears, then the season wasn't a total loss. And the Bears felt exactly the same.

In 1957, the Packers were still searching for a way out of the abyss. Bart Starr and Forrest Gregg had shown up the year before, but Jim Taylor, Jerry Kramer, Ray Nitschke, Herb Adderley and Dave Robinson hadn't arrived yet. No one knew about an obscure line coach for the New York Giants named Vince Lombardi, and the concept of "Titletown" was unknown.

All these Packers had to fight for was right there in front of them. Win a game, build some momentum and hope it continued. But it wasn't easy, and it hadn't been for a long time.

And while the Packers were coming off a pallid 4-8 season, optimism burned bright because there was a chance to start fresh, and why not start it against the Bears?

It began, and ended for that matter, just like a typical Bears-Packers brawl. Chicago scored the first points in the new stadium when quarterback Ed Brown ran in for a touchdown from five yards out. But the Packers came right back to tie it when backup quarterback Babe Parilli, subbing for the injured Starr, threw 37 yards to Billy Howton.

The Bears went back up on a Brown-to-Harlon Hill touchdown pass, and the Packers answered back with a one-yard touchdown run by fullback Fred Cone to tie the game at halftime.

The only scoring in the third quarter was a 13-yard George Blanda field goal for the Bears, though the Packers had their opportunities to score, too. The rookie Paul Hornung, however, missed two long field goal attempts. That set up the drama of the fourth quarter.

After the Packers' defense stopped the Bears on fourth down, Parilli came right back and connected with Howton on a 41-yard pass to the Bears' eight. Two plays later, Parilli eluded a strong pass rush, faded to his right and found tight end Gary Knafelc on his knees deep in the end zone for the touchdown and a Packers lead.

Chicago still had eight minutes to rally, but one drive ended when Bobby Dillon intercepted a Brown pass, and Larry Lauer later recovered a fumbled punt. The Packers had pulled off the upset, opening their new stadium by beating the only team that ever really mattered.

It was, of course, the perfect start to what would be a great season, except that it wasn't. The next week, in the second game at the new stadium, Green Bay lost to Detroit.

The Packers lost the only other game they played at the new stadium that year, too—to the New York Giants—and finished with another dismal record of 3-9. Blackbourn resigned after that season, and assistant coach Ray "Scooter" McLean took over. He lasted one season after the Packers limped in with a 1-10-1 record in 1958. That's when the Packers turned to the obscure line coach from the New York Giants.

It was 1965 when the Packers organization decided to rename the stadium in honor of the team founder and perhaps the most seminal figure in its development—Curly Lambeau. Since then, Lambeau Field has become one of the most recognized sports venues in the world.

But it wasn't a decision that thrilled everyone. Vince Lombardi, who had brought the Packers back from oblivion in 1959, couldn't understand why Lambeau got the honor when it was clear Lombardi had done much of the most recent work. Indeed, 1965 would mark the year the Packers won their first of three straight NFL titles, and those would be tacked on to the two Lombardi had already won.

But he didn't want to make a massive issue of the move and was placated when the Packers decided to rename Highland Avenue, which ran next to the stadium, "Lombardi Avenue."

# WHAT BECAME OF RON KRAMER?

To this day, Ron Kramer has no regrets about the decision he made to leave the Packers after the 1964 season. In truth, there was really no decision to make.

"People got the impression that Vince got rid of me, and he didn't," Kramer said. "I told him, 'I don't want to leave you because you're the best coach I've ever been around.' I still love Green Bay, but family came first. Family is much more important."

Kramer was still at the height of his career in 1964. He had missed the 1958 season due to military obligations, but when he returned in 1959, he became an integral part of the Packers' building juggernaut. From 1961 to 1964, he caught 138 passes and scored 15 touchdowns and was named All-Pro in 1962 and 1963. He was also part of two NFL championship teams in 1961 and 1962.

He could see as well as anyone that the Packers were still a powerhouse in 1964 and he wanted to be a part of it. But circumstances changed dramatically prior to the 1965 season when Kramer's seven-year-old son Kurt lost an eye playing with a pair of scissors. The family was living in Detroit at the time and would not move to Green Bay under those circumstances, so Kramer did the only thing he felt he could do—he joined them. Kramer played out his option with the Packers and signed with the hometown Detroit Lions.

But he didn't leave without making sure the tight end position was in good hands.

"I told Vince that I would not leave Green Bay without teaching everything I know to [rookie] Marv Fleming," he said. "I said that Marv Fleming will know everything about playing tight end here."

Kramer played three years for the Lions with something less than terrific results. He caught 59 passes and scored one touchdown in that time, but while the Packers were winning three more championships, the Lions won a grand total of 15 games.

"I could have had five championships," he says now. "But I don't regret anything."

Kramer retired after the 1967 season and dabbled in many business ventures, some successful and some not. He was in the steel business for a while, and in 1981 he went bankrupt and lost seven million dollars. Then he went into the advertising and public relations business, where he's been ever since. He has been president of Ron Kramer Industries for the past 23 years, and his life continues to revolve around football in general and the Packers in particular.

He rarely misses a chance to meet up with his old friends and recall the good old days when they were all part of what was the best team in pro football. He may not raise hell like he did in his youth with his running buddy Hornung, but none of them ever miss a chance to remember what it used to be like.

"I'll never forget playing for the Packers," said Kramer, who also owns 130 acres of land south of Flint, Michigan. "Those were some of the best days of my life." Kramer, who remained a Packers fan long after leaving football, died September 11, 2010 at his home in Fenton, Michigan. He was 75.

# CHAPTER 11

# SANTANA DOTSON

*"It was like a lion walking through a slaughterhouse."*

**Name:** Santana Dotson
**Birthdate:** December 19, 1969
**Hometown:** New Orleans, Louisiana
**Current residence:** Houston, Texas
**Position:** Defensive tackle
**Height:** 6-foot-5
**Playing weight:** 285
**Years:** 1996-2001
**College:** Baylor University
**Accomplishments:** Signed as an unrestricted free agent with the Packers in 1996...Began his pro career with the Tampa Bay Buccaneers where he was NFL Defensive Rookie of the Year in 1992...Played in 121 consecutive games from 1992-99.
**The game:** San Francisco 49ers, January 4, 1997, at Lambeau Field

# THE LIFE OF SANTANA DOTSON

Named after the great Native American chief, the name Santana means "With unity there's strength" and it is a creed that has always been a part of the essential makeup of Santana Dotson.

He came from good stock; that was a given, since his dad was a former NFL lineman in his own right—Alphonse Dotson, who was a second-round draft pick of the Packers in 1965 out of Grambling but who chose to play for Kansas City of the rival AFL instead. So young Santana had the bloodlines, but he also knew there were no guarantees of anything in the game. And he found he had to prove himself everywhere he went.

He was born in New Orleans. The family moved to Houston when he was a kid, and he became a three-year star football player at Jack Yates High School. A prep All-American, he decided to attend Baylor University, where he continued his steady development. He was a three-year starter for the Bears as well as a three-time All-Southwest Conference pick. As a senior, he was an All-American, a finalist for both the Outland and Lombardi trophies, and the conference Defensive Player of the Year.

He finished his college career with 193 tackles and 18 sacks, and he was a fifth-round draft pick of the Tampa Bay Buccaneers in 1992.

As a rookie, he led the Bucs in quarterback sacks with 10, and he added 71 tackles and earned NFL Defensive Rookie of the Year honors. The sky, it appeared, was the limit for Dotson.

But as Dotson discovered, the things that are worth having are often the things that are the toughest to get and usually require the longest road to find.

He learned that more quickly than he ever figured he would in Tampa Bay. One year, he was the next great defensive lineman on a team still trying to find its foothold. The next year the rumors began, in back halls and in hushed tones at first, that Dotson didn't play hard every down. Then they grew a little louder, that he was lazy, that he had a bad attitude, that he thought he was better than the talent around him.

Santana Dotson. *Harry How/Getty Images*

Rumors like that can be a disaster for any player, especially one still trying to prove himself. The rumors hurt and confused Dotson, because those were sins he had never, ever been accused of before. Not playing every down? Please. Lazy? Me? He was shocked and angry and, in a kind of self-fulfilling prophecy, his play did start to trail off and the Bucs continued to struggle.

After four years in Tampa, it seemed obvious he couldn't stay. The atmosphere was poisonous and he had worn out his welcome. Despite racking up 23 quarterback sacks and 195 tackles in four seasons, he jumped at an offer to sign with the Packers in 1996.

"I have to give credit to [Packers general manager] Ron Wolf," Dotson said. "I always had a belief in myself that I could do the job. What came from Tampa about me not playing every down and not holding up the whole season wasn't true. But as soon as I stepped in the building in Green Bay, they made it clear I was their guy. They said that if I went there, I was their guy and they felt I was the missing piece on the defense. I had a chance to stay in the same division [as Tampa Bay] and the biggest suitors were Minnesota and Green Bay. And when I watched the Packers lose the NFC championship the year before, I knew they could use my services. There was never any doubt from the Packers."

# THE SETTING

The Packers had barely returned to their locker room in Texas Stadium after losing the 1995 NFC title game to the Dallas Cowboys when the talk already turned to the next season.

The Packers knew they were close. The loss to the Cowboys, in which Green Bay had dominated for three quarters before collapsing in the final 12 minutes, proved that they were on the verge of greatness. And on the plane ride home, coach Mike Holmgren pleaded with his guys not to forget how this loss felt and do something about it.

They did. With the addition of Dotson and safety Eugene Robinson, the defense was set. With a year's maturity in Brett Favre, the offense was in good hands. There was also the practically ignored signing of a former Heisman Trophy winner who was a too-small wide receiver who returned kicks. He was looking for a new opportunity in Green Bay—his name was Desmond Howard.

So the pieces were clearly in place, and when *Sports Illustrated* announced in August that the Packers would play the Chiefs in Super Bowl XXXI in New Orleans, the expectations tripled.

"It was hard to be picked right out of the blocks like that," Dotson said. "But I knew on paper the defense was going to be good. The only thing that was missing was the lack of a bad guy, a rebel, somebody who wasn't going to take anything from anybody."

But the Packers found some of those guys too. Dotson recalled a game in the Metrodome where the Vikings hit Favre out of bounds.

"We looked at each other and said, 'You know we have to answer that,'" Dotson said. "So on the next series [linebacker] Wayne Simmons took [Vikings running back] Amp Lee and just twirled him around. That's how we answered, and from there on we outhit everybody we played."

But there was still that hurdle to overcome. Despite a 13-3 record and domination of the NFC Central, the Packers really hadn't proven anything. They needed to reach the Super Bowl and win it. But first, the 49ers stood in their way.

# THE GAME OF MY LIFE
### *By Santana Dotson*

The biggest thing that sticks in my mind is leaving my situation in Tampa and going to Green Bay. Everybody will always talk about the offense [during the 1996 season] and how formidable they were. But the thing that sticks out in my mind was how strong the defense was. That sticks out to me as being a part of the best defensive line I've ever seen. Gilbert Brown, Reggie White, Sean Jones, those were great players and we loved looking at the offensive linemen and seeing the looks on their faces every play as they tried to decide who they were going to double-team. It was like a lion walking through a slaughterhouse. You knew somebody was going to eat.

We were the kind of defense that year that we felt if somebody scored more than 17 points on us, it was a problem. We took a lot of pride in that. What a lot of people didn't know was that it was 22 guys who were in that room together and who enjoyed being around each other. If we were done with practice at three, we stuck around until four-thirty or five. We genuinely enjoyed the game and being around each other.

We knew that whole season that we could be something special, but we also knew we hadn't really proven anything until we beat the teams we had to beat in the playoffs and got to the Super Bowl. I remember that besides the Super Bowl that year, I didn't sleep the night before the game with San Fran. I recall so much of the hoopla from that game. We had beaten them earlier in the season at home, and it's very difficult to beat Super Bowl-caliber teams.

That morning I remember it was 35 degrees and rainy, and it was the coldest game I'd ever played at Lambeau. I remember I just couldn't get warm. But it was cold and so wet they turned off the seat warmers on the bench because they didn't want anybody to get shocked. And we thought, "Yeah, we're cold, but the other team is even colder," and we used that to our advantage. I remember [49ers wide receiver] Jerry Rice went in at halftime and changed his whole uniform and he came out all nice and clean. We made a point on the first play of the second half to get him dirty again. And on that first play I looked up and there was [cornerback] Craig Newsome and [linebacker] Wayne Simmons knocking him to the ground just to make sure he was muddy again.

It was the mud bowl, and to me it was perfect Packers weather. You had the sushi eaters from California with their nice suits and they had to come to Lambeau Field. It was perfect weather for us because you had to peel yourself out of your uniform afterward.

We were a defense that took it one quarter at a time, and we talked about being dominant all the time. We'd say how we had to win one quarter and then this half and then this game and we're

In 1996, tackle Santana Dotson proved to be the final piece in the NFL's most dominant defense. *Brian Bahr/Getty Images*

going to do the things we're supposed to do. We talked each week about every game being a stepping stone, and that 49ers game was a huge one.

# GAME RESULT

If it had been five degrees colder, perhaps 15 inches of snow would have fallen on this miserable January day. Instead, a cold, miserable, unforgiving rain pounded down, soaking everything and everyone.

It was great.

The Packers had earned home field advantage and planned to take full advantage of it against a 49ers team that still harbored serious doubts about how good the Packers really were. Several 49ers had been quoted that week saying that the Packers had proven nothing to anyone until they won it all. And, in truth, the Packers couldn't argue the point.

But in front of a packed house at Lambeau Field, the Packers made believers even of the 49ers.

Desmond Howard brought a punt back 71 yards for the first touchdown, and the next time he touched the ball, he returned a punt 46 yards to the 49ers' seven-yard line, setting up a Favre-to-Andre Rison touchdown. An Edgar Bennett touchdown run made it 21-0 before San Francisco cut that lead to 21-7 by halftime.

After a mix-up on the opening kickoff of the second half that resulted in a fumble, the 49ers closed to 21-14 on an Elvis Grbac touchdown run. That's when the Packers found the extra gear that champions always discover.

Favre took the Packers on a 72-yard drive, throwing the ball only twice in a 12-play march, and the Packers scored a touchdown to recapture the momentum. Later in the fourth quarter, after a 49ers turnover, Bennett scored again and the Packers had the decisive 35-14 win.

Green Bay gained just 210 total yards in the slop, but that's all that was needed. Favre threw for just 79 yards, and the ground game came up big with 139 yards between Bennett and Dorsey Levens.

The next step had been accomplished.

# WHAT BECAME
# OF SANTANA DOTSON?

Over and above everything else, football is a business, and no one knew that better than Santana Dotson. The Packers had given him another chance after Tampa Bay. They had ignored the rumors and made their own decisions, and the result was that Dotson helped the Packers to two straight Super Bowls, two division titles and five trips to the playoffs. But times change, as they always must.

In 1999, he missed his first game ever with an injury, and in 2000 he suffered a torn quadriceps muscle. In 2001 a serious neck injury early in the season made him ineffective. The years were catching up to him.

Because of the injuries and the Packers' unwillingness to pay the unrestricted free agent what he wanted, the Packers released Dotson in July 2002. The consummate team player who had seen his career reborn in Green Bay was out of work, though not for long. He signed with the Washington Redskins, but in training camp he tore his Achilles tendon.

"The first nine years of my career I didn't miss a game, and then all this started happening," he said. "But my grandmother put it best. She said, 'The game has been good to you. You're 34 and your body's telling you something.'"

So, reluctantly, Dotson retired.

"You want to do it forever, but you can't," he said. "I miss it, but I don't miss Monday mornings and the pain that came with it."

He remains among the Packers' all-time leaders in sacks with 26, and he finished with 248 tackles. But Dotson's contributions went far beyond the statistics. He was the steadying force and the versatile athlete the Packers needed to solidify the defensive line.

"I just made a point to show my teammates what I could do," he said.

Dotson lives in Houston with his family and spends much of his time running his charitable Santana Dotson Foundation that also has a chapter in Milwaukee. He's trying to take time to expand the foundation regionally and, he hopes, nationally.

Dotson also stays busy in real estate ventures and coaching his nephew, Alonzo Dotson, who played football at Oklahoma.

"Things have been good," he said. "My son [Khari] is 11 and my daughters are 10 and six. My boy loves Lambeau Field and he misses it. I have season tickets to the Houston Texans, but he'd much rather sit on the couch and watch."

# CHAPTER 12

# JOHN BROCKINGTON

*"I could do no wrong."*

**Name:** John Stanley Brockington
**Birthdate:** September 7, 1948
**Hometown:** Brooklyn, New York
**Current residence:** San Diego, California
**Position:** Running back
**Height:** 6-foot-1
**Playing weight:** 230
**Years:** 1971-77
**College:** Ohio State
**Accomplishments:** All-Pro in 1971 and 1973...First-team All-NFC in 1972...Named to Pro Bowl in 1971, 1972 and 1973...NFC Rookie of the Year in 1971...Inducted into Packers Hall of Fame in 1984.
**The games:** November 1, 1971, against the Detroit Lions at Milwaukee County Stadium; November 7, 1971, against the Chicago Bears at Soldier Field; November 14, 1971, against the Minnesota Vikings at Metropolitan Stadium

# THE LIFE OF JOHN BROCKINGTON

From New York City, John Brockington was something to see for the fans of Ohio State football. He had the size of a fullback but the moves and speed and agility of a halfback. He was one of those classic players who would just as soon gain yardage by running over you than running around you. And he found himself part of some of the best college football teams in history.

"[Ohio State coach] Woody Hayes was so positive," Brockington said. "He'd say, 'This is how you'll execute,' and we did. In three years on the varsity, we never went into a game thinking somebody was better than we were. We never went into a game thinking we were going to lose. That's a hell of a mind-set."

And in three seasons, from 1968-70, few were better than the Buckeyes. Ohio State won the national title in 1968, finished fourth nationally in 1969 with an 8-1 record and won a disputed national title in 1970 after going through the regular season 9-0 before losing to Stanford in the Rose Bowl. Brockington pounded his way to 1,142 yards and 17 touchdowns that season and was named one of four Ohio State All-Americans.

The senior class of 1970, which featured Brockington, line-backer Jim Stillwagon and defensive back Mike Sensibaugh, finished their three-year varsity careers with a 27-2 record, three Big Ten titles and two national championships.

In the 1971 NFL draft, the Packers had the ninth pick over-all and knew they needed to overhaul their rushing attack that was beginning to break down. With first-year coach Dan Devine, who favored the more conservative running attack anyway, Brockington was the ideal choice.

# THE SETTING

It was a shock in more ways than one for Brockington as he went from the supremely confident, almost arrogant, world of Ohio State to the NFL. In Columbus, Brockington had been told,

**John Brockington.** *Vernon J. Biever photo*

and had come to believe it with his entire being, that no one was better. But in Green Bay, the mood shifted dramatically.

"I get to the pros and Dan says, 'They're quicker than you are and they're faster than you are,'" he said. "He was the most mealy-mouthed coach I'd ever had. He was always criticizing things."

Packers fans found it hard to believe that they were just four years removed from the iconic and mourned Vince Lombardi, who could make his players fly through a wall and smile while doing it.

But Devine was a far different animal. Quiet and oh-so-conservative, Devine replaced Phil Bengtson, a Lombardi lieutenant, after Bengtson decided three years was enough trying to outrun a shadow.

Bengtson's three years had produced just one winning season, and Devine was brought in from the University of Missouri to instill a new attitude that had no particular ties to the Green Bay Packers of the previous decade.

He brought in a run-the-ball-first mentality and emphasized defense. He slowly started to phase out all the Packers from the previous era, including quarterback Bart Starr, in favor of the young, smart Scott Hunter. He also slipped youngster Jim Carter in at middle linebacker to replace legendary Ray Nitschke, and Brockington stepped in as the featured runner.

A new era had begun, whether anyone wanted it to or not.

# THE GAME OF MY LIFE
### By John Brockington

My game was really three games. Monday night in Milwaukee against the Lions and against the Bears and Vikings. Those games are what put me on the path to my first 1,000-yard year. They really didn't run me that much in 1971 [216 carries in 14 games], but I remember I really got into a groove. I had my first 100-yard game against the Bengals [on October 3], and that's when I said, "OK, now I'm getting warmed up."

But then came the Detroit game on Monday night in the rain. It was awful. It was rainy and nasty. It was so wet and slushy I wondered what kind of game we'd have. The first play was a draw play and there was such a big hole that I thought, "Man, I could've gotten a big one," but I was tripped up in the hole.

But we ran 37 Slant, off-tackle to the right, all night. That was the bread and butter play for my career. It seemed every time I got the ball, there was a hole. I had a really big night for the amount of carries I had.

The Bears game was next. I remember the night before the game [quarterback] Scott Hunter, [cornerback] Charlie Hall and I went out to dinner in downtown Chicago. It was this overblown Chicago restaurant and there was a beefeater at the door and he'd always say, "Welcome, senator." He called everybody "senator." This restaurant had a great bar and this two-pound steak, and after we were done I thought we wouldn't be worth a damn the next day.

**John Brockington's three-game outburst against Detroit, Chicago, and Minnesota established him as one of the NFL's top young running backs.**
*Vernon J. Biever photo*

But it was a big rival for us, and I had a great game. Everything I touched, it worked. I was running through some serious holes. One play, it was like third down and 19 and we called a draw play. I went through the hole, cut to the right and got like 20 yards. On the closing drive [to win the game] it was pitch right, pitch left, and I was getting yards. I said, "This is easy."

Then came the Vikings game. The first time we played them that season [a 24-13 loss in Green Bay] I couldn't get to the hole. The Vikings defense was super fast. But by the second game, I was more mature and things started slowing down in my mind. I'd get 10 yards, five yards a carry. It was like I was greased.

Those games were so significant to me because they put me on the track for 1,000 yards. I was in a serious zone for those three games. I could do no wrong. That's when the season really got fun.

I remember once listening to this speech from the National University Center for Peak Performance and they talked about all these athletes and when they're trying to get to their peak performance. They talked about being in a zone and it's an amazing thing. Everything slows down. You're running and you can do no wrong. I can see things. I can cut back. When you're like that you just want the ball. But I never had a string of games like that again.

# GAME RESULTS

When John Brockington entered his three-game "zone," the Packers were effectively going nowhere in a hurry. Through six games, Green Bay was sputtering along with a 2-4 record that had included wins over two of the AFC's weakest entrants—Denver and Cincinnati—and an ignominious 42-40 opening-day loss to the Giants in which Devine had his leg broken after a sideline collision.

Into County Stadium came the Detroit Lions for a Monday night game that had to be played in a constant, dreary downpour. But a national audience got to see the new, young back out of Ohio State who was going to make the Packers relevant again.

Knowing the weather wasn't going to cooperate, Devine was at his conservative best, allowing Hunter to throw just five passes all night. The bulk of the offense would fall to Brockington, and he came through superbly.

He rushed only 16 times, but he gained 111 yards in a game that ended up 14-14. In fact, it was 14-14 at halftime thanks to a last-second 49-yard Greg Landry-to-Charley Sanders touchdown pass. The Packers' two scores came on short runs by Dave Hampton and Hunter.

Green Bay had opportunities in the second half, but 36-year-old field goal kicker Lou Michaels missed from 39 and 44 yards in the muck. In the end, the Packers gained just 218 total yards, all on the ground, while the Lions managed just 290 yards. But for the Packers, at least, a tie wasn't a loss. And the Lions came away impressed with Brockington.

"I'll tell you," All-Pro linebacker Mike Lucci said afterward. "The Packers didn't waste their first draft pick."

The following Sunday at Soldier Field, Brockington was even better. He plowed over the Bears for 142 yards on 30 carries and scored on a seven-yard run. His 30 carries were just two shy of the club record set in 1967 by Jim Grabowski.

Green Bay led the game 14-0 at halftime before the Bears tied it late in the fourth quarter. But on the kickoff, Hampton, who had already fumbled four times in the game, brought the kick back 62 yards to the Bears' 39. That's when Brockington took over, carrying six straight times down to the Chicago 15. Michaels then connected on a 22-yard field goal with 59 seconds left to win the game, 17-14.

The last game in his remarkable journey came in Minneapolis against the powerful Vikings. And while the Packers dominated nearly every aspect of the game, they also made a ton of mistakes and ended up losing 3-0.

Brockington pounded out 149 yards on 23 carries, which may have been the best accomplishment of the three 100-yard games, since the Vikings had easily the toughest defense in the NFC. The Packers ended up with 245 rushing yards, an unheard-of total against the Vikings. The defense also held the Vikings to five first downs and 87 total yards.

Unfortunately for the Packers, they also committed four turnovers, including a Donny Anderson fumble deep in Minnesota territory, two missed field goals by Michaels and failing on two shots from the Vikings' one.

The decisive play came with eight minutes left when, again deep in Minnesota territory, Hunter decided against the safe run and tried to hit tight end Rich McGeorge for a touchdown. The ball was intercepted by Charlie West and brought back to mid-field. Eventually Fred Cox kicked a 25-yard field goal that ended up being the final score.

It was a frustrated and angry Packers locker room afterward, and Brockington said it best: "God must not dig somebody on this team."

Brockington's three-game total was 402 yards and he finished the season with 1,105 yards, earning him NFC Rookie of the Year honors. But the Packers' fortunes weren't any brighter as they finished 4-8-2, their worst mark since 1958.

# WHAT BECAME
# OF JOHN BROCKINGTON?

There was no reason to believe 1972 would be any better, but in the bizarre world of the NFL, nothing is ever as it seems. The Packers caught lightning in a bottle, got steady play from Hunter, superb seasons from rookies Willie Buchanon and Chester Marcol, and used the tandem of Brockington and MacArthur Lane in the backfield to dominate teams.

With Brockington rushing for 1,027 yards and Lane adding another 821 yards, the Packers won the NFC Central Division with a 10-4 record. In the playoffs, though, the Washington Redskins employed a five-man front to shut down the Packers' running game and made them throw. The Packers never did.

Brockington was held to nine yards on 13 carries, and Washington prevailed 16-3. That result still rankles Brockington.

"We'd run into that five-man front two weeks earlier and [offensive coordinator] Bart Starr said, 'If they do that again, run two backs out of the backfield and throw it.' But Dan never did it because he decided he wanted to coach that day. Nobody could believe we let that happen. I ran into [Redskins linebacker] Chris Hanburger a few weeks later and he said, 'Why didn't you guys throw the ball? We didn't expect to stay in that defense all day.'"

Brockington didn't know it at the time, but that would be his first and last taste of the playoffs. He ran for another 1,144 yards in 1973, but the Packers fell back to 5-7-2. In 1974, he managed just 883 yards and Green Bay was just 6-8, and that cost Devine his job.

Starr took over and made changes of his own, including trading Lane to Kansas City and reducing Brockington's role in the offense. The former 1,000-yard rusher squeezed out just 434 yards in 1975, and Green Bay sank to 4-10. Brockington was clashing with new offensive coordinator Paul Roach, and he decided a change of scenery was needed. He asked for a trade in 1977 and the Packers complied, dealing him to Kansas City.

He finished out the 1977 season with the Chiefs, gaining 161 yards and finishing his pro career with 5,185 yards and 30 touchdowns. By 1978, he was out of football.

Immediately after leaving football, he got into the financial services business in San Diego and he's been there ever since.

# CHAPTER 13

# JAMES LOFTON

*"We felt we had something good."*

**Name:** James David Lofton
**Birthdate:** July 5, 1956
**Hometown:** Los Angeles, California
**Current residence:** San Diego, California
**Position:** Wide receiver
**Height:** 6-foot-3
**Playing weight:** 192
**Years:** 1978-86
**College:** Stanford University
**Accomplishments:** Inducted into Pro Football Hall of Fame in 2003…Named to eight Pro Bowls, seven with the Packers, including six in a row in Green Bay from 1980-85…Named All-Pro four times…Named All-NFC three times…Inducted into Packers Hall of Fame in 1999.
**The game:** New York Giants, September 20, 1982, at The Meadowlands

# THE LIFE OF JAMES LOFTON

It almost seems James Lofton was born to be an NFL wide receiver the way William Shakespeare was born to be a writer. Blessed with ideal size, great speed, and the kind of languid athleticism that made it look like he was hardly even trying sometimes, Lofton set the standard for what would become the prototypical pro wide receiver that we see today. But in the 1970s, he was considered something extraordinary.

Born in Fort Ord, California, he was a standout athlete at Los Angeles' Washington High School. He took that ability to Stanford University and blossomed into one of the nation's best college receivers. While at Stanford, he caught 68 passes for 1,216 yards and he set a single-season NCAA record in 1977 with 12 touchdown receptions. But he was more than a football star as he earned All-America honors four straight years in the long jump. Perhaps most important of all, Lofton earned his bachelor's degree in industrial engineering.

But as well rounded as Lofton already was coming out of college, everyone knew his future was in football. Certainly the Green Bay Packers knew it, and they made him their first of two first-round draft picks in 1978, the sixth pick overall. And immediately he made that pick pay off.

In 1977, the Packers' top receiver was fullback Barty Smith, who caught just 37 passes. With Lofton, the Packers could actually become a wide receiver-oriented offense again and caught 46 passes, averaged nearly 18 yards a catch and caught six of the 11 touchdown passes Packers quarterbacks managed to throw that season. That would be the last season (except for the strike-shortened 1982 season) that Lofton would catch fewer than 50 passes for the Packers.

In 1983 and 1984, he led the NFL in receptions with 58 and 62 catches, respectively, and he became perhaps the NFL's most dangerous deep threat.

**James Lofton.** *Vernon J. Biever photo*

# THE SETTING

The NFL owners and the players, quite simply, were in the midst of a civil war as the 1982 season began.

The threat of a strike had loomed for a while, but as with most unsavory topics, nobody really wanted to deal with the reality of the situation until it was too late. The issues were as simple, and as complicated, as free agency and salaries. The NFL had fought the concept of one player leaving his team to join another for a long time. But times were changing, and NFL players had seen how successful baseball players had been in their quest for free agency.

So the topic finally bubbled to the surface in 1982, and when the current NFL Players Association contract ran out and no agreement was reached, a strike date was set. Players knew what the future held, and it wasn't pretty.

Remember, this wasn't the NFL of today, the NFL that was made possible in a large part by the walkout that occurred in 1982. Players then did not make millions of dollars in signing bonuses that could be deferred, if necessary, forever. This was a strictly salary business, and if you didn't play, you didn't get paid.

But the cause was important enough that most of the players were solid behind the union and walked out willingly when the time came. And this was an especially contentious strike, with charges and countercharges being leveled by both management and players alike.

For the Packers, this was a critical time. The pieces seemed to be in place for this team to do some damage in the NFC Central Division. The offense had found its stride and was as dangerous as any in football. The defense could do the job, but it was going to be the offense that led this team.

Lofton knew, like players on so many other teams knew, that solidarity was key to being successful once the strike ended. Players needed to hang together, stay in town, practice together and support each other, because if they didn't, the results could be disastrous.

Once the strike was called, the Packers did indeed stay together.

"I remember we got back on our charter plane and got back to Green Bay in the wee hours of the morning," Lofton said. "We met the next day in a local park and we talked as a team. I remembered we practiced at a high school in DePere and the media came out a little at the beginning. Mike Douglass and I officiated Pop Warner football games and other guys were trying to do a lot of things just to stay active."

But no one knew how long the strike would last, and with no paychecks coming in, it was a tough time, especially for younger players who had almost nothing.

"I'm sure there were some landlords who were lenient with the rents," Lofton said.

Finally, after 57 days, an agreement was reached. The last game had been played September 21 and the walkout lasted until November 16. In the interim, seven games had been lost and could not be made up. As it was, the Super Bowl had to be pushed back to January 30 and the divisions had to be scrapped in favor of a "tournament" in which eight teams from each conference would earn playoff berths.

The Packers finished third with a solid 5-3-1 record and hosted the No. 6 St. Louis Cardinals. In Green Bay's first playoff game since 1972 and its first at home since 1967, the Packers blasted St. Louis 41-6 before going to Dallas and losing to the Cowboys, 37-26. Green Bay's next playoff game would not come for another 10 years.

# THE GAME OF MY LIFE
### By James Lofton

The reasons I believe this game was significant are twofold — No. 1, I was on the executive committee of the NFL Players Association and I knew that following the game we'd go on strike. We'd started off with a win the very first week of the regular season, and I knew that since we were going to go on strike, one of the most important things to keep our team together was to win this game. If you don't win then everybody drops their heads for a couple of days and they take off for different parts of the country. We were able to win, and qualifying for the playoffs was important.

We had beaten the Rams in a comeback win in Milwaukee and then we turned around and beat the Giants 27-19. I had a couple of big plays—a reverse and a long catch. But it was a game we felt like we could give away. It was Monday night. It was the national stage. With so much fooling around between the players and owners, the game took on a bigger magnitude.

We had had so many meetings leading up to the strike, and I tried to keep the guys abreast of the negotiations and the offers. It was a real taxing time for me personally. When you're trying to get 50 guys in a consensus, it's tough. They had a strike fund set up, but in 1982, the average salary was $50,000, so most guys would come back after the strike without money.

I remember we were pretty well united as a team. The guys were behind me. I had great support. At the time we were trying to get a system in place, we were trying to get free agency, a wage scale. But the owners were saying, "We're never going to allow you to get free agency; we'll never let you be free."

So the game was in New York, and it was the final game before the strike deadline. I think the strike actually started while the game was still being played, because it was a midnight deadline. The other significant thing about the game was that the lights went out twice. You think about the unions who were supporting the players, and you always wonder if they had something to do with it. But there were 68,000 fans there, and I don't recall them being adversarial toward us.

I really think that if we had lost that game the guys would have splintered, so we talked about it before the game and said how we needed to win. We felt we had something good. I think if we had 16 games that season we would have 11. That's how good we thought we were.

I remember once the strike ended, it was the best feeling to be back on the field. And we hadn't even played in Green Bay yet. We

James Lofton (80) was an integral part of one of the most powerful and innovative offenses the NFL had ever seen. *Vernon J. Biever photo*

started the season in Milwaukee and then went to New York and our next game [after the strike ended] was in Milwaukee against the Vikings. Then we went to New York to play the Jets. Playing was a gift we were allowed to have for a short period, and then to have it taken away from us for almost half the season. But we stayed together.

# GAME RESULT

Both the New York Giants and Green Bay Packers understood the significance of what was about to occur that night. It was the last game before a strike—potentially debilitating—was about to be called. It could last a week, it could last a month, or it could last the entire season. No one really knew.

But this much every player did know—they had to show solidarity to the cause, and while 62,000 or so fans hooted from the stands, players from both teams went to midfield prior to the game and shook hands in a show of strength that the owners surely didn't want to see.

The game itself was important, as Lofton said. But in other ways, it was just an afterthought, an event that had to be completed only because it was on the schedule. More than a few players were already thinking about the next day, and the day after that. Still, if it was going to be played, it might as well be played the best way possible.

The Giants took command early and led 19-7 late in the third quarter when Lofton made the play that turned the game around. With 1:37 left in the third quarter, Lofton took an end-around hand off from Lynn Dickey and went practically untouched for an 83-yard touchdown. That changed the momentum completely.

In the fourth quarter, Eddie Lee Ivery ran for an 11-yard touchdown and Jan Stenerud kicked field goals of 37 and 22 yards as Green Bay rolled to the 27-19 win.

Dickey completed 13 of 20 passes for 203 yards, and Lofton finished with four receptions for 101 yards. Overall the Packers outgained New York 363 total yards to 267. But for many the result was lost in the fact that the next day they would be on strike. And while they didn't know it then, the strike would last nearly two months.

# WHAT BECAME OF JAMES LOFTON?

The mid-1980s proved to be turbulent years both on and off the field for the Packers. As their fortunes continued to flounder in the standings, a series of brutal public relations disasters off the field continued to sully the reputation of one of pro sports' most storied franchises.

In 1986, coach Forrest Gregg, now in his third season, decided to cut loose some popular veteran players like tight end Paul Coffman, defensive end Mike Butler, and linebacker Mike Douglass. Defensive end Charles Martin was suspended by the NFL for two games for his body slam and subsequent injury of Bears quarterback Jim McMahon. To come later was the holdout of quarterback Randy Wright and first-round draft pick Brent Fullwood, continued problems with Martin, and the conviction of cornerback Mossy Cade for second-degree sexual assault.

Caught up in the web, to the shock of nearly everyone, was James Lofton. He was a model citizen, a terrific player, a record-setting wide receiver and one of the few bright spots for a franchise desperate for anything to go right.

But late in the 1986 season he was charged with second-degree sexual assault for an incident in a Milwaukee hotel, forcing the Packers to keep Lofton from playing in the season finale in New York against the Giants—a game the Packers tanked 55-24.

Though he was cleared of all charges, the Packers decided it was best to cut ties with the receiver. So despite catching what was then a club-record 530 passes for 9,656 yards (still a team record) and 49 touchdowns, in April 1987 Green Bay traded him to the Los Angeles Raiders for a third- and fourth-round draft pick.

Lofton proved that, even after nine seasons in Green Bay, he still had plenty left in the gas tank. After two seasons in Los Angeles, he signed with the Buffalo Bills in 1989 and was part of three AFC championship teams and three Super Bowl appearances. He closed out his career with short stints with the Rams and Eagles before retiring in 1993.

He became the first player to surpass 14,000 yards in receptions, and he was the first NFL player to score touchdowns in three decades. He finished with 764 receptions (10th all-time) and 75 touchdowns.

After retirement Lofton joined CNN as a pro football analyst from 1994-96, then went to NBC in 1997, returned to CNN in 1998 and then was a game analyst for Fox from 1998-2001. He also handled the preseason color commentary for the Carolina Panthers from 1995-2001.

But despite all that TV work, Lofton could never shake the feeling that he wanted, and needed, to coach.

"I had always known that but I was just delaying it to spend more time with my family," he said. "I was coaching my kids a little bit, and I wanted to have an impact on their lives."

Indeed, football has been passed down to his kids, as his son David is a quarterback at Stanford, and Daniel is a highly regarded high school receiver. Youngest daughter Rachel is a quality middle school athlete.

Lofton was lured back to coaching and will begin his third season as wide receivers coach for the San Diego Chargers. And after 18 years of playing, Lofton believes he has a unique ability to get the best out of today's young receivers.

"You're compiling the information you got as a player and as a broadcaster," he said. "I think I've got a good handle on what players are thinking."

Lofton's future goals consist of becoming a head coach, either at the pro or college level.

"We'll see," he said.

# CHAPTER 14

# DAVE ROBINSON

*"As well as I played, I didn't get the game ball."*

**Name:** David Richard Robinson
**Birthdate:** May 3, 1941
**Hometown:** Mount Laurel, New Jersey
**Current residence:** Akron, Ohio
**Position:** Linebacker
**Height:** 6-foot-3
**Playing weight:** 240
**Years:** 1963-72
**College:** Penn State
**Accomplishments:** Named to Pro Bowl 1966, 1967, and 1969...Named All-Pro 1967, 1968, and 1969...Inducted into Packers Hall of Fame in 1982.
**The game:** Baltimore Colts, December 12, 1965, at Memorial Stadium

# THE LIFE OF DAVE ROBINSON

Like so many players at the time, Dave Robinson was more than just a football player. He was another of the long line of athletes who could excel in anything they did. And, oh yeah, he was another in a long line of serious mamas' boys.

Growing up without a father, he adored his mother, Mary, and like so many other moms, she didn't like her child playing football. But he was exceptional at it and earned a scholarship to Penn State, where he was not only an All-America defensive end but an All-America offensive end as well. But as he was thriving on the football field, he was also a star basketball player who managed to find time to earn his degree in engineering.

The Packers made him their first-round draft pick in 1963 with plans to move him from defensive end to linebacker. After studying for a year behind Dan Currie at left linebacker, Robinson stepped in as a starter in 1964 and never relinquished the role.

He became known for his uncanny ability to make the right play at the right time. When the Packers needed something big to happen on defense, he was there to make the play. He would come up with the interception or the fumble recovery or the quarterback pressure just when the Packers needed it most. And that often meant in games against the Colts, who were one of the Packers' great rivals in those days.

# THE SETTING

Indeed, as the Dallas Cowboys were the great rivals a few years later, the Colts and Packers waged their share of epic battles earlier in the 1960s. These were two proud franchises that never gave an inch to each other because they didn't have to. But 1965 was clearly a year of war.

The Packers had already beaten the Colts once that season, a 20-17 victory in Milwaukee. They played again in Baltimore later that year with the Packers again winning 42-27. But that wouldn't be the end of it.

On December 26, the two teams met again for the Western Conference Championship in Green Bay, and it was a game that would change the very way football was played and a game still talked about today.

"The reporters were asking us how difficult it was going to be to beat the Colts three times in one year," Robinson said. "Lombardi said, 'If you're better than they are, you can beat them 10 times in one year.' We thought, 'He's right. Let's beat them and get out of here.'"

And it figured to be easy, especially since Baltimore would have to play without both starting quarterback Johnny Unitas and backup Gary Cuozzo, both of whom were out with injuries. That forced the Colts to use halfback Tom Matte, who hadn't played quarterback since high school. With plays taped to his wrist, Matte did little more than hand the ball off or run it himself.

"We went into the game so confident," Robinson said. "Then Bart Starr went out and we went, 'Uh-oh.'"

Sure enough, Starr left the game after only 21 seconds with a rib injury, forcing backup Zeke Bratkowski into the game. Now in a battle of survival, the Colts, with Matte frantically running the show, led 10-0 at halftime before Green Bay finally scored on a Paul Hornung run. That set up the play Colts players and fans still squawk about.

With time running out in regulation, Don Chandler kicked a 22-yard field goal that many, including Chandler, thought was wide right. But the kick was high above the upright, and the officials on the end line couldn't tell definitively if the kick was wide or right over the uprights. They called the kick good, and the Colts howled. To this day, Robinson insists the kick was good.

"I was on the field goal team and my eyes were a lot better then than they are now," he said. "Chandler knew he hit it bad and the kick kind of hung. But it was good. Back then the NFL had a rule that they wouldn't allow a TV camera behind the goal post, so you only had a two-dimensional view. You couldn't tell. But I knew."

**Dave Robinson.** *Vernon J. Biever photo*

In overtime, Chandler left no doubt, drilling a 25-yarder to win the game. The controversy swirled, though, and the next season, the uprights were lengthened so such indecision might be avoided in the future.

In 1966, the Colts had another chance to take out the Packers late in the season as Unitas drove them to what figured to be a late, game-winning touchdown. But Robinson hit Unitas and forced a fumble, and the Packers held on for the 14-10 win in Baltimore.

# THE GAME OF MY LIFE
## By Dave Robinson

It's a funny thing because all those games were big to me. But the biggest game to me was the 1965 game in Baltimore in the fog. That means a lot to me, and I still think about it a lot and what happened in that game.

I remember my mother was going to take a bus down to Baltimore [from the Philadelphia suburb of Mount Laurel, N.J.] and she said she needed 42 tickets for the game. I really had to scurry around to find 42 tickets. Then she called that weekend and said she'd sold all her tickets and didn't have any for herself or my two brothers. So I called my friend [and Colts tight end] John Mackey and he got more tickets for my brothers and my mother. She sat right in the middle of the most die-hard Colts fans, along with my brothers Leslie and Byron.

They said that the Colts fans were boisterous but fun people. I remember just before halftime we were up 13-3 or something like that and Jim Taylor fumbled on the [Packers'] six-yard line. My brother Byron said, "Don't worry, my brother's going to stop them," and he bet $50 on it. The next play [Colts quarterback] Gary Cuozzo tried to lob it into the end zone and I intercepted it and ran it back 80 yards to the Colts' 10. Then Bart Starr threw a little pass to Boyd Dowler to score.

The guy paid off the bet, but that guy—I never did find out his name—insisted that my brother sit in the same seat every time we came to Baltimore to play.

That was a big game for me, because my family was there. That interception was the longest ever against the Baltimore Colts at the time, but I didn't score. Lenny Moore caught me. I remember on that play that the fullback flared out and he was my man. Cuozzo tried to lob it to him, and I just cut in front and intercepted it. I took it down the sideline and I slowed up to let somebody block Cuozzo. I got razzed [for not scoring] immediately if not sooner after I got to the bench. There was always somebody giving me a hard time.

But I had a good game. That same game, Paul Hornung scored five touchdowns, so as well as I played, I didn't even get the game ball.

# GAME RESULT

While Paul Hornung will be remembered for his five touchdowns, it was that Robinson interception that turned the course of the game.

It was a horrendously foggy day in Baltimore, so bad in fact that many fans and the viewers on national TV simply couldn't see what was going on down on the field.

But the players knew only too well.

The Packers led the Colts 14-13 when Taylor fumbled the ball deep in Packers territory. A Baltimore score could be disastrous for the Packers, allowing the Colts to take a halftime lead and steal away the momentum.

On second down and two from the Packers' two, Cuozzo tried to hit fullback Jerry Hill out of the backfield, and that's when Robinson made his interception and returned the ball 87 yards to the Colts' 10. Two plays later Starr hit Boyd Dowler for the touchdown and a critical 21-13 lead.

"That was the big play," Lombardi said afterward. "They didn't score and we did. It changed the game."

Of course, Hornung had his say, too, scoring on three runs and two long passes from Starr. The defense held the Colts to 231 total yards while forcing three interceptions and two fumbles.

# WHAT BECAME
# OF DAVE ROBINSON?

Dave Robinson always figured he'd retire as a Green Bay Packer.

"I didn't want to be one of those guys who had four or five teams behind his name," he said. "I wanted to retire as a Green Bay Packer."

But sometimes plans don't work out like you want them to. In 10 years with the Packers, Robinson redefined the outside linebacker position. He intercepted 21 passes and recovered nine fumbles and was the kind of athletic force that turned the position into what it is today.

After moving in as the starting left linebacker in 1964, Robinson didn't budge from that spot until 1970 when he missed 10 games with a ruptured Achilles tendon. He recovered and took back his spot in 1971 and 1972. But after the '72 season, coach Dan Devine wanted a younger and faster player in that position, and Robinson, despite his wishes to stay a Packer forever, was dealt to Washington for a second-round draft pick.

He seriously contemplated retirement, but Redskins coach George Allen, who was looking for veteran players to help revitalize the franchise, convinced him to play and he had two more solid seasons.

Robinson retired after the 1974 season and went to work for Schlitz Brewing in Akron.

"Schlitz was going to be a three-year assignment, and we've been here ever since," he said.

He said his years as a Packer helped him get into the business, of which he knew very little when he got started.

"The only thing I had was the Super Bowl rings," he said. "Because I was a member of the Packers, it allowed me to get in and see people. But if you didn't know what you were doing, you were out the door. Some people thought I was just a jock who didn't know a damn thing about business. I had to prove myself. I had to sell people on the fact that I knew what I was talking about."

Robinson did just that.

He formed Mars Distributing in 1984, but he has since sold the stock in the company. Now he calls himself "semiretired" and has a hand in selling field turf for a Montreal-based company. One of his assignments is trying to sell the turf to Milwaukee city high schools.

"It's always good to come back to Wisconsin," he said.

# CHAPTER 15

# PAUL COFFMAN

*"We pulled out all the stops."*

**Name:** Paul Randolph Coffman
**Birthdate:** March 29, 1956
**Hometown:** St. Louis, Missouri
**Current residence:** Peculiar, Missouri
**Position:** Tight end
**Height:** 6-foot-3
**Playing weight:** 225
**Years:** 1978-85
**College:** Kansas State
**Accomplishments:** All-Pro 1984...First-team All-NFC in 1983 and 1984...Named to Pro Bowl 1982-84...Inducted into Packers Hall of Fame in 1994.
**The game:** Washington Redskins, October 17, 1983, at Lambeau Field

## THE LIFE OF PAUL COFFMAN

He was a big farm kid from Kansas who wanted nothing more than a chance to prove himself.

At Kansas State, Coffman, with the endearing nickname "Hog," majored in grain milling and figured his future might lie somewhere on the farm. But he just wanted a chance. One chance.

So when Kansas State teammate and friend Gary Spani, a linebacker, was set to try out for Green Bay Packers assistant coach John Meyer, Coffman tagged along and asked Meyer to take a look at him, too.

Meyer was impressed with Coffman's athleticism and determination and the fact that he caught everything in sight. But he still went undrafted in 1978. A little while later, when the Packers needed a tight end to fill out the roster, Meyer remembered Coffman and the Packers signed him as a free agent. It was one of the great free agency decisions in team history.

He didn't catch a pass that season, but in 1979 he took over the spot from Rich McGeorge and became one of the game's most prolific pass-catching tight ends.

## THE SETTING

By 1983, Bart Starr had used up nearly all of the good will and fond memories that he had built up in his 16 years as Packers quarterback. The fans remembered the good old days when he threw his strikes to Boyd Dowler and Max McGee, but good old days are just what they were—old. And with each passing year, the memories grew fainter and the frustration grew deeper.

Starr had taken over as head coach in 1975 from Dan Devine, and in the eight years that followed, he had taken the Packers to just one playoff berth and two winning records. It seemed with every step forward there were three steps back, and patience was running out on everybody's part. Were it any other coach besides the sainted Starr, he wouldn't have lasted four seasons. But Starr

**Paul Coffman (82).** *Vernon J. Biever photo*

was given an extra long leash with the hope that one day it would pay off.

The signs were there in 1982 when, despite a strike that cancelled half the season, the Packers cobbled together a 5-3-1 record, earned a playoff berth for the first time in 10 years and actually won in the postseason for the first time since the Ice Bowl.

All the pieces were in place for the Packers to make their return to the NFL's elite, and it would be even more perfect with Starr in charge.

But it never happened. The season started badly and only got worse. The Packers couldn't sign left end Mike Butler, and starting safety Maurice Harvey was waived. The Packers lost linebacker Randy Scott and nose tackle Rich Turner to season-ending injuries.

It was no coincidence that the damage all came to the defensive side of the ball and the Packers simply didn't have enough fingers for all the leaks sprouting in the dam. For most of the season, the Packers had to play defense with guys who didn't belong in the NFL. Sure there were the warriors like linebackers Mike Douglass and John Anderson and safety Johnnie Gray, but it simply wasn't enough, and these Packers set a record for futility on defense that went unmatched for years.

One of the highlights was certainly the Washington game, but the next week the Packers lost to Minnesota in overtime and then went to Cincinnati and got clobbered by the Bengals.

Despite the fact that Green Bay couldn't stop anybody on defense, they still amazingly had a shot at the playoffs in the final week. But leading the Bears in the final minute, Starr refused to call his available timeouts and Chicago marched to the Packers' five, where Bob Thomas kicked a 22-yard field goal. Gray fumbled the kickoff and the season was done.

The next day Starr was fired, and Forrest Gregg, another voice from the golden past, took over.

# THE GAME OF MY LIFE
## By Paul Coffman

It seemed like in that era we were an average team, but we always thought we were better than that. We thought we should have won some of the games we were losing, but we could never get over that 8-8 situation we put ourselves in.

But this was one of the elite teams in the NFL coming into Lambeau Field on Monday night. What more could you ask for when you're an average team trying to prove yourself? It was exciting.

That week we saw something on film we thought we could take advantage of. [Offensive coordinator] Bob Schnelker was so detailed that he made sure you knew everything. He was that detailed. We knew we needed to hit on all cylinders and we knew we couldn't even punt if we wanted to win. We had to play lights-out.

And we had the athletes to do it. We had an offensive line that, because we didn't win much, they didn't get the recognition they deserved. But they really protected Lynn. We scored quite a few points that season, but we never had the killer defense that stuffed people. At times that came back to hurt us because Lynn would sometimes take chances he shouldn't have taken. He'd get a bad rap for throwing an interception when he should've taken a sack. But we had to take the chance because our defense wasn't going to stop anybody. They practiced hard, they did what they were supposed to do, but we just didn't have the horses to stop people. They just weren't big enough, strong enough, fast enough to make it happen.

But just the fact that it was the Super Bowl champions and *Monday Night Football*, that was enough. That scenario on *Monday Night Football* was exciting. I'd been to the Pro Bowl and watched Monday night games and I knew everybody would be watching, and I wanted to have a good game.

In pregame warmups people were already in their seats. It seemed from the get-go that the stadium was packed. People were hanging out of the stadium and we pulled out all the stops. We even had a play where we actually threw the ball back to Lynn. We had a short-yardage play where we handed it to Eddie Lee Ivery and he threw it back to me. We tried some things and they worked, and the Redskins had a pretty darned good defense.

I remember one play. Bob Schnelker was on the sidelines and he said, "Give me a fullback, give me a fullback" and a guy named Mike Meade stepped up. He gave Meade the play and sent him in. It's a play that would go to him if it worked out, and Schnelker realized it and said, "No, no, no." Lynn threw it to him in the flat, Meade ran for a touchdown, and Schnelker went from "No, no, no" to "Go, go, go." Everybody got into the act that night.

Down the stretch Gerry Ellis was going on an out route. Lynn hit him in the middle of the field, and there was no one around. It was like the seas parted. [Washington cornerback] Darrell Green finally caught him at the five. But the thing is, if he'd scored, it probably would have left another 45 seconds on the clock and Washington could have probably scored again. If that happened we wouldn't be talking about this now.

After the game, it was late and people have to go to work, but the whole stadium was still packed. After we dressed and were ready to go there were still people in the parking lot. All the bars and restaurants in Green Bay were packed. Nobody wanted the night to end.

## GAME RESULT

For every player who was there, the memories come back in a flood. And everybody remembers something different.

For example, quarterback Lynn Dickey remembers the early-week taunt by a Redskins player who said the game would be a rout. That would prove impetus for not only Dickey, but for coach Bart Starr.

Coffman remembered no such comment and said he wouldn't have needed it anyway.

Paul Coffman's 322 receptions remains a Packers all-time record for tight ends. *Vernon J. Biever photo*

"I played hard no matter what," he said. "You're a professional and you should play hard every week. I went out and caught passes and ran over people."

Coffman needed no motivation because he had a first half that would be a season for some players. Paired up one on one against Redskins safety Curtis Jordan, Coffman ran wild and it was only after a halftime adjustment that Coffman was corralled. In the second quarter alone Coffman abused the Redskins' secondary, scoring on receptions of 36 and nine yards as the Packers built a 24-20 halftime lead.

The Redskins, with a fairly prolific offense of their own, appeared to take command in the third quarter and led 33-31, but another wave of scoring in the fourth quarter brought the game into the final minute when Jan Stenerud kicked a 20-yard field goal with 57 seconds left. And with this game, in which seven of the 16 scores came on drives of less than a minute, 57 seconds were several lifetimes. And that's exactly what happened as Washington moved from its 27 to the Green Bay 23 before Mark Moseley missed the 39-yard field goal on the final play.

# WHAT BECAME
# OF PAUL COFFMAN?

He played eight seasons in Green Bay, and four of them were 8-8 campaigns. Today those numbers bemuse Coffman because it spoke to just how average the Green Bay teams were that he played for. But he always did his part. A free agent nobody from Kansas State, he went on to catch 322 passes, average 13 yards per catch and grab 39 touchdown passes. He remains the all-time leader among Packers tight ends, and it's a statistic he guards with pride.

He left the Packers after the 1985 season and spent two uneventful seasons with the Kansas City Chiefs and one more with the Vikings before he retired.

He bought 80 acres of land and put his college degree to work farming the land. But soon he decided to go to work for a friend of his, and today he's a salesman for Meyer Labs, a company that makes chemical cleaners. It allows him to stay around his family in the Kansas City area and offers him opportunities to do other things like coach freshman football at the local high school and watch his athletically gifted kids develop.

Two of his older sons, Chase and Carson, are superb high school football players in their own right. Chase is a wide receiver who has Big 12 schools keeping an eye on him, and Carson is a quarterback. His daughter, Camille, plays volleyball and basketball, and the youngest, Cameron, is a wrestler and basketball player.

Paul Coffman got out of his career everything he could have hoped for, and probably a little more.

"Just to be part of all that was great," he said.

# CHAPTER 16

# DON MAJKOWSKI

*"Everything was clicking."*

**Name:** Donald Vincent Majkowski
**Birthdate:** February 26, 1964
**Hometown:** Depew, New York
**Current residence:** Duluth, Georgia
**Position:** Quarterback
**Height:** 6-foot-2
**Playing weight:** 203
**Years:** 1987-92
**College:** Virginia
**Accomplishments:** All-Pro 1989...Pro Bowl 1989.
**The game:** New Orleans Saints, September 17, 1989, at Lambeau Field

# THE LIFE OF DON MAJKOWSKI

There was always that swashbuckling look to Don Majkowski. Blonde and blue-eyed with an ever-present smirk on his face that made it seem like he always knew a little bit more than you did. It was the perfect persona for the NFL quarterback, and he played to the hilt for as long as he could. And for one remarkable season, he was the best quarterback in the league, and that's more than a lot of players can claim.

He came out of the Buffalo suburbs of Depew, N.Y., relatively unknown. He went to Fork Union Academy in Virginia before enrolling at the University of Virginia, where he would offer enticing glimpses of what he would provide in later years for the Packers.

In fact, it was in his sophomore season with the Cavaliers that he engineered his first dramatic comeback. He led Virginia to the 1984 Peach Bowl against Purdue, but the Cavs found themselves trailing by 10 points at halftime.

In the third quarter, though, Majkowski pulled the offense together and capped a touchdown drive with a one-yard scoring run. After tying the game on a field goal, Majkowski spearheaded a fourth-quarter drive that led to a field goal and a 27-24 win.

He was a capable, if unimpressive, quarterback for a Virginia program still trying to find itself. He led the team in total offense for three straight seasons from 1984-86 and is still seventh all-time in school history in passing with 3,901 yards, 22 touchdowns, and 29 interceptions.

He was one of those 'tweeners that either intrigue NFL pro personnel directors or send them screaming into the night. He had decent size, some running ability, and a good enough arm to make the Packers decide to grab him in the 10th round of the 1987 draft. After all, the Packers had struggled through Randy Wright, Vince Ferragamo, and Chuck Fusina in 1986, and those three managed to throw for barely 3,700 yards while heaving just 18 touchdowns and 27 interceptions. So it was no great gamble taking a project like Majkowski.

**Don Majkowski.** *Scott Halleran/Getty Images*

In 1987, Wright held out at the beginning of training camp; then the strike hit and the season finished with a 5-9-1 mark with Majkowski throwing for 875 yards and three scores.

In 1988, under new coach Lindy Infante, he battled with Wright again, and after leading the Packers to wins over New England and Minnesota, Majkowski seemed ready to take command. But the Packers went on a seven-game losing streak and scored just 53 points while they were at it. The disastrous conclusion led Infante to realize that he needed one guy in charge of his offense. In 1989, Majkowski would run the show, and oh, what a show it would be.

# THE SETTING

It was a season unlike any the Packers had ever known before and, frankly, haven't seen since. Every game was a dance on the knife's edge, every play a study in human psychodrama. And in the middle of it all was Majkowski, the guy who was dubbed, wisely or not, "The Majic Man."

That season, the Packers won 10 games and came from behind to win seven of them. They also set an NFL record with four one-point wins. They won with the help of replay and they won with the help of stupid players on the other team. They won with incredible plays and with boneheaded maneuvers.

And everywhere there was Don Majkowski, blonde locks flowing and footballs flying. He was the quarterback who came practically from nowhere. In those days, Joe Montana and Randall Cunningham were king. They were quarterbacks who could make amazing plays out of nothing. Not some guy from Virginia whose name looked like a typographical error.

But that season no one was better than Majkowski at generating last-minute, jaw-dropping finishes that included one-point wins over New Orleans, Chicago, and back-to-back wins over Tampa Bay and Minnesota.

Yet as incredible as the season was, the Packers were still the Packers. They closed the season with a flourish, beating the

Vikings and Bucs and closing with wins over the Bears and Cowboys. But sandwiched in the middle was a lackluster loss to the Kansas City Chiefs at Lambeau Field.

That loss would prove crushing as the Packers finished tied with the Vikings for the Central Division title. But the Vikings had a better division record overall, and these were still the days before the extra wild-card berth. As a result Minnesota went to the playoffs and the Packers stayed home.

# THE GAME OF MY LIFE
## *By Don Majkowski*

Obviously I have one game that's more publicized and famous. That Bears game (the replay game on November 5) was the one everybody remembers, but before that there was the second game of the season against the New Orleans Saints. We came back from a 24-3 deficit against them. We had a rough first half and came back with a nice second half. I completed 18 consecutive passes to tie Lynn Dickey's record, and that was the first big comeback game of my career. That was the most memorable game of my career.

The first game of the season we had lost a tough, close game to Tampa Bay where I'd thrown a last-minute interception. So it was kind of a bad taste in my mouth spilling into the next week. And in the first half of the Saints game, we didn't have a lot of things going for us and the fans were getting on me pretty good. I had to suck it up and block everything out of my mind, and that's what made the game extra special.

At halftime, I spent all my time with [coach] Lindy [Infante] and he told me to just relax and play my game. We had a great game plan in the first half, but we had some unfortunate penalties that stalled drives. But if there was any game I can ever remember being in the zone and throwing the ball the best I ever had, it was definitely that game.

We had a perfect game plan, and Lindy did an unbelievable job of play calling. Everything was just there. I just had to get the ball to the open guy. Everything was clicking.

We had made a nice comeback and I think there was 1:22 left to play, and we needed a touchdown to win the game. During the course of that last drive, I got sacked and fumbled, and we ended up in that fourth-and-17 situation. I remember coming to the sideline and I asked Lindy what he wanted me to run. So we called a deep comeback on the far sideline. I remember throwing a perfect pass to Jeff Query. Fourth and 17 is a tough pass to complete. It was a great throw, and Jeff did a great job of keeping his feet inbounds. One official had called it out of bounds and then [referee] Ben Dreith overruled it.

Then on the touchdown to Sterling [Sharpe], it was designed to be a rub play. We thought they'd play man to man, so we sent Aubrey Mathews in motion to set up some interference and run Sterling's guy into coverage. But they played zone instead. Sterling did his slant route and got behind the guy. It wasn't designed that way, but he did a nice job. That was the icing on the cake.

That game set the tone for that whole season. It was a game that was kind of forgotten, but it was an unbelievable comeback. The Saints were on a roll in that game with [quarterback] Bobby Hebert and [running back] Dalton Hilliard. And to come back in the second half like that—it gave our team the confidence it needed. We were 4-12 the year before and we had lost our season opener, so that game was the start of it all in my opinion. That was the first year the job was mine.

# GAME RESULT

The boos cascaded down on Majkowski and the Packers as they ran off the field at halftime. And, in truth, it had been an abysmal performance as New Orleans pushed the Packers all over the field.

In a season never to be duplicated, Don Majkowski threw for 4,318 yards and 27 touchdowns and was named to his only Pro Bowl in 1989.
*Vernon J. Biever photo*

But Majkowski, after a quick pep talk from Infante, was about to enter a realm he had never been before and would never see again.

The Packers scored on every possession in the second half as Brent Fullwood ran in from four yards out and Majkowski threw touchdown passes of three and 17 yards to tight end Ed West. Majkowski had completed his final two passes of the first half and then hit on 16 straight to begin the second half, tying a club record established by Lynn Dickey.

Even with all those fireworks, New Orleans appeared to wrap up the game when Morten Anderson kicked a field goal with 2:21 to play. But Majkowski wasn't done. He brought the Packers back down the field and, facing fourth and 17 from the Saints' 48, the end seemed to have come.

But Majkowski found Jeff Query, a tiny, speedy wide receiver from little Millikin University, on the sideline for a 23-yard catch. The officials did indeed confer after one said it was out of bounds. But the catch was ruled good and the drive continued. Majkowski hit Query two more times down to the Saints' three when Majkowski connected with Sharpe for the game-winning score with 1:26 to play. For the game Majkowski completed 25 of 32 passes for 354 yards with Sharpe catching eight passes and Query four.

It was the start of a season few would ever forget. Majkowski went on to throw for an astounding 4,318 yards and 27 touchdowns and earn a Pro Bowl berth.

# WHAT BECAME
# OF DON MAJKOWSKI?

This was the same season, of course, that featured the infamous replay game against the Bears when Majkowski, seemingly over the line of scrimmage, threw a winning touchdown pass to Sharpe.

First ruled a penalty, the official consulted replays and said he was not over the line of scrimmage and ruled it a touchdown.

"That Bears game, personally, I didn't have a good game statistically," Majkowski said. "But team-wise, it was the biggest team win I was ever associated with. What was so rewarding in that game is that they were so good. Talk about a flair for the dramatic."

But the magic didn't last. In 1990, Majkowski held out for 45 days at the start of training camp in a bitter contract dispute. He returned at the beginning of the season, but it was never the same.

He did engineer another comeback win early in the season, but on November 18 he suffered a shoulder injury that affected him the rest of the season. In 1991 the injuries continued and the Packers continued to fade. Infante was fired and Mike Holmgren was hired, and along with him came a young hotshot quarterback named Brett Favre.

Though Majkowski began 1992 as the starter, it was clear Holmgren saw the future was with Favre. That future began on September 20, 1992, against Cincinnati when Majkowski was knocked out with an ankle injury. Favre took over, led the Packers to a last-second win, and never left the lineup.

Majkowski left Green Bay after that season and went to Indianapolis for two years and Detroit for two more. But he never recaptured the brilliance he had known in 1989.

"I finally had to retire because of that ankle injury," he said. "It kind of lingered for a couple of years."

In fact, Majkowski went through some difficult years following his retirement. That ankle required three different surgeries over three years.

"I had teams calling me, and it was difficult," he said. "That was the frustrating thing. I was just 34 and I was in great shape. But I had tried to come back way too soon after the 1996 season."

He left football and went to work with a friend as an area manager in computer data storage.

"I absolutely hated it and was bored out of my mind," Majkowski said.

Then he met Mark Benson, who suggested to Majkowski he team up with him in real estate investment. Now they own Hotlanta Homebuyers in suburban Atlanta. Majkowski has other irons in the fire as well, though he says now nothing is definite.

# CHAPTER 17

# BART STARR

*"Everyone knew exactly what was at stake."*

**Name:** Bryan Bartlett Starr
**Birthdate:** January 9, 1934
**Hometown:** Montgomery, Alabama
**Current residence:** Birmingham, Alabama
**Position:** Quarterback
**Height:** 6-foot-1
**Playing weight:** 190
**Years:** 1956-71
**College:** Alabama
**Accomplishments:** Inducted into Pro Football Hall of Fame in 1977...Named to Pro Bowl 1960-62 and 1966...League MVP in 1966...MVP in Super Bowl I and II...Inducted into Packer Hall of Fame in 1977...Highest quarterback rating in NFL playoff history.
**The game:** Dallas Cowboys, December 31, 1967, at Lambeau Field

# THE LIFE OF BART STARR

Before he became one of the NFL's all-time great quarterbacks and perhaps the most enduring figure as a Green Bay Packer, Bart Starr was just like everybody else. It might have seemed as though he had sprung fully formed and ready to play quarterback at the highest levels, but that was far from the case.

There was a stretch as a youngster when Starr went almost three years without seeing his father, whose National Guard unit was called up for WWII. Perhaps those were the years when he developed the quiet confidence and steely resolve that would one day make him a Hall of Famer.

Starr grew up in Montgomery, Alabama, where as a junior at Sidney Lanier High School he took over as starting quarterback when the other quarterback broke his leg. As a senior, Starr was an All-State selection, and when it came time to choose a college, he selected Alabama.

He seemed on his way to a superb college career when, as a sophomore, he led the Crimson Tide to the Cotton Bowl (a loss to Rice). But the upward movement did not continue. As a junior, he was plagued by back problems, and with a change in coaching staff the next year, Starr and numerous other seniors watched from the sidelines as Alabama staggered in with a 0-10 record.

Despite those disappointments, Starr hoped the NFL would still take a look, and in 1956, the Packers, coming off a 6-6 season and in need of a quarterback, took Starr in the 17th round of a draft that in those days went 30 rounds.

In his first three pro seasons, Starr did nothing to make anyone think he'd be the answer to the Packers' prayers. He completed barely half of his passes and threw only 13 touchdowns while throwing 25 interceptions, and the Packers won only eight games in his first three years.

But all of that was about to change.

**Bart Starr.** *AP Images*

# THE SETTING

Bart Starr remembered his first encounter with Vince Lombardi, but only after he learned the obscure New York Giants offensive line coach would become the Packers' new head coach in 1959.

"I didn't know who he was until recognizing a picture of him in one of the Green Bay papers," he said. "I recognized his face immediately because the year before in a preseason game at Fenway Park, we had scored a touchdown and, just as it was at Milwaukee County Stadium, the benches were on the same side of the field. While jogging off after holding for the extra point and going past the Giants' bench, I see this guy who is ranting and raving at defensive players for the Giants. Then I recognized him. To show you his aggressiveness and intensity, he was yelling at the defensive players and he was the offensive line coach."

Starr got a better idea of what the future held in his first meeting with Lombardi.

"He looked us in the eye and said, 'Gentlemen, we are always going to relentlessly chase perfection, knowing full well we will not catch it because nothing is perfect. In the process we will catch excellence.' He paused and said, 'I'm not remotely interested in being just good.' We knew immediately there would be a change. I called my wife back in Alabama and said, 'Honey, we're going to begin to win.' It was an absolutely wonderful experience."

Lombardi understood immediately that Starr's strength was intelligence and poise and the ability to make decisions at the right time, and he played to those strengths. Starr never threw more than 295 passes in a season, but he also never completed fewer than 52 percent of his passes, either, and that was in Lombardi's first season.

Starr choreographed NFL titles in 1961 and 1962 and again in 1965 and 1966, when he was named the NFL MVP when he threw for 2,257 yards, completed 62 percent of his passes and threw only three interceptions.

# THE GAME OF MY LIFE
*By Bart Starr*

Foremost in my mind is the Ice Bowl because of its significance on several levels. Football fans remember the weather, which was no doubt a key element. What some observers forget is that we were a team competing for our third consecutive NFL championship and our fifth title in the decade of the 1960s, yet we were playing with several starters on the injured list. That's what stands out in my mind even more than the weather.

There are a couple of things about the game that people may not remember. The change in the weather from Saturday to Sunday was one. When we went out for our light Saturday workout, the field was in great condition. The temperature was zero, but there was no wind. The problem developed overnight as a cold front moved in and led to a damaged heating system under the field. At kickoff the footing was tolerable, but as the game progressed it deteriorated to the point where we were skating rather than running.

In addition, few football experts wrote about the quality of the Cowboys' team. They were talented, physical, and well prepared. We were more experienced, but they had earned the right to be there. Despite the brutal weather, the Cowboys nearly matched us that day, and it took every bit of creativity and determination on our part to win the game.

As we ran onto the field to start what would be our last drive, I stepped into the huddle and looked into the eyes of my teammates. I knew instantly that nothing needed to be said regarding the importance of that opportunity. Everyone knew exactly what was at stake and what would be required.

I do not believe we can single out any play as the most important of that drive, because the very nature of a game-winning drive is that every play is crucial. I prefer to focus on the tremendous contribution from a couple of players who never received enough credit. We had a dedicated, committed group of guys who were also very bright. For example, Donny Anderson, our halfback, observed that the linebacker covering him was dropping off into deeper than normal coverage, which meant I could safely pass the ball to him for modest but steady gains. Chuck Mercein, our fullback, noted that the linebacker covering him was staying too far toward the middle of the field, which allowed us to achieve a large gain on a relatively simple swing pass.

Equally important was a play we planned for but had not yet used. We waited until it was perfect for that drive. I handed the ball to Chuck Mercein on what was called an "influence" play. If you were looking at the back of our offensive line, our left guard pulled to the right. (Cowboys defensive tackle) Bob Lilly was opposite him and charging at an angle almost parallel to the line, which meant that we could not block him cleanly. We decided to use Lilly's tremendous quickness and anticipation to our advantage. We pulled our guard, Gale Gillingham, to the right, hoping that Lilly would try to beat him to the point of attack. This would take Lilly out of the play, which was going to be run in the spot where he originally lined up. This was a risky call, but I believed

One of the most famous photos in sports history: Bart Starr sneaking into the end zone to beat the Cowboys in the "Ice Bowl." *AP Images*

the time had come to try it, as the adrenaline was running full tilt and Lilly would likely try to make a decisive play for their defense, which he had done so many times.

There was a second aspect to this play, without which we could not have succeeded. If Lilly took himself out of the intended hole, we knew that the Cowboys' defensive end, George Andre, would cover the area unless our left tackle, Bob Skoronski, could cut him off. I asked Bob if he could make that block and he said yes. That was all I needed to hear.

The play was a huge success, the highlight of the drive. Mercein gained eight crucial yards, and if the field had been better he might have scored. Had that occurred, the quarterback sneak on the goal line would have been moot. It was the most memorable play I ever called. It perfectly illustrated how important it was for every player to execute his block, because if Skoronski had failed to cut off Andre, we would have achieved only a one- or two-yard gain. In my opinion, Skoronski should be in the Hall of Fame. He was an outstanding offensive tackle. Had he not been overshadowed by his teammate, Forrest Gregg, one of the best tackles ever to play the game, he would already be in Canton.

That game certainly helped our spirit. We'd had the toughest year imaginable. We were two-time defending NFL champions, badly banged up, and everybody wanted an extra piece of us. Each team was at its very best when we played them.

# GAME RESULT

Anyone with even a passing interest in pro football knows the details of this one. It was, perhaps, the game that turned the NFL from a sport America enjoyed to a sport America devoured.

There were so many subplots coming into play from the weather—which was 13 degrees below zero—to the significance of the game to the competition that saw the reigning kings, the Packers, facing the new rising power in the Dallas Cowboys.

And the fact is, the Cowboys played well enough to beat the Packers despite the weather conditions.

Early on, the Packers were in command, taking a 14-0 lead on two Starr-to-Boyd Dowler touchdowns—one of eight yards and the other of 46. But the Cowboys climbed back in when the Cowboys' Willie Townes sacked Starr and he fumbled, and George Andrie picked up the ball for the touchdown. After another Packers fumble, Danny Villanueva kicked a 20-yard field goal and Green Bay led 14-10 at halftime.

The weather grew even colder and the field hardened, and the game became a study in survival as much as anything else.

After a scoreless third quarter, the Cowboys stunned the Packers on the first play of the fourth quarter when halfback Dan Reeves took a pitch and threw 50 yards for the score to Lance Rentzel.

The Packers got the ball back with 4:54 to play and the ball on the Green Bay 32-yard line. The rest is the stuff of history. Starr completed key passes to Dowler, Donny Anderson, and Chuck Mercein. Then Mercein, on the "give" play touted by Starr, rolled up the middle for an 18-yard gain to the Cowboys' three. Then it was third down from one with 13 seconds to play.

"I asked the linemen if they could get their footing for one more wedge play, and they said yes," Starr said.

He called a timeout and went to the sideline to confer with Lombardi.

"I told him the linemen could get their footing but the running backs were having trouble getting their footing and that I was upright and could shuffle my feet and get in on the wedge play," Starr said. "Lombardi said, 'Well, run it, and let's get the hell out of here.' And I went back to the huddle chuckling."

Starr wedged in over center Ken Bowman and right guard Jerry Kramer, and the game took its frozen place in history. Again, lost in all of that was the fact that the Packers still had to play the Oakland Raiders in Super Bowl II in Miami. But, in almost an afterthought, the Packers prevailed 33-14 and Starr was the MVP.

# WHAT BECAME OF BART STARR?

He was around so long that many Packers fans could hardly imagine a time when Bart Starr wasn't the quarterback. After Super Bowl II, though, changes started to come.

Lombardi left the sidelines and moved in solely as general manager, leaving his top assistant Phil Bengtson as the new coach. But it was an uncomfortable arrangement at best, and after one season away from coaching, Lombardi left Green Bay to coach the Washington Redskins. A year later, he was dead of cancer.

Meanwhile Bengtson had no hope of escaping Lombardi's considerable shadow, and the Packers stumbled. Starr did complete a career-best 64 percent of his passes in 1968, but the Packers missed the playoffs with a 6-7-1 record. He remained the starter two more years and played four games in 1971 before retiring in training camp prior to the 1972 season.

He came back in 1972 to help coach a new batch of Packers quarterbacks before leaving after a year to do some TV work for CBS. Starr had been in the automobile business since 1969, and after his television stint, he devoted his full attention to that.

But the NFL called again, and when the Packers asked him to take over as head coach in 1975, even though he had no head coaching experience, he couldn't refuse. He lasted nine seasons, his teams went 52-76-3, and he was fired after the 1983 season. It's a period in his life he politely chooses not to talk about.

After living for a time in Phoenix, where he was part of a group that tried unsuccessfully to get an NFL expansion franchise, he moved back to Birmingham, where he is now in the health care real estate business. Starr is chairman of the services arm of HealthCare Realty Trust, and though the publicly traded company is based in Nashville, he's able to stay in Birmingham with his family.

"It's been an absolutely joyful experience," he said.

As for his years with the Packers, they remain some of the best of his life.

"It's indescribable," he said. "It's a blessing and a thrill you'll treasure the rest of your life. Cherry and I will always consider Green Bay our adopted home. We lived 31 years in Wisconsin and it was fabulous."

# Chapter 18

# MARV FLEMING

*"This was going to be easy."*

**Name:** Marvin Xavier Fleming
**Birthdate:** January 2, 1942
**Hometown:** Compton, California
**Current residence:** Marina del Ray, California
**Position:** Tight end
**Height:** 6-foot-4
**Playing weight:** 232
**Years:** 1963-69
**College:** University of Utah
**Accomplishments:** Packers' 11th-round draft pick in 1963...Part of what at the time was a record five Super Bowl teams (two in Green Bay and three in Miami).
**The game:** Baltimore Colts, October 27, 1963, at Memorial Stadium

# THE LIFE OF MARV FLEMING

There are some guys who just happen to be in the right place at the right time. And in his pro career, Marv Fleming was one of those guys. He never shied away from pushing the envelope, from doing things that other guys couldn't, or wouldn't, do. Maybe that's why a kid from inner-city Los Angeles decided to play college football at a place like the University of Utah, a world away from where he came from.

But he learned then what it was like to get along with everybody. In 1963, the Packers were already well into their era as one of the NFL's most dominant franchises. They had already won world titles in 1961 and 1962, so there were precious few openings on a team that would go on to win three more titles. Still, the Packers needed a backup for Ron Kramer at tight end, and in a draft that also produced starters Dave Robinson, Tom Brown, and Lionel Aldridge, the Packers took an athletic and sometimes outspoken tight end from Utah in the 11th round. He would prove the perfect complement to a team that was already loaded.

# THE SETTING

Green Bay remains, by a wide margin, the smallest city in the nation to host an NFL franchise. It is part of the allure that is the Green Bay Packers that a city of 90,000 not only has an NFL franchise but can be as consistently strong as it's been the last decade or so.

So just imagine the Green Bay of the early 1960s. It was even smaller, even more insular, and if players live in the proverbial fishbowl today, they lived in a coffee cup back then. Everybody knew the Packers, and the joke, though it really wasn't all that funny, was when a black man was seen walking through all-white Green Bay, he had to be a Packers player.

But there was little racial tension, if any, on those Packers teams because they knew that anyone who could help them win

**Marv Fleming.** *Vernon J. Biever photo*

would have a place in the huddle. And Lombardi wouldn't abide such dissension anyway.

"On Vince Lombardi's teams, there were no racial overtones," Fleming said. "If there were—boom—they were out there. But that didn't mean we didn't have to be careful. I remember one of the players told Lombardi one night that I was out with a white girl, so Lombardi called me into his office the next day. He said, 'Marvin, I know you were popular at Utah and we like you here, but you have to be discreet.' I said, 'Is that all?' and he said, 'Yeah,' and I said, 'OK.' Everybody was on equal terms with Lombardi."

In fact, Fleming would go on to develop a strong and enduring friendship with his fellow tight end, Ron Kramer, a Kansas boy who played at Michigan. It's a friendship as strong today as it was 40 years ago to the point that they still talk three times a week.

"If it wasn't for Ron Kramer, I wouldn't be the football player I am today," Fleming said. "I idolized him. I saw what type of football player he was, I saw how he blocked, how he caught passes and what his motivation was."

But in 1963, Fleming still had to earn his stripes—not because of his skin color but because as a unit, the Packers knew what they had. Every player had a role and did it to the best of his ability. If one player broke down, the whole team could. That's why Fleming was greeted so skeptically that first time on the field. But once you passed your test with teammates, there was never another question about your ability.

# THE GAME OF MY LIFE
## *By Marv Fleming*

My biggest game was when I played in Baltimore. [Starting tight end] Ron Kramer was hurt and here I am on the sidelines with [backup running back] Elijah Pitts and I hear my name, "Fleming, Fleming." And I think to myself, "Oh no, this is not special teams unit time." I'm so excited I almost run out there without my helmet. I'm thinking "Ron's hurt? Ron never gets hurt." But I ran out there on the field and we're playing the Baltimore Colts. One of my good friends was [Colts All-Pro tight end] John Mackey, and I always thought I was as good as he was.

So I run into the huddle and the veterans look at me, and one of the veteran guys said, "Marvin, you better know the plays, because if you don't, I'm going to kick your butt." I said, "You do your job and I'll do mine," and that's when everybody in the huddle said, "Whoa."

Several plays later I caught a big pass that set up a touchdown, and after that I guess you could say I was invited to the party. I won their confidence.

The Packers had already won [NFL titles] once or twice before I'd gotten there, and it's true what they say that you take on the mentality of your peers. That's what I did. I was a winner already. Being with the Green Bay Packers, it instilled winningness in me, and that goes on today. Being with Herb Adderley, Willie

Marv Fleming (81) played in two Super Bowls with Green Bay and three more in Miami—winning four of them—and earned a special place in NFL history. *AP Images*

Wood, and Bart Starr, having seen all these guys on TV, I wanted to be just like them. I wanted to be a winner.

But that first catch was the highlight—when you get that first call. A lot of times when that happens, you get flustered. But I caught that huge pass and I threw the ball on the ground and said, "This is going to be easy."

# GAME RESULT

The Packers did well just to get out of this game alive. This was a team that had chalked up two straight NFL titles, but they were in a war for a third straight with the Chicago Bears (who would end up winning the Western Division by a half-game over the Packers). But coming up quickly were the Baltimore Colts, a team that had dipped since its heyday in the late 1950s but was starting to rebuild a powerhouse.

In 1963, the Packers had already beaten the Colts in Green Bay and needed this one to at least stay close to the Bears. But it wouldn't be easy.

Heading into the game in Baltimore, starting quarterback Bart Starr didn't play after breaking a hand the week before in St. Louis. Also absent was halfback Tom Moore. Then early in the game, All-Pro tight end Ron Kramer injured his leg and didn't return. Those were three key spots that required three key replacements, and somehow, the Packers muddled through.

John Roach, a journeyman quarterback from SMU, got the start in place of Starr and was efficient enough, completing nine of 20 passes for 156 yards. Elijah Pitts, who would take over as a starter in later years, stepped in for Moore and was solid as well, with 74 yards on 10 carries.

And then there was the rookie Fleming, something of an unknown who had done little up to that stage of the season except play on special teams. But he made his mark on this day with three catches for 51 yards, including an 11-yard touchdown catch in the second quarter that put the Packers up 17-3 at halftime.

The Colts did come back to tie the game at 20-20 with six minutes to play, but Green Bay turned the tide two minutes later when Willie Davis and Jerry Norton blocked a field goal. Pitts then ran 34 yards for a touchdown, and Jim Taylor scored again later to seal the 34-20 win.

Fleming caught only four more passes the rest of that season, though that was hardly the point. He had been called on to do a job and he did it, and everything else would take care of itself.

# WHAT BECAME OF MARV FLEMING?

Ron Kramer played through the 1964 season in Green Bay before family considerations convinced him to sign with the hometown Detroit Lions. That meant the starting tight end job belonged to Fleming. Before Kramer left, though, he imparted all the knowledge and wisdom he could to the young replacement.

And over the next five seasons, Fleming would become a solid, dependable tight end who could block and catch and get downfield. His best season in Green Bay was 1966 when he caught 31 passes. He caught 109 passes and 12 touchdowns in his seven seasons in Green Bay before coach Phil Bengtson traded him to Miami for wide receiver Jack Clancy. Fleming didn't know it at the time, but he went from a declining NFL power to a rising force.

He became the blocking tight end for a surging Miami Dolphins running game, and he would go to three more Super Bowls in 1971, 1972, and 1973 for the Dolphins—winning two of them. He is part of the undefeated 1972 Dolphins team that still holds celebrations when the last team in the current NFL season loses.

Actually, Fleming has made something of a career since he retired selling that 17-0 Dolphins' season in 1972.

"One night I said to myself that I can sell this idea," he said. "I can sell the perfect season. So I started calling a lot of the players and they liked the idea. I got $1,000 and I bought $1,000 worth of footballs and jerseys and helmets. We sign them and we have a reunion and everybody became part of the company. I became chairman of the 1972 Perfect Season Team."

And every year, when the last unbeaten team falls, all the team members celebrate their longstanding accomplishment.

"When the Bengals played the [unbeaten] Chiefs, I couldn't watch," Fleming said. "But the Bengals ended up winning and I went outside and screamed and all my neighbors could hear me."

Fleming is also a motivational speaker, and most of his talks are about growing up and the influence Vince Lombardi had on his life.

"No one leaves," he said of audiences.

# CHAPTER 19

# JIM CARTER

*"I did my job well."*

**Name:** James Charles Carter
**Birthdate:** October 18, 1948
**Hometown:** St. Paul, Minnesota
**Current residence:** Eleva, Wisconsin
**Position:** Linebacker
**Height:** 6-foot-3
**Playing weight:** 235
**Years:** 1970-78
**College:** University of Minnesota
**Accomplishments:** Pro Bowl 1973.
**The game:** Philadelphia Eagles, October 25, 1970, at Milwaukee County Stadium

# THE LIFE OF JIM CARTER

Jim Carter is still outrunning his demons. After all these years away from football, the pressure, the anger, and the uncertainty, he is finally at peace with himself and his turbulent, exhilarating years with the Green Bay Packers.

"I'm a recovering person," he said. "I quit drinking 21 years ago and I've had some other addictions. And while most people will tell you addictions go back to childhood, the experience I had with the Nitschke situation exacerbated the situation. I was ill-equipped emotionally to deal with it. I probably didn't have a strong enough self-image."

Carter was likely a ticking bomb from his earliest years as high school star from South St. Paul, Minnesota. He decided to attend the hometown University of Minnesota, where he was a terrific fullback, earning All-Big Ten honors. He was also an exceptional hockey player and was drafted by the Minnesota Fighting Saints of the World Hockey Association. But there was no doubt in his mind where his future was.

He wanted to play in the NFL, and it had been his hope that if, and when, he was drafted that he'd get the opportunity to be a running back again. Those hopes died quickly, however, when the Packers made Carter their third-round pick in 1970 and immediately moved him to linebacker.

"I thought I was a pretty good running back in college," he said. "I was hoping to get a chance at running back, but I never played a down."

That's because these Packers of a new decade were reformulating and seeking a new identity. The players from those championship days of the 1960s were retiring or being traded, and new blood had to step in to fill the vacuum.

One player from the golden years was still doggedly holding on and still playing good football. Ray Nitschke had been a force at middle linebacker for the Packers since 1958. He had already been a three-time All-Pro, a Pro Bowler and was voted to the NFL's

**Jim Carter.** *Vernon J. Biever photo*

All-50 Year Team. His ticket to the Hall of Fame had already been bought and paid for.

But in 1971, Nitschke still wasn't ready to move aside. He was convinced he still had plenty of good football left in him and that, if he didn't, it was up to the next young stud to beat him out.

In 1970, Carter had stepped in for one legend when he took over for the injured Robinson. In 1971, new coach Dan Devine was impressed enough with Carter's play to move him into the middle linebacker spot in training camp. The promotion should have made Carter ecstatic. Instead, it was just the beginning of a nightmare that simply would not end.

# THE SETTING

Nitschke was a proud man who didn't feel his job should be handed to a second-year guy. And Packers fans, who had grown to love Nitschke's relentless, take-no-prisoners style on the field, were angry that a kid had taken his place. So every time Carter took the field, he was greeted with a torrent of boos.

"The booing wasn't about who I was as a person; it was about replacing somebody like Nitschke," Carter said.

He understands that now. He didn't then.

"It bothered me so much that I drank more, smoked more grass, got laid more," he said. "I knew I wasn't emotionally or psychologically prepared. And once it started, it was tough the whole time. It never got any better."

And Nitschke didn't do much to help his young replacement. There would be times during games when Nitschke would be on the sidelines and would start to stretch as though he was getting ready to enter the game. When fans saw that, they went nuts. But instead Carter remained, infuriating fans even more. Nitschke finally retired after the 1972 season.

"At first it wasn't about me, and then it was about me, because I didn't handle it very well," Carter said. "I had a TV show in 1972 and there was this question-and-answer period where this woman asked me if I ever thought I'd be good enough to fill the shoes of

Ray Nitschke," he said. "Now I'd had a few drinks before the show and I had heard enough of this. So I told her to go to hell. I just reacted badly. In 1973 I was an All-Pro. I wasn't at Nitschke's or Dick Butkus' level, but to be a middle linebacker starting in the NFL, you have to be fairly good. I was good enough to play, good enough to be a starter, good enough to be a team captain for four years. But I wasn't Nitschke. Plus our teams weren't that good."

# THE GAME OF MY LIFE
## By Jim Carter

The game I really remember that year was when we played Philadelphia and we played them in Milwaukee. The Eagles had a tight end named Steve Zabel, and he went on to become a linebacker and became a very, very good player. But at that time he was a tight end and our starting left linebacker, Dave Robinson, had torn his Achilles tendon and they started me at outside linebacker.

Now Robby was such a great player even late in his career. I never saw anybody do such a great job on tight ends as he did. He was an artist. I tried to emulate him, but I was nowhere near the player he was. I was told in that game that my job was to stand Zabel up. I knew Zabel was tough and strong and I was pretty successful at doing that in that game. I did my job well. I think then I knew after that game that I could play in this league. I think [defensive line coach] Dave Hanner and [new head coach in 1971] Dan Devine, probably thought the same thing, and maybe that's why they put me in the middle after that. I did a pretty good job in that game and that helped them make that decision. I don't remember if I made any tackles in that game, but I felt I could control him and that's what they wanted.

# GAME RESULT

Even if the 1970 Packers weren't the powerhouse of two years earlier, fans still had expectations. And when the Packers skidded to an ugly 30-17 victory over the winless Eagles, it was further evidence that the good old days were gone for good.

Carter did indeed play well and held Steve Zabel without a catch. He had four tackles overall and proved to any objective observer that he was a linebacker to be taken seriously.

The Packers jumped on the Eagles quickly when Doug Hart returned an interception 76 yards for a touchdown and Green Bay went on to force four other Philadelphia turnovers.

There was very little remarkable about a midseason game between the now average Packers and the hopeless Eagles. Bart Starr, nearing the end of his career as well, threw for 129 yards, and the Packers' defense held the Eagles to 241 total yards.

# WHAT BECAME OF JIM CARTER?

What should have been the crowning moment of his life—playing middle linebacker for the storied Packers—was instead, quite literally, a hell on earth for Carter.

Even after Nitschke's retirement and his plea to fans to take it easy on Carter, the fans never let up. Certainly Carter's surly, sullen attitude didn't help, but chances are anyone replacing a legend would have struggled just as much.

"I talked too much and drank too much," Carter said. "What could have been a great experience turned into a pretty sour experience for me. But that's how I handled it."

He has come to grips with his years in Green Bay and many fans today who remember him apologize for the awful treatment he received. But even though he has lived just across the state since he retired, he has yet to return to watch a game or for an annual player reunion.

"I've always been afraid to go back," he said. "If there are 60,000 people there and there are 59,900 cheering, I'd only hear the boos. I've had teammates tell me to come back, but it's too tough on my emotional makeup."

After retiring after the 1978 season, Carter took a year off to recuperate. His father and brother owned automobile dealerships in Eau Claire, and Carter decided to go that route. He expanded his dealership into Ford, General Motors, Chevrolet, Audi, and others, and he built one of the largest dealerships in the region.

"I actually had too much," Carter said.

He sold the dealerships five years ago, and though he still dabbles in real estate, he is all but retired to a large spread in rural Eau Claire, where he and his family raise llamas.

"I'm more a landlord now," he said.

He understands, at least a little, why his years in Green Bay were so difficult and, if he could, he would do a lot of things differently.

"It's hard to complain much about it because most people would give their right arm to play in the NFL," he said. "I know that now."

# CHAPTER 20

# LARRY McCARREN

*"We did what we did best."*

**Name:** Laurence Anthony McCarren
**Birthdate:** November 9, 1951
**Hometown:** Park Forest, Illinois
**Current residence:** Green Bay, Wisconsin
**Position:** Center
**Height:** 6-foot-3
**Playing weight:** 240
**Years:** 1973-84
**College:** University of Illinois
**Accomplishments:** Pro Bowl 1982 and 1983...All-Pro 1982...
Inducted into Packers Hall of Fame in 1992.
**The game:** Washington Redskins, October 17, 1983, at Lambeau
Field

# THE LIFE OF LARRY McCARREN

He is one of the great overachievers on a franchise where there have been many.

Even back in the early to mid-1970s when McCarren was slamming away at rival defensive tackles, he was considered undersized for the position. But through doggedness and an innate toughness, he battled through all the odds and earned one of the great nicknames in Packers history: "Rock." Its genesis was simple enough. It was awarded to him for his rock-steady play, game in and game out.

Over a 12-year career he played in 162 games, and even when he shouldn't have played, he did. In 1980, for example, he had a hernia operation during training camp. He had all but recovered but was far from 100 percent when the season opened. Still, coach Bart Starr put him in just to keep his consecutive games started streak alive. Then he'd remove him. But after the first play, McCarren waved off his replacement and he played the entire game.

He played through a broken hand and, in one especially bizarre incident, his family was overcome by carbon monoxide fumes one morning, but he played later that day. And, oh yes, he played center in the NFL at the relatively puny weight of 240 pounds.

"He's the toughest player I've ever been around," quarterback Lynn Dickey said.

# THE SETTING

McCarren joined the Packers at what could charitably be called the beginning of the franchise's dark ages. A relatively obscure 12th-round draft pick, he labored on the old taxi squad his first season before taking over the starting center job from another holdover from the golden era, Ken Bowman, in 1974. He would hold the job for the next 11 years.

**Larry McCarren.** *Vernon J. Biever photo*

But in that time, he would see some of the most mediocre football this franchise could produce. In his 12 seasons, the Packers reached the playoffs once, in 1982. He didn't see a .500 mark until 1978 when the Packers went 8-7-1, and while hope always blossomed every season, it was always crushing disappointment by the end.

The optimism seemed justified late in McCarren's career when, after earning the strike-shortened playoff berth in 1982, the Packers welcomed back most of the team in 1983.

But while the offense was more that adequate, the defense was a shambles. Inconsistency plagued the team from beginning to end, and often it was because the defense could be counted on to collapse spectacularly. The Packers' final playoff gasp ended with a regular season-ending loss to the Bears.

In 1984, Forrest Gregg replaced Bart Starr and managed to carve out an 8-8 record, including three straight wins to end the season. But McCarren missed those final three games with a pinched nerve in his neck.

# THE GAME OF MY LIFE
### By Larry McCarren

It was a special night for an offensive player, and I remember a couple of things leading up to it. We had a big-play offense that year and we could light it up, but we didn't have much on defense. In previous games we had tried to slow the game down to help the defense, and that just wasn't our offense.

So Bill Meyer, the offensive line coach, came up to us the week before the game and said enough of that ball-control stuff. [Offensive coordinator] Bob Schnelker said, "The defense is just going to have to fend for itself. We're cutting loose." And we ran everything we had. Overall we played really well. We just said to heck with that ball control and we did what we did best. We went for home runs and got huge chunks of yardage. It was one of those games that whoever got the ball last was the one who's going to win the thing.

Then it came to the final field goal attempt, and Schnelker, after orchestrating that offensive explosion, couldn't bear to watch. He just turned his back on the field. That missed field goal was probably the highlight of all the highlights.

You could look at that one as a team effort. The blocking was there, the coaching was there, the play-calling was there. These were the defending Super Bowl champs and we beat them. You have to look at it as an overall team effort.

It was, comparatively speaking, a very memorable moment in Packers history. It was a good opponent and it was on Monday night. Walking off the field, I've seen pictures, and I remember how great it felt to win a game like that.

# GAME RESULT

Much has been written about the unforgettable offensive display in this game. There were 771 total yards gained and 95 points scored, and the two teams combined to run for 254 yards.

But what is often forgotten is the play of the Packers offensive line that protected Lynn Dickey from what was considered a fearsome Redskins pass rush. McCarren, of course, anchored the line at center, but it was also a line that had to be rebuilt for the Redskins game.

Regular right guard Leotis Harris was hurt, and that forced normal right tackle, Greg Koch, over to Harris' spot. To replace Koch, the Packers signed Charlie Getty. Karl Swanke was the left tackle, and Dave Dreschler was the left guard. Those five kept Dickey vertical most of the night despite a pass rush that featured the NFL's most feared rusher, Dexter Mann, and massive tackle Dave Butz. It's a tidbit from the game few acknowledge.

"You don't ring up that kind of yardage without someone blocking some folks," McCarren said.

Dickey was sacked three times, but more importantly, he threw for 387 yards in a game that, more than 20 years later, is still regarded as a classic.

To McCarren, who had suffered through his share of awful seasons and even worse games, the only reason it became significant is because the Packers won.

"Up until that point, it was just a game where, yeah, we were moving the football," he said. "But until we won, that's when it became special. The end result made it special. We went to Atlanta later in the season and we lost 40 something to 40 something [47-41] and that wasn't anything special. This was special. Everything worked."

# WHAT BECAME
# OF LARRY McCARREN?

After 162 games and 12 seasons, even Larry McCarren couldn't defy time. He was the only center many Packers fans had ever known, and while he wasn't the most high profile of players, his presence was still comforting. He had been there. He knew what to do. And you could count on him.

But his streak of consecutive games finally ended at the end of the 1984 season when a pinched nerve forced him out of the lineup. He tried to come back in 1985, but it wasn't to be, and he retired during training camp, ending one of the most remarkable careers in Packers history.

But he wouldn't stray far. He moved immediately into television work and he has been a mainstay at WFRV-TV in Green Bay, where he has earned numerous awards. In 1995, he also moved into the radio booth with veteran announcers Jim Irwin and Max McGee. In 1999, when Wayne Larrivee was hired as the new play-by-play announcer, McCarren took over as the sole color analyst. And, just like in his playing days, he's been there ever since.

# CHAPTER 21

# BRETT FAVRE

*"I really thought I was done."*

**Name:** Brett Lorenzo Favre
**Born:** October 10, 1969
**Hometown:** Kiln, Mississippi
**Current residence:** Hattiesburg, Mississippi
**Position:** Quarterback
**Height:** 6-foot-2
**Playing weight:** 224
**Years:** 1992-present
**College:** Southern Mississippi
**Accomplishments:** Three-time NFL MVP 1995-97...Eight-time Pro Bowler 1992-93, 1995-97, and 2001-03...All-Pro 1995-97... Led NFL in touchdown passes four times...Started 257 straight games, an NFL record for quarterbacks...Holds NFL record for completions (5,021)...Second in the NFL in touchdown passes (414), career attempts (8,223), and career passing yards (57,500).
**The game:** Minnesota Vikings, November 2, 2003, at the Metrodome

# THE LIFE OF BRETT FAVRE

It has been a journey of wondrous myth, remarkable talent, and head-shaking luck for Brett Favre, and it all came together to the point where he is now the most identifiable Packer in the team's long and storied history.

All Packers fans, and even those who aren't necessarily Packers fans, have a favorite Brett Favre story. They remember a game he played or a pass he threw or a play he made that no one should make, but which Favre, somehow, did.

It is a story of a young, hotshot quarterback who fell out of favor in Atlanta, the team that drafted him in 1991, and landed in Green Bay with a new coach and a franchise desperately trying to regain the magic of 30 years earlier. And it's the story that says, sometimes, dreams really do come true.

Brett Favre was always one of the kids who was bigger than life. Even as a little kid he was the quarterback who led his pee wee team to the prestigious "Mullet Bowl." At North Central High, where he played for his dad, Irvin, he was an option quarterback who yearned to throw the ball but played within a system.

At Southern Mississippi, he was known as much for his remarkable recuperative powers as his ability to play football. Indeed, his national profile increased dramatically in July 1990, when he was in a serious car accident and had to have 30 inches of his intestines removed. Not even a month later, he was on the field and leading the Golden Eagles to an upset win over Alabama.

So anyone who didn't know how tough Favre was before learned quickly after that. In four seasons at Southern Miss, Favre (whose name was frequently and horrendously mispronounced, mostly by Easterners) led the Golden Eagles to 29 wins, two bowl victories and an MVP award in the East-West Shrine Game.

He also caught the eye of a New York Jets scout by the name of Ron Wolf, who badly wanted his team to draft the young quarterback. But the Jets never got the chance as he was taken in the second round by the Falcons, the 33rd pick overall and third quarterback selected behind Dan McGwire and Todd Marinovich.

Favre languished with the Falcons as a rookie, frequently raising the ire of coach Jerry Glanville for his carefree ways. Often, Favre would stun observers that year by taking footballs and firing them into the upper decks of stadiums. It was the only action Favre really saw.

When Wolf took over in 1992 as the Packers' general manager, one of his first moves was to trade for Favre, and on February 10, he gave up a first-round pick to get him. The rest, as they say, is history.

# THE SETTING

The legend began on September 20, 1992, when Favre subbed for the injured Don Majkowski and led the Packers to a last-minute win over Cincinnati. There would be many, many other games like that—too many, in fact, to recount.

But Favre proved early on that injuries wouldn't stop him from playing the game he loved. In one of his greatest performances, he shook off a severely sprained left ankle in 1995 to play against the Bears.

"I didn't practice at all the whole week," Favre said. "Usually I do something just to get a feel for it, but that week I didn't do anything. The ankle wasn't broken, but it was purple and yellow. I've actually had surgery on that ankle since, and while I'm not saying what happened on that particular day caused the surgery, it didn't help. But my ankle has never been the same."

In a key game at home against Chicago, Favre, with an ankle taped so heavily it resembled a cast, threw five touchdown passes in a 35-28 win.

"I'm not the most mobile guy to begin with, but I really couldn't move in that game," he said. "I really had to rely on stuff I've got in my arsenal but never want to use. In fact it made me be a pocket passer, and I'm never quite sure if I can do that."

That sprained ankle had come the week before in another demoralizing loss to the Minnesota Vikings in the Metrodome.

**Brett Favre.** *Jonathan Daniel/Getty Images*

Even then, that dome had developed into a house of horrors for the Packers.

In 1992, with a playoff berth on the line, the Packers were clobbered 27-7. In 1993, a last-second desperation completion to a guy named Eric Guliford had led to a last-second loss. In 1994, the Packers lost in overtime.

And in 1995, it was even worse. With Favre and backup Ty Detmer both out with injuries, the quarterbacking duties fell to journeyman T.J. Rubley. Still, somehow, the Packers were in control and had the ball and the lead late in the game. But inexplicably, Rubley called an audible on a Holmgren run play and tried a pass that was intercepted. The Vikings came back to tie the game and then win it with a field goal in overtime.

Rubley was gone the next day.

"It just seemed like we were cursed," Favre said.

# THE GAME OF MY LIFE
### By Brett Favre

I don't know. For other guys it might be easy to pick one game. The obvious choice would be the Super Bowl, but even games we didn't win or games where I didn't play as well as others, every one of them has been memorable. That's probably why I've been as successful as I have been for so long—I've enjoyed the hell out of every one.

But the 2003 year in Minnesota may rank, in my opinion, as one of the all-time best. When I've felt my best I've had terrible games over there, so of all the games I played in Minnesota, this past would have been the easiest one for everyone to say, "Well, they ain't got a chance. Favre can't play when he's healthy, and now he's going to try to play with a broken thumb?"

We had just gotten beaten in St. Louis in a dome and I'd heard all the talk about domes, but I never paid much attention to it. But the stats don't lie. So I was determined I was going to play. I was telling myself most of the time, "You're stupid. Of all the times you could actually back out of a game and no one would question it, this is it. You've got a broken thumb. You obviously can sit this one out and not catch any grief over it." But I really wanted to play and redeem myself, broken thumb or not.

When I knew I was going to play, I thought, "How am I going to play with a splint? Hell, you can't play with a splint on your throwing hand. And of all places in Minnesota."

And Mike Sherman, he's telling me all week and putting pressure on me saying, "If you can play, great, because you've always played great coming off injury." And I said, "Mike, now you're putting pressure on me of all places." He was real optimistic. I wasn't as optimistic, but I was confident. I said that if I'm going to play, I'm going to play. But to play the way I did, and obviously win the game, which we haven't done there a lot, ranks as one of the best.

I went out early that morning and went out for a walk-through and we were just trying some different stuff, because the previous week we were off. The splint was not my idea, but they wanted to tape it up, and I said that I needed the least amount of tape, because I need to be able to try to feel the ball as much as I possibly could. I knew the splint would keep the thumb from moving. So I said let's Super Glue the splint to the back of my thumb. That way if the tape comes off, it should keep me from using a lot of tape. And it did do that. It took us three days to get that splint off, and we never did it again. We used nail polish remover, you name it. It got to the point where it almost pulled my thumbnail off.

But that morning, messing around with different tape jobs, I was able to throw the ball fine. But throwing with a broken thumb and no one chasing you and you're able to just kind of concentrate is one thing. It's different than when they're chasing you and all eyes are upon you. It's a different ballgame, even with a good thumb. I was confident I could throw the ball. But it's just a different ballgame when they're shooting live bullets at you.

But as the game progressed, I was making plays I hadn't attempted in practice. I was probably as surprised as anyone afterwards with the throws I made. I was able to kind of go through the game without really thinking about it. Six or seven games into wearing the splint I thought back to that Minnesota game, and I thought, "I have no idea how I did it," because my thumb bothered me the whole year. It got a little bit better and a little bit better, and a little bit better, but I don't know how I did it because it hadn't even been two weeks since I'd broken it. And six or seven weeks after I'd broken it, the X-rays looked the same as the day after I'd broken it. So, for a lot of reasons, that win was important, because the odds were definitely against me that game.

I put a lot of thought into that week, really the two weeks. So much went through my mind those two weeks. When the game was over against St. Louis, I was upset that we'd lost and I had no idea my thumb was broken until the next day. But I played, for the most part, fairly well. My thumb was killing me, but I figured it was just bruised.

In a career with innumerable highlights, leading the Packers to a win over the Vikings at the Metrodome despite a broken thumb in 2003 rates the highest. *AP Images*

But going back on the plane I was thinking that it was not looking good this year and that's not even knowing my thumb was broken. When I found out it was broken, I thought, "This ain't good; it's going to be one of those years." I really thought I was done. That's the first broken bone I'd ever had, and in my throwing hand at that.

But I told Mike and [team doctor] Pat [McKenzie] and [head trainer] Pepper [Burruss] that I thought I could play. They said, "You have a broken thumb." And I said, "Well, I had a broken thumb the whole day yesterday." Had I known it, I probably wouldn't have played. But now that I knew I could play and actually played fairly well against St. Louis, I thought I could play [against the Vikings]. Had I known in St. Louis, I would have played differently, protected it and stuff.

But more than anything, I just wanted to go over there and win. Hell, I hadn't had much success in there, and I considered it a huge challenge, good thumb or not, to go over there and win. I didn't look at it like, "Well, if we lose, everybody will say he had a broken thumb and this time he has an excuse." I didn't look at it that way. The easy games, everyone wants to play in those, and I knew the odds were against me. But I just considered it a huge challenge.

# GAME RESULT

To understand the importance of the Vikings game, it's important to go back two weeks to Edward Jones in St. Louis where the Packers lost 34-24 and where Favre broke his thumb after hitting the helmet of guard Mike Wahle.

Favre broke the thumb in the second quarter, yet continued to play. And though the Packers lost, Favre played well, completing 23 of 32 passes for 268 yards with two touchdowns and one interception.

With the bye week looming, Favre figured he could play against the Vikings, who had led the NFC North comfortably but were now starting to lose steam. Favre knew if he could play, it would provide an emotional lift the team desperately needed.

And it wasn't as though he put up terrific numbers against the Vikings. He completed 18 of 28 passes for 194 yards and threw two touchdown passes to Javon Walker and one to Ahman Green. But it was more how he managed the game, took the plays that were available to him and never put himself, or the team, in trouble. Then he relied on the running game that piled up 261 yards, including 137 by Green.

It wasn't an easy win, because it never is in the Metrodome, where half the crowd is for the Packers and the other half is ramped up to a fever pitch to see the Packers lose.

But Favre's touchdown pass to Walker and a Ryan Longwell field goal with 2:37 to play gave the Packers a seemingly comfortable 30-20 lead. The Vikings scored again to make it close, but the Packers got away with a 30-27 victory.

The importance was obvious. It showed the Packers could win in a dome against their longtime nemesis. It showed Favre could play with a bad thumb. And it showed that the division race, which had seemed over, was far from it. The win brought the Packers within two games of the Vikings, and they had the easier schedule down the stretch.

And in the end, it made all the difference as the Packers slipped in to win the title on the last day of the season.

## WHAT BECAME OF BRETT FAVRE?

That's actually a simple question. Brett Favre was, is, and always will be a Green Bay Packer. In 17 seasons, he has become the most identifiable player this organization has ever known and, indeed, during the 2007 season, he will eclipse Bart Starr as having played more games than any other player in team history.

He continues to raise millions of dollars through his charitable foundations, including a golf tournament in his native Mississippi and a softball tournament in Wisconsin. But with all the accolades and success Favre has known in his career with Green

Bay, the last few seasons have been a struggle, and he has brought much of that on himself. He has seen his mortality in recent seasons and has watched as the Packers have fallen off the perch as one of the NFL's premier franchises.

As far back as the 2003 season, Favre talked about retiring, but in recent years the talk has heated up even more.

In 2004, the Packers had another solid season as Favre threw 30 TD passes, leading Green Bay to the second round of the NFC playoffs. In that game, a stomach-churner against the Philadelphia Eagles, Favre threw a costly interception in overtime that eventually led to an Eagles victory.

In 2005, the final season under coach Mike Sherman, Favre had an abysmal campaign, throwing 29 interceptions and just 20 touchdown passes as the Packers collapsed to 4-12, the worst record in his Packers career.

Sherman was fired after the season and a new, young coach, Mike McCarthy, took over. And even though Favre was familiar with McCarthy (he had been Favre's quarterbacks coach during Ray Rhodes' short-lived tenure), he wasn't sure he wanted to play under another new coach. Meanwhile, the Packers drafted California quarterback Aaron Rodgers to become, presumably, Favre's heir apparent.

In the summer after the '05 season, a disheartened and confused Favre toyed with fans, teammates, and the organization when he refused to let anyone know if he planned to return for the '06 season.

It got so bad that during Favre's midsummer golf tournament in Mississippi, rumors spread that the athlete would announce his decision. As the media descended on the tournament, Favre was incredulous. He told the gathered reporters that he'd made no decision and that they had all wasted their time. It was an embarrassing episode for all concerned, including Favre, who was beginning to take on the appearance that he was somehow bigger than the franchise.

Finally, he decided he was excited enough to come back for the 2006 season and, under the guidance of McCarthy, he played better. With a young offense, Favre only threw 18 touchdown passes, his fewest since his first season in Green Bay 1992. But he also threw only 18 interceptions.

He played smart and controlled, and he helped a young team learn about itself. The result was an 8-8 record and renewed hope for the future. Favre didn't repeat the same mistake after the 2006 season. So, despite a tearful farewell to the crowd after the Packers' season-ending win over Chicago, he soon announced he would return for the '07 season.

That season, he was rejuvenated, throwing for 4,155 yards and leading the Packers to a 13-3 record and the NFC title game, where his ill-timed interception in overtime led to a loss to the New York Giants.

The following March, he dropped the bombshell many Packers fans had expected—and dreaded. Saying "I know I can still play, I just don't know if I want to," he announced his tearful retirement. Some long-time observers never believed it and they were right.

He changed his mind in July and said he wanted to return, even though the Packers had moved on and handed their started job to the once and future king, Aaron Rodgers. In an ugly divorce that still reverberates around Packerland, Favre was traded to the New York Jets, where he played one season before retiring again.

In 2009, he was brought back out of retirement to play for the Packers dreaded rivals, the Minnesota Vikings. That season Favre was spectacular, throwing for 4,202 yards, 33 touchdowns and just seven interceptions, sending the Vikings into the NFC title game. But another costly interception against the Saints left Favre, and Vikes fans, in despair.

Another retirement followed, as did another change of heart, but 2010 was far different from the magical season of '09. Wracked by injury and inconsistency, Favre's consecutive games played streak finally ended on December 13, 2010, when he could not play in a Monday night game against the Giants due to a damaged shoulder. His streak, probably untouchable, lasted 297 games and 19 seasons. He did not play the rest of the season and finally retired for good.

His relationship with the Packers remains raw, though team officials insist, when the time is right for all parties, he will be invited back to Lambeau Field and his No. 4 will be retired.

# CHAPTER 22

# AARON RODGERS

*"That's about as well as I could play."*

**Name:** Aaron Charles Rodgers
**Birthday:** December 2, 1983
**Hometown:** Chico, California
**Current residence:** Chico, California
**Position:** Quarterback
**Height:** 6-2
**Weight:** 225
**Years:** 2005-present
**College:** California
**Accomplishments:** Named NFL Most Valuable Player in 2011 after throwing 45 touchdown passes and just six interceptions and leading the Packers to a 15-1 regular season…Named MVP of Super XLV in 2010 season…His career passing rating of 98.4 is first all-time in NFL history…Became the first quarterback in NFL history to throw for more than 4,000 yards in his first two years as a starter (2008-09)…Pro Bowl selection in 2009 and 2011 and All-

Pro in 2011…Green Bay's first-round draft pick in 2005.
**The game:** Atlanta Falcons, NFC Divisional Playoffs, January 15, 2011, at the Georgia Dome.

# THE LIFE OF AARON RODGERS

Maybe because Aaron Rodgers has rarely taken anything for granted, he has an appreciation for his circumstances few athletes of his caliber can grasp.

He was always considered a good athlete, never a great one. In high school, he was a good enough quarterback to intrigue colleges but not good enough to get those schools to offer him a scholarship. And after college, after setting the Pac-10 on fire for two seasons at the University of California, his descent down the 2005 draft board is still the stuff of painful legend.

Then, once in the NFL, his purgatory on the bench in Green Bay left many to assume that he was just another in a long line of Packers backup quarterbacks who would never get a sniff of an opportunity, much less success, in Green Bay.

But, every time, Rodgers accepted the circumstances, worked hard and bided his time, knowing his opportunity would come… one day.

The saga truly begins when Rodgers, after spending one season at Butte College, a junior college near his Chico, California hometown, caught the eye of University of California head coach Jeff Tedford, an offensive guru and an impressive developer of quarterbacks.

Rodgers ended up being a two-year starter for the Golden Bears, completing 64 percent of his passes for 5,469 yards with 43 touchdown passes and just 13 interceptions. He was a first team All-Pac-10 choice and an honorable mention All-American and was given consideration for the Heisman Trophy and other major college awards. He didn't win.

But as the 2005 draft dawned, Rodgers was considered one of the top quarterbacks in a relatively mundane class. Utah's Alex Smith was expected to be the top pick in the draft, going to the quarterback-starved San Francisco 49ers. But Rodgers wasn't expected to be far behind.

**Aaron Rodgers.** *Associated Press*

Yet there were questions about him. He had a funky throwing motion and he came from a college offense that didn't translate well to the NFL. Those concerns seemed to take root on draft day. So as the draft dragged on, pick after pick, Rodgers sat in the NFL's waiting room in New York City…waiting. The cameras caught every excruciating moment as players from all different positions—linebackers, running backs, defensive tackles, cornerbacks—were taken. Yet Rodgers just sat and waited, his anger and humiliation growing.

Finally, with the 24th pick, the Green Bay Packers, stunned that Rodgers was still available, didn't hesitate. They grabbed him without a thought. Sure, Green Bay still had the mercurial and legendary Brett Favre, but for how much longer? He'd been making noises for two years about retiring and while the Packers had gone 10-6 and reached the playoffs in 2004, cracks were appearing in the team's foundation.

Rodgers appeared to be the perfect bridge from past to present to future and Rodgers seemed genuinely appreciative that the Packers drafted him. And while Favre and Rodgers enjoyed a cordial working relationship, the veteran did little to instruct the new kid on what was required to be an NFL quarterback. As Favre said time again back then, he was there to play, not to teach the youngster. Rodgers played little his first three seasons in Green Bay, throwing just 35 passes.

But everything changed in 2008. Favre finally followed through with his threat, stunning the NFL community and sending Packers fans into confusion and mourning, when he announced his retirement in March. The starting job now belonged to Rodgers whose patience, again, had paid off.

As training camp opened that summer, though, it was clear Favre was having second thoughts. What followed was a scene worthy of any soap opera. He wanted to return, as the starter, but Packers coach Mike McCarthy and general manager Ted Thompson had already committed to Rodgers.

Sensing a public relations disaster, the Packers invited Favre back to compete with Rodgers for the starting job—an offer made after an especially surreal all-day meeting between Favre, McCarthy and Thompson. Insulted and furious, Favre said no. Instead, the Packers traded perhaps the most iconic player in team history to the New York Jets on August 7, 2008.

In the midst of the maelstrom, Rodgers remained calm and focused. The Packers had committed to him, he took them at their word and he would make them happy they did.

Rodgers took his first snap as the Packers first new starting quarterback since 1992 in the preseason opener against the Cincinnati Bengals at Lambeau Field. He was greeted with a standing ovation by most of the sellout crowd, a memory Rodgers still holds dear. And all he did that first season was throw for 4,038 yards and 28 touchdowns, despite a nagging shoulder injury, and slid seamlessly into a position he seemed born to play.

He has fought through criticism, uncertainty and injury and has delivered everything he said he would, including a Super Bowl title.

More amazingly, Rodgers has done what few in the NFL, and even fewer Packers fans, thought was possible – he has relegated the larger-than-life Brett Favre to the dusty annals of Packers history.

# THE SETTING

The foundation for Aaron Rodgers' success in that epic January playoff game in Atlanta may well have been laid nearly two months earlier when the Packers played, and lost, to the Falcons in a terrific regular season game at the Georgia Dome.

On November 28, the Packers and Falcons engaged in one of the season's most entertaining games when Green Bay, behind Rodgers' fourth-quarter heroics, rallied to tie the game at 17-17 on a touchdown pass to Jordy Nelson with 56 seconds remaining.

"I was thinking overtime at that point," Rodgers said at the time.

But a good kickoff return by Atlanta's Eric Weems got even better thanks to a Packers penalty, putting the Falcons in field goal range. With six seconds remaining, Matt Bryant nailed a 47-yard kick for the game-winner for Atlanta.

Rodgers was superb in that game, completing 26 of 35 passes for 344 yards and running for a season-high 51 yards. He completed every kind of pass imaginable to eight different receivers and though it didn't result in victory, it was another step in Rodgers' progression.

For Green Bay, it was a season on the edge. Tough late-season losses had left the Packers with no margin for error in terms of reaching the playoffs. But they beat the New York Giants and Chicago Bears in the final two regular season games to post a 10-6 record and slide in as the sixth, and final, seed. They then went to Philadelphia and held off the Eagles for Rodger's first-ever playoff victory.

That set up the second round game in Atlanta against the NFC's top-seeded Falcons. But the Packers knew, not only from their strong performance in November but from their win in Philly the week before, that they can play with anyone and, more important, anything was possible.

# THE GAME OF MY LIFE

### *By Aaron Rodgers*

I always feel confident going into games so when we went to Atlanta, I felt really good. That was a great week of practice and we had a strong expectation of playing well. In the regular season game down there, we had played really well and we knew that if the Falcons played the same way against us on defense that they did in that game, that we might have some opportunities. Sure enough they did and we picked them apart.

It's always difficult to play on the road but we had a lot of confidence because we had to go to Philly the week before and that's always a difficult environment to go in. But we won there and we knew going into the playoffs anything could happen. So we felt really confident going back to Atlanta. And a lot of things happened in that game and we made some plays early.

For whatever reason, I felt I had eyes in the back of my head in that game. More than usual, I was able to get around. I got out of sure sacks. I think the biggest play was our first drive of the second half. We had a sack on first down—John Abraham got to me—and then we had a short completion on second so we were facing a pretty long third down. I somehow got away again when I should have been sacked and I hit James (Jones) for a big first down and it got the crowd back out of the game. Then we went down and scored again. That play was kind of indicative of the game. It was a good momentum switch.

That was a big drive because not only did we double up on them (cornerback Tramon Williams had returned an interception 70 yards for a score on the last play of the first half), then we scored on that drive coming out of halftime and that broke their will.

I'm always striving for that perfect game and I played a nearly flawless game in college when I completed 23 passes on a row. But other than that, the Atlanta game was as well as I could play. One that stage, in that situation, that's as well as I can play.

Now we have a lot of expectations every year, but that was the key game to get us into the NFC Championship against the Bears and then we knew anything could happen from there. That game, personally, gave me a lot of confidence. I knew I could play at a high level when my best was needed.

# GAME RESULT

The domination came swiftly, unexpectedly. One minute it was a tight game between two evenly matched teams and it seemed the next it was over.

Indeed, the Falcons were in charge early, forcing a Packers turnover on their first possession and turning it into a Michael Turner 12-yard touchdown run.

But Rodgers set his tone for the day too, bringing the Packers right back, eluding Atlanta's swarming, blitzing defense and eventually throwing a six-yard scoring pass to Jordy Nelson to tie the game at 7-7.

But Eric Weems, who had done the Packers in with a great kickoff return in the Falcons' November win, did it again, this time bringing a kickoff back 102 for the touchdown.

From that point on, the Packers, and Rodgers, would take command. Coolly, Rodgers led the Packers back, eluding another certain sack from safety William Moore along the way to complete a 34-yard pass to James Jones. The eventual result was a 1-yard John Kuhn touchdown run.

With just 42 seconds left in the first half, the Packers took the lead for good when Rodgers completed a 20-yard scoring pass to Jones.

Then came the thunderbolt when, on the final play of the half, cornerback Tramon Williams intercepted a badly throw Matt Ryan pass and brought it back 70 yards for the touchdown, stunning the crowd and the Falcons.

Getting the ball to start the second half, Green Bay kept up the pressure, marching 80 yards and scoring on Rodgers' seven-yard run. The route was on.

By the time it was over, the Packers owned a resounding 48-21 win. Rodgers completed 31 of 36 passes for 366 yards and three touchdowns (and two of his incompletions were dropped). He directed the Packers on touchdown drives of 92 and 81 yards and two of 80 yards, frustrating the Falcons at every turn.

It was as complete a performance as any Packers quarterback had ever put together in the playoffs and it was the first time in team history that it had won two road playoff games in a row.

If there was any doubt about Rodgers' ability to perform in the playoffs, they were dashed after that masterful performance.

# WHAT BECAME OF AARON RODGERS?

Quite simply, Aaron Rodgers has become the face of the Green Bay Packers. And that's no easy task for a franchise that has seen its share of such mythic figures over the years as Curly Lambeau, Vince Lombardi, Bart Starr, Ray Nitschke, Reggie White and, yes, Brett Favre.

But Rodgers won over a skeptical fan base, uncertain teammates and a dubious league by simply playing at a level few had ever seen.

After the Packers missed the playoffs in Rodgers' first season as a starter in 2008, they went back to the postseason in 2009, losing in overtime to the Arizona Cardinals despite Rodgers throwing for a Packers playoff record 423 yards and four touchdowns.

But there were still nagging questions about Rodgers. The knock was that he made bad mistakes at the worst time. He seemed uncertain with the game on the line. He couldn't produce when it was required.

All that changed in 2010. He shook off a late-season concussion and led the Packers to three road playoff wins—over the Eagles, the Falcons and then in the NFC title game against the Bears—before capping Green Bay's remarkable resurgence with an MVP performance against the Pittsburgh Steelers in Super Bowl XLV. On the game's biggest stage, Rodgers was cool and confident, completing 24 of 39 passes for 304 and three scores and the Packers won their fourth Super Bowl.

"I think the Super Bowl win validated each of us as individuals," Rodgers said. "That was the ultimate validation. That put us on the map league wide."

But, apparently, he was only warming up. In 2011, Rodgers had a season most quarterbacks don't even dream about. In 15 games (he sat out a meaningless season finale), he threw for 4,643 yards, 45 touchdowns and just six interceptions as the Packers rolled to 15-1 record. The record was more incredible considering the Packers defense surrendered an NFL record for passing yardage, forcing Rodgers to be more accurate and thorough on offense.

The Packers were upset in the first round of the playoffs by the New York Giants, but Rodgers was still named the NFL Most Valuable Player in a season that also saw record-setting quarterback performances from the likes of New Orleans' Drew Brees and the Giants' Eli Manning.

Today, Rodgers is the veteran and confident leader the way Favre was in 2005 when Rodgers first arrived. He triggers one of the game's most prolific offenses for one of the NFL's most respected franchises and he accepts the role without complaint.

"The attention on me has really ramped up," he said. "From the endorsement to charities to appearances, there are events and being able to do some really cool things," he said. "I was able to present an award at the ESPYs. That was pretty cool. The drawback is the loss of any semblance of private time. People are always wanting something."

But when he thinks about that, he also remembers a draft room in New York City in 2005 and the sickening feeling then that no one wanted him. So he understands to be where he is now is the price for success—and he's willing to pay it.

"I ultimately ended up in such a good spot," he said. "It's a special feeling."

# Genocide and the Modern Age

# Genocide and the Modern Age

## ETIOLOGY AND CASE STUDIES OF MASS DEATH

EDITED BY

## Isidor Wallimann

AND

## Michael N. Dobkowski

AFTERWORD BY
Richard L. Rubenstein

CONTRIBUTIONS TO THE STUDY OF WORLD HISTORY, NUMBER 3

GREENWOOD PRESS
NEW YORK • WESTPORT, CONNECTICUT • LONDON

LIBRARY OF CONGRESS CATALOGING-IN-PUBLICATION DATA

Genocide and the modern age.

  (Contributions to the study of world history,
ISSN 0885-9159 ; no. 3)
    Bibliography:  p.
    Includes index.
    1.  History, Modern—20th century.  2.  Genocide—
History—20th century.  3.  Crimes against humanity—
History—20th century.  I.  Walliman, Isidor, 1944-
II.  Dobkowski, Michael N.  III.  Series.
D445.G36  1987    909.82   86-9978
ISBN 0-313-24198-8 (lib. bdg. : alk. paper)

Library of Congress Catalog Card Number:  86-9978
ISBN:   0-313-24198-8
ISSN:   0885-9159

First published in 1987

Greenwood Press, Inc.
88 Post Road West
Westport, Connecticut 06881

Printed in the United States of America

The paper used in this book complies with the
Permanent Paper Standard issued by the National
Information Standards Organization (Z39.48-1984).

10  9   8   7   6   5   4   3   2   1

To Raphael Lemkin
(1901-1959)


International lawyer, scholar, activist, and principal
drafter of the 1948 U.N. Convention for the Prevention
and Punishment of Genocide

# CONTENTS

# ACKNOWLEDGMENTS

In the course of preparing this volume, we have incurred many debts, some of which we are at last able to acknowledge publicly. We are particularly grateful to the contributors for the prompt submission of their essays and the high quality of their work. To those who offered editorial advice, we give special thanks. The editors, of course, assume final responsibility for the text.

The staff members of the libraries we utilized were unfailingly helpful in making materials available. We would like to offer special thanks to Gary Thompson of the Hobart and William Smith Colleges Library staff and the reference librarians at the University of Rochester Rush Rhees Library, Margaret Beckett, Janet Prentice, Brad Smith, David Legel, and Shirley Ricker. A Faculty Research Grant from Hobart and William Smith Colleges facilitated the completion of the work.

To colleagues in our respective institutions and to other friends and students who have provided an intellectual environment that was conducive to productive work, many thanks. A special acknowledgment to Dr. James T. Sabin, Vice-President, Editorial, of Greenwood Press, who supported this project from its inception and to the dedicated Greenwood Press staff.

Credit for typing goes to Karen Wigden and Mary Watkins.

Finally, but not least, we would like to thank Karen Gabe Dobkowski for her unfailing support, patience, sensitivity, and hospitality, and for creating the conditions that made the compiling of this book possible. And our thanks to Batsheva, Jonathan, and Tamar and to all children.

# INTRODUCTION

*Isidor Wallimann and*
*Michael N. Dobkowski*

Millions have died from poverty, millions from war and, as will become evident in this book, millions have been victims of genocide. While the social sciences have long been concerned with poverty—its effects, causes, and prevention—much less attention has been given to the nature of social conflicts and their possible escalation into war and the destruction of human lives. Attempts to increase our understanding of the nature of social conflicts and ways to de-escalate them (e.g., Kriesberg 1973) are part of a relatively recent endeavor to use social science insights for the prevention of war and the maintenance of peace. Still, despite the growing number of individuals and research institutes devoted to "peace research," efforts to successfully destroy life through war far outweigh those to preserve it. When it comes to genocide, the situation is even more precarious. Although genocide has been a recurring social phenomenon and has become ever more devastating in terms of lost human life as we have moved into the twentieth century, little effort has been spent in assessing its causes in the hope of better preventing it. It is as if events of genocidal proportions have—for whatever psychological or sociological reasons—been suppressed and excluded from the researchers' agenda. Yet, it is our opinion that genocide, like poverty, war, and all other events and processes destructive of human life, should gain top attention from scholars. With this collection of essays, we wish to enhance and facilitate this process in the hope that knowledge and "scientific" effort will increasingly be directed toward and serve the preservation of life.

If such scholarly efforts are to contribute to the improvement of the human condition by preserving life, in the case of genocide we can no longer conceive of it as a random (although relatively rare) historic phenomenon. Instead, we are compelled to look for patterns which lead to and are associated with these annihilations. Difficult as it may be to accept such a notion, we must also look upon the history and nature of societies giving rise to genocides as man-made and thereby influenceable. Any other perspective would preclude the human agency necessary to act preventively. Thus, postulating that the social and historic circumstances making genocide possible are man-made, and that genocides, far from being random events, may be associated with certain social patterns, we must begin to penetrate the circumstances under which human beings have been annihilated in the past so that we can establish criteria for the prevention of similar destructions in the future.

This volume is divided into two parts. The first part contains contributions of a general nature. They are primarily concerned with definitions, typologies, and explanations of genocide. The essays in the second part focus more heavily on special aspects of the phenomenon. On the one hand, they illuminate processes or special characteristics associated with a particular genocide. On the other hand, they attempt to test specific hypotheses or to explain the emergence of a given event of genocide. Ultimately, both the more general and the specific articles complement and draw from each other. In no way can they be treated as mutually exclusive. Both parts, we believe, bring us a step further in the "scientific" analysis and understanding of genocide as a modern social and historical phenomenon.

Any disciplined analysis of genocide requires that certain definitional issues and problems be clarified. Even if such problems cannot immediately be resolved, they must nevertheless be articulated. This we have attempted to do at the outset. Here the discussion centers around such issues as the groups that should be subsumed under any discussion of victims of genocide. In addition to racial groups, for example, should the annihilation of ethnic, religious, economic, or political groups also be included in a definition of genocide? Other points concern the question of numbers killed, intent, and plan. How many or what percentage of members of a group must be destroyed before an event should be called genocidal? Must this destruction be intentional or should any comparable destruction, intentional or not, be categorized as genocide? The important question also arises concerning when, if at all, war is genocide and genocide is war.

Not unrelated to definitions of genocide is the attempt to classify events of genocide. In fact, classifications and typologies are a necessary prerequisite if genocide is to be understood and explained at all. Again, we have chosen to place contributions aiming to develop and justify typologies of genocide in Part I, which investigates how genocides have varied throughout history and to what extent this variance may have been "caused" by differences in modes of production; differences in warfare; economic competition; the tendency to accumulate economic power and wealth; differences in state power; the need to maintain political control; or bureaucratization, ideology, and technology.

In many ways, typologies imply explanation because events of genocide are grouped according to criteria which in themselves can serve as explanation. Nevertheless, the first part of this volume also includes contributions which focus, aside from any explanatory power inherent in typologies, on more general explanations of genocide. Thus, it is discussed how genocide could be a technique of dealing with surplus populations, implying that if the rise of surplus populations could be prevented genocide might not occur. Other endeavors look for an explanation of genocide in the existence of severe social cleavages, and in the outright support of (or lack of constraints placed on) totalitarian regimes by other nations. Also, it is postulated that the inability to carry through structural social and political readjustments induces genocide, particularly when drastic changes might be called for as a result of defeat in war, national independence, revolution, and so on. Finally, it is suggested that we should begin to understand modern genocides not as examples of a rather impersonal process of technological rationality, or as the results of structurally induced crises, but rather as acts of societal madness. The entire notion of purposeful intentionality is critically explored.

More specific studies characterize Part II. By focusing on the corruption of the law as it preluded genocide, by examining the Jewish Holocaust, and by looking at other instances of genocide such as the Armenian case or the "genocide" perpetrated against the Aborigines in connection with colonialism and imperialism, it is possible to improve our understanding of mass death. In addition, the question of the uniqueness or universality of genocide(s) can fruitfully be dealt with in this manner. For should the Holocaust, for example, prove to be unique, the criteria making it thus can be drawn upon as explanatory variables for a better understanding not only of the Holocaust but also, by inference, of other examples of mass death. Thus, it is postulated that the Holocaust is unique because of its scope, its unprecedented involvement of the legal and administrative apparatus, the horrible treatment meted out to the individuals to be annihilated, and the concerted ideological campaign directed against the population targeted for destruction. Yet these destructions do not occur in a vacuum. In as much as it is individuals who carry out these atrocities, it also is important to pose certain questions on the social psychology level. For example, which ideology, mind sets, and personalities must already exist or be created for individuals or even major segments of a society to feel unashamed and justified in being part of an extermination enterprise?

It has been suggested that middleman minorities, due to their peculiar position, and to the cleavages and conflicts in which they partake or become involved, are particularly likely to be discriminated against. Could it be that, since such discrimination has often assumed high levels of intensity, middleman minorities are therefore likely to become victims of genocide? Is there a connection between middleman minority status and genocide? For, should such a connection exist, we may have come a step closer to understanding the phenomenon and possibly being able to devise ways of preventing it.

Given the issues and questions raised in this collection, where do we go from here? What points need further clarification, and what problems still are to be solved? Admittedly, they are many, and if we, as editors, now enter the discussion by pointing out some of the issues we believe need further attention, we are fully aware of the selective nature of our attempt. Yet, we maintain that these issues are pressing and important. They concern the connection between genocide, surplus population, economic gain, and middleman minorities, and the question of intentionality as it pertains to genocide.

We believe that it is of great importance to further investigate the connection between genocide and the presence or absence of surplus populations, just as it has been important to investigate the evolution of societies, their stratification systems, and the corresponding existential conditions in a manner that includes population size in relation to available resources (Lenski 1966). However, in studying the connection between genocide and surplus population, we need not necessarily confine ourselves solely to the question of how so-called surplus populations have been and are being eliminated. We can equally inquire how society has "constructively" rather than "destructively" dealt with surplus populations throughout history. For instance, we can study, as Mizruchi (1983) shows, how potentially troublesome surplus populations, far from being annihilated, have been socially controlled and regulated. Thus, by inference, ways might be found which preempt genocidal strategies of surplus population management.

Whenever the notion of surplus population is being used, it is important to distinguish between absolute and relative surplus population, something Lenski and Mizruchi fail to do. For a portion of the society may appear to us as superfluous while in fact it is not. Appearances can be misleading and superficial; our observation that some people can no longer maintain themselves or lack sufficient integration into the economic system may tempt us to conclude that a surplus of people exists. However, taking appearances for reality has more often than not been a source of great error. If, as is the case in capitalist societies, for instance, millions go hungry, are unemployed, underemployed, or on welfare while factories run at much lower than full capacity and land remains uncultivated or inappropriately used, the problem is not one of having too many people. The problem lies instead in the structure of the economy and the entire mode of production and distribution. The apparent surplus population is, under these circumstances, only relative, not absolute, and should not even be called a surplus population. This term itself tends to blame the victims, i.e., those negatively affected by the politics inherent in a given mode of production. It tends to single them out as the problem's source, overlooking the real sources of the apparent overpopulation located in the economic system as a whole. In short, the problem of relative surplus population is one of political economy, not one of individuals reproducing at a rate faster than economic means can be made available. Even if one were able to show that a society or segments thereof reproduce in excess of what can be produced to maintain everyone, it must be kept in mind that fertility rates themselves are influenced by existing economic conditions. This can be observed in those cases in which some elements of the population who are marginalized economically distribute their risks by increasing the number of offsprings. All this goes to demonstrate that so-called surplus populations are rarely absolute. Should the presence of a relative surplus population, therefore, be connected with events of genocide, it follows that in order to prevent the latter, structural economic changes preventing the rise of relative surplus populations must be brought about.

The present tradition (see, for instance, Rubenstein 1983) of linking relative surplus population with genocide postulates that this surplus population consists of the chronically unproductive and generally unemployable who, in times of crisis, might be eliminated. Since large-scale elimination has been witnessed under Joseph Stalin as well as under Adolf Hitler, it is concluded that these genocides served as a means to reduce or eliminate the existing relative surplus population perceived to be problematic. It is our opinion, however, that the population eliminated in both cases should not be characterized as chronically unproductive and generally unemployable, and when they showed such "traits," as in part was the case in Germany, this was the result of a policy that systematically cut Jews off from economic activity. What we are confronted with here, therefore, seems to be a problem involving the categories employed. This problem deserves further attention and scrutiny. The following questions must be asked: Why were other groups not eliminated who readily appeared as superfluous, i.e., as chronically unproductive and generally unemployable? Why should the relative surplus population be eradicated indirectly? What can be gained, and who benefits (politically and economically) from an elimination of middleman minorities or otherwise situated economically integrated segments of a population in order to "solve" the relative surplus population problem? In a larger economic and political context, what could be the function of generating "vacancies" by eliminating groups that would not usually be called chronically unproductive or generally unemployable? Why is it that programmed and planned annihilation, historically speaking, seems to be directed more often against economically integrated non-wage labor groups (such as middleman minorities) while wage laborers, the marginalized, and the poor of all ages seem to perish without explicit effort and intention on the part of the remaining society?

The related idea that only intentional or planned massive destruction of human lives should be called genocide can also be a very difficult and, in our opinion, an inadequate notion. As such it has the tendency to gloss over structural violence which through various mechanisms can be equally as destructive of human life as many an intentional and planned program of annihilation. In addition, the presence of structural violence promotes the use of planned violence. The problem here lies not in the difficulty of demonstrating what intentionality means psychologically speaking, but rather in the neglect of those processes of destruction which, although massive, are so systematic and systemic, and that therefore appear so "normal" that most individuals involved at some level of the process of destruction may never see the need to make an ethical decision or even reflect upon the consequences of their actions. What prevents people from stepping outside of their particular situations and from reflecting upon the consequences of their actions or inactions? Has society, a product of human activity, become so objectified, so alien to its source, that its creators feel no part of its operation, feel no possibility of affecting its course of movement? Why is it that individuals do not seem to be able to reflect upon the processes that have made them anonymous actors, cogs in the system, and that have nudged many of them to participate in genocide?

In a world that historically has moved from domination based primarily on the will of given individuals (in the Middle Ages, for example) to one in which individuals are dominated by anonymous forces such as market mechanisms, bureaucracies, and distant decision making by committees and parliaments, the emphasis on intentionality almost appears anachronistic. To be sure, we are not suggesting that the individual actor qua actor, be it Eichmann, a Turkish nationalist, or a soldier sitting in a missile silo, is not responsible and should not be held accountable for his or her actions. Neither do we say that they would not be capable of making existential decisions. People do have a choice. Neither are we suggesting that a specific nation or group engaged in genocide is involved in a process that has a degree of inevitability about it, hence mitigating the issue of accountability. Rather, we are pointing to the fact that in the modern age, the issue of intentionality on the societal level is harder to locate because of the anonymous and amorphous structural forces that dictate the character of our world. Technically speaking, individuals have a will and retain the capacity to use it, but how often is their agency the product of their will and intentions? Where in these market mechanisms and decision-making processes lies the origin of intent, and whose intentions are being carried out? If, as a result of worldwide market involvement and market pressures, slaves in the eighteenth century began to be worked to death within some seven or eight years, down from a much longer life expectancy, where can the plan for this large-scale destruction of members of the black race be located? And why was there no serious reflection on the part of slaveholding society concerning the long-run economic consequences for the slave system as a whole, to say nothing of the humanitarian and moral considerations, dictated by the waste of such a cruel and seemingly "irrational" system? And where was the rest of the world? Ideology, racism, and the availability of surplus labor to exploit, be it in the American South or in the Nazi slave labor camps, are certainly operative and important factors, but they are only partial explanations.

These are important questions since they force us to probe more deeply and fundamentally into the nature of social structures and systems. Aside from the presence or absence of intentions and plans, it must be investigated which forms of social organization are more likely to guarantee the preservation rather than the systematic destruction of lives through structural violence. Which forms of social organization also make it less likely for a massive genocide to occur? Along these lines it can be hypothesized that the less a society is permeated by structural violence, the lower will be the likelihood of genocide and mass destruction, for societies with lower levels of structural violence are also less likely to allow for planned large-scale genocide. The less individuals' lives are ruled by anonymous forces, i.e., the less they are subject to structural violence of any kind, the less likely it is that they will become involved as perpetrators in an event of genocide. Conversely, in societies where all are perpetrated upon, all become perpetrators in one way or another. Therefore, freedom from structural violence and the anonymous forces that dominate modern man seems to be one precondition for overcoming our age of genocide. For, if in history we have increasingly moved to more frequent and massive forms of genocide as anonymous and impersonal domination increased, it follows that, aside from personal domination and intentions, the structural domination—that anonymous domination exerted by the character of an entire social system—would have to be reversed. Not necessarily eliminating genocide resulting from personal domination or the exercise of that power (by dictator, tyrant, king, tribal chieftain, for example), this reversal may contribute to the mitigation of the massive and frequent genocides that have been part of the landscape of modern human intercourse. Making genocide by definition dependent on the existence of any intention and plan to destroy lives, therefore, seems historically and politically too limiting.

What is required, then, is a greater degree of reflection upon and awareness of the anonymous societal forces that frame and propel our existence so that we can begin the arduous task of eliminating the structural violence that leads to domination, inequality, and the possibility of genocide. Ultimately what seems to be needed is a society that can provide an equal access to power and resources for all with a minimum degree of personal or structural coercion. We are fully aware of the utopian nature of our suggestions and recognize that such a world order may never be achieved. Nevertheless, we stress our conviction that efforts in this direction must begin. We believe that the clarification of this predicament must be attempted so that the struggle to eliminate structural violence and domination can be initiated. Correct action requires understanding. Whatever progress is made in this pursuit, be it modest or radical, will contribute to diminishing the possibility that in the future we will engage in genocide, this most pernicious of anti-life-affirming behaviors.

## BIBLIOGRAPHY

Kriesberg, Louis. *The Socioloy of Social Conflicts*. Englewood Cliffs, N.J.: Prentice-Hall, 1973.

Lenski, Gerhard E. *Power and Privilege: A Theory of Social Stratification*. New York: McGraw-Hill, 1966.

Mizruchi, Ephraim H. *Regulating Society: Marginality and Social Control in Historical Perspective*. New York: The Free Press, 1983.

Rubenstein, Richard L. *The Age of Triage: Fear and Hope in an Overcrowded World*. Boston: Beacon Press, 1983.

# PART I

# Conceptualizing, Classifying, Defining, and Explaining Genocide: Some Macro Perspectives

# A TYPOLOGY OF GENOCIDE AND SOME IMPLICATIONS FOR THE HUMAN RIGHTS AGENDA

## *Kurt Jonassohn and Frank Chalk*

## INTRODUCTION

To begin with, such a title requires an explanation. Why would anyone try to construct a typology of genocide? The great majority of serious studies that deal with genocide deal with a single case, usually the Holocaust, less often with the Armenians in Turkey, and very rarely with other cases. In doing a study of a single case no typology is required, either because the case is treated as a unique event, or because the argument involves the internal sequence of circumstances that led to the genocide.

The need for some method of classification becomes apparent only when one is trying to deal with a large number of cases comparatively. In fact, in so doing one even becomes aware of the need for a rather rigorous and unambiguous definition; how else will one decide which cases belong in the study and which ones really represent a quite different phenomenon and thus should not be included? But even after this first step has been taken, the question arises whether all of the cases that do meet the criteria of the definition should be considered as falling into one large group. This question tends to answer itself after some preliminary work on some of the cases has been done. It is quickly appar-

We want to thank Norman Cohn, Helen Fein, Leo Kuper, and Anton Zijderveld for discussing our work on genocide with us, though they are not responsible for the contents of this chapter. An earlier version of this paper was presented at the Seventeenth World Congress of Philosophy, August 21-27, 1983, held in Montreal, Canada.

ent that genocides occur in quite different societies, under vastly varying circumstances, confronting quite different people, and resulting in dramatically different outcomes. Thus, treating all such cases as if they represented an undifferentiated phenomenon seems unlikely to lead to the kinds of results that are the aim of scholarly research. What we need is to group together those cases that appear to have some crucial characteristics in common. If we can fit all observed cases into one of several such classes, then we can talk about a process of classification, the end result of which will be a typology.

The textbooks on research methods tell us that the classes in a typology must be exhaustive and mutually exclusive. Such a requirement is difficult enough to meet but is not sufficient. We are not interested in imposing on our data some typology for the sake of order and neatness. A typology is a tool of research; unless it can be used as a tool in the analysis of the data, it is merely a frill that looks elegant but leads neither to meaning nor to explanation. If our aim is to satisfy such requirements, then the question arises as to what to use as a basis of building a typology. It soon appears that typologies could be built around several criteria. Thus, one could look at minority-majority relations within a society as well as power relations between societies; one might classify genocides by the means employed as well as by the results achieved; or one could consider causes as well as intentions. No doubt other bases for developing a typology could be added. And good reasons for using any of these could probably be developed. The choice will depend on the kinds of questions we want to explore. But the answer is really based on a hunch about the nature of the research to be undertaken. The very word "research" tells us that we are entering the realm of the unknown; if we knew the answers beforehand, we would not be searching for them. Thus, the adequacy of any particular typology can only be assessed in terms of the research results it helps to produce.

The typology to be proposed here is based on the hunch that intent is one such crucial criterion. If a definable group of people was almost or wholly eliminated, but nobody intended this to occur, is this genocide? Some definitions of genocide do not include the intent of the perpetrator. However, the case made here is that such events, although equally regrettable, are not genocides and therefore should be called something else. This leaves us with the task of trying to classify the kinds of intentions of the perpetrators and leads directly to a major difficulty: how does one prove or infer intent?

One of the major reasons for engaging in the study of genocide from a historical and comparative perspective is to find out whether some kinds of societies are more likely to commit genocide than others. From this perspective, it seems that a typology based on intent might have a great deal of analytic utility. However, there are two problems with the criterion of intent: first, it is rarely easy to get good evidence on conscious intent and, second, intent may be either explicit or implicit. However, the criterion of intent seems so important, and other criteria for constructing a typology seem to yield so little analytic gold, that these difficulties will simply have to be dealt with to the best of our ability. With these remarks in mind, the present chapter will discuss the need to examine events within the context in which they occurred, examine the reasons why genocidal events have been largely ignored in the literature until the middle of the twentieth century, and propose a typology of genocide.

## THE BRUTISHNESS OF THE PAST
## AND COLLECTIVE DENIAL

Our study of genocide has forced us on many occasions to confront the brutishness of most human societies in the past and the changing value placed on human life. It was not very long ago that many human societies sacrificed human beings to propitiate the gods, to protect the living against their displeasure, and to reassert the corporate unity of society. Human sacrifice existed throughout the ancient world, buttressed by religions that promised a good life in the afterworld to the sacrificial victim as well as the favor of the gods in this world for those who carried out the ritual slayings. The most recent discovery by archeologists excavating at Carthage of the remains of 6,000 infants sealed in individual sacrificial urns gives credence to the reports of commentators in the ancient world that the Carthaginian aristocracy gave its youngest sons to the priests for sacrifice to win the favor of the gods of war. In many societies human sacrifice continued until the society embraced an ethic that ennobled the individual in this world and adopted a code of behavior that placed this new ethic above the need to satisfy the grim appetite of the old gods for human blood.[1] Nigel Davies, who traces this change among the ancient Hebrews, credits them with transforming the "concept of life-giving . . . into that of self-giving." He contends that once the ancient Hebrews came to see God as good and just, human sacrifice ceased entirely.[2]

Yet even in those societies which abandoned human sacrifice, daily life was coarse and brutal for all but the very few. The great French historian Fernand Braudel reminds us that famines and epidemics were so common that "they were incorporated into man's biological regime and built into his daily life."[3] In Western Europe, which was favored by nature, "famine only disappeared at the close of the eighteenth century, or even later."[4] Sixteenth-century European towns worked out elaborate stratagems to divert armies of starving peasants from their gates. In the sixteenth and seventeenth centuries, France and England developed new institutions to control the poor displaced peasants who flocked to their cities and to harness their labor. The physically fit poor of Paris were often chained together in pairs and forced to clean the drains, while the poor of London were held in poorhouses under the new authority of the Poor Laws and put to work at menial labor. Conditions for the mass of the people were even worse, according to Braudel, in China and India, where famines struck more frequently and with greater severity than in Europe.

Peasants in Europe who reacted to their misery by stealing food or property felt the full vengeance of the law. Death or maiming were the usual penalties until the late Middle Ages. Medieval penalties for such crimes were codified in the German Empire in the *Constitutio Criminalis Carolina* of 1532, which was representative of European practice. After specifying such penalties as hanging in chains, beheading or burial alive, and impaling for the graver crimes, the *Carolina* takes up less serious crimes such as theft. For these offenses it "prescribes afflictive punishments—flogging, pillorying, cutting off the ears, chopping off the fingers, cutting out the tongue—usually accompanied by a sentence of banishment."[5] In Western Europe, following the enormous population losses of the Thirty Years' War and the start of the effort to populate overseas colonies, human life came to be more highly valued. In the mid-seventeenth century, England and France moderated their use of capital punishment in cases of crimes against property.[6] As the number of executions in England diminished, the English turned to the transportation of convicts to the colonies for terms of labor as indentured servants.[7] At the same time, France and other Mediterranean countries found it increasingly useful to sentence physically fit convicted felons to life sentences as oarsmen on naval galleys. (The argument in this paragraph follows Langbein, chapter 2.)

This coarseness and brutality of human existence throughout much of history was a subject that hardly ever appeared in the curricula of our schools. The good news was reported; the bad news was not. The great massacres of the past lay beyond the range of the telescopes designed to focus upon evidence that justice always triumphed. In high school and university-level textbooks, Athens flourished, but the massacre of the men of Melos was barely mentioned. The Romans destroyed Carthage and Corinth, but the fate of their peoples was not discussed. The authors of history textbooks hardly ever reported what the razing of an ancient city meant for its inhabitants. In other words, the fate of millions of human beings who died unnatural deaths as defenseless civilians was invisible.

Our review of the history of mass extermination and its neglect has led us to the conclusion that until very recently scholars participated in a process of pervasive and self-imposed denial. Many factors entered into the process of collective denial. Throughout most of recorded time, it was the victors who wrote the history of their conquests, and even the victims of mass extermination accepted their fate as a natural outcome of defeat. The idea of human rights is relatively new in Western society; even today, many parts of the world still emphasize duties more than rights. The Enlightenment tradition of viewing human beings as inherently good and rational also played a part in the denial, as did the rise of nationalism. The slaughter of people of *other* races, religions, and nationalities barely offended anyone's sensibilities.

It took the shocks of the twentieth century to reverse the process of collective denial; the gap between practice and ideals simply became too great to support the intellectual foundations of such denial. The Jews who survived the Holocaust refused to accept meekly the Nazis' assault on their right to exist. They recorded their experiences for posterity. At the end of World War II, the victorious Allied powers tried and executed top Nazi leaders judged guilty of crimes against humanity, an action which created a new interest in the history of crimes against civilians. Parochialism and nationalism were undermined by the spread of the democratic ideal after the war and the increasing sophistication of the mass of the people that resulted from greater access to higher education. Increasingly, journalists in the West have cast themselves in the role of adversaries to the holders of power and as spokesmen for the underdog in national and international affairs. Emboldened by this freer, more sympathetic atmosphere, other victims of past exterminatory campaigns —the Ukrainians, the Armenians, and the Gypsies—have begun to tell their stories. Ultimately, even scholars awakened to the paucity of studies examining and analyzing the phenomenon of mass extermination in history.

## A REVIEW OF THE LITERATURE

When we began our work on genocide in 1978, we could count on the fingers of one hand the number of scholars who had written comparatively about genocide. A small group of writers, taking up the challenge of Raphael Lemkin's work, contributed to this literature.[8] The pioneering scholarly study of genocide published by Lemkin in 1944, *Axis Rule in Occupied Europe,* established a definition of genocide which laid out the approximate boundaries of the concept and identified a number of specific historical events within its perimeter. Lemkin defined genocide as the coordinated and planned destruction of a national, religious, racial, or ethnic group by different actions through the destruction of the essential foundations of the life of the group with the aim of annihilating it physically or culturally. What we call ethnocide was a form of genocide in Lemkin's all-inclusive definition. After the war, the French coined the term ethnocide to deal with the extermination of a culture that did not involve the physical extermination of its people.[9]

Writing as news of the Nazis' depredations flowed in from Europe, Lemkin defined genocide to include attacks on political and social institutions, culture, language, national feelings, religion, and the economic existence of the group. Acts directed against individuals because they were also members of a group came within his definition of genocide. These included killing the members of the group or the destruction of their personal security, liberty, health, and dignity.

Lemkin incorporated a three-part typology of genocide based on the intent of the perpetrator in *The Axis Rule in Occupied Europe.* The aim of the first genocides—which he situated in antiquity and the Middle Ages—was a total or nearly total destruction of nations and groups. In the modern era, Lemkin argued, a second type of genocide emerged, involving the destruction of a culture without an attempt to physically annihilate its bearers. Nazi genocide comprised the third type of genocide in Lemkin's analysis. It combined ancient and modern genocide in a hybrid version characterized by the Nazi strategy of selecting some peoples and groups for extermination in the gas chambers and others for ethnocidal assimilation and Germanization. What Lemkin did not realize was that twentieth-century genocide was increasingly becoming a case of the state physically liquidating a group of its own citizens. Had he paid more attention in his 1944 book to the case of the Armenian genocide of 1915 or the genocide of the German Jews, this facet of modern genocide might have played a more prominent role in his analysis.

Until the early 1970s, there was almost no scholarly comparative output on genocide. Since then, several authors have produced books and articles renewing serious theoretical discourse on the subject. Hervé Savon's typology, which appeared in his book *Du Cannibalisme au Génocide,* consists of genocides of substitution, devastation, and elimination. These types of genocide take their meaning from the outcome of genocidal killings.[10] While Savon's work revived interest in the problem of genocide, his typology based on outcomes fails to illuminate the events leading up to the genocide and the possible methods of interrupting the process.

In 1976, Irving Louis Horowitz tackled the subject in a short volume titled *Genocide* which he revised and reissued in 1980 under the title *Taking Lives: Genocide and State Power.* As the new title suggests, Horowitz views genocide as a fundamental policy employed by the state to assure conformity to its ideology and to its model of society. His discussion of the role of the state in genocide and his critique of the failure of modern social science to tackle the most pressing social issues of the day ring true.

Horowitz devises a continuum of modern societies in which the level of state-induced repression of the right to dissent and to be different is the key variable.[11] This continuum ranges from genocidal societies at one extreme, through less repressive and more liberal societies, to permissive societies at the other extreme. Horowitz' typology is based primarily on twentieth-century cases. His approach focuses on outcomes and does little to explain the process whereby an authoritarian state resorts to genocide, nor does it account for pre–twentieth-century genocides. Moreover, as Horowitz himself admits, a typology based on internal repression cannot explain by itself those genocides conducted in foreign countries.

Vahakn Dadrian, who followed Lemkin in emphasizing the intent of the perpetrator, published a somewhat confusing typology at about the same time that Horowitz' book appeared. He posits five types of genocide: (1) cultural genocide, in which assimilation is the perpetrator's aim; (2) latent genocide, which is the result of activities with unintended consequences, such as civilian deaths during bombing raids or the accidental spread of disease during an invasion; (3) retributive genocide, designed to punish a segment of a minority which challenges a dominant group; (4) utilitarian genocide, using mass killing to obtain control of economic resources; and (5) optimal genocide, characterized by the slaughter of members of a group to achieve its total obliteration, as in the Armenian and Jewish holocausts. Dadrian's lumping together of intended and unintended genocide serves to weaken the rigor of his typology. It seems to us that Dadrian has blended together the motives of the perpetrators, unintended outcomes, ethnocide, and non-genocidal massacres.[12] We learned a great deal from his discussion of the importance of perpetrator intent but have not been able to use his typology effectively in our work.

Helen Fein included two thoughtful pages on types of genocide in her 1979 book on the Holocaust, *Accounting for Genocide*.[13] Before the rise of the nation-state, Fein argues, there were two types of genocide: genocides intended to eliminate members of another faith and genocides designed to exterminate other tribes because they could not be subdued or assimilated. In her view, the nation-state has given birth to three new types of genocide: in the first, the state commits mass extermination to legitimate its existence as the vehicle for the destiny of the dominant group; in the second, the state kills to eliminate an aboriginal group blocking its expansion or development; and, in the third, the state reacts spontaneously to rebellion by totally eliminating the rebels.

Understandably, there are omissions and gaps in Fein's typology, which is only incidental to her major task. She does not provide a place for mass exterminations intended to instill terror in others to facilitate conquest, or for mass killings to further economic enrichment. These are categories that we have found helpful in our work.

Leo Kuper has contributed more to the comparative study of the overall problem of genocide than any scholar since Raphael Lemkin. In his 1981 monograph on the subject, Kuper wrestles with the problems of genocidal process and motivation. His discussion of past genocides

clusters the motives of the perpetrator around three categories: (1) genocides designed to resolve religious, racial, and ethnic differences; (2)
genocides intended to terrorize a people conquered by a colonizing empire; and (3) genocides perpetrated to enforce or fulfill a political ideology.[14] Kuper is especially concerned with the increasing frequency of
genocidal events in the modern period. Since modern genocides occur
within nation-states that have the character of plural societies, the
creation of new plural societies during the period of colonization and
decolonization becomes of particular significance for his analysis.
Under the heading of "related atrocities," Kuper discusses two groups
which are excluded under the U.N. definition of genocide.[15] These are
the victims of mass political slaughter and attempts to decimate an economic class. He examines three exterminations in this category: in
Stalin's Russia, the decimation of the peasants, the Party elite, and the
ethnic minorities; in Indonesia, the slaughter of Communists in 1965;
and in Cambodia, the mass murders of the Kampuchean government led
by the Khmer Rouge. Kuper concludes that each of these cases would
have been labeled genocide if political groups had been protected by the
U.N. Convention.

In examining a large number of cases, Kuper insists on the need to
refer to specific conditions in each case. He does not think that it is
possible to write in general terms about the genocidal process. "The
only valid approach would be to set up a typology of genocides" and to
analyze the genocidal process in each type and under specific conditions.[16]

Kuper's book is the most useful contribution to the literature on
genocide thus far, but we have two major problems with it. One,
because he does not have a rigorous definition of genocide, he includes a
number of cases in his discussion which have no salient characteristics in
common. This is a serious handicap in attempting a comparative study
of genocide. Although Kuper is aware of this problem, instead of
excluding certain cases of large-scale killing, he includes them under the
category of genocidal massacre and related atrocities. Two, in his analysis, he treats plural societies as particularly vulnerable to genocide. We
think that the plural character of a society is at best an intervening
variable. It is new states or new regimes attempting to impose conformity to a new ideology that are particularly likely to practice genocide.
When tensions between the traditional society and the new regime
escalate, it is the plural character of a society which is most likely to
provide the social cleavages that define the perpetrator and victim
groups.

## A DEFINITION AND TYPOLOGY OF GENOCIDE

In order to distinguish genocide from the various misfortunes that befall people, it is important to include the criterion of planning and intent to destroy in its definition.  The most widely accepted definition of genocide is that contained in the 1948 United Nations Convention on Genocide:

> In the present Convention, genocide means any of the following acts committed with intent to destroy, in whole or in part, a national, ethnical, racial or religious group, as such:
> (a)  Killing members of the group;
> (b)  Causing serious bodily or mental harm to members of the group;
> (c)  Deliberately inflicting on the group conditions of life calculated to bring about its physical destruction in whole or in part;
> (d)  Imposing measures intended to prevent births within the group;
> (e)  Forcibly transferring children of the group to another group.[17]

While this definition certainly does include the criterion of intent, it does not cover the extermination of political and economic groups—an exclusion made necessary in order to assure the passage of the Convention. In our own work, we have broadened the United Nations definition to include political and economic groups.

We propose to use this amended United Nations definition in our work although it has serious shortcomings:  it does not adequately define the victim groups;  it includes acts which we would consider ethnocide rather than genocide; and it obfuscates the distinction between genocides, massacres, and wartime casualties.  However, since this definition is the most widely known one and since no better definition has been devised, we shall use it for the time being.  But in our usage, we shall exclude those killings which are not the deliberate physical extermination of a defenseless group, in whole or in part.

In devising a typology of genocide, we had no difficulty in deciding that it should be based on intent, but the actual categories posed a much harder problem.  We have tried a number of typologies only to discard them later.  When we examined actual cases, it turned out that almost all of them could fit into more than one category and thus required decisions as to what should be considered the dominant intent.  The present typology is offered as a heuristic device and not as a final product.  It may well be modified as a result of our own further research or in response to such critiques as interested readers are prepared to contribute.

We have classified genocides in terms of those committed (1) to eliminate the threat of a rival; (2) to acquire economic wealth; (3) to create terror and (4) to implement a belief, a theory, or an ideology. In looking at actual cases, the motives tend to be more complex than such a relatively simple scheme allows for; therefore, we have assigned cases to one of these types on the basis of what we consider to have been the dominant intent of the perpetrator.

We do not know when the first genocide occurred. It seems unlikely that early man engaged in genocide during the hunting and gathering stage. While we have no direct evidence, this seems a reasonable assumption because men lived in quite small groups and overall population densities were extremely low (1 per 10 km$^2$ of habitable terrain according to the estimates of McEvedy and Jones).[18]

After the discovery of agriculture, the world divided into nomads and settlers. This marked the start of systematic conflict in the form of food raiding by the nomads. The nomads quickly learned to raid their settled neighbors at harvest time for their food stores; however, they had no interest in exterminating them because they planned to repeat their raids in subsequent years. The settlers may have had much better reason to do away with the nomads, but they had neither the means nor the skills to do so.

As the settlers improved their agricultural techniques and produced significant surpluses, they were able to support cities, rulers, and armies. They accumulated wealth and engaged in significant trade. With these developments, the scene changed dramatically. Conflicts arose over wealth, trade, and trade routes. Wars were fought over the access to wealth and over the control of transportation networks (to use a modern term). At first, these conflicts were probably in the nature of brigandage and robbery. Soon they escalated to wars between city-states. However, these warring peoples soon discovered that their victories were mostly temporary: the defeated peoples withdrew long enough to rebuild their resources and their armies, and then tried to recoup their losses and to avenge their defeat. This pattern became so common that it soon appeared that the only way to assure a stable future was to eliminate the defeated enemy once and for all. People that were not killed during or after the battle were sold into slavery and dispersed. This *elimination of a potential future threat* appears to be the reason for the first genocides in history.

Genocides of this first type seem to have been common throughout antiquity, especially in the Middle East, where trade routes between Asia, Africa, and Europe crossed. The Assyrians were expert practitioners; about a number of the peoples whom they vanquished we know little more than their names.[19] When the empire of the Hittites was destroyed, it was done so efficiently that not even the location of their capital was known until an inspired German archeologist unearthed it almost by accident in the nineteenth century.[20] Perhaps the best-known example of this type of genocide is the destruction of Carthage.[21] The so-called Punic Wars between Carthage and Rome lasted well over a century (264-146 B.C.) and were fought mostly over the control of the Mediterranean trade and economy. These wars were incredibly costly in terms of material and lives, even by modern standards. After Rome just barely won the Second Punic War (218-201 B.C.), it decided that Carthage had to be eliminated once and for all. Those who were not killed in the Third Punic War (149-146 B.C.) were sold into slavery, and the city was destroyed. Looking at the available evidence from antiquity, one might even develop a hypothesis that most wars at that time were genocidal in character.

The evidence from antiquity is often contradictory, ambiguous, or missing. Such evidence as we have consists almost exclusively of written materials that were produced either by the victims or by the perpetrators; in those rare cases where we have accounts from both sides, they tend not to confirm each other's evidence. It may well be that as yet undiscovered evidence will shed new light on how and why entire peoples have disappeared. Such disappearances in themselves are not evidence of genocide because they may have been due to a variety of processes, from migration to assimilation. However, if we should ever develop an archeology of genocide, we may acquire more conclusive proof of what happened to the populations of cities that were destroyed and to whole peoples that have disappeared. One case illustrating such possibilities is the extermination, reported by Iranian historians, of whole populations by the Mongols under Genghis Kahn; these reports were thought to be exaggerated because they originated from the victims. They gained renewed credibility, however, when archeologists unearthed the pyramids of skulls that Iranian historians had described.[22]

The second type of genocide is one committed primarily *to acquire economic wealth*. It probably also originated in antiquity. People looking for greater wealth than their own territory could provide found it in the possession of others. When such wealth was in the form of fertile land and other primary resources, it could not be carried off as loot, but could only be acquired by occupying the land and enslaving and/or exterminating the indigenous population. This type of genocide has continued to occur throughout history up to the present day. It has often been associated with colonial expansion and the discovery and settlement of new parts of the world. The Tasmanians[23] disappeared in the same way that some of the peoples of the interior of Brazil are disappearing today.[24]

The third type of genocide is a somewhat later invention and was associated with the building and maintaining of empire. To conquer others and to keep them subjugated requires large armies and a permanent investment in a large occupying force. Genghis Khan probably

present a set of particularly difficult problems. This is not the place for
exploring these problems in detail. However, four kinds of problems
should be mentioned that make such study especially difficult:

1. The evidence is by its very nature difficult to obtain because throughout
   most of history relevant records either were not kept or did not survive;
2. Where records do exist, they either originate with the perpetrators or with
   the victims, but rarely do we find records from both;
3. When we do have records from the perpetrators and the victims, they are
   often so divergent that it is difficult to decide what actually did occur, and
   the intentions of the perpetrator may be the most difficult evidence to
   discover; and
4. The reliability of the records presents another problem, especially in the
   premodern period. Thus, we have evidence for genocides that occurred
   but were not reported;  but we also have those that were reported but never
   occurred.

## IMPLICATIONS FOR THE HUMAN RIGHTS AGENDA

In our century, the increasing prevalence of the conditions leading to
type four genocide is becoming a matter of serious concern to those of us
who care about human rights. If we look at societies from Horowitz'
perspective, then we must ask how they deal with deviance and non-
conformity. It seems to us that the crucial dimension in a society's
handling of deviants is the way it defines and maintains their membership in the society itself. This is not a purely conceptual distinction,
because it has wide-ranging consequences not only for the victims but
also for the way the world responds to the victims and the perpetrators.

Insofar as a given society responds to its deviants and dissenters with
something other than tolerance and permissiveness, the first question to
be asked is whether such groups are defined as continuing members of
the society or whether they are deprived of such membership. Loss of
membership can be implemented in only two ways, that is, by deportation or by extermination. Any other form of repression or punishment
implicitly acknowledges the victim's continuing membership.

Torture and harassment are ways of physically punishing "deviant"
groups and individuals. But punishment is incidental to intimidating and
terrorizing the rest of society:  when victims remain at large or eventually
rejoin their erstwhile groups, their membership in society remains
unquestioned precisely because they are intended to serve as a dire warning to other actual or potential "deviants." It is also precisely because
they have retained their membership and their citizenship that it is possible to take action on their behalf under various human rights legis-
lations and conventions.

Deportation and extermination pose a different problem. In the case of deportation, the victims may be helped by being granted a new membership status and the associated civic rights in another society that is willing to welcome them. However, in the case of extermination assistance is, by definition, too late to help the victims. Thus, in these cases any meaningful action would have to address the search for methods of early warning and prevention. Such a search faces daunting problems of theory and practice. Prediction and early warning of mass exterminations and deportations have barely been raised as a theoretical problem, and a great deal of work remains to be done before any such prediction can be made with some assurance of correctness. But even after such theoretical problems are solved, there still remains the practical problem of the sovereignty of the perpetrator. The history of the United Nations, with all of its conventions, stands as mute testimony to the discouragement of those of us who still believe in the worth and dignity of all human beings.

Against this background, it is understandable that human rights activism addresses itself to torture and harassment much more than to deportation and extermination. With respect to torture and harassment, much more is known about help for the victims and the possibility of prevention. Success, when achieved or seen as attainable, reinforces further activism. No such encouragement seems to be available to those concerned with genocide and deportation. While mass deportations seem to be decreasing due to growing populations which are too large to transport, the spread of the nation-state, and the disappearance of relatively empty territories, genocides in the twentieth century seem to have been increasing in number and in scope. (To cite just one example, while it was possible for England, France, Spain, and Portugal to expel the Jews at different times, it was not possible for Hitler to expel the millions of Jews living in Germany and its occupied territories.)

In discussing the persecution and extermination of individuals and groups, it is important to remember the distinction between theory and practice. Many countries have declared judicial torture to be illegal; an even larger number of countries have signed the United Nations Convention on Genocide. Yet this has clearly not meant that either practice has disappeared or even diminished. There is a huge gap between declarations of good intentions and their application and realization.

The twentieth century has seen a tremendous increase of new states, the majority of which are ruled by one-party totalitarian or military regimes. Totalitarian or military regimes usually have to deal with dissenting groups, which leads inevitably to various forms of repression and persecution, and, with increasing frequency, to genocidal massacres and to outright genocide.[30] Such states are particularly prone to engage in what we have called type four genocides, that is, genocides based on the implementation of a belief, a theory, or an ideology.

Individual activists and protest groups, assisted by several international conventions on human rights, have learned a great deal about the various ways of assisting the victims of persecution in different countries. Such help, while not always successful, is usually initiated by specific reports of incarceration and torture while the victims are alive. Similar reports of killings and genocides do not elicit the same kind of action for the obvious reason that the victims are already beyond help.

Why are human rights efforts not more successful? The first reason is that the very notion of human rights is foreign to most cultures of the world. It is often seen as another Western export that is being imposed on the rest of the world from outside. Implementation of human rights legislation is possible only in a democratic regime based on the rule of law. Where military and/or totalitarian regimes are in power, the whole notion of human rights is a contradiction in terms. The second reason is that the nation-state is both the guardian and the violator of human rights. Therefore, action from within is either impossible or fruitless, and action from without conflicts with the much too widely accepted definition of sovereignty. A further consequence of military and authoritarian regimes is that they can control access to and distribution of information, with the result that violations may not even become known or that proof may not be accessible. The third reason is that international bodies and international agreements, largely supported by the West, continue to exist mostly for symbolic reasons. Their continued existence is dependent upon the degree to which they serve the interests of all sides. However, their efficacy will remain largely symbolic because no supra-national body exists that can enforce their terms. The participants are sovereign nations that will not accept any diminution of their sovereignty, especially when they are also the offenders.

For these reasons, human rights actions will have to continue to rely on publicity and on shaming campaigns, where these are successful. In addition, their mission should be to spread the ideology of human rights and to encourage and support research into the conditions and situations which seem to increase or decrease the probability of human rights violations in various countries.

Any worthwhile activism with regard to genocide will have to be radically different from other human rights efforts. In order to be of help to the potential victims, it will have to focus solely on prevention. Theo van Boven, the former Director of the United Nations Division of Human Rights, has recently made a similar plea with regard to political assassinations and extra-judicial executions. However, in order to prevent such lethal crimes, we would have to be able to predict their occurrence—something that our present state of knowledge does not yet permit. Thus, any efforts at preventing future genocides will have to start with the kind of research capable of yielding predictive indicators that would then allow concerted efforts at prevention; in addition, research will be needed to uncover those conditions and techniques of external pressure that are likely to be the most effective means of prevention.

## NOTES

1. Nigel Davies, *Human Sacrifice in History and Today* (New York: William Morrow, 1981), p. 280.

2. Ibid., p. 66.

3. Fernand Braudel, *Capitalism and Material Life: 1400-1800* (New York: Harper and Row, 1967), p. 38.

4. Ibid., p. 39.

5. John Langbein, *Torture and Law of Proof* (Chicago: University of Chicago Press, 1977), p. 40.

6. Ibid., p. 44.

7. Ibid., p. 40.

8. Raphael Lemkin, *Axis Rule in Occupied Europe* (Washington, D.C.: Carnegie Endowment for International Peace, 1944).

9. Jean Girodet, *Dictionnaire du Bon Français* (Paris: Bordas, 1981), p. 269.

10. Hervé Savon, *Du Cannibalisme au Génocide* (Paris: Hachette, 1972), Chap. 1.

11. Irving Louis Horowitz, *Taking Lives* (New Brunswick, N.J.: Transaction Books, 1980), Chap. 4.

12. Vahakn Dadrian, "A Typology of Genocide," *International Review of Modern Sociology* 5 (1975), pp. 201-12.

13. Helen Fein, *Accounting for Genocide* (New York: The Free Press, 1979), pp. 7-8.

14. Leo Kuper, *Genocide: Its Political Use in the Twentieth Century* (New Haven: Yale University Press, 1982), pp. 11-18.

15. Ibid., pp. 138-60.

16. Ibid, p. 105.

17. Reprinted as Appendix I in Kuper.

18. Colin McEvedy and Richard Jones, *Atlas of World Population History* (New York: Penguin Books, 1978), p. 14.

19. Morris Jastrow, *The Civilization of Babylonia and Assyria* (New York: Benjamin Blom, 1971).

20. O. R. Gurney, *The Hittites* (London: Book Club Associates, 1975).

21. B. H. Warmington, *Carthage* (London: Robert Hale, 1960).

22. J. A. Boyle, ed., *The Cambridge History of Iran*, Vol. 5 (Cambridge, England: Cambridge University Press, 1968).

23. Robert Travers, *The Tasmanians* (Melbourne: Cassell Australia, 1968).

24. Shelton Davis, *The Victims of the Miracle* (Cambridge, England: Cambridge University Press, 1977).

25. J. J. Saunders, *The History of the Mongol Conquests* (London: Routledge and Kegan Paul, 1971).

26. According to Chernyk as cited in Christina Larner, *Enemies of God* (London: Chatto & Windus, 1981), p. 196.

27. Dickran Boyajian, *Armenia* (Westwood, N.J.: Educational Book Crafters, 1972).

28. Anton Antonov-Ovseyenko, *The Time of Stalin* (New York: Harper and Row, 1981).

29. Raul Hilberg, *The Destruction of the European Jews* (Chicago: Quadrangle Books, 1961).

30. Kuper, *Genocide,* pp. 57-59.

# 2

# HUMAN DESTRUCTIVENESS AND POLITICS: THE TWENTIETH CENTURY AS AN AGE OF GENOCIDE

## Roger W. Smith

We can no longer choose our problems; they choose us.

Albert Camus

Genocide has existed in all periods of human history, but prior to the contemporary period it was rare except as an aspect of war, or, in the sixteenth and nineteenth centuries, as an aspect of development. To a large extent genocide also appeared in a form specific to a given period —conquest, religious persecution, colonial domination. In the twentieth century, however, genocide has been a common occurrence; moreover, the forms it has taken are diverse and spring from different motives: there has been a convergence of destructive forces in our period.

Camus called the twentieth century an age of murder, but it is, more precisely, an age of politically sanctioned mass murder, of collective, premeditated death intended to serve the ends of the state. It is an age of genocide in which 60 million men, women, and children, coming from many different races, religions, ethnic groups, nationalities, and social classes, and living in many different countries, on most of the continents of the earth, have had their lives taken because the state thought this desirable. Such an age should perhaps be condemned out of hand, but it must also be understood: for we have to live as well as die in that world, and, to be realistic, a great many persons alive today have contributed to that genocide, mainly through passivity, but often through more active involvement.

There have been other ages of genocide—Assyria engaged in genocide almost annually for several hundred years and turned deportation

and forced labor into routine instruments of public policy, and millions
of lives were taken in the sixteenth and nineteenth centuries in the name
of progress. Yet there are unique aspects to genocide in the twentieth
century—the scale, the range of victims, the technology, the variety of
genocidal forms, even the motives—that set it apart from earlier ages of
human destructiveness. It is these that this chapter will explore, but
without neglecting elements of repetition and continuity in the politics of
death.

## I

Genocidal precedents exert pressure, yet each occurrence of genocide
is separate: the specific victims, perpetrators, motives, methods, and
consequences differ. Nevertheless, each genocide is related to all others
in certain ways. Genocide must be legitimated by tradition, culture, or
ideology; sanctions for mass murder must be given by those in authority;
the forces of destruction have to be mobilized and directed; and the
whole process has to be rationalized so that it makes sense to the perpetrators and their accomplices.[1] Victims, however else they may differ,
will be vulnerable to attack and will be perceived as lying outside the
universe of moral obligation. They will be dehumanized: "Cargo, cargo"
is the way Franz Stangl described his victims at Treblinka; "Guayaki," a
term meaning "rabid rat," is how the Paraguayans refer to the Aché
Indians.[2] They will be viewed not as individuals but only as members
of a despised group, blamed for their own destruction, and held accountable in terms of the ancient notion of collective and ineradicable guilt.
Then, too, there is the ever present cruelty; this must be discussed at
greater length, however, since it is often either ignored or misunderstood.

One is tempted to say that in the contemporary period genocide is a
crime of logic, whereas in earlier ages it was a crime of passion. But
this would distort both the present and the past: much gratuitous cruelty
accompanies genocide today, and most of the genocide from the twelfth
century B.C. forward has been premeditated, a rational instrument to
achieve an end. What is proper, though, is to recognize that because
much contemporary genocide aims at the total elimination of a group,
which even with modern means of destruction takes time, sheer passion
is not likely to sustain the participants beyond the initial destruction.[3]
Thus, the fabricators of genocide today have created the image of an
"ideal killer": the "dispassionate, efficient killer, engaged in systematic
slaughter, in the service of a higher cause."[4] Nevertheless, all genocide,
over and above the actual killing of persons, appears to contain a large
measure of cruelty. Not all of this is gratuitous, however. Some of it in
earlier society stemmed from the sheer exhilaration of power that accompanied destruction, or was calculated to create terror or to exact retribu-

tion; more recently (though this also occurred in earlier societies), some cruelty has been ritualistic, expressive of good triumphing over evil, as in the slaying of the Indonesian Communists.[5]  In many respects, then, the brutality that accompanies genocide is culturally patterned.  In more modern, secular cultures, however, there is little or no support for torture, as opposed to the taking of lives, yet much sadistic behavior still occurs.  Here the cruelty can perhaps be understood as the dehumanization—loss of compassion, psychic numbing, detachment—that results from the prolonged participation in mass slaughter.[6]  But however one is to explain it, cruelty is everywhere the twin—not the father—of genocide.

There is another element that is found in many genocides, though there are important exceptions in earlier ages:  the refusal to accept responsibility for one's acts.  The refrain is familiar:  we knew nothing, we only obeyed orders, it was God's will, we were defending ourselves, they had it coming.  On the other hand, while most twentieth-century genocide has been preceded by crisis or great frustration, this seems not to be the case historically, except perhaps where religious genocide has occurred.  Indeed, the relationship between crisis and genocide is almost the opposite of what some scholars have taken it to be.[7]  And even in the twentieth century, crisis has not always existed: the Indians of Paraguay, Brazil, and Peru, for example, have been destroyed out of cold calculation of gain (and in some cases, sadistic pleasure) rather than as the result of economic or political crisis.  While context and situation are important, genocide is never an accidental feature of society.

## II

Genocide is almost always a premeditated act calculated to achieve the ends of its perpetrators through mass murder.  Sometimes, however, genocidal consequences precede any conscious decision to destroy innocent groups to satisfy one's aims.  This is most often the case in the early phases of colonial domination, where through violence, disease, and relentless pressure indigenous peoples are pushed toward extinction. With the recognition of the consequences of one's acts, however, the issue is changed: to persist is to intend the death of a people.  This pattern of pressure, recognition, and persistence is typically what happened in the nineteenth century.  Today, however, when indigenous groups come under pressure, the intention to destroy them is present from the outset; there are few illusions about the likely outcome.  The distinction, then, between premeditated and unpremeditated genocide is not decisive, for sooner or later the *genocidal* is transformed into *genocide*.

Rather than being simply an expression of passion, genocide is a rational instrument to achieve an end.  While these ends have varied from perpetrator to perpetrator and, to a large extent, by historical period, they have typically included the following: revenge, conquest, gain, power, and purification/salvation. From these we can construct a grammar of motives which, in effect, asks the perpetrator: What are you trying to do and why is it so important that you are willing to sacrifice thousands, even millions of lives (including those of children) to achieve it? Formal, but nevertheless useful, answers to these questions are contained in the different types of genocide, arranged in terms of the grammar of motives. Classified in this manner, the pure types of genocide are retributive, institutional, utilitarian, monopolistic, and ideological.[8]

### Retributive Genocide

Retribution may play a role in all genocide, but it does so mainly as a rationalization: it is a way of blaming the victim. Though it draws from the vocabulary of justice and of judicially administered punishment, genocide destroys persons most often for what they are rather than for anything they have done. In this sense, retribution flows from the dehumanization that has been fastened to the victims before they are attacked. As a principal motive in genocide, retribution is rare, but it does seem to figure prominently in accounts of conquerors like Chingis-khan (Genghis Khan).[9] Nevertheless, it is difficult to see how the "Conqueror of the World," as he called himself, differed in his actions when inspired by revenge than he and others did when they engaged in the institutional genocide associated with warfare until about the fifteenth century.

### Institutional Genocide

Institutional genocide was the major source of politically sanctioned mass murder in the ancient and medieval worlds. The massacre of men, the enslavement of women and children, and, often, the razing of towns and the destruction of the surrounding countryside, were universal aspects of conquest: genocide was embedded in the very notion of warfare.[10] As such, no explicit decision had to be made to commit genocide —it had become routinized. In part, institutional genocide was motivated by the desire to create terror, to display one's power, and to remove the possibility of future retaliation. But it was also due to a failure of political imagination: genocide was a substitute for politics. Instead of ruling a city or territory, extracting tribute from it, and perhaps even incorporating it into one's own system of power and authority, the society was devastated. By the late medieval period this practice had largely ended in the West (indeed, it had begun to change with the Romans, who understood that only through politics could one build an empire), yet it became a prominent part of the Crusades and was made all the more deadly because of religious passion.[11] In any case, institutional genocide continued in the East with figures like Timur Lenk until the fifteenth century. For some 500 years thereafter, the genocide of conquest disappeared. It is possible, however, that both guerrilla warfare and the use of nuclear weapons signify a revival of this early form of genocide. If the means are different, the motives seem not that dissimilar, and the consequences include both widespread devastation and the massive taking of innocent life by those in authority.

## Utilitarian Genocide

If utility played a role in institutional genocide, it became particularly prominent in the genocide of the sixteenth and nineteenth centuries, when colonial domination and exploitation of indigenous peoples in the Americas, Australia, Tasmania, parts of Africa, and elsewhere became pronounced. It has continued in the twentieth century, especially in Latin America, where Indians have been subjected to genocidal attacks in the name of progress and development. Apart from the more sadistic aspects of this kind of destruction, the object has been Indian land—for the timber it contains, the minerals that can be extracted, and the cattle it can feed—and, at the turn of the century, Indian labor to harvest, under conditions of forced labor, the sap of the rubber tree.[12]

Richard Rubenstein has recently argued that development leads to a population "surplus," which in turn leads to programs to eliminate the superfluous population.[13] What is happening with the remaining indigenous population of Latin America, and what was the fate of millions in various areas of the world earlier, has nothing, however, to do with a surplus population (whatever that is, for Rubenstein never defines his basic term). They are being killed, were killed, because of a combination of ethnocentrism and simple greed. The basic proposition contained in utilitarian genocide is that some persons must die so that others can live well. If that proposition no longer claims a large number of lives, it is because the previous genocide was so effective and the remaining tribes so small, with at most a few thousand members each. Yet precisely because of the tenacity of the assaults against them, and the small size of the groups, utilitarian genocide, although somewhat rare in the twentieth century, tends to be *total*.

## Monopolistic Genocide

Most genocide prior to the twentieth century was external—it was exacted of groups that lived outside one's territorial boundaries. There are some important exceptions—most of which are connected with religious persecution—but for the most part genocide was directed outward: its goals were conquest and colonial exploitation. Today almost all genocide is domestic—groups within one's borders are destroyed. Again there are exceptions—Hitler committed both domestic and external genocide—but most examples of genocide in the twentieth century have been directed inward. Issues that were not at stake in external genocide are central today: who belongs, who is to have a voice in the society, what is to be the basic shape of the community, what should its purposes be?

While these questions obviously lend themselves to ideological solutions, the genocide that has emerged as a means of shaping the basic structure and design of the state and society has been more inclusive than that. Examples of such attempts come from those that are ideologically motivated (Cambodia), those that are not (Pakistan), and those that combine elements of both (Armenia). In fact, whatever the shape of the regime, the most frequent source of genocide in the twentieth century has been the struggle for the monopolization of power. While issues of international dominance, of the distribution of power, of who rules can be raised in any political system, they have been crucial to conflicts that have emerged in Pakistan, Burundi, Nigeria, and other societies that have pervasive cleavages between racial, religious, and ethnic groups. These plural societies are in large part a legacy of nineteenth-century colonialism, but their genocidal struggles take place today within the framework of self-determination.[14] Having been subjected to colonial exploitation and genocide, these societies now butcher themselves.

### Ideological Genocide

Most genocide in the twentieth century has not been ideological but, where it has, the results have been catastrophic: ideology under modern conditions tends toward holocaust.[15] Most genocide in the past was also not ideological: it was an instrument not for the restructuring of society according to some blueprint of the mind, but for gaining, on the ideal plane, revenge, and on the more tangible one, booty, women, territory, public slaves, or the exploitation of "native" labor and resources. Ideology, in the form of religion, did contribute to human destructiveness—it provided rationalization to the Spanish for conquering and enslaving Indians, it formed the background for repeated attacks on Jews, and was one, but only one, ingredient in the so-called wars of religion in the sixteenth and seventeenth centuries. On the other hand, the Inquisition, which is sometimes cited as an example of genocide, was nothing of the kind: cruel as it was, the Inquisition took the form of a judicial inquiry, with those suspected of either heresy or of insincere belief receiving scrutiny; those convicted (and not all were) were burned en masse, but they were tried as individuals.[16] Nevertheless, some genocide before the twentieth century certainly was ideological: the destruction of unholy cities in ancient Israel and of the Albigensians in the thirteenth century. The Crusades also to some extent had a religious basis, though many other elements (political ambition, desire for material acquisitions) became entangled in it. In all these cases, however, the aim was essentially conservative: genocide was used to protect and defend a particular religious faith, not as contemporary ideology is, to transform society. With us the attempt has been to eradicate whole races, classes, and ethnic groups—whatever the particular ideology specifies—in order to produce a brave new world free of offensive human material.

At the heart of contemporary ideology is what Camus called a "metaphysical revolt" against the very conditions of human existence: plurality, mortality, finitude, and spontaneity.[17] It is, as it were, an attempt to re-establish the Creation, providing for an order, justice, and humanity that are thought to be lacking. At the same time that it strives for a kind of salvation, it is often motivated by a profound desire to eliminate all that it perceives as being impure—be it race, class, or even, in the case of the Khmer Rouge, cities. The revolt is metaphysical, but it is also deeply moral in an ancient way: the rejection of the unclean, the fear of contamination. How else explain the constant references in Nazism to purification and the Cambodian references to the cleansing of the people? When one attempts to bring about a "perfect" society, much of the human material must be jettisoned; and since humans are going to be killed for what they are rather than for what they have done, the most primitive, but still basic, moral category surfaces, that of the unclean, the impure. Indeed, one contemporary philosopher suggests that the "dread of the impure and rites of purification are in the background of all our feelings and all our behavior relating to fault."[18] When defilement is understood ideologically, it is literally true, as Paul Ricoeur notes in a different context, that "we enter into the reign of Terror."[19] Yet it is possible to substitute one symbol of evil for another; in the Soviet Union the idea of guilt, especially the objective guilt of class origins, assumes the role played elsewhere by defilement. At bottom, ideology turns politics into a variety of the sacred. Yet holocausts are born, not in the name of God, but of biology, history, and peasant simplicity.

Tendencies, however, are not necessarily results; holocaust is not a matter of deduction. Ideology seldom exists in a pure form: its relationship to culture is of particular importance. Does the culture reinforce the ideology, as in Nazi Germany and the Soviet Union, or does it come into conflict with it, as in Italy and Cuba? That culture can humanize and restrain ideology gives hope; that it does not always succeed and may even buttress ideology is part of the contemporary uncertainty about the future of genocide in its most extreme form, holocaust.

**III**

A recent study of genocide begins with this statement: "The word is new, the crime ancient." This should read, "The word is new, the phenomenon ancient," for while the slaughter of whole groups has occurred throughout history, it is only within the past few centuries that this has produced even a sense of moral horror, much less been thought of as "criminal." Indeed, from ancient times to well into the sixteenth century, genocide was not something that men were ashamed of, felt guilt for, or tried to hide; it was open and acknowledged. Massacre, deportation, forced labor, the transfer of children from one group to another, torture—all are laid out in the Bible, in the official records and monuments of empires, in epic and dramatic poetry, in histories and memoirs. The early Hebrews, the Assyrians, Greeks, and Romans, the Church with its heretics, the Crusaders, the Mongols, and the Spanish in America—each went to great lengths to leave public records of their acts of human destructiveness. Some went further—they boasted of the number of persons killed, the amount of booty gained, the prisoners deported for forced labor, the terror their attacks had inspired.[20] In Assyria public festivals were held in celebration of the destruction of yet another people, with prisoners slaughtered as an offering to the gods. Stelae, bas-reliefs, obelisks, monuments of every sort were then erected by the king to commemorate his deeds.[21] Like us, but for different reasons, the kings thought that no act of genocide should be forgotten. But one does not have to look only at the Assyrians: similar accounts of revelling in destruction could be taken from the memoirs of the Crusaders and others.[22]

In the twentieth century, however, no country has acknowledged that it engaged in genocide. Monuments have sometimes been raised for victims, but not by perpetrators to commemorate their deeds. Turkey not only did not acknowledge publicly that it killed over 300,000 Armenians between 1895 and 1908 and over a million between 1915-1917, but even sixty years later it still denies that genocide was committed: people were relocated as a wartime security measure and some died in the war, but that, it says, is all. Nazi Germany attempted to hide its own massive destruction of the Jews, Gypsies, Slavs, and other groups, including those Germans who were, for reasons of health, considered unfit to live. The most noble chapter in German history, according to Heinrich Himmler, would never be written.[23] Civil war, the destruction of terrorists, or the repulsion of external invasion are the terms used by contemporary regimes to describe their genocidal activities. The United Nations, moreover, has only once detected an instance of genocide (despite the fact that its own trucks were used in Burundi to transport victims to their death) and that was of Communist China before it was a member of the United Nations.[24] While the Khmer Rouge was destroying the lives of 3 million of the inhabitants of Cambodia and turning others into refugees, it consistently denied that it had engaged in genocide; rather, it accused other countries of major rights violations. Occasionally, the leaders of a country have admitted privately what was taking place, and years after the event some examples of genocide have been lamented by a new leadership—for example, Nikita Khrushchev's condemnation of Stalin's destruction of various nationality groups and, especially, the members of the Party.[25] Yet he also mentioned with approval the destruction of the kulaks. So genocide in the twentieth century, while justified in the eyes of its perpetrators, is not open and is not acknowledged except privately, or for reasons that reject some genocide but fully endorse other examples of it.

In the twentieth century, we find genocide to be horrifying, morally unjust, and criminal, yet we go on committing it. For us the formula goes something like this: It never happened, and besides, *they* deserved it. Prior to the sixteenth century, when the Spanish in America began to have doubts about killing men whose souls they claimed they wanted to save, the formula would have read: *We* did it, and *they* deserved it.[26] Even so, responsibility could still be assigned to a god or, better yet, the victim. But with us, as genocide has become more repugnant, as it has come to seem unthinkable, it has actually become commonplace. Contemporary man deals in bad faith as well as death.

## IV

The scale of genocide in the twentieth century is staggering and helps to account in part for the sense of the incomprehensible and the unreal that conditions contemporary responses to genocide. Although genocide has claimed many victims throughout history, in terms of scale, there has never before been a century like ours: in less than one hundred years some 60 million persons have been murdered to meet the needs of the state. And with the exception of the destruction of small groups of indigenous peoples, or the admonitory genocide (a version of the struggle for power) that claims the lives of several hundred persons, genocide in the twentieth century almost never claims less than 100,000 victims—that is the minimum, and the scale quickly goes up from there. Turkey destroyed the lives of a million or more Armenians; Nazi Germany destroyed 6 million Jews, but it is often forgotten that it went on to murder other groups as well, so that a reasonable estimate for the total number of its victims, apart from war deaths, is 16 million; Pakistan slaughtered 3 million Bengalis; Cambodia brought about the death of 3 million persons; and the Soviet Union first destroyed 20 million peasants in the 1930s and then went on to take hundreds of thousands of other lives in the 1940s with its assaults on various nationality groups suspected of disloyalty.

In some ways, of course, it is a mistake to discuss numbers of victims. Every life and every group is unique, and deaths can thus never be compared. Also, numbers have the effect of dissolving the solidarity that victims might otherwise feel for each other; instead of sensing a common plight, questions of who has suffered the most come to the fore.[27] And numbers lead us into thinking that genocide is defined by some magic number of victims, whereas legally and morally that is not what genocide means. Nevertheless, numbers do indicate the massiveness of the problem of genocide in the current period. They can also help us to see some qualitative differences between genocide as it is practiced now and as it was until at least the nineteenth century, which in its often total assault on indigenous peoples began to resemble the twentieth century, with its attempts to annihilate groups as a whole.

Genocide for most of its history has been local—the conquered city, the particular group of Muslims or Jews before one, the Indians within easy reach of exploitation. It was also segmental—except for groups of heretics or, occasionally, out of desire for revenge, there was no attempt to destroy an entire group (all Jews, all Muslims, all members of a particular race or class). The reason usually given for both the local and segmental quality of genocide prior to the nineteenth century is that dominant groups lacked the means: the instruments of violence were limited and the means of communication and transportation difficult at best. While this is true, it also misses an important point: genocide previously had a *finite* quality to it; there was no aspiration to eliminate a group totally. In the nineteenth century, Alexis de Tocqueville, for example, still viewed genocide as rooted in a finite world: tied to appetite, limited in its goals, a world without demand for totality or infinity.[28] But contemporary theories of genocide (Hannah Arendt, Erich Fromm, Albert Camus) characteristically present a radically different image of genocide, coinciding with a changed set of experiences with human destructiveness. It remained for the nineteenth and twentieth centuries to generate both the *means* and the *desire* to destroy entire groups.

## V

Genocide of any magnitude requires a sizable number of participants, but it does not necessarily follow that a large increase in victims requires an equally large increase in perpetrators. This partly depends on the technology of destruction that is employed (some forms are, so to speak, labor-intensive, others less so); on whether the victims are concentrated in one area or must be rounded up over a large territory; and on the extent to which the victims are able to resist. It also depends on what might be called the style of destruction. Some regimes, such as that of Idi Amin, concentrate the task of destruction in the hands of specially created units, with almost no participation by wider segments of society.

Others, such as Turkey, deliberately involve the army, local officials, selected tribal and ethnic groups, and in the case of both Turkey and Indonesia, large numbers of peasants. The decision to involve a large number of groups is not due primarily to the availability of technology, but to certain political objectives. In acting as Turkey and Indonesia have, the regime satisfies the passions and greed of elements of the society, thus building support for its actions; destroys the victim group in the most vicious way possible in order to emphasize the subhumanity of the dominated; and, by plunging a large part of the population into murder, binds them to the regime.[29] In other cases still, such as that of Nazi Germany, the intended magnitude of destruction is so great, and the victims so scattered, that most social and political institutions are harnessed to one overriding aim—the taking of lives.[30]

The large-scale genocide of the twentieth century does require numerous participants, but the extent to which this is true varies from case to case. The scale of genocide in the twentieth century is unprecedented with regard to victims; with regard to the percentage of the population that participates in the actual process of destruction, it would appear to be no greater than in previous ages of genocide. But given the frequency of genocide in this century, this means that an enormous number of our contemporaries, with the support and permission of political authority, have committed mass murder.

# VI

At all times, genocide has claimed a wide range of victims, but in the twentieth century it has become more extensive. Before our own period, victims came from one or more of the following categories: those subjected to conquest, those destroyed for religious reasons, and those exploited in a colonial relationship. Only a small number of these were killed because of *who* they were.

Until the early modern period, one was typically subjected to genocide simply because of *where* one was. Most of the victims of genocide in the past became such because they were on a conqueror's line of march. They died or were enslaved because they were there, not because of any special selection process that singled them out in terms of race, religion, political convictions, or the like. They were victims of institutional genocide. On the other hand, victims of religious genocide, though few in number, were chosen because of *who* they were: their views and practices were considered a threat to unity and truth. And with the beginnings of colonial domination in the sixteenth century, a much larger set of victims was killed because of *who* its members were (they came from a different race and a less technologically advanced culture) and *what they had* (land, gold, labor power). They became victims of utilitarian genocide.

In the twentieth century the range of victims has greatly increased; moreover, almost all of them have been selected for genocide because of *who* they are, because in the eyes of the stronger group (whether majority or minority) they do not deserve to live. The victims, otherwise so different, have only three attributes in common: for historical, situational, or ideological reasons they have been defined as beyond the circle of moral obligation and thus as inhuman; they are vulnerable to genocidal attacks, whether sporadic or sustained, selective or indiscriminate; and if they do survive, they often carry a greater burden of guilt than the victimizers do for attempting to take their lives.[31] The diversity and range of those who have fallen victim to genocide in this century can be suggested by the simple device of naming names and listing categories: Armenians, Gypsies, Jews, Slavs, Bengalis, Cambodians, Tibetans, Hutus, Ibos, Chinese, Achés; Buddhists, Hindus, Christians, Muslims; Communists, non-Communists; kulaks, intellectuals, workers, stone age hunters, national groups, homeless peoples; persons who are black, brown, red, yellow, white; the sick and the well; those who resist and those who are compliant; those who are killed because of their race, religion, ethnicity, physical condition, political opinions, class origins, or stage of historical development.

Falling victim to genocide has been so widespread and varied in the twentieth century that few groups can be reasonably sure that they will not be next. Even the most powerful nations—those armed with nuclear weapons—may end up in struggles that will lead (accidentally, intentionally, insanely) to the ultimate genocide in which they destroy not only each other, but mankind itself, sealing the fate of the earth forever with a final genocidal effort. Human history would assume this form (though it would never be written): mankind would have moved from the mortality of the individual (who could be murdered or, like Abraham, "die old and sated with life") to the genocidal destruction of human groups (large or small, completely or incompletely) to the extermination of the species itself.[32] The will to genocide, which began as the will to power, revenge, wealth, salvation, would have become (what perhaps in some deep sense it had been all along) the will to nothingness.

## VII

All the elements of the technology of death that we associate with twentieth-century genocide—bureaucracy, modern communications, rapid transportation, even the concentration camp in a primitive form—had emerged by the late nineteenth century. But apparently the first to perceive the possibilities of this new technology to eliminate a whole group of persons numbering in the millions was the ruling clique in Turkey, which in 1915 began the systematic extermination of the Armenians, an extermination that is the prototype of genocide in the twentieth century. It was premeditated, centrally planned (though carried out by local officials to a large extent), and intended to be total. It was also, to the extent possible, to be carried out without the knowledge of the outside world. As Michael Arlen notes, "The Armenian genocide was based on the imperfectly utilized but definitely perceived capacities of the modern state for politically restructuring itself, which were made possible by the engines of technology." In fact, he suggests, "In virtually every modern instance of mass murder, beginning, it appears, with the Armenians, the key element . . . which has raised the numerical and psychic levels of the deed above the classic terms of massacre has been the alliance of technology and communications."[33]

If modern forms of technology do not cause genocide, they facilitate it, extend its range, sustain its actions, and make it possible to destroy huge numbers of victims in a relatively short time. Yet it appears that Hitler's gas chambers were developed not only for the sake of efficiency, but to reduce the moral and psychological burdens that his soldiers had experienced in shooting large numbers of women and children on the Eastern Front.[34] The means that contemporary bureaucracy develops to destroy whole groups are calculated not only to kill, but to neutralize any sense of guilt or responsibility for what is done. Ideology can help overcome any feeling of revulsion or any sense of guilt, but only a few of those who are part of the apparatus of destruction may be ideologically motivated. More decisively, modern forms of organization can distance most persons from the actual killing and can routinize the work which supports the killing.[35] Most bureaucrats in Germany, for instance, "composed memoranda, drew up blueprints, signed correspondence, talked on the telephone, and participated in conferences." Yet, as Raul Hilberg indicates, they "could destroy a whole people while sitting at their desks."[36] Routinization reduces the occasions on which moral questions can arise and encourages the job holder to focus on the technical details of his work rather than on its meaning.[37] Moreover, the sharp division of labor fragments the act of destruction—those who decide to commit genocide, those who organize it, and those who carry it out are not the same persons; no one, therefore, accepts responsibility for the final result. Finally, because of the hierarchical structure of the organization, everyone can insist, not insincerely, that they were only obeying orders.[38] If organization, communications, transportation, and various new implements of violence (among them the gas chambers) have played central roles in the technology of genocide, their capacity to reduce moral awareness has also been important.

Nevertheless, highly developed organization and sophisticated means of destruction are not always employed in the twentieth century: often there is a mixture of the primitive and the modern. Indian tribes are hunted, like any other prey, in Latin America, but are also bombed from the air; they are given sugar laced with arsenic and blankets that contain the bacilli of fatal diseases, but are also relocated to reservations that are little more than concentration camps. In Turkey and Indonesia, socially induced hate and dehumanization are substituted for the bureaucratic neutralization of moral responsibility. In Cambodia, ideology allows the cadres of the Khmer Rouge to destroy parents in front of their children, to desecrate age-old religious institutions, and, in place of means of destruction that distance the perpetrator from the victim, to resort to direct and brutal means of disposing of the "impure" portions of the population: beating persons to death with hoes, driving nails into their heads, and carving them open with knives. And in Uganda, victims would often be strangled slowly and then killed with a sledgehammer blow to the chest; thereafter, they would be driven in trucks for hours to a river where they were thrown to crocodiles.[39]

While the capacity for organization varies—the Young Turks were more efficient than the Sultan, the Nazis more sophisticated in the production of mass deaths than either—the use of a low level of technology to destroy hundreds of thousands of victims is done by choice in the twentieth century. Cambodia did have bullets; peasants armed with ritual knives was not the most efficient means of destruction available in Indonesia. Rather, the technology chosen was a mirror of the purposes of the perpetrators (to inflict as much suffering as possible, to gain support for the regime by satisfying the appetites of groups long hostile to the victims) and the culture of the particular society (to invoke the symbolism of an autonomous peasant society, which when it kills uses hoes, or, with Indonesia, emphasizes the ritual triumph of good over evil).

The technology of genocide in the twentieth century thus offers the perpetrator a choice of means that can be tailored to a specific situation. This kind of choice in itself makes contemporary genocide unique, as does its enormous capacity to destroy human life.

Prior to the twentieth century, however, there was little choice in the technology of mass death. For several thousand years the technology of genocide was relatively static. Weapons used were hand-held (clubs, swords, bows) and could be used only in close contact with the victim. The introduction of firearms increased the efficiency of killing and made the work of destruction less physically tiring, but it still involved direct contact. Yet if I am correct in thinking that there were few, if any, moral barriers to genocide until the sixteenth century, this proximity to the victim would not have generated the burdens it would for us. It is odd, then, that those who stress the distancing from violence that is required for contemporary man to destroy his fellows have not explored the more direct, and bloody, genocides of the past.[40] The work was slow and tiring; it went on for days; and in the end, sometimes literally wading in blood, one knew what one had done.[41]

They were able to carry out these acts (which an Eichmann would not have had the stomach for) because, like us, they tended to obey orders, but mainly because—and here they are unlike us—they were not burdened with moral inhibitions against killing those outside the group. The ancient Hebrews, for example, did not worry about killing those who had betrayed the faith, but only about ritual defilement—whether, say, a man had had sexual intercourse before going into the *herem* (a term usually translated "holy war," but which means "a pact with the deity by which everything animate was devoted for destruction").[42]

In addition to various weapons of the sort mentioned, fire was used to destroy large groups. This was one of the favorite methods of the Spanish in America, but was also used by the Crusaders. Another technique, later used by Stalin, was to induce starvation: prisoners were locked up without food and left to die; crops were burned; and, not uncommonly, the available crops were seized and used by the dominant group, allowing the producers to die in a genocidally induced famine.

All of the techniques of destruction in use before the twentieth century were relatively primitive compared to what is available to us. Yet, given the finite goals of earlier genocide, smaller populations, and the absence of moral restraints, it was sufficient unto the day.

## VIII

In the end, though, it is the concentration camp that is the symbol of the technology of evil in the twentieth century. It is here, in the world of the dying, that the Nazis, Stalinists, and those like them pursue their beliefs that everything is permitted and everything is possible, and thus aim at the total domination of man, stripping him initially of everything except his body, and finally of even that. Yet we know from Bruno Bettelheim, Alexsander Solzhenitzyn, and Elie Wiesel, and thousands of other survivors, that the attempt fails; under sustained assault and the most grotesque conditions, human beings can still maintain decency, can share with others, and can continue to respect life.[43] One looks for parallels to the concentration camps, but, as Hannah Arendt indicates, there are none: "Forced labor in prisons and penal colonies, banishment, slavery, all seem for a moment to offer helpful comparisons, but on closer examination lead nowhere."[44] Whether the camps serve as places of detention, forced labor, or extermination (the usual classification, but misleading since most inmates do, after all, die in the camps), they are places in which "punishment is meted out without connection with crime . . . exploitation is practiced without profit, and . . . work is performed without product."[45] It is here that one confronts what Arendt calls "radical evil": an absolute evil that cannot be punished, forgiven, or comprehended in terms of any recognizably human motives. Not surprisingly, therefore, the metaphor of pain and endless torment that

most of us fall back on is one that secular society knows only at second
hand and abstractly, the image of Hell. In fact, it is through the medieval
depiction of Hell, where

> The very weeping there forbids to weep,
> And grief finding eyes blocked with tears
> Turns inward to make agony greater

that the literary critic George Steiner believes we can begin to grasp the
horror and meaning of the concentration camp.[46] For it is here that we
find the "technology of pain without meaning, of bestiality without end,
of gratuitous terror. . . . In the camps the millenary pornography of
fear and vengeance cultivated in the Western mind by Christian doctrines
of damnation was realized."[47] Quite true, yet the comparison is
dangerously flawed: for Hell, as traditionally understood, was a place of
justice, and neither those readied for mass execution in Treblinka nor
those left to a Darwinian struggle against exhaustion and gradual
starvation in Kolyma deserved their fate.

The fact that the analogies fail is not without its own significance.
For the failure of imagination indicates that we are in the presence of a
unique form of human destructiveness, one that in itself separates the
twentieth century from all that has gone before.

## IX

The twentieth century, then, is an age of genocide. Moreover, in
terms of the number and range of victims, the variety of forms that
genocide has taken, the urge toward total destruction of whole groups,
the elaborate technology that facilitates death and eases conscience, the
concentration camp, and the radical evil that is inseparable from it, it is a
unique age of genocide. But to speak of "uniqueness" in the context of
political death is, at bottom, to call attention to the acuteness of the
problem; it is, in human terms, to indicate the necessity of finding means
to prevent further genocide. The massiveness of genocide in this
century, however, makes us feel that the task of prevention is futile.
Despair stands in the way of action, knowledge leads to a sense of
hopelessness. Yet we know from Sören Kierkegaard that despair is a
sin, whether against God or man, and sin exists to be overcome. We
cannot bring back to life the dead of this century or those who have been
victims of political mass murder throughout the ages, but we can act. It
is not true, as some have thought, that "he who saves the life of one,
saves the world," but it is a good beginning.

## NOTES

1. Cf. Neil J. Smelser, "Some Determinants of Destructive Behavior," in Nevitt Sanford and Craig Comstock, eds., *Sanctions for Evil* (San Francisco: Jossey-Bass, 1971), Chap. 2.

2. Gitta Sereny, *Into That Darkness* (New York: Vintage Books, 1983), p. 201; Eric R. Wolf, "Killing the Achés," in Richard Arens, ed., *Genocide in Paraguay* (Philadelphia: Temple University Press, 1976), p. 53.

3. Cf. George M. Kren and Leon Rappoport, *The Holocaust and the Crisis of Human Behavior* (New York: Holmes and Meier, 1980), pp. 4-8.

4. Leo Kuper, *Genocide: Its Political Use in the Twentieth Century* (New Haven: Yale University Press, 1982), p. 122.

5. On ritual slaughter in Indonesia, see the Amnesty International report, *Political Killings by Governments* (London: Amnesty International, 1983), p. 36, and Clifford Geertz, *The Interpretation of Cultures* (New York: Basic Books, 1973), pp. 417-21, 451-53. On the role of cruelty in early society, see Friedrich Nietzsche, *The Birth of Tragedy and The Genealogy of Morals,* trans. Francis Golffing (Garden City, N.Y.: Doubleday Anchor, 1956), especially pp. 189-202.

6. Herbert C. Kelman, "Violence Without Moral Restraint: Reflections on the Dehumanization of Victims and Victimizers," *Journal of Social Issues* 29 (1973), pp. 50-52.

7. Cf. Helen Fein, *Accounting for Genocide* (New York: Free Press, 1979), pp. 8-9.

8. For other types of classifications, see Vahakn N. Dadrian, "A Typology of Genocide," *International Review of Modern Sociology* 5 (1975), pp. 201-12, and Leo Kuper, *International Action Against Genocide* (London: Minority Rights Group Report No. 53, 1982), pp. 5-9.

9. René Grousset, *Conqueror of the World: The Life of Chingis-Khan,* trans. Marion McKellar and Denis Sinor (New York: Viking Press, 1972).

10. Cf. Thomas Alfred Walker, *A History of the Law of Nations,* Vol. 1 (Cambridge, England: Cambridge University Press, 1899).

11. Antony Bridge, *The Crusades* (New York: Franklin Watts, 1982).

12. Arens, *Genocide in Paraguay;* Shelton H. Davis, *Victims of the Miracle: Development and the Indians of Brazil* (Cambridge, England: Cambridge University Press, 1977); and an older, but important account, W. E. Hardenburg, *The Putumayo/The Devil's Paradise* (London: Unwin, 1912).

13. Richard L. Rubenstein, *The Age of Triage: Fear and Hope in an Overcrowded World* (Boston: Beacon Press, 1983).

14. Kuper, *Genocide,* Chap. 4.

15. If this is the tendency, it may not, for reasons suggested later, always be the result. Yet, with one partial exception, all holocausts have been

associated with deeply ideological regimes. The Armenian holocaust was motivated in equal parts by ideology and the quest for dominance, but retribution and even utility played important roles, especially at the local level. I am uncertain whether a holocaust could ever come about wholly apart from ideology, but it may be that a strong convergence of motives could produce such a result.

16. Cf. Kuper, *Genocide*, p. 13. A. S. Turberville, *The Spanish Inquisition* (Oxford: Oxford University Press, 1932), provides an excellent factual account.

17. Albert Camus, *The Rebel*, trans. Anthony Bower (New York: Vintage Books, 1956).

18. Paul Ricoeur, *The Symbolism of Evil*, trans. Emerson Buchanan (Boston: Beacon Press, 1969), p. 25.

19. Ibid.

20. See the Assyrian text in James B. Pritchard, *The Ancient Near East: An Anthology of Texts and Pictures* (Princeton, N.J.: Princeton University Press, 1958), pp. 188-201.

21. Georges Contenau, *Everyday Life in Babylon and Assyria* (New York: Norton, 1966), pp. 147-56, and L. Delaporte, *Mesopotamia: The Babylonian and Assyrian Civilization*, trans. V. Gordon Childe (New York: Barnes and Noble, 1970), p. 248.

22. Bridge, *The Crusades*, pp. 237-38; Grousset, *Conqueror of the World*, p. 261.

23. Raul Hilberg, *The Destruction of the European Jews* (New York: Harper and Row, 1961), p. 648.

24. On the United Nations and its response to genocide, see Kuper, *Genocide*, Chap. 9.

25. For the conversations between the Turkish leaders and the American ambassador at the time of the worst of the atrocities against the Armenians, see Henry Morgenthau, *Ambassador Morgenthau's Story* (New York: Doubleday Page, 1918), pp. 307, 333-39, 342, 351-52, 391-92. For Khrushchev's speech and commentary on it, see Bertram D. Wolfe, *Khrushchev and Stalin's Ghost* (New York: Praeger, 1957).

26. On the growing uneasiness in Spain about the conquest of the Indians, see Charles Gibson, *Spain in America* (New York: Harper and Row, 1966), Chaps. 2-3.

27. Irving Louis Horowitz, *Taking Lives*, 3rd ed. (augmented) (New Brunswick, N.J.: Transaction Books, 1982), Chap. 11.

28. Alexis de Tocqueville, *Democracy in America*, ed. J. P. Mayer and George Lawrence (New York: Harper and Row, 1966), p. 312.

29. On crime as a binding element, see Fyodor Dostoevsky, *The Possessed*, trans. Andrew T. MacAndrew (New York: New American Library, 1962), p. 368.

30. Hilberg, *The Destruction of the European Jews*, pp. 32-39.

31. On "survivor guilt," see Robert J. Lifton, "The Concept of the Survivor," in Joel E. Dimsdale, ed., *Survivors, Victims, and Perpetrators: Essays on the Nazi Holocaust* (New York: Hemisphere Publishing Co., 1980), Chap. 4.

32. Cf. Gunther Anders, "Reflections on the H Bomb," *Dissent*, 3 (1956), pp. 146-55.

33. Michael J. Arlen, *Passage to Ararat* (New York: Farrar, Straus and Giroux, 1975), pp. 243-44.

34. Kren and Rappoport, *The Holocaust and the Crisis of Human Behavior*, pp. 58-59.

35. Stanley Milgram, *Obedience to Authority* (New York: Harper and Row, 1974), pp. 121-22.

36. Hilberg, *The Destruction of the European Jews*, p. 658.

37. Milgram, *Obedience to Authority*, pp. 7, 157; Kelman, "Violence Without Moral Restraint," pp. 46-48.

38. Milgram, *Obedience to Authority*, p. 11; Kelman, "Violence Without Moral Restraint," pp. 38-46.

39. Horowitz, *Taking Lives*, pp. 74-75.

40. If one starts from the present, one asks what weakens and erodes the moral restraints against genocide. If, on the other hand, one starts with the ancients, one has to ask how these restraints came about in the first place and when, and subsequently consider why they have not been more effective. If we just assume that such moral inhibitions have always existed, we distort the history of both genocide and society. On the historical nature of morality and the invention of guilt, see Nietzsche, *The Genealogy of Morals*.

41. Bridge, *The Crusades*, p. 111.

42. On the meaning of *herem*, see Josh. 6:17-21; Norman H. Snaith, *The Distinctive Ideas of the Old Testament* (New York: Schocken Books, 1964), p. 33; and *The Interpreter's Dictionary of the Bible*, Vol. 4. (New York: Abingdon Press, 1962), p. 804. On ritual and *herem*, see Num. 31: 1-24; Deut. 23: 9-14; 1 Sam. 21: 4-6.

43. Cf. Terrence Des Pres, *The Survivor: An Anatomy of Life in the Death Camps* (New York: Oxford University Press, 1976).

44. Hannah Arendt, *The Origins of Totalitarianism*, new ed. (New York: Harcourt, Brace and World, 1966), p. 444.

45. Ibid., p. 457.

46. George Steiner, *In Bluebeard's Castle: Some Notes Towards the Redefinition of Culture* (New Haven: Yale University Press, 1971), pp. 53-55. The quotation is from the thirty-third canto of Dante's *Inferno* as translated by Steiner.

47. Ibid., pp. 54-55.

# THE ETIOLOGY OF GENOCIDES

## *Barbara Harff*

One of the most enduring and abhorrent problems of the world is genocide, which is neither particular to a specific race, class, or nation, nor rooted in any one ethnocentric view of the world. Genocide concerns and potentially affects all people. Some people have found refuge in the idea that the Holocaust was particular to the inhuman Nazis. Thus, all barbarous activities perpetrated by these subhumans had to be judged by different standards. However, evidence suggests that the many who participated in the extermination of a people were not sadistically inclined.[1] Israel Charny argues that in many societies "traditions of humanitarian concerns for victims" coincide with "the role of killer . . . or of accomplice to other more vicious genociders."[2] Often democratic institutions are cited as safeguards against mass excesses. In view of the treatment of Amerindians by agents of the U.S. government, this view is unwarranted. For example, the thousands of Cherokees who died during the Trail of Tears (Cherokee Indians were forced to march in 1838-1839 from Appalachia to Oklahoma) testify that even a democratic system may turn against its people.

It is tempting to exaggerate the role of individuals, to blame leaders for leading their citizens to genocide. But is it not the case that citizens and leaders are able to make choices? Although powerful elites in a democratic society are able to inject their political preferences into the democratic process, sometimes not consistent with the preferences endorsed by the majority, that likelihood is far greater in a totalitarian system. But the capabilities for implementing ruthless decisions are always hampered or aided by the decisions made in countless bureaucracies. Thus, all people associated with the decision-making process lend their own motives, rationalization, and legitimation to the genocidal outcome. Although most of these people are not directly involved in executing their victims, their ability to halt the process makes them equally responsible for the executions. Clearly, the decision to destroy a certain people is a product of the many involved, and although some decisionmakers are more important than others, the role of the "helpers" surely facilitates the larger choice which delivers others to death.

Throughout the course of history genocides or massacres have been directed against specific groups in the context of larger political aims. Thus, the Nazis' aim of eliminating "foreign" elements from within by targeting Jews, Gypsies, Communists, and the mentally handicapped for annihilation was advanced by stressing mystical qualities of the dominant group. Similarly, the Turkification efforts, aided by the cry for "holy war" of the Young Turks, may have led to the destruction of the Armenians. A more recent example is Kampuchea, where under the leadership of Pol Pot all potential political adversaries were eliminated, which included the children of those perceived as reactionary elements. Though some massacres could be explained as acts of violence in the course of widespread mass hysteria, most genocides are devoid of the emotional climate which is conducive to a compulsion to murder those who are perceived as enemies of the dominant interests. In contrast, murderous leaders are voted into office, are allowed to propagate their pathological ideas, and often have ample time to plan and meticulously execute genocidal policies. What environment allows for organized officially sanctioned violence? What enables individuals to shed their responsibilities and become part of the murderous machine? In the absence of that passion which sometimes kills, how do "normal" people become vicious killers of children, old and infirm people, and the many others who have died in the genocides of modern times?

The following analysis investigates the conditions under which some genocides have taken place. The theoretical framework is provided by the author's previous efforts to shed light on why states engage in genocide.[3]

## ASSUMPTIONS AND PROPOSITIONS

Scholarly persuasion has it that the state is the ultimate obstacle to a just world order, while others see ideological identity or class solidarity as the one true path to that envisioned order. Some attempts to overcome these predominant modes of analysis in international relations, such as the Club of Rome's "doom project," have met with criticism and sometimes ridicule. It is not my purpose to assess in detail the ecologists', realists', or Marxists' contribution to the analysis of international relations. Instead, this modest effort attempts to incorporate various elements of different modes of analysis into a framework which allows for an assessment of why past genocides have occurred and why future ones will occur. Ecological challenges and the international security dilemma have greatly contributed to the erosion of the state as the central actor in the world. In contrast, the durability of the state is demonstrated through its expanding role in providing social services to its citizens. The often conflicting roles of the state as provider and entrepreneur have sometimes led to increased elite domination internally or increased military/ economic adventurism abroad.[4] Here elite domination refers to people who hold the controlling positions in the state structure; in other words, they are the political elite. Under exceptional circumstances this elite domination may lead to genocide. The following identifies the conditions conducive to the occurrence of genocide in national societies. National societies are those coincidental with the emergence of the modern state system during the early seventeenth century. This does not mean that genocides are confined to modern times. But "historical" genocides are of lesser importance to my argument, which claims that the "legitimate" authority structure, i.e., the state, is the predominant culprit in genocides (for an extended discussion on the subject, see Chapter 2).

One of the emphases of my theoretical argument is on structural change as exemplified in the concept of national upheaval. National upheaval is an abrupt change in the political community, caused, for example, by the formation of a state through violent conflict, when national boundaries are reformed, or after a war is lost. Thus, lost wars and the resultant battered national pride sometimes lead to genocide against groups perceived as enemies. Post-colonial and post-revolutionary regimes are prone to internal violence during times of national consolidation, when competing groups/tribes fight for leadership positions.

Structural change is a necessary but not sufficient condition to promote the likelihood of genocide. A second factor leading to the development of genocide is the existence of sharp internal cleavages combined with a history of struggle between groups prior to the upheaval. The stronger the identification within competing groups the more likely that extreme measures will be taken to suppress the weaker groups. Polarization is usually intensified by such factors as the extent of differences in religion, values, and traditions between contending groups, and their ideological separation. There are numerous examples from past genocides in which group polarization provided the background to genocides. Gentiles versus Jews, Muslims versus Hindus, Fascists versus Communists, Germans versus Gypsies, whites against blacks and Indians— such are the genocides of Nazi Germany, Bangladesh, Uganda, German Southwest Africa, and countless others.

A third factor triggering genocide against national groups is the lack of external constraints on, or foreign support for, murderous regimes. At present, lack of international sanctions and/or interventions against massive human rights violators is the norm rather than the exception. Unless national interest combined with the ability to interfere dictates intervention, few efforts are made to ameliorate the suffering of local populations.

Who are the genociders? Here genocide is defined as public violence —by some political actor—aimed at eliminating groups of private citizens. Sometimes genociders are state officials, e.g., soldiers, police, or special *Einsatzgruppen;* sometimes genociders are less openly linked with state power, e.g., death squads. Usually genocide is the conscious choice of policymakers, one among other options for repressing (eliminating) opposition. However, the likelihood of genocide occurring is rare compared to the likelihood that officials will use sporadic violence and/or torture to repress opposition. Thus, we have to differentiate between sporadic violence used against opposition groups, i.e., state terrorism, and systematic, Draconian attempts to eliminate or annihilate them. Additional incentives to settle scores through lesser means are the avoidance of regime instability and/or sometimes the threat of regional/ international sanctions or other forms of interference. Genocide is not just another policy instrument of repression; genocide is the most extreme policy option available to policymakers.

International wars are not genocides, because victims have no specific group identity and are often unintended, i.e., civilians. The crime of fighting an aggressive war, though outlawed as an instrument of international policy, is sometimes used as a coercive means to bring about structural changes in the target state, not to eliminate the total population. More difficult is the distinction between civil strife (wars) and genocides—civil wars are contributing factors to the possible occurrence of genocides but are not genocides themselves. In civil wars the legitimate authority structure is weak and is opposed by strong opposition forces. Again, as in wars, though atrocities may become a pattern on both sides, the intent to destroy the opposition in part or as a whole is the crucial variable in determining the onset of genocide. Burundi is a good example, one in which civil war eventually turned into a genocide, given an array of other contributing factors, such as previous tribal rivalries, and lack of regional and international intervention.

In addition, my definition of genocide differs from the official definition (Convention on the Prevention and Punishment of the Crime of Genocide/Declaration by the General Assembly of the United Nations, Resolution 96, dated December 11, 1946, article 2) insofar as it broadens the scope of the victims and perpetrators. Thus, political opponents are included in my definition, though they lack the formal legal protection of the Convention on Genocide. The official definition includes those acts leading to the physical destruction of the group when "such acts are committed with intent to destroy, in whole or part, a national, ethnical, racial or religious group," but says nothing about political groups. The Kampuchean mass slaughter under Pol Pot (1975) testifies to the need to include political opponents in the definition, thereby allowing the Kampuchean tragedy to be properly called genocide and thus to enjoy the unfortunately limited protection of the Convention. Political victims are not political as in contrast to religious or ethnic victims; rather, it is their *political affiliation* which singles them out as victims, not their ethnic identity. Thus, a Jew in Stalin's Russia who opposed Stalin would have been a likely victim during the murderous campaigns of the 1930s because he opposed Stalin, not because he was a Jew. Furthermore, in my conception the Holocaust is the ultimate instance of genocide, rather than a unique event defying comparison. Only through comparison with other similar or dissimilar cases of genocide can we begin to understand what triggered that monstrous episode. This is not to deny Holocaust survivors and victims their place in the conscience of humanity; rather, it is to remind us of our special responsibility to its millions of dead children, women, and men in finding ways to anticipate and eliminate future holocausts.

What follows is an analysis of information about twentieth-century governments which have engaged in genocidal activities. It describes the systemic properties, external environment, and internal conditions of states at the time of genocide. It is based on the cases listed in Table 3.1, a list which is by no means complete. What is attempted here is only the beginning of a systematic ordering of specific cases into categories. The cases are selected because they are relatively recent and well known, and because information is readily available about them; thus, their analysis should foster the kind of international reaction envisioned in the United Nations Charter. The cases may also make it possible to test the plausibility of my argument that national upheaval and prior internal struggle, combined with lack of constraints in the international environment, are conducive to genocide. It should be noted that the estimated numbers of victims vary greatly, often because "statistics" were not kept (with the exception of the Holocaust) or because population data were inadequate or dated. However, I do not believe that the *number* of victims makes a great difference: the important factor is that they were the victims of genocidal policies.


## TYPES OF NATIONAL UPHEAVAL

Genocide happens in different types of political society—what types of society? The classification scheme follows from the theoretical framework and distinguishes between types of societies formed after major national upheavals. The task of differentiating among societies with ongoing fundamental political change is difficult. Obviously a successful revolution with clearly defined ideological goals is much more likely to

lead to a restructuring of society than anticolonial rebellions with "reformist" goals. In other words, the greater the changes affecting society through new governments, the likelier it is that genocidal policies are implemented to insure total obedience. Thus, the extent of structural change is a major factor underlying my typology.[5]

Revolutions are a type of national upheaval. Revolutions always involve the overthrow of the ruling political elite and aim at bringing about fundamental social change.

Anticolonial rebellions, which are similar to separatist conflicts, are a type of national upheaval. Anticolonial rebellions are internal struggles with mass participation, directed against the ruling foreign power, seeking autonomy. In the case of separatist conflicts, the major struggle takes place between two movements, one trying to break away, the other to prevent it.

Coups may constitute a type of national upheaval. Coups involve the total or partial replacement of the ruling elite and lack mass participation. Thus, coups which involve the total replacement of the ruling elite are more likely to induce fundamental social change.

A special case is a takeover by duly elected or appointed political elites who endorse extreme ideologies (right-wing or left-wing). There is no abrupt structural change, but rather a move to exert total control. Such changes may lead to the creation of a climate in which people are absolved from making personal judgments and are rewarded for their total obedience to authority.

Another crucial factor in the development of genocide is the existence of sharp internal cleavages. In some societies internal violence is a way of life,[6] and some societies are preconditioned to accept political violence (coups, for example) because they frequently do occur (for example, in Bolivia). However, genocide needs more than reinforcement through societal acquiescence. Genocide is a product of state policy, with an involvement and commitment of massive resources, and is only marginally beneficial to people involved in the process.

National upheaval always intensifies internal cleavages. Depending on the preferences of policymakers, some groups may become targets of genocidal policies. Groups which are most "different" from the dominant group are more likely to become targets than those which more closely resemble the dominant group. Thus, groups different in religion, culture, wealth, education, and/or ideology have a greater chance to be singled out for genocide. Economic preponderance by some groups may be enough to induce genocidal policies against them. These cleavages usually pre-exist, but in some cases they are introduced by the new elite. Thus, for example, the targeted group may involve all those opposed to the new regime (Kampuchea), or rich peasants (Communist Russia).[7]

The structural precondition of national upheaval combined with societal receptiveness for internal violence targeted against "most different" groups may pave the path to genocide, but a third condition may ultimately provide the final incentive for the occurrence of genocide. Here we are talking about external support for either the genocider or the target group. Sometimes the genociders are foreign powers, for example, colonizers; sometimes genocidal elites enjoy support/protection from powerful neighbors. In modern times the overt or covert support of one of the superpowers is a warrant for the survival of regimes involved in repression or genocide. In other cases, states may neither condemn nor praise other states engaged in internal repression. The state in question may be too unimportant to warrant international attention, thus enjoying the kind of freedom which comes from lack of automatic sanctions in cases of extreme human rights violations.

Support of a different kind may come for the genocidal target. Thus, fellow religionists or ethnic groups may induce their governments to intervene on behalf of the potential victims. A more limited kind of support may come from international organizations in the form of protests or boycotts. In some cases irredentist movements elsewhere may lend military support.

## COMMON ELEMENTS IN DIFFERENT GENOCIDES

The merits of this theoretical argument can be demonstrated by analysis of the characteristics of cases of genocide categorized according to their political circumstances.

### Post-War, Post-Imperial Genocides

The Holocaust is undisputably the most abominable instance of modern genocide; however, it has many structural, societal, and external similarities with lesser genocides. Hitler's rise to power, though by constitutional means, came in the wake of a worldwide depression. The post-war economic crises and the inability of the new democratic government to cope with massive unemployment and extreme currency inflation greatly strengthened the radical left and the extreme right. Fear of a Communist takeover led to the bare victory of the National Socialist Party, and the "Enabling Act" left Hitler with dictatorial powers, which he used to bar any opposition. (See Chapter 10.)

The emergence of the nationalist movements of the "Young Turks" came in the wake of a disintegrating Ottoman Empire. A prior rebellion in 1908, which briefly restored a constitutional monarchy, led to a coup in 1913 and the total takeover by the Young Turks under their leader, Enver Pasha. During the Balkan wars (1912-1913) the Ottoman Empire lost almost all its territory in Europe, which left the new nationalist movement with little sympathy for the national aspirations of the remaining ethnic minorities in Turkey. (See Chapter 11.)

Both countries—Turkey and Germany—did experience a major re-structuring of their respective governments following loss of territory in war and a rapid succession of different versions of government. The German Empire was replaced by a democratic government, which lacked the strength to unite the warring factions of Communists and Monarchists. In Turkey the Sultan was briefly replaced by a constitutional Sultan, who, however, was in no position to halt the nationalist movement of the Young Turks, who tried to propel Turkey into the twentieth century with sweeping reforms. The national upheavals following the takeover by both nationalist movements had disastrous consequences for some ethnic/religious minorities in both countries—Armenians in Turkey and Jews and Gypsies in Germany.

The annihilation of Jews and Gypsies in Germany and the genocide against Armenians in Turkey followed a similar pattern. In both countries domination of the state apparatus by a tightly controlled political elite was complete. Both the Young Turks and the Nazi movement introduced a kind of myth, exalting the likeness of the dominant group, i.e., "Aryan"-Germans and Turks. Germanization and Turkification both emphasized pureness of race and common cultural/ethnic and religious values. Thus, all "real" Germans were to be Christian, Aryan, and non-Communist, as all Turks were to be Muslim, Turkoman, and pro Young Turk. Both Jews and Armenians were easy targets, for they were different in religion, "racial" heritage, and culture. The age-old division between Christians and Muslims and Christians and Jews accelerated receptiveness for a renewal of a crusade against infidels and the people of the book. The readiness to massacre Jews and Armenians was not new to either society. Sporadic violence or planned massacres had taken place prior to both genocides. But the Holocaust and the Genocide of 1915 against the Armenians were exceptional, because they were premeditated acts by policymakers to eliminate a people. Why?

I have argued that once preconditions such as structural changes, lack of external constraint, and internal cleavages combine, *the stage is set for genocide*. In both cases external constraints were either nonexistent or too late and too little to halt the slaughters of thousands of innocent victims. Neither meager German protest in 1915 (Turkey's major ally) nor an international boycott by World Jewry did much to stop impending disaster. Russian threat of intervention against Turkey was superseded by World War I, similar to Allied lack of intervention due to World War II. International sympathy for Jews was virtually nonexistent, evidenced by the refusal of other countries to grant entry permits to fleeing Jews. Armenians fared little better in the wake of competing nationalist movements elsewhere in Europe and the impending Russian Revolution, and the making of new alliances culminating in World War I.

But neither structural change nor external conditions *fully* explain why policymakers decide to eliminate or annihilate a people rather than engage in *sporadic* violence, i.e., why they resort to genocide rather than state terrorism to suppress opposition. Internal conditions may provide the final clues to why states engage in genocide. Often the strength of a new government greatly depends on its ability to mobilize mass support. Often divisions within culturally heterogeneous societies are overcome by declaring one group responsible for the other's misfortunes. Sometimes that is the case in socialist revolutions, where capitalists serve as scapegoats for the misery of the workers. Turkification and Germanification both served to unite people in their pride of belonging to a people, both inheritors of a long history, i.e., heirs of the Holy Roman Empire and the Ottoman Empire. Armenians may have been a legitimate threat to the Young Turks because they were collectively organized and demanded limited autonomy within the new state. Jews, however, were no threat to the Nazis; they were neither politically organized nor particularly visible as a group—Germany boasted a more assimilated "enlightened" (non-religious) Jewish population than most other European countries. Yet Nazi propaganda had singled out the Jew from its beginning. If Jews in Germany were at all special as a group they were so because of achievements in the professions. A disproportionate number of them were doctors, scientists, literary greats, and artists. Leading lights of Marxism/Socialism included many Jews, e.g., Karl Marx, Rosa Luxembourg, Ferdinand Lassalle, and Eduard Bernstein. Why did the Nazis single out the Jews? Anti-Semitism has long been part of European history. It was probably the single most appealing prejudicial doctrine available to the Nazis, who were trying to consolidate their power. Different groups in Germany may have had different animosities, but the Jews offered more value as scapegoats than other groups such as Gypsies or Communists. Communists were after all "genuine Germans," whereas Gypsies were too small in number and not a settled people. The successful merchant image of the Jews spelled competition for the average shopkeeper in Germany; the dominance of Jewish scientists may have caused envy among their colleagues; legendary Jewish international finance connections added to the image resented by others. The liberal image of artists residing in the capital did nothing to persuade the provincial German that the Jew was part of their world. Hitler's claim that Marxism/Communism was after all a Jewish invention thus was easily absorbed into an ideology offering an escape for many. The Jews had something for everyone, and those enlightened enough to realize the demagoguery thought that Hitler could be controlled. Once the Nazis realized the appeal of anti-Semitism, propaganda made full use of it. Nazis, once in power, fulfilled their promises to put people to work and "clean" the towns of Jews. Once the Nazis realized that the world was not eager to take "their" Jews, the "final solution" was to take care of the Jewish "problem." Who was to stop the murderous engine? In 1944 the Germans, their cities bombed, were losing the war, yet the death camps were working to full capacity.

Killing the Jewish population of Europe may have been the rational choice of the Nazis, yet the utility of doing so was utterly irrational. The costs of keeping the camps going despite the war effort were immense. Thousands of people were involved in killing Jews; trains transporting Jews had priority over those aiding the war effort.[8] The fanatic pursuit of "finishing the job" was part of the robot-like performance of those selected to serve the "higher cause" of Nazi ideology.

## Post-Colonial Genocides

The genocides of Southern Sudan, Biafra, Bangladesh, Burundi, and East Timor all took place following massive internal rebellions. Bangladesh, Biafra, East Timor, and the Southern Sudan sought to secede —from Pakistan, Nigeria, Indonesia, and the Northern Sudan, respectively. Bangladesh was successful; Biafra, East Timor, and the Southern Sudan were not. In Burundi the Hutus tried unsuccessfully to throw off the minority rule of the Tutsis. All five genocides happened in the wake of colonial liberation. In each case euphoria over liberation soon gave way to a *reemphasis* of existing cleavages.

The Northern Sudanese, Muslims who claim Arab descent, saw their future tightly bound to the Arab world. For the Southern Sudanese, mostly Negroid, animist (though including many Christians), and multiethnic, the traditional societies of East Africa seemed a more likely ally. The racial division is somehow arbitrary, since many Northerners who claim to be Arabs are Negroid in appearance and many Southerners called Negroid have non-Negroid features.[9] More important, Southern economic development was grossly inferior to the North. It was no surprise that the politically and economically powerful (and more populous) North should dominate the South after independence in 1956. Thus, domination by the British was replaced with domination by the North. Even before independence came to the country the South revolted against the North, which resulted in the slaughter of many thousands of innocent people.

Nigeria after independence in 1960 was united under a federal system. But unity was fragile among the three dominant ethnic groups, the Hausa-Fulani (about 15 million), the Yoruba (about 10 million), and the Ibos (about 10 million). The three were different in language, religion, and social organization.[10] The Ibos who became the targets of genocide, were mostly Christians and animists, in contrast to the Hausa-Fulani, who were Muslim and organized in the traditional Arab way under a strong central authority. Adding to the problem was the Ibos' dominance in education and industrialization. The North, with a high illiteracy rate and a largely agrarian economy, nevertheless controlled the federation by sheer weight of numbers (the total Northern region numbered about 35 million people).[11] The Ibos who attempted to secede in 1967 capitulated to the federal government of Nigeria in 1970. During the years of warfare hundreds of thousands died either in battle, during massacres, or by starvation.

The process of decolonization in India brought the division of India and Pakistan, strongly fostered by religious cleavages. Pakistanis were largely Muslims, and most Indians were Hindus; intermingling between the two groups was prohibited because of the caste system of the Hindus. Caught between the two groups were the Sikhs, who were divided between the emerging states of India and Pakistan. Before partition the Sikhs were embroiled in a "holy war" against the Muslims. Communal strife during this time took on mass proportions as an estimated 1 million people lost their lives. Upon partition Pakistan was divided into West and East Pakistan, separated by 1,000 miles of India. As in the Sudan, one region, West Pakistan, was considerably more industrialized, whereas the East was predominantly agricultural. In addition to economic domination, political domination was secured by a bureaucracy consisting largely of West Pakistanis. Negotiations for greater autonomy for the East in 1971 ended in massive retaliations by the West Pakistani government. During the following months genocidal policies were implemented which resulted in the indiscriminate deaths of men, women, and children numbering well over 1 million.

Burundi became independent in 1962 after years of extended rebellions against Belgian authorities. The country has a majority of Hutus—about 85 percent of the population—ruled by a minority government composed of Tutsis, who make up about 15 percent of the population. This domination by a minority was over 400 years old, established when the warrior Tutsis invaded the country from Ethiopia. Three aborted coups in 1965, 1969, and 1972 against the unwanted minority government led to severe reprisals by the Tutsis and in 1972 to genocide against the Hutus which claimed about 200,000 lives.

East Timor was a Portuguese colony which was to become independent in 1978 but preempted that step in 1975 by unilaterally declaring independence. The people are largely of Malay and Papuan stock, with a majority of Christians and some Muslim minorities. Past rivalries were confined to interparty conflicts. The most popular party, FRETILIN, which enjoyed 60 percent of the popular vote, was anticolonial and anti-Indonesian and was thought to be left-leaning. Two other parties, APODETI and UDT, called for union with Indonesia. This division erupted into violence during August 1975. Indonesia immediately reacted by initiating a blockade against East Timor and subsequently invaded the country in December 1975. With the help of UDT and

APODETI forces, independence was exchanged for union with Indonesia; the invasion resulted in looting, torture, and slaughter, with the result that nearly 10 percent of the population was killed.[12]

In all five cases foreign intervention significantly added to the success or failure of the secessionist movement. The intervention by India in December 1971 ended the genocidal massacres and also secured the independence of the new state of Bangladesh. Not so typical was the international support given to Nigeria/Biafra. China, France, Portugal, Israel, and South Africa supported Biafra, while Great Britain and the Soviet Union supported Nigeria. The latter "alliance" was probably due to Britain's effort to curtail growing Soviet influence in Nigeria. Biafran support came in the midst of conflicting European and big-power politics (e.g., France's oil interest in Biafra and China's tensions with Moscow), while Israel mostly confined its support to humanitarian relief efforts. The United States paid lip service to a united Nigeria. The Organization for African Unity (OAU) also supported Nigeria.[13] The Southern Sudanese enjoyed almost no support from outside sources, while Egypt, Libya, Algeria, Kuwait, East Germany, and the Soviet Union were said to have armed the North. In Burundi, no international action was taken to halt the massacres, although protests through diplomatic channels were plentiful. So, for example, the OAU supported the Burundi government, as did China, North Korea, and France. The greatest concern was shown by the former colonial power, Belgium, which early on protested against Burundi's genocidal policies. East Timor received verbal support from Australia and Portugal, and Indonesia received military support from the United States, while others claimed ignorance about accusations of genocide in East Timor. In all cases United Nations actions were confined to humanitarian relief efforts.[14]

## Post-Coup and Post-Revolutionary Genocides

The genocides of Kampuchea, Uganda, and Indonesia took place after a revolution in Kampuchea, after a coup in Uganda, and after an attempted coup in Indonesia, each conflict causing massive internal upheaval.

With the deposal of Prince Norodom Sihanouk in 1970 a relatively tranquil period ended in Cambodia. Increased involvement in the Vietnam War led to increased turmoil in the Khmer Republic. Forces of the Khmer Republic fought the Khmer Rouge in a civil war, which ended in the takeover by the Khmer Rouge Communists in 1975 and the establishment of Democratic Kampuchea. From 1975 to 1979 the Khmer Rouge expelled all foreigners and instituted one of the bloodiest regimes known in the twentieth century. Under the leadership of Pol Pot the urban population was sent to the countryside to become part of the "new" productive forces. He designated as expendable all those unable to perform the task. Pol Pot's "Marxist" revolution was but a peasant uprising against the feudal class represented by the townspeople.[15] Though his fury was mainly directed against townspeople, former collaborators including loyal peasants were also eliminated; thus, all perceived as opposing the regime were targets of genocidal policies. The failure of the regime was sealed with the invasion by Vietnamese forces in 1979; Vietnam is still occupying the country.

In January 1971 Idi Amin overthrew Milton Obote of Uganda in a coup, setting in motion a regime which ruled with unprecedented brutality. Amin, the dictator of Uganda who is often compared with Hitler, during his first three months in office was responsible for the deaths of 10,000 civilians and 2,000 soldiers. Like Pol Pot, Amin immediately chose to expel all foreigners from the country. His genocidal policies extended to all perceived as opposing his regime. His henchmen were members of his own tribe, the Kakwa, Nubians inside Uganda, and mercenaries from the Southern Sudan. In the effort to consolidate his power, Amin was responsible for the slaughter of an estimated 500,000 people. His regime ended with an invasion by Tanzanian forces in 1979, leaving behind a legacy of tyranny.[16]

On October 1, 1965, six Indonesian generals and a lieutenant were murdered in an uprising against President Sukarno. Although the truth may remain forever a secret, the events were thought to be Communist inspired and/or initiated.[17] In a predominantly Muslim society, the Communist party was something of an enigma (membership estimated at 10 million or one-quarter of the adult population). The short-lived uprising was crushed a few days later and led to the *systematic* slaughter of hundreds of thousands of Communists over a period of two years. Participating in the slaughter were soldiers and civilians trained for the purpose. Some officials of the Suharto regime later explained the slaughter as the "people's revenge," suggesting a spontaneous mass reaction to avenge the death of some of their leaders—hardly convincing in light of the fact that the slaughter continued over two years.

International support for the revolutionaries in Kampuchea came from Vietnam and China, while the regime was supported by American arms and aid. The faltering United States effort in Vietnam led to an abandonment of the pro-American Lon Nol regime, which enabled Pol Pot to take over. The subsequent fall of the Pol Pot regime was in part due to the growing antagonism between China and Vietnam, eventually leading to the invasion by the latter, whereupon Pol Pot fled to China. Uganda's Amin received full support from Libya but was criticized by the leaders of Tanzania, Zaire, and Zambia. By and large, however, the OAU remained silent about the indiscriminate killings of Ugandans. Only after Uganda invaded Tanzania did Tanzania respond with a counterinvasion. Supported by renegade Ugandan soldiers, the invasion successfully removed the murderous regime, and Amin fled to Libya. In Indonesia the coup was thought to be inspired by Peking, though no direct link with China could be detected. American sympathies went to the Suharto regime. In all cases the United Nations did little other than express its dismay and verbally condemn these flagrant violations of human rights.

### Genocides of Conquest

During the imposition of German colonialism in what is today Namibia, the Hereros became the target of genocidal policies. In the early 1970s "the International League for the Rights of Man, joined by the Inter-American Association for Democracy and Freedom, charged the government of Paraguay with complicity in genocide against the Guayaki Indians."[18]

In the short-lived colonial history of the German Empire (ending in 1918), early efforts of peaceful colonization in Southern Africa were soon replaced by measures which reduced the indigenous people to serfdom. The Hereros, a pastoral people noted for their large cattle herds, saw themselves slowly stripped of their land by German settlers. From 1903 to 1907 they revolted against the German colonizers—with devastating results. Successful at first, the Hereros were eventually defeated by superior technology and firepower. Thousands lost their lives in the actions following the uprising. The Germans "hunted them down like wild beasts all during 1905."[19] An estimated 65,000 Hereros lost their lives.

The Guayaki (Aché) Indians, a hunting and gathering people, were targets of genocide when "modern" Paraguayans encroached upon their traditional lands. During 1974 the Paraguayan government was blamed for allowing the slaughter, torture, and enslavement of the Indians by hunters and slavetraders.

International action was negligible in the first case. Wars against native Africans warranted no attention from other colonizers. There was some international attention given to the Aché Indian case, and verbal condemnation of Paraguayan policy eventually resulted in some response by the government.

## CONCLUSIONS

In all the cases considered here genocides were preceded by some attempt to change the existing power structure. It should be obvious that any attempt to change existing power relations carries a certain amount of risk for the challenger. Though most potential revolutionaries accept the calculus of losing some lives, genocide would be an unacceptable risk to anyone.

Successful rebellions (Kampuchea, for example) more often resulted in massive internal upheavals than did failed attempts (Indonesia, for example). Moreover, unsuccessful coups often resulted in the slaughter of those affiliated with the rebelling faction, for example, in Indonesia and East Timor. Evidently governments utilize genocidal policies to eliminate the opposition in an attempt to maintain the existing power structure. In some cases these processes may extend to include attempts to annihilate a people, i.e., a holocaust. This does not mean that holocausts result in more deaths; it simply means that the pursuers seek the total destruction of a people rather than their partial destruction. The difference is especially apparent in cases where the victims belong to the political opposition—often the slaughter stops short of family members. The child of a Communist may not necessarily become one himself, but the child of a Jew cannot escape his/her Jewishness, as a result often becoming the victim of a holocaust. Utilizing genocide to eliminate political opposition thus appears to be a more rational choice than the attempt to annihilate a people. As such, policymakers sometimes make the argument that political victims are legitimate targets of governmental violence which aims to prevent further violence, e.g., future civil war. In contrast, one may argue that ethnic/religious victims are illegitimate targets of governmental violence because they have neither the means to fight back, nor do they compete with government, and thus are truly innocent of any wrongdoing. But what is at stake is not the characteristics of the victim group, but the motives of the perpetrators. The killing of a people for attempting to change the existing government structure cannot be based on the collective character of a group, simply because not everybody is involved in the struggle. The only public offense which warrants the execution of an individual is the murder of another (in some societies even murder does not result in death). Excluded from this principle are killings done in the process of war, although many people view war and the resulting human carnage as an unacceptable means of international interaction. In cases of no war and where no individual crime has taken place, any killing either done by or conspired in by public authorities against a group of people is a crime.

The theoretical argument advances the proposition that structural challenges result in upheavals, polarize existing internal cleavages, and —with external help or the lack of it to either the dominant group or the rebelling faction—sometimes lead to genocide. In all cases cited above the genocides were preceded by challenges to the dominant power strata. In all cases genocidal processes were accelerated through the polarization of internal cleavages. The most distinct cases are those of the Holocaust, the Armenian genocide, and Burundi, where the groups were targets of prior discrimination and/or random violence, and also were easily identified by differences in culture, religion, and ethnicity. The Southern

Sudan, Biafra, and Bangladesh similarly saw incidences of random violence and/or repression against target groups who were culturally, ethnically, and/or religiously different.  In East Timor, Kampuchea, and Indonesia the victim groups shared similar ethnic characteristics with the dominant group, but, though prior internal rivalries existed in all cases, the victims were considered enemies mainly because of their political affiliations.  Uganda is something of a special case, because victims were neither clearly political enemies nor did they belong to one specific religious or ethnic group.  The killings, although systematic, seemed to be instituted to consolidate the despotic power of a tyrant, similar to the "Enabling Act" which gave Hitler the license to kill.  The genocides against the Hereros and the Aché Indians were policies designed to extend the control of the dominant "civilization."  In the case of the former, the Germans encountered a new type of warfare in the guerrilla tactics of the Hereros, which they responded to in kind.  Thus, random incidents of "savagery" by the Hereros led to their wholesale, systematic slaughter by the Germans.  The Achés, although part of the same racial stock as their persecutors, were culturally separated from the dominant stratum of Paraguay.  Malign neglect by the government led to their genocide, perpetrated by those acting on behalf of the dominant interest, in a march toward their version of civilization.

In all cases external support for either the dominant group or a rebellious faction added significantly to the success or failure of the undertaking.  The Herero genocide is the exception, probably because the slaughter of "savages" in 1904 by the colonizers was more acceptable then.  Today, the "savages" of the past are replaced by either the *Untermenschen* or enemies of the dominant group.  Nowadays, the drive toward civilization is replaced by the search for a better world, in which those perceived as standing in the way of "progress" are liquidated.

If we are able to explain past genocides and thus to anticipate future genocides, the next logical step is their prevention.  International organizations such as the United Nations have failed to halt the use of genocidal policies by sovereign states.  Internal bickering and competing interests have prevented the effective use of international diplomacy to prevent or stop genocides.  Yet, the emergence of numerous private organizations, in combination with a few U.N. efforts, gives the impression that something may yet be done.

## NOTES

1. For an extended discussion see Israel W. Charny, *How Can We Commit the Unthinkable? Genocide: The Human Cancer* (Boulder, Colo.: Westview Press, 1982), and Herbert C. Kelman, "Violence Without Moral

Restraint: Reflections on the Dehumanization of Victims and Victimizers," *Journal of Social Issues* 29 (1973).

2. Charny, op. cit.

3. Barbara Harff, *Genocide and Human Rights: International Legal and Political Issues* (Denver: University of Denver Monograph Series in World Affairs, 1984).

4. Richard Falk, *The End of World Order: Essays on Normative International Relations* (New York and London: Holmes and Meier, 1983).

5. D. E. H. Russell, *Rebellion, Revolution and Armed Force: A Comparative Study of Fifteen Countries with Special Emphasis on Cuba and South Africa* (New York: Academic Press, 1974).

6. Helen Fein, "A Formula for Genocide: Comparison of the Turkish Genocide (1915) and the German Holocaust (1939-1945)," *Comparative Studies in Sociology*, 1 (1978).

7. Leo Kuper, *Genocide: Its Political Use in the Twentieth Century* (New Haven: Yale University Press, 1981).

8. Fein, op. cit.

9. Cecil Eprile, *War and Peace in the Sudan 1955-1972* (London: David and Charles, 1974).

10. Peter Schwab, ed., *Biafra* (New York: Facts on File, 1971).

11. Ibid.

12. This discussion draws in part upon an unpublished paper by Christian C. Mattioli, "Invasion and Genocide in East Timor," Department of Political Science, Northwestern University, 1983.

13. Schwab, op. cit.

14. Mattioli, op. cit.

15. Michael Vickery, *Cambodia 1975-1982* (Boston: South End Press, 1984), and Kuper, op. cit.

16. Dan Wooding and Ray Barnett, *Uganda Holocaust* (Grand Rapids, Mich.: Zondervan Publishing House, 1980).

17. Kuper, op. cit., and Brian May, *The Indonesian Tragedy* (London: Routledge and Kegan Paul, 1978).

18. Kuper, op. cit., p. 33.

19. Jon M. Bridgman, *The Revolt of the Hereros* (Berkeley: University of California Press, 1981).

# 4

# GENOCIDE AND THE RECONSTRUCTION OF SOCIAL THEORY: OBSERVATIONS ON THE EXCLUSIVITY OF COLLECTIVE DEATH

*Irving Louis Horowitz*

The subject of genocide in general and the Holocaust in particular threatens to become a growth industry in the Western cultural apparatus. Books, plays, and television dramatizations on the subject pour forth relentlessly. Sometimes they are presented soberly, other times scandalously; but all are aimed at a mass market unfortunately more amazed than disturbed by their implications. There is danger in this massification of Holocaust studies. Western culture is inclined to adopt fads; even Holocaust studies may become a moment in commercial time—interest in them may decline as well as grow, and even peak out, leaving in its wake a void. The residual debris will probably be summarized in musical comedy; we have already seen examples of this in *The Lieutenant* (Lieutenant Calley) and *Evita* (Eva Peron) on Broadway. Peter Weiss' play *The Investigation* led one commentator to suggest that the major character in the play, in order to elicit shock from the audience, read lines "as if he were saying: 'Let's hear it for genocide.'"[1] This may be a sign of things to come.

One of the least attractive features of post-Holocaust studies is the effort of a few to monopolize the field. As a consequence, a linguistic battle looms among survivors over which exterminations even deserve the appellation "holocaust" (the total physical annihilation of a nation or a people). Such a bizarre struggle over language remains a grim reminder of how easy it is for victims to challenge each other and how difficult it is to forge common links against victimizers.[2] I do not wish to deny Jewish victims of the Nazi Holocaust the uniqueness of their experience. But there are strong elements of continuity as well as discontinuity in the process of genocide, in the evolution of life-taking as an essential dimension by which state power can be measured in the twentieth century.

Writing with compelling insight, Elie Wiesel personifies the mystic vision of the Holocaust. Those who lived through it "lack objectivity," he claims, while those who write on the subject but did not live through it must "withdraw" from the analytic challenge "without daring to enter into the heart of the matter."[3] More recently, it has been suggested that "for Jews, the Holocaust is a tragedy that cannot be shared" and "it may be unrealistic or unreasonable or inappropriate to ask Jews to share the term holocaust. But it is even more unreasonable and inappropriate not to find a new name for what has taken place in Cambodia."[4] Since what took place in both situations is a holocaust—from the demographic point of view—we need not invent new terms to explain similar barbaric processes. Those who share a holocaust share a common experience of being victim to the state's ruthless and complete pursuit of human life-taking without regard to individual guilt or innocence. It is punishment for identification with a particular group, not for personal demeanor or performance. These are not theological, but empirical criteria. To seek exclusivity in death has bizarre implications. The special Jewish triumph is life. All too many peoples—Jews, Cambodians, Armenians, Paraguayans, Ugandans—have shared a similar fate for victims to engage in divisive squabbles about whose holocaust is real or whose genocide is worse.

Those who take an exclusive position on the Holocaust are engaging in moral bookkeeping, in which only those who suffer very large numbers of deaths qualify. Some argue that the 6 million deaths among European Jews is far greater than the estimated 1 million deaths among Armenians. However, the number of Armenian deaths as a percentage of their total population (50 percent) is not much lower than the percentage of Jewish losses (60 percent). Others contend that the deaths of Ugandans or Biafrans are too few to compare to the Holocaust; yet here, too, tribal deaths in percentage terms rival the European pattern of genocide. In certain instances high death rates (approximately 40 percent of all Cambodians, or 3 million out of 7 million) are indisputable; then one hears that such deaths were only random and a function of total societal disintegration. Yet it has been firmly established that such deaths were targeted against intellectuals, educators, the foreign-born, and literate people—in short, the pattern was hardly random; anyone who could potentially disrupt a system of agrarian slave labor flying under Communist banners was singled out and eliminated. Even making the definition a matter of percentages risks creating a morality based solely on bookkeeping.

There is need to reaffirm the seriousness of the subject. The problem of genocide must be rescued from mass culture. It must not be returned to academic preserves, but it must be made part and parcel of a general theory of social systems and social structures.  The positions which I would like to discuss, examine, and criticize perhaps have been articulated best by theologian Emil L. Fackenheim[5] and sociologist Leo Kuper.[6]  In some curious way they represent the extremes that must be overcome if an integrated approach to the study of genocide is to become a serious subject for scientific analysis.  On the one hand Fackenheim speaks with a thunderous theological certitude that approaches messianic or at least prophetic assuredness.  On the other hand is Kuper, who is extremely modest in his approach, to the point where some fundamental distinctions between severe strife and mass destruction are entirely obliterated.  This is not to suggest that the truth lies somewhere in the middle but rather that the need for a social scientific standpoint in the study of genocide may convince all to move to a higher ground in this area—an area of research that has truly replaced economics as the dismal science.

Fackenheim's propositions have come to represent the main trends in the theological school of Holocaust studies.  They carry tremendous weight among mass culture figures for whom theological sanction provides legitimation to their endeavors and respite from critics.[7]  Fackenheim does not remotely intend his views to become part of mass culture. Quite the contrary.  His eight propositions distinguishing the Holocaust in particular from genocide in general represent a tremendous effort to transcend journalistic platitudes, to move beyond an articulation of the banality of evil and into the evil of banality.  This deep respect for Fackenheim registered, it must also be said that an alternative perspective—a social science framework—is warranted.

Fackenheim presents his eight propositions with direction and force. A general theory of genocide and state power, which accounts for the specifics of the Holocaust, can have no better baseline.

One: The Holocaust was not a war.  Like all wars, the Roman War against the Jews was over conflicting interests—territorial, imperial, and religious—waged between parties endowed, however unequally, with power.  The victims of the Holocaust had no power.  And they were a threat to the Third Reich only in the Nazi mind.

The Holocaust was a war; but a modern rather than a medieval variety.  Earlier wars redistributed power by military means.  Genocide redistributes power by technological as well as military means.  Robert Lifton recently stated the issue succinctly.

The word holocaust, from Greek origin, means total consumption by fire. That definition applies, with literal grotesqueness, to Auschwitz and Buchenwald, and also to Nagasaki and Hiroshima.  In Old Testament usage there is the added meaning of the sacrifice of a burnt offering.  That meaning tends to be specifically retained for the deliberate, selective Nazi genocide of six million Jews—retained with both bitterness and irony (sacrifice to whom

for what?). I will thus speak of the Holocaust and of holocausts—the first to
convey the uniqueness of the Nazi project of genocide, the second to suggest
certain general principles around the totality of destruction as it affects survivors. From this perspective, the holocaust means total disaster: the physical, social, and spiritual obliteration of a human community.[8]

The precedent for this war against the Jews was the Turkish decimation
of the Armenian population. Like the Nazis, the Ottoman Empire did not
simply need to win a war and redistribute power; it had an overwhelming
amount of power to begin with.[9]  A war of annihilation is a war.  To
deny the warlike character of genocide is to deny its essence:  the destruction of human beings for predetermined nationalist or statist goals.

The Holocaust is also modern in that it is an internal war, waged with
subterfuge and deception by a majority with power against an internal
minority with little power.  Here too the Armenian and Jewish cases are
roughly comparable.  Although one can talk of genocide in relation to the
bombing of Hiroshima and Nagasaki, genocidal conflict involves internal rather than external populations.  But this is an unambiguous point
on the nature of war rather than a denial of the warlike nature of the
Holocaust per se.

The victims of the Holocaust did have a certain power:  they represented a threat to the Nazi Reich.  The Jew as bourgeois and the Jew as
proletarian represented the forces of legitimacy and revolution in Weimar
Germany.  They had modest positions in universities, in labor, and in
industry.  Regarding state power itself, where there were scarcely any
Jews, they were powerless.  Jews were locked out from the German
bureaucratic apparatus much as the Turkish Beys locked out Armenians
from the Ottoman administrative apparatus, except to use them in a Quis-
ling-like manner.  The Jews posed a threatening challenge to the legitimacy of the Nazi regime.

Two:  The Holocaust was not part of a war, a war crime.  War crimes belong
intrinsically to wars, whether they are calculated to further war goals, or are
the result of passions that wars unleash.  The Holocaust hindered rather than
furthered German war aims in World War II.  And it was directed, not by
passions, but rather by a plan devoid of passion, indeed, unable to afford this
luxury.

This argument rests on a peculiar and misanthropic rendition of the
Hilberg thesis.  The Holocaust did hinder the Nazi war effort in the
limited sense that troop transportation took second priority to transporting Jews.  But in the longer and larger perspective, there were
advantages.  Slave labor was itself an advantage; unpaid labor time was
useful.  The expropriation of goods and materials was an economic gain
for the Nazi Reich.  People were liquidated at marginal cost to the

system. The gold taken from extracted teeth became a proprietary transfer.[10] Fackenheim questions whether war goals were furthered by the Holocaust; this is not answered simply. As a mobilizing device linking military and civil sectors of the population, war ends were enhanced by the conduct of the Holocaust. The Nazi attempt to exterminate the Jews was motivated by passion, as evidenced by the fact that troop movements to the Russian front took second priority.

Raul Hilberg makes clear the direct collusion of the German Wehrmacht and the German Reichsbahn with respect to the systematic deportation of Jews and the front-line servicing of the armed forces. The management of the German railroad illustrates how irrationality can become rationalized, how a "true system in the modern sense of the term" was employed for the unrelenting destruction of human lives. As Hilberg notes, to the extent that the technification of mass society was exemplified by the transportation network, such human engineering considerations cannot be viewed as ancillary.

It illuminates and defines the very concept of "totalitarianism." The Jews could not be destroyed by one Führer on one order. The unprecedented event was a product of multiple initiatives, as well as lengthy negotiations and repeated adjustments among separate power structures, which differed from one another in their traditions and customs but which were united in their unfathomable will to push the Nazi regime to the limits of its destructive potential.[11]

The question of passion is a moot point at best; undoubtedly there was a collective passion undergirding the conduct of the Holocaust. It was not simply a methodical event.

Fackenheim and many other theologians overlooked parallels in the pursuit of a genocidal state following defeat. After the Turkish defeat at the hands of Bulgaria in 1912, the most massive genocide against Armenians occurred. After the Nazi defeat at Stalingrad in 1943, the most massive destruction of Jews ensued. Whatever the vocabulary of motives—fear of discovery, of reprisal, or of judgment—the use of state-sanctioned murder to snatch victory from the jaws of defeat is evident.

The largest part of European Jewry was destroyed after Germany had in effect lost the war. When the major object of the war, defeat of the Allied powers, was no longer feasible, the more proximate aim, destruction of the Jewish people, became the paramount goal. War aims have manifest and latent elements. The manifest aim was victory in the war, but the latent aim was defeat of the internal "enemy," the Jews. The near-total destruction of the Jewish population might be considered the victory of the Third Reich in the face of the greater defeat they confronted by the end of Stalingrad.

Three: The Holocaust was not a case of racism, although, of course, the Nazis were racists. But they were racists because they were anti-Semites, not anti-Semites because they were racists. (The case of the Japanese as honorary Aryans would suffice to bear this out.) Racism asserts that some human groups are inferior to others, destined to slavery. The Holocaust enacted the principle that the Jews are not of the human race at all but "vermin" to be "exterminated."

Here Fackenheim represents a considerable body of thought. But the Holocaust was a case of racism. It is not a question of which comes first, anti-Semitism or racism; that philosophical dilemma is secondary. Assignment of special conditions of life and work to Jews implies what racism is all about: the assumption of inferiority and superiority leading to different forms of egalitarian outcomes. Ultimately racism is not about institutionalizing inferiority or superiority, but about denial of the humanity of those involved. Jewish vis-à-vis Aryan physical characteristics were studied by German anthropologists to prove that there was such a thing as race involved. These stereotypes were the essence of European racism, as George Mosse has fully documented in a recent work.

Racism had taken the ideas about man and his world which we have attempted to analyze and directed them toward the final solution. Such concepts as middle-class virtue, heroic morality, honesty, truthfulness, and love of nation had become involved as ever against the Jew: the organs of the efficient state helped to bring about the final solution; and science itself continued its corruption through racism. Above all, anthropology, which had been so deeply involved in the rise of racism, now used racism for its own end through the final solution. Anthropological studies were undertaken on the helpless inmates of the camps. Just as previously non-racist scientists became converted by the temptation to aid Nazi eugenic policies, so others could not resist the temptation to use their power over life and death in order to further their anthropological or ethnographic ambitions.[12]

The fact that American racism has a clear-cut criterion based on skin color does not mean that the physical and emotional characteristics attributed to Jews were less a matter of racism than the characteristics attributed to American blacks. To deny the racial character of the Holocaust is to reject the special bond that oppressed peoples share, the special unity that can bind blacks and Armenians and Jews. To emphasize distinctions between peoples by arguing for the uniqueness of anti-Semitism is a profound mistake; it reduces any possibility of a unified political and human posture on the meaning of genocide or the Holocaust. The triumphalism in death implicit in this kind of sectarianism comes close to defeating its own purpose.

Four: The Holocaust was not a case of genocide although it was in response to this crime that the world invented the term. Genocide is a modern phenomenon. For the most part in ancient times human beings were considered valuable, and were carried off into slavery. The genocides of modern history spring from motives, human, if evil, such as greed, hatred, or simply blind xenophobic passion. This is true even when they masquerade under high-flown ideologies. The Nazi genocide of the Jewish people did not masquerade under an ideology. The ideology was genuinely believed. This was an "idealistic" genocide to which war aims were, therefore, sacrificed. The ideal was to rid the world of Jews as one rids oneself of lice. It was also, however, to "punish" the Jews for their "crimes," and the crime in question was existence itself. Hitherto, such a charge had been directed only at devils; Jews had now become devils as well as vermin. And there is but one thing that devils and vermin have in common: neither is human.

Here Fackenheim has a problem of logical contradiction. First we are told that the Holocaust is not a case of genocide, and then we are reminded of the Nazi genocide of the Jewish people. But more significant is the contradiction within this framework, an inability to accept the common fate of the victims. Whether they are Japanese, Ugandans, Gypsies, Cambodians, Armenians, or Jews, their common humanity makes possible a common intellectual understanding. Insistence upon separatism, that the crime was Jewish existence and that this makes the Jewish situation different from any other slaughter, whatever its roots, contains a dangerous element of mystification. It represents a variation of the belief in chosenness, converting it from living God's commandments into chosenness for destruction. This approach is dangerously misanthropic. It misses the point that being chosen for life may be a unique Jewish mission, but being selected for death is common to many peoples and societies.

The description of Jews as devils was not the essence of Nazi anti-Semitism; it was only the rhetoric of Nazism. The Ayatollah Khomeini and other Iranian clerics constantly refer to Americans as devils. The essence of the Jewish problem for Nazism was the Jew as a political actor, and beyond that, the Jew as a cosmopolitan, universalistic figure in contrast to Fascist concepts based on nationalism, statism, and particularism. The Jewish tradition of social marginality, of reticence to participate in nationalistic celebrations, makes anti-Semitism a universal phenomenon, as characteristic of France as of the Soviet Union. The special character of Jewish living cannot be easily converted into the special nature of Jewish dying. Dying is a universal property of many peoples, cultures, and nations.

Five: The Holocaust was not an episode within the Third Reich, a footnote for historians. In all other societies, however brutal, people are punished for doing. In the Third Reich, "non-Aryans" were punished for being. In all other societies—in pretended or actual principle, if assuredly not always in practice—people are presumed innocent until proved guilty; the Nazi principle presumed everyone guilty until he had proved his "Aryan" innocence. Hence, anyone proving or even prepared to prove such innocence was implicated, however slightly or unwittingly, in the process which led to Auschwitz. The Holocaust is not an accidental by-product of the Reich but rather its inmost essence.

Response to this proposition must acknowledge the basic truths of the first part of the statement. The Holocaust was not merely a passing moment within the Third Reich. It did not occur in other Fascist countries, like Italy, for example, where death itself was alien to the Italian culture, where not only the survival of Jews but the survival of Communists was tolerated and even encouraged. Antonio Gramsci's major works were written in a prison that had been converted into a library by his jailers. The nature of national culture is a specific entity. The Italian people, the Turkish people, the German people all had a distinctive character. Social analysts do not discuss this kind of theme in public. It is not fashionable; we have become even a bit frightened of the concept of national character. Any notion of national character as that advanced by Fackenheim carries within itself the danger of stereotypical thought. But how else can we understand these phenomena? How can we understand the character of reaction, rebellion, and revolution in Turkey without understanding Turkish character, especially the continuity of that kind of character in the moral bookkeeping of development?

Ascribing guilt through proving innocence fits the framework of the Nazi ideology. But to construct a general theory of historical guilt may have pernicious consequences, in which the sins of the fathers are bequeathed to the children and further offspring. That the Holocaust was an "inmost essence" makes it difficult to get beyond phylogenic memories, beyond a situation in which a society might be viewed as having overcome its racism. When guilt is generalized, when it no longer is historically specific to social systems and political regimes, then a kind of irreducible psychologism takes intellectual command and it becomes impossible to stipulate conditions for moving beyond a genocidal state. The Holocaust becomes part of a rooted psychic unconsciousness hovering above the permanently contaminated society. To be sure, the Holocaust is the essence of the Third Reich. However, such an observation is not necessarily the core question. Does the destruction of the Jews follow automatically upon a nation that is swallowed up by the totalitarian temptation? In which forms of totalitarianism does a holocaust or genocide take place? Is anti-Semitism the essence of the Soviet Union as is now claimed? Does the existence of anti-Semitism prove a theory of totalitarian essence?

The uncomfortable fact is that genocide is the consequence of certain forms of unbridled state power. But whether anti-Semitism or other forms of racism are employed depends on the specific history of oppressor groups no less than oppressed peoples. States which demonstrate their power by exercising their capacity to take lives may be termed totalitarian. Totalitarianism is the essence of the genocidal process. This in itself provides an ample definition. If the Holocaust is unique to the Third Reich, the question of genocide loses any potential for being a general issue common to oppressive regimes. It is parochial to think that the Third Reich somehow uniquely embodied the character of the Holocaust, when since then we have seen many other societies adopt similar positions and policies toward other minorities and peoples.

Six: The Holocaust is not part of German history alone. It includes such figures as the Grand Mufti of Jerusalem, Jajj Amin al-Husseini, who successfully urged the Nazi leaders to kill more Jews. It also includes all countries whose niggardly immigration policies prior to World War II cannot be explained in normal terms alone, such as the pressure of the Great Depression or a xenophobic tradition. Hitler did not wish to export national socialism but only anti-Semitism. He was widely successful. He succeeded when the world thought that "the Jews" must have done something to arouse the treatment given them by a German government. He also succeeded when the world categorized Jews needing a refuge as "useless people." (In this category would have been Sigmund Freud, had he still been in Germany rather than in America; Martin Buber, had he not already made his way to the Yishuv [Palestine].) This was prior to the war. When the war had trapped the Jews of Nazi Europe, the railways to Auschwitz were not bombed. The Holocaust is not a parochial event. It is world-historical.

Curiously there is no mention of any other kind of history. Is, for example, the genocide of the Armenian people part of world history or is it simply part of Turkish history? This is a very complicated point; at the risk of sounding impervious to moral claims, one has to be history-specific if anything serious is to emerge. If one blames the whole world for what took place at Van, one can construct such a theory. But it is more pertinent, more appropriate, more pointed, to blame the Turks and not the universe, and to blame the Germans and not the whole world, including the Grand Mufti. The issue is implementation, not rhetoric. The issue is neither the Grand Mufti nor the insecurities of Ambassador Morgenthau.

Fackenheim's idea that Hitler neither exported national socialism nor wished to do so represents a special reading of events. As Gideon Hausner reminds us,[13] as late as April 1945, when the Soviets were penetrating Berlin for the final assault and Hitler was imprisoned in his bunker, his last will and testament concluded by enjoining "the government and the people to uphold the racial laws to the limit and to

resist mercilessly the poisoner of all nations, international Jewry."
Hausner makes it plain that national socialism was an international movement whose linchpin was anti-Semitism. Fackenheim presumes that
World War II was all about anti-Semitism, but at a more prosaic level it
was about conquest. There was a Nazi government in Rumania; there
was a Nazi government in Yugoslavia—all these regimes were exported.
The idea that Hitler was not interested in exporting national socialism is
curious. It would be more appropriate to note that wherever national
socialism was exported, so too did anti-Semitism follow. However, in
conditions where the Jewish population was not a factor, Nazism still
sought to establish a political foothold, either with or without direct
military aggression. The relation between national socialism as an
ideology and anti-Semitism as a passion is one that the Nazis themselves
were hard put to resolve. The linkage between the ideology and the
passion, which seems so close in retrospect, was far less articulated
policy than felt need in the earlier states of the Nazi regime.

Fackenheim slips in a subtle point that Jews were "trapped" in
Europe. But Jews were not trapped in Europe. They were of Europe
and had been of Europe for a thousand years. One of their dilemmas is
one rendered in almost every history where those who are to be exploited
or annihilated overidentify with their ruling masters. The Jews of
Europe were entirely Europeanized. Only a small fragment remained
outside the framework of Europeanization. The great divide of German
and Russian Jews was participation in European nationalism, identification with enlightenment. Fackenheim's idea that the Jews were
trapped in Europe is a clever misreading of the facts. The added horror
of the Holocaust is that it happened to a people who were endemic to that
part of the world.

Seven: The Jews were no mere scapegoat in the Holocaust. It is true that
they were used as such in the early stages of the movement. Thus Hitler was
able to unite the "left" and "right" wings of his party by distinguishing, on the
left between "Marxist" (i.e., Jewish) and "national socialism" (i.e., "Aryan")
and, on the right, between raffendes Kapital ("rapacious," i.e., "Jewish"
capital) and schaffendes Kapital ("creative," i.e., "Aryan" capital). It is also
true that, had the supply of Jewish victims given out, Hitler would have been
forced (as he once remarked to Hermann Rauschning) to "invent" new
"Jews." But it is not true that "The Jew [was] . . . only a pretext for
something else." So long as there were actual Jews, it was these actual Jews
who were the systematic object of ferreting-out, torture, and murder. Once,
at Sinai, Jews had been singled out for life and a task. Now at Auschwitz,
they were singled out for torment and death.

The difficulty with this exclusivist formula is that while Jews were
singled out, so too were Gypsies, Poles, and Slavs. Hitler's appeal was
to state power, not to unite left and right; not to unite bourgeoisie and

proletariat, but to make sure that the bourgeoisie and the proletariat of Germany were purified of Jewish elements. If one considers the national aspects of the Third Reich rather than the mystical aspects of Jewish destruction it becomes a lot easier to fathom. German Jewish concentration points were the bourgeoisie and the proletariat, in leftist socialist politics and in high bourgeois economics. Liquidation of the Jews enabled the German bureaucratic state to manage the bourgeoisie and the proletariat of Germany without opposition.[14] The destruction of socialism was attendant to the destruction of the Jews. Without socialist opposition, the German proletariat was an easy mark for Third Reich massification. The first two legislative acts of the Third Reich were bills of labor, work, and management. The liquidation of the Jewish population, within both the bourgeoisie and the proletariat, permitted the Nazis to consolidate state power. The Holocaust, from a Nazi standpoint, was an entirely rational process, scarcely a singular act of mystical divination. It was the essential feature of Nazi "domestic" policy in the final stages of the Third Reich.

Eight: The Holocaust is not over and done with. Late in the war Goebbels (who needless to say, knew all) said publicly and with every sign of conviction that, among the peoples of Europe, the Jews alone had neither sacrificed nor suffered in the war but only profited from it. As this was written, an American professor has written a book asserting that the Holocaust never happened, while other Nazis are preparing to march on Skokie in an assault on Jewish survivors. Like the old Nazis, the new Nazis say two things at once. The Holocaust never happened; and it is necessary to finish the job.

On this point, Fackenheim is on sound ground. Still, the point that he does not make and that requires emphasis is that the Holocaust did happen and could happen again, but is now more likely to happen to people other than Jews and Armenians. It was more likely to happen to Ugandans, and it did; to Cambodians, and it did; to Paraguayans, and it did; to Biafrans, and it did. It is correct to say that the Holocaust is not over and done with. But it is not over and done with because there are other peoples victimized by the very model created by the Turkish and Nazi genocides.

It is important not to fit peoplehood into theories; theories must fit the realities of people. If the restoration of human dignity is to become a theme for social research, it becomes imperative to understand the unified character of genocide, the common characteristics of its victims, and ultimately the need for alliances of victims and potential victims to resist all kinds of genocide. To insist on universalism, triumphalism, or separatist orientations is self-defeating. If there is to be any political consequence of research into genocide, and if victim groups are to do more than pay for annual memorials and remembrances, understanding of the unity needed to confront state oppression must be made paramount; otherwise little will have been accomplished and nothing will have changed.

Although my analysis has sharply demarcated theological from sociological viewpoints, it should be appreciated that Jewish religious thought is itself far from unanimous on the special nature of the Holocaust. Orthodox segments in particular have cautioned against an overly dramaturgical viewpoint, urging instead a position in which the Nazi Holocaust is but the latest monumental assault on the Jewish people— one that is neither to be ignored nor celebrated, but simply understood as part of the martyrdom of a people. In a recent essay, William Helmreich has finely caught the spirit of this "strictly orthodox" view—which may be shared by larger numbers than either the mystifiers or the celebrationists may recognize.

He notes that this orthodox wing rejects paying special homage by singling out the victims of the Holocaust on both philosophical and practical grounds.

In their view, the Holocaust is not, in any fundamental way, a unique event in Jewish history, but simply the latest in a long chain of anti-Jewish persecutions that began with the destruction of the Temple and which also included the Crusades, the Spanish Inquisition, attacks on Jews led by Chmielnicki, and the hundreds of pogroms to which the Jewish community has been subjected to over the centuries. They do admit that the Holocaust was unique in scale and proportion but this is not considered a distinction justifying its elevation into a separate category.[15]

Helmreich goes on to note that the ethical problem, in view of orthodox believers, is the same if one Jew is murdered or if 6 million meet such a fate. Since Judaism is a *Gemeinschaft* ("a community of fate"), the sheer volume killed, while awesome, does not in itself transform a quantitative event into a unique qualitative phenomenon.

The significance of this minority theological report is to call attention to the fact that in the problem of the Holocaust, while there are some strong clerical-secular bifurcations, there are also cross-cutting patterns across disciplinary boundaries. For example, certain sociological lessons can be drawn from the Holocaust: the breakdown in egalitarian revolutions of the nineteenth century, the subtle abandonment of the Palestinian mandate after the Balfour Declaration, the lofty assertion followed by a total revocation of Jewish minority rights in the Soviet Union. For orthodoxy the Holocaust is more a function of the breakdown of Jewish solidarity than of any special evils of the German nation or the Nazi regime.

The sociological view attempts to transcend sectarian or parochial concerns and develop a cross-cultural paradigm that would permit placing the Holocaust in a larger perspective of genocide in the twentieth century rather than seeing the former as entirely distinctive and the latter as some weaker form of mass murder. For example, with the liquidation of roughly 40 percent of the Cambodian population, even the quantitative indicators of the Nazi Holocaust have been approached in at least one other situation. In the past, it has been argued that genocide of other peoples—Armenians, Ugandans, Paraguayans, Indians—has been too random and sporadic to be termed a holocaust. It has also been claimed that the atomic attacks on Hiroshima and Nagasaki were highly selective and refined military targets and not efforts at the total destruction of a people. Whatever the outcome of such contentions, the Cambodian case would indicate the risks in vesting too much intellectual capital in the sheer numbers involved—although it is clearly a factor to be contended with.

Having argued thusly, let me note that qualitative differences do exist which distinguish the Jewish Holocaust from any other forms of genocide. First, there is the systematic rather than random or sporadic nature of the Holocaust: the technological and organizational refinement of the tools of mass slaughter which ultimately reduced all morality to problems of human engineering—development of the most effective methods for destroying and disposing of large numbers of people by the fewest cadres possible in the shortest amount of time. Second, there was an ideological fervor unmatched by any other previous variety of genocide. So intent were the Nazis in their policy of extermination of the Jews that they dared contact other nations, especially Axis powers and neutral countries, to repatriate Jews back to Germany to suffer the ultimate degradation. Third, genocide against the Jewish people represented and rested upon a national model of state power: the purification of the apparatus of repression by a total concentration of the means of destruction in a narrow military police stratum unencumbered by considerations of class, ethnicity, gender, or any other social factors affecting Nazi response to non-Jewish groups. The liquidation of plural sources of power and authority made easier, indeed presupposed, the total liquidation of the Jewish population.

With all these inner disputations and disagreements accounted for, there are still those who—too guilt-ridden to face the monstrous consequences of the Holocaust against Jews in particular and victims of genocide as a whole—have chosen the path of evading reality. An isolated voice like that of Arthur R. Butz[16] is now joined in a quasi-intellectual movement, with all the paraphernalia of historical scholarship,[17] denying this massive crime. Denials of gas chambers, rejection of photographic evidence, equation of indemnification of the victims with Zionist beneficiaries are all linked to the rejection of the Holocaust's occurrence. The Nazi "revisionists" dare not speak of Nazism, but of national socialism; not of Germany under Hitlerism, but of a Third Reich. The Nazi epoch is even spoken of in remorseful terms: "Overwhelming British, American, and Soviet forces finally succeeded in crushing the military resistance of a Germany which they accorded not even the minimum of mercy."[18]  Pity the poor victim!

Even the New Nazi "intelligentsia" does not deny mass murder, but only the numbers murdered.[19]  If it is not 6 million, then what number is it?  No matter, those massacred were Zionists, Communists, or a hyphenated variety of the two—Jewish-Bolsheviks—any euphemism for Jews other than the admission of a special assassination of Jews as a people.  The need for exacting scholarship—the sort that has begun to emerge—with respect to all peoples victimized for their existence is not simply a matter of litanies and recitations, but of the very retention of the historical memory itself.  The scientific study of genocide is not a matter of morbid fascination or mystic divination, but of the need to assert the historical reality of collective crime.  Only by such a confrontation can we at least locate moral responsibility for state crimes even if we cannot always prevent future genocides from taking place.

With all due weight given to the different traditions involved in the theological and sociological arguments concerning genocide, they do have a strong shared value commitment to the normative framework in which greater emphasis is placed on the protection of life than on economic systems or political regimes.[20]  Both traditions are committed, insofar as their dogmas and doctrines permit, to the supreme place of life in the hierarchy of values.  This is no small matter.  Nazism witnessed the breakdown of religious and scientific institutions alike; and those that could not be broken down were oftentimes simply corrupted, as in decadent and exotic notions of a Teutonic Church and the equally ludicrous belief in an Aryan Science.  In the larger context of world history and in the wider picture of centuries-old barbarisms, we bear witness not to a warfare of science versus theology but rather to a shared collapse of any sort of normative structure in which either could function to enhance the quality or sanctity of life.

Leo Kuper, born and banned in South Africa, is professor emeritus at the University of Southern California and the author of several excellent monographs in social stratification and race relations in African contexts. He is a good man writing about an awful subject who has produced, unfortunately, a mediocre book.  The author of *Genocide: Its Political Use in the Twentieth Century* manages to skirt just about every major issue which has arisen in the field of investigation:  the relationship between the Holocaust and genocides in general; the relationship between civil conflict and state destruction; and the reasons for the ineffectiveness of international peace-keeping agencies in reducing genocide.  The last omission is particularly glaring since Kuper describes this as an essential task.

On a different level, however, it is an excellent basic text, especially for individuals who are not familiar with the subject of genocide.

Definitions are invariably fairminded and essentially sound; the appendices, especially on United Nations resolutions and areas of backsliding (such as its attitude toward the Turkish genocide against Armenians), are particularly revealing. The role of the United Nations, or its lack thereof, has been discussed often but understood rarely. At such descriptive levels the book provides a welcome contribution. The selected cases are for the most part helpful and demonstrate a keen sense of the magnitude of the problems of genocide. When we talk in terms of roughly 800,000 Armenians, 6 million Jews, and 3 million Cambodians, we have clear-cut examples of an enormous portion of a national population decimated by the authorities, giving a sober reminder that our century hovers dangerously between creativity and destruction.

The book's problems are less those of sentiment than of method. Equating such phenomena as civil strife between Catholics and Protestants in Northern Ireland with the destruction of German Jewry or the destruction of urban Cambodia just does not work. Even the author acknowledges that in Northern Ireland, victims have been numbered in the hundreds over a long stretch of time, whereas in most clear-cut cases of genocide the numbers destroyed are in the millions. Then there is the too simplistic equation of civil war and genocide. Equating the Nigerian Civil War or even the struggle against apartheid in South Africa with cases of undisputed genocide blurs and confuses rather than clarifies what genocide is about—namely, the vast, near-total destruction of large numbers of noncombatants innocent of any specific crime. Furthermore, burdening the United Nations as the source of the failure to control genocide is unconvincing since, as Kuper explains at length, this organization is primarily a composite of nations and not in itself a sovereign power. Underneath the demand to strengthen the United Nations is an implicit assumption that nationalism should be weakened—something that clearly has not taken place, nor is likely to take place, certainly not under the aegis of the United Nations.

In the balance of this critique, let me take up some of the thornier issues. The problem of genocide is not a new one, and the need for a scholarship to move beyond horrors and into analysis becomes increasingly critical. It is risky to equate genocide with arbitrary death. Two examples which Leo Kuper has given illustrate a problem rather than indicate a solution. He raises, for example, the case of India during the partition. Hindus and Moslems constituted majorities in different parts of the country, each with the capacity to engage freely in what he calls reciprocal genocidal massacre. However terrible and tragic that mutual destruction was, to speak of it as genocidal in the context of religious competition and conflict risks diluting the notion of genocide and equating it with any conflict between national, religious, or racial groups. This error also appears in his analysis of Northern Ireland, where Protestants and Catholics engage in the meanest and most dangerous kinds of assaults on one another. If one were to tally the numbers of deaths since 1920, they would total about 10,000, surely a terrible human loss and an indicator, according to Kuper, of the risks involved in the removal of the British presence in Ulster before a political solution is achieved. One might indicate, as have many leaders from both the Catholic and Protestant camps, that the British presence is itself a source of violence and that the removal of the occupying power would overcome a major obstacle to resolution of the civil conflict. Whether this belief is correct or not, we are dealing within the realm of political tactics and international relations, but surely not with genocide—unless we reduce the term to a fatuous notion of the cultural elimination of certain groups and ideologies.

Kuper also confounds legal identification between apartheid and genocide in South Africa with the empirical problem: the place and condition of the blacks within South Africa. As the author himself well appreciates, there is a demographic restraint to annihilation. The black African population in South Africa grew from roughly 8 million in 1945 to 19 million in 1980. The Asian population grew from 285,000 to 765,000; and the white population from 2.4 million to roughly 4.4 million. The demographics alone indicate that genocide simply has not occurred. What may have happened is the fragmentation of the African population and the consequent denial of blacks' citizenship rights. South Africa is also a classic case of exploitation of the majority by a racial minority, in a very specialized context. But it does not benefit the victims or anyone else to present South Africa as a case of genocide —which implies the absolute destruction of a people, if not completely, then in such large numbers as to affect their future survival potential.

Relativizing the issue of genocide particularly damages efforts to understand the Nazi Holocaust against the Jews. The major problem in such relativizing is that it completely fails to distinguish between the systematic, total, scientific engineering of death, and the more random occurrences that are characteristic of other events. If others were to operate under a veil of anonymity such as the Nazis did, they might also attempt a kind of "final solution." But whether that is so or not, the notion of the final solution, the sources and consequences of the Nazi destruction of the Jews, is absent in the work of Professor Kuper. While I myself have argued against celebrating the exclusivity of death, one must consider seriously differences between the almost total destruction of a population, reducing it to a remnant, and the selective, random elimination of political or religious opposition. The very concept of the Holocaust as something unique fails to appear in Kuper's work and is mentioned only in relation to a book title. It is as if the author were consciously and deliberately attempting to relativize the Jewish case as one of many, and consequently disregarding the specificity and peculiar characteristics involved in the Nazi Holocaust. This undermines not only the moral basis of Kuper's work but also weakens his appreciation of the full meaning of the Turkish assault on Armenians. The latter was not merely an event that took place in the Ottoman Empire but is characteristic of the Kemalist democracy that followed. The genocide against Armenians, like the Holocaust against Jews, was special in its totality as well as in its movement beyond the boundaries of nationalism and rationalism. Both cases are not characteristic of any others—until we get to Cambodian communism.

Underlying his failure to distinguish between genocide and civil strife on the one hand, and genocide and total destruction such as the Holocaust on the other, is a peculiar inability to distinguish between theory and action and, more specifically, an unwillingness to deal with German and Turkish cultures. Kuper, along with others, has dedicated a great deal of futile time to problems of ideology. There is sufficient confusion within Marxism and Fascism to make one wary of this line of approach. Perhaps Marxism, in its acceptance of a theory of class polarization, yields to a Manichean vision of a world torn apart; but even a Marxism predicated on guilt by social origin may or may not translate into genocidal behavior. It certainly does in terms of the Gulag Archipelago and the years of Stalinism; it certainly does not in such places as Yugoslavia. Likewise, even with Fascism there seems to be no doubt that the Nazis analogized European Jewry to a cancer which had to be excised and identified Jews with world conspiracy. Fascism in Italy did not have the same genocidal potential. When Jewish enclaves in Asia came under Japanese dominion during World War II the genocidal pattern did not follow. Any comprehensive analysis of genocide must deal seriously with cultural canons which permit or forbid genocidal behavior. This total absence of cultural analysis—of both those who were and were not given to genocide—seriously weakens Kuper's book. Ideology rather than culture is held responsible and accountable for genocidal behavior. This is a difficult thesis to prove. The republican developmentalism of Ataturk in Turkey is absolutely at odds with imperial notions derived from the Ottoman Empire, yet both republican and anti-republican forces within Turkey carried on genocide against the Armenians. The peasant egalitarianism of the Khmer Rouge did not spare us a major genocide. Wherever one seeks an answer based on ideology the same kind of confusion presents itself, issues which Kuper unfortunately does not address.

Kuper charges the United Nations with having done much less than it should have. He argues that its capacities to curtail genocide, much less prevent or punish atrocities, have been blunted. He gives several reasons for this laxity: first, the punitive procedures of the United Nations are weak; second, the United Nations is committed to the sanctity of state sovereignty; and third, the United Nations has established commissions to deal with complaints about human rights violations which are themselves highly politicized and controlled by a clique of powerful nations whose vested interests are in stilling the voices of opposition. One could hardly argue with Kuper's analysis of the weaknesses of the United Nations, but from an analytical point of view, it is an extremely thin reed on which to hang an analysis of the problem of genocide. The sources of genocide are certainly not in the United Nations. The limits of the organization are well understood by most. Kuper might then have analyzed different kinds of national cultures as well as how punishment and law emerge in various countries.

There is now a burgeoning literature on just these subjects. It might be possible to develop an early warning signal, a concern about problems of law and democratic order, that might limit the possibility of future genocides taking place. But if the genesis of the problem is not in a world organization, then it is hard to believe that the solution will be found there. As Kuper knows quite well, the United Nations is itself the source of so much amoral self-righteousness that its very existence strengthens nationalism and the national ideal.

The treatment of the Holocaust as a dialogue between God and Golem, as ineffable and unspeakable, serves to return the matter of death into the antinomic and Manichean tradition of original sin versus original goodness, or, as it is more fashionably called, historical pessimism versus historical optimism. On the other hand, the treatment of genocide as a problem for the United Nations makes it a rather tepid organizational affair, denying to this "dismal science" its full meaning and significance.

If social science is to make its own serious contribution to Holocaust studies, it must get beyond the mystery of silence or the silence of mysteries. However limited the clinical analysis of collective death may be, we may at least be spared the repetition of some forms of genocide. To incorporate in the Jewish psyche the phrase "never again" requires an antecedent commitment to explain why genocide happened in the first place. Theologians must not presume an exclusive monopoly on meaning by insisting upon the mystery and irrationality of taking lives. The task of social science remains, in this area as in all others, a rationalization of irrationality. Only in this way can the victory be denied to Golem and the struggle against evil be understood as a task God assigns to humanity. This is far greater than standing in silent awe at the tragedies that have befallen our tragic century.

## NOTES

1. John Vincur, "In West Berlin: A New Curtain Rises on Auschwitz," *New York Times,* 7 April 1980, p. 2.
2. Yehuda Bauer, *The Holocaust in Historical Perspective* (Seattle: University of Washington Press, 1978), pp. 39-49.

3. Elie Wiesel, *Legends of Our Time* (New York: Holt, Rinehart and Winston, 1969), p. 6. For an analysis of this see Terrence Des Pres, "The Authority of Silence in Elie Wiesel's Art," in *Confronting the Holocaust: The Impact of Elie Wiesel,* ed. Alvin H. Rosenfield and Irving Greenberg (Bloomington: Indiana University Press, 1978), pp. 49-57.

4. Peter J. Donaldson, "In Cambodia, A Holocaust," *New York Times,* 22 April 1980, p. 17.

5. Emil L. Fackenheim, "What the Holocaust Was Not," *Face to Face* (an interreligious bulletin issued by the Anti-Defamation League of B'nai B'rith) 7 (Winter 1980), pp. 8-9. This set of propositions is derived from Fackenheim's Foreward to Yehuda Bauer's *The Jewish Emergence from Powerlessness* (London: Macmillan, 1979).

6. Leo Kuper, *Genocide: Its Political Use in the Twentieth Century* (New Haven: Yale University Press, 1981).

7. For a fuller version of what has become the dominant and most widely respected Jewish viewpoint on the Holocaust, see Emil L. Fackenheim, *God's Presence in History* (New York: Schocken Press, 1972), pp. 70-73.

8. Robert J. Lifton, "The Concept of the Survivor," in *Survivors, Victims, and Perpetrators: Essays on the Nazi Holocaust,* ed. Joel E. Dimsdale (Washington, D.C.: Hemisphere Publishing Co., 1980), pp. 113-26.

9. Literature on the Armenian subjugation is uneven, and scholars are only now facing up to the herculean research tasks involved. An excellent compendium of available materials for 1915-1923 is contained in Richard G. Hovannisian, *The Armenian Holocaust* (Cambridge, Mass.: Armenian Heritage Press, 1978).

10. Anna Pawelczynska, *Values and Violence in Auschwitz* (Berkeley and Los Angeles: University of California Press, 1979), pp. 101-5.

11. Raul Hilberg, "German Railroads/Jewish Souls," *Transaction/ SOCIETY* 14 (November-December 1976), pp. 60-74. For a general introduction to this subject see *Captured Germans and Related Records: A National Archives Conference,* ed. Robert Wolfe (Athens: Ohio University Press, 1974).

12. George L. Mosse, *Toward the Final Solution: A History of European Racism* (New York: H. Fertig, 1978), pp. 226-27.

13. Gideon Hausner, "Six Million Accusers," in *The Jew in the Modern World: A Documentary History,* ed. Paul R. Mendes-Flohr and Jehuda Reinharz (New York: Oxford University Press, 1980), pp. 521-23.

14. Irving Louis Horowitz, *Foundations in Political Sociology* (New York: Harper and Row, 1972), pp. 245-46. See in this connection D. L. Niewyk, *Socialist, Anti-Semite, and Jew: German Social Democracy Confronts the Problems of Anti-Semitism* (Baton Rouge: Louisiana State University Press, 1971).

15. For a full discussion of the orthodox (minority) viewpoint on the Holocaust in the context of Yeshiva life, see William Helmreich, "Making the

Awful Meaningful: Understanding the Holocaust," *Transaction/SOCIETY* 19, no. 6 (September-October 1982), pp. 62-66.

16. Arthur R. Butz, *The Hoax of the Twentieth Century* (Torrance, Calif.: Institute for Historical Review, 1976).

17. See Austin J. App, "The 'Holocaust' Put in Perspective," *Journal of Historical Review* 1 (Spring 1980), pp. 81-82.

18. Charles E. Wever, "German History from a New Perspective," *Journal of Historical Review* 1 (Spring 1980), pp. 88-94.

19. The most authoritative estimate of the number of Jews killed by the Nazis—5,978,000 out of a prewar population of 8,301,000, or 72 percent —is contained in Leon Poliakov and Josef Wulf, eds., *Das Dritte Reich und die Juden: Dokumente und Aufsaetze* (Berlin: Arani, 1955), p. 229.

20. For an articulate statement of legal and social issues at an individual level which have direct relevance to our discussion at the collective level, see George Z. F. Bereday, "The Right to Live and the Right to Die: Some Considerations of Law and Society in America," *Man and Medicine* 4 (November 4, 1979), pp. 233-56.

# 5

# GENOCIDE, THE HOLOCAUST, AND TRIAGE

## John K. Roth

Since its historical entry into world history the German people has
always found itself in need of space. . . . Our people has never been
able to settle this need for space, except through conquest by the sword
or through a reduction of its own population.

Adolf Hitler, 1928

In May 1984, the Associated Press wired to American newspapers the
recent findings of the Population Reference Bureau, a Washington-based
research group that studies population trends.[1] Beyond announcing that
nearly 4.8 billion human beings now inhabit the earth, the bureau indicated that our planet's population has doubled since World War II. Not
only did the world's population increase by almost 85 million in the past
year, the report went on to say, but there will be 5 billion persons here
by 1987. That number will rise to 6 billion by the end of the twentieth
century. Within forty years, the world's population will double.
Strangely, however, the AP's story took no notice of forces that could
disrupt these trends. Such interruptions, hastened by exploding population growth, ought not to be taken lightly. Nuclear threats make that fact
obvious. So does the history of genocide. More people exist than anyone needs. That condition—more or less—has always held. It makes
history, as Hegel deftly said, a slaughter-bench.

Where more people exist than are wanted, man-made death is never
far behind. One of the most persuasive teachers of that lesson was Adolf
Hitler. Although not sufficient, his leadership was a necessary condition
for the Holocaust, the Nazi attempt to exterminate the Jews. As suggested by the quotation with which this essay begins, Hitler believed that

the world's population was too large, and that therefore space, entailing opportunity as well as geography, was lacking for the German people. His self-proclaimed mission was to lead them to their rightful increase and dominion.

Significantly, Hitler's statement comes from his so-called *Zweites Buch*.[2] Drafted in 1928, this sequel to *Mein Kampf* was suppressed by Hitler himself. It is not necessary to assess the various explanations that have been offered to account for that fact—the work was identified in 1958 and published in German three years later—but the issue that provoked Hitler to write is noteworthy. As Telford Taylor tells the story, "the question of the South Tyrol was an especially sharp thorn in the Nazi flesh" (p. xvi). For more than a century preceding the end of World War I, this Alpine region south of the Brenner Pass, much of it German-speaking, lived under Austrian rule. Thanks to the Treaty of St. Germain, Italy gained control of the area. Its policy toward the German population was benign until Benito Mussolini's Fascist regime introduced a program of Italianization. By March 1928, for example, Italian had become the language of religious instruction in South Tyrol, prompting strong criticism from the Austrian Chancellor, Ignaz Seipel. When Mussolini returned the favor by recalling his ambassador from Vienna, the anti-Italian reaction in Germany as well as in Austria was considerable.

Hitler, however, did not profit from this feeling. On the contrary, having praised Mussolini in *Mein Kampf,* where he also asserted that unrest in the South Tyrol was a Jewish-inspired scheme to discredit Il Duce and to threaten German-Italian cooperation, Hitler found himself "attacked from the 'folkish' and nationalist quarter as 'soft' on an issue of German irredentism" (p. xvii). Ironic though the facts just mentioned may be, Hitler's *Zweites Buch* concentrated on the status of South Tyrol. If the passing of the crisis influenced him to withhold the book when it became apparent that nothing could be gained by publishing a work that would "belabor an issue on which he and his Party were on the defensive," Hitler's *Zweites Buch* still shows that the problem of not enough space and too many people, or at least not enough space for the right kinds of people, was never far from his mind at the time (p. xx). Nor would those issues dwindle in importance as Hitler came to power and unleashed genocide in his quest for *Lebensraum.* After the *Anschluss,* Hitler may have been content to leave South Tyrol under Mussolini's jurisdiction, even though he was unsuccessful in urging its German population to emigrate to the Reich, but both outcomes drove home the governing principles Hitler had written down in 1928:

Politics is history in the making. History itself is the presentation of a people's struggle for existence. I deliberately use the phrase "struggle for existence" here because in truth that struggle for daily bread, equally in peace and war, is an eternal battle against thousands upon thousands of resistances just as life itself is an eternal struggle against death. (P. 5)

No people have ever been wanted less than the Jews were by Hitler. His anti-Jewish campaign was so virulent that it reduced Jews to sub- or non-human status, thus making their elimination easier. Under Hitler, then, the Nazis unleashed their genocide on the Jews. The success of this attack is corroborated by the fact that even now debate rages about whether *genocide* is a category that is adequate to encompass the Holocaust. At issue in those debates is the Holocaust's uniqueness. Consider, therefore, the useful distinctions that Yehuda Bauer makes by designating the Holocaust as "the extreme case" of genocide.[3]

To Bauer, genocide suggests a continuum, each instance aimed at destroying a people in one way or another. The Holocaust belongs at its "farthest point" because, as Hitler's targets, "every Jew—man, woman, and child—was to be killed" (pp. 331-32). Genocide includes a multitude of sins, but heretofore its instances have not aimed at the total annihilation Hitler eventually directed against the Jews.[4] Hence, the Holocaust is unique. Yet, owing to the possibility that total annihilation might in some time or place become the aim again, Bauer contends that the term "Holocaust" can be "not only the name by which the planned murder of the Jewish people is known," but also "a generic name for an ideologically motivated planned total murder of a whole people."[5] Just as history contains a variety of Holocaust-related events, such as the Armenian massacres, there may also be Holocausts in the offing, a possibility made all the more real since *the* Holocaust occurred.

If genocide is a continuum with Holocaust at its farthest point, how are genocide's victims to be understood? If there is not some universal characteristic that they all share, do they at least have what the philosopher Ludwig Wittgenstein would have called a family resemblance? The import of such questions is more than historical; it also directs us toward the future. For if people become potential targets of genocidal campaigns for reasons that at least resemble one another, that knowledge can alert the endangered and those who care about them.

Such concerns are among those that orient the scholarship of Richard L. Rubenstein, whose writings are as far-ranging as they are controversial, as perceptive as they are discomforting. An authorship taking him from *After Auschwitz* (1966) to *The Cunning of History* (1975) has recently been enhanced by *The Age of Triage* (1983), his most disturbing and hence most important work to date. There will be more to say about that book, but first *The Cunning of History*. It not only focused on the Holocaust but did so by accenting motifs already noted in this essay.

For example, while impressed by the unprecedented features of the Holocaust, Rubenstein affirmed that more understanding is to be gained by regarding Auschwitz as part of a continuum of human action than by putting it in a category entirely its own. Next, although *The Cunning of History* makes no mention of Hitler's *Zweites Buch,* Rubenstein knew the importance of Hitler's conviction that Germany "was always an overpopulated area."[6] Rubenstein further understood that Hitler's appraisal along those lines was not limited to quantitative considerations. Overpopulation was a qualitative matter for Hitler as well. In fact, a witches' brew of quantitative and qualitative concerns about population was not only what drove Hitler to establish the death camp as one of the twentieth century's fundamental realities. That melange could also reveal the Holocaust's significance in light of the recognition that the world's population is nearly 4.8 billion and escalating at a startling pace. With the Holocaust as the precedent, mass murder—if not genocide or Holocaust—might well be the remedy of choice to achieve a "final solution" to the problems created by hordes of people who are unwanted by the powers that be.

Stressing that the power of a political state is essential for Holocaust, if not for every form of genocide, *The Cunning of History* packs an incisive array of views into little more than a hundred pages. But none drew more vigorous response than Rubenstein's simplest and most fundamental thesis: "The Nazi elite clearly understood that the Jews were truly a *surplus people* whom nobody wanted and whom they could dispose of as they pleased. . . . In terms of German ideology, the Jews were a *surplus population* because of the kind of society the Germans wanted to create."[7] He would expand those claims in *The Age of Triage,* but already Rubenstein's point was that established interests had for centuries engaged in the riddance of redundant populations. The Nazis' handling of the Jews implemented an extremely calculated procedure for dealing with an old problem. It also involved a host of particular features—typically involving the blending of ancient strands of religious anti-Semitism with modern ideologies of nationalism and racism. But Rubenstein's major insight was that the category of "surplus people" was a crucial one to employ in relation to the Holocaust because it could help us understand not only how that event is unique but also how it is *symptomatic* of features that may be endemically destructive in our current ways of life.

Lest he be misunderstood, Rubenstein carefully stated that "the concept of a surplus population is not absolute. An underpopulated nation can have a redundant population if it is so organized that a segment of its able-bodied human resources cannot be utilized in any meaningful economic or social role" (p. 10). That qualification, however, did not prevent criticism for introducing population redundancy into an interpretation of the Holocaust. Even going on to clarify that "a surplus or redundant population is one that for any reason can find no viable role in the society in which it is domiciled," Rubenstein is still attacked for holding that the Holocaust—though exceptional—is still one of many instances of state-sponsored population elimination.[8]

A theory is only as good as its ability to cope with the objections brought against it. By indicating some typical challenges directed against Rubenstein's view about the Holocaust and surplus populations, responding to each, and then elaborating other dimensions of his vision, Rubenstein's contributions to an understanding of the age of genocide can be appraised. As to the criticisms—some explicit, others implied—the first of seven examples comes from Jacob Katz. Responding to statements made by Rubenstein at a conference on "The Holocaust—A Generation After," he asserted that Rubenstein was mistakenly trying to analyze the Holocaust "in Darwinian terms."[9] Specifically, contended Katz, the hypothesis that the Jews were a surplus people was not credible because the Nazis, even during the intensity of the Holocaust itself, "used Jews very profitably in SS factories" (ibid.). Variants of this argument have frequently been raised against Rubenstein from time to time, but they are not telling. Katz, for instance, undermines his own analysis by acknowledging that decisions to use Jews for slave labor were often overturned and instead those workers were dispatched to the gas chambers. Or, it could be added, many others were simply worked to death, as *The Cunning of History* testifies. Coupling these notes with Rubenstein's basic qualification that population redundancy is not simply a matter of numbers, Katz' objection remains beside the point.

In the same forum, Alice A. Eckardt took a different approach. She concurred with Rubenstein that the Nazi treatment of the Jews was not adequately handled by calling it an irrational aberration. Instead there was a kind of rationality in the Nazis' anti-Jewish campaign. But, she insisted, that rationality was not to be located in any Nazi perception that the Jews were superfluous. Rather, the Nazis looked on the Jews "as an absolute hindrance, a virus, a cancer" (p. 260). They were, in short, "the incarnation of evil" (ibid.). From the Nazi perspective, then, it could have made good sense to be rid of the Jews. To suggest, however, that the Jews were targets simply because they were superfluous will not do.

Not much more than Katz' remarks do Eckardt's undermine *The Cunning of History*. Indeed, they reflect it, for her argument, ironically, has the unintended consequence of supporting Rubenstein's analysis. The concept of a surplus population is not absolute; instead it encompasses the factors that Eckardt rightly stresses. People—and the Nazi outlook did not simply deny that Jews were people—do not become classified as viruses and cancers unless those beings are already regarded as unwanted in the extreme. Propaganda and ideology utilizing such classifications do so to underscore the more effectively how radically these people are unneeded, how they have no viable role in the scheme of things controlled by the powers that be in the region where they happen to dwell.

A third criticism has been advanced by Shlomo Avineri. He takes Rubenstein to task for being "a functional structuralist" (p. 262). Rubenstein, claims Avineri, tries too hard to subsume particular events under universal categories. Such attempts may be part of a noble tradition, but in the case of the Holocaust, avers Avineri, they will not enable Rubenstein to do what he wants. For there simply is not evidence to substantiate the claim that the Nazis regarded the Jews as surplus and therefore decided to exterminate them. On the other hand, there is abundant evidence that the Nazis were fundamentally anti-Semites. The Jews became targets not because they were superfluous but because the Nazis hated Jews so thoroughly. The full measure of that hatred was taken at Auschwitz.

One ought not trifle with a scholar of Avineri's deserved stature. Thus, it is welcome that Rubenstein can accept his points and find that the surplus people hypothesis is not jeopardized but strengthened. Rubenstein would be the first to agree with Avineri's observation that "Nazi antisemitism was not instrumental to Nazi aims but basic and immanent to them" (ibid.). Genocide, on the other hand, is instrumental. "Seldom elected by a government as an end in itself," Rubenstein has since pointed out, "genocide is always a means of eliminating a target population that challenges an economic, political, cultural, religious, or ideological value of the politically dominant group."[10] Hence, Avineri's stress on Nazi anti-Semitism indicates *why* the Jews were targeted, but in being targeted, the Jews also revealed themselves to be a surplus people as far as the Nazis were concerned. Rubenstein's point is rightly a functional one. Practically speaking, Nazi anti-Semitism meant Jewish superfluity. Already we have noted that Hitler had much to say about overpopulation, but even if Nazi rhetoric did not speak directly and consistently about the Jews as surplus people, actions spoke louder than words. Moreover, since there is no genocide without human redundancy of one kind or another, Nazi actions do support the contention that the Holocaust belongs on Bauer's continuum of genocide, albeit at its extremity. In spite of Avineri's contention to the contrary, the perspective of a functional structuralist, if the term is apt, can illumine the Holocaust's place in the larger scheme.

The previous objections find fault with Rubenstein's account because its emphasis on surplus people seems to overlook certain economic considerations and features of Nazi ideology. If those objections are much weaker than purported, the plot thickens when Berel Lang questions the explanatory power of Rubenstein's appeal to "the superfluity of a certain proportion of the population."[11] Lang does not elaborate his objection, but it seems to entail the belief that the surplus people category is itself rather superfluous when it comes to telling us how or why mass murder takes place in particular circumstances. If Lang's briefly stated position were expanded, it might claim that Rubenstein's concept says both too much and too little. We do not know what "surplus" means until we look at particular cases where allegedly surplus people are to be found. When we do such looking, moreover, we find that "surplus" is indeed not an absolute idea but so extremely relative that its meaning incorporates any number of specific reasons why a particular people might be targeted and killed. In the process, the concept covers so much as to become nearly meaningless.

Lang's criticism, implicit as well as explicit, has not gone unnoticed by Rubenstein. The best evidence for that claim is that the author of *The Cunning of History* planned early on to produce the sequel, *The Age of Triage,* that would buttress the propositions about surplus populations that were offered only in germinal form in the earlier study. As will be pointed out in more detail below, the latter book analyzes numerous historical examples to show that man-made mass death is linked with perceptions of population redundancy. That redundancy is not merely a matter of semantics, either. Historically, people tend to be killed en masse when dominant powers deem them unnecessary and unwanted. The factors that can put people into that risk are myriad, and hence the utility of Rubenstein's theory about surplus populations emerges. If one focused only on the many and varied particulars that lead to man-made mass death, the continuities among those events would be overlooked. Genocide and even Holocaust are concepts that help us to see the links. Rubenstein's contribution, vastly meaningful, is to show that the specific reasons for genocide also involve a pattern, one to which his intentionally elastic concept of surplus population directs us. The explanatory power of the concept may not be its primary hallmark—for explanation one must go more to the details in particular cases. The concept's strength is instead in its synthesizing capacity, which in turn enables us to see before it is too late the diverse ways and places in which people might find themselves functionally redundant and destined to be targets for riddance.

Other interpreters have taken *The Age of Triage* into account and still find Rubenstein vulnerable where his theories about surplus people are concerned. John Patrick Diggins, for example, echoes Berel Lang by wondering whether Rubenstein's appeal to the problem of surplus populations really tells us why genocide happens. "For all his admirable research," Diggins says of Rubenstein, he "cannot establish the precise cause, or even causes, of genocide, and this is profoundly disturbing."[12] This critic reasons that a historian "must demonstrate that causes originated in man's conscious intentions and purposes" before claiming to know why human consequences turned out as they did. On Diggins' reading, then, population superfluity could only be a cause of genocide if awareness of such a superfluity existed and the superfluity yielded a conscious motive that led people to kill accordingly. Such evidence, he implies with Avineri, is hard to come by not only in the Holocaust but in other genocidal scenarios as well.

Rubenstein, I believe, would be agreeable to Diggins' insistence on documentation. One issue between them, however, is where such documentation can or must be found. Again, Rubenstein's methodology places less emphasis on what people say than on what they do. People do not have to be overtly labeled "surplus" in order to be redundant; nor do the powers that be have to pronounce that there is a problem of surplus population in order for them to document through their actions that they do, in fact, think one exists. The ultimate documentation is extermination. Diggins may wish to wait for more explicit documentation, but if he does so, it is not clear that his historical positivism will show itself superior to Rubenstein's willingness to let practice document belief.

Incidentally, Diggins' skepticism notwithstanding, Rubenstein has boldly asserted that the Holocaust "can be *fully* comprehended in terms of the normal categories of history, social science, demography, political theory and economics."[13] The credibility of that claim, of course, will depend on what is meant by "*fully* comprehended," but at this juncture Rubenstein's Hegelian reach may well exceed an existential grasp. For if human experience cannot ultimately account for itself—and it cannot —then it is hard to see how "the normal categories of historical and socio-political analysis" can fully comprehend the Holocaust or anything else, for that matter. Yet, even if Rubenstein's assertion on this particular issue is not well-founded, a major point in his favor remains. He defends the Holocaust's comprehensibility to contest perspectives that mystify the Holocaust by stressing that the event eludes rational comprehension. Probably the truth is closer to Rubenstein's side than not. Admitting that we lack the requisite metaphysical certainty to comprehend fully any historical occurrence, the disciplines of history, social science, demography, political theory, and economics nevertheless do tell much about how and why Auschwitz appeared. The Holocaust's "incomprehensibility" is more in the beholder's eye than in the facts themselves.

Where the Holocaust is concerned, however, the nature of the facts remains in question, and to some extent that will probably be true forever. An example is found in the research of Steven T. Katz, who by implication disagrees with some of Rubenstein's economic emphases in interpreting how and why the Jews became a redundant population destined for mass death.[14] Particularly in *The Age of Triage,* Rubenstein has held that the West's modernization process tended to render Jews surplus as it turned them away from being an economically complementary class, rendered them instead a source of instability and

conflict, and thus set them up for the kill. Not so, says Katz. The decisive turning point on the road to Auschwitz was instead a specific kind
of anti-Semitic racism. Close to Alice Eckardt's perspective, Katz' suggests that this racism was "microbial" and "parasitological." Such
racism reflects and inculcates the belief that inferior races will destroy
superior ones in ways analogous to those that exist when deadly disease-
causing agents invade human life. Racism of this kind brooks no com-
promise. Be killed or kill—completely—is its imperative.

Once more, nothing in Rubenstein's theory would require him to
deny that Katz' analysis has much in its favor. But Rubenstein can also
reply that Katz' account itself would be more credible if it took
economics with greater seriousness. Katz stresses that the content of the
Nazis' anti-Semitic racism had very little relationship to any empirical
realities. Its irrationality was a major characteristic, one that gave this
ideology peculiar power because it was beyond disconfirmation.
Rubenstein, however, urges a second look. Perhaps this anti-Semitism
is not quite so irrational, not quite so much a thing unto itself, if we see it
more than Katz does as an effect of economic relationships gone sour.
Understanding that "no single cause can explain a historical phenomenon," Rubenstein invites us to consider that realities of all kinds are more
interrelated and continuous than they are discrete and disparate.[15]
Rubenstein's approach has the advantage of fitting that pattern better than
Katz'. It does so by illuminating the economic factors in Nazi anti-
Semitic racism, thus making the latter no less hideous but more intel-
ligible than Katz' stress on its irrationality can do.

Although Richard Rubenstein's critics contest much that he says,
even they are likely to agree that he is on target in asserting that ours is
the age of triage. How we arrived there and what we might do about that
outcome are two of his main concerns as his book by that title assesses
the extent of fear and hope in an overcrowded world. Having explored
several major objections with which Rubenstein's Holocaust theories
have had to contend, plus some of the rejoinders that can appropriately
be made to them, it will be well to conclude with an overview of *The
Age of Triage*, drawing out of Rubenstein's total vision of our past and
future his accent on the importance of religious as well as social scientific
reflection.

A socioeconomic sorting that saves some ways of life by dispatching
others, triage testifies to the ascendancy of a powerfully practical form of
human rationality. Casting his point in economic terms, Rubenstein
stresses how decisive it has been that people discovered how to produce
a surplus. For thereby, he asserts, they also took *"the first step in
making themselves superfluous."*[16]

Already we have observed that current concerns about global population find the world containing many more people than anyone needs.
Rubenstein recognizes, in turn, that this perceived population redun-

dancy exists partly because of sheer numbers but even more because the dominant intentions that energize modern society tend to be governed by the belief that money is the measure of all that is real. More than any other, he claims, that belief drives the modernization process, which has been under way and intensifying for centuries. One effect of this process is that the intrinsic worth of people diminishes. Their worth is evaluated functionally instead. Hence, if persons are targeted as non-useful—they can be so regarded in any number of ways, depending on how those in power define their terms—a community may find it sensible to eliminate the surplus from its midst. In modern times, that action has been facilitated, indeed instigated and promoted, by governmental power. Triage, then, entails state-sponsored programs of population elimination: through eviction, compulsory resettlement, expulsion, mass warfare, and outright extermination—roughly in that order. This winnowing process, more or less extreme in its violence, enables a society to drive out what it does not want and to keep what it desires for itself.

Persistently intrigued by history's continuity as well as by its cunning, Rubenstein links modernization and mass death in a study that encompasses such *apparently* diverse events as the enclosure movement in England during the Enlightenment, the nineteenth-century famine years in Ireland, and a variety of twentieth-century events—a non-exhaustive list would include the Armenian genocide, the slaughter of Soviet citizens under Stalin, the destruction of the European Jews under Hitler, and the devastation of Cambodia. Taken alone, Rubenstein's political interpretation is stunning enough, but *The Age of Triage* does more because its author has not abandoned his grounding in religion and theology to turn exclusively to socioeconomic analysis. On the contrary, an age of triage makes the vitality of religion and theology more critical than ever. It is within this perspective that Rubenstein should be understood when he states that "no theological enterprise, that is, no consideration of the ultimate values that move men and women, can be adequate to its task if it ignores critical political and social theory, especially insofar as these modes of inquiry seek to comprehend the conditions under which men attempt to conduct their lives both individually and collectively" (p. v).

Explicitly and implicitly, God is both absent and present in *The Age of Triage*. Historically, for example, Rubenstein argues that Western monotheism desacralized the world, leaving human power free to exploit nature and to kill far too much with impunity. Ironically, the same God found in the theologies that were instrumental in unleashing the modernizing process has also been its victim, eclipsed by an advancing civilization that has produced in tandem benefit and destruction, both in unprecedented abundance. Yet, looking toward the future, Rubenstein hints at—indeed he yearns for—a religious revival that might transmute humanity's propensity to move, as Benjamin Nelson put it, "from tribal brotherhood to universal otherhood" (p. 7). Such a revival, hopes Rubenstein, would convert us so that we are "born again as men and women blessed with the capacity to care for each other here and now" (p. 240). God's place in an age of triage ought not to be the least of our concerns. Consider, then, four of Rubenstein's fundamental propositions. Each merits a governing role in late twentieth-century theology and religious reflection.

1. "Modern civilization is largely the unintended consequence of a religious revolution" (p. 230). Western monotheism, contends Rubenstein, replaced magic and belief in a spiritualized nature by insisting that there is one and only one God who is the sovereign creator of heaven and earth. The success of Judaism and Christianity inadvertently paved the way for the secular outlooks that result in triage. True, these traditions affirmed that the earth is the Lord's. Men and women, moreover, were to be obedient to God's will. That will, in turn, would make itself known in history, and there not everything was to be permitted. Bonds of moral obligation, underwritten by God's judging power, were claimed to be in force. Human life, formed in God's image, appeared to be even more sacred than it had been prior to monotheism's eminent domain.

Neither in practice nor in theory, however, does history conform entirely to conscious intention. In spite of and even because of monotheism's moral components, a course unfolded in which nature and even human life itself came to be regarded as subject to the mastery of politics and economics. Religions predicated on revelation within history unleashed reason in ways that transmuted the moral authority of revelation itself. A biblical God inspired a secular consciousness, and at times God disappeared in the process. Providence became Progress. Progress meant the triumph of a calculating, functional rationality whose Golden Rule was *Efficiency*.

My account, if not Rubenstein's, is overly simple. Still, the power of its drift remains. Religions and theologies are loaded dice because they always contain more options for development than the limitations of immediate consciousness can comprehend. In an age of triage, we have learned that lesson to our sorrow. Yet Rubenstein's point is that we can be aware of it now. That awareness enjoins a warning, which takes us to a second proposition deserving of attention.

2. "In a crisis, a secularized equivalent of the division of mankind into the elect and the reprobate could easily become a controlling image" (p. 216). Western monotheism's emphasis on a God of History has typically included the idea that some groups or persons are specially called. They are linked together and with God in relations of covenant. At their best, these convictions have singled people out for service, but nearly all of these doctrines of election and covenant have also been

extremely volatile. Separating people, they have induced a host of rivalries. Those rivalries and their offspring, Rubenstein avers, have more than a little to do with triage.

Unintended consequences are no less real than those that are consciously desired. The former, in fact, may be the more devastating precisely because their full power remains hidden until the effects are felt. In our religious context, the crucial link between theology, religious reflection, and triage lurks in the fact that Western monotheism has much to do with economic versions of divine election and covenant. Within such perspectives, poverty and wealth are much more than economic conditions. They entail divine judgment and just desert. Thus, their driving force can be not one of ministering to the poor but rather of eliminating them so that the position of the elect remains unthreatened.

The theology of election and covenant sketched here sounds perverse. It is. But Rubenstein's point is that it is too simple, too convenient, only to protest that a tradition has been distorted. No doubt distortion exists, but perhaps the more important point is that what we say about God is usually a two-edged sword. That fact holds with respect even to the best examples of theology and religious reflection that we can cite. For the seeds that sprouted into destructive versions of election and covenant were not sowed first by the spiritually bankrupt or by the intellectually corrupt. They are gifts from the giants of Western religion. The issue that remains, then, is whether theology and religious reflection can speak in ways to avert the crises that fuel forces bent on triage because they see the world in terms of the elect and reprobate.

3. "We are by no means helpless in meeting the challenge confronting us" (p. 224). Economically, argues Rubenstein, the basic remedy for triage would be to create a social order that provides a decent job for any person who is willing to work. His optimism is muted, however, because he knows that the implementation of his economic remedy is anything but an economic matter alone. In fact, the forms of practical rationality that govern modern economic thinking tend to mitigate against policies of full employment. The challenge that confronts us, then, is largely a spiritual one. Unless men and women are resensitized religiously, the resources to avert triage are likely to be hopelessly inadequate.

Rubenstein thinks that we need nothing less than "an inclusive vision appropriate to a global civilization in which Moses and Mohammed, Christ, Buddha, and Confucius all play a role" (p. 240). To call Rubenstein's vision demanding understates the case. For, their universalizing tendencies notwithstanding, the major religious traditions have themselves been instrumental in "triaging" people "into the working and the workless, the saved and the damned, the Occident and the Orient" (p. 240). Rubenstein, of course, hopes that a new religious consciousness will build on the inclusive aspects of the major religious traditions, excluding the exclusive features in the process. Yet a further difficulty is that, while the thinker and the theorist can point out the needed direction, they cannot manage the achievement of such a vision.

If the so-called death of God theologies have had their moment in the limelight and have now largely faded from view, the radical secularization of our time remains. Functionally, human reason in history tends toward Godlessness, a pattern that theology and philosophy may check but seem unlikely to reverse. It is Rubenstein's conviction that the needed reversal, one that would substantially reduce the prospects of triage, depends on "authentic religious inspiration" (p. 239). Such inspiration is not absent, but it cannot be called into being at will, least of all by intellectuals. Nor are religion's presently dominant forms characterized chiefly by the inclusiveness that Rubenstein advocates. If the age of triage is one in which God's best defense may be that God does not exist, our religious situation is truly a season of advent, of expectant waiting and seeking for the religious transformation we need.

4. "Theology seeks to foster dissonance-reduction where significant items of information are perceived to be inconsistent with established beliefs, values, and collectively sanctioned modes of behavior" (p. 132). Every religious tradition has to cope with evidence that disconfirms it. Triage itself is a case in point, for the experience of the death of God in our time has everything to do with the mass wasting of human life. Typically, theologians have apologized for God when the problem of evil has taken center stage. Specifically, they attempt to reduce the dissonance that arises when traditional claims about God's power and goodness collide with history.

The pertinent point here, however, is that Rubenstein's description of theology's function, whatever its validity, is not propounded by him as normative. On the contrary, his use of this description helps to identify meaningful work that remains for thinkers and theorists to do, even if they do not have the charisma to control the floodgates of religious inspiration. Rubenstein's *Age of Triage* is a theological statement, but his reflection does little to reduce dissonance. Its mood is instead quite the opposite. By calling attention to the Holocaust, to triage, to the reality that men and women too often kill with impunity, and by doing so in a way that questions the functional status of God in the world, Rubenstein's book is an exercise in dissonance production.

At least indirectly, Rubenstein suggests that an age of triage calls for more, not less, theology and religious reflection in that vein. Yet a note of caution should intrude. For the dissonance production that is needed today, Rubenstein implies, is not the kind that will intensify individualism and isolation. Rather, it ought to shatter such barriers and extend the boundaries of mutual social obligation. To move in that direction, however, is a task that will tax the best brain power we can muster, for powerful indeed are the drives and interests that find triage tempting because such sorting offers a solution as rational as it is final.  Political and economic sophistication will need to join hands with theological acumen if religious thinkers are to do their dissonance-producing responsibly.

God's fate, as well as that of humankind, hangs suspended in an age of triage.  Should God be real in any sense at all, God joins humankind in responsibility for history's destruction.  Yet realistic hope against fear in an overcrowded world ought not to pronounce God dead.  For history itself may induce shame and sorrow in some quarters, but if the age of triage is literally a Godless time altogether, the net effect of the defenseless victims will be to testify that the powers of death are irredeemably victorious.  Hence the pages of *The Age of Triage,* particularly those that deal with the Holocaust, set an agenda for Western theology and religious reflection.  In sum, it consists of at least these four imperatives: (1) Deconstruct the ties between Providence and Progress.  (2) Destabilize distinctions between the elect and the damned.  (3) Discern, as far as thought permits, ways beyond the self-regarding individualism that so often drives propensities toward triage.  (4) Deploy the right kinds of dissonance.

In his *Zweites Buch,* Adolf Hitler had a different vision.  Proclaiming himself a German nationalist, he announced a National Socialist foreign policy predicated on "folkish, racial insights" and "determined by the necessity to secure the space necessary to the life of our people."[17] Knowing that vestiges and variants of that outlook are still very much a part of our world long after Hitler's demise, Richard Rubenstein assays genocide, the Holocaust, and triage to find ways beyond them.  Admittedly there is little that is totally novel in that agenda, any more than Richard Rubenstein's account originated with him alone.  The pieces have been lying there for some time.  Yet, to Rubenstein's credit and for our benefit, he has worked the puzzle in a way that shows with particular urgency the vital tasks that must be attempted if catastrophe is to be forestalled in our overcrowded world.

## NOTES

1. "World Population Nearing 4.8 Billion," *Pomona Progress Bulletin,* 9 May 1984, p. 5.

2. See Adolf Hitler, *Hitler's Secret Book,* trans. Salvator Attanasio, with an Introduction by Telford Taylor (New York: Grove Press, Inc., 1983), p. 50.  Additional references to this work and to others cited in this chapter are found in parentheses within the text.

3. Yehuda Bauer, *A History of the Holocaust* (New York: Franklin Watts, 1982), p. 332.

4. For further discussion on Hitler's intentions concerning the Holocaust, see my article "How to Make Hitler's Ideas Clear?," *The Philosophical Forum* 16, nos. 1-2 (Fall-Winter 1984-1985), pp. 82-94.

5. Bauer, *History*, p. 332.

6. Hitler, *Secret Book*, p. 50.

7. Richard L. Rubenstein, *The Cunning of History: The Holocaust and the American Future*, with an Introduction by William Styron (New York: Harper Colophon Books, 1978), pp. 18, 83. Rubenstein's italics.

8. Richard L. Rubenstein, *The Age of Triage: Fear and Hope in an Overcrowded World* (Boston: Beacon Press, 1983), p. 1.

9. See the section entitled "Discussion: The *Judenrat* and the Jewish Response," in *The Holocaust as Historical Experience*, ed. Yehuda Bauer and Nathan Rotenstreich (New York: Holmes and Meier, 1981), p. 249. The conference referred to was held in March 1975, about the time that *The Cunning of History* first appeared.

10. Rubenstein, *Triage*, p. 124.

11. Bauer and Rotenstreich, *Historical Experience*, p. 266.

12. John Patrick Diggins, review of *The Age of Triage* by Richard L. Rubenstein, in "The Book Review," *Los Angeles Times*, 20 February 1983, pp. 3-4.

13. Richard L. Rubenstein, "Naming the Unnameable; Thinking the Unthinkable: A Review Essay of Arthur Cohen's *The Tremendum*." (Typewritten.)

14. See Steven T. Katz, *The Uniqueness of the Holocaust* (forthcoming). Useful background for Katz' views can be found in his *Post-Holocaust Dialogues: Critical Studies in Modern Jewish Thought* (New York: New York University Press, 1983). His chapter on "The 'Unique' Intentionality of the Holocaust," pp. 287-317, is especially relevant.

15. Rubenstein, *Triage*, p. 146.

16. Ibid., p. 3. Rubenstein's italics.

17. Hitler, *Secret Book*, p. 45.

# 6

# GENOCIDE AND TOTAL WAR: A PRELIMINARY COMPARISON

*Eric Markusen*

## INTRODUCTION

Of all the problems confronting humankind during the last quarter of the twentieth century, none is more significant or urgent than the mass killing of defenseless citizens by human beings acting as agents of, or with the tolerance of, their governments.

This chapter seeks to contribute to greater understanding of this problem by comparatively analyzing two major types of state-sanctioned mass killing—genocide and total war. Since several of the other chapters in this volume address definitions, causes, and examples of genocide, the focus here is on the phenomenon of total war. Then a preliminary analysis of differences and similarities between the two types of mass killing is offered. The central thesis of this chapter is that there are important similarities between the two types. Specifically, it is suggested that ideology, bureaucracy, and technology play comparable facilitating roles in both genocide and total war. Finally, tentative lessons from this analysis of mass killing in the past and present are drawn in order to shed light on the seemingly inexorable momentum toward nuclear war.

Humankind has been afflicted by the problem of mass killing since early prehistory. Archeologists have discovered indications that lethal conflict among groups of human beings may have originated as early as a million to a half-million years ago.[1] As an organized social institution, however, warfare is a relatively recent development. According to Arnold Toynbee, the institution of war did not emerge until approximately 5,000 years ago, in the lands of what are now Iraq and Egypt.[2]

Since that time, the human and material costs of war have tended to increase steadily, despite some temporary respites. In his survey of warfare from the end of the fifteenth century through the early 1960s, Quincy Wright notes: "War has during the last four centuries tended to involve a larger proportion of the belligerent states' population and resources and, while less frequent, to be more intense, more extended, and more costly. It has tended to be less functional, less intentional, less directable, and less legal."[3]

It is perhaps not surprising, therefore, that an unflinching review of past centuries—with their mounting death tolls from wars, revolutions, massacres, as well as famine and disease resulting from human malevolence and negligence—led William James in his celebrated 1910 essay, "The Moral Equivalent of War," to conclude that "history is a bath of blood."[4]

However, a number of analysts have concluded that the number of human beings deliberately killed by other human beings during the twentieth century is far greater than for any other equivalent period of time in history. The "bath of blood" that James discovered in his study of many past centuries has become a veritable ocean of blood in just a few decades.

For example, Pitirim Sorokin, in his study of wars from the twelfth to the twentieth centuries (which was published in 1937, two years before World War II began), calculated war casualties in relation to the populations of the combatant nations and concluded:

If we take the relative indicators of the casualties, probably the most important criterion of war, they tell definitely and unequivocally that *the curse or privilege to be the most devastating or most bloody war century belongs to the twentieth; in one quarter century, it imposed upon the population a "blood tribute" far greater than that imposed by any of the whole centuries compared.*[5]

The most detailed and comprehensive attempt to identify those killed by their fellow human beings during the twentieth century is British sociologist Gil Elliot's *Twentieth Century Book of the Dead,* published in 1972. On the basis of his carefully documented review of historical sources, Elliot estimates that there have been approximately 100 million "man-made" deaths during the first three-quarters of this century. Elliot asserts: "It is possible—in my view certain—that in a future perspective this explosion of human lives will be seen as the significant 'history' of this period."[6]

But even more ominously, the most powerful nations on the planet are currently devoting prodigious resources to the preparations for the ultimate mass killing project—nuclear holocaust. The United States and the Soviet Union are each annually spending billions of dollars to maintain and expand their nuclear arsenals. At present, these arsenals combined contain approximately fifty thousand nuclear warheads with a collective explosive force equivalent to more than 3.5 tons of high explosive for each of the 4.5 billion people on earth.[7] Current plans for both nations call for adding thousands of new warheads to their arsenals during the next decade. While the United States and the Soviet Union are increasing their stockpiles of weapons of mass destruction, the other nuclear-armed nations, like Great Britain, France, and China, are also making additions and refinements in their nuclear arsenals, while several nations without nuclear weapons are struggling to acquire them.[8]

If even a small portion of current arsenals is actually used in a nuclear war, the ensuing holocaust will dwarf the worst atrocities of history. A recent World Health Organization study, for example, concluded that a nuclear war fought with about one-half of present arsenals could result in 1 billion prompt deaths and an additional 1 billion serious injuries, most of which would eventually result in death due to lack of medical care, the effects of radiation exposure, shortages of food, and other lethal after effects of the initial carnage and destruction.

To these findings must be added those from recent studies of the possible climatic and long-term biological consequences of nuclear war. Among the most shocking is the possibility that the detonation of even a very small portion of existing arsenals (as few as 1,000 of the 50,000 warheads) could produce a so-called nuclear winter, which would entail plunging temperatures and a pall of darkness resulting from smoke and other atmospheric pollution generated by fires. This nuclear winter could spread across the entire Northern Hemisphere and last for months.[9] So grave could these and other consequences of nuclear war be that the researchers concluded:

Combined with the direct casualties of over 1 billion people, the combined intermediate and long-term effects of nuclear war suggest that eventually there might be no human survivors in the Northern Hemisphere. . . . In any large-scale nuclear exchange between the superpowers, global environmental changes sufficient to cause the extinction of a major fraction of plant and animal species on Earth are likely. . . . In that event, the possibility of the extinction of Homo Sapiens cannot be excluded.[10]

In view of the terrible toll of human lives due to governmental mass killing in the past, the present, and, very possibly, the future, one might expect that a life-affirming species would have mounted a massive effort to confront and reduce this problem. Unfortunately, such a massive effort has not yet been made. Despite the vital contributions of a number of individuals and organizations, the attention and energy devoted to understanding and preventing state-sanctioned mass killing have been negligible when compared with the scale and urgency of the problem.[11]

Avoiding this disturbing topic may well assure peace of mind and contentment with the status quo over the short term. On the other hand, such avoidance may also serve to encourage the social forces favoring continued reliance on mass killing as an acceptable tool of national security and thus increase the risk that government leaders may resort to mass killing in the future. If that mass killing takes the form of nuclear war, then the final price of short-term peace of mind will be oblivion.

## GENOCIDE

Although the wholesale destruction of groups of human beings has been practiced for millennia, the concept of genocide, which depicts certain forms of such destruction, has been in existence for less than fifty years. The term was coined by Raphael Lemkin, a Polish emigré to London who lost seventy members of his family to the Holocaust. In 1943, he wrote *Axis Rule in Occupied Europe,* one of the earliest and most comprehensive accounts of Nazi persecutions of the Jews and other citizens of occupied nations. It was in this book that he introduced the term "genocide," which he derived from the Greek word *genos,* meaning race or tribe, and the Latin word *cide,* meaning killing. According to Lemkin, "By 'genocide' we mean the destruction of a nation or of an ethnic group."[12]

Thanks in large part to Lemkin's indefatigable lobbying efforts, on December 9, 1948, the General Assembly of the United Nations unanimously adopted the Convention on the Prevention and Punishment of the Crime of Genocide. The Convention listed specific actions which constitute the crime of genocide. Article 2 states:

In the present Convention, genocide means any of the following acts committed with intent to destroy, in whole or in part, a national, ethnical, racial or religious group, as such:
    (a) Killing members of the group;
    (b) Causing serious bodily or mental harm to members of the group;
    (c) Deliberately inflicting on the group conditions of life calculated to bring about its physical destruction in whole or in part;
    (d) Imposing measures intended to prevent births within the group;
    (e) Forcibly transferring children of the group to another group.[13]

More recent analysts of genocide have incorporated features of the U.N. Convention in their own definition while at the same time criticizing its limitations. Leo Kuper, for example, states that "genocide . . . is a crime against a collectivity, taking the form of massive slaughter, and carried out with explicit intent."[14] He notes also that "genocide is pre-eminently a government crime."[15] However, Kuper also questions the Convention for its exclusion of political groups from among those protected. Such an omission leaves out such cases as the murder of tens of millions of Soviet citizens under the Stalinist regime and the extermination of millions of their own citizens by the Khmer Rouge forces in Cambodia during the 1970s.[16]

Likewise, Irving Louis Horowitz defines genocide as "a special form of murder: state-sanctioned liquidation against a collective group, without regard to whether an individual has committed any specific and punishable transgression."[17] Horowitz goes beyond the "standard" type of deliberate, intentional mass killing to include "one shadowy area of genocide that permits the state to take lives by indirection, for example by virtue of benign neglect, or death due to demographic causes."[18]

A final contemporary definition is provided by Vahakn Dadrian, who defines genocide as "the successful attempt by a dominant group, vested with formal authority and/or with preponderant access to the overall resources of power, to reduce by coercion or lethal violence the number of a minority group whose ultimate extermination is held desirable and useful and whose respective vulnerability is a major factor contributing to the decision of genocide."[19] As will be discussed below, Dadrian includes a wide range of actions within his definition, including military activities that cause high casualty levels among civilians, even if the targeting of the civilians is not deliberate.[20]

Despite inconsistencies evident among these and other definitions of genocide, and despite disagreements among analysts regarding whether or not particular cases of mass killing constitute genocide, there does appear to be a strong consensus on several crucial features of genocidal acts.

First, genocide is undertaken by and for governments. The official ruling elite of a sovereign state either undertakes a deliberate campaign of intentional extermination; permits subnational groups to slaughter other subnational groups; or implements (or tolerates) practices that result in mass deaths among members of certain groups, even if such deaths are not the explicit policy objective.[21]

Second, the individual identity of the victims is in general irrelevant, as are distinctions among sex and age. What concerns the state is that the individual belongs to the group targeted for destruction. A wide range of groups has been targeted throughout history, including racial, ethnic, and religious groups; the mentally handicapped; homosexuals; citizens of enemy nations; and members of political groups. The vast majority of victims of genocide have been civilians.

Third, while the methods employed vary considerably, direct mass killing is the most characteristic form of genocidal destruction, although many additional deaths have resulted from hunger, disease, and other sequelae of direct killing and the destruction of resources necessary for survival.

## TOTAL WAR

Like the concept of genocide, the concept of total war encompasses a wide range of cases and subsumes a number of components.[22] Two features of total war—a high degree of societal mobilization for war and an extremely high level of death and destruction—have been emphasized in most definitions and analyses of this type of mass killing. In considering the destructiveness of total war, most commentators note the tendency to deliberately attack noncombatant citizens of the enemy nation or group. Moreover, the direct or indirect participation of the entire nation in the war, combined with the targeting of civilians, tends to result in wars in which the very survival of one or more of the belligerents is at stake. Thus, strategist Edward Luttwak defines total war as "a war in which at least one party perceives a threat to its survival and in which all available weapons are used and the distinction between 'military' and 'civilian' targets is almost completely ignored."[23]

No recent war, even World Wars I and II, has been completely "total" in the sense that literally all of the available resources of the combatant nations have been devoted to the conflict or that the destruction of the enemy has been complete. (However, as noted above, a nuclear war could conceivably result in the latter condition, not only for the belligerents, but for uninvolved nations as well.) In practice, the concept of total war applies to conflicts in which either or both of these conditions—societal mobilization and destructiveness—exist to extreme degrees. As Frederick Sallagar notes, "What characterizes an all-out, or total, war is that it is fought for such high stakes that the belligerents are willing, or compelled, to employ, not *all* weapons they possess, but *any* weapons they consider appropriate and advantageous to them."[24]

Throughout human history, many wars have been characterized by one or both of the features now associated with the concept of total war. As J. F. C. Fuller notes in *The Conduct of War, 1789-1961,* "Primitive tribes are armed hordes, in which every man is a warrior, and because the entire tribe engages in war, warfare is total."[25] The price of defeat in such conflicts was not simply the concession of territory to the victor, but the mass slaughter of the vanquished, with the possible exception of those dragged off into slavery. Religious wars have often been total wars. Edwin Corwin, noting that most people think of total war in terms of extreme degrees of ruthlessness, observes: "While the phrase itself is of recent coinage, total war in this primary sense is at least as old as recorded history and enjoys, at times, the most exalted sanction."[26] To illustrate his point, Corwin cites a passage from the Bible, in Deuteronomy 20: "Of the cities of these people, which the Lord thy God doth give thee for an inheritance, thou shalt save nothing alive that breatheth: But thou shalt utterly destroy them."[27]

Subsequent wars of religion, including the Crusades, involved the mass slaughter of noncombatants as a routine practice. Such total wars culminated in the Thirty Years' War (1618-1648) in which as many as 8 million civilians (as compared with "only" 350,000 combatants) were killed, and the destruction of property and crops was so pervasive that many survivors were reduced to cannibalism.[28]

In the aftermath of the Thirty Years' War, a trend toward more civilized, limited warfare developed, although there were many relapses and exceptions. For nearly 150 years, most European wars were fought between relatively small mercenary armies sponsored by absolute monarchs. Killing of noncombatants was significantly curtailed, and the casualty levels among soldiers were reduced, in part to keep the financial burden on the sponsoring monarchs as low as possible. Rather than ending in the annihilation of the loser, wars tended to end in settlements that left the structure of all societies largely intact.[29]

This respite from total war began to end at the close of the eighteenth century with the French Revolution, the rise of Napoleon, and the beginning of the era of wars waged between entire nations. Napoleon's chief contribution to the revival of total war was his utilization of huge armies of conscripted soldiers. However, while the scale and intensity of military conflicts increased precipitously with the advent of mass armies, the other practice of total war, deliberate mass killing of noncombatants, remained relatively constrained.

Following the final defeat of Napoleon at Waterloo in 1815, a war-weary Europe entered another period of relative peacefulness. Indeed, in his survey of warfare over the centuries, Sorokin found the overall intensity of war during the nineteenth century to have been exceptionally low.[30] Nations strove to prevent and limit wars through such efforts as the Vienna Congresses which, beginning in 1815, attempted to facilitate peaceful resolution of disputes, and the Rush-Bagot Agreement of 1817, in which the United States and England agreed to limit warships on the Great Lakes. Also, as Richard Preston and Sydney Wise note in their history of warfare, the nineteenth century witnessed "the restoration of the conservative military system of the eighteenth century in place of the mass nationalistic armies of the Revolutionary era."[31]

Unfortunately, however, such restraints on war began to weaken during the latter half of the nineteenth century, and the twentieth century was to witness the resurgence of both aspects of total war to a degree that would compress the carnage of the Thirty Years' War into little more than a decade and multiply it severalfold.

In modern total wars, mobilization of the combatant nations is accomplished in several ways, including the conscription of citizens to serve in mass armies, the widespread use of propaganda to maintain morale and support for the war, and the calculated exploitation of the national economy in the service of the war.

Conscription results in large numbers of citizens being obliged to leave their peacetime positions, often for the duration of the war. This can have a disruptive effect on individuals and families, and on the economy as well. In the case of the *levée en masse* imposed by the French revolutionary government in 1793, it has been noted that "the forced withdrawal of such great numbers from the normal pursuits of daily life disturbed the social economy profoundly, while the task that was put upon the depleted society of supplying and equipping such numbers aggravated the disturbance."[32] Conscription by one belligerent generally compels the others to adopt a similar system for building up comparable forces. In the American Civil War, for example, both sides initially relied on volunteers, but the high rates of attrition required first the Confederacy and then the Union to resort to conscription.

Mass conscription has affected not only the degree to which the nation is involved in war but also the nature of warfare itself. In the case of the Napoleonic wars, casualties among combatants increased considerably in comparison with the preceding 100 years. As Fuller observes, "Conscription changed the basis of warfare. Hitherto soldiers had been costly, now they were cheap; battles had been avoided; now they were sought, and however heavy the losses, they could rapidly be made good by the muster-roll."[33] The vastly increased size of the revolutionary French army, which grew with conscription to include 750,000 soldiers, rquired changes in administration and logistics. The army was broken up into smaller, more mobile units, and long supply lines gave way to "compulsory requisition" of shelter and food, which often entailed officially sanctioned plunder of the contested territory.[34] Similar measures were employed by the German military forces during World War II in their campaigns against Poland and the Soviet Union.

To maintain the morale of the conscripted soldiers and the support of the citizens, government propaganda tends to be widely utilized in total wars. Such propaganda, which frequently takes the form of vilifying the enemy nation, can raise passions to the point where it becomes difficult to end wars on a basis that would promote a lasting peace. In his analysis of the Napoleonic wars of the late 1700s, Fuller emphasizes how difficult it was "for a conscripted nation—that is, a nation in arms —a nation fed on violent propaganda, to make an enduring peace. The peace treaties wrung from the vanquished were generally so unreasonable that they were no more than precarious armistices; the losers only signed them through duress, and with the full intention of repudiating them at the first opportunity."[35]

During the same period that conscription was radically altering both the impact of warfare on society and the nature of war itself, the Industrial Revolution was moving both European society and warfare in the direction of ever greater mechanization. As Hans Speier notes, this trend necessitated "a particularly close interdependency between the armed forces and the productive forces of the nation."[36] As the size of armies increased, and as armies became increasingly mechanized, the number of noncombatants needed to keep the army provided with equipment and supplies increased as well. Under such conditions, much of the adult population tends to be directly or indirectly involved in supporting the war effort. The coordination of the many sectors of the economy requires greater centralization of governmental authority. "Such a gearing-in," observes Wright, "of the agricultural, industrial, and professional population to the armed forces requires a military organization of the entire society."[37] Or, as stated by Raymond Aron in *The Century of Total War,* "the army industrializes itself, industry militarizes itself; the army absorbs the nation: the nation models itself on the army."[38]

Such processes tend to blur the distinctions between democratic and totalitarian forms of government. Noting the centralization of authority among all the involved nations in World War II, Marjorie Farrar suggests that "as a result institutional and ideological distinctions among the belligerents were reduced and the democratic regimes increasingly resembled their totalitarian counterparts."[39]

Just as industrialization decisively affected the mobilization of the society for total war, it has also had a profound impact on the second basic component of total war—the extreme levels of destruction and death affecting civilian and soldier alike. Such destructiveness reflects two trends in the era of modern total war. First, the close interdependence of the military and the economic-industrial sectors of society has created a steady expansion in the types of targets considered legitimate by military forces. Second, the long-range and highly destructive nature of modern weapons has made it difficult, if not impossible, to discriminate between noncombatants and combatants, thereby resulting in high levels of civilian casualties even when traditional "military" targets are attacked. When civilians are deliberately attacked, the death tolls are of course far higher.

The dependency of the mechanized military forces on civilian industry has meant that whole nations have become targets. As Gordon Wright observes in his analysis of World War II, "the battlefield, no longer limited or defined, was everywhere; it was occupied by civilians and soldiers alike."[40]

Some military policymakers, recognizing that total wars are fought between entire societies, rather than between armies, have urged and engaged in deliberate attacks against enemy civilians. During the American Civil War, for example, Union General W. T. Sherman conducted a campaign of killing and destruction against the civilians of Georgia. In World War I, although most of the fighting was confined to the battlefield, toward the end of the war the Germans began using submarines to sink civilian ships. Bombing of cities, which had begun early in the war, had steadily escalated during its course, although the armistice was signed before its full potentialities were realized. Still, the noncombatant death tolls were relatively low. According to Gordon Wright, civilians accounted for only one in twenty deaths during World War I.[41] By World War II, however, such practices as the scorched earth campaign of the Nazis and the Nazi and Allied practice of firebombing population centers contributed to far greater overall casualty rates, especially among civilians, who, according to Elliot, accounted for two-thirds of the approximately 60 million deaths.[42]

It should be noted that many commentators have deplored the practice of deliberate attacks on civilians as a profound moral retrogression. In his essay "The Morality of Obliteration Bombing," John Ford argues that many, if not most, civilians killed in bombing raids were "innocent noncombatants," especially children and the elderly, who made no contribution to the war effort and therefore could not be regarded as legitimate targets.[43] The practice of targeting civilians for mass destruction, like the total mobilization of the society for war, tends to narrow the gap between democratic and totalitarian forms of government. Quincy Wright observes that "the development of the airplane by the totalitarian states in the twentieth century first extended their empires and then compelled the democracies to adopt their techniques."[44] Lewis Mumford, in his essay "The Morals of Extermination," asserts:

By taking over this method [obliteration bombing] as a cheap substitute for conventional warfare—cheap in soldiers' lives, costly in its expenditures of other human lives and in the irreplaceable historic accumulations of countless lifetimes—these democratic governments sanctioned the dehumanized techniques of fascism. This was Nazidom's firmest victory and democracy's most servile surrender.[45]

## GENOCIDE AND TOTAL WAR: A PRELIMINARY COMPARISON

Genocide and total war have consumed many tens of millions of human lives during the twentieth century and many hundreds of millions of lives throughout history. The preparations are now being made for a nuclear war that could destroy billions of lives and possibly extinguish our species.

The following comparative analysis is offered in the hope of generating insights into mass killing in the past and in the hope of increasing understanding of the momentum toward mass killing in the present and future. It should be emphasized that this comparison is preliminary, tentative, and necessarily brief; it attempts to discern important differences and similarities between two ostensibly distinct types of state-sanctioned mass killing. It is hoped that it will stimulate others—including those who disagree with its findings as well as those who find them plausible—to undertake further study along these lines.

Perhaps many others share with Horowitz the assumption that "it is operationally imperative to distinguish warfare from genocide."[46] One of his reasons for advocating this distinction is his belief that genocide involves mass killing in an intrastate, or domestic arena, whereas warfare involves lethal conflict between two nation-states. His decision to emphasize the distinction, he states, is "warranted by the weight of current empirical research that indicates that domestic destruction and international warring are separate dimensions of struggle." In further support, he cites political scientist R. J. Rummel: "There are no common conditions or causes of domestic and foreign conflict behavior."[47]

Others differentiate between genocide and warfare on moral grounds. Genocide is unequivocally evil, an entirely unjustifiable atrocity perpetrated against helpless and innocent victims by cowards who face little personal risk. On the other hand, warfare can be seen as evil or heroic, depending upon one's perspective. It has been noted above that some commentators regard the practice of bombing cities as moral retrogression. Indeed, prior to their involvement in World War II, both Great Britain and the United States issued statements condemning the practice as immoral. They expressed righteous outrage when Germany bombed such cities as Warsaw, Rotterdam, and, later, London. Both nations decried the bombing of cities as a reversion to barbarism and beneath the dignity of a democratic nation. Yet, in the course of the war, both countries—first Great Britain in Europe and then the United States in Japan—engaged in firebombing of crowded population centers on a scale far greater than the Nazis. It is perhaps noteworthy that after the war, Great Britain appeared to have second thoughts about its obliteration bombing policy; the airmen who managed to survive their extremely hazardous missions were never awarded a campaign medal, and the individual most responsible for the policy, Sir Arthur Harris, slipped into an obscurity that amounted to virtual exile.[48] In contrast, Curtis LeMay, the individual most responsible for the decision to shift American bombing policy in Japan from precision attacks on military targets to the deliberate creation of vast firestorms in the highly flammable, densely populated Japanese cities, was widely touted as a hero after the war and was rewarded with the command of the elite Strategic Air Command, the nation's atomic-armed military unit.[49]

Another basis for distinguishing between genocide and total war is the relation between goals and means. While both phenomena utilize similar means—the production of very large numbers of dead bodies—the goals are quite different. For example, Mumford suggests that, "in principle, the extermination camps where the Nazis incinerated over six million helpless Jews were no different from the urban crematoriums our air force improvised in its attacks by napalm bombs on Tokyo. . . . Our aims were different, but our methods were those of mankind's worst enemy."[50]  The difference in aims is crucial.  The Nazis, as Michael Sherry points out in "The Slide to Total Air War," would not have stopped mass killing Jews if they had won the war; in fact, they had hopes and plans of intensifying their "Final Solution" to additional areas they might have conquered.[51]  Some scholars suggest that the ability to exterminate the Jews was among the chief motives for Nazi aggression that led to World War II.[52]  So vital was genocide as a primary goal during the war that the Nazis carried on their extermination program even at the expense of their military efforts against the Soviets and Allies.  In contrast, the Allies continued their mass bombing operations only until the surrender of their enemies:  as soon as their primary goal was attained, they had no reason to continue employing the means.

While these and other differences between genocide and total war support the assumption that they represent two distinct phenomena, much of the literature on mass killing is more equivocal. Even Horowitz, who was cited above as an advocate of maintaining the distinction, is inconsistent.  At a later point in his pioneering study, he appears to contradict himself by suggesting that "the end of an era when formal declarations of warfare were made signifies the beginning of a new era in which the line between war and genocide becomes profoundly blurred."[53]  As an example, he cites the U.S. war in Vietnam, an undeclared war which has been alleged by some critics to have had genocidal dimensions, and by others as being a case of actual genocide.[54]  After citing arguments on both sides of the issue of whether or not the war was genocidal, Horowitz states, "the distinction between internal and foreign people who are being killed helps little, since it must be confessed that all genocidal practices involve a definition by the perpetrators of mass violence of those destroyed as outsiders."[55]  Thus, he appears to be acknowledging the existence of an important process, depersonalization of victims, that occurs in state-sanctioned mass killing in both domestic and foreign conflicts.

Likewise, Kuper, while emphasizing that the sovereign state is the main arena for genocide, refers to both conventional and atomic bombings as genocidal when he notes that:

the changing nature of warfare, with a movement to total warfare, and the technological means for instantaneous annihilation of large populations, creates a situation conducive to genocidal conflict. This potential was realized in the Second World War, when Germany employed genocide in its war for domination; but I think the term must also be applied to the atomic bombing of the Japanese cities of Hiroshima and Nagasaki by the U.S.A. and to the pattern bombing by the Allies of such cities as Hamburg and Dresden.[56]

Finally, it has been noted that Dadrian, in developing his conceptual schema of types of genocide, explicitly identifies strategic bombing as an example of what he terms "latent genocide."[57]

Just as careful analysts of genocide have implicitly or explicitly included certain operations of total warfare within their definitions of genocide, some definitions of war have included situations that have been regarded as genocidal. For example, in "The Social Types of War," Hans Speier develops the concept of "absolute war," which has many of the same characteristics as genocide. Absolute war, according to Speier, "is not waged in order to conclude peace with the vanquished foe. Peace terminating an absolute war is established *without* the enemy. The opponent is an existential enemy. Absolute war is waged in order to annihilate him."[58] Such wars feature a lack of moral restraint; one or both of the belligerents regard the other as subhuman or even as an animal. As examples of absolute wars, Speier mentions the wars of the ancient Greeks against the barbarians and the wars between Christians and Muslims during the Middle Ages. In the latter case, weapons and techniques that were prohibited in conflicts with other Christians were freely employed against the Mohammedans. Speier also includes clashes between heavily armed colonizers and poorly armed indigenous peoples in this category, which would appear to move it within the realm of genocide.

Thus, there does appear to be some overlap between the definitions of genocide and total war. In terms of actual practice, several common features are evident, three of which are particularly salient for this analysis.

First, both genocide and total war involve mass killing of human beings, the majority of whom are civilians. The mass nature of the killing reflects the fact that large numbers of people are killed more or less simultaneously and as anonymous members of a targeted group or inhabitants of designated areas. Second, in both cases mass killing tends to be done in a deliberate, planned, premeditated fashion. The goal of the perpetrators or implementors is clearly to kill large numbers of people, either as an end in itself, or else as a means to a different end. Finally, in both genocide and total war, mass killing is undertaken by the state as a national security measure. Both are organized and administered, or at least facilitated, by officials of the government for the ostensible purpose of assuring the well-being and security of the majority of citizens.

Another approach to comparison involves examining the role of three factors—ideology, bureaucracy, and technology—that have been cited by several analysts as significant elements in both genocide and total war.[59]

If ideology is defined as a system of psychological and political rationalizations for adopting a particular policy or engaging in a particular practice, then it is evident that the twentieth century has featured abundant ideological incentives to participate in mass killing projects.[60] In this respect the twentieth is no different from past centuries: there have always been ideological justifications for mass killing. One of the most potent of these has been religion, which has inspired some of the most savage cases of organized mass slaughter.

In the modern world, however, religious ideologies have often been replaced by political ideologies, particularly the "religion of nationalism," to use Toynbee's phrase. This powerful ideology has been used to justify some of the most atrocious mass killing projects of the century. "Intense nationalism," notes Horowitz, "is itself an essential characteristic of the genocidal society. It instills not only a sense of difference between those who belong and those who do not, but also the inhumanity of those who do not belong, and thereby the rights of the social order to purge itself of alien influence."[61] Nationalistic ideologies have also inspired wars of increasing scale and intensity. Toynbee states that "the increasing fanaticism of nationalism has exacted an increasing oblation of military human sacrifice."[62]

When the advocates of mass killing are able to justify their policies on the basis of national security, they increase the likelihood of cooperation by citizens, both in the role of direct perpetrator/implementor and in that of compliant bystander. In some cases, the official claim of a threat to national security is clearly specious, as has been the case with recent genocides. For example, the Jews in Nazi Germany certainly did not pose a real threat to the German state. But to the extent that Nazi propagandists were able to convince German citizens that the Jews were to blame for Germany's many grave problems, they were able to secure active complicity and passive compliance with respect to the "Final Solution." In other cases, especially total wars like World War II, the threat to national survival posed by the enemy is real. But in both cases, specious and real, the ideology of nationalism and the authority of government is used by leaders to promote citizen cooperation in state-sanctioned mass killing projects.

When the authority of national government is invoked, many individuals are willing to subdue any moral reservations they might have about a particular policy or practice in order to continue service to their nation. This was the defense of many of the war criminals on trial at Nuremberg; however, the Tribunal consistently refused to respect their claims of having had to obey "superior orders." As the infamous "Obedience to Authority" experiments conducted by Stanley Milgram disclosed, normal individuals are willing to inflict severe pain on other people when induced by a convincing authority figure.[63]

If the government begins to fear waning support for its policies, it can employ propaganda or outright deception. During World War II, there is evidence to suggest that bomber crews were given briefings that intentionally exaggerated the military significance of such targets as Dresden.[64] The British government attempted to restrict information about the Dresden raids from the general public to avoid "jeopardizing public support for the war."[65]

In addition to capitalizing on the tendency of both civilians and soldiers to defer personal scruples in favor of conforming to authority, the invocation of national security can create a "kill or be killed" mentality. The targets of the government killing project, whether members of a despised minority group or citizens of an enemy nation, must be eliminated in order for the vitality of one's own group or nation to be preserved. In his study of Nazi doctors, "Medicalized Killing in Auschwitz," Lifton notes that "killing was done in the name of healing. It is not too much to say that every action an SS doctor took was connected to some kind of perversion or reversal of healing and killing. For the SS doctor, involvement in the killing process became equated with healing."[66] Likewise, Charny states, "Incredible as it may seem, virtually every genocide is defined by its doers as being on behalf of the larger purpose of bettering human life."[67] In his article, "American Military Ethics in World War II: The Bombing of German Civilians," Ronald Schaffer cites excerpts from a wartime memo by U.S. Army Air Forces commander Henry H. Arnold in which Arnold stated that the bomber, "when used with the proper degree of understanding . . . becomes, in effect, the most humane of all weapons."[68] Schaffer comments:

These sentiments appear to conflict with Arnold's willingness to burn down cities, his desire to see robot bombers fall indiscriminately among the German people. . . . Yet they are more than lip service or words for the historical record. They represent a moral attitude inherent in air power theory, a position that goes back to World War I—the idea that the bomber is a way of preserving lives by ending wars quickly and by providing a substitute for the kind of ground warfare that had killed so many soldiers a quarter century earlier.[69]

Among the most important forms of ideological justification for mass killing is the dehumanization of the victims. "Dehumanization," according to Kuper, "might be conceived as the relegation of the victims to the level of animals or objects or to a purely instrumental role."[70] Herbert Kelman suggests that dehumanization entails the removal of two fundamental qualities from the victims, identity and community; the individual identity of each victim is submerged in the group to which he or she belongs, and the group as a whole is considered as subhuman or nonhuman.[71] In Helen Fein's terms, the victims are placed "outside the sanctified universe of obligation—that circle of people with reciprocal obligations to protect each other whose bonds arose from their relation to a deity or sacred source of authority."[72] If the invocation of national security and official authority provide initial inducement for both participants and bystanders to accept the necessity of harsh measures against a targeted group, dehumanization of that group further erodes any moral or empathic restraints on the willingness to perpetrate massive and indiscriminate violence. As Kelman notes: "Thus when a group of people is defined entirely in terms of a category to which they belong, and when this category is excluded from the human family, then the moral restraints against killing them are more readily overcome."[73]

Both total war and genocide are characterized by the dehumanization of victims. When the victims are members of a different religion or race, dehumanization is greatly facilitated. For example, when the United States shifted its bombing policy in Japan from "precision" attacks against military targets to deliberate efforts to create huge firestorms in urban areas, accounts of the raids in the popular media were replete with images suggesting that the Japanese were more similar to insects than people and that the bombing campaign was closer to pest extermination than a traditional military operation. The image of pest extermination was also frequently used by Nazis who were involved in the attempt to exterminate the Jews.

A final element in the ideological justification of mass killing to be considered in this preliminary analysis is the role of the academic and scientific communities. In the case of the Holocaust, the entire campaign against the Jews—from the earliest official persecutions in 1933 through the implementation of the "Final Solution"—was intellectually rationalized by members of the German academic and scientific community. The medical profession, for example, as has been documented by Lifton, played very important roles, both by contributing to such legal measures against the Jews as the Nuremberg Laws of 1935, which made it illegal for Jews and non-Jews to be married or have sexual relations (on the assumption that interbreeding with Jews would pollute and weaken the German-Aryan "blood"), and by direct participation in the mass killing operations.[74] Scientific authority was also invoked to justify the shift from precision to area bombing by the British during World War II. The military and political leaders who favored such a shift in targeting policy eagerly seized on the fact that certain prestigious scientists had purportedly found evidence indicating that such a policy would significantly help the war effort. Other scientists, who reached a contradictory conclusion—that "de-housing" the German workers was less efficient than continuing to attack specific industrial targets—found far less receptivity among the policymakers.[75]

A second contributing factor emphasized by analysts of contemporary mass killing is the pervasiveness of bureaucratic political and social organization. According to Richard Rubenstein in his study *The Cunning of History: The Holocaust and the American Future:*

Usually the progress in death-dealing capacity in the twentieth century has been described in terms of technological advances in weaponry. Too little attention has been given to the advances in social organization that allowed for the effective use of the new weapons. In order to understand how the moral barrier was crossed that made massacre in the millions possible, it is necessary to consider the importance of bureaucracy in modern political organization.[76]

Sociologist Randall Collins sees bureaucracy as a reason for the "ferocious" face to face cruelty of the past to have been replaced by a new kind of cruelty: callousness, or "cruelty without passion." While he notes that callous cruelty has existed throughout history, he suggests that it is "especially characteristic of large-scale, bureaucratic organization," and that "the structural organization of bureaucracy seems uniquely suited for the perpetration of callous violence."[77]

Ongoing mass killing projects—like the operation of killing centers or the undertaking of a sustained incendiary bombing campaign against densely populated cities—require a complex and efficient organization. For every individual who is directly involved with the mass killing (e.g., operating the gas chamber or serving as crew on the bomber), there are many others who must decide and promulgate the policy; design, build, and service the necessary machinery; coordinate the logistics of transport and supply; generate, distribute, and file paperwork; monitor and evaluate.

Several features of bureaucratic organizations serve to promote the overall efficiency of mass killing projects as well as to enable individual participants to carry out their tasks with a minimum of questioning or doubt. Insofar as the positions within a bureaucracy are arranged in a formally hierarchical structure, individuals at the lower levels tend to have a reduced sense of personal responsibility for either the policy they are helping to implement or its final outcome. They are, after all, only "following orders" that have descended through all the levels of the organization above their own. This is particularly true of the military with its strongly indoctrinated tradition of unquestioning loyalty to authority. Another feature of bureaucracy, division of labor, breaks down complex tasks into compartmentalized sub-tasks. "Microdivision of labor," according to sociologist Don Martindale, "has made the goal of activity invisible, depriving it of meaning for the individual."[78] For example, the distinguished physicist and U.S. defense consultant Freeman Dyson, reflecting on his involvement as a scientific analyst in Bomber Command, the organization responsible for British strategic bombing during World War II, notes:

Bomber Command was an early example of the new evil that science and technology have added to the old evils of soldiering. Technology has made evil anonymous. Through science and technology, evil is organized bureaucratically so that no individual is responsible for what happens.[79]

A further diminishment of personal responsibility results from the formal separation of the individual from the position which he or she occupies within the organization. According to Collins, this separation is "the fundamental principle of bureaucracy."[80] The assigned task is performed during working hours, after which the individual is free to pursue other activities and interests.

Bureaucracy facilitates the crossing of the "moral barrier" to which Rubenstein referred by its deliberate effort to render humane considerations irrelevant with respect to the performance of the task at hand. As Max Weber noted, a bureaucratic organization, "develops the more perfectly the more the bureaucracy is 'dehumanized,' the more completely it succeeds in eliminating from official business love, hatred, and all purely personal, irrational, and emotional elements which escape calculation. This is the specific nature of bureaucracy and it is appraised as its special virtue."[81]

Such amoral rationality augments the effects of the other features to help create technically proficient functionaries who perform their specialized assignments with a minimized tendency to concern themselves with the fundamental nature of the overall project or its ultimate goals and results. As Fein observes, "Bureaucracy is not itself a cause of the choice of destructive ends, but it facilitates their accomplishment by routinizing the obedience of many agents, each trained to perform his role without questioning the ends of action."[82]

Technology is the third factor that has contributed decisively to the unprecedented death tolls of the twentieth century. It has made this contribution by providing killers with weapons of ever-increasing lethality and by creating a physical and emotional distance between killers and victims.

Throughout history, technology has always had a powerful impact on warfare. In his analysis of the historical development of weaponry from preliterate peoples through the 1950s, Francis Allen concludes that technology is "the clearcut, outstanding *variable* of importance" in determining the nature of war.[83] This conclusion is shared by Quincy Wright, who states that "the outstanding characteristic in which modern war has differed from all earlier forms of war has been in the degree of mechanization."[84]

The lethality of weapons has increased tremendously during the modern era. In his classic study of the increasing rate of social change, sociologist Hornell Hart has documented several dimensions of the "accelerating power to kill and destroy." These include the range over which weapons can be projected and, as a function of this range, their "killing area." Hart notes that from 1 million B.C. until approximately A.D. 1450, the maximum range of available weapons remained under one-third of a mile and the killing area under one square mile. The only weapons developed during this entire period capable of attaining these results were the catapult and the ballista (a giant crossbow). Between 1453, with the invention of cannons, and 1912, with the development of coastal artillery, the range increased from 1 mile to 11.4 miles and the killing area from 3 square miles to 408 square miles. However, between 1915, with the first Zeppelin raid on London during World War I, and 1954, with strategic bombers and in-flight refueling, the range grew from 200 miles to 12,500 miles and the killing area from 126,000 square miles to 200 million square miles. This killing area exceeded the total surface area of the earth, approximately 10 million square miles.[85]

Hart also traced the increase in the killing power of the explosives that can be delivered over the above ranges. One measure that he uses is deaths per ton of explosive. During the German bombing raids on London during World War I, for example, about 3 people were killed for each ton of TNT bombs dropped. By World War II, the rate had risen precipitously; in the American incendiary bombing raid on Tokyo on March 9, 1945, deaths per ton was 50. By the end of the war, the invention of the atomic bomb had raised the death toll per ton of explosive even higher, up to "about 10,000 persons killed per ton of normal bomb load for the B-29 that made the raid."[86] Hart concludes his analysis of increased killing power by noting that "the five centuries from 1346 to 1875 saw several times as much increase in explosive power as had been achieved in the previous million years. The 70 years from 1875 to March, 1945, saw several times as much increase in explosive power as the previous five centuries."[87] With the development during the war of atomic weapons, and after the war of thermonuclear weapons, destructive capabilities have climbed even higher.

The combination of long-range delivery capability and high levels of destructiveness has made modern weapons indiscriminate. During World War II, even efforts to precisely target key industries frequently created large death tolls among civilians living in the vicinity, as the result of either errant bombs or conflagrations that started in the designated target areas and then spread to surrounding residential areas.

Warfare is not the only type of mass killing that has been vitally affected by technological developments. As Horowitz notes, "What makes genocide a particularly malevolent practice in this century, with wide-ranging consequences, is the role of modern technology in the systematic destruction of large numbers of innocents."[88] In the case of the Holocaust, technology played a crucial role in at least two ways. First, existing technology was utilized by the killers to facilitate their tasks. For example, communications technology enabled them to coordinate a killing project that involved millions of intended victims scattered throughout Europe, and transportation technology was exploited to ship the Jews and other victims from their far-flung homes to the killing centers. Second, new technologies of killing and corpse disposal were developed in order to increase the "output." This included gas chambers with a capacity of 2,000 people at one time, huge ventilation systems designed to evacuate the poisoned air from the gas chambers, and crematoria capable of disposing of thousands of corpses per day. While none of this technology was particularly sophisticated or esoteric, its efficient exploitation definitely helped the perpetrators to attain higher "body counts" than would have been the case had they continued to resort to more "primitive" methods like shooting, drowning, and burying victims alive.

In addition to affecting contemporary mass killing by increasing the destructiveness of the tools used by the killers, technology has also decisively affected the mass killing process by imposing physical and emotional distance between killers and their victims. Not only can killers annihilate great numbers of people in short periods of time, but they can do this often without even seeing their victims. As Allen notes, "The increasing tendency is to wage war at a distance. . . . Modern scientific war thus becomes depersonalized."[89] For example, during World War I, the crews of heavy artillery pieces fired across no man's land into the area of enemy trenches rather than at individually sighted enemy soldiers. During World War II, many of the bombing raids were obscured by cloud cover or by smoke rising from fires started by earlier strikes. In the Holocaust, the heavy psychological toll on the *Einsatzgruppen* killers engaging in the face-to-face mass shooting of men, women, and children was greatly reduced when the killing methodology shifted to the large gas chambers into which technicians would pour gas crystals through openings on the roof, without having to watch the victims die.[90]

An important effect of technologically imposed distance between killers and victims is an increased tendency to dehumanize the victim.[91] "In general," notes sociologist Lewis Coser, "the perception of the humanness of the 'other' decreases with the increase in distance between perceiver and perceived."[92] Such dehumanization further erodes any moral restraints that might intrude upon the effective performance of function by the killer. A case in point is provided by the strategic bombing campaigns of World War II. Kennett observes:

The escalation of the air war was made easier by the fact that those who directed the bombing offensives and those who carried them out remained curiously insulated and detached from the consequences of their work. Photographs taken at thirty thousand feet gave no clue to the human effects of a raid, nor did other sources. In this vacuum, imagination and extrapolation could picture the population of an enemy town deprived of its homes but not of life and limb. . . . Anodyne, antiseptic phrases such as "dual target" and "area attack" further served to mask the fact that human lives were being destroyed.[93]

## SUMMARY AND CONCLUSIONS

Despite apparent differences between genocide and total war as forms of state-sanctioned mass killing, this preliminary comparison has disclosed several significant similarities and parallels.

Both genocide and total war are undertaken by the nation-state as national security measures. Democracies as well as totalitarian governments have perpetrated genocides and engaged in total wars. Indeed, participation in a total war tends to narrow the gap between the two forms of government by centralizing authority and encouraging governmental propaganda and secrecy.

Ideological elements such as dehumanization of the targets of violence are common to both genocide and total war, as is the conviction that the vitality of one's own group or nation can be preserved only by willingness to destroy masses of people in a different group or nation. The invocation of a threat to national security, and governmental authorization for measures that would ordinarily be considered atrocious, facilitate the suppression of moral and empathic restraints among citizens who participate directly in the mass killing, as well as those who tacitly support it as "good citizens."

In the modern era, both genocide and total war tend to be bureaucratically organized. This form of social organization results in a diminished sense of personal responsibility for those who are directly or indirectly involved in the mass killing project. It also routinizes the performance of specialized tasks that are removed from the reality of the end results, but which collectively and cumulatively contribute to those results.

Technology plays an extremely important role in both forms of mass killing in at least two ways. First, it makes the task of killing large numbers of people easier and more efficient, and second, it eases any potential mental burden on the killers by interposing physical distance between them and their victims. This distancing reinforces the effects of dehumanizing ideology noted above.

The result of all three facilitating factors is to create a momentum that tends to increase levels of destructiveness until the goal has been reached or an outside force prevents continuation of the policy.

This comparative analysis has been admittedly preliminary and brief. The roles of such facilitating factors as ideology, bureaucracy, and technology need to be explored in greater detail, and other differences and similarities need to be identified and analyzed.

On the basis of this initial effort, however, it does appear that the line between genocide and total war has become very blurred in many cases. Warfare in the twentieth century has become increasingly genocidal, and several genocides—with the German genocide against the Jews as the exemplary case—resemble military campaigns and utilize military forces in the killing process.[94]

The lessons of this study for the problem of the nuclear threat are very ominous. The same facilitating factors that expedite genocide and total war also characterize the preparations for nuclear war. The build-up of nuclear arsenals and the willingness to use them are justified on the grounds of national security. Elaborate ideological rationalizations are used to convince citizens of the need for more and better nuclear weapons. In both the United States and the Soviet Union, government propaganda and secrecy surround the making of nuclear policy and the plans for nuclear combat. Those who are closest to the policies and the weapons see them as being absolutely essential for the preservation of their nations, even to the point of being willing to risk destruction of those nations. The leaders and citizens of each "side" are vilified and dehumanized by official rhetoric and propaganda on the other side. The Soviets are demonized as "Godless monsters" dwelling in an "evil empire," while citizens of the United States are caricatured as "evil imperialists" and "heartless capitalists."

The preparations for nuclear war take place in vast bureaucracies in which many thousands of patriotic individuals make their livings by performing compartmentalized tasks that contribute to the readiness to engage in nuclear holocaust. The destructive capacity of nuclear weapons technology is beyond the comprehension of most, if not all, potential victims of nuclear war, which decreases their ability to recognize and confront the risk that such technology poses. The weapons themselves will be launched by young men and women buried in underground missile silos, submerged beneath the ocean in submarines, or flying high above the ground in airplanes. Most of those who will be responsible for actually using the weapons do not even know their precise destination.

These and many other features of the nuclear threat make it very difficult for human beings to comprehend and confront it. Yet, if they fail to even try, then factors that contribute to the growing likelihood will be allowed to grow stronger, and the efforts of the minority of the people who have dedicated themselves to trying to prevent the holocaust will be in vain. The problem of state-sanctioned mass killing—in the past, present, and future—must be elevated to the highest level of our priorities as citizens, scholars, and parents. We must confront the ugly issue of mass killing in order to avoid becoming victims ourselves.

Although the following words of Bruno Bettelheim were originally addressed to the question of why the Jews became ensnared in the unimaginable madness of the Holocaust, they have much to say to us in an era of genocide, total war, and the preparations for nuclear holocaust:

When a world goes to pieces and inhumanity reigns supreme, man cannot go on living his private life as he was wont to do, and would like to do; he cannot—as the loving head of a family, keep the family living together peacefully, undisturbed by the surrounding world; nor can he continue to take pride in his profession or possessions, when either will deprive him of his humanity, if not also of his life. In such times, one must radically reevaluate all that one has done, believed in, and stood for in order to know how to act. In short, one has to take a stand on the new reality—a firm stand, not one of retirement into an even more private world.[95]

## NOTES

1. Quincy Wright, *A Study of War,* 2nd ed. (Chicago: University of Chicago Press, 1965), p. 30.

2. Arnold Toynbee, "Death in War," in Arnold Toynbee et al., *Man's Concern With Death* (St. Louis: McGraw-Hill, 1968), p. 145.

3. Quincy Wright, *A Study of War,* p. 248.

4. William James, "The Moral Equivalent of War," in Richard Wasserstrom, ed., *War and Morality* (Belmont, Calif.: Wadsworth Publishing Co., 1970), p. 5.

5. Pitirim A. Sorokin, *Social and Cultural Dynamics,* Vol. 3 (New York: The Bedminster Press, 1962), p. 342. Emphasis in original.

6. Gil Elliot, *Twentieth Century Book of the Dead* (New York: Charles Scribner's Sons, 1972), p. 1.

7. Ruth L. Sivard,*World Military and Social Expenditures 1982* (Leesburg, Va.: World Priorities, 1982), p. 15.

8. See, for example, Lewis A. Dunn, *Controlling the Bomb: Nuclear Proliferation in the 1980s* (New Haven: Yale University Press, 1982).

9. International Committee of Experts on Medical Sciences and Public Health, *Effects of Nuclear War on Health and Health Services* (Geneva: World Health Organization, 1984), p. 5. R. P. Turco et al., "Nuclear Winter: Global Consequences of Multiple Nuclear Explosions," *Science* 222 (December 23, 1983), pp. 1283-91.

10. Paul R. Ehrlich et al., "Long-term Consequences of Nuclear War," *Science* 222 (December 23, 1983), p. 1299.

11. For example, Robert Jay Lifton, a psychiatrist who has undertaken pioneering studies of such holocausts as the atomic bombings of Japan and the Nazi attempt to exterminate the Jews of Europe, notes that, until recently, Western society was reticent on the subject of death itself, let alone mass death and mass killing. "Next it became permissible to speak about individual death and dying," observes Lifton, "but not holocaust. Now holocaust is increasingly discussed, but mainly in terms of the past, not in relationship to future holocausts or to our own capacity for mass murder." Robert Jay Lifton, "Witnessing Survival," *Society* 15 (March/April 1978), p. 41. Like-

wise, Israel Charny, on the basis of his detailed study of the psychosocial dimensions of genocide, concludes: "At this point in its evolution, mankind is deeply limited in its readiness to experience and take action in response to genocidal disasters. Most events of genocide are marked by massive indifference, silence, and inactivity." Israel Charny, *How Can We Commit the Unthinkable? Genocide: The Human Cancer* (Boulder, Colo.: Westview Press, 1982), p. 284.

12. Raphael Lemkin, *Axis Rule in Occupied Europe* (Washington, D.C.: Carnegie Endowment for International Peace, 1944).

13. International Military Tribunal, "Charter of the International Military Tribunal," *Trials of War Criminals Before the Nuremberg Military Tribunals under Control Council Law Number 10,* Vol. 1 (Washington, D.C.: U.S. Government Printing Office, 1950), p. xii.

14. Leo Kuper, *Genocide: Its Political Use in the Twentieth Century* (New Haven: Yale University Press, 1981), p. 96.

15. Ibid., p. 113.

16. Ibid., pp. 97, 154-60; see also Richard Rubenstein, "The Agony of Indochina," in Richard Rubenstein, *The Age of Triage: Fear and Hope in an Overcrowded World* (Boston: Beacon Press, 1983), pp. 165-94.

17. Irving Louis Horowitz, *Taking Lives: Genocide and State Power* (New Brunswick, N.J.: Transaction Books, 1980), p. 1.

18. Ibid., p. 34.

19. Vahakn N. Dadrian, "A Typology of Genocide," *International Review of Modern Sociology* 15 (1975), p. 204.

20. Ibid., p. 206.

21. Kuper, *Genocide*, pp. 138-60. See also Robert Payne, *Massacre* (New York: The Macmillan Company, 1973).

22. For a valuable discussion of the origins and history of the concept of "total war," see Berenice A. Carroll, *Design for Total War: Arms and Economics in the Third Reich* (The Hague: Mouton, 1968), pp. 9, 17-36.

23. Edward Luttwak, *A Dictionary of Modern War* (New York: Harper and Row, 1971), p. 203.

24. Frederick Sallagar, *The Road to Total War* (New York: Van Nostrand Reinhold Company, 1969), p. 3. Emphasis in original.

25. J. F. C. Fuller, *The Conduct of War, 1789-1961* (New Brunswick, N.J.: Rutgers University Press, 1961), p. 31.

26. Edwin Corwin, *Total War and the Constitution* (New York: Alfred A. Knopf, 1947), p. 3.

27. Ibid.

28. Fuller, *The Conduct of War*, p. 15.

29. Ibid., p. 15-25.

30. Sorokin, *Social and Cultural Dynamics*, Vol. 3, pp. 340, 345, 349.

31. Richard A. Preston and Sydney F. Wise, *Men in Arms: A History of Warfare and Its Interrelationships with Western Society* (New York: Praeger, 1970), p. 207.

32. Corwin, *Total War and the Constitution*, p. 7.

33. Fuller, *The Conduct of War*, p. 35.

34. Ibid.

35. Ibid., p. 36.

36. Hans Speier, "Class Structure and Total War," in Hans Speier, *Social Order and the Risks of War* (Cambridge, Mass.: M.I.T. Press, 1971), p. 254.

37. Quincy Wright, *A Study of War*, p. 305.

38. Raymond Aron, *The Century of Total War* (New York: Doubleday and Company, 1954), p. 88.

39. Marjorie Farrar, "World War II as Total War," in L. L. Farrar, Jr., ed., *War: A Historical, Political, and Social Study* (Santa Barbara, Calif.: ABC-Clio, 1978), p. 175.

40. Gordon Wright, *The Ordeal of Total War* (New York: Harper and Row, 1968), p. 236.

41. Ibid., p. 264.

42. Elliot, *Twentieth Century Book of the Dead*, p. 88.

43. John Ford, "The Morality of Obliteration Bombing," in Richard Wasserstrom, ed., *War and Morality* (Belmont, Calif.: Wadsworth Publishing Co., 1970), pp. 15-41 (especially pp. 21-23).

44. Quincy Wright, *A Study of War*, p. 302.

45. Lewis Mumford, "The Morals of Extermination," *The Atlantic* 204 (October 1959), p. 39.

46. Horowitz, *Taking Lives*, p. 32.

47. Ibid.

48. See, for example, Max Hastings, *Bomber Command* (New York: Dial Press, 1979), p. 347.

49. For LeMay's role in the firebombing of Japan, see, for example, Martin Caidin, *A Torch to the Enemy* (New York: Ballantine Books, 1960), and Lee Kennett, *A History of Strategic Bombing* (New York: Scribner's, 1982), pp. 163-77. For LeMay's postwar role with nuclear weapons, see Fred Kaplan, *The Wizards of Armageddon* (New York: Simon and Schuster, 1983), pp. 42-44, 104, 134.

50. Mumford, "The Morals of Extermination," p. 39.

51. Michael Sherry, "The Slide to Total Air War," *The New Republic* (December 16, 1981), p. 25.

52. See, for example, Lucy Dawidowicz, *The Holocaust and the Historians* (Cambridge, Mass.: Harvard University Press, 1982), p. 12, and Yehuda Bauer, "Genocide: Was It the Nazis' Original Plan?" *The Annals of the American Academy of Political and Social Science* 450 (July 1980), p. 40.

53. Horowitz, *Taking Lives*, p. 56.

54. Ibid. For further analysis of the genocidal dimensions of the Vietnam War, see also Richard Falk, Gabriel Kolko, and Robert Jay Lifton, eds., *Crimes of War* (New York: Random House, 1967); and Hugo Adam Bedau, "Genocide in Vietnam?" and Richard Falk, "Ecocide, Genocide, and the

Nuremberg Tradition of Individual Responsibility," both in Virginia Held, Sidney Morgenbesser, and Thomas Nagel, eds., *Philosophy, Morality, and International Affairs* (New York: Oxford University Press, 1974), pp. 3-47 and 123-37, respectively.

55. Horowitz, *Taking Lives,* p. 56.

56. Kuper, *Genocide,* p. 46.

57. Dadrian, "A Typology of Genocide," pp. 205-7.

58. Hans Speier, "The Social Types of War," in Speier, *Social Order and the Risks of War,* p. 223.

59. Professor David Cooperman, University of Minnesota, personal communication, June 1982; Jack Nusan Porter, "What Is Genocide? Notes Toward a Definition," in Jack Nusan Porter, ed., *Genocide and Human Rights* (Washington, D.C.: University Press of America, 1982), pp. 2-32.

60. For several valuable discussions of the meaning of ideology and its role in national security policy, see George Schwab, ed., *Ideology and Foreign Policy* (New York: Cyrco Press, 1978).

61. Horowitz, *Taking Lives,* p. 65.

62. Toynbee, "Death in War," p. 148.

63. Stanley Milgram, *Obedience to Authority* (New York: Harper and Row, 1974).

64. David Irving, *The Destruction of Dresden* (New York: Ballantine Books, 1963), p. 165.

65. Mark A. Clodfelter, "Culmination Dresden: 1945," *Aerospace Historian* 36 (September 1979), p. 139.

66. Robert Jay Lifton, "Medicalized Killing in Auschwitz," *Psychiatry* 45 (November 1982), p. 292.

67. Charny, *How Can We Commit the Unthinkable?,* p. 113.

68. Ronald Schaffer, "American Military Ethics in World War II: The Bombing of German Civilians," *The Journal of American History* 67 (September 1980), p. 333.

69. Ibid.

70. Kuper, *Genocide,* p. 86.

71. Herbert C. Kelman, "Violence Without Moral Restraint: Reflections on the Dehumanization of Victims and Victimizers," *Journal of Social Issues* 29 (1973), p. 49.

72. Helen Fein, *Accounting for Genocide* (New York: Free Press, 1979), p. 4.

73. Kelman, "Violence Without Moral Restraint," p. 51.

74. Lifton, "Medicalized Killing in Auschwitz."

75. Hastings, *Bomber Command,* pp. 122-40.

76. Richard Rubenstein, *The Cunning of History: The Holocaust and the American Future* (New York: Harper Colophon Books, 1978), p. 22.

77. Randall Collins, "Three Faces of Evil: Towards a Comparative Sociology of Evil," *Theory and Society* 1 (1974), p. 432.

78. Don Martindale, *Institutions, Organizations, and Mass Society* (Boston: Houghton Mifflin Company, 1966), p. 144.

79. Freeman Dyson, *Disturbing the Universe* (New York: Harper and Row, 1979), p. 30.

80. Collins, "Three Faces of Evil," p. 433.

81. Max Weber, "Bureaucracy," in H. H. Gerth and C. Wright Mills, trans. and eds., *From Max Weber: Essays in Sociology* (New York: Oxford University Press, 1958), pp. 215-16.

82. Fein, *Accounting for Genocide*, p. 22.

83. Francis R. Allen, "Influence of Technology on War," in Francis R. Allen et al., *Technology and Social Change* (New York: Appleton-Century-Crofts, Inc., 1957), p. 353.

84. Quincy Wright, *A Study of War*, p. 303.

85. Hornell Hart, "Acceleration in Social Change," in Allen et al., *Technology and Social Change*, pp. 35-38. For a more recent discussion of the destructiveness of modern weapons, see J. P. Perry Robinson, "Neutron Bomb and Conventional Weapons of Mass Destruction," *Bulletin of the Atomic Scientists* 34 (March 1978), pp. 42-45.

86. Ibid., pp. 41-43.

87. Ibid., p. 43.

88. Horowitz, *Taking Lives*, p. 2.

89. Allen, "Influence of Technology on War," p. 381.

90. Robert Jay Lifton, in his recent study of Nazi doctors and the role of the German medical profession in the Holocaust, reports on an interview with a German physician who treated a number of soldiers attached to *Einsatzgruppen* who were incapacitated by various forms of psychological stress. Lifton's book is entitled *The Nazi Doctors: Medical Killing and the Psychology of Genocide* (New York: Basic Books, 1986). For a preliminary report on his approach and findings, see "Medicalized Killing in Auschwitz," referred to above.

91. Group for the Advancement of Psychiatry, *Psychiatric Aspects of the Prevention of Nuclear War*, Report Number 57 (September 1964), pp. 222-317. (See especially "Dehumanization—Another Psychological Factor Bearing on Modern War," pp. 237-46.)

92. Lewis Coser, "The Visibility of Evil," *Journal of Social Issues* 25 (1969), p. 105.

93. Kennett, *A History of Strategic Bombing*, p. 187.

94. Henry Mason, "Imponderables of the Holocaust," *World Politics* 34 (October 1981), pp. 89-120.

95. Bruno Bettelheim, "The Ignored Lesson of Anne Frank," in *Surviving and Other Essays* (New York: Vintage, 1980), p. 257.

# 7

## SOCIAL MADNESS

### *Ronald Aronson*

## I

In *The Dialectics of Disaster: A Preface to Hope* I have analyzed the "Final Solution to the Jewish Problem" as an act of societal madness.[1] We ordinarily use this term "madness" quite freely in conversation, but then abandon it upon moving into serious discourse and study—perhaps in trying to be more precise, objective, or scientific, perhaps to avoid a contentious descriptive term. I would argue, however, that sophisticated thought has ignored an important spontaneous insight. Used carefully and self-consciously, the term "madness" illuminates much of the century's genocidal history, including above all the Nazi project to exterminate Europe's Jews.

Mad: untutored and casual reflection contains an insight to be preserved and deepened, not suppressed, by systematic and scientific study. Nazi policies toward the Jews were mad, as were Stalin's attacks upon Russian society, as was the American near-destruction of Vietnam. And in the dynamic structures of these and other quite different madnesses we can find guides for understanding and perhaps combatting the nuclear madness menacing all of us.

Yet to describe social policies as mad immediately exposes one to a raft of doubts: about indulging in rhetorical excess, about being imprecise, about confusing the social with the individual, injecting normative conceptions that have no place in social analysis. For example, even if we grant that individuals may be described as mad—and this language is contestable as being value-charged, unscientific, and obsolescent—how can psychological terms appropriate to individual mental functioning be

applied to collective behavior? After all, don't societies function according to different processes than do individuals?

This and similar objections are reinforced by the functionalist premise
that generally guides studies of social life. It is no great leap from assuming, quite appropriately, that all social policy is intentional, to seeing
that intentionality as rational—thus gilding rulers' acts with the rationality of those studying them. If it had a *function* and *purpose,* the "Final
Solution" was done "in order to . . .": to unite Germany, say, or to
divert it. It had a particular function, then, a logic. The executioners
were guided by or manipulated according to this logic. But such formulations tend to cast genocide as another human project among the
universe of projects—whose rationality is either assumed or lies beyond
the specific study in question—rather than as a policy whose logic is
fundamentally rooted in illogic. Yes, it was just another human act, but
it was also an insane one. Yes, understanding it demands that we use
customary explanatory categories, but it also stretches them to their limit.

The Nazi policy and practice of extermination was—in spite of its
overwhelming technical rationality, in spite of the palpable reality of the
extermination-camp universe—as supremely irrational as can be
imagined. Yet its madness, if felt and intuited, is difficult to locate, more
difficult to argue. Was it in the decision to exterminate, in the machinery
itself, in the mental functioning of those who ordered it or those who
carried out their orders, in the society that made it possible? Although
the debate continues, it is at least plausible for us to see an organizer of
the "Final Solution," Adolf Eichmann, as did Hannah Arendt, as banal
and mediocre rather than as pathologically mad.[2] And it is at least possible to argue, as did Richard Rubenstein, that the key to the Holocaust
is not a crazed intentionality but a rather indifferent and impersonal
process of twentieth-century technological rationality.[3]

Certainly I agree that "madness" is a methodologically troubling term
—a culturally bound concept whose use for socio-historical processes is
so problematic and controversial that it would be preferable to avoid it
altogether. But discarding the term will not dispel what it would convey.
How else can we preserve what is essential to it—the systematically and
radically *deranged* character of the "Final Solution"? How do justice to
the intuition that at its core it was insane, beginning to end?

Yet aren't these *subjective* responses? Rubenstein has argued that we
should bracket our emotional responses as interfering with our objective
understanding of this event.[4] Is not our sense of its madness similarly
subjective and distortive? Won't dwelling on it slant our discussion in a
hopelessly colored personal direction? Shouldn't we limit ourselves to
presenting and understanding the facts without adding any such personal
evaluation to them?

On the contrary, if the Holocaust commands our attention it is because
we cannot separate data—the numbers of dead, for example—from our

definition of their meaning. The event's impact and significance is indeed *subjectively* based: the sheer scale of the catastrophe cannot be disentangled from our sense of its grotesque character. The "Final Solution" was an end in itself. There is no value-free way of characterizing the Holocaust—its very definition as the worst catastrophe imaginable short of nuclear war is rooted in our respect for life, our sense of what humans should be and how they should and should not treat each other. Objectivity, insofar as history and society are concerned, is an intersubjective product constituted by those who share this same space, the earth. It is assumed, perhaps elaborated, as our sense of the collective conditions for survival, let alone well-being. In its utter gratuitousness, the Nazi extermination program so violates even the most minimal of these norms—proper behavior in wartime—that we cannot help but perceive it by using such terms as "unspeakable," "evil," "barbaric," "horrifying," or "demonic."

We *perceive* it this way: our lenses are inescapably emotional—subjective *and* objective, and give us the event already laden with meaning. We perceive it this way: it *is* this way. In the human world "subjective" reactions are indeed objective: they claim to illuminate not our feelings about the Holocaust but its very structure and character. Conversely, as a human project it has a structure and character only within the human world whose norms it so systematically outraged. Our objective-subjective reactions claim to mark it off from other historical events and tell us how and why it is unique. In this sense such terms do not call for being bracketed out at the start, but rather for being retained—clarified and understood, in order to better guide us to the event itself.


# II

But what does it mean to call social policy and collective behavior "mad"? How can the intuition be preserved and rendered usable for research and analysis?

Let us be clear what we do when we call an act "mad." First, our assertion may be of various strengths, and our emphasis may vary accordingly. We may simply mean that it is severely and systematically abnormal—that it departs considerably from our sense of the normal. "Normal," of course, is a subjective-objective notion which, strictly speaking, conveys our judgment of the range of proper human behavior —the norm we apply. But even if we try to restrict this judgment to behavior, it is hard to escape an accompanying reference to the psychological state underlying the behavior. In other words, in addition to considering a "mad" act as extremely abnormal, we imply that its source is in a mind that is somehow deranged. A mad action, we may suggest, proceeds from a disordered psyche. Indeed, if we call an act "insane" we complete this shift and our emphasis falls more heavily on the mental state of the actor. Between the milder emphasis on an action's abnormality and the stronger focus on its subjective source, I propose to explore "madness" in the middle sense, as suggested by "deranged"—as judgment of an act which opens toward, but does not immediately insist on focusing on, its subjective source.

Second, we must insist on the normative claim implied at each stage so far. When we speak of individuals as mad/deranged, we may have in mind three possible areas: systematic derangement of perception, systematic derangement of intention, or systematic derangement of affect. The individual may claim to see things that are not there or not see things that *are* there, may seek to do things that are inconceivable, or may show feelings or responses that are seriously and systematically inappropriate. In each type of madness, a standard is implied against which the act is measured: what is really there to be perceived, what is really possible to do, what is normal for human beings to feel. Obviously we cannot restrict ourselves to common-sense judgments of reality for our standard— revolutionaries, inventors, and poets constantly break beyond and redefine what are assumed to be the limits of reality and are frequently falsely thought to be mad. This does not deny that there are standards, however; just that a given society's definition of what is real—as in the case of Nazi Germany—must in turn be judged against more solid standards.

What is their source? Daily life is underpinned by a shared sense of the real world, its structures and limits. Science uses but sees beyond this, remains guided by its own, and corresponding, shared sense of reality, which is continuously and collectively refined and redefined just as is that of common sense. Even a revolutionary social philosophy, Marxism, which projects social transformation—a radically different reality which, if glimpsed, has not yet been achieved—bases its claim to truth on its *scientific* character. In other words, it is no more than utopian speculation if its projections are not based on actual, observable tendencies and possibilities of *this* society.

Even if it is now regarded as intersubjectively based rather than independent and external to us, a structured real world is central to all our experience. The rebellious—or revolutionary—rejection of the common-sense version of these structures is not mad, nor are the transcending visions of great poets, artists, and scientists. *Their* visions have seen through to deeper layers of the reality and have allowed future generations access to them. To be sure, sometimes we cannot tell for sure whether we are witnessing a transcendence of common sense or a mad break with reality—a vision of a madman. But then no normative concept is without its gray areas. Despite these, judgments of abnormality/

derangement still rest on a shared and demonstrable sense of objective reality, its spheres including intention and feeling as well as perception.


## III

The three categories of individual madness demand closer examination to see which are useful for societal analysis. First, what does it mean to see what is not really there? The Nazis saw the Jews as the source of Germany's problems: they perceived them as sub- and super-humans, as a danger, a pollutant, a parasite, an evil.[5] I do not mean "see" and "perceive" literally in terms of the physiological/optical fact of perception, but inferentially, as in the case of a belief. When someone sees the devil we assume not a perceptual but a mental malfunctioning: madness is not color-blindness but a mental disorder in which we believe our world of experience to form a causal pattern which is radically false. Patently absurd connections or processes of causation are invented, beings are created for which there is no basis in reality. *These* specific people, the Jews, were endowed by large numbers of Germans with certain menacing qualities and were linked mentally to their actually experienced problems.

To see this as madness is to concede that at its core were not the manipulators and the manipulated, but rather, more disturbingly, people who believed the inanities they spoke. Like the madman who sees the devil, those who thought the Jews were racially defiling them were sincere. They believed in their fantasies.

To see what is not there is also to *not* see what is there. If one looks at nuclear weapons and does not see danger but instead security we may speak of a similar double, and similarly radical, misperception. Again, the term "perception" is used loosely: the derangement lies in the mental, not the optical, process.

Why not simply speak of an *error?* Why is it not enough simply to label as *mistaken* the man who sees the devil or the Nazi who sees the Jew as the devil? After all, we are first of all talking about a mistake. The problem is that to call misperception a mistake locates it within the realm of reason and evidence we presume in all discourse and indeed perception. Within that realm a mistake may be corrected, for example, by demonstrating it to be false. But to call it madness underscores on the one hand its depth and seriousness, on the other its psychological roots and quality of being beyond reason and demonstration. If we regard a belief as mad we see it as being both willful *and* beyond reach.

This is a remarkable combination of opposites: a mad belief is beyond control, unreachable by any customary process of evidence or reasoning, yet it is willful. It proceeds with determination and from a definite intention.

Madness of the first sort, then, suggests a willful turning away from both normal perception and inference and its standards of evidence and truth, and a turning away which proclaims—and acts on—the inexistence of what is real and the existence of what is not. Of course, no individual or social movement turns completely from reality. Hitler not only showed normal perceptual capacities when he ate and drank, but in rising to power he demonstrated a brilliant grasp of the political situation down to the smallest detail of timing. If he was deranged it was only in certain specific areas. The same is true for those judged and treated as clinically insane: however far from normal reality they may be in specific areas, they know where and how to eat, how to walk, what it means to sleep. Total derangement, if possible, would deprive the would-be pathological killer of the very capacity to kill: *every* reality would be scrambled. Derangement is always selective and limited, leaving intact most of the vast web of one's other ties to reality as well as abilities to function within it.

Which is why we must see madness as lying along a continuum which stretches from the impossible extreme of seeing and acknowledging reality completely to the other impossible extreme of breaking with it totally. If the second is inconceivable for the reasons just given, Sigmund Freud has made clear why the first is also conceivable: civilized life demands repression and neurosis. If sane people stand somewhere along the continuum, the insane stand further along, having broken with *more* of reality. It is, however, a quantitative change which becomes qualitative. To speak of "madness" implies that reality is being denied more fully and in an area that is decisive for functioning. One could scarcely imagine functioning without denying *some* aspects of reality—this is the meaning of repression and neurosis as Freud articulated them. Repression is necessary to civilized life as such—for example, generating the sublimations that yield culture as well as protecting humanity from the impulses that would threaten it. Neurosis, differentiated from madness only by degree, afflicts every member of Western society in *some* way(s) which at *some* time(s) may become disruptive. Madness is more pronounced, more disruptive, more systematic.

If the phenomenon of denial characterizes all neurosis and suggests the (relatively) easy reversability that treatment or time can bring, a stronger term is needed to describe the willful, radical, systematic departure from reality we mean by "madness": a *rupture* with reality. This formulation captures all of the meanings I have been exploring: the fact that madness involves a relationship with reality; the normative character of the description; the seriousness of the derangement; its willful character; and the difficulty of return.

A second meaning of "madness" emphasizes the derangement not of perception but of intention. Of course, the two are linked: belief is an act whose derangement proceeds from an *intention* to rupture with reality and so believe. Moreover, madness has consequences—and is thus talked about and studied—only when it becomes yet more active and produces practical results. Nevertheless, "madness" has still a further implication, within the practical sphere, of an act that is undertaken contrary to evident possibility and in spite of that evidence. To attempt unaided flight from a tall building is so patently pursuing the impossible and courting death as to be mad. Of course, as with the earlier qualifications of misperception, acts that seek to "do the impossible" are regarded as mad when they are sustained, serious, and far-reaching. If this madness indeed contains strong elements of misperception, the emphasis falls on the misperception of causal relations between act A and intended result B. "If I leap I will fly." The absence of any conducting path between A and B is rejected, replaced instead with magical belief. B can be accomplished by doing A, in the face of all contrary evidence and experience. Reality is defied.

The intention is mad not insofar as it is felt or desired, but insofar as it is *willed against reality*. I focus on this as a distinct kind of madness because the intention dominates so wholly as to be pursued in spite of its patent impossibility. My desire to fly goes against reality, but instead of submitting to that reality I attack and disregard it by jumping from the window. If I disregard it with reference to the laws of physics, I attack it with regard to my own body. In this sense the realities in and through which the action takes place are violated in decisive ways—my body in particular—in hope of achieving B. Madness: an extreme and systematic violation of reality in the intention of achieving an impossible result.

And yet common sense tells us that many things are impossible which are later accomplished. Was flight impossible in 1900? Black-white equality in the American South in 1950? I select a technical *and* a sociopolitical example, both of which were susceptible to change over time. Yesterday's impossibility becomes tomorrow's common sense: space travel, for example, or women's equality with men. This implies that special caution is necessary when talking about madness. Moreover, systematic analysis of social structures and tendencies may reveal certain possibilities which are roundly denied by established ideologies: social movements sometimes suddenly and momentously extend the field of possibilities, as when Russian workers created the Soviets in 1905.[6]

Thus the intention for social change—even for revolutionary change—cannot be *a priori* characterized as mad any more than can the impulse to invent what has not yet been invented. Defenders of the status quo may see a given project as mad because of interests which understandably limit their sense of what is possible. Here it is important to note not that "madness" is and can be falsely applied—true of any normative term—but that it is used, and with a precise but incorrectly applied meaning: to attempt what is plainly contrary to possibility.

A third meaning of "madness" needs to be considered: systematic and radical estrangement from oneself. Psychopathic mass murderers are often regarded as mad not only because they kill but also because they do so without normal affect. "Cold-blooded murder": the assumption is of an appropriate complex of motivations and feelings which *this* killer utterly lacks. We see him as having thus ruptured with *his own* moral sensibilities and human fellow-feeling. He does not feel or react as one is *supposed to,* meaning in turn that he is not only abnormal but quite probably radically separated from *himself.* Acts of extreme cruelty which spread beyond specific acts of self-defense or revenge can be easily seen to express this divorce between the person's actions and underlying feelings.

Rather than exploring the various problematic aspects of this meaning of "madness," it will be useful to note that, like the others, it rests on demonstrable standards of reality and normality and makes no sense without them. Like the others, it may be arguable, but those who employ it as a normative concept would willingly shoulder this burden of argument.


## IV

I have so far been discussing "madness" as we usually use it—to describe individuals. In what ways, and with what qualifications, can it be applied to the social world? Certainly if we focus on a given ruler we can assess his mental state and describe his acts using the definitions just developed: Hitler's "Final Solution" was mad. To the extent that an individual decides policy, we might conclude that any and all analysis of individual behavior can be used. Was Hitler's perception deranged? His intention, or his affect? How are these reflected in Nazi policy?

But if we make no distinction between individual and social we would ignore the specifically *societal* character and determinants of the acts of even the most powerful dictator. Hitler matters not because he was an individual but as the one who managed to become absolute ruler of that specific society. He became absolute dictator in the most intimate relation with those specific social and historical conditions—his character expressing and focusing that situation, right down to and including his insanity. Moreover, his individual qualities themselves were produced in and through a specific history of a specific social class in a specific society. Above all, they became reflected in policy only as Hitler took power: insofar as he led the movement that became the dominant political force in Germany.

The point is that every step and layer of the madness that became the "Final Solution," even the most individual, was *social.* This suggests that the above meanings of "madness" cannot simply be grafted from individual to social process without prior reflection on their suitability. Hitler may have been mad in all the senses described above: our question turns on the madness of the social policy and collective behavior he directed.

This difference between the individual and the societal becomes clear as soon as we ask how political behavior can be mad in the third sense used above, as systematic and radical estrangement from self: derangement of affect. What is the "self" of a society from which it would become estranged in acting madly? Certainly it might be possible to describe a "sane society" or a "sick society" in terms of specific internal relations and standards of health. But such an exercise would require a totally new definition of categories rather than a translation of the individual into the social. Such a redefinition would mark the considerable difference, *pace* Plato, between character structure and social structure.[7]

Political behavior is not individual behavior writ large—the body politic is a rather different animal than the individual human being. The affective character that is inextricable from relations between individuals, for example, has a wholly different place, if any, in collective relations these individuals direct or participate in.

John F. Kennedy and Nikita Khrushchev confronted each other in the Cuban Missile Crisis of 1962 not as individuals but as leaders of nations. That the difference was decisive can be gathered from a reading of Robert Kennedy's memoir on the near-catastrophe.[8] It was a *political* conflict which, however it may have used or been reinforced by individual feelings, was conducted in political terms, according to a political logic, for political ends. Kennedy and Khrushchev acted not as private individuals might—concerned above all, for example, about their children—but as rulers of nations—concerned about power. For example, the political consequences of being seen to be backing down were central in Kennedy's calculations *because of* his self-conscious role as president of the country that saw itself as the most powerful in the world. As such, an abstraction as remarkably distant from the fate of the world's people—or of his own children—as "national interest" largely controlled Kennedy's behavior in the conflict. However we interpret this psychologically, we must clearly put its peculiar political character at the center of our interpretation.

Thus the example suggests that the third area of our definition of individual madness, estrangement from self, offers serious resistance to being applied to political behavior. But the other two meanings can be more readily applied. When its rulers organize a society against false enemies, when they believe and propagate the view that the society is being mortally threatened although it is not, when they organize to combat the threat—then we may speak of madness as surely as when an individual does the same. For systematic misperception is involved.

But how can we say that the *society* perceives or misperceives? Especially when a society is fragmented into warring classes or groups? Here the shift from individual to societal "madness" may complicate our efforts but not cancel them. In speaking of a ruler we may say, simply, that he sees what is not there and does not see what is there. Rulers' perceptions of themselves and their situation may be so deranged as to merit the term "madness."

In certain situations, however, this deranged perception is not theirs alone, but rather becomes *collective* madness. I would cite as an example, insofar as it has been believed, the Communist "threat" to the United States, or Soviet society's organization against Leon Trotsky's "threat" to the Bolshevik Revolution, or (taking a less controversial example) the Jewish "threat" to Germany. In each case—however different from each other—the character and extent of a societal derangement was so extreme as to at least arguably warrant the description of "madness." What makes it a matter of a specifically *societal* derangement is not only the obvious fact that it was shared by vast numbers of people, but that this sharing, beyond being an imposition by a powerful ruler or dominant class, had deep social roots. The "Final Solution" became policy as a response to what vast numbers crazily regarded as a real threat to their society. To be sure, along the road to Auschwitz there had to be manipulators and manipulated—those who, for reasons of power, consciously *used* paranoid anti-Semitism without sharing it, as well as those who acted according to it because they saw no alternative. But the manipulations of and obedience to authority were not the secret of the Nazi madness but only its inevitable corollary. Bullying and manipulation, submission and obedience may have a place in any social movement, but they never explain it.[9]

But isn't everything we have been saying served adequately by the term "ideology"? Nazism was an ideology—a class-centered vision of social reality which was offered, and accepted, beyond the German lower middle class because it made sense of the experience of vast numbers of people and gave them a program of action. As such it had to distort aspects of reality, just as it had to render aspects of it adequately. Nazism, anti-Communism, Stalinism—in speaking of madness am I not really describing ideologies which in these key respects are similar to all other ideologies?

Where I quarrel with such analysis is in emphasizing that some ideologies must be seen as mad. A central question, in spite of all relativism, is how far ideology corresponds to reality. At what point do we call it deranged? Granted, all ideologies distort in service of specific social classes; granted, also, that Marxism set itself up as the scientific critique of ideology but in power has become just another ideology. The original Marxist distinction between a more or less distorted and a more or less accurate vision of social reality is decisive. The psychological spectrum, stretching from (impossible) complete sanity to (impossible) complete madness, requires only slight alteration to become as relevant to the discussion of societies as of individuals. The rulers of any society may impose a more or less distorted vision of reality on all other social groups and classes, but at a certain point along the continuum ideological distortion can become so severe as to fundamentally lose touch with reality. The image of the Jew in Nazi ideology is an example. Quantity becomes quality: the degree of willful yet believed obfuscation is so great as to merit description as "madness." Even in class societies, then, ones governed by grotesque lies and absurdities, a point may be reached when the ruling vision crosses a line, the line of madness.

To explain Auschwitz means looking at those who *believed* that the Jews were menacing German society, and humanity, and were a threat that could only be eliminated by extermination. A "misperception" on this scale, as I have said, stems from an intention: the various stresses and traumas of their experience were shaped by the Nazis and their supporters into a deranged vision which placed the evil Jew at its center and called for action. The Nazis who so believed ruptured with the reality before them to create instead a fantasy-universe which "explained" their problems and directed them toward a "solution." That it was evil, that it was barbaric and ultimately self-destructive, did not deter (and perhaps attracted) those who chose it. It motivated and united them, gave them moments of victory and indeed mastery, successfully propelling them far from their original pain and stress. Since they were able to re-shape the world around them according to their mad vision, we might say that their madness "worked"—the mental rupture led to an actual physical rupture in which the menacing subhuman parasites were progressively deprived of human rights and human treatment, and then were exterminated.

## V

I have differentiated derangement of perception from that of intention, but the "Final Solution" certainly crosses the line. In perceiving, then treating, people as people-who-are-not-human, the Nazis clearly acted contrary to reality. Yet they *succeeded* whenever they exterminated a Jew, insofar as they did remake reality according to their mad fantasy. Nevertheless, testimony of survivors indicates that they failed, utterly. Not only did many of these people retain their sense of humanity while in the camps, as was demonstrated in acts of solidarity, compassion, cunning, and outright resistance, most dramatically in the successful destruction of Treblinka. But afterwards, even those who felt themselves nearly reduced to subhumans by the Nazis but survived *returned:* to reconstitute their sense of humanity, to testify, to remember, to remind us. Those who later demonstrated—or whose children demonstrated—

against wars they saw as inhumane testified to a resilience of human fellow-feeling and moral sense which will forever mock the Nazis' effort to redefine their reality as human beings. Indeed, the only way the Nazis were successful in remaking reality according to fantasy was by committing genocide.

I originally spoke of the madness of intention in relation to an individual trying to do the impossible. We are dealing with *action*, the category where analyses of individuals have the easiest societal application. As with the individual, so with social policy: trying to do what cannot be done is mad. I have emphasized that it must be clearly differentiated from trying to do what *common sense* says is impossible, for common sense always sets its boundaries in keeping with the prevailing social structures and their accompanying universe of discourse. But the criterion remains valid nevertheless: it is not madness to seek to transform society in keeping with its possibilities and tendencies, according to its demonstrable capacities. It was not madness to attempt to enslave another people when the differences of power and of culture were so great as to render this possible. It is madness to seek to realize a vision which has no basis in fact, actual tendencies, human relations, or human capacity.

And so we may judge the Nazi vision: the Reich sought to subjugate other "Aryans," to destroy the national identity of "non-Aryans" like Slavs or others judged "inferior," and to exterminate the "subhumans." Even if extermination could be carried out—and it was the most successful of all the Nazi policies—the rest of the vision could not. Indeed, even without the Normandy invasion, the Soviet Union alone eventually would have destroyed Nazi Germany.

It is not mad to attempt a brutal or benevolent social policy whose success is unlikely, nor to attempt an action in order to test its possibility. The madness, rather, lies in going against reality, willfully and obdurately, when it is quite clear that success is impossible. Great destruction is a likely corollary in such cases, because those bent on changing what is unchangeable easily seek to coerce it if they have the means. In *The Dialectics of Disaster* I have explored the dynamic whereby impotence, in power, can lead to genocide. Societal mass murder, in our century, has been rooted in ruptures with reality in which the project of transformation can only be achieved through violence. Human reality may be recalcitrant, even to those with political and military power, but human beings can be *forced:* threatened, beaten into submission, destroyed if they refuse. Violence is indeed the only way of reshaping what resists. Thus was "socialism" created by Stalin; thus was an "independent non-Communist South Vietnam" pursued by the United States after its unattainability became clear in late 1964. In each case reality was madly assaulted by those with power to do so, violently made over to resemble the guiding vision. In each case a grotesque mutant was created, and at frightful human cost.

## VI

I have tried to develop a working notion of "madness" as a rupture with reality and to indicate how it might be useful for understanding catastrophic events like the Holocaust. A number of unresolved questions remain, above all regarding the kinds of societal processes that can produce mad societal behavior. If a society is not an individual writ large, how does it become deranged to the point of producing the kinds of acts we have indicated? And how is this derangement different from the "normal" social conflicts and class struggles that make up so much of history?

In *The Dialectics of Disaster* I have explored the dynamics of uneven historical development within and between societies in search of an answer. For now, however, a more immediate question involves staying on the terrain of the concept and its application: how to employ the meanings of "madness" described above to clarify *current* political behavior? It may be possible to reflect fruitfully on the past, but can the understanding help us to clarify the far more volatile and difficult world in which we ourselves are immersed? Above all, I have in mind the impending nuclear holocaust. How are we to regard the casual intuition that the current process of nuclear escalation is mad?

Certainly the notion of radical misperception can be our starting point. Do the nuclear planners, we may ask, not see what is there and see what is not there? The question may be posed from two directions—one regarding their perception of the Soviet Union, its behavior and its intentions; the other concerning how they perceive danger and security vis-à-vis the spread of nuclear weapons. The point is not to fall into labeling a given policy "mad" just because it is unpalatable, but to use the notion rigorously as a significant evaluation. It is possible that social policies are mad; it is possible that *this* policy is mad. The task is to evaluate the policy of nuclear escalation to determine whether it is indeed a rupture with reality of the sort we have been describing.

Second, we may ask whether it displays a madness of intention: trying obdurately to achieve what is demonstrably impossible, assaulting reality in doing so. Here our terrain would be the supposed quest for security involved in increasing and diversifying nuclear arsenals: "peace through strength." Does this in fact only increase the general *insecurity?* Is this not self-evident to all but those who insist on building more weapons? Again, the point is not whether the policy is mistaken, but rather whether it systematically flouts what is possible and falsely redefines reality in doing so. To destroy a village "in order to save it," as was done during the Tet offensive in 1968 (and indeed describes much of American conduct during the war in Vietnam), is more than a violation of sense. It is a madness of intention, trying to do the impossible and then resorting to destruction.

We cannot yet talk about the nuclear planners actually destroying the world in order to achieve its security, because they have not done so *yet*. Still, we must not be mystified by the peculiar character of nuclear destruction: it is all prepared, waiting to happen, the missiles ready to be launched. If a mistake sets off the holocaust it will not only, or even primarily, be the fault of the mistaken machinery or persons, but of the entire process which lies waiting at this very moment. If the world's destruction depends on a computer error, we are justified in exploring whether the human process leading to this state of affairs was mad. In other words, *then* (and only then, alas, after the fact) will the intuition about the systematic rupture with reality be proven incontrovertibly true. The question now is, how do we regard the system that endangers us? How do we analyze this derangement of intention *now,* before the catastrophe? In short, the intention to achieve security by expanding nuclear arsenals can and must be evaluated *today,* before the holocaust.

Finally, I have left aside the question of estrangement of self as offering too many difficulties for societal analysis. Trying to assess the possible madness of nuclear war would force us to reconsider this. It may well be that the structure and governing logic of states are drastically different than the structure and governing logic of individuals, and that this makes it extremely difficult to diagnose a political rupture with normal human fellow-feeling. After all, states have quite "normally" engaged in wars, and virtually all have habituated their young men to fight and die and their people to support their killing. But adequately describing nuclear policy brings a new perspective to such questions.

Ultimately, the purpose of a society is to further the well-being of its people. I say "ultimately" understanding that most societies have been marked by class and other social struggles—because they have also been characterized by class and other social consensus. When the consensus has totally broken down—and the rulers decide to survive by permanently suppressing a major part of the population—the society is ripe for revolution. Most often a state apparatus has contradictory functions—it serves all of its people in some fashion even while guaranteeing the exploitation of some by others. The point is that even slaves must be fed and kept alive at a human level adequate to their functioning. The slave-owners who declare all-out war on their slaves are destroying *their own* conditions of survival. Mad? Our earlier reservations about the psychological origins of the concept no longer apply because we are dealing with a self-rupture which is far more basic. They would be made in a structural sense similar to the estrangement from self discussed earlier.

Similar, yet more profoundly so: actions which attack one's own survival itself are the most radical rupture with one's own reality.

Of course, to return to the individual level, suicide is not necessarily mad, even if it is the most extreme possible rupture with self. Great pain or suffering or a loss of all purpose can lead one to choose death over life, just as death in struggle may rationally be preferable to a life of subjection. The Warsaw Ghetto uprising, although suicidal, asserted for all time the dignity of the fighters and their refusal to die passively. It was a sane act. Their suicidal struggle was self-consciously seen as a *testimony:* it implied a world that would continue beyond this battle and even the Nazis, and it spoke to that world.

Are those who declare "better dead than Red" threatening the same courageous battle to the death? Not at all. First, nuclear policymakers are choosing not only their own death, but that of tens of millions of others. Certainly the Warsaw Ghetto fighters brought German retribution down upon the entire ghetto, but this happened in the process of the Nazi attack on the resistance. The primary targets of nuclear war are civilian population centers themselves, *because* they are population centers. Thus he who would save Americans from an alleged Communist victory would "save them" by having them killed. Moreover, the threat itself is an absurdity. The belief in the Communist or Soviet threat is one of those madnesses of perception which has operated, and continues to be revived, against all evidence, by those whose perception is systematically deranged. But above all, the nuclear planners are mad because nuclear war would destroy the world as we know it. Even assuming for a moment that their cause were real, the war they plan on its behalf would leave no one alive to struggle for a better social system than the one they would combat.

Are there no conditions under which it would make sense to risk destroying all human life for an end superior to life itself? Or is it mad to risk destroying all of life? We can find our direction in answering this by asking how we would respond if the Soviet Union were indeed Nazi Germany and threatened the rest of the world with nuclear weapons unless it surrendered. This is the deranged perception of some anti-Communists, notably the Committee on the Present Danger; let us suppose it were true. Even then, it would be mad to deprive tens of millions of people who had made no such decision, as well as virtually all of humankind, present and future, of the chance of struggling against and overthrowing such a monster. Yes, surrender under such conditions would not only be the best course, it would be the only *sane* course. Even the mass suicide at menaced Masada left Jewish communities intact *elsewhere:* otherwise no one would recall it today. It would then have had no meaning at all. Destroying the outside world as well as those locked in a struggle, however righteous, against an evil system would render their own struggle absurd. A continuing existence is a presupposition of every struggle, just as the continuing existence of an outside world is a presupposition of every individual suicide.

In short, omnicide—the destruction of everything—is mad in a way that individual or group suicide is not. It is mad without regard to its reason, mad because it attacks the basis of all life, all value, all meaning. To risk this—virtually unimaginable—total death is totally different than risking death amidst an abiding world. Today, "better dead than Red" points us toward the ultimate rupture with reality, the nuclear planners' flirtation with destroying the human adventure as such. Or rather, we must say that they have *already* decided to do so—under such and such determinate conditions.

I have willy-nilly begun characterizing nuclearism while still in the process of asking whether our categories could be useful in describing it. The reason lies in the nature of omnicide itself—it is unlike any evil humans have yet encountered in that it promises destruction without appeal, the world at an end. It alone threatens the premise of continuing human existence implied by other, more partial disasters, indeed, by suicide itself. Madness, in all forms, suggests a partial but significant and systematic rupture with reality. How, then, to characterize the preparation for total and ultimate rupture, the destruction of reality per se? We can understand the relevance of the category as we have done only by briefly exploring the situation itself.

The rigorous use of "madness" is deeply disturbing, of course, which is perhaps one reason why it has been so conspicuously avoided in a century so rife with madness. The functionalist bias of most systematic thought assumes that there is a reason for every societal act, a more or less rational intention behind political action. It offends the intellect to suggest that there is *no* reason behind a major policy—or that indeed its reason is profoundly and systematically irrational. "Madness" is even more unsettling in suggesting that we may be living admist a profound and destructive irrationality, one which lies beyond the traditionally understood irrationalities of history—those of mad individual leaders, for example, or of irrational class societies in a state of crisis. Moreover, our conventional political sense is deeply troubled by ascriptions of such madness: what political countermeasures will move the crazy leaders of mad societies? To describe a major social policy as "mad" and to suggest that it is rooted in fundamental societal dynamics is to rule out the hope of simple reforms improving the situation, of leaders seeing the light.

Above all, as if these implications were not disturbing enough, much of this essay, and the study where these reflections began, points to *our* society, today, in the United States and the West. If it can be seriously discussed whether the Vietnam War was mad, whether nuclear escalation is mad, then all of the above problems may apply to us, our social structures, our daily life. Not that they do not or have not applied else-where—in the Soviet Union, for example, or in the genocidal transfor-mation of Kampuchea—but we who study and think and act here have responsibility for understanding the situation we would influence. Did most Germans between 1933 and 1945 see the sickness of their society, or were some of them too deeply immersed to even question it, others deluded by false hopes? What assumptions did they share with those who ruled them, and with the genocidal policies they themselves carried out? Can the same question be asked, today, by ourselves, of our-selves? Can we afford to wait until the blinding flash to acknowledge that the nuclear planners are mad?

Such are some of the challenges of pursuing, rather than abandoning, a term like "mad" to describe events such as the "Final Solution." Daunting to the intellect, certainly, and to the will as well. But too much is at stake to ignore the challenge.

## NOTES

1. Ronald Aronson, *The Dialectics of Disaster* (London: Verso, 1983).

2. Hannah Arendt, *Eichmann in Jerusalem* (New York: Viking Press, 1965).

3. Richard Rubenstein, *The Cunning of History* (New York: Harper and Row, 1978).

4. Ibid., p. 2.

5. See Eberhard Jackel, *Hitler's Weltanschauung: A Blueprint for Power* (Middletown, Conn.: Wesleyan University Press, 1972).

6. See Jean-Paul Sartre's interview with Daniel Cohn-Bendit on the events of May 1968 in *The French Student Revolt*, trans. B. Brewster (New York: Hill and Wang, 1968).

7. See Plato, *The Republic*, trans. F. M. Cornford (Oxford: Clarendon Press, 1941).

8. Robert Kennedy, *Thirteen Days: A Memoir of the Cuban Missile Crisis* (New York: Macmillan, 1969).

9. This is Stanley Milgram's error in the famous experiments described in *Obedience to Authority* (New York: Harper and Row, 1973).

## PART II

## Understanding Occurrences of Genocide: Some Case Studies and Investigations of Related Social Processes

# WAS THE HOLOCAUST UNIQUE?: A PECULIAR QUESTION?

## *Alan Rosenberg*

The question of the "uniqueness" of the Holocaust has itself become a unique question.  However, when we approach the Holocaust we are at once confronted with the following dilemma:  if the Holocaust is the truly unique and unprecedented historical event that it is often held to be, then it must exceed the possibility of human comprehension, for it lies beyond the reach of our customary historical and sociological means of inquiry and understanding.  But if it is not a historically unique event, if it is simply one more incident in the long history of man's inhumanity to man, there is no special point in trying to understand it, no unique lesson to be learned.[1]  Of all the enigmas, paradoxes, and dilemmas facing Holocaust scholarship,[2] the "uniqueness question" is surely the most vexing and divisive, the one question most likely to evoke partisan debate and to generate emotional heat in discussion.[3]

In my own efforts at analysis of the issues underlying the "uniqueness question" I have been struck by the very oddity of the question itself, for it is strange that there should be argument about it at all.  What strikes me as peculiar about it is the fact that the legitimacy of the question as such is so taken for granted, that it is so readily assumed that the uniqueness of the Holocaust is not merely a fit subject for analysis but is a problem of the very first rank in importance.  The anomaly here is just that the "uniqueness question" itself is taken to be crucially relevant to an understanding of the Holocaust although it is relevant to few—if any—other landmark events of history.  One finds little discussion, for example, of the "uniqueness" of the Protestant Reformation or the Industrial Revolution.  The atomic destruction of Hiroshima and Nagasaki—surely qualified as "unique" and "unprecedented" in terms of their implications for the future of mankind—is simply not the subject of debate concerning its "uniqueness" involving controversy and serious divisions of opinion. While scholars often draw comparisons and mark the contrasts of the American and French revolutions, little time is spent in analysis or discussion of the "uniqueness question" with respect to either. If the "uniqueness" of such events as these, events that have radically altered our world, is not in question, why is it that the "uniqueness question" has assumed such prominence in the context of Holocaust studies? Why is the question itself so hotly contested? Why do some authorities on the history of the Holocaust go so far as to claim that the stance that one takes with respect to the "uniqueness question" determines the way in which one relates the Holocaust to the rest of human history, influencing every dimension of one's interpretation and evaluation of the event itself?

According to Saul Friedländer, for example, before we can begin analyzing any number of the central issues surrounding the Holocaust we must first deal with "a preliminary issue of crucial importance for every aspect of the Holocaust: are we dealing with a phenomenon comparable with some other historical event or are we facing something unique not only within any traditional and historical context, but even within Nazism itself?"[4] George Kren and Leon Rappoport call the "uniqueness question" very important, for, "depending upon how it is answered, the general orientation of interpretive analysis will obviously vary a great deal."[5] And again, insistence upon its historical uniqueness may, according to Yehuda Bauer, render the Holocaust irrelevant except as a specifically Jewish tragedy. Here is the thrust of Bauer's argument:

If what happens to the Jews is unique, then by definition it doesn't concern us, beyond our pity and commiseration for the victims. If the Holocaust is not a universal problem, then why should a public school system in Philadelphia, New York or Timbuktu teach it? Well, the answer is that there is no uniqueness, not even of a unique event. Anything that happens once, can happen again: not quite in the same way, perhaps, but in an equivalent form.[6]

In what follows I shall be addressing the problems and issues that are raised by texts like these, texts cited here simply as evidence that—for Holocaust studies—the "uniqueness question" is at once paramount and problematic.

It is clear, moreover, that the "uniqueness question" has become a matter of concern to the Jewish and Christian lay community as well as to the professional scholars in the field. One need only think of the public debate over the issues of the inclusion of the Holocaust in the social studies curriculum of the New York City school system or the U.S. Holocaust Memorial Council to see how sensitive the issue has become, especially within the Jewish community itself.[7] We may ask if this special sensitivity is not itself an impediment to more widespread dialogue, thus hampering the very cause of understanding which Jews support. For, as Professor Ismar Schorsch states, the Jews' "obsession" concerning the uniqueness claim "impedes genuine dialogue, because it introduces an extraneous, contentious issue that alienates potential allies from among other victims of organized human depravity. Similarly, our fixation on uniqueness has prevented us from reaching out by universalizing the lessons of the Holocaust."[8]

Considerations such as these clearly imply that, if we are to widen and deepen our understanding of the Holocaust, we must deal with the claim of "uniqueness" by developing a strategy that will free us from the conceptual muddles that presently cloud the issue. We must be clear as to the *meaning* of the claim itself if we are to escape the mystification that frequently has surrounded it.[9] We appear to have three principal options: (1) We can dismiss the whole question of "uniqueness," as Schorsch suggests that we should, simply on the grounds that it adds nothing of value to our understanding of the Holocaust. (2) We can attempt to account for why it is that the "uniqueness" claim has become integral to the discussion of the meaning of the Holocaust while it has been treated as merely peripheral to the analysis of other historical events of major consequence. (3) We can concentrate our analysis upon how the "uniqueness question" helps as well as hinders us in our quest to elucidate the meaning and significance of the Holocaust.

Though I am sympathetic with those who confine their strategy to the first option, I shall reject it as unrealistic. For, while it is true—as Schorsch points out—that the claim to uniqueness sometimes does pose a difficulty for those who would gain a better understanding of the Holocaust by comparing it with other cases of mass human destruction, it does not seem to me that we can duck the "uniqueness question" by simply disregarding it. The "uniqueness question" is much too central to the Holocaust to be ignored. Since, as I shall go on to show, an adequate strategy for dealing with the "uniqueness question" will *include* —rather than *preclude*—grounds for developing comparative historical analysis and evaluation, the second option is of decisive import, for it is always helpful to understand what lies behind any particular perspective on an event, and especially so when the range of perspectives on the event is so much a part of the event itself and gives rise to so much controversy. Although I shall be exercising the third option, since it builds upon the second—depending as it does upon clarification of the meaning of the claim of "uniqueness" with respect to the Holocaust—so it will be necessary for me to say something about this issue, though a full account of the matter lies beyond the scope of this chapter. In the end I shall try to show why "unpacking" the "uniqueness question" is the strategy that is most fruitful in understanding the Holocaust itself. However, although I shall be adopting this third option, let me first sketch some of the factors that have tended to make the "uniqueness question" itself a part of the problem in understanding the Holocaust. Before we can see how it can be treated as part of the "solution," so to speak, we must see why it has become "part of the problem."

It seems to be beyond question that the peculiar role that the "uniqueness question" has come to play in relation to the historical accounts and understanding of the Holocaust is largely due to the insistence of the Jewish community that the Holocaust *must* be viewed as unique.[10] It was a segment of the Jewish community, in fact, that devised and accepted the very label "Holocaust" in order to express the uniqueness of the event,[11] literally *defining* it as such by the name that they gave it.[12] The process by means of which a series of historical incidents becomes known as an "event" is well known, for it is only by gathering into meaningful clusters the apparently separate and unrelated facts of historical happenings that we are able to form coherent concepts of what has happened in the past. The naming of such a cluster is but one step in the process of self-understanding, and so it is easy to see why a segment of the Jewish community has come to view the naming of the Holocaust as an attempt to capture and preserve the uniqueness of meaning which is implicit in the facts so named. As those facts became known in the aftermath of World War II they immediately gave rise to a numbing horror in which the human mind seemed to be incapable of dealing with them, of grasping them in the normal fashion that we deal with the factual materials of history. The awful depth and scope of these "incidents," of these particular historical facts, were of such horrible dimensions as to seem completely incomprehensible. It is from this response that the claim to the "uniqueness" of the Holocaust is generated.[13] And it is in the context of this response that the search for those characteristics and traits that mark the Holocaust as unique must be understood. For it is precisely this search, and the various proposals which have issued from it, that is responsible for making the "uniqueness question" a part of the event which the "Holocaust" names: it has become part of the problem of the understanding and comprehension of what happened. The peculiar question of "uniqueness" may not have been an inevitable component of the problem, but it is clearly, at this point, an inescapable one.

Quite aside from the origins of the "uniqueness question" and its integration into the total problematic of the Holocaust, there are at least three other substantive problems concerning the characterization of the Holocaust as "unique." They can be readily stated, though not so readily solved. We must, first of all, be clear about what we mean when we claim an event to be unique. Secondly, we must be clear as to what element or elements of the event make it unique. And, lastly, we must at least try to be clear about the implications of the decision to classify the Holocaust as unique and try to understand how that decision may affect our interpretation of the event itself.

Existing Holocaust scholarship, surprisingly, is of little help in determining criteria for what constitutes "uniqueness" with respect to a historical event, whether it be the Holocaust or any other. And, should we consult ordinary language, we are helped even less. The *American College Dictionary* gives three possible definitions of "unique": (1) "of which there is but one"; (2) "having no like or equal"; and (3) "rare and unusual." In such terms, *every* event can be called unique, for *no* event of history is ever literally duplicated or "happens" twice, or is exactly "like" any other event, or its "equal." Moreover, it would seem to trivialize the importance of an event such as the Holocaust to call it simply "rare" or "unusual." In order to avoid such trivialization we must look at the actual use of the claim itself, we must analyze the intentions of those who have insisted upon the "uniqueness" of the Holocaust, and we must try to grasp the point of the claim. In this way, it seems to me, we can make sense of the question. For it is clear that what the claim of "uniqueness" is intended to do is to set apart from other historical events just that singular event that has the potential of transforming a culture, or altering the course of history, in some profound and decisive way. If the Industrial Revolution, for example, is said to be a "unique event" in the history of the West, it is because it is viewed in this transformational light; it changed our Western culture, altered its values, and so can be viewed as a cause of a major "turning point in history."[14] Such a way of defining the "uniqueness" claim corresponds closely to the definition offered by Emil Fackenheim, for his "epoch making event"[15] is just what is meant by terming an event as actually—or potentially—"transformational" of the *status quo ante,* as radically altering the course of history.[16] Given such a definition we can see how it is possible to claim that the Holocaust, as well as other events, such as the atomic bombing of Japan, can be classified as "unique."

And yet we must be cautious about such claims. I have used the words "see how it is possible to claim" since it must be emphasized that no historical event comes with its meaning already attached. As Walter Wurzburger has said:

Historic events possess only the kind of meaning which historians assign to them. Since there is no objective meaning inherent in any historic event that awaits discovery, meaning is not given but is created. The meaning of any particular event is not a function of its objective properties but hinges upon the choices of categories selected by a given subject for its interpretation. Hence, history teaches only the lessons that people choose to learn.[17]

For my own part, even Wurzburger's statement puts the matter too weakly and accounts for only a small portion of the process whereby meaning accrues to a historical event. For it is not merely the ascription of meaning by "historians" that counts, but the *construction of meaning*

by the culture that matters. It is by means of those processes that we
have come to understand, after Peter Berger and Thomas Luckmann, as
the "social construction of reality," that the past can become meaningful.[18] It is not the ascriptions of historians that make certain events
rather than others "transformational" events or "turning points" in history. It is only through the actions of the individual members of a culture and the consequences of those actions—both intentional and unin-
tentional—that any event becomes transformational of meanings and
values. Only through those practices which Anthony Giddens has called
acts of "structuration" can events of transformational *potential* become
*actual* transformations of culture.[19] And yet, while these are undoubted
features of the historical process of change and the acquisition of meaning, we find interpreters of the Holocaust seriously divided over the *preliminary* question of uniqueness—a question that must surely be
resolved if the event itself is to be transformational.

In the first instance, there are those who view the whole issue of
uniqueness as unimportant, for there is, as we have seen, a trivial sense
in which *all* historical events are unique.[20] They see the Holocaust as
unique only to the extent that every historical event is necessarily different from every other historical event; since "history never repeats
itself"—contrary to what has sometimes been popularly believed—it
follows that the "uniqueness" of the Holocaust is affirmed. But such an
affirmation is clearly a "trivialization" of the "uniqueness question."

There is yet a second group that falls within the camp of the "trivialists." They are quite willing to see the Holocaust as an event of major
importance, but they nevertheless agree that the claim of uniqueness
cannot be sustained in any non-trivial form. They argue that too much
has been made of what have been called the "exceptional" features of the
Holocaust. Without denying the existence of these features, this group
concentrates on showing that these features are just what might have
been expected to follow from the events leading up to the Holocaust as
such. In their view the Holocaust may simply be regarded as just one
more incident—albeit a flagrant one—of man's inhumanity to man, one
more horrible atrocity in a century filled with them. They cite such
precedents as the destruction of the Armenians by the Turks[21] and
pogroms in Poland and Russia, even reaching back to the genocidal
near-extermination of the American Indians for parallel cases. Some of
these critics grant that whatever uniqueness the Holocaust may possess
can only be seen within the context of Jewish history.[22] But some
Jewish intellectuals, Jacob Neusner[23] and Arnold Eisen[24] for example,
go so far as to hold that even within the context of Jewish history the
Holocaust cannot be viewed as unique. They contend that the Holocaust
should be understood as one event in a succession of events, one link in
a long chain of events aimed at the elimination of the Jews as a people
commencing with the destruction of the Second Temple in 70 C.E.

In sharp contrast, those that I have called "absolutists" are certain that
no other event in history even remotely resembles the Holocaust or
furnishes a precedent for understanding it. Its singularity is such that it
exceeds the power of language to express; its meaning is such that it
belongs to "another planet." It is incomprehensible, completely outside
the normal dimensions of our terrestrial history, beyond all historical
explanation and appraisal. It is, they say, not merely unique; it is, to use
the Eckhardts' phrase, "uniquely unique."[25]

Menachem Rosensaft sums up this view succinctly: "Holocaust
stands alone in time as an aberration within history."[26] And Elie Wiesel
writes that "the universe of concentration camps, by its design, lies
outside if not beyond history. Its vocabulary belongs to it alone."[27] In
Bauer's striking characterization, the Holocaust is viewed by these
writers as an "upside down miracle."[28] These absolutists see the Holocaust as unique simply because it happened, and concerning their view
nothing needs to be added.

Those reluctant to accept either the trivialist or the absolutist position
may be termed "relativists." Other turning points in history, other great
crises, they suggest, contain elements comparable to and related to the
Holocaust. Accordingly, they view it as "*relatively* unique," for there
will always be distinct features of the Holocaust that set it apart and
which remain of more importance than its similarities and resemblances
to other events. Approached from this angle the Holocaust is neither
"extra-historical," in the sense claimed by the absolutists, nor yet just
another atrocity, as the trivialists maintain. It is central to the relativist
thesis that the Holocaust must be viewed *contextually*. This means that it
is possible to view the Holocaust as unprecedented in many respects,
that it is an event of critical and transformational importance in the
history of our world, and yet it is still an event that must be addressed as
a *part of that history*. It can and should be compared to other genocidal
incidents, described and analyzed in language free from the "mystification" which only blocks our understanding, and made as accessible to
explanation as possible. It should not be assumed, on *a priori* grounds
of its absolute "uniqueness," that what *caused* the Holocaust is forever
beyond the reach of the tools of historical analysis, or that the consequences cannot be explored by means of social theory. For, if we fail in
our efforts at historical comprehension, and if our social theories are
inadequate to the task of *explaining* such events, we are almost sure to
experience similar catastrophes in the future. Indeed, if our conceptual
tools and analytical methods are baffled by the Holocaust, we must devise new concepts and new methods.

It would be misleading to claim that all those scholars that I have
categorized as relativists—possibly the term "contextualists" would be
more appropriate—speak with a single voice concerning the "uniqueness
question." Steven Katz[29] and Saul Friedländer,[30] for instance, take an

"intentionalist" approach. They hold the view that it is the "intention" of
the Nazis with respect to the *total elimination of Jewry* that marks the
Holocaust as unique among comparable pogroms and genocides.
Others, such as Richard Rubenstein[31] and Henry Friedlander,[32] take a
more "methodological" point of view. They see the uniqueness of the
Holocaust more in terms of the distinctive bureaucratic and technological
*methods* of destruction employed. These very sharply defined differences of focus on what accounts for the uniqueness of the Holocaust are
responsible for serious divergences of interpretation of the event itself.
For it is clear that both the intentionalists and the methodologists employ
their respective views of the "uniqueness question" as interpretive frame-
works for understanding the Holocaust itself. The preliminary question
of uniqueness helps to determine, by the way in which it is solved, the
conceptual apparatus for exploring the other problems of the Holocaust.

Some idea of how decisively this preliminary step figures in the eventual perspective upon the character of the event itself can be gained from
comparing the following texts. In "Whose Holocaust?" Yehuda Bauer
takes the intentionalist approach:

The uniqueness of the Holocaust does not . . . lie in numbers. It does not
lie in the method of mass murder. . . . What makes it unique is the existence of two elements: planned total annihilation of a national or ethnic group,
and the quasi-religious, apocalyptic ideology that motivated the murder.[33]

By contrast, here is Robert E. Willis representing the approach from the
methodology standpoint:

For whatever similarities are present between Auschwitz and other
cases—and there are many—the former is distinguished by being the first
instance of a situation in which the full bureaucratic and technical apparatus of
the state was mobilized for the primary purpose of extermination.[34]

With these very different approaches to the Holocaust locked into the
different interpretive grids through which the event itself is to be viewed
and interpreted, from the preliminary stage on, it is small wonder that the
eventual interpretations that are reached should themselves be widely
variant.

What concerns me here is not that we should accept any one approach
to the "uniqueness question" as *true*—and the others as *false*—but that
we should try to discover which of these approaches yields the most coherent and intelligible results, which framework elucidates the problems
of understanding the Holocaust most clearly and is the most promising
for understanding its historical and moral significance. It is not a simple
matter to decide, and the fact that there are subtle differences within each
of the two basic types of approach does not make the task any easier.
Some methodologists, for example, make it clear that they fully recog-

nize the important role which the intentionalists ascribe to the "uniqueness" of the Nazis' emphasis on "total extermination," while insisting
that the special bureaucratic and technological means employed in that
destruction are the more decisively unique feature of the event.[35]  Both
forms of relativist interpretation have great appeal owing to their common stress upon understanding the Holocaust in contextual terms, and
the great illumination that results from such analysis of the "uniqueness
question" leads to a preference for both over either the trivialist or absolutist stands.  And yet between them, I lean most to the methodologist
explanation as providing the framework that most clearly helps in com-
prehending both the uniqueness of the event and the event itself.  For it
is the emphasis upon *method* in the apparent "madness" of the event that
helps us most to grasp the significance of the event for our own lives and
for the world we live in.  After all, we *do* live in a depersonalized bureaucratic world, a world in which almost every facet of public and
private life is subject to the mindless influence of bureaucratic methods.

But it is not merely that the methodologists appear to shed more light
upon the relevance of the Holocaust to our own situation that leads to my
rejection of the intentionalist approach.  For there are internal problems
with the intentionalist position itself, problems of internal coherence, as
well as problems with the facts and assumptions upon which it is predicated.  In order to show the dimensions of some of these difficulties, I
have chosen to analyze them in the context of Yehuda Bauer's position,
for he is clearly the strongest exponent of the intentionalist view and the
most popular of its recent defenders.  It is not my purpose to refute
Bauer—for both "proof" and "refutation" are hardly apposite when we
are dealing with frames of reference such as these—but I do intend to
show how Bauer's insistence that it is the intention of the Nazi state—the
policy of *total* annihilation of the Jews—that determines the uniqueness
of the Holocaust can be more of a hindrance than a help in dealing with
the meaning of the Holocaust.

Bauer's argument is most forcefully presented in his important book,
*The Holocaust in Historical Perspective,* in which he devotes his second
chapter to an analysis of the various implications of the "uniqueness
question."  Titled "Against Mystification:  The Holocaust Phenomenon,"
this chapter puts the central dilemma of uniqueness this way:

If what happened to the Jews was unique, then it took place outside of history, it becomes a mysterious event, an upside down miracle, so to speak, an
event of religious significance in the sense that it is not man-made as that term
is normally understood.  On the other hand, if it is not unique at all, then what
are the parallels and precedents?[36]

Bauer wants to escape the dilemma by developing a conception of the
Holocaust that will account for its uniqueness by placing it *within* the

context of history.  He argues that the historical uniqueness of the Holocaust does not consist in the fact that it involves the practice of genocide, for he acknowledges that there are precedents and parallels where genocidal practices have been politically instituted.  He does, however, find that there is something unique and unprecedented in certain special features of the genocidal policies and practices of the Holocaust.  These features, he claims, show that what happened to the Jews is different from what befell other victims of mass murder, both within the Nazi "universe of death" and outside it.  For it is clear that Bauer wants to give full weight to the fact that mass murder as practiced by the Nazis—as well as by others—has not been confined to attempts specifically aimed at the elimination of the Jews as a people.  But he also wants to claim that there is something quite different about the Nazi policy with respect to the Jews.  Bauer argues that *only* the Jews were the victims of a deliberate policy of total extinction.

He acknowledges that some two and a half million Soviet prisoners of war were killed by Nazi practices and policy, by ill-treatment in the prison camps, malnutrition, and starvation.  He points out that "tens of thousands of Poles were brutally murdered as resistants, real or imagined."[37]  But he goes on to argue that the policies which sponsored these atrocities, while "genocidal" in character, were not aimed at the *total* extinction of either the Poles or the Soviets.  Bauer cites Raphael Lemkin, coiner of the term "genocide," in order to support his contention that "clearly, what was happening to quite a number of people in Nazi Europe was genocide."[38]  But he goes on to distinguish such general Nazi practices from the *intentions* embodied in the Holocaust:

The difference between that and the Holocaust lies in the difference between forcible, even murderous, denationalization, and wholesale total murder of every one of the members of a community.  Contrary to legend there never was a Nazi policy to apply measures used against the Jews to other national communities.[39]

In short, Bauer's contention is that the only group that the Nazis intended to *totally* annihilate was the Jews.  Accordingly, he concludes, the term "Holocaust" should only be used with reference to the extermination of the Jews so that its uniqueness does not become blurred and the Holocaust confused with other mass murders committed by the Nazis, murders to which the term "genocide" also applies.

It is this last contention that weakens Bauer's argument by introducing into it an element of conceptual confusion and incoherence.  When Raphael Lemkin first introduced the term "genocide" he intended that it should be used to denote only those instances of mass murder directed at the total extermination of a people, and not merely intended to bring about their "denationalization."  Lemkin states:

Denationalization was the word used in the past to describe the destruction of a national pattern. The author believes, however, that this word is inadequate because: (1) it does not connote the destruction of the biological structure; (2) in connoting the destruction of one national pattern, it does not connote the imposition of the national pattern of the oppressor; and (3) denationalization is used by some authors to mean only deprivation of citizenship.[40]

Bauer does not appear to recognize that Lemkin himself was fully satisfied that the Nazi policy of genocidal destruction *was* aimed at total annihilation, whether directed at the Jews or at the Czechs or the Poles. Lemkin specifically stated that "genocide is directed against the national group as an entity, and the actions involved are directed against individuals, not in their individual capacity, but as members of a national group."[41] Genocide is instituted, Lemkin argued, as "a coordinated plan of different actions aiming at the destruction of essential foundations of the life of national groups, with the aim of annihilating the groups themselves."[42]

The incoherence of Bauer's use of the term "genocide" as applicable to the policies aimed at less than total annihilation is made even more perplexing when it is recalled that, in an earlier work, he employed the term—as Lemkin did—to denote the intended total destruction of a people. There he stated: "The Holocaust was a crime of genocide—that is, an attempt to exterminate all members of a particular national or racial group simply because they were members of that group."[43] It is clear that in this statement the "Holocaust" and "genocide" are not seen as denoting two different types of event. One can, of course, argue, as Bauer does, that the Holocaust was a unique event, distinguishable from other events of Nazi mass murder. One might even be able to argue that the Nazi *intention* was different in kind, with respect to the Jews, from what it was with respect to other national groups. But one cannot, as Bauer has done, cite Lemkin as sponsoring authority for such arguments. For it is undeniable that Lemkin views what happened to the Gentile populations that fell victim to Nazi genocide as more, rather than less, like what happened to the Jews. Lemkin sees the Nazi intent in all such cases as the same, i.e., total destruction.

On the factual side, Bauer's argument is similarly weak. He argues, for example, that the Nazis' intention with respect to the Gypsies and other groups was very different from that toward the Jews. Although debate over this matter cannot be entered into here, there is substantial evidence to indicate that the Nazis did indeed intend the total elimination of the Gypsy population. As Bauer himself had earlier acknowledged: "History records other actions which qualify as genocide by the strictest definition. Hitler himself sought to annihilate the Gypsies as well as the Jews."[44]

Assuming that my criticism has cast doubt upon the adequacy of

Bauer's thesis as to the "uniqueness question" and shows that there are serious difficulties to be overcome in the intentionalist position, we now have to ask about the alternative methodological view. Is it, perhaps, a more adequate perspective in terms of which to approach the "uniqueness question," and from which to proceed to the substantive interpretation and understanding of the Holocaust itself? Can it be said, for example, that the Holocaust is a *unique form of genocide*—using that term, indeed, as Lemkin originally defined and used it? As we have seen, Lemkin treated genocide as the intentional attempt to destroy a group in its ethnic and biological totality. With that definition in mind are there discernable features of the Holocaust that distinguish it from other such genocidal events?

I believe that these questions can be answered affirmatively. Although I cannot deal with the evidence here in detail,[45] I can suggest at least *four kinds of evidence* that can be offered as showing how and why the Holocaust should be understood as a unique genocidal event, genuinely unprecedented in the annals of our world and its history. First, there is evidence of uniqueness in the simple fact of the size and scope of the destruction, in the enormity of the numbers alone, which are of an entirely new order of magnitude when compared with other genocides. Second, there is the far more complex fact of the means employed in the Holocaust, for no other genocidal event has so deeply involved the entire structure of the legal and administrative machinery of a government in its implementation. There are simply no similar instances of a legally constituted government adopting anything like the extensive bureaucratic and technological apparatus that was created to carry out the genocidal intention of the Holocaust. Third, the Holocaust is unique in the varied physical and psychological qualities used to reduce the intended victims to their barest physical qualities as "objects" in order that they might be more efficiently processed in the mechanical production line of the death camps. And, finally, the Holocaust is unique in the vast and determined attempt by the Nazis to transform the victims into the image that the Nazis had of them. The scope of this massive effort at creating an "image" of the intended victims of genocide is such that it vastly exceeds similar efforts; its scale is literally unprecedented.

It will be evident, then, that I am among those who believe that it is the various processes, techniques, and methods of destruction characteristic of the Holocaust that justify the ascription of "uniqueness" to it. And it is because of these same features of the Holocaust, features that help us to understand not merely why the Holocaust is unique but also features that help us to understand how it was possible that such an event could occur in our history and in the context of our age, that I reject the absolutist view. That view, I believe, tends to render the Holocaust incomprehensible by putting the event outside of our history, by treating it as outside the context of our age, our language, and our capacity for analysis and understanding.[46] This rejection of the Holocaust as something that *could* occur in our time, and which could clearly occur again for much the same political and sociological reasons, seems to me simply unacceptable. It virtually amounts to the denial that it *did* occur, a denial that seems to me almost an invitation for it to happen again. For if we are to avoid such an event in the future we must surely attempt to grasp its meaning in political and sociological terms. If the Holocaust seems somehow to be beyond the grasp of our usual categories of political and sociological analysis, to be beyond the reach of our normal concepts of historical interpretation and explanation, the lesson is *not* that we should give up the attempt at analysis and explanation. The lesson is that we must develop *more adequate categories and concepts.*

Finally, it is for this last reason that I reject all forms of trivialism with respect to the "uniqueness question." By drawing attention away from just those novel features of the Holocaust process that *are* unprecedented, by trivializing them, the trivialists divert our attention from the very features of the Holocaust that we ought to be trying to understand and explain, features that we must be able to cope with if we are to avoid such events in the future. By taking the view that the Holocaust is just one more atrocity, we are unlikely to see its deep and unique significance as an event with potential transformational consequences for our culture and our age. We are unlikely to see the possible implications of the Nazi abuse of science and technology, the application of bureaucratic techniques, principles of managerial efficiency and "cost-benefit" analysis, and all such unique features of the Holocaust process for our own situation, our own lives. For there *are* analogies to be drawn between our own situation and that of the victims of the Holocaust, analogies that depend upon understanding as clearly as possible how such things as science and technology, bureaucracy and managerial "efficiency" were employed in the destruction of the Jews and how they might well be employed for our own destruction somewhere down the road. Moreover, as I have emphasized, we cannot accept the simple situation of the Jews and the special "intention" of the Nazis with respect to their total extinction. Not only does this emphasis on the particularity of the Jewish situation tend to obscure relevant analogies with the predicaments of other groups—possibly even with our own situation as hostages to the threat of nuclear war—but it also obscures the more universal implications for the future of *all* mankind that the Holocaust raises. For, as even Bauer himself once asked, if the Holocaust has no universal lesson for all men, why should anyone study it?[47] In the end it is those who emphasize the uniqueness of the methods, processes, and techniques of the Holocaust that best enable us to draw the analogies and explicate the event itself. In the end it is possible that by understanding those methods, techniques, and processes by means of which an oppressed population can be destroyed we can avoid such destruction in the future.

If we can succeed in this purpose, the Holocaust will truly have been a transformational event.


## NOTES

1. For different formulations of this problem, see Emil Fackenheim, *To Mend the World: Foundations of Future Jewish Thought* (New York: Schocken Books, 1982), p. 20; Henry L. Feingold, "How Unique Is the Holocaust?," in *Critical Issues of the Holocaust,* ed. Alex Grobman and Daniel Landes (Los Angeles: Simon Wiesenthal Center and Rossel Books, 1983), p. 397; and Robert McAfee Brown, "The Holocaust as a Problem in Moral Choice," in *When God and Man Failed: Non-Jewish Views of the Holocaust,* ed. Harry James Cargas (New York: Macmillan Publishing Co., Inc., 1981), p. 99.

2. For a more detailed analysis of the enigmas and paradoxes facing Holocaust scholarship, see Alan Rosenberg, "The Problematic Character of Understanding the Holocaust," *European Judaism* (forthcoming); and Alan Rosenberg, "The Crisis in Knowing and Understanding the Holocaust," in *The Holocaust: Its Philosophical Impact,* ed. Alan Rosenberg and Gerald Myers (Philadelphia: Temple University Press, forthcoming).

3. See Pierre Papazian, "A 'Unique Uniqueness'?," and the symposium it generated, "Was the Holocaust Unique?: Responses to Pierre Papazian," *Midstream* 30, no. 4 (April 1984), pp. 14-25.

4. Saul Friedländer, "On the Possibility of the Holocaust: An Approach to a Historical Synthesis," in *The Holocaust as Historical Experience,* ed. Yehuda Bauer and Nathan Rotenstreich (New York: Holmes and Meier, 1981), p. 1.

5. George Kren and Leon Rappoport, "Failure of Thought in Holocaust Interpretation," in *Towards the Holocaust: The Social and Economic Collapse of the Weimar Republic,* ed. Michael N. Dobkowski and Isidor Wallimann (Westport, Conn.: Greenwood Press, 1983), p. 380.

6. Yehuda Bauer, "Right and Wrong Teaching of the Holocaust," in *The International Conference on Lessons of the Holocaust,* ed. Josephine Z. Knopp (Philadelphia: National Institute on the Holocaust, 1979), p. 5.

7. See Ismar Schorsch, "The Holocaust and Jewish Survival," *Midstream* 17, no. 1 (January 1981), p. 39; and Paula E. Hyman, "New Debates on the Holocaust," *The New York Times Magazine* (September 14, 1980), pp. 80-82.

8. Schorsch, "The Holocaust and Jewish Survival," p. 39.

9. For the significances of the issue, see Henry Friedlander, "Toward a Methodology of Teaching about the Holocaust," *Teacher's College Record* 80, no. 3 (February 1979), pp. 524-25; and Rosenberg, "The Crisis in Knowing and Understanding the Holocaust."

10. Schorsch, "The Holocaust and Jewish Survival," p. 39.

11. Lucy S. Dawidowicz states, "The Holocaust is the term that Jews themselves have chosen to describe their fate during World War II." *The War Against the Jews: 1933-1945* (New York: Holt, Rinehart and Winston, 1975), p. xv.

12. For a brilliant historical analysis of how the term "Holocaust" became the name for what happened to the Jews under Hitler, see Gerd Korman, "The Holocaust in American Historical Writing," *Societas* 2, no. 3 (Summer 1972), pp. 259-62.

13. Rosenberg, "The Problematic Character of Understanding the Holocaust."

14. On the question of transformational events, see George M. Kren and Leon Rappoport, *The Holocaust and the Crisis of Human Behavior* (New York: Holmes and Meier, 1980), pp. 12-15; and Alan Rosenberg and Alexander Bardosh's critique of the same in *Modern Judaism* 1, no. 3 (December 1981), pp. 337-46.

15. Emil Fackenheim, *The Jewish Return into History* (New York: Schocken Books, 1978), p. 279.

16. For an analysis of what has been radically altered in history by the Holocaust, see Kren and Rappoport, *The Holocaust and the Crisis of Human Behavior,* pp. 131-43; and Alan Rosenberg, "The Philosophical Implications of the Holocaust," in *Perspectives on the Holocaust,* ed. Randolph L. Braham (Boston: Kluever-Nijhoff Publishers, 1983), pp. 8-16.

17. Walter S. Wurzburger, "The Holocaust Meaning or Impact," *Shoah* 2, no. 1 (Spring-Summer 1980), p. 15.

18. Peter L. Berger and Thomas Luckmann, *The Social Construction of Reality: A Treatise in the Sociology of Knowledge* (New York: Doubleday and Company, Inc., 1967).

19. Anthony Giddens, *Central Problems in Social Theory: Action, Structure and Contradiction in Social Analysis* (Berkeley and Los Angeles: University of California Press, 1979).

20. For an incisive analysis of the problem, see Carey B. Joynt and Nicholas Rescher, "The Problem of Uniqueness in History," in *Studies in the Philosophy of History,* ed. George H. Nadel (New York: Harper and Row, 1965), pp. 3-15, and Alice L. Eckhardt and A. Roy Eckhardt, "The Holocaust and the Enigma of Uniqueness: A Philosophical Effort at Practical Clarification," *The Annals of the American Academy of Political and Social Science* 450 (July 1980), pp. 166-67.

21. See Papazian, "A 'Unique Uniqueness'?," p. 14.

22. Ibid.

23. Jacob Neusner, *Stranger at Home: "The Holocaust," Zionism and American Judaism* (Chicago: University of Chicago Press, 1981), pp. 6-8.

24. Eisen's remarks appear in "The Meaning and Demeaning of the Holocaust: A Symposium," ed. Hillel Levine, *Moment* 6, no. 3-4 (March/April 1981), p. 3.

25. Eckhardt and Eckhardt, "The Holocaust and the Enigma of Uniqueness," pp. 167-69.

26. Menachem Rosensaft, "The Holocaust: History as Aberration," *Midstream* 28, no. 5 (May 1977), p. 55.

27. Elie Wiesel, "Now We Know," in *Genocide in Paraguay,* ed. Richard Arens (Philadelphia: Temple University Press, 1976), p. 165.

28. Yehuda Bauer, *The Holocaust in Historical Perspective* (Seattle: University of Washington Press, 1978), p. 31.

29. Steven T. Katz, "The 'Unique' Intentionality of the Holocaust," *Modern Judaism* 1, no. 2 (September 1981), pp. 161-83.

30. Saul Friedländer, "On the Possibility of the Holocaust," pp. 1-6.

31. Richard Rubenstein, *The Cunning of History* (New York: Harper and Row, 1975), pp. 6-7, 22-35.

32. Henry Friedlander, "Toward a Methodology of Teaching About the Holocaust," pp. 530-31.

33. Yehuda Bauer, "Whose Holocaust?," *Midstream* 26, no. 9 (November 1980), p. 45.

34. Robert E. Willis, "Confessing God after Auschwitz: A Challenge for Christianity," *Cross Currents* 28, no. 3 (Fall 1978), p. 272.

35. See Leo Kuper, *Genocide* (New Haven: Yale University Press, 1981), pp. 120-22, 135.

36. Bauer, *The Holocaust in Historical Perspective,* p. 31. For a more complete assessment of Bauer's book, see Mark Rosenblum and Alan Rosenberg, "Holocaust Scholarship: Breaking New Ground,"*Cross Currents* 29, no. 3 (Fall 1979), pp. 344-49.

37. Bauer, *The Holocaust in Historical Perspective,* p. 33.

38. Ibid., p. 35.

39. Ibid.

40. Raphael Lemkin, *Axis Rule in Occupied Europe* (Washington, D.C.: Carnegie Endowment for International Peace, 1944), pp. 79-80.

41. Ibid., p. 79.

42. Ibid. In a paper published some two years after *The Holocaust in Historical Perspective,* Bauer attempted to respond to this criticism. He argued that Lemkin's "definition" of genocide "contains a contradiction," for if it is total annihilation that is intended it makes "no sense" for Lemkin to talk about such methods as "interfering with the activities of the Church," or the "debasement" of morality through dissemination of pornography and the encouragement of alcoholic consumption. The fact of the matter is that Lemkin mentions such factors as these as constituent elements of planned total destruction because he recognized that such planning "does not necessarily mean the *immediate* destruction of a nation." (Emphasis added.) By failing to acknowledge Lemkin's carefully drawn distinctions in the body of his text, and by limiting himself merely to the outline of Lemkin's thesis in the preface to the book, Bauer once again distorts Lemkin's position. (See Bauer, "Whose Holocaust?," p. 43-44, and Lemkin, *Axis Rule in Occupied Europe,*

pp. 79-82.) It is clear that the elements that "make no sense" to Bauer in Lemkin's description of genocidal techniques are all part of the "coordinate plan" to weaken "the essential foundations" of various groups with the *long-run* "aim of annihilating the groups themselves."

43. Yehuda Bauer, *They Chose Life: Jewish Resistance in the Holocaust* (New York: The American Jewish Committee, 1973), p. 11.

44. Ibid., pp. 11-12. See also Donald Kenrick and Grattan Puxon, *The Destiny of European Gypsies* (New York: Basic Books, Inc., 1972), pp. 76-100, and Leon Poliakov, *Harvest of Hate: The Nazi Program for the Destruction of the Jews of Europe* (New York: Holocaust Library, 1979), pp. 263-80. Bauer also claims in *The Holocaust and Historical Perspective* "that the Holocaust is unique in intent when compared with the Armenian Massacres" (pp. 36-37). For a refutation of this position, see Papazian, "A 'Unique Uniqueness'?," pp. 14-18; and for Bauer's response, see "Was the Holocaust Unique?: Responses to Pierre Papazian," pp. 19-20.

45. For more extensive analysis, see Alan Rosenberg, "The Genocidal Universe," *European Judaism* 13, no. 1 (Autumn 1979), pp. 29-34, reprinted in *Genocide and Human Rights,* ed. Jack Nusan Porter (Washington, D.C.: University Press of America, 1982), pp. 46-58.

46. For an excellent analysis of the problem of incomprehensibility, see Dan Magurshak, "The Incomprehensibility of the Holocaust: Tightening Up Some Loose Usage," *Judaism* 29, no. 2 (Spring 1980), pp. 233-42, and Papazian, "A 'Unique Uniqueness'?," p. 18.

47. See note 6.

# 9

# THE HOLOCAUST AND HISTORICAL EXPLANATION

## *Robert G.L. Waite*

I

Those who reflect on the nature of the Holocaust will confront the question of its uniqueness. Was the Holocaust the culmination of over 2,000 years of active anti-Semitism and persecution, or was it unique, forming a radical break from the past?

Both sides of this ancient historical debate, continuity versus change, are important. Certainly there is much continuity with the past. Indeed, the Holocaust was made possible, in large part, because German history had shown a continuum of virulent anti-Semitism. It is of course true that anti-Semitism existed in every country of the Western and Slavic worlds. But in no country in the world did so many influential leaders over so long a time champion so vicious a hatred of the Jewish people.

Martin Luther, for example, preached hatred and persecution of the Jews 400 years before Hitler. As early as 1543 Luther demanded that Jewish synagogues and schools be set afire, that their silver and gold be taken from them, their houses and prayer books seized and destroyed, that brimstone and pitch should be thrown upon them, and that they be driven away "like mad dogs"[1]—a program which Adolf Hitler would put into practice on a national scale beginning with the infamous *Reichskristallnacht* of November 9-10, 1938, a date which, by a quirk of chronology, fell on Luther's birthday.

For centuries Catholic bishops and priests joined Lutheran pastors in thundering against an imaginary "Jewish menace." Indeed, the anti-Semitic record of both Christian confessions is one of the most appalling chapters in the entire history of religion. Published statements made by saints of the Catholic Church were later used as texts for scurrilous anti-Semitic broadsides. Saint Gregory of Nyssa (d. 396) described Jews as "slayers of the Lord, murderers of the prophets, haters of God, advocates of the devil, a brood of vipers." St. Ambrose, Augustine's teacher, said that Jewish synagogues should be burned to the ground and boasted that he personally had set fire to one. St. John Chrysostom (d. 406) called Jews "lustful, rapacious, greedy, perfidious bandits." He preached that "it is the duty of Christians to hate the Jews" and concluded that the Jews are "fit for slaughter."[2] Saint Thomas Aquinas, the most influential theologian in the history of the Catholic Church, argued that it was morally justifiable for Jews to serve Christians as slaves because, as the slayers of God, they were bound to "perpetual servitude."[3]

The Church practiced what its Fathers preached. Official Church councils set forth decrees which clearly foreshadowed Hitler's infamous Racial Laws. The Synod of Elvira of 306, for example, forbad intermarriage and sexual relations between Christians and Jews. The Synod of Claremont (535) decreed that Jews could not hold public office. The Third Synod of Orleans of 538 made it illegal for Jews to walk in public streets during Passion Week. The Fourth Lateran Council of 1215 decreed that Jews must mark their clothing with a special badge. The Council of Oxford (1222) forbad the construction of new synagogues. The Council of Basel of 1434 prohibited Jews from obtaining academic degrees.[4]

One day in April 1933 when Catholic bishops protested to Hitler that his government was mistreating Jews, Hitler replied that he was "only putting into effect what Christianity had preached and practiced for 2000 years."[5] He had a point.

The historian Uriel Tal is therefore probably justified in concluding that the Christian church bears heavy responsibility for the virulent anti-Semitism of the Third Reich.[6] German Christians agree. In January 1980, the Synod of the German Evangelical Church of the Rhineland, the most populous of the twenty-seven regional units of the EKD, passed overwhelmingly the official declaration, *Zur Erneurung des Verhältnisses von Christen und Juden* (For the Renewal of Relations between Christians and Jews). The first sentence of this historic declaration reads: "Stricken, we confess the co-responsibility and guilt of German Christendom for the Holocaust."[7]

Religious anti-Semitism, it bears repeating, had shown great continuity in Germany. But it was only in the Second Reich—Imperial Germany after 1871—that religious persecution gave way to a *racial* anti-Semitism which explicitly anticipated the Third Reich.

When Adolf Hitler was still a babe in his doting mother's arms, Germany's most influential thinkers were inciting racial anti-Semitism with slogans which Hitler would later take over as his own. In the 1890s, for example, the prodigious scholar Paul de Lagarde (whom

Thomas Mann hailed as "one of the giants of our people")[8] coined portentous metaphors: "Jews are decayed parasites . . . usurious vermin" and warned that "with bacilli one does not negotiate: one exterminates them as quickly as possible."[9] The long list of racial anti-Semites includes Germany's most popular historian, Heinrich von Treitschke, a best-selling novelist, Gustav Freytag, and probably the most influential Jew-baiter of them all, Richard Wagner.[10]

Hitler exploited this legacy of hatred. But while showing continuity with the past, Nazi anti-Semitism was different from its predecessors. Here was not merely prejudice, persecution, and invective. Here, for the first time, was a calculated program of mass murder set forth by the legal government of Germany—a government unique in all history.

This was no mere "authoritarian state" of which we have so many and varied examples in world history. This was a government conceived in oppression and dedicated to the proposition that all men are created unequal. This was social and moral cannibalism. This was the very "negation of God erected into a system of government."

This government promised that Jews would be traduced, persecuted, vilified, destroyed. Such was the promise and such was the practice. The horror of Hitler was this: he was no hypocrite; he meant what he said; he practiced what he preached; he kept his promises. Indeed, as Elie Wiesel has noted with bitter irony, "Hitler is the only one who kept his promises to the Jewish people."[11]

Hitler's policy of genocide was not designed to remove subversives who were a threat to the German state. Quite to the contrary, German Jews through the centuries had proven their devotion to the Fatherland by supporting its government and fighting gallantly in its wars. Their loyalty was shown even after Hitler came to power in 1933. One example: the *Reichsbund jüdischer Frontsoldaten* (National Association of Jewish War Veterans) hailed the advent of Hitler in 1933 and publicly promised support of his government.[12] (They soon changed their minds.)

Nor were the Nazi executions designed to punish criminals and malefactors. The Jews were killed not because they had *done* anything but merely because they existed—because they had been born. Jews were criminals *by definition*. In occupied Russia, for example, the Nazi conquerors decreed death for the following crimes: (1) sabotage, theft, espionage, and (2) also for "*Judenverdacht*"—those suspected of *being Jewish*.[13]

The Nazi Holocaust was also different in the extent of the cooperation it received from the German social infrastructure. The Holocaust enjoyed the support or the benevolent neutrality of Christian churches, the civil service, the judiciary, educators, and thousands of the railroad officials who handled the complex logistics of transporting millions of people to their death. Army generals—the evidence is now incontrovertible—also knew of the mass murders and gave their approval.[14] Thus this genocide succeeded because its perpetrators could count on the cooperation or acquiescence of German state officials, of religious, civic, and military leaders, and of the German public at large. Recent studies have shown that the German people really did know about the genocide and reacted with "a mixture of private sympathy and public passivity."[15] A German historian of public attitudes toward Jews during the Third Reich has concluded that there was "scarcely another country whose population accepted the carrying away of its Jewish fellow citizens with so little opposition."[16]

There is another reason why the Holocaust could take place: the victims cooperated with their executioners; they collaborated in their own destruction. I find this to be one of the most disturbing and least understood problems of the Holocaust. But here we must sound a clear note of warning about the use of the words "cooperative" and "collaboration." If they suggest a voluntary desire to be helpful, the words are badly misused. As Lucy Dawidowicz has emphasized in her valuable studies, there was no voluntary Jewish cooperation; there were no Jewish collaborators in the sense of the word made infamous by Quisling and Laval. Not one Jew wanted to cooperate with the Nazis. No Jew wanted Hitler's "New Order" in Europe.[17] The *Judenräte* (the Jewish Councils approved by the Nazis and elected by the Jews themselves) cooperated with the SS by selecting Jews for transport to their deaths, but they did so only under the most extreme duress. When the Nazis threatened more drastic enlargement of the death quotas they were obliged to fill, the councils had little choice but to obey. Constantly they confronted soul-destroying decisions: choose for extinction either the young or the old. The *Judenräte* —it must be repeated—had virtually no choice. They tried desperately to do the very best they could under impossible circumstances. They were *coerced* into compliance. That much needs to be said and remembered. And yet the hard conclusion reached by eminent Jewish authorities on the Holocaust must be squarely faced and carefully pondered: however compelling the reasons, however extreme the duress, the fact is that Jews actually did become tragic accomplices in their own extinction. Raul Hilberg, Hannah Arendt, and Isaiah Trunk have demonstrated beyond dispute that leaders of the Jewish communities in Berlin, as in Amsterdam, Antwerp, and Warsaw, cooperated with the Nazis and smoothed the way to deportation and death. It is true that there were notable exceptions among the Jewish Councils, but the predominant pattern is clear. Most of the *Judenräte* implemented SS directives, published benign Nazi cover stories, denied warnings given by the Jewish underground, selected those who were to die, arranged their transportation, and collected money to pay their transportation to the death camps—thereby helping the Nazis achieve their goal of making the Final Solution "self-financing." The Councils generally opposed sabotage and active resistance and ordered compliance with Nazi directives.[18] Most Jews followed the orders of their leaders, and many displayed what Hilberg has called "anticipatory compliance": in pathetically futile efforts to pacify the Nazis, they sedulously collected and turned in their jewels and gold and arrived well ahead of time at the designated staging areas, having paid their railway fare in advance. "They attempted to tame the Germans," Hilberg writes, "as one would attempt to tame a wild beast. They avoided 'provocation' and complied instantly with decrees and orders."[19]

The Nazis were surprised and pleased by the passivity and cooperation they received from their victims. It made their job much easier. Adolf Eichmann, the SS official chiefly in charge of the mass murders, testified during his trial in Jerusalem that the Jewish Councils were so effective in implementing SS orders that German personnel could be released for other service.[20] Hannah Arendt concludes bitterly that without Jewish help, the murder of millions of Jews would not have been possible: "To a Jew, this role of the Jewish leaders in the destruction of their own people is . . . the darkest chapter of the whole dark story."[21]

An even darker role was played by the Jewish Police of the ghettos, an agency which the Nazis created with Satanic cunning to implement their orders and to shatter and demoralize the Jewish community by setting it against itself. After the war, Jewish "Courts of Honor" established that the Jewish Police actively participated in the destruction of their fellow Jews. They ferreted them out of their hiding places, arrested them in the middle of the night, beat them up in the streets, and filled their own pockets with bribes from their victims. A Jew who was to pay with his life for their vicious treachery angrily recorded in his diary: "Every Warsaw Jew, every woman and child, can cite thousands of cases of the inhuman cruelty and violence of the Jewish Police. Those cases will never be forgotten by the survivors, and they must and shall be paid for."[22]

Later we must consider some of the explanations which Jewish writers have given for the extent of Jewish cooperation with their executioners. But first something else must be said. For it is true, as Reuben Ainsztein has shown in his massive book on Jewish resistance to the Nazis, that many, many heroic Jews fought back at hopeless odds. Their gallant resistance was most tragically demonstrated in the uprisings against their oppressors in the Warsaw ghetto during the spring of 1943 —was it not the *only* urban uprising against the Nazis in Europe?—and in the death camp of Sobibor in October 1943.[23]

And yet it must be recorded that the overwhelming majority of the Jews of Europe, by the hundreds and hundreds of thousands, did indeed go, as furious Jewish activists charged at the time, "like sheep to the slaughter." Shortly before he and his family were killed, one of the heroes of the Warsaw ghetto noted "the passivity of the Jewish masses" and asked some anguished questions: "Why are they all so quiet? Why does the father die, and the mother, and each of the children without a single protest? . . . Why did everything come so easy to the enemy? . . . This will be an eternal mystery—this passivity of the Jewish populace even toward their own police."[24]

These questions of Emmanuel Ringelblum and the mystery he could not solve will continue to haunt historians of the Holocaust.

The Holocaust differed from other genocides in other ways as well. For the first time in history, a cultivated and articulate people, confronted by unimaginable suffering and death, left records of immense value to survivors who seek to understand what happened. Philip Friedman has called the details of these harrowing experiences "test tubes . . . in a vast psycho-sociological laboratory such as had never been set up before."[25] These records do indeed provide insight into the ways in which the human psyche reacts to stress. They also cast new light into the human soul, probing not only the depth of wickedness and evil, but also—in the memoirs of Anna Frank, Emmanuel Ringelblum, Viktor Frankl, Chaim Kaplan,[26] and thousands of others—the light that human courage, faith, and goodness can shed in the darkest pits of hell.

In short, these precious records display the human capacity both for evil and for good. There is a *political* as well as a moral and a psychological lesson here, for the duality of human wickedness and human goodness proclaims the dangers of dictatorship and the saving promise of democracy. The political lesson of this human duality was best stated in Reinhold Niebuhr's memorable aphorism:

> Man's capacity for good makes democracy possible;
> Man's inclination to evil makes democracy essential.

The Nazi genocide was also unique in its senselessness. Yehuda Bauer has well asked, where else in history has a government of a civilized nation set out to kill *everyone* whose grandfather was of a particular religion or ethnic group? "For the first time in history a sentence of death had been pronounced on anyone guilty of having been born."[27] And where have mass murders been so injurious to the perpetrator's own self-interest? In 1943, 1944, 1945, beleaguered Germany desperately needed railway transport and skilled labor supply. Yet Hitler allocated billions of work hours and massive amounts of transportation to one purpose: the killing of a nonexistent "menace." For the Jews were not then and had never been a threat to the German Reich. The whole thing was quite literally senseless.

But was this genocide really *unique?* Was there no historical precedent or parallel? Historians will recall other mass murders, other slaughters of the innocent. One thinks of Herod and Genghis Khan, or of Stalin's murder of some 15 million kulaks, minority groups, and Russian prisoners of war.[28] We recall the massacres perpetrated by Idi Amin Dada of Uganda[29] and the calculated starvation in Cambodia, where over 50 percent of the entire population was killed between 1975 and 1980.[30]

Two parallels to the Holocaust of the Jews seem particularly close. In 1915 Turkish authorities ordered the annihilation of the entire Armenian people. The proportion of Armenians killed was about the same as that destroyed in Hitler's Holocaust of the Jews: two out of every three people died.[31] The Nazi genocide of the Gypsies also shows close parallels to the murder of the Jews. Gypsies too were killed for no other reason than the alleged threat of "racial pollution" of German blood. As with the Jews (and unlike the Poles) *all* Gypsies were to be executed. They too (unlike other Nazi victims) were gassed at Auschwitz.[32]

So what can be concluded on this issue of continuity versus change? Many eminent Jewish authorities insist that this Holocaust was *unique*— it alone deserves a capital letter. Alvin Rosenfeld has called it an event without analogy, "something new in the world, without likeness or kind."[33] Yehuda Bauer has said that any comparison with other genocides is misleading and inaccurate.[34]

An American sociologist, John Murray Cuddihy, has noticed something revealing about the very intensity of Jewish insistence that it is only *their* genocide which is worthy of the name "Holocaust." He finds that this affirmation of uniqueness and denial of universality is a modern reworking of the ancient "Chosen People" concept: "Chosenness is found ... even in such horrible context as the Holocaust in the attempt to define victimization in such a way as to exclude all other groups besides Jews."[35]

Elie Wiesel illustrates Cuddihy's point. When historians refer to other holocausts, such as the massacre of the Armenians or the Gypsies, Wiesel is disturbed because such parallels question the special status of the Jewish victims. He is sorely afraid, he says, that "they are stealing the Holocaust from us ... [which] we need to regain our sense of sacredness."[36]

There are obviously differences of opinion on this question, but I would say that despite close parallels, the uniqueness of the Jewish Holocaust is striking. It was unique in Hitler's avowed purpose of killing *all* members of a religious, cultural, ethnic community—a calculated effort to annihilate one of the most creative people on earth.[37] This genocide was unique in the endorsement of leading social institutions and agencies; unique in the senselessness of the whole program; unique in the help the victims gave to their murderers; unique in the consequence it has had on both Jewish and Christian thought.

**II**

Let us turn to a second group of questions that highlight the problem. *How adequate are the explanations and theories that attempt to account for the Holocaust? What approaches seem most fruitful? What new approaches are needed?*

First, how adequate are the explanations? The answer to this is simple: there is no adequate explanation of the Holocaust. This event will continue to stagger the mind and trouble the soul of anyone who investigates it.

Yet several approaches are particularly helpful in leading us to a deeper understanding—though we shall never know the full and final truth about it, just as we shall never know the final truth about any historical problem that is worth its intellectual salt.

In our search for understanding, insights can be gained from sociological and psychological studies. Helen Fein,[38] for example, following closely the monumental work of Raul Hilberg, has examined the social setting for the Holocaust and found answers to such questions as: What made the social environment congenial to genocide? She provides careful comparative statistics from different countries to show that the extent of cooperation with the SS depended upon a number of factors, but the most important of these was the amount of anti-Semitism that existed historically in each country (thus the importance of the first question about continuity). Fein shows, for example, that there is a direct relationship, a positive correlation, between the amount of anti-Semitism —and the support it received from church, army, and the civil service— and the number of Jews killed. Where anti-Semitism was extensive, as in Germany, Rumania, Hungary, and Poland, genocide was extensive. Where anti-Semitism was not strong historically, and where popular sentiment and civic and religious leadership did not support it, as in Denmark and Bulgaria, killing was minimal. Bulgarians and Danes refused to carry out SS orders and helped thousands of Jews to escape death.

Thus the congeniality of the social environment helped determine the extent of the Holocaust. So too did the degree of effective political power. Where political power is overwhelming—as in Stalin's Russia, Amin's Uganda, or Hitler's Germany—where opposition is silenced and bureaucracy is obedient, mass murder can become routine.

Fein's comparative approach, which encompasses sociological and quantitative analysis, is a valuable aid to a fuller understanding. So too are the contributions made by psychologists and psychoanalysts.[39] We particularly need their help because the very irrationality of the Holocaust makes traditional political and historical explanations distressingly inadequate.

Psychologists can tell us a great deal about the personalities of the perpetrators. What kinds of people, yes, what kinds of *human beings,* were the Nazis? For it is important, though admittedly distasteful, to remember that the Nazis were human. To dismiss them as "monsters" or "freaks" or "demons" is too easy and far too dangerous. We shall learn little about this historic event until we recognize that the Holocaust was a *deeply human phenomenon.*

In all people there is a propensity for murderous aggression. Even the unspeakable events of the Holocaust are not "bestial" in the literal sense of the word. To call the Nazis beasts is to defame beasts. Animals in the jungle do not kill except for food or self-defense. Such events as the Holocaust, Heinz Kohut has written, are "decidedly human, an intricate part of the human condition."[40] That is a disturbing and unpalatable thought, but it is a basic fact of psychological life. Hannah Arendt reached the same conclusion. In her brilliant study of Eichmann in Jerusalem she observed that Eichmann was no monster—if he *had* been, the entire case against him would have collapsed immediately. "The trouble with Eichmann was precisely that so many were like him and that the many were neither perverted nor sadistic, that they were and still are terribly and terrifyingly normal. . . . This normality was much more terrifying than all the atrocities put together."[41] Elie Wiesel found the same things to be true about Franz Stangl, commandant of the Sobibor and Treblinka death camps: "It is not the murderer in Stangl that terrifies us—it is the human being."[42] We need to know more about the mechanisms which permit normal people to commit such awful crimes, and psychologists can help provide some answers.

Psychologists have also helped by demonstrating what the "anti-Semitic personality" is like.[43] Germany has no monopoly on such twisted human beings. Hitler, Heinrich Himmler, Eichmann, and the rest were very much like American anti-Semites: they too reveal infantile personalities incapable of development; they too swing radically between swaggering confidence and abject despair. Like American anti-Semites, the Nazis exalted the strong and despised the weak. They too projected their personal problems onto others, namely, the Jews. They too tended to be sado-masochists with inclinations to perversion.

Psychologists can help us understand the anti-Semitic person. So too can philosophers. Jean-Paul Sartre, quite without realizing it, has painted a discerning picture of Adolf Hitler and his vicious but frighteningly human colleagues:

We are now in a position to understand the anti-Semite. He is a man who is afraid. Not of the Jews, to be sure, but of himself. . . . He is a coward who does not want to admit his cowardice to himself; a murderer who represses and censures his tendency to murder without being able to hold it back. . . . The existence of the Jew merely permits the anti-Semite to stifle his anxieties. . . . The anti-Semite is a man who wishes to be pitiless stone, a furious torrent, a devastating thunderbolt—anything except a man.[44]

Biographers, aided by psychology, can reach a deeper understanding of the individual perpetrators of the Holocaust. One recalls Peter Loewenberg's penetrating study of Himmler,[45] Richard Hunt's pioneering work on Joseph Goebbels,[46] Gidda Sereny's sensitive insights into Franz Stangl,[47] as well as Hannah Arendt's study of Eichmann.

Certainly we need to know a great deal more about the personality of the one person who was finally responsible for the Holocaust: Adolf Hitler.[48] We need to understand the psychodynamics of the process by which his personal hatred of the Jews was rationalized and projected into public policy. We need to see how the personal prejudice of one demented person was transmuted into a horrendous historic force.

Psychologists have also widened our horizons and deepened our knowledge of how it is possible for average people to follow orders which debase and destroy their fellow human beings. Here, two studies by two American social psychologists offer insights—only partial insights, it is true, but nevertheless revealing glimpses of an answer—to that simple but terribly complex question: How could decent people commit such evil crimes? *How could they possibly do it?* Stanley Milgram at Yale and his colleagues in several other American universities have reached deeply disturbing conclusions about the propensity of ordinary people—in this case hundreds of American citizens—to follow brutal orders commanding them to turn on electric currents which appeared to inflict suffering on fellow citizens. Professor Milgram concludes:

Subjects will obey the experimenter no matter how vehement the pleading of the person being shocked, no matter how painful the shocks seem to be and no matter how much the victim pleads to be let out. This was seen time and again in studies and has been observed in several universities where the experiment was repeated. It is the extreme willingness of adults to go to almost any lengths on the command of an authority that constitutes the chief finding of the study and the fact most urgently demanding explanation.

This is perhaps the most fundamental lesson of our study: ordinary people simply doing their jobs and without any particular hostility on their part can become agents in a terrible destructive process.[49]

If this is true of average American citizens, how much more it is true of German Nazis whose attitude and inclinations were powerfully reinforced by an environment which not only permitted the destruction of their fellow men, but demanded it.

Philip Zimbardo of Stanford University has demonstrated that college students carefully selected for their normality can become perverted by the pathology of power. These students illustrate Stendhal's assertion that "power is the greatest of all pleasures." In his experiment, Zimbardo simulated a prison situation and had students act out the roles of prison guard and prisoner. The experiment showed how much American students delighted in that greatest of all pleasures and used it to humiliate and hurt their fellow students. It also showed that the victims of this power—also normal college students—became depressed and disoriented, and meekly followed the commands of their persecutors.

Zimbardo's experiment, which was planned to last two weeks, was aborted after six days because in those few days Professor Zimbardo was alarmed by a frightening metamorphosis he witnessed in the students. Those who were serving as guards grew increasingly abusive and sadistically cruel to the "prisoners"; the students who were prisoners became so depressed that they were on the verge of psychological disintegration and suicide. Zimbardo concluded that

in the contest between forces of good men and evil situation, the situation triumphed. Individuals carefully selected for their normality, sanity, and homogeneous personality traits were, in a matter of days, acting in ways that out of this context would be judged abnormal, insane, neurotic, psychopathic and sadistic.[50]

If that can happen to average American college students in six days, it is small wonder that Germans who had been carefully conditioned to Nazi ideology could become brutal instruments of Hitler's "wicked will," or that humiliated, frightened, starving, and disoriented Jews who felt the utter futility of resistance should yield to brute force and passively obey commands.

Psychoanalysts such as Bruno Bettelheim have further increased our understanding of the difficult question—and to Jews a very sensitive question—of why the Jewish people cooperated in their own destruction. Bettelheim believes that the aggressive-destructive drive so obvious in the SS was also present in their Jewish victims. Feeling helpless and abandoned, they were unable to direct aggressive impulses outward against their hated oppressors. They therefore made both an excuse and a virtue out of futility and used it as a psychological defense against self-accusations of cowardice. Thus they continually exaggerated their own utter helplessness and the total omnipotence of the enemy, and then turned aggressive-destructive drives *inward* against themselves, thereby cooperating in their own destruction. Bettelheim concludes that Jews were already suicidal before they walked toward the death chambers.[51]

Such analysis, not surprisingly, has brought a storm of protest and denial from Jewish writers. But it is ironic that these writers who denounce the conclusions reached by Bettelheim, Arendt, and Hilberg, and who vehemently deny that the Jews died with meek resignation, nevertheless in their own books offer explanations of *why* the Jewish people were compelled to do just that. They give a number of reasons, all of which have considerable merit.

*First,* they argue that Jewish tradition did not encourage active resistance to persecution. They point out that for centuries Jews had been conditioned to obey, to suffer, and to survive. As Lucy Dawidowicz has written, "[their] religious tradition elevated powerlessness into a positive Jewish value. It fostered submissiveness."[52] Jews believed that their vaunted capacity to submit and yet to endure would carry them through even this persecution, as it had so often in their past. They made a catastrophic mistake. As Richard Rubenstein has noted, "The Jewish reaction to the Nazis was one of the most disastrous misreadings of the character of an opponent by any community in all of human history."[53] Jews did not understand that Hitler did not plan merely to humiliate them; he planned to kill them. This sensible, legally minded, and cultivated people simply could not believe that the German government really meant to murder them all. That just did not make sense. In this the Jews were quite correct. It did not make sense. But it happened.

*Second,* Jewish writers argue that to this tradition of "suffer and survive" was added the psychological defense of denying. Jews denied that they were to be transported to death camps. Such horror stories could not be true. Gladly they accepted the Nazi fiction that they were merely being "resettled" in the East. Their psychological *need* to believe that fantasy led them to cooperate and obey SS orders because to do so was a way of denying what they dreaded might be true. Notice how psychological denial is reflected in their euphemisms. Jews did not talk of killing centers, of gas ovens or death camps; they referred to them as "bakeries"; a person who had given up all hope was a "Moslem"; a depot holding the belongings of recently gassed victims was called "Canada."[54]

*Third,* as Helen Fein has noted, there was a general belief—particularly among Western Jews—that the Nazis were "punishing" only Eastern Jews, not the rest. Many German Jews, for example, said that Polish Jews must have done something terribly wrong to merit their fate.[55]

*Fourth,* Yisrael Gutman believes that thousands of devout Jews went quietly to their death with prayer shawls gathered about them in the faith that they were participating in a *Kiddush Hashem*—a sanctification rite in which they bore witness to their devotion to God. They agreed with a revered rabbi who said, "The quintessence of martyrdom is dying for one's Jewishness."[56] And psychologically it was easier to believe that they were dying as martyrs to their faith in God than it was to entertain the awful thought that their God had forsaken them.

*Fifth,* to many Jews, death in Hitler's gas chambers was atonement for individual or collective sin. Devout Jews found it more bearable to believe that it must be they themselves—and not the God of Abraham and Sarah, Isaac and Jacob—who had broken the sacred covenant which Jehovah had made with his Chosen People.

*Sixth,* historically, Jews tended to trust their spiritual leaders. As we have noted, official *Judenräte* urged Jews to obey orders for shipment to the East and not to resist. As Dawidowicz has written, they feared—with ample justification—that any act of resistance would only increase the wrath of the SS.[57]

Finally, and this is the point that needs most emphasis, we must recognize that European Jews, like the kulaks of Russia or Idi Amin's victims in Uganda, yielded to a *force majeure.* The Jews, isolated, intimidated, and confronted by the institutionalized terror of a modern police state, had no other effective choice. They were overwhelmed by sheer power.

It seems to me that all these explanations—including Bettelheim's—deserve an examination that is as careful, as courageous, and as dispassionate as this emotion-laden issue will allow.

The Holocaust clearly required perpetrators; and we need to understand the psychodynamics which drove them. Here, by and large, were frighteningly normal people who were given great power and trained to exploit universal human frailties for horrendous purposes. The Holocaust also required victims, and they too can teach us much about the human condition—how even under the most brutal tyranny, people can retain their humanity and refuse to be broken. But the Holocaust also shows how the cowed and frightened and disoriented can succumb to brutal power and cooperate in their own psychic and physical destruction. The Holocaust is indeed a terrifying but profoundly revealing laboratory of human behavior.

Which is to say that the Holocaust was a human event—an event of shattering and unspeakable inhumanity, but one perpetrated by humans upon humans. It was an event unique in history and yet within the human experience.

## III

Historians, as well as psychologists and sociologists, can also contribute to our understanding of the Holocaust because of their long experience with a third issue: the role of the commanding personality.

We see in the Holocaust yet another example of the ancient historical interplay of man and circumstance. But it is doubtful if ever in the past there has been so close a relationship, so fateful an interconnection, as there was between this peculiarly compelling man and these peculiarly receptive circumstances.

First consider the man, Adolf Hitler, the originator and mover of the Holocaust, the one person without whom this event could not have been possible.[58] He was both a consummately cunning political opportunist and a pathological fanatic. And both aspects determined his program for the Jews. As an astute political operator he recognized the appeal of anti-Semitism to Germans of the 1920s and 1930s. This "Terrible Simplifier" offered a simple explanation for all difficulties: Jews were responsible for the defeat and humiliation of 1918, for the economic disasters of 1923 and 1930-1933, for all the political and moral problems of the time. It was not "our" fault: the Jew was to blame. There have been other racists, other political anti-Semites before Hitler. Three things made Hitler special: the depth and intensity of his hatred for the Jews; the extent of his effective political power; the opportunity given to him by a compliant and cooperative society.

Hatred of the Jews and the desire to murder them was a lifelong obsession of Hitler, the organizing principle of his life. One can feel the venom of his hatred in an early conversation, now recorded in the archives of the Institut für Zeitgeschichte, Munich.

As soon as I have power [he said in 1922] I shall have gallows erected, for example in Munich in the Marienplatz. Jews will be hanged one after another and they will stay hanging until they stink ... then the next group will follow ... until the last Jew in Munich is exterminated. Exactly the same procedure will be followed in other cities until Germany is cleansed of the last Jew.[59]

This personal obsession became his political program. His promise was kept. Both his last and his first political statements confirmed his obsession with a nonexistent "Jewish Menace." His last political statement, delivered on April 30, 1945, was dictated just before taking a lethal dose of cyanide: "Above all I enjoin the leaders of the Reich to scrupulous observance of the Racial Laws defending against the universal poisoner of mankind, international Jewry." In his first public speech, of which we have one faded shorthand report dated August 7 or 8, 1920, Salzburg, Hitler had sounded the same ominous note:

Don't be misled into thinking that you can fight diseases without killing the carrier! ... Don't think you can fight racial tuberculosis without ridding the nation of the carrier of racial tuberculosis! This Jewish contamination will not subside, this poisoning of the nation will not end until the carrier himself, the Jew, has been banished from our midst.[60]

That promise was also kept.

The extent of Hitler's anti-Jewish phobia is manifest. The psychological reasons for it are complex and cannot concern us here.[61] Let us simply reiterate that the Holocaust was not possible without Hitler. It was also not possible without a supportive society. For, once again in history, man and circumstances worked together to produce the event.

German society exhibited attitudes and values recognizable in any country. What made German circumstances peculiar was the intensification and distortion of those attitudes and values through the force of unusual historic pressures and the manipulative skills of the man, Adolf Hitler. We should consider some of these attitudes and notice the way Hitler used them to his advantage. His program required anti-Semitic racism, and German history, as noted, obliged him with a particularly virulent variety. He manipulated it with diabolical cunning. Anti-Semitism not only provided a simple explanation for all Germany's recent disasters, it allowed Hitler to fulfill his contradictory claims that he was, at the same time, a conservative and a revolutionary; that he would preserve traditional society and transform it through a New Order; that he was the champion of both capitalism and socialism. "The Jew" enabled him to have it both ways and to win both capitalist and proletariat to his banner. He convinced capitalists that he was the enemy only of "Jewish finance capitalism"; he persuaded socialists that his program of National Socialism fought only "Jewish Marxist Socialism." He also applied anti-Semitism in another way. His success as mass leader was due in part to his psychological insight that man is both evil and good, beset by two conflicting tendencies: an impulse for aggression, destruction, hatred; and a capacity for creation, cooperation, sacrifice, and service. Hitler appealed to both impulses. His regime institutionalized brutality and aggression, channeling them against the Jews. But we do not understand his appeal, particularly to the youth of Germany, unless we understand that he also inspired them with faith and hope—a shining hope for the future, faith in him as their Messiah. Through the magic of his charisma and the cunning of his propaganda he convinced millions that barbarism was heroic, brutality was strength, and nihilism was an exalted ideology. And the lofty goals of Germany strong and triumphant could be achieved only when the country was cleansed and purified by removing the Jews who defiled the Fatherland.

Hitler manipulated German anti-Semitism to his own advantage. He also gained mightily from another national tradition: obedience to the state. Surely the German people have no monopoly on obedience and capacity to obey inhuman orders, as Milgram's chilling experiments have shown. Yet in Germany, since Luther and the Prussian kings and the Imperial Army, obedience to *Obrigkeit* (authority) was raised to the highest virtue of citizenship. At Nuremberg, as at a score of Nazi trials since, the phrase *Befehl ist Befehl!* (an order is an order) was recited as a litany.

Hitler's Holocaust was helped along by yet another circumstance: general indifference to the suffering, humiliation, and murder of the Jews. Here again a common human phenomenon was intensified in

Germany. People in most societies are indifferent to the existence of social evil in their midst. Edmund Burke's justifiably famous warning about evil prospering because of the indifferent silence of good men and women is, unfortunately, true of most good people. Certainly the silence of many good and influential people—people like Pope Pius XII, Franklin Roosevelt, Winston Churchill, Felix Frankfurter, and Rabbi Stephen Wise[62]—helped Hitler carry out the Holocaust. Silence was international. But the indifference of the elite of German society was particularly pronounced and peculiarly helpful to Hitler, as Rainer Baum and Dieter Hartmann have graphically shown.[63]

Hitler was also aided by the psychological phenomenon of defensive denial. People have a remarkable capacity to deny what they prefer not to believe. Turks deny that an Armenian massacre took place in 1915; Englishmen denied the existence of concentration camps in the Transvaal; Americans denied the Christmas bombing of Hanoi; Israelis denied all responsibility for massacres of Palestinians. But denial was pandemic during the Holocaust. And Jews joined the chorus of those who insisted that the genocide was not actually taking place. Since they could not believe they were being transported East to their deaths, they denied it, and their denial expedited their extinction. To a large degree, as was noted, Jews accepted their own victimization. But attitudes of resignation and cooperation with one's oppressor are emphatically not an exclusively Jewish trait. As Barrington Moore has demonstrated, human beings in vastly different social, religious, and political settings all display a remarkable tendency to accept maltreatment and make a virtue out of humiliation. Such is true of Christian ascetics and saints, the Untouchables of India, Chinese coolies, and German steel workers in the Ruhr in the 1890s. Acceptance is a social norm, Moore has observed; resistance is an acquired taste.[64] But here again, during the Third Reich there were specific psychological, social, and political reasons *why* the Jews put up so little resistance and helped Hitler to direct a human condition to inhuman purposes.

We seek to understand the Holocaust, to explain it, and to establish the truth about what happened. We shall never explain it adequately, never find the final truth. But there is no cause for despair. We can find comfort in the words of a wise old rabbi:

Who says the Truth was meant to be revealed?
It has to be *sought*, that's all.

I have suggested that we begin our search by considering the interplay of a peculiar man with peculiarly fortuitous circumstances; that we seek enlightenment from such disciplines as sociology, psychology, and history; and that we recognize this event both as a part of a historical continuum and as a phenomenon with distinctive features of its own.


## NOTES

This chapter draws upon papers originally presented to the International Scholars' Conference on the Holocaust held at Indiana University, November 3-5, 1980, and at Tel Aviv, Israel, June 20-24, 1982. The present version revises those remarks and incorporates comments made at the conferences.

1. Martin Luther, "The Jews and Their Lies," in *Luther's Works,* vol. 47 (St. Louis: Concordia, 1971), pp. 135, 258, 266-68, 272, 292.

2. Larry E. Axel, "Christian Theology and the Murder of Jews," *Encounter* 40, no. 2 (Spring 1979), pp. 135-36, and Rosemary Radford Ruether, *Faith and Fratricide: The Theological Roots of Anti-Semitism* (New York: Seabury Press, 1974), pp. 179-80. See also Edward H. Flannery, *The Anguish of the Jews: Twenty-three Centuries of Anti-Semitism* (New York: Macmillan, 1965), pp. 47-51.

3. Thomas Aquinas, *De Regimine Principum* (Westport, Conn.: Hyperion Press, 1979), as quoted by Axel, "Christian Theology," p. 136.

4. Ibid., p. 135.

5. Hitler's *Tischgespräche* as quoted by Ruether, *Faith and Fratricide,* p. 224.

6. Uriel Tal, *Christians and Jews in Germany: Religion, Politics, and Ideology in the Second Reich, 1870-1914,* trans. Noah Jonathan Jacobs (Ithaca, N.Y.: Cornell University Press, 1975), pp. 304-5.

7. As quoted in A. Roy Eckardt, "Preparatory Paper: Indiana University Conference, November 3-5, 1980" (unpublished), p. 13.

8. Fritz Stern, *The Politics of Cultural Despair: A Study in the Rise of Germanic Ideology* (Berkeley: University of California Press, 1961), p. 87.

9. Paul de Lagarde, *Deutsche Schriften,* 5th ed. (Göttingen: Dieterich, 1920), pp. 33-37, 348; Stern, *Politics of Cultural Despair,* pp. 62-63.

10. For a brief discussion of Wagner's influence on Hitler, see Robert G.L. Waite, *The Psychopathic God: Adolf Hitler* (New York: Basic Books, 1977), pp. 99-113. It is, of course, true that many German intellectuals opposed anti-Semitism, championed Jewish emancipation, and paid tribute to Jewish thought and culture. This list includes Gotthold Lessing, Johann Herder, Johann Schiller, Johann Wolfgang von Goethe, and Friedrich W. Nietzsche. But other Germans were vocal and influential anti-Semites. The great Prussian liberal reformer Baron vom Stein wanted to ship all the Jews out of Germany. Johann Gottlieb Fichte, professor of philosophy at the University of Berlin, spoke—jokingly, he later said—of "cutting off all Jewish heads." Kant asserted that Jewish thought was devoid of spirituality; Hegel said it amounted to a "dunghill." For a general survey of the problem

see Alfred D. Low, *Jews in the Eyes of Germans: From the Enlightenment to Imperial Germany* (Philadelphia: Institute for the Study of Human Issues, 1979), and Nathan Rotenstreich, *The Recurring Pattern: Studies in Anti-Judaism in Modern Thought* (London: Weidenfeld and Nicolson, 1963).

11. As quoted by Alvin Rosenfeld, International Scholars' Conference on the Holocaust, Bloomington, Indiana, November 5, 1980.

12. Ulrich Dunker, *Der Reichsbund jüdischer Frontsoldaten, 1918-1938: Geschichte eines jüdischen Abwehrvereins* (Düsseldorf: Dreste, 1977).

13. Raul Hilberg, *The Destruction of the European Jews* (Chicago: Quadrangle Books, 1961), p. 657.

14. See Heinz Artzt, *Mörder in Uniform: Organisationen die zu Vollstreckern nationalsozialistischer Verbrechen wurden* (Munich: Kindler, 1979).

15. Lawrence D. Stokes, "The German People and the Destruction of the European Jews," *Central European History* 6, no. 2 (June 1973), pp. 182, 191. See also the perceptive article by Dietrich Strothmann, "Die Schrift an der Wand," *Die Zeit* 6 (February 9, 1979).

16. Gerhard Schoenberner, ed., *Wir haben es gesehen. Augenzeugenberichte über Terror and Judenverfolgung im Dritten Reich* (Hamburg, 1962), p. 8, as quoted in Stokes, "The German People," p. 182.

17. Lucy Dawidowicz, *The War Against the Jews: 1933-1945* (New York: Holt, Rinehart and Winston, 1975), p. 348.

18. Hilberg, *Destruction,* pp. 122-25, 297, 316, 343, 662-69. See also three later essays by Hilberg: "The *Judenrat:* Conscious or Unconscious 'Tool,' " *Proceedings of the Third Yad Vashem International Historical Conference 4-7 April 1977* (Jerusalem: Yad Vashem, 1979),"The Ghetto as a Form of Government," *Annals of the American Academy of Political and Social Sciences* 450 (July 1980), and his introductory essay in Joel Dimsdale, ed., *Survivors, Victims and Perpetrators: Essays on the Nazi Holocaust* (Washington, D.C.: Hemisphere Publishing Co., 1980). Hannah Arendt, *Eichmann in Jerusalem: A Report on the Banality of Evil,* rev. ed. (New York: Viking Press, 1964), pp. 18, 284. Isaiah Trunk, *Judenrat: The Jewish Councils in Eastern Europe under Nazi Occupation* (New York: Macmillan, 1972), pp. 550-57, 570-73, the same writer's *Jewish Responses to Nazi Persecution: Collective and Individual Behavior in Extremis* (New York: Stein and Day, 1979), p. 53, and his essay, "The Typology of the *Judenräte* in Eastern Europe," *Proceedings of the Third Yad Vashem International Historical Conference* (Jerusalem: Yad Vashem, 1979), p. 29. Yehuda Bauer disputes the conclusions reached by Hilberg, Arendt, and Trunk and argues that some Council members did in fact resist the Nazis—a point which can be accepted without destroying what he calls the "myth" of Jewish passivity. See his valuable collection of essays, *The Holocaust as Historical Experience: Essays and Discussion* (New York: Holmes and Meier, 1981). This volume reprints comments made orally at a conference of scholars of the Holocaust. In the midst of a heated debate on the role of the Councils, a judicious observation was made by Saul Friedländer, who suggested that the

"polemics" over the *Judenräte* were due to a confusion between the objective *function* of the Councils and the *intentions* of the Council leaders. He noted that Hilberg and Trunk stress the former while Bauer emphasizes the good intentions of the Councils and implies that their function was benign—it was actually not to abet the Nazis but to safeguard their communities. Friedländer concludes with a question: "Could we not say ... that *objectively* the Judenrat was probably an instrument in the destruction of European Jewry, but that *subjectively* some of them—or even most of them—tried to do their best ... in order to stave off destruction?" I would agree with that point and accept the conclusion reached by Hilberg: "That the Council was pained we are convinced. That in desperation Council members committed suicide is a matter of record. But that notwithstanding, ... they went on doing what they were asked—that is a matter of record too." (Discussion reprinted in Bauer, *Holocaust as Historical Experience*, pp. 236-37, 254-55. Emphasis in original.)

19. Hilberg, *Destruction*, p. 343; see also Yisrael Gutman and Livia Rothkirchen, eds., *The Catastrophe of European Jewry: Antecedents, History, Reflections* (Jerusalem: Yad Vashem, 1976), pp. 423-32, and Trunk, "Typology," p. 29.

20. George M. Kren and Leon Rappoport, "Resistance to the Holocaust: The Idea and the Act," in Bauer, *Holocaust as Historical Experience*, p. 214.

21. Arendt, *Eichmann*, p. 118.

22. Emmanuel Ringelblum, *Notes from the Warsaw Ghetto: The Journal of Emmanuel Ringelblum*, ed. and trans. by Jacob Sloan (New York: McGraw Hill, 1958), pp. 331-32.

23. See Reuben Ainsztein, *Jewish Resistance in Nazi-Occupied Eastern Europe: With a Historical Survey of the Jew as Fighter and Soldier in the Diaspora* (New York: Barnes and Noble, 1974), Miriam Novitch, *Sobibor: Martyrdom and Revolt* (New York: Holocaust Library, 1980), and, for a brief account, Yisrael Gutman, "Rebellions in the Camps: Three Revolts in the Face of Death," in *Critical Issues of the Holocaust*, ed. Alex Grobman and Daniel Landes (Los Angeles: Simon Wiesenthal Center, 1983).

24. Ringelblum, *Notes*, pp. 332-33.

25. Philip Friedman, "Problems of Research on the European Jewish Catastrophe," in Gutman and Rothkirchen, *Catastrophe*, p. 644.

26. See, among many, many memoirs, the following: Viktor Frankl, *Man's Search for Meaning* (New York: Pocket Books, 1971), Chaim A. Kaplan, *The Warsaw Diary of Chaim A. Kaplan*, ed. Abraham I. Katsh (New York: Schocken Books, 1965), Terrence Des Pres, *The Survivor: An Anatomy of Life in the Death Camps* (New York: Oxford University Press, 1980), and Ringelblum, *Notes*.

27. Yehuda Bauer, *The Holocaust in Historical Perspective* (Seattle: University of Washington Press, 1978), p. 32.

28. The numbers killed during Stalin's reign of terror have been variously estimated. Nicholas Riasanovsky sets the figure at about 5 million

in his *History of Russia* (New York: Oxford University Press, 1963), p. 551, but that figure seems much too low. Alexander I. Solzhenitsyn, *The Gulag Archipelago* (New York: Harper and Row, 1974-1978), vol. 3, p. 350, says that some 15 million peasants alone were murdered. Alec Nove in *Stalinism and After* (London: Allen and Unwin, 1975), estimates between 12 and 15 million (p. 56). Robert Conquest, in his huge monograph, *The Great Terror: Stalin's Purge of the Thirties* (New York: Macmillan, 1968), says that the total number, including kulaks, political "opponents," and those worked to death in the gulag system, almost certainly reached 20 million (p. 533).

29. Idi Amin Dada, according to the International Commission of Jurists, probably killed over 250,000 people in a population of some 9 million. See Samuel Decalo, *Coups and Army Rule in Africa: Studies in Military Style* (New Haven: Yale University Press, 1976), p. 213, and Thomas and Margaret Melady, *Idi Amin Dada: Hitler in Africa* (Kansas City: Sheed, Andrews and McMeel, 1977).

30. Peter J. Donaldson, *The New York Times,* 22 April 1980.

31. Marjorie Housepian, "The Unremembered Genocide," *Commentary* 42 (September 1966), pp. 55-61.

32. Bohdan Wytwycky, *The Other Holocaust: Many Circles of Hell, A Brief Account of the 9-10 Million Persons Who Died with the 6 Million Jews under Nazi Racism* (Washington, D.C.: Novak Report on the New Ethnicity, 1980).

33. Alvin H. Rosenfeld, "The Problematics of Holocaust Literature," in *Confronting the Holocaust: The Impact of Elie Wiesel,* ed. Alvin H. Rosenfeld and Irving Greenberg (Bloomington: Indiana University Press, 1978), p. 12.

34. Bauer, *The Holocaust in Historical Perspective,* p. 36.

35. As quoted by Paula E. Hyman, "The New Debate on the Holocaust," in *The New York Times Magazine* (September 14, 1980), p. 82. For a thoughtful and critical commentary on Cuddihy's observation, see Henry L. Feingold, "How Unique Is the Holocaust?" in *Critical Issues of the Holocaust,* pp. 397-401.

36. Quoted in Hyman, "The New Debate . . . ," pp. 82, 109.

37. Dawidowicz, *War Against Jews,* pp. xiv-xv.

38. Helen Fein, *Accounting for Genocide: National Responses and Jewish Victimization During the Holocaust* (New York: The Free Press, 1979).

39. See Lita Linzer Schwarts, "A Psychohistorical Perception of the Holocaust," a valuable paper prepared for a symposium on Hitler, The Citadel, April 25, 1980.

40. Heinz Kohut, *The Search for the Self: Selected Writings of Heinz Kohut, 1950-1978* (New York: International Universities Press, 1978), vol. 2, p. 635.

41. Arendt, *Eichmann,* p. 276.

42. Wiesel in a review of Gitta Sereny's book, *Into That Darkness: An Examination of Conscience* (New York: Vintage Press, 1974), in *Midstream: A Monthly Jewish Review* 3, no. 9 (November 1975), p. 73. See also Peter Loewenberg, "The Unsuccessful Adolescence of Heinrich Himmler," *American Historical Review* 76, no. 3 (June 1971).

43. See Nathan W. Ackerman and Marie Jahoda, *Anti-Semitism and Emotional Disorder: A Psychoanalytic Interpretation* (New York: Harper, 1950), Martin Wangh, "National Socialism and the Genocide of the Jews: A Psychoanalytic Study of a Historical Event," *International Journal of Psycho-Analysis* 45 (1964), pp. 386-95, and the essays in Ernst Simmel, ed., *Anti-Semitism a Social Disease* (New York: International Universities Press, 1946).

44. Jean-Paul Sartre, *Anti-Semite and Jew,* trans. George J. Becker (New York: Schocken Books, 1948), pp. 26-27, 54-55.

45. See note 42.

46. Richard M. Hunt, "Joseph Goebbels: A Study of the Formation of His National-Socialist Consciousness (1897-1929)" (Ph.D. dissertation, Harvard University, 1960).

47. See note 42.

48. I have attempted such a study in *The Psychopathic God: Adolf Hitler* (New York: Basic Books, 1977), and have commented on the historical question of the extent to which Hitler was personally responsible for the Holocaust in my chapter, "The Perpetrator: Hitler and the Holocaust," in *Human Responses to the Holocaust,* ed. Michael D. Ryan (New York: E. Mellen Press, 1981).

49. Stanley Milgram, *Obedience to Authority* (New York: Harper and Row, 1974), pp. 5-6.

50. Philip G. Zimbardo, "Transforming Experimental Research into Advocacy of Social Change," in *Applying Social Psychology: Implications for Research, Practice and Training,* ed. Morton Deutsch and Harvey A. Hornstein (Hillsdale, N.J.: Halsted Press, 1975), pp. 33-67.

51. Bruno Bettelheim, *The Informed Heart: Autonomy in a Mass Age* (New York: Avon Books, 1971), pp. 243-45, and *Surviving and Other Essays* (New York: Knopf, 1979), pp. 100-101.

52. Dawidowicz, *War Against Jews,* pp. 343, 346.

53. Richard Rubenstein, *The Religious Imagination* (Indianapolis, Ind.: Bobbs-Merrill, 1968), p. xvii.

54. Hilberg, *Destruction,* p. 668, and Bettelheim, *Informed Heart,* pp. 253-54.

55. Fein, *Genocide,* p. 317.

56. Gutman, *Catastrophe,* p. 377.

57. Dawidowicz, *War Against Jews,* pp. 287-88, 348.

58. Gerald Fleming's decisive monograph, *Hitler und die Endlösung: "Es ist des Führers Wunsch ..."* (Wiesbaden and Munich: Limes, 1982),

proves Hitler's direct responsibility for the Holocaust and puts finally to rest
the spurious claims of the so-called revisionists that Hitler was ignorant and
innocent of the mass murders.  For a different approach to the same problem,
but one that reaches the same conclusion, see my chapter, "The Perpetrator:
Hitler and the Holocaust," in Michael D. Ryan, ed., *Human Responses to the
Holocaust: Perpetrators and Victims, Bystanders and Resisters: Papers of
the Scholars' Conference on the Church Struggle and the Holocaust*  (New
York: E. Mellen Press, 1981).

59.   Quoted in Waite, p. 16.

60.   Ibid.

61.   See Waite, *Psychopathic God,* and his article, "Adolf Hitler's Anti-
Semitism:  A Study in History and Psychoanalysis," in Benjamin Wolman,
ed., *The Psychoanalytic Interpretation of History* (New York: Basic Books,
1971).  See also Norbert Bromberg, *Hitler's Psychopathology* (New York:
International Universities Press, 1983).

62.   Henry L. Feingold, *The Politics of Rescue:  The Roosevelt Admin-
istration and the Holocaust, 1938-1945*  (New Brunswick, N.J.: Rutgers
University Press, 1970), Walter Laqueur, *The Terrible Secret: An Investiga-
tion into the Suppression of Information about Hitler's Final Solution*
(London: Weidenfeld and Nicolson, 1980), Martin Gilbert, *Auschwitz and
the Allies* (New York: Holt, Rinehart and Winston, 1981), and especially
David S. Wyman, *The Abandonment of Jews: America and the Holocaust*
(New York: Panther Books, 1984).

63.   Rainer C. Baum, *The Holocaust and the German Elite:  Genocide
and National Suicide in Germany, 1871-1945* (Totowa, N.J.: Rowman and
Littlefield, 1981), and Dieter D. Hartmann, "Anti-Semitism and the Appeal of
Nazism," paper presented at the Oxford Conference of the International Society of Political Psychology, July 1983.

64.  See Barrington Moore, Jr., *Injustice:   The Social Bases of
Obedience and Revolt* (New York: Harper and Row, 1975).

# 10

# DISCRIMINATION, PERSECUTION, THEFT, AND MURDER UNDER COLOR OF LAW: THE TOTALITARIAN CORRUPTION OF THE GERMAN LEGAL SYSTEM, 1933-1945

## Gunter W. Remmling

The German dictatorship did not materialize quite as suddenly as Pallas Athena, who sprang fully armed from the forehead of Zeus. The Third Reich, something the German resistance fighter Ernst Niekisch called the "realm of the lower demons,"[1] had numerous links with the past.

## SOCIAL ORIGINS OF THE GERMAN DICTATORSHIP

The anti-Semitic rabble-rousers of imperial Vienna kindled Adolf Hitler's murderous hatred of the Jews. "Then I came to Vienna," he wrote in his political autobiography *Mein Kampf,* as he set out to explain the origin of his anti-Semitism.[2] The chief designer of the National Socialist death machine was never in the mood for hiding his megalomania: "So I believe today that I am acting in the spirit of the Almighty Creator," Hitler raved. *"By struggling against the Jew I am fighting for the Lord's work."*[3] When the Austrian moved across the northern border he joined the strident chorus of German anti-Semites.

World War I and its aftermath influenced the political drift toward authoritarian regimes in Germany. When Hitler entered the political scene in Weimar Germany, he promised to restore the power of the military and garnered support among the warlords.[4] When the ex-corporal promised to "tear up" the Treaty of Versailles, he won over many nationalistic and conservative voters.[5] When Hitler echoed the *"Dolchstoss"* legend he appealed to chauvinists and militarists who peddled the fantasy that radical Social Democrats, pacifists, and Jews in Berlin had plunged a dagger into the back of the victorious army.[6]

The National Socialist German Workers Party (NSDAP) received financial support from German industrialists and bankers who were convinced that Hitler could destroy the trade unions and the Communists.[7] In the crucial election of July 31, 1932, the inhabitants of upper-class and upper-middle-class residential districts of large cities cast a disproportionately high Nazi vote.[8] Available statistics show that the social "elite" was overrepresented in the party leadership and membership.[9]

The Nazi party, however, was not the movement of a single class. All strata of German society contributed to the growth of the Nazi vote and the buildup of the NSDAP. The National Socialist program offered something to some Germans in every segment of society—with the exception of the German Jews.[10]

## FREE CORPS ACTIVITIES AND VEHMIC TRIALS

Apart from the wider connections between the Nazi phenomenon and the German past,[11] there are two developments which directly influenced the course of events leading to the totalitarian corruption of the legal system.

The first development began in World War I, when German Army commanders built up Storm Troops (*Sturmbataillone*). These highly trained "princes of the trenches" had a special mission. They were to tear apart the unity of the enemy's defenses and open the way for the regular infantry attack.[12] According to G. S. Graber, the storm battalions of World War I were the forerunners of the SS or *Schutzstaffel* (Protective Squad). They anticipated the Nazi SS as regards recruitment and the relationship between the men and their leader. The storm battalions also left their imprint on the SS in other ways: in the creation of an elitist self-image and in the practice of a "blind savagery which was taken over from the heightened conditions of war into peacetime bourgeois life."[13]

Unwilling to lay down their weapons after the war, many members of storm battalions enthusiastically supported the formation of the Free Corps (*Freikorps*). These paramilitary volunteer units brutally went to war against the German Communists and against the Poles, Latvians, and Russians on the country's eastern borders. *Freikorps* soldiers used the German salute (*Heil!*), the brown shirt, and the swastika.[14] When the government disbanded the volunteer units in 1921, thousands of *Freikorps* fighters joined the SA and the SS.[15]

The second development which is especially important for the corruption of the law began after World War I with a series of illegal Vehmic trials—imitations of secret medieval blood trials or *Vehmegerichte*.[16]

In 1920, ex-*Freikorps* leader Hermann Ehrhardt founded a secret society in Munich: *Organisation Consul.* This organization of right-wing conspirators held Vehmic trials of postwar political leaders and others who were condemned to death as traitors.

On August 26, 1921, two members of *Organisation Consul* killed Matthias Erzberger, Catholic Center politician and chief signer of the armistice. Another famous victim of the Vehmic trials was the Jewish industrialist and German foreign minister Walther Rathenau; members of *Organisation Consul* murdered him on June 24, 1922.[17] In 1922 and 1923, Major Buchrucker's nationalistic *Schwarze Reichswehr* or Black Army conducted Vehmic trials of so-called traitors which resulted in numerous brutal murders.[18]

Ehrhardt's and Buchrucker's roles were not limited to the sphere of Vehmic murder (*Fememord*). Both men were involved in attempts to overthrow governments which the German people had elected.[19]

The German judicial system treated the right-wing extremists who had participated in Vehmic murders and political insurrections with great leniency. The legal liquidations of political insurrections such as the Kapp, Küstrin, and Hitler putsch created a pattern that became typical for the treatment of right-wing offenders: law breakers were allowed to flee the country or go into hiding; highly placed offenders were never brought before a court; cases against defendants were dropped; convicted criminals received light sentences; prisoners only served a fraction of their time.[20] After the Beer Hall putsch, Hitler was sentenced to serve five years at *Festung* Landsberg; he was paroled after a few months. In the preface to *Mein Kampf,* he described his comfortable stay at Landsberg prison as a chance to relax and start work on his autobiography.[21]

While the courts treated right-wing extremists very leniently, they handed out severe—often unjustified—sentences to left-wing Germans.[22] The operation of this double standard revealed the fatal flaw of the entire judicial system: tacit approval of Fascist and anti-Semitic terrorism. Over the years most jurists proved to be disloyal to the Weimar Republic.[23] The same lack of loyalty characterized the behavior of many civil servants, administrators, and military officers who had sworn to uphold the republic.[24]

## BATTLE LAW AND SECRET POLICE TERROR

The National Socialists knew that they could count on the cooperation of most established jurists and civil servants when they set out to create law in their own image. The totalitarian corruption of the German legal system began as soon as the NSDAP came to power on January 30, 1933. The Vehmic courts provided a murky background as Nazi jurists began to demolish the existing legal system. The National Socialists called their new law *Kampfrecht,* or battle law.

"*Heil,* Comrade jurists!" wrote Hans Frank, the *Führer* of the German Law Front (*Deutsche Rechtsfront*), ushering in the year of the bloody Röhm Purge, "you are gathering around the flag of Adolf Hitler . . . you have committed your entire being . . . to the battle against the enemies of our State and Community."[25]

In 1935, Frank told a meeting (*Gautagung*) of the National Socialist Jurists League: "There is only one source of law . . . the sovereign National Socialist people, and there is only one center of will for Reich and people and the Movement, and that is the *Führer.*"[26]

In this roundabout way German jurists were ordered to accept blindly the will of Hitler as the only legitimizing principle. Now one man's pathological hatred and thirst for revenge came to determine what was considered justice in Germany. The National Socialists transformed the German legal profession into an army of soldiers taking its orders from Hitler, the supreme commander. On January 30, 1934, Roland Freisler wrote: "So we also have our task. We, the soldiers of law. . . . We must create a law, a German, a National Socialist law . . . Therefore criminal law must be combat law. . . . like the weapon's tip which in battle is pointed at the enemy . . . it must view the lawbreaking will of the . . . antisocial and antinational . . . individual as the object of . . . destruction."[27]

Nazi battle law changed all parts of Germany's legal system; the transformation was most lethal in the area of criminal law. The National Socialists invented a plethora of nebulous new crimes such as "insulting the people," "affront to the folk tradition," "economic treason," and "assaults upon the racial continuance of the German people."[28] The National Socialists also escalated the severity of punishment—death penalties became as common as fines for littering.

With unprecedented ruthlessness and brutality, the dictator and his henchmen used all the levers of power to transform Germany into the monstrous thing Hitler liked to call the "total state." Battle law served the purposes of the new rulers well—but they wanted more. Therefore the Nazis accepted *SS-Gruppenführer* Reinhard Heydrich's idea to institutionalize protective custody (*Schutzhaft*): a dreadful penal twilight zone supervised by the SS Main Security Office (*Sicherheits-Hauptamt*). Now official pseudo-law was linked with the naked terror of secret police activity. Graber has described the sequence of events. Under the guise of *Schutzhaft* any local Gestapo official could suddenly arrest anybody he viewed as an "enemy of the state." The victims of protective custody were never brought to trial: without ever finding out what crimes they were charged with they languished in police prisons until they were herded into cattle cars and transported to concentration camps.[29]

Among the first victims of protective custody were the leaders and

members of Germany's workers' mass movements and so-called pacifists. On March 9, 1933, the Nazi Minister of the Interior, Wilhelm
Frick, proclaimed gleefully that Communists and Social Democrats were
being sent to concentration camps.[30] On March 20, 1933, *Reichsführer-
SS* Heinrich Himmler announced the opening of Dachau concentration
camp during a news conference in Munich.[31]

The destruction of the workers' movement entailed the arrest, torture,
and murder of proletarian leaders and activist workers, the theft of all
properties and funds belonging to trade unions, workers' organizations,
the German Communist Party (KPD), and the Social Democratic Party
(SPD), and the prohibition of all working-class activities. On March 31,
1933, the National Socialist government decreed that "crimes against
public safety" were punishable with death by hanging. The last blow fell
on June 22, 1933, when the Nazis used Article 48 of the Weimar Constitution to outlaw the SPD. With the "voluntary" dissolution of the
Catholic Center Party on July 5, 1933, all political parties—with the
exception of the NSDAP—ceased to exist.[32]

The Nazi leaders used battle law and secret police terror to destroy
their opponents, to cow the people, and to accelerate the establishment of
a totalitarian social system. Nazi totalitarianism was a reign of terror
benefiting only a few: Hitler, the National Socialist leadership, high-
ranking military officers, large landowners, the big capitalists, and the
top civil servants.[33] The rest of humanity paid an exorbitant price for the
twelve-year rule of the Nazi mass murderers. When World War II
ended, 50 million people had been killed, 30 million were crippled, and
half of Europe lay in ruins.[34]


## THE ASSAULT ON GERMAN JEWRY

When the destruction of the workers' movement and the demolition of
the democratic political structure were in their final phase, the Nazis intensified their official assault on the German Jews. On March 28, 1933,
the leadership of the NSDAP organized the nationwide *Judenboykott,*
centered around the long-standing Nazi slogans "Don't buy from the
Jews" and "The Jews are our misfortune." The boycott took place on
April 11, 1933. This anti-Jewish action unleashed members of the SA
and SS who terrorized Jewish retail merchants, physicians, professors,
lawyers, and their clients. Uniformed Nazis also prevented Jews from
entering universities, libraries, and law courts.[35] During the boycott
many Jewish merchants and professionals were taken into "protective
custody" and sent to concentration camps.[36]

The continued oppression and persecution of the German Jews deepened the corruption of the legal system. During the period 1933-1939,
the National Socialists created a huge body of anti-Jewish law—their

*Judengesetzgebung,* which they published in its entirety in 1939.[37]  As Joseph Walk and his co-workers have shown in their recent collection of anti-Jewish laws, decrees, ordinances, secret orders, etc., the legal transformations took place during the entire Nazi period, continuing until the last year of World War II.[38]  The fate of the roughly 565,000 German Jews[39]—eventually shared by the other victims of the Holocaust throughout Nazi-ruled and Nazi-occupied Europe—indicates that modern large-scale genocide must be prepared for.  And among the prerequisites of genocide, the corruption of the law occupies a prominent place.

## THE FIRST PHASE OF ANTI-JEWISH LEGISLATION

The first phase of the Nazi anti-Jewish legislation began on January 30, 1933, with the National Socialist seizure of power, and ended on September 15, 1935, with the enactment of the "Nuremberg Laws."[40]

The anti-Jewish measures belong to a body of laws made possible by actions of the *Reichstag* which met for one day on March 23, 1933.  The Nazi-dominated legislative body suspended all constitutional provisions protecting the political and civil equality of all German citizens.  On the same day, the *Reichstag* transferred its legislative powers to the cabinet, thereby giving the Hitler government unquestioned authority to issue any kind of dictatorial edict.  The enabling law (*Ermächtigungsgesetz*), which empowered the government to enact laws deviating from the constitution, provided the legal smoke screen for this drift into totalitarianism.  By a vote of 441 the *Reichstag* adopted the law—a creation of the NSDAP and the *Deutschnationale Volkspartei.*  Only the Social Democrats cast their 94 votes against the enabling law.  The KPD had already been forced to leave the *Reichstag* on March 8, 1933.[41]

The drift into extraconstitutionality which began in the final phase of the Weimar Republic had been speeded up by the Reich President's Emergency Decree on the Protection of People and State of February 28, 1933.  The provisions of Paul von Hindenburg's decree included the revocation of the citizens' basic constitutional rights.[42]  With the subsequent enabling law of March 24, 1933, the extraconstitutional power passed into the hands of Hitler.[43]

During the first phase of the anti-Jewish drive, German government authorities enacted numerous laws and issued many decrees, regulations, ordinances, directions, and explanations.  In keeping with the Party Program of the NSDAP[44] this "legal" onslaught was designed to publicly humiliate Jews, baptized Jews, non-Jews of Jewish descent, non-Jewish spouses of Jews, and persons of "doubtful Aryan descent."[45]  The term "Aryan" formerly designated groups of languages.  The Nazis arbitrarily used the term in their crackpot racial theory claiming that "non-

Aryans" were inferior to "Aryans." Nazi agitation and legislation was programmed to brand all "non-Aryans" as pariahs.

The National Socialists combined the public humiliation of the Jews with their campaign of discrimination and persecution. On April 7, 1933, shortly after the boycott of Jewish business, Reich Chancellor Hitler, Reich Minister of the Interior Wilhelm Frick, and Reich Minister of Finances Count Schwerin von Krosigk promulgated the Law for the Restoration of the Professional Civil Service. Paragraph three of the law, the so-called Aryan paragraph, began with the statement, "Civil servants who are not of Aryan descent are to be retired; honorary officials are to be dismissed from office."[46] Many Germans of Jewish descent were deprived of their jobs by a stroke of the dictator's pen.

On April 11, 1933, the Minister of the Interior and the Minister of Finances promulgated the First Decree to the Law for the Restoration of the Professional Civil Service. The second paragraph of this decree extended the expulsion to civil servants with only one Jewish grandparent. The decree also appointed an "expert on racial research" (*Sachverständiger für Rasseforschung*) in the Ministry of the Interior to whom persons of "doubtful Aryan descent" had to apply for an opinion. Paragraph one of the decree ordered the dismissal of all civil servants with Communist affiliations of any kind—an afterthought in view of the earlier mass arrests of German Communists and Socialists.[47]

The Second Decree to the Law for the Restoration of the Professional Civil Service of May 4, 1933, annulled all service contracts of "non-Aryan" clerks and workers in civil service organizations such as health insurance and social work.[48]

On May 6, 1933, the Third Decree to the Law caused the dismissal of "non-Aryan" judges, notaries, public school teachers, and salaried and unsalaried university teachers.[49]

The National Socialists deployed the "Aryan paragraph" as a major "legal" weapon in their offensive against the economic underpinnings of the Jewish community: a tidal wave of discriminatory legislation followed the attack on Jewish civil servants.

When the Nazis enacted the Law on Patent Lawyers on September 28, 1933, they completed a series of laws which excluded Jews from all forms of legal practice and all positions in the judiciary.[50]

The beneficiaries of this campaign quickly responded with a public display of their servile obedience to the Nazi rulers. On October 1, 1933, the judges of the Reich donned their blood-red robes and assembled in front of the law court in Leipzig. There the judges and other jurists swore an oath of loyalty to Nazi battle law.[51]

The arbitrary and inhuman expulsions of Jews from the civil service, education, and law were coordinated with other ousters to bring about the blighting effect upon Jewry which the Nazis had been planning from the start.

Other laws which the Nazis enacted to surround their illegitimate campaign of Jewish annihilation with the mantle of legality removed and excluded Jews from tax assessment and tax consultancy. The anti-Semitic legislation destroyed the likelihood of Jewish physicians, dentists, and dental technicians working with social health plans which covered almost the entire population. Other laws removed and excluded Jews from journalism, literature, the film industry, the theatre, broadcasting, music, the plastic arts, the ownership of hereditary rural homesteads, public orders and contracts, the stock exchange, the produce exchange, and executive positions in trade unions.[52]

On July 14, 1933, the cabinet passed the Law Regarding the Seizure of Anti-folkish and Subversive Assets, which was aimed at Marxist organizations. However, the Nazis also used this law to steal Jewish property; later they promulgated specific anti-Semitic laws designed to rob Jews of their possessions.[53]

The Nazis used boycotts, forced sales, and terror to oust Jews from commerce and trade. The Law Concerning the Ordering of National Labor of January 20, 1934, intensified the process of excluding Jews from executive positions in the German economy.[54]

During the Party Day rally of September 1935 (Parteitag der Freiheit), Hitler ordered officials of the Ministry of the Interior to Nuremberg, where they had to draft legislation which became known as the "Nuremberg laws." On September 15, 1935, the Nuremberg law on citizenship (Reichsbürgergesetz) officially transformed Jews into second-class citizens. Unlike "Aryans," Jews were not allowed to attain the new status of "citizen of the Reich" (Reichsbürger) and consequently lost all political rights.[55] The blood protection law (Blutschutzgesetz) of September 15, 1935, prohibited marriages and extramarital relations between Jews and "citizens of German or kindred blood." Jews were not allowed to employ "Aryan" females below the age of forty-five in their households, and they could not display the German flags.[56]

## THE ROAD TO GENOCIDE

The second phase of anti-Jewish legislation began on September 15, 1935, with the Nuremberg laws and ended on November 9, 1938, with the start of the officially prompted pogrom which the Nazis dubbed the night of crystal (Kristallnacht).

During this period the Nazis intensified the anti-Jewish drive by using the weapon of prohibition of profession (Berufsverbot). The ousters devastated additional occupational groups such as construction engineers, cattle dealers, auctioneers, arms dealers, realtors, nurses, etc.[57]

The Nazis continued to expropriate Jewish companies and enacted oppressive measures which excluded Jews from doctoral examinations;

imprisoned Jewish violators of racial laws and returning emigrants in concentration camps; prohibited changes of Jewish names; enforced the registration of Jewish businesses, assets, and persons; and ordered Jews to carry special identity cards and to use the middle names Sarah or Israel.

After the annexation of Austria, the Nazis disenfranchised the Austrian Jews on March 16, 1938. On October 5, 1938, the German government seized all Jewish passports. The Minister of the Interior also limited the issuance of new passports, which had to be marked with the letter J. On October 26, 1938, Himmler ordered the deportation of all Polish Jews. Two days later the Gestapo arrested these Jews and transported them to the border, where SS officials brutally forced them into an unhospitable Poland.[58]

The third phase of anti-Jewish legislation extends from the pogrom night of November 9-10, 1938, to the start of World War II on September 1, 1939. During the November pogrom Hitler unleashed hordes of sadistic SA and SS hooligans who murdered Jews, burned down their synagogues, demolished their stores and apartments, and carried out mass arrests.[59]

A wave of legislation followed the pogrom which accelerated the isolation and impoverishment of the Jews. On November 11, 1938, Jews had to surrender all weapons in their possession to the police. On November 12, 1938, Hermann Göring signed three decrees in his capacity as plenipotentiary for the (economic) Four-Year Plan. The first decree and subsequent legislation levied a punitive payment in the amount of 1 billion marks upon all Jews. The second decree excluded Jews from cooperatives and forbade them to engage in business, artisanry, or management. The third decree forced Jews to pay for the enormous damages which Nazi hoodlums had inflicted upon Jewish property during the November pogrom and to surrender all insurance claims to the Third Reich.[60]

The discriminatory legislation of the third phase sharpened the isolation and confinement of the Jews. On November 12, 1938, the president of the Reich Chamber of Culture, Joseph Goebbels, issued an order barring Jews from theatres, movie houses, concerts, exhibitions, etc. Subsequent legislation forbade Jewish children to attend public schools, subjected Jews to curfews, limited their freedom of movement, invalidated their driver's licenses and automobile registrations, expelled them from non-Jewish apartments and houses, and forced them to move into buildings occupied solely by Jews.[61] On July 4, 1939, the Minister of the Interior, Wilhelm Frick, established the SS-controlled Reich Association of Jews in Germany and decreed that all Jews inside Nazi territory had to belong to the association.[62]

The fourth phase of anti-Jewish legislation and activity extends from the start of World War II to the destruction of the Jews in Nazi-dominated Europe and covers the period September 1, 1939 to May 8, 1945.

The legislation of this phase aimed at the complete impoverishment and isolation of the Jews and their physical destruction. On September 12, 1939, Heydrich issued an edict which limited the access of Jews to food stores and subjected their apartments to police searches.[63] Other measures forbade Jews to do the following: leave their apartments after eight in the evening; own radios; buy clothes; have telephones; use public transportation without restrictions; move without permission; write checks; own typewriters, bicycles, cameras, binoculars, etc.; use public telephones; keep pets; subscribe to newspapers and magazines; receive an education; purchase meat, meat products, eggs, milk, and books; send letters abroad.[64] These measures and others of similar nature dissolved the everyday world of Jews.

Behind this nightmarish scene smoldered the Polish horizon; there the SS was herding Jews into city ghettos. By December 1939, Poles and Jews were pouring into Nazi-dominated Poland, where the SS was carrying out executions of hundreds of thousands.[65]

On March 4, 1941, the Nazis subjected German Jews to forced labor; on September 1, 1941, they ordered them to wear a yellow Star of David; on October 23, 1941, they forbade them to emigrate; on November 4, 1941, the transportation (*Abschiebung*) of Jews to Nazi-occupied Eastern Europe went into high gear and the Minister of Finances, Schwerin von Krosigk, organized the seizure of the deportees' assets.[66]

On July 31, 1941, Göring, as head of the Four-Year Plan, charged the chief of the Security Police and the Security Service (SD), *SS-Gruppenführer* Heydrich, with the preparation of the Final Solution of the so-called Jewish question.[67] On January 20, 1942, Heydrich summoned top officials of all ministries and offices involved in anti-Jewish activities to a villa in Wannsee, a swank Berlin suburb. Under SS direction the assembled civil servants developed a plan for the Final Solution. Authorized by Hitler and supported by the Nazi leadership, the Wannsee planners developed a detailed schedule for the destruction of Europe's 11 million Jews.[68]

After the Wannsee Conference Nazi legislation and policy operated in support of genocide. The consequences were horrendous and bestial: Jews became the slave workers of German corporations, which profited enormously from their misery; Jews were systematically worked to death by the SS; Jews were murdered in the torture chambers and gas chambers of the concentration camps.

The Nazi program of large-scale genocide, resulting in the death of 6 million Jews and millions of Poles, Russians, and other non-Jews, conjured up a final wave of legislation. On April 25, 1943, the Minister of the Interior cynically decreed that Jews and Gypsies—who were continually being destroyed in Nazi death factories—could not become German citizens.[69] On June 9 and 10, 1943, the Nazis dissolved the

Reich Association of Jews in Germany and seized the assets of the organization.[70] On July 1, 1943, Jews officially lost all legal protection and were subjected to the power of the police and Gestapo. In the event of death, Jewish assets were seized by the Reich.[71]

And so the Nazi death machine rattled on. The horrifying operation of the machine of mass extermination was supervised by brutal SS hordes and accompanied by the dry pronouncements of miserable bureaucrats. These debased representatives of a perverted legal and administrative system continued their lethal labor to the last moments of the Hitler regime—down to that *Runderlass* of the Minister for Economics, Walther Funk. The minister's circular of February 16, 1945, ordered the destruction of all files containing references to anti-Jewish activities in order to prevent the capture of these documents.[72]

The Nazi technicians of hell tried to shroud the scenes of mechanized mass murder with an impenetrable veil of secrecy. Against concealment, ignorance, and indifference a united humanity must set the watchword of the Italian anti-Fascists: *Non dimenticare!* Don't forget!

## NOTES

1. See Ernst Niekisch, *Das Reich der niederen Dämonen* (Hamburg: Rowohlt, 1953). In 1937, Niekisch was sentenced to lifelong imprisonment. He left the penitentiary in 1945 as a cripple. He was not alone. In April 1939, Nazi concentration camps were filled with more than 300,000 Germans. Approximately 35,000 non-Jewish Germans left the country as émigrés between 1933 and 1941. The figures are cited in David Schoenbaum, *Hitler's Social Revolution: Class and Status in Nazi Germany, 1933-1939* (New York: Doubleday, 1966), p. xiii.

2. Adolf Hitler, *Mein Kampf* (Munich: Franz Eher Nachfolger, 1925-1927), p. 55.

3. Ibid., p. 70 (emphasis in original; my translation). The last paragraph of Hitler's testament of April 29, 1945, ordered all Germans to continue their "merciless resistance" against "international Jewry." The last page of the testament is reproduced in Helmut Eschwege, ed., *Kennzeichen J: Bilder, Dokumente, Berichte zur Geschichte der Verbrechen des Hitlerfaschismus an den deutschen Juden, 1933-1945* (Frankfurt a.M.: Röderberg-Verlag, 1979), p. 286.

4. See John W. Wheeler-Bennett, *The Nemesis of Power: The German Army in Politics, 1918-1945* (New York: St. Martin's Press, 1954).

5. Hitler attacked the Treaty of Versailles, which concluded World War I, at the start of his political activity. For his early speeches and writings on the treaty see Hitler, *Sämtliche Aufzeichnungen, 1905-1924*, ed. Eberhard Jäckel and Axel Kuhn (Stuttgart: Deutsche Verlags-Anstalt, 1980), pp. 92-94, 113-15, 143-46, 157-63, 237-41, 265-69, 305-11, 398-400, 897-901.

6. See Hitler, *Mein Kampf*, pp. 216-25. In reality sailors of the imperial battle fleet at Kiel started the German revolution. Rebellious soldiers joined the navy mutineers in early November 1918. The military revolt made possible the formation of the armed Workers' and Soldiers' Soviets that supported Friedrich Ebert's "social republic." For the chronicle of these events see Cuno Horkenbach, ed., *Das Deutsche Reich von 1918 bis Heute* (Berlin: Verlag für Presse, Wirtschaft und Politik, 1930), pp. 27-35.

7. See Ulrike Hörster-Philipps, "Conservative Concepts of Dictatorship in the Final Phase of the Weimar Republic: The Government of Franz von Papen," in Michael N. Dobkowski and Isidor Wallimann, eds., *Towards the Holocaust: The Social and Economic Collapse of the Weimar Republic* (Westport, Conn.: Greenwood Press, 1983), p. 120. See also Fritz Thyssen, *I Paid Hitler* (New York: Cooperation Publishing, 1941). Thyssen expanded his father's steel company into the giant *Vereinigte Stahlwerke*. The authoritarian magnate wrote his revelations after his flight from the Nazi Germany he had helped to create. Many industrialists and bankers subsidized Hitler and his NSDAP (*Nationalsozialistische Deutsche Arbeiterpartei*), including Krupp, Siemens, Bosch, Flick, Vögler of the United Steelworks, and Schacht of the *Reichsbank*. See Daniel Guerin, *Fascism and Big Business*, 2nd ed., trans. Frances and Mason Merrill (New York: Monad Press, 1973).

8. See Richard F. Hamilton, *Who Voted for Hitler?* (Princeton: Princeton University Press, 1982), pp. 121, 137, 219, 223-25, 228.

9. See Michael H. Kater, *The Nazi Party: A Social Profile of Members and Leaders, 1919-1945* (Cambridge, Mass.: Harvard University Press, 1983), pp. 155-61, 229-33.

10. See Schoenbaum, *Hitler's Social Revolution*, pp. 1-42.

11. Prager and Telushkin view Nazi anti-Semitism as the outgrowth of practically all the popular ideologies which influenced the course of German history: "Christianity, the Enlightenment, Marxism, nationalism, and racism." For this statement see Dennis Prager and Joseph Telushkin, *Why the Jews? The Reason for Antisemitism* (New York: Simon and Schuster, 1983), p. 157. See also Fritz Stern, *The Politics of Cultural Despair* (Berkeley: University of California Press, 1961), Peter Viereck, *Metapolitics: From the Romantics to Hitler* (New York: Alfred A. Knopf, 1941), and Rohan Butler, *The Roots of National Socialism, 1783-1933* (New York: Dutton, 1942).

12. See G. S. Graber, *History of the SS* (New York: David McKay, 1978), pp. 24-25.

13. Ibid., p. 25.

14. Ibid., p. 31.

15. Ibid., p. 30. SA or *Sturmabteilung* means Storm Detachment. See also Robert G.L. Waite, *Vanguard of Nazism: The Free Corps Movement in Post-War Germany, 1918-1923* (Cambridge, Mass.: Harvard University Press, 1952). On November 8, 1933, delegations of the Free Corps handed over their flags to the SA in Munich's Königsplatz. The ceremony and the speech of SA *Stabschef* Röhm are reported in Cuno Horkenbach, ed., *Das*

*Deutsche Reich von 1918 bis Heute* (hereafter cited as *Reich*) (Berlin: Presse-und Wirtschafts-Verlag, 1935), p. 533.

16. The modern German word for *Vehme* is *Feme*.

17. See Cuno Horkenbach, ed., *Das Deutsche Reich von 1918 bis Heute* (Berlin: Verlag für Presse, Wirtschaft und Politik, 1930), pp. 131, 143-45.

18. See Erich Eyck, *A History of the Weimar Republic*, Vol. 1, trans. Harlan P. Hanson and Robert G.L. Waite (New York: Atheneum, 1970), p. 263. See also Emil J. Gumbel, *Vom Fememord zur Reichskanzlei* (Heidelberg: Schneider, 1962).

19. Captain Ehrhardt's brigade supported the Kapp Putsch in March 1920; Ehrhardt also assisted Hitler's Munich Beer Hall Putsch of November 8, 1923. Major Buchrucker was guilty of the Küstrin Putsch of October 1, 1923. For these events see Eyck, *A History of the Weimar Republic*, Vol. 11, pp. 147, 263, 272.

20. Ibid., pp. 160, 263.

21. Hitler, *Mein Kampf*, p. xxvii.

22. See Karl Dietrich Bracher, *Die Deutsche Diktatur: Entstehung, Struktur, Folgen des Nationalsozialismus* (Cologne and Berlin: Kiepenheuer & Witsch, 1969), p. 112. See also Heinrich Hannover, *Politische Justiz 1918-1933* (Frankfurt: Fischer Bücherei, 1966).

23. For the problems of German interwar society see Gunter W. Remmling, "Prologue: Weimar Society in Retrospect," in Dobkowski and Wallimann, *Towards the Holocaust*, pp. 3-14.

24. See Uwe Dietrich Adam, *Judenpolitik im Dritten Reich* (Düsseldorf: Droste Verlag, 1972), pp. 38-46; Gotthard Jasper, *Der Schutz der Republik* (Tübingen: Mohr Verlag, 1963).

25. Hans Frank, "Deutsche Juristen," *Deutsches Recht* 4, no. 1 (January 1934), p. 1 (my translation). The old system of law, Frank gloated, has been replaced by the "crystalline hardness of the decision-making power of National Socialist fighters." For this statement see Frank, "Das ewige deutsche Recht ist unser Ziel," *Deutsches Recht* 4, no. 11 (June 1934), p. 250. In this speech a power-drunk Frank frequently refers to battle law and the role of jurists as servants of Hitler and the NSDAP. In another speech Frank referred to Hitler as "our highest leader who is also our highest judge (*Gerichtsherr*)." For this statement and other comments on the subordination of the Nazi legal system under Hitler's will, see Frank, "Aufgabe des Rechtslebens nicht die Sicherung der Paragraphenanwendung, sondern vor allem Sicherung des Volkslebens," *Deutsches Recht* 4, no. 18 (September 1934), p. 427 (my translation). In 1933, Frank became a *Reichsminister* and *Reichsleiter*. He was also *Reichsjuristenführer* and leader of the League of National Socialist German Jurists, which had replaced the German Bar Association. He directed the "coordination" of the legal system as *Reichskommissar für die Gleichschaltung der Justiz*. The Nazis quickly formed their own organizations and outlawed all other associations of the legal profession. From 1939 to 1945, Frank was overlord of the General Government of

Poland, where he dedicated himself to the eradication of the Jews. Convicted by the International Military Tribunal, he was executed in 1946.

26. Cited in *Frankfurter Zeitung*, October 29, 1935.

27. Roland Freisler, "Deutsches Strafrecht, Vermächtnis und Aufgabe," *Deutsches Strafrecht*, Neue Folge, 1, no. 1 (January/February 1934), pp. 2, 5 (my translation). Freisler achieved notoriety as the Nazi judge presiding over the bloody People's Court which "tried" many German army officers and civilians accused of involvement in the attempt on Hitler's life of July 20, 1944. For the development of the totalitarian legal system in Nazi Germany, see the following legal periodicals: *Die Juristische Wochenschrift; Zeitschrift der Akademie für Deutsches Recht; Schriften Der Akademie fur Deutsches Recht; Das Recht der Nationalen Revolution; Deutsches Recht; Jahrbuch der Akademie für Deutsches Recht.* See also Ernst Brandis, *Die Ehegesetze von 1935* (Berlin: Verlag für Standesamtswesen, 1936); Hans Frank, *National-sozialistisches Handbuch für Recht und Gesetzgebung*, 2nd ed. (Munich: Zentralverlag der NSDAP, 1935); Hans Frank, *Nationalsozialistische Strafrechtspolitik* (Munich: Zentralverlag der NSDAP, 1938); Hans Frank, *Rechtsgrundlegung des nationalsozialistischen Führerstaates*, 2nd ed. (Munich: Zentraverlag der NSDAP, 1938); C. Haidn and L. Fischer, *Das Recht der NSDAP* (Munich: Zentralverlag der NSDAP, 1936); Ernst Rudolf Huber, *Verfassungsrecht des Grossdeutschen Reiches* (Hamburg: Hanseatische Verlagsanstalt, 1937-1939); Otto Meissner and Georg Kaisenberg, *Staats- und Verwaltungsrecht im Dritten Reich* (Berlin: Verlag für Sozialpolitik, Wirtschaft und Statistik, 1935); Karl-Friedrich Schrieber, ed., *Das Recht der Reichskulturkammer* (Berlin: Junker and Dünnhaupt Verlag, 1935); E. Volkmar, A. Elster, and g. Küchenhoff, eds., *Die Rechtsentwicklung der Jahre 1933 bis 1935/36* (Berlin: Walter de Gruyter, 1937); Wissenschaftliche Abteilung des NS. -Rechtswahrerbundes, ed., *Der Deutsche Rechtsstand* (Berlin: Deutscher Rechtsverlag, 1939). For a recent analysis of the Nazi judicial system see Ilse Staff, ed., *Justiz im Dritten Reich* (Frankfurt: Fischer-Taschenbuch-Verlag, 1978).

28. See Hans Frank, "Zur Strafrechtsreform," *Deutsches Recht* 4, no. 3 (February 1934), p. 49. Writing in his capacity as *Reichsjustizkommissar,* Frank demanded the "severest punishments" for the perpetrators of these "terrible crimes."

29. See Graber, *History of the SS*, pp. 88-95.

30. *Reich*, p. 106.

31. Ibid., p. 123. Oranienburg concentration camp opened on March 21, 1933.

32. *Reich*, pp. 41, 74, 83, 106, 115, 120, 150, 209, 220, 255, 258, 260, 263, 271, 274, 275.

33. See Reinhard Kühnl, *Faschismustheorien: Ein Leitfaden* (Hamburg: Rowohlt, 1979), p. 209. For the names of the top civil servants, bankers, and industrialists closely linked with the Nazi leadership, see *Reich*, p. 439. On totalitarianism see Hannah Arendt, *Elements and Origins of Totalitarian*

*Dictatorship* (New York: Harcourt, Brace and World, 1951); Carl J. Friedrich and Zbigniew K. Brzezinski, *Totalitarian Dictatorship and Autocracy* (Cambridge, Mass.: Harvard University Press, 1956); Karl Dietrich Bracher, *The German Dictatorship* (New York: Praeger, 1970).

34. See Kühnl, *Faschismustheorien*, p. 9.

35. See *Reich*, pp. 145-46, 153. For connections between anti-Nazi demonstrations and boycotts in the United States, England, Poland, France, etc., and the Nazi and anti-Jewish boycott, see Edwin Black, *The Transfer Agreement* (New York: Macmillan, 1984), pp. 7-68.

36. See Eschwege, *Kennzeichen J.*, p. 38.

37. Hans Peter Deeg, ed., *Die Judengesetze Grossdeutschlands* (Nuremberg: Der Stürmer Verlag, 1939).

38. See Joseph Walk, ed., *Das Sonderrecht für die Juden im NS-Staat: Eine Sammlung der gesetzlichen Massnahmen und Richtlinien—Inhalt und Bedeutung* (hereafter cited as *Sonderrecht*) (Heidelberg: Karlsruhe: C. F. Müller Juristischer Verlag, 1981).

39. See American Jewish Committee, *The Jews in Nazi Germany: A Handbook of Facts Regarding Their Present Situation,* reprint (hereafter cited as *Jews*) (New York: Howard Fertig, 1982), p. 3. *Jews* was first published in 1935. The official census of June 1925 indicated that the Jews in Germany numbered 564,379 or 0.9 percent of the total population. The census of June 16, 1933, revealed that the number of Jews had dropped to 499,682 or 0.77 percent of the total population. In 1933, about 60,000 Jews emigrated from Germany. In 1934, Jewish emigrants numbered approximately 23,000; in 1935, they numbered about 21,000; in 1936, about 25,000; in 1937, about 23,000. Between January 1, 1938, and the start of World War II on September 1, 1939, about 157,000 Jews emigrated from Germany. By May 17, 1939, forced confiscatory emigration, deportation, and murder had reduced the Jewish population in Germany to 213,930. On May 8, 1945, there were about 15,000 German Jews who had survived the Holocaust in Nazi-ruled and Nazi-occupied Europe. In Europe the Nazis had murdered about 6 million Jews. These statistics are cited in *Jews*, pp. 3, 116, and in Eschwege, *Kennzeichen J.*, pp. 349, 350, 351, 354, 355, 363.

40. For the distinction of the different phases of the Nazi anti-Jewish legislation I am indebted to Eschwege and Walk. See Eschwege, *Kennzeichen J.*, p. 5, and *Sonderrecht*, p. xi.

41. See *Jews*, p. 75; *Reich*, pp. 106, 140.

42. The decree of February 28, 1933, based on Article 48, paragraph 2 of the Weimar Constitution (*Reichsverfassung*), was the fundament of the Nazis' totalitarian police state. See *Verordnung des Reichspräsidenten zum Schutze von Volk und Staat, Reichsgesetzblatt* (hereafter cited as RGB1) I, 1933, p. 83.

43. *Gesetz zur Behebung der Not von Volk und Reich* (*Ermächtigungsgesetz*), RGB1 I, 1933, p. 141. Article 3 of this enabling law empowered the

chancellor, i.e., *Reichskanzler* Hitler, to engross and promulgate the laws of the Reich.

44. Points four and five of the Party Program of February 24, 1920, declared that Jews could not be German citizens and that they should be subject to alien legislation. Cited in *Sonderrecht*, p. 3.

45. The American Jewish Committee uses the concept non-Jews of Jewish descent. See *Jews*, p. 76. The Nazis publicized their intention to cause "the humiliation of the Jews of Germany." See *Völkischer Beobachter*, April 3, 1933.

46. For the "Aryan paragraph" and its consequences see *Gesetz zur Wiederherstellung des Berufsbeamtentums*, RGB1 I, 1933, pp. 175-77. See also *Jews*, pp. 123-29. Exceptions concerning Jewish war veterans and their families were rendered nugatory in practice.

47. *Erste Verordnung zur Durchführung des Gesetzes zur Wiederherstellung des Berufsbeamtentums*, RGB1 I, 1933, p. 195. Paragraph 2 of this decree defined as "non-Aryan" anybody "who is descended from non-Aryan, in particular Jewish parents or grandparents. It is sufficient that one parent or one grandparent is non-Aryan. This shall be deemed to be so, in particular, if one parent or one grandparent belonged to the Jewish religion."

48. *Zweite Verordnung zur Durchführung des Gesetzes zur Wiederherstellung des Berufsbeamtentums*, RGB1 I, 1933, pp. 233-35. In contrast to many other countries, health insurance and social work are civil service organizations in Germany.

49. *Dritte Verordnung zur Durchführung des Gesetzes zur Wiederherstellung des Berufsbeamtentums*, RGB1 I, 1933, pp. 245-46. In Germany judges, notaries, public school teachers, and university professors are civil servants. See also Hans Mommsen, *Beamtentum im Dritten Reich* (Stuttgart: Deutsche Verlagsanstalt, 1966).

50. The restrictive laws excluded Jews from admittance to the profession of law, juries, commercial judgeships, labor and arbitration courts, the lawyers' and patent lawyers' association, etc. See RGB1 I, 1933, pp. 188-89, 217-18, 522-23, 669-77. See also *Jews*, pp. 139-48.

51. See *Reich*, pp. 436-37.

52. These discriminatory laws, decrees, ordinances, orders, instructions, and rulings were promulgated in 1933. For the text of this legislation see *Jews*, pp. 149-77. Subsequent legislation increased the severity of these measures and extended their range to all other professional activities.

53. See RGB1 I, 1933, pp. 479-80. For subsequent legislation see RGB1 I, 1937, p. 1161; RGB1 I, 1938, pp. 404, 414-16, 973, 1579-81, 1638-40, 1709; RGB1 I, 1939, pp. 282-86. See also *Sonderrecht*, p. 233, No. 503; p. 263, Nos. 52, 53; p. 264, No. 57.

54. See *Reichsarbeitsblatt* I, 1934, pp. 45-56.

55. See RGB1 I, 1935, p. 1146.

56. For the Law for the Protection of German Blood and German Honor *(Gesetz zum Schutze des deutschen Blutes und der deutschen Ehre)* see RGB1 I, 1935, pp. 1146-47.

57. See RGB1 I, 1935, pp. 1524-25; RGB1 I, 1936, pp. 11-12, 317-18, 347-58, 524-26, 563-64; RGB1 I, 1937, pp. 28-29, 191-202; RGB1 I, 1938, pp. 40-44, 115, 202, 265-69, 823-24, 1309-15, 1403-6, 1545-46.

58. See *Sonderrecht,* p. 187, No. 290; pp. 191-92, No. 310; p. 203, No. 363; p. 210, No. 400; p. 222, Nos. 452, 453; p. 223, Nos. 457, 458; p. 226, No. 471; p. 227, No. 475; p. 229, No. 487; p. 233, Nos. 503, 506; p. 237, Nos. 524, 526; p. 244, Nos. 556, 557; p. 247, No. 569.

59. See Herrmann Graml, *Der 9. November 1938: "Reichskristallnacht,"* 6th ed. (Bonn: Bundeszentrale für Heimatdienst, 1958).

60. See RGB1 I, 1938, pp. 1573, 1579-81, 1638; *Reichssteuerblatt,* 1938, pp. 1073-75. See also Adam, *Judenpolitik im Dritten Reich,* pp. 211-12.

61. See *Sonderrecht,* p. 255, No. 12; p. 256, No. 17; p. 260, Nos. 34, 37; p. 262, No. 47; p. 292, No. 190; p. 293, No. 192.

62. See RGB1 I, 1939, pp. 1097-98. The *Reichsvereinigung der Juden in Deutschland* was controlled by Heydrich, chief of the SS Main Security Office. In 1938 and 1939, the Nuremberg laws were extended to Nazi-dominated Czechoslovakia.

63. See *Sonderrecht,* p. 304, No. 10.

64. Ibid., p. 305, Nos. 12, 16; p. 306, No. 17; p. 307, No. 24; p. 312, No. 48; p. 325, No. 115; p. 350, Nos. 241, 244; p. 355, No. 264; p. 360, No. 287; p. 364, Nos. 308, 310; p. 377, No. 376; p. 379, No. 386; p. 387, No. 426; p. 389, No. 437; p. 402, No. 501.

65. See Graber, *History of the SS,* pp. 137-39.

66. See *Sonderrecht,* p. 336, No. 174; p. 347, No. 229; p. 353, No. 256; p. 354, No. 261.

67. See Eschwege, *Kennzeichen J.,* p. 148.

68. Ibid., p. 228.

69. See RGB1 I, 1943, pp. 268-69.

70. See *Sonderrecht,* p. 398, No. 485; p. 399, No. 487.

71. See RGB1 I, 1943, p. 372.

72. See *Sonderrecht,* p. 406, No. 525.

# 11

# THE ULTIMATE REPRESSION: THE GENOCIDE OF THE ARMENIANS, 1915-1917

## *Gerard J. Libaridian*

## INTRODUCTION

Exterminations of families, tribes, and ethnic or religious groups have been known to occur since the dawn of history. The particular heinousness of mass death, however, has brought the gradual recognition of such acts as crimes against humanity. Planned and systematic genocides have even acquired a wider scope, while technology has increased their efficiency. Given the technological advances in military and biological hardware, the degrees to which many groups depend on governmental policies for their survival, the abrupt changes which traditional societies undergo when facing the challenge of modernization, and the increase in tensions between nations due to the diminishing resources available for distribution, one can expect governments to have recourse to radical solutions such as genocide to solve real or imaginary problems. Genocide thus may become merely another manifestation of what differentiates a state from other institutions: its monopoly of the right to kill enemies of society and to ask its citizens to kill enemies of the state or to be killed doing it.

A corollary to the above hypothesis is that certain groups that seek change in a system, particularly a traditional one, are more likely to be victims of genocide. This is especially true when the ideology of the state characterizes a potential victim as both an enemy of society (of the internal order) and of the state.[1]

The genocide of the Armenian people during World War I is the earliest case of a documented modern day extermination of a nation. Planned and carried out by the Ittihadist (Ittihad ve Terakke Jemiyeti, or the Committee of Union and Progress) government of the Ottoman

Empire, this first genocide of the twentieth century may also be a paradigm for a type of "political" genocide likely to become the pattern of twentieth-century genocides.

The purpose here is to suggest the possibility that twentieth-century genocides may have become radical means used by governments to resolve political problems. This chapter will briefly present the facts and impact of the Armenian genocide, discuss the generally accepted explanations of the holocaust as the final solution to a thorny national problem, introduce some newly discovered evidence on the relations between Armenian and Turkish leaders preceding the genocide, and suggest that the Ittihadist government perceived Armenians not only as an unwelcome ethnic group but also as a social group which threatened the traditional authoritarian order of Ottoman society.

The events between 1915 and 1917, the worst years of the genocide, are quite clear and documented in gruesome detail.[2] In early 1913, the Young Turk government was taken over by its militaristic and chauvinistic wing led by Enver, Talaat, and Jemal Pashas.[3] This triumvirate led the country into World War I on the side of Germany. Sometime in early 1915 that same government developed and put into effect a plan for the extermination of its Armenian population, variously placed at between 2 and 3 million subjects. Most Armenians lived in the rural and small-town environment of historic Western Armenia, a part of the Ottoman Empire since the sixteenth century.[4]

The plan was carried out in phases. In April 1915, the religious, political, educational, and intellectual leadership of the Armenian people, close to 1,000 individuals, most educated in the Western tradition, were taken into custody throughout the Empire and killed within a few days. Then Armenian draftees of the Ottoman army, estimated at 200,000, were liquidated through mass burials, burnings, executions, and sheer exhaustion in labor battalions. Finally, the remainder of the population, now composed largely of elderly people, women, and children, was given orders for deportation in all parts of the Empire (except the capital and a few cities with European presences).[5] While a few cities and districts resisted the orders, most followed them, with the faint hope that they might be given a chance to come back.[6]

The fate of the deportees was usually death. Caravans of women and children, ostensibly being led to southern parts of the Empire, became death marches. Within six months of the deportations half of the deportees were killed, buried alive, or thrown into the sea or the rivers. Few reached relatively safe cities such as Aleppo. Most survivors ended up in the deserts of Northern Mesopotamia, where starvation, dehydration, and outright murder awaited them. Subsequent sweeps of cities ensured the elimination of the Armenian people from the western and largest portion of their historic homeland.

The extermination was accomplished under the supervision of a secretive organization which functioned as part of the government, the *Teshkilat-i Mahsusa* or Special Organization, run by the highest government officials, manned by convicts released from jail, and acting under the immediate supervision of select members of the Ittihad Party.[7] The release of the vilest, unbridled animal passions served well the government's purpose of ensuring extermination in the most humiliating, dehumanizing fashion. The torture of thousands of women and children became a source of satisfaction for hundreds who sought and found official sanction from government officials as well as Muslim clergymen, since the murder of Armenians was characterized, like the war against the Entente, as a *jihad* or holy war. Human imagination labored to devise new ways of mutilating, burning, and killing. The suicide of hundreds of women and children attests to the particular brutality of the methods used.

The carnage took place in full view of the military and diplomatic representatives of governments allied with the Ottoman state, such as Germany, and neutral ones, such as the United States (until 1917). In addition, Western missionaries, journalists, travellers, and even sympathetic officers of the Ottoman army described the death marches and atrocities in daily letters and accounts. Reports of the extermination and its methods forwarded to Washington, Berlin, and other capitals by eyewitnesses confirm the stories told by thousands of survivors in subsequent memoirs and oral history interviews.[8]

The methods used to bring about the extermination of the Armenians are very significant, since they attest to the participation of an important segment of the general population. The acquiescence of Turkish, Kurdish, and, to a limited extent, Arab civilians was made easier by the promise of loot, of appropriation of children and women, and of an afterlife in heaven. A governmental decree making it illegal to assist refugees or orphans might ultimately have been responsible, however, for the absence of wholesale assistance from Turks to their former neighbors and friends. The penalty for such assistance was death by hanging in front of one's own house and the burning of that house.[9] This did not stop some, nonetheless, from resisting orders. A number of Turkish governors and sub-governors were removed from office for their unwillingness to follow orders. Many Turks and Kurds, especially in the Dersim region, risked their lives to save straggling Armenians, and Arabs throughout the Empire's southern provinces accepted and helped the survivors.[10]

It is not clear whether it was the absence of technologically viable means to exterminate swiftly or the desire to keep the appearance of "deportations" that led the government to achieve extermination through such methods. The Ottoman government had a record of massacres, some against Armenians. Of these, the 1894-1896 and 1909 are the best known.[11] But this was the first time such a wholesale operation was conducted, ending in the uprooting of a whole nation.

The impact of the genocide was devastating. Of the 2 to 3 million Western Armenians, 1.5 million perished during the holocaust. Up to 150,000 of those who had accepted Islam or had been kept, stolen, or protected by Turks and Kurds survived in Western Armenia without, however, any possibility of preserving a sense of religious or national identity. Close to 400,000 survived by fleeing to Russian Armenia and the Caucasus (where many more died as a consequence of disease and starvation) or Iran; perhaps 400,000 survived by reaching the southern or Arab provinces of the Ottoman Empire.[12]

In addition to the death of some 50 to 70 percent of Armenians living under Ottoman Turkish rule, Armenians lost the right to live as a community in the lands of their ancestors; they lost their personal property and belongings. They left behind the schools, churches, community centers, ancient fortresses, and medieval cathedrals, witnesses to a long history. Survivors were forced to begin a new life truncated, deprived of a link with their past, subject to upheavals in the new lands where they suddenly found themselves as foreigners. The remnants of the largely peasant and rural population were now a wretched group of squatters on the outskirts of cities poorly equipped to handle an increase in population.

The genocide constituted a radical break with the past for Western Armenians. The normal transmission of ethical and cultural values was cut off. The traditional ways of explaining tragedies could not accommodate the final solution. Orphans grew to remember and tell the stories of childhood years; they did not know what to think of their Turkish neighbors and found it difficult to imagine that they had once lived together in relative peace.

## ENEMIES BY DEFINITION

The victims of twentieth century premeditated genocide—the Jews, the Gypsies, the Armenians—were murdered in order to fulfill the state's design for a new order. . . . War was used in both cases (an opportunity anticipated and planned for by Germany but simply seized by Turkey after World War I began) to transform the nation to correspond to the ruling elite's formula by eliminating groups conceived of as alien, enemies by definition.[13]

So argues Helen Fein in *Accounting for Genocide.* This provides a basic and adequate explanation for the dynamics of the Armenian genocide. Whatever political, sociological, and other explanations one may end up accepting as part of the causal process, only such an encompassing, exclusive characteristic of the human mind can account for the radical nature of the "solution," for the act of genocide. It is when man plays God and wants to recreate the world in his own image—however perverted man or the image—that the *other* can be reduced to a nuisance, to an enemy that by definition must be destroyed regardless of his or her actions and policies.

Explanations of the Armenian genocide have generally agreed with Fein's conclusion. The "formula" which historians have ascribed to the Ittihadist elite may vary; some stress a Pan-Islamist vision at work, others a Pan-Turanian one. Most have focused on the rise of an exclusive Turkish nationalism underlying or in the service of Pan-Turanian and/or Pan-Islamic dreams.[14] This nationalism was tied to Anatolia, the "birthplace" of Turkism, a last bastion after the loss of European Turkey. In some cases, as if to moderate the burden of the crime, some have argued that the genocide was the violent manifestation of an otherwise predictable and historically natural clash of two nationalisms in conflict, Armenian against Turkish; this explanation allows for the equation of the motivations of the two groups, with a difference only in the means used by each to achieve their goal.[15]

Evolving Turkish nationalism was, in fact, the major factor which determined the course of Ottoman history during the first two decades of this century. Whatever subjective satisfaction Pan-Islamic and Pan-Turanian dreams gave to its adherents, whether under Sultan Abdul Hamid II or the Young Turks who replaced him, these ideologies remained vehicles by which energies outside Turkish nationalism could be harnessed to its service. The Young Turk-Ittihadist elite cared not under what ideology it continued its domination. Religion worked for a while, in some places. It was particularly potent in moving the ignorant masses, in ensuring the support of the *mollahs* (priests) and the *softas* (students of religion) for the Holy War. The idea of unification of Turkish groups across Asia had some success as well; but Pan-Turanism too remained an abstraction for most of the people it was supposed to inspire.

By the time the Ittihadist triumvirate decided to sign an alliance with Germany, its members had determined that whatever ideology emerged, and regardless of who won the war, drastic measures were needed if the Turkish elite were to continue to rule over the remains of the Empire. Long before the war, the Ittihadists were already pursuing a policy of Turkification which went beyond Pan-Islamism.[16] Arabs and Albanians were to speak Turkish; it was not sufficient that they were largely Muslim. The problem with the Ittihadists was that they had not as yet given up on the idea of an empire, which required an ideology and a basis of legitimation wider than Turkish nationalism or dynastic allegiance.

Conditions were ripe for genocide to occur during a period of transition from the concept of an empire based on dynastic allegiance to that of a nation-state. Pan-Turanian and Pan-Islamic ideologies were stages that helped the Ottomans accept the break from a tradition of conquest. One of the vehicles for the building of Turkish nationalism was the identification of "enemies" of the yet to be born nation; a second vehicle was its resistance to the loss of territory and dignity to Western imperialism. The self-definition in relation to the Armenian enemy was convenient, since Armenians were neither Turks nor Muslims; and the long history of the Armenian Question as an integral part of the Eastern Question made identification with outside enemies, in this case France, Great Britain, and Russia, easy.[17]

The Ottoman government had used wholesale massacres before against "enemies" of the state. Wartime conditions provided justification for extraordinary measures. Western governments, traditionally the only ones interested in and capable of intervention, were already at war, on the wrong side, as far as the Ottoman Empire was concerned. Germany, the Ottoman Empire's major ally, was capable of making a difference but opted not to.[18] Armenians, based on their history of past victimization, could easily be perceived as enemies of society or the state, given the paranoia of Ittihadist leaders.[19]

It is possible to paraphrase Helen Fein, then, and reconstruct a Turkish "design for a new order." This would be based, on the one hand, on the assertion of sovereignty vis-à-vis the West by reversing the series of losses of territories; on the other hand, this design would insist on the establishment of "order" within the country, an order which was threatened by elements for whom the symbols of Turkism, Islamism, or Turanism could not mean much and who were seeking an alternate framework for identification with the state. In addition, these elements, i.e., Armenians, could be charged with collusion with the traditional enemy, Russia.[20]

The basic explanation provided by Fein, however, does not preclude the further elaboration of the vision of the criminal state in its specific and more complex historical context. Many scholars have contributed to the understanding of genocide and to the identification of factors leading to genocide. Leo Kuper and Irving L. Horowitz have developed new perspectives on genocide as a political weapon in the twentieth century and argued for its study as a new category in social research.[21] Vahakn Dadrian, a sociologist pioneering in studies on the Armenian genocide, has concentrated on the victimization theory and has pointed out sociological factors involved in the process of dehumanization leading to genocide resulting from the search for power.[22]

The Kurdish historian Siyamend Othman, in his doctoral dissertation and a subsequent article, attempted to explain the reasons why Kurds played such a prominent role in the deportations and massacres. His argument is that for Kurds within a feudal structure the tribe provided group identity and therefore allegiance was to the chief, who was manipulated by the Ottoman government. Othman also points out that the common Kurd may have been harboring some resentment toward Armenians, who tended to be the usurers and capitalists in the marketplace.[23]

In a recent paper Ronald Suny attempted an analysis of the sociological makeup of both Turks and Armenians and suggested that the existence of an Armenian upper class in control of many critical sectors of the economy might in fact have accentuated antagonisms.[24]

Of major importance is the analysis provided by Robert Melson. Melson has recently argued that one must go beyond victimization theories that generally point to victims of genocide as scapegoats or as provocateurs. He found instead that groups that have social mobility and adaptability to modernization, and thus tend to disturb the traditional orders, may tend to become victims in times of crisis. Melson has called for a somewhat more complex model within which the paranoia of the victimizer is as important in understanding—and foreseeing—genocide as the "success" of the victim.[25]

These recent points of view can be seen as suggestive and important efforts that provide specificity to the case of the Armenian genocide and help shed light on the "formula" operative in the minds of the Turkish leaders that made possible the dehumanization and, eventually, the extermination of Armenians.

## A Populist Agenda and the Alienation of the State

To the extent that the Ittihad decision to exterminate Armenians in the Ottoman Empire can be explained by the history of relations between the two, the period from 1908 to 1914 is obviously the most important. Armenian political parties, the revolutionary Hunchakians and Dashnaktsutiune, had opposed the Sultan's government until 1908, as had the various Turkish groups known as the Young Turks, of which the Ittihad ve Terakke was the most important. When the Young Turks took over the government in 1908 and restored the Constitution that had been promulgated in 1876 and prorogued in 1878, Armenian revolutionaries ended their armed struggle and pledged allegiance to the new regime and kept their pledge until the beginning of the genocide.

Thus, the first point to be made regarding the pre-genocide period is that Armenian political parties functioned as legitimate Ottoman institutions, whose goals and bylaws were recognized by the Ottoman government. While they differed in their assessment of the chances for successful reforms under the Ittihad government, there was and there could have been nothing in their programs or actions which could have been considered illegitimate or detrimental to the Constitution.

The second important fact with regard to these relations is that, along with a change in the ruling elite of the Ottoman Empire, the 1908 Constitution also produced a change in the representation of the Armenians. To negotiate Armenian demands for reform the Ottoman Turkish government had to deal with Armenian leaders of the revolutionary and guerrilla movement. The new spokesmen for the Armenians had won the right to represent Armenians by waging an armed struggle on behalf of economic and political rights; their religion had been Enlightenment. These new leaders supplanted the largely conservative clergymen of the Patriarchate who were bound by the dictates of the *millet* system which defined Armenians as a religious community and denied them an essentially political character.

A third important characteristic of the pre-genocide Armeno-Turkish relations is that they evolved between 1908 and 1914. The major factor which determined this change was the gradual elimination of the liberal program which some Young Turks had advocated prior to and immediately after the 1908 takeover. As a whole, the Young Turks had linked the imperative of preserving the territorial integrity of the Empire with the need to introduce general reforms. This willingness to recognize the importance of domestic social, economic, and political policies affecting the larger population had satisfied Armenians in their struggle to improve their situation, particularly the lot of the peasant and rural populations. Generally speaking, the Ittihad government discarded its liberal democratic ideals; it moved toward despotism and began relying, as its predecessor had done, on the reactionary classes, repressive measures, and symbols to secure its position in power.

Based on documents being studied for the first time, it is possible to argue that the critical period when the fundamental change occurred was between 1909 and 1911.[26] By 1909, the excitement of the first days was over. Elections for the first Parliament were completed. The Ittihad Party had run on a platform with the Armenian Revolutionary Federation (ARF) or Dashnaktsutiune, and won. Furthermore, following the massacre of Adana, the government promised to take concrete steps to introduce long promised reforms, consolidate the constitutional regime, and resolve domestic issues which caused hardship to Armenians.

An agreement signed between the Ittihad and the Turkish Section of the Western Bureau (highest executive body) of the Dashnaktsutiune seemed a secure path toward the realization of reforms throughout the Empire. In 1911 the Sixth World Congress of the Dashnaktsutiune reached the conclusion that the party could no longer hope that the Ittihad would realize the reforms and consequently it could no longer remain in an alliance with the Ittihad.[27]

According to the agreement, the two parties were to develop a joint committee, above and beyond formal contacts and parliamentary negotiations. This committee would be composed of high-level officials whose task it was to find ways to strengthen the Constitution, educate the public on political issues and against the reaction, educate the Turkish masses on anti-Armenian prejudices, and increase political rights for all. In addition to the main committee in Constantinople, regional and district joint committees were also to be organized. The agreement was reached at a meeting between representatives of the Turkish Section of the ARF Bureau and the Central Committee of the Ittihad held in Salonika in August 1909, four months after the massacres of Adana. These negotiations may have been the price paid by the Ittihad in return for the willingness of the Dashnaktsutiune to ascribe the massacres to the reaction, when in fact at least local Ittihad members were implicated.

The institutionalization of contacts at all levels appeared a good way to avoid future misunderstandings, to decrease tensions, and to open the way to important reforms. However, from the beginning, the Dashnaktsutiune had difficulties in ensuring the functioning of the committee. The first and most important committee, to be established in the capital, did not get its Turkish appointees until early 1910. In addition, the Ittihad avoided regular meetings from March to June 1910, and none of the important issues, foreign or domestic, was placed on the agenda by the Ittihad.

The Dashnaktsutiune had its own agenda, which constituted basically its minimum and practical program. The party demanded:

1. The end of feudal structures, laws, and practices in Anatolia.
2. A change in the government's policy of total indifference toward social and economic development and the concomitant crises affecting all segments of society; economic development was necessary to provide opportunities for the improvement in the standard of living.
3. The solution of the most critical issue, the agrarian crisis, which resulted both from inherent inequities and the feudal system as well as from the conscious policies of officials to expel Armenians from their farms, expropriate their lands, and give them to *muhajirs* or Muslim immigrants. The latter, often coming from the formerly Ottoman Balkan districts, were systematically directed into Armenian districts for resettlement, which would then take place at the expense of Armenian farmers.
4. The end of regressive, extralegal, and illegal taxes, which particularly affected Christians, but generally had a negative impact on all subjects.
5. The end of insecurity of life, honor, and property, particularly for Armenians whose communal existence was threatened by continuing pillaging, lawlessness, and renewed overt aggression and discrimination.[28]

These issues, and especially the agrarian crisis and the tax laws, were pointed to as threatening the economic foundation of the Armenian community.[29]

The Dashnaktsutiune placed these and other, more specific, items on the agenda on many occasions. None of the issues, however, received satisfactory solutions. A second trip was needed to Salonika to determine why there was no action. In March 1911 two party plenipotentiaries went to meet again with the Ittihad Central Committee. The result was renewed promises for reform, once a new study was completed by two Ittihad leaders who were sent on a tour of the provinces. The Ittihad leaders seem to have agreed with the Dashnaktsutiune representatives that the problem was not between Armenians and Turks or Kurds but between the poor and the rich, and that Turkish and Kurdish peasants often suffered as much as Armenians. Despite the agreement in principle and the promise to seriously confront the problem, the tour by the two dignitaries produced no changes in government policies. Reporting from Van, a member of the Dashnaktsutiune's local Central Committee echoed the observation of many Armenians when he wrote: "[The two representatives] are here now and, frankly, we cannot understand what they are doing. They have shied away from all contacts with the popular masses and the rural folk; they are constantly surrounded by the local notables and government officials."[30]

Following two years of intense efforts and accommodation to an Ittihad agenda which seemed to be lacking focus, the Dashnaktsutiune came to the conclusion that it no longer could expect basic changes to come from the Ittihad. A Memorandum accompanying the Report to the Congress listed a number of reasons for the inability of the Ittihad to respond:

1. Feudalism was still not such an abhorrence to the Ittihad; at any rate, its leaders did not wish to alienate the Kurdish chieftains and local landlords, whose support they ultimately considered more important, and safer—since they demanded nothing in return—than that of the Armenians.

2. The Ittihad allowed reactionary elements, such as great landowners and *mollahs,* to become members of the local Ittihad clubs, changing the liberal character of the organization; it was gradually taken over by those forces which constituted the backbone of the previous regime and which had opposed constitutional change and parliamentary government.

3. The fear ascribed by Ittihad leaders to Kurds but in fact shared by some Turks that should Armenians have an equal chance in the system they would overwhelm others by their numbers and achievements.

4. The Ittihad did not wish to see the Dashnaktsutiune or any other Armenian party strengthened.

5. The Dashnaktsutiune's unqualified support of the Ittihad allowed them to take that support for granted; the Ittihad did not need to return any favors for the support.

6. The Ittihad did not wish to see an element in Asia Minor strengthened which might be favored by the Russians, particularly

when the more important friend, Germany, had other plans for Asia Minor.

7. The disagreement between two Dashnaktsutiune members of the Ottoman Parliament on the best methods to develop the proposed railroad in Eastern Anatolia.

8. Instability in the cabinet and its inability to make decisions.

In addition to the absence of reforms and the Ittihad's disregard for its own pledges, the authors of the Memorandum listed the following governmental actions to support their conclusions:

1. The Ittihad government had stopped prosecuting Kurdish chieftains accused of crimes against Armenians; one prominent criminal, Huseyin Pasha, had in fact been invited back into the country with a pardon.

2. The Ittihad had favored the Bagdad railway line which, in the view of the Dashnaktsutiune, would only enrich foreign capitalists; the party had recommended instead the Anatolian railway, which would help the economic development of this poor region.

3. No concrete steps were taken to return to Armenian peasants and farmers their lands, their principal means of livelihood. Such a distribution would hardly have affected the Kurdish or Turkish peasant, but it would have hurt the large landowners and *muhajirs*. The Dashnaktsutiune's proposal to achieve such a return through administrative decisions was frustrated by the Ittihad's recommendation that the regular courts be used for that purpose; pleas that the courts had not yet been reformed since the revolution and that peasants did not even have money to go to court or to bribe the corrupt officials were hardly heeded.

4. Where joint committees had been formed, the CUP representatives had on occasion made unreasonable and suspicious demands, such as assimilation of the Dashnaktsutiune into the Ittihad ve Terakke or turning over the lists of party members to the Committee of Union and Progress.[31]

The Sixth World Congress of the Dashnaktsutiune determined that the party could no longer be in alliance with the Ittihad, and that it would continue its efforts as a party in friendly opposition in Parliament.

Thus, during the period of intense relations following the revolution, when the two groups were able to know each other and act on this knowledge, Armenian leaders discussed security of life, land reform, economic development, and political equality, rather than autonomy or independence. Their disagreements and ultimate break were over bread and butter issues rather than over boundaries. Simon Zavarian, one of the founders of the party and a member of the Buro's Turkish Section, argued in 1912 that of all the elements in the Ottoman Empire, Armenians had been the most supportive of the Constitution:

This sympathy was not the consequence of [the Armenians'] high morals, [their] pro-Turkish inclination, or [their] political maturity. Rather, it is a question of geo-political realities and the current situation. Dispersed all over Asia Minor and mixed with Turks and other nationalities over the centuries, Armenians could not seek their future in a territorial autonomy, to lead an even more isolated political life. Armenians have tried to create [favorable] conditions for all Ottomans by supporting reform for the Ottoman state, [and to change] for the better the status of Armenians and Armenia.[32]

He observed, however, that Ottoman subjects had very little to show for the four years they had lived under a Constitution: "End of the internal identification cards, a few students to Europe, and some road projects. ... But what do peasants and craftsmen have to show? ... One also cannot hope much from the new Parliament, since most new deputies have titles such as *beys, zades, pashas* and *mufties*."[33] The alienation of the Armenians from the state was most dramatically illustrated in the final defense statement of the Hunchakian Paramaz in 1915, who after having been accused of plotting against the government, was hanged along with twenty other Hunchakian leaders. "I am not a separatist," said Paramaz. "It is this state which is separating itself from me, unable to come to terms with the ideas which inspire me."[34]

It seems, then, that long before the beginning of World War I the Ittihad, as well as the Armenian parties, had concluded that the Young Turk revolution had failed. Jemal Pasha, one of the triumvirate, argued in his memoirs that the Ittihad failed to take root.[35] In 1912 Zavarian had been more explicit in his explanation of the failure of the Ittihad:

Instead of waging a struggle, of establishing a popular militia, of creating a democratic party, a party with [political] principles, [the Ittihadists] went the way of their predecessors: they chose "the easy path." They kissed and allied with all the dignitaries and created a "union" of coreligionists.[36]

Armenian political parties wavered between clear signs that the liberal era had ended and the hope that they were mistaken. Meeting in Constanza in September 1913 for its Seventh World Conference, the Hunchakian Party had perceived the dangers inherent in Ittihad mentality. A new party policy was based, among other arguments, on

the fact that the fundamental principles [of the Ittihad] call for the preservation of a Turkish bureaucracy and that they do not allow for the emergence of a new state, and that it is the [Ittihad's] obvious goal not only to assimilate but also to eliminate, and if need be, exterminate, constituent nationalities.[37]

The Hunchakians concluded that Armenians should at least be ready for self-defense. Nonetheless, they, along with others, were determined to pursue the search for peaceful solutions. The Dashnaktsutiune continued to advocate reform, whatever the source. In 1914 the Dashnaktsutiune was still insisting on the need for reforms advocated in a June 1912 editorial published in the party organ, *Droshak*. That editorial had listed six critical issues, in addition to land reform:

1. Better administration throughout the Empire;
2. Decrease in taxes on the poor and implementation of progressive taxation;
3. Abolition of all feudal taxes;
4. Balanced budget by decreasing the number of officials and building up an economic infrastructure;
5. End to acts and policies which create fear of Turkification and Islamization of minorities;
6. Safeguarding of freedoms.[38]

After 1912, Armenians welcomed the renewed Western, and especially Russian, interest in pressuring the Ottoman government for reforms in the Armenian provinces of the Empire, reforms which would be realized under the supervision of European governors.[39] This, however, did not change the fundamental relationship between the leaderships of the Ittihad government and Armenians and the political program each represented for the other.

## LIMITATIONS OF THE NATIONALIST PERSPECTIVE

While the issues raised by Armenians were in the area of social and economic development and political equality, general interpretation of the genocide which followed this period remains mired in the limited and limiting perspective of Turkish and Armenian nationalisms.

The nationalist perspective creates many obstacles to an understanding of the full and real picture of Armeno-Turkish relations and mutual perceptions during the period preceding the genocide. It is true that the nature of the crime and its inhumanity are such that it is difficult to imagine that the Armenians and Turks were able to have a relationship other than that of victim and victimizer; it seems that it was always in the nature of the relations of these two peoples to massacre and to be massacred; that it was in the spirit of the times for both peoples to develop traditions of modern nationalism; that these two nationalisms were bound to clash as they did; and that it was natural for the Turks to be the killers and for the Armenians to be the victims. Moreover, the current domination of the theme of genocide in Armenian life, the bitterness and resentment in the absence of international recognition, and the increasing intensity of the Turkish denial of the genocide strengthen the misleading impression that all events preceding the genocide led to the genocide, and all events succeeding the genocide have been caused by it.

Turkish historiography has had particular difficulties with the Young Turk period, which remains little studied. While critical of the Ittihad ve Terakki on many grounds, Turkish historians have followed the policy of recent Turkish governments in either denying the genocide or justifying "deportations" during which "unfortunate" deaths occurred.[40] More so than is the case with Armenian writers, Turkish historians have denied Armenians any role in Ottoman politics except to assign them dreams of "independence," of which pre-genocide Armenians had to be disabused. Charges of separatism have become convenient vehicles to avoid discussion of the real problems then facing Ottoman society and the failure of the Young Turk government to solve them by means other than war and genocide.

The absence of Armenian life in Western Armenia (now Eastern Turkey), the success of the genocide, and the depoliticized existence of a contemporary Armenian community denied its memory in Istanbul make it easier for some Turkish historians to characterize Armenians and their aspirations as they do the Balkan peoples: once happy Ottoman subjects who were carried away by romantic nationalism. Turkish historians treat Armenians as an important political factor only in the context of a separatist threat that had to be dealt with.[41]

In other words, students of the period have difficulty imagining that Armenians were an integral part of Ottoman society for many centuries. This integrality was based on more than the physical occupation of lands under Ottoman dominion. It involved parallel developments in folk cultures, integration through a single economy, and mutual adjustments of social mores and values between Armenian and Turkish as well as Kurdish societies.[42] Thus Armenians constituted an integral part of the political life of the Ottoman Empire, whether defined as a *millet* or as an ethnic group with parliamentary representation under the Young Turks.[43]

Yet terms such as nationalism and independence have re-created a reality which places Armenians outside Ottoman history, just as the genocide placed Armenians outside Ottoman society; and analysis revolving around conflicts over irreducible categories such as race and religion turn history into a field where, instead of human beings interacting, abstract concepts do battle. It is as if hordes of individuals think and act as prescribed by ideologies of nationalism, religion, or race. Terminology then comes to reconfirm the view imposed by the genocide that, ultimately, one need not account for real Armenians leading real lives whose disappearance from their homes and from history must be accounted for; one is comforted by the thought that Armenians can be reduced to a corollary of a concept. The politician dehumanizes a nation in order to get rid of it; the historian does so to explain it away. Genocide becomes its own explanation; ultimately, it becomes its own justification.

The Young Turks, including the Ittihad ve Terakke, evolved in opposition to the despotic, reactionary, and corrupt rule of Sultan Abdul Hamid II as well as in reaction to his ineptness in protecting the territorial integrity of the Ottoman Empire against separatist tendencies and Western imperialistic encroachments. The latter were often justified in the name of persecuted minorities in the Empire. Therefore there evolved a linkage between domestic reforms, particularly those that might affect non-Muslims and non-Turks, and the defense of the territorial integrity of the Empire.

While all Young Turks agreed that the Sultan must go and that the prorogued Constitution of 1876 must be reestablished, it was obvious from the start that not everyone agreed on the best possible solution to the problem of territorial disintegration. One group, led by Prince Sabaheddine, promoted the idea of a multinational empire, with not only equal rights to the non-dominant groups, such as Armenians, but also a decentralized government which recognized a degree of regional autonomy to these groups.[44] Ahmed Riza, on the other hand, whose views became the more dominant after the revolution, believed in an Ottomanism which minimized differences, in a centralized state which, while recognizing the equality of all under the law, would promote the evolution of a homogeneous, corporate body politic. According to one historian:

[Ahmed Riza] used the word "Ottoman" freely in connection with individual inhabitants of the Empire, Muslim and Christian, as did Sabaheddine, but in Riza's vocabulary the word did not connote so much an individual with supra-national citizenship as a person who, if he was not already a Turk, must be hammered into a reasonable likeness to one.[45]

In 1908 the Young Turks took over the government and restored the 1876 Constitution. An era of brotherhood and renovation was thought to have begun; there was popular support for the move, and all problems were expected to be resolved soon with a new parliament.[46] Parliamentary elections were held twice during this period, in 1909 and 1912. These parliaments included representatives of various religious and ethnic groups, including Armenians, although there seems to have been constant haggling over the number of deputies each group was allotted, the Turks always retaining a comfortable majority.

But the Ittihad government, already weak in its commitment to democratization, was frustrated in its attempts to implement significant reforms. Between 1908 and 1914 the Ottoman Empire had to fight two

wars against Balkan states during which it lost the remainder of its
European holdings; the Ottomans also lost Libya to Italy. Thus, their
revolution had not guaranteed the territorial integrity of the Empire. The
Young Turks were particularly irritated by France and England, the two
bastions of liberalism and the principal external sources pressuring for
internal reform, who stood by while more and more Ottoman lands were
taken away. The Ittihad ve Terakke was also naive in its belief that a
parliament in and by itself constituted reform and could change a society.
Impatient about criticism and unwilling to undertake reforms which they
thought would weaken the authority of the state, the Ittihad ve Terakke
itself moved toward despotism, just as Abdul Hamid II had done over
three decades earlier. The Ittihad leadership gradually eliminated not
only opposition parties but also elements within the Ittihad who still
linked the salvation of Ottoman society to domestic reforms and a
vigorous constitutional life.[47] The coup d'etat in 1913 led by Enver,
Talaat, and Jemal Pashas came as the logical conclusion of the evolution
of the Ittihad toward a dictatorship. The three continued to believe that
they embodied all the wisdom necessary to lead the Empire toward
salvation; and the salvation of the Empire was couched in terms of
molding the character and thoughts of the citizens of the Empire in the
image of some ideal Ottoman.

From the promise of reform and equality and political rejuvenation
springing from the dedication to the ideal of a state which provided
equality under the law, the Ittihadids had moved to the position of a
corporate state within which not only non-Turks would be designated
"enemies" by definition, but also all liberals who insisted on a different
vision than the one articulated by the Ittihad, however vague and shifting
that may have been. Liberalism, which sought to reject the use of ethnic,
religious, or national identity as the basis for legitimation of power, was
seen as a weakness, as the lot of the forces of particularism and dissent,
as a source of chaos and further disintegration, unworthy of the various
visions of greatness that were motivating the Ittihad—the "true"
successor of the once powerful sultans.[48]

The Ittihad distaste for liberalism is critical for the understanding of
their policies before and during the war. In the Ottoman Empire liberalism and ethnic issues had been intertwined since the nineteenth century. Western pressures for reform always focused on the status of
Christians. The Turkish and Kurdish masses in the Empire had been
denied a systematic exposure to the need for reform from their own
revolutionaries.[49] They consequently viewed the Ottoman Constitution
as a privilege only for Christians.[50] Moreover, the Turkish people felt a
false sense of power through identification with the ruling dynasty and
ruling elite. Ramsaur, who tends to see all minorities as budding
nationalists, nonetheless recognizes that

the Moslem minorities, such as those Albanians who professed Islam, were beginning to feel the sweep of nationalism as well, but they were somewhat weakened in their aspirations by the fact that they enjoyed better treatment than did the Christian minorities and because they had a religious bond with the dynasty that the latter did not possess.[51]

Naturally, non-Turks found it easier to understand and appreciate reforms. Being more affected by the corrupt and decrepit taxation and legal systems than others, Armenians had long developed a tradition of political thought of their own in reaction to Ottoman misgovernment, Turkish superiority, and despotic rule.

Nonetheless, these non-Turkish parties constitute as much a part of Ottoman history as those founded by Turks. The Armenian focus of their parties, for example, is a reflection of the religious/ethnic structure created by the Ottoman government, not a natural result of Armenian nationalism.[52]

By 1914 the idea of liberal reforms had been eliminated from the agenda of the Ittihad. By 1914 as well, Armenians were the only significant non-Muslim people left in the Empire, the only non-Turkish political element in Anatolia capable of measuring the actions of the government beyond the rhetoric of Pan-Turkism and Pan-Islamism—a rhetoric which certainly could not inspire Armenians. Armenians were also the only segment of the electorate still supporting the parliamentary system and the Constitution. While the promise of Russian-sponsored reforms may have diminished the need to see political reform for the majority in the Armenian vilayets (administrative divisions) of the Empire, Armenians in central Anatolia, Cilicia, and the western provinces had no other hope.

## A CONTRACTUAL AGREEMENT

Armenian liberalism was the legacy of the revolutionary movement which developed following the failure of the signatories of the Congress of Berlin in 1878 to deliver on their promise of reforms for Ottoman Armenia. Armenians developed a liberation movement which, while having as an inspiration the Balkan movements, grew in reaction to Ottoman policies and Armenian realities and needs. Armenian groups were motivated much more by the socioeconomic disintegration of their society than by dreams of a renewed Armenian dynasty.[53] Even the Hunchakian Party, the first revolutionary party and the only one to advocate independence when founded in 1887, did so because it argued that since there were no positive results to be seen decades after the promise of internal reforms and almost a decade after the Congress of Berlin, Armenians could no longer hope to see reforms general enough to bring a change in their status.[54] The Dashnaktsutiune, founded in 1890, which in 1892 advocated a degree of autonomy and the opportunity to create "political and economic freedom," made clear that their purpose was not the replacement of a Turkish sultan with an Armenian one.[55] It was not surprising, therefore, that neither the Church nor the wealthy classes in Armenian society supported the revolutionaries; both remained very much part of the *millet* mentality fostered by the Ottoman government and, ultimately, were manipulated by it.

The liberation movement among Armenians, which turned into an armed struggle in the 1890s, acquired depth and an inter-ethnic scope in the 1900s. This included prodding Young and liberal Turkish groups into action against despotism and cooperation among the anti-sultan forces. One of the issues raised by the Armenian political parties during these early years was the need for Turkish liberalism to acquire a popular basis by addressing social and economic issues and by being ready to engage in an armed struggle to achieve the goal of a democratic and parliamentary regime. They also urged Turks to provide for a popular defense mechanism against any possible reaction following a revolution. In other words, the Young Turks were urged to make a revolution rather than a coup d'etat. These positions were articulated clearly over a decade of relations between Armenian revolutionaries and Turkish liberals in Europe and in the Ottoman Empire.[56] The last time the Dashnaktsutiune had insisted on the need for an Ottoman revolution was in 1907, during the second congress of Ottoman opposition forces, which had been convened on its initiative. Armenians did not have much faith in revolutions from above.

Although in 1908 it was the Ottoman army and not the people that toppled the Sultan, the move was radical enough to invite the support of many segments of Ottoman society, and particularly Armenians for whom liberalism and reform had become political solutions as well as ideological tenets. The Young Turk revolution of 1908 produced important changes in the Armenian political scene. The oldest of the political parties, the quasi-Marxist and revolutionary Hunchakians, met in 1909 for their Sixth General Convention and decided to discard the party's demand for political independence for Armenia and voted to realize their ultimate goal, socialism, within the Ottoman context. Nonetheless, the Hunchakians registered their distrust of Ittihadist nationalism and absence of commitment to reforms.[57] The Dashnaktsutiune put into place a mechanism for realizing the federal structure it had envisioned in its Fourth World Congress in 1907, in collaboration with the Young Turks.[58] Finally, the Armenian bourgeoisie and well-to-do, who had never felt comfortable with the armed struggle and socialistic rhetoric of the two existing parties, created a third party, the Ramgavar-Sahmanatragan or Democratic-Constitutional Party, which rejected violence and adopted capitalism as the proper form of economic development for the Ottoman Empire and the appropriate way to solve Armenian socio-economic problems.[59]

All three parties worked within the bounds of the Constitution to achieve gains and to realize their goals. The coalition of the Dashnaktsutiune and the Ittihad produced parliamentary victories for both. The Hunchakians formed an alliance with the Ittilaf Party of Prince Sabaheddine. More important, all three Armenian political parties shared a vision of the society which they wanted to see evolve in the Ottoman Empire. This vision was based primarily on the need to address the problems facing a disintegrating Armenian rural society and a frustrated middle class. Equality, reform, and progress were slogans which everyone used and no one found to be against the interests of the state in 1908.[60] They were inspired by what educated Armenians considered the universal values of the Enlightenment. Armenians believed in progress and in change at the expense of the traditional because, to paraphrase what has been said of German Jews, these attitudes facilitated emancipation from the political and social disabilities that had oppressed them for centuries; the Enlightenment gave them optimism, faith in themselves and in humanity. It was this general belief that led the Armenians, but especially the Hunchakians and Dashnaktsutiune, not only to participate vigorously in the first Russian revolutionary movement in 1905 but also to play a role in the Persian Constitutional movement before World War I. This role was critical enough for one of the leaders of the Dashnaktsutiune, Yeprem, who had led his guerrilla fighters into many battles, to end up with the responsibility for the security of Tehran until his death in 1912.[61]

Among the Turks, enlightenment and progress were adopted by Prince Sabaheddine and the Liberal Party. However, they were small in number and lacked a popular base. Even the nascent Turkish bourgeoisie supported the Ittihad policies of economic nationalism and placed their hopes on a strong central government which might find it easier to make room for the growth of Turkish capital, as opposed to the traditional Ottoman capital that had been accumulated in trade by Armenians, Greeks, and Jews. The masses were more easily swayed by the rhetoric of glory, whether of the imperial or religious variety. When faced with the Western challenge, the Turkish reformers, whose liberalism was "ill digested," were more likely to be impressed by the technological and military advances—advances which, when borrowed, could have resolved the Ottoman problem as seen by Turks: military weakness against European powers and humiliation at the hands of former subjects.[62] Some also internalized Social Darwinism, which made it possible for them to rationalize their insistence on the primacy of Turks in the Empire, their internal imperialism.[63]

Even in 1908, therefore, there were two visions of society at work, both in opposition to the Sultan, both favoring the Constitution, both based on the dual principles of internal reforms and territorial integrity of the Empire. It was the first time since the articulation of Armenian political demands that so much common ground existed and that there was an opportunity for the solution of both problems. Yet for those in the Ittihad who had believed in some degree of equality and justice, the promise of reforms may have been the price to be paid in return for territorial integrity, and possibly aggrandizement. With the continued loss of territories in the Balkans and the threatened loss of the Arab provinces, the Ittihad lost even its weak interest in limited reforms and sought its aggrandizement elsewhere.

Armenian political parties, meanwhile, had been willing to make all the necessary adjustments to strengthen the Constitution: it was a welcome alternative to an otherwise difficult position. Armenians, particularly the Hunchakians and Dashnaktsutiune, made serious compromises on the degree of socioeconomic reform needed in order to provide the best possible support to the liberal elements in Turkish politics. And while among the Young Turks they had always associated with Sabaheddine, the Dashnaktsutiune agreed to run joint election campaigns with the Ittihad, which, as the party in power, the Dashnaktsutiune thought needed the largest dose of liberal presence.

The Armenian parties made it clear, however, that their commitment to the Ottoman fatherland, their willingness to defend its territorial integrity and the search for Armenian reforms in the context of the empire-wide changes, were contingent upon one condition: the Ottoman Empire had to be a "democratic and parliamentary state."[64] This feeling was shared by the larger Armenian population as well. A letter to the editor of the *Droshak* stated it clearly:

For citizens states are not goals. They are means to develop, to progress, to become strong. If a means to reach a goal is inappropriate, inadequate or weak, it becomes necessary to exchange it for a better and more appropriate form. . . . The issue is not separation or inclusion in the Ottoman state, since these are fundamentally related to the larger purpose—our welfare. We, Turks, Armenians, Greeks, Bulgars, Kurds and other citizens like to remain and live and even, yes, sacrifice and be sacrificed, in a state where our welfare is [considered]. We shall shed our blood only for the flag which knows how to keep our heads up. Flags which are miserable, shameful, often defeated, subject to derision and mockery do not deserve our blood.[65]

The Hunchakians in 1913 reaffirmed their intention not to seek a separate homeland; but they also made it clear that they did not intend to accept a regime where any group dominated the others.[66] In October 1913 all Armenian parties functioning in the Ottoman Empire signed a joint statement which, in addition to promising an end to internal conflicts, also reasserted their dedication to the Ottoman Parliament and Constitution.[67]

In other words, for Armenians allegiance was to basic forms of political association or organization rather than to a dynasty, a nationalism, a religion, or a race. They were ready to support a political system which allowed for the equitable and just solution to ethnic and religious as well as social and economic problems.[68] This was a form of social contract which was reminiscent of what Sabaheddine had come to learn and respect from contemporary readings.[69] With their concern for social, economic, and agrarian reforms and a democratic system of government, Armenians were thus part of the Ottoman political spectrum. But they occupied the left wing of the spectrum.

Two other issues were problematic for the Ittihad government. First, Armenian parties had strong popular bases due both to their long struggle and sacrifices and to their populist platforms. Secondly, given the socialistic nature of their programs, they had also made serious efforts, beginning in 1900, but especially after 1908, to spread the liberal creed among Turks, and even Kurds in Anatolia.[70] While they had had very limited success, there always was a danger that Armenian revolutionary parties with socialistic tendencies could create politically viable coalitions of peasants and rural craftsmen, supported by a liberal bourgeoisie.

## WAR AND THE TRANSFORMATION OF THE STATE

It was no accident that the Ottoman Empire entered World War I and did so on the side of Germany. A crisis situation, martial law, and war conditions in general would change the rules of politics and the need for accountability for failures, while creating the possibility of territorial expansion. Siding with Germany was in character with an elite in power increasingly hostile toward any element which reminded them of their promises and failures. Fighting the war on the side of Germany could free the Ittihad from its commitment to reform just as the Russo-Turkish war of 1877-1878 had freed Abdul Hamid II from the pledge he made in 1876 to create a constitutional government.[71] A war which was to be fought against France and England, the liberal states of Europe, allowed the linkage between external threats and internal reform to be articulated in the measures taken against Armenians, now seen as the main threat, the enemy of the Ittihad "vision"; the Turkish elite considered Armenians ideological allies of the French and British or as a population sympathizing with the traditional enemy, Russia, which in 1912 had resumed its role as the sponsor of Armenian reforms. The war provided an opportunity for the Ittihad to create a coherent world: an opportunity to prove Turkish military prowess by fighting on the side of a strongly militaristic non-liberal empire such as Germany, and against the bastions of liberalism, France and England.

But the war also made it possible to eliminate the particularities and dissent in the political arena by eliminating Armenians, who could never be part of the new vision since they were not Turks or Muslims, and who, by their political consciousness, were bound to become a permanent source of dissent and discontent, a particularity in a society which was expected to find solace in the Pan-Turanian, Pan-Islamic creeds or in Turkish nationalism rather than in the search for equality, justice, and a dignified human existence. Jemal Pasha, one of the Ittihad triumvirate and Minister of the Navy, conceded a fundamental relationship between the decision to enter the war, domestic policy, and the Armenian "problem":

Of course, it was our hope to free ourselves through the World War from all conventions, which meant so many attacks on our independence. . . . Just as it was our chief aim to annul the capitulations and the Lebanon Statute, so in the matter of Armenian reforms we desired to release ourselves from the agreement which Russian pressure had imposed upon us.[72]

Jemal certainly did not imply that reforms were not needed, since in these memoirs he confesses having promised Armenians reforms as soon as the war was over, if Armenians functioned as a fifth column in Russian Armenia against Russia.[73] In a strange but intriguingly vague style, Jemal stated that "it was an active domestic and foreign policy" that drove the Ittihad to war. The most important domestic problem was the question of the minorities, Jemal asserted, and, among the minorities, the Armenians were the most critical.[74] Subsequent justifications of the deportations and massacres clarify the meaning of "active" policy. It seems to have been nothing less than the domestic equivalent of war on enemy states.

The desire to proceed with state building unfettered by any external or internal accounting was, according to Jemal, one of the reasons for the Ittihad's decision to enter the war. Of course, as soon as the war started, the two European governors who had just arrived in the country to supervise reforms in Armenian provinces were sent back. But the war allowed the Ittihad to do more. The purpose of the deportations and massacres, wrote the German missionary and eyewitness Johannes Lepsius, "seems to be to drive the idea of reforms out of the Armenians' minds once and for all."[75] Perhaps this will explain why the murder of the intellectuals took on such a gruesome character. It is said by eyewitnesses that on more than one occasion their skulls were crushed with stones and the brains were thrown to the ground with an invitation to the victim to dare to "think again."

When the news of the deportations and massacres reached Europe, many Turks dissociated themselves from the policies of the Ittihad. Attempting to do so publicly, Mehmet Sherif Pasha, the son of the first

Grand Vizier of the constitutional regime in 1908, described the Armenians as industrious and peaceful people. Attempting to explain the carnage taking place in his homeland, Mehmet Sherif added that "the Armenians' agitation against despotisms in Turkey and Persia [is a quality] one suspects has not endeared them to the autocratic 'reformers' of the Young Turk regime."[76]

## GENOCIDE: A RADICAL FORM OF POLITICAL REPRESSION?

The relationship between genocide and domestic change is a theme which precedes the Young Turks in Ottoman history. Evaluating the meaning of the Constitution first introduced by Midhat Pasha under the young Sultan Abdul Hamid II in 1876, Harry Luke wrote that, "[Midhat Pasha] was sufficiently shrewd and realistic a statesman to know that only by drastic internal reform, self administered, could the rapidly dissolving Empire stave off the coup de grace which Russia was impatient to administer."[77] Soon after he felt secure, the Sultan exiled Midhat Pasha and replaced the Constitution with an administration repressive enough to invite a revolution from his most resilient subjects, the Turks. In the introduction to an unsigned study published in 1913, "Turkey: The Situation of Armenians in Turkey Introduced with Documents, 1908-1912," a commentator discussed the repression of the massacres of 1894-1896 in the following way:

The top officials of the old regime were convinced that repression is essential to despotism and reforms are deadly weapons. Seeing the determination of Armenians to obtain reforms and to make their Turkish compatriots companions in their aspirations, they preferred to massacre the Armenians as the ones responsible for the situation, instead of undertaking general reforms which could have brought the end of despotism and their rule.[78]

Given this strong sense of the relationship between repression and wholesale massacre felt by Armenian leaders and nurtured by events, it is not surprising that both major parties as well as conservative leaders could see by 1913 that the Young Turks might be moving in the same direction as the Sultan. "Turkey is promising reforms for European consumption," argued a *Droshak* editorial in June 1913, "but is actually aiming at the destruction of the Armenian element in Anatolia." Only the method would be different from the Hamidian massacres, argued the editorialist.[79] The Hunchakians thought that the scope would be different too.[80]

They were both correct, although it seems that none wanted to believe that the worst actually could happen. The parties did caution the Armenians not to give any reason for provocations. During the initial stages of the roundups of leaders, the drafting of young men into the army, the inspections for caches of arms, and other preliminaries to the actual deportations and massacres, Armenians tended to accede to demands, avoided any actions which might have been construed as opposing the state, and hoped that the whole episode would ultimately be forgotten and that the community would survive with minimum damage. Local measures such as the murder of a few hundred intellectuals or a few thousand enlistees were nothing compared to what had been predicted. In most communities where any self-defense was possible the realization that the small incidents were part of the larger event came too late to be of any use. Where communities acted early, such as in Van, Shabin Garahisar, Musa Dagh, and Urfa, the self-defense became part of the justification for the genocide while the genocide was progressing.[81]

To complete the preliminary stages of the genocide, the emasculation of the nation without risking much resistance, the planners of the genocide had, in fact, counted on the infinite belief of Armenian leaders in the possibility of political solutions to their problems. Armenians were, after all, students of the Enlightenment and devotees of political discourse once discourse had been made possible by the elevation of the "revolutionary" Young Turks to power. To believe that their colleagues from the days of exile in Europe and from the Ottoman Parliament could in fact use the methods of the Sultan and improve on them was to undermine the basic motivation for their adoption of the best that the West had to offer: belief not only in progress by man but also progress in man, in his perfectibility, in his ability to reason and to do what is reasonable.

When the Young Turks determined to exterminate the Armenians, they were not just ridding themselves of another ethnic group; they were also eliminating the social basis for a substantial change in the regime. They were not guaranteeing just a turkified Turkey, but also a Turkey which was closer to the model of the Empire in its heyday: virile and run by elites who were inspired by ideas beyond the reach of common men and women, particularly those of a lower race and religion, by ideas beyond the reach of discourse, abstracted from reality and, ultimately, from humanity.

The genocide of the Armenian people may be a paradigm for twentieth-century "political" genocides, where the elite's vision was predicated upon the political and sociological dimensions of the society they wanted to rule over. The return to a traditional order where hierarchies are in place and unchallenged may be one such vision. Recent genocides, especially the Indonesian, the Cambodian, and the Ibo, have been more brazenly political in nature, confirming the worst fears that knowledge of evil does not necessarily result in abhorrence of evil; that human reasoning can always find ways to characterize evil as being something else and to conclude that some societies must be destroyed or must destroy parts of themselves to be saved.

## NOTES

The transliteration system used in this text is based on the phonetic values of Western Armenian.

1. The relationship between genocide and modernization has been discussed by George L. Mosse, *German Jews Beyond Judaism* (Bloomington: Indiana University Press/Hebrew Union College Press, 1985), with regard to the Jewish holocaust, and by Robert Melson in a recent paper entitled "Neither Scapegoats Nor Provocateurs: A Preface to a Study of Genocide with Special Reference to the Armenian Genocide of 1915 and the Holocaust," presented at the Conference on Genocide at Harvard University, April 13, 1985.

2. The best reference work for non-Armenian sources on the Armenian genocide is Richard G. Hovannisian, *The Armenian Holocaust: A Bibliography Relating to the Deportations, Massacres, and Dispersion of the Armenian People, 1915-1923* (Cambridge, Mass.: National Association for Armenian Studies and Research, 1978 and 1980). Other sources include Aram Andonian, *The Memoirs of Naim Bey: Turkish Official Documents Relating to the Deportations and Massacres of Armenians* (London: Hodder and Stoughton, 1920; repr. Armenian Historical Research Association, 1964 and 1965); Dickran H. Boyajian, *Armenia: The Case for a Forgotten Genocide* (Westwood, N.J.: Educational Book Crafters, 1972); Gerard Chaliand and Yves Ternon, *The Armenians: From Genocide to Resistance* (London: Zed Press, 1983); Irving Louis Horowitz, *Taking Lives: Genocide and State Power* (New Brunswick, N.J.: Transaction Books, 1980); Leo Kuper, *Genocide: Its Political Use in the Twentieth Century* (New Haven: Yale University Press, 1981); Henry Morgenthau, *Ambassador Morgenthau's Story* (Garden City. N.Y.: Doubleday, Page, and Co., 1926; French ed., Paris: Payot et cie., 1919); Martin Niepage, *The Horrors of Aleppo, Seen by a German Eye-witness* (London and New York: Fisher Unwin, 1917 and George H. Doran Co., 1918; repr. New Age Publishers, 1975); Gerard J. Libaridian, ed., *A Crime of Silence: The Genocide of the Armenians. The Permanent People's Tribunal* (London: Zed Press, 1985); Jack Nusan Porter, *Genocide and Human Rights* (Washington, D.C.: University Press of America, 1982); Yves Ternon, *The Armenians: History of a Genocide* (Delmar, N.Y.: Caravan Books, 1981); Arnold Toynbee, *Armenian Atrocities: The Murder of a Nation* (London: Hodder and Stoughton, 1915; reissued New York: Prelacy of the Armenian Apostolic Church of America, 1975); Arnold J. Toynbee, *The Treatment of the Armenians in the Ottoman Empire, Documents Presented to Viscount Grey of Falloden* (London: J. Causton and Sons, 1916).

3. For the early history of the movement, see Ernest E. Ramsaur, *The Young Turks: Prelude to the Revolution of 1908* (Princeton: Princeton University Press, 1957); for the prewar years see Feroz Ahmad, *The Young Turks: The Committee of Union and Progress in Turkish Politics, 1908-1914* (Oxford: Clarendon Press, 1969).

4. Historic Armenia was divided between the Ottoman and Safavid Persian empires, once in the sixteenth century and finally in the seventeenth century. The eastern, and smaller, part was occupied by Persia until the Russo-Persian war of 1827-1828, when it became part of the Russian Empire. That segment of historic Armenia became independent in 1918 and was sovietized in 1920.

For the social makeup of Western Armenian society, see Gerard J. Libaridian, "The Changing Self-Image of the Armenian in the Ottoman Empire: *Rayahs* and Revolutionaries," in *The Image of the Armenian in History and Literature,* ed. R. G. Hovannisian (Malibu Beach, Calif.: Undena Press, 1981).

5. Because of the presence of the diplomatic corps and an international community, Armenians in the capital were spared deportations, although their leadership there was rounded up and murdered. The regions of Izmir and Adrianople were spared because the chief of the German Military Mission during the war in the Ottoman Empire, General Liman von Sanders, threatened to use force against the Turkish soldiers and gendarmes should they implement the deportation orders. He told his story in Otto Liman von Sanders, *Fünf Jahre in der Türkei* (Berlin: A. Scherl, 1920), and repeated it during his testimony at the trial of Talaat Pasha's self-confessed executor, Soghomon Tehlirian, in Berlin in 1921. See *The Case of Soghomon Tehlirian* (Los Angeles: ARF Varantian Gomideh, 1985), pp. 83-85.

6. The cities and districts which resisted included Van, Musa Dagh, Urfa, Shabin Karahisar, and Hajin. Only the first two were able to survive long enough to receive assistance from the outside and save their people: Armenians in Van were saved by the Armenian volunteers with the Russian army; those in Musa Dagh were rescued by French ships off the coast of the Mediterranean. Resistance in most cases was not undertaken with the hope of ultimate salvation but rather to have a choice in the manner of death.

7. Information on the role of this organization is fragmentary, often from oral history sources. The only substantial research on the subject, done as a doctoral dissertation by Philip Hendrick Stoddard, is silent on the organization's role in Anatolia and the Armenian provinces where the deportations occurred; see Philip Hendrick Stoddard, "The Ottoman Government and the Arabs, 1911-1918: A Preliminary Study of the Teshkilat-i Mahsusa" (Ph.D. diss., Princeton University, 1963).

8. Over 4,000 interviews have been taped on cassettes with eyewitnesses and survivors of the Armenian genocide. Significant numbers of interviews have been conducted by Professor V. L. Parseghian (Rensselaer Institute),

Professor Richard G. Hovannisian (University of California at Los Angeles), and their associates as well as by organizations such as the Armenian Library and Museum of America (Belmont, Mass.) and the Armenian Assembly of America (Washington, D.C.).  The Armenian Film Foundation of Los Angeles has a collection of filmed interviews with survivors, while the Zoryan Institute for Contemporary Armenian Research and Documentation (Cambridge, Mass.) has over 300 videotaped interviews.

Some press accounts of the deportations and massacres have been re-published in *The Armenian Genocide, as Reported in the Australian Press* (Sydney: Armenian National Committee, 1983), *The Canadian Press and the Armenian Genocide* (Montreal: Armenian National Committee, 1985), and Richard Kloian, ed., *The Armenian Genocide: News Accounts from the American Press* (Berkeley, Calif.: Anto Printing, 1985).

9. Cipher telegram, Mahmud Kiamil, Commander of the Third Army to Governors General, July 10, 1915; cited in Gerard J. Libaridian, "The Ideology of the Young Turk Movement," in *A Crime of Silence,* ed. Gerard J. Libaridian (London: Zed Books, 1985), p. 49.

10. See, for example, Yves Ternon, "Report on the Genocide," in *A Crime of Silence,* p. 116.

11. The 1894-1896 massacres claimed over 200,000 Armenian victims throughout the Ottoman Empire; for an analysis of the events, see Robert Melson, "A Theoretical Inquiry into the Armenian Massacres of 1894-1896," in *Comparative Studies in Society and History* 24, No. 3 (July 1982), pp. 481-509.  The 1909 occurrence, known as the massacre of Adana, was in fact a series of massacres in many Cilician cities.  It claimed over 20,000 Armenian lives.  Coming less than a year after the revolution, the outbreak was embarrassing to the Young Turks trying to project a new image in Europe. The government sent Enver Pasha to participate in joint ceremonies condemning the massacres; see Msgr. Mouchegh, *Les Vêpres Ciliciennes* (Alexandria: Della Rocca, 1909), and the report of an Armenian deputy of the Ottoman Parliament, a member of the Ittihad, Hagop Babigian, *Deghegakir* [Report] (Paris: N.p., 1919).

12. There are no exact numbers or reliable census figures with regard to the various peoples of the Ottoman Empire. Figures proposed by the Armenian Patriarchate or the Turkish census have been challenged on various grounds. Figures used here are on the conservative side. See Hovannisian, *Armenia,* pp. 34-37; Turkish census figures have more recently been used by Justin McCarthy, *Muslims and Minorities*  (New York: New York University Press, 1983).

13. Helen Fein, *Accounting for Genocide* (New York: The Free Press, 1979), pp. 29-30.

14. This has been the dominant view among Armenian writers for decades.  The most widely known works in this category are Haygazn Ghazarian, *Tseghasban Turke* [The Turk, Author of Genocide] (Beirut,

1968), and Zarevant, *Miatsyal ev angakh Turania gam inch ge dsrakren turkere* [United and independent Turanian or what the Turks are planning] (N.p., 1926).

15. The most prominent scholar to advance this view is Bernard Lewis, *The Emergence of Modern Turkey* (Oxford: Oxford University Press, 1961), p. 356. As Robert Melson has pointed out in his recently delivered paper (see note 1), the equation between the nationalism of a Turkish elite with access to resources such as an empire and that of a relatively small and altogether unarmed subject people as the Armenians is not a valid one.

16. Bernard Lewis, *The Emergence of Modern Turkey*, 2nd ed. (Oxford: Oxford University Press, 1968), pp. 218-19.

17. The Armenian Question, i.e., the interest which the Great Powers had regarding the Armenians of the Ottoman Empire as part of their imperialistic designs or occasional humanitarian concern should not be equated with the Armenian revolutionary movement, however the two were connected for tactical or strategic considerations. The revolutionary movement involved Armenians in Russia and Persia in addition to those in the Ottoman Empire; it also developed its own dynamics, which included cooperation with non-Armenian and non-Muslim peoples. See Gerard J. Libaridian, "Revolution and Liberation in the 1892 and 1907 Programs of the Dashnaktsutiune," in *Transcaucasia: Nationalism and Social Change,* ed. Ronald Grigor Suny (Ann Arbor: University of Michigan, 1983).

18. Tessa Hofmann, "German Eyewitness Reports of the Genocide of the Armenians, 1915-1916," in Libaridian, *A Crime of Silence,* pp. 61-92; Susan K. Blair, "Excuses for Inhumanity: The Official German Response to the 1915 Armenian Genocide," *Armenian Review* 4 (1984), pp. 14-30; Ulrich Trumpener, *Germany and the Ottoman Empire, 1914-1918* (Princeton: Princeton University Press, 1968).

19. Melson, "Neither Scapegoats Nor Provocateurs."

20. Armenian sympathy for Russia has a long history. In some respects it is the continuation of a medieval belief that Armenians would be freed of the rule of the infidel by a Christian savior; particularly for Armenians in border provinces such as Erzerum and Van, which were constantly ravaged by Ottoman armies during intermittent wars with Russia, and given the inability of the Ottoman government to implement reforms, Russian Armenia seemed a better place to be than Ottoman Armenia. Russia, of course, used these feelings for its own expansionist purposes. But Russia was also concerned that a revolutionary movement among Armenians inspired by the principles of democracy and equality might turn against the Romanov regime, which in fact did occur in 1903 and later, when the tsar's government adopted an assimilationist policy toward Armenians and fomented Armeno-Tatar clashes between 1905 and 1907.

It should also be pointed out that there were large segments of the Armenian population who thought the Ottoman system was preferable to the Russian, since the Ottomans had allowed a *millet* structure to develop, had given more privileges to the Church, and had not tried to assimilate the Armenians. A debate on this issue raged in the newspapers intermittently.

21. Despite the fact that the genocide of 1915-1916 has a central position in Armenian consciousness and history, there is as yet no comprehensive, systematic history of the genocide.

22. Vahakn N. Dadrian, "A Theoretical Model of Genocide, with Particular Reference to the Armenian Case," *Armenian Review* 2 (1979); idem, "The Structural-Functional Components of Genocide: A Victimology Approach to the Armenian Case," in *Victimology*, vol. 3, and "The Common Features of the Armenian and Jewish Cases of Genocide: A Comparative Victimological Perspective," in *Victimology*, vol. 4, ed. Israel Drapkin and Emilio Viano (Lexington, Mass.: D. C. Heath and Co., 1974 and 1975); idem, "A Typology of Genocide," *International Review of Sociology* 2 (1975).

23. Siyamend Othman, "La participation des kurdes dans les massacres des Arméniens, 1915," *Critique Socialiste* 13 (1982), pp. 31-48.

24. Ronald Suny, "Background to Genocide: New Perspectives on the Armenian Massacres and Deportations of 1915," paper presented at the Conference on Genocide, Harvard University, April 13, 1985.

25. See note 1.

26. Studies of the 1908-1918 period are rare; existing works also have made rare use of existing Armenian sources; historians have functioned under the assumption that Armenians could not have been that important in the minds of the Turkish leaders, even when the issue was the state's attitude toward the Armenians. See, for example, Tarik Z. Tunaya, *Turkiyede Siyasi partiler, 1859-1952* [Political parties in Turkey, 1859-1952] (Istanbul: N.p., 1952).

For brief discussions of this period see Hovannisian, *Armenia,* pp. 28-34, and Mikayel Varantian, *H. H. Dashnaktsutian Batmutiun* [History of the Armenian Revolutionary Federation], vol. 2 (Cairo: N.p., 1950), pp. 183-235.

27. This agreement has been referred to briefly by Varantian, ibid., pp. 203-4. Members of the Turkish Section of the Dashnaktsutiune's Bureau were asked by the Sixth World Congress of the Dashnaktsutiune in 1911 to prepare a comprehensive report on the relations between the party and the Ittihad. The resulting study consists of two documents. The first is a diary-like notebook of about forty-six pages with entries on meetings between ARF and CUP leaders between 1909 and 1911 (Archives of the Dashnaktsutiune, File 78/a-1). The second is entitled a "Memorandum" on the same issue; the document has forty-six pages (File Number 78/a-2). These archives contain extensive files on the period under study and are certain to yield much critical information once studied. Both documents mentioned here are drafts; it is hoped that further research may unearth the final versions, although drafts often provide clues on difficult points which may be covered in the final draft.

28. Archives of the Dashnaktsutiune, File 78/a-1.

29. Simon Zavarian, "Asdijanagan vochnchatsum" [Gradual extermination], *Azadamard*, August 9 and 26, 1911. The article provides statistical evidence of the dramatic decrease in the number of Armenians and Armenian-owned houses, farms, and farm utensils in a number of districts over a period of thirty years.

30. Shamil, to Western and Eastern Bureaus of the Dashnaktsutiune, August 10, 1911. Archives of the Dashnaktsutiune, File 671, Doc. 46.

31. Archives of the Dashnaktsutiune, File 78/a-2. For the last point, see also Jemal Pasha, *The Memoirs of a Statesman* (New York: Dial, 1919), p. 254. Jemal states that the Ittihad asked the Dashnaktsutiune to come under the umbrella of the Ittihad as should all other parties. The argument was that there was no need for divisions when everyone was now an Ottoman.

32. Simon Zavarian, "Paregamutian Artunke" [Result of friendship], *Azadamard*, April 19, 1912.

33. Simon Zavarian, "Himnagan vdanke" [The fundamental danger], *Azadamard*, May 17, 1912. The titles indicate either large landownership, other great wealth, or positions of traditional authority.

34. Arsen Gidur, *Batmutiun S. T. Hunchakian gusagtsutian* [History of the Social Democratic Hunchakian Party], vol. 1 (Beirut: N.p., 1962), p. 389.

35. Jemal Pasha, *Memoirs*, p. 256.

36. "Azadakrutian janabarhe" [The path to liberation], unsigned editorial, *Azadamard*, May 18, 1912.

37. Gidur, *Batmutiun S. T. Hunchakian*, p. 365.

38. Unsigned lead article, *Droshak*, June 1912.

39. Hovannisian, *Armenia*, pp. 38-39.

40. The denial/justification pattern was set during the genocide itself and consecrated by none other than Talaat Pasha, the Minister of Interior of the Ittihad most responsible for the holocaust, in his memoirs, "Posthumous Memoirs of Talaat Pasha," *Current History* (November 1921), pp. 287-95.

41. It is difficult to find in Turkish historiography a serious treatment of the history of Armenians in the Ottoman Empire. In addition to limitations to archival sources imposed by the Turkish government even to some Turkish historians, the discussion of the genocide is a politically dangerous undertaking, unless one is denying it. To justify silence on the genocide, historians must also remain silent on pre-genocide relations.

42. To prove his humanitarian concerns, Jemal Pasha remembers having argued against deporting and killing all Armenians since these actions would have disastrous effects on the economy, especially the agriculture of Anatolia (*Memoirs*, p. 278). Zavarian had characterized the role of the Armenians in the Empire as "the milking cow" (*Azadamard*, August 5, 1911).

It should be noted that Armenians were involved in the reform movement, although in a different way, in the first constitutional period too, under Midhat Pasha. Krikor Odian, a Paris-trained lawyer who had played a major role in the development of the Armenian "National Constitution" for the *millet* in

1860-1863, was an advisor of Midhat Pasha, and is thought to have been instrumental in the writing of the 1876 Ottoman constitution.

The integration was particularly strong in folk culture, where language and other barriers break down; comparative studies in folk music and dance should be revealing.

43. Benjamin Braude and Bernard Lewis, eds., *Christians and Jews in the Ottoman Empire, Volume 1, The Central Lands* (New York: Holmes and Meier, 1981).

44. Prince Sabaheddine, who was related to the Sultan and whose family went into exile, became one of the leading figures of the Young Turk movement. He became the founder of the Hurriyet ve Ittilaf Firkasi (Freedom and Private Initiative Party), which included Greeks, Turks, Armenians, Arabs, and Bulgarians. See Ahmad, *Young Turks*, p. 99, and Ramsaur, *Young Turks*, pp. 82-83.

45. Ramsaur, *Young Turks*, p. 92.

46. Ibid., p. 44.

47. Ahmad, *Young Turks*, p. 163.

48. Ibid., p. 158.

49. Ramsaur points out that one of the reasons why the Young Turk Damad Mahmud's critique of the Sultan's regime was effective with Turks was that "he was a Turk and a Muslim himself, as well as a member of the royal family" p. 59.

50. *Droshak* (Geneva), October-November 1909; Garo Sasuni, *Kurd azkayin sharzhume ev hay-krdagan haraperutiunnere* [The Kurdish national movement and Armeno-Kurdish relations] (Beirut: Hamazkaine Press, 1969), pp. 155-57.

51. Gidur, *Batmutiun,* p. 319; Ramsaur, *Young Turks,* p. 73.

52. It seems to this writer that had the political, economic, and social reforms supported by Armenian political parties been part of the program of Turkish parties, Turkish historians would have found them relevant for understanding Ottoman history; some of them also might have found echoes in the concerns of more contemporary perspectives.

53. The most readily available studies of the subject are Louise Nalbandian's *The Armenian Revolutionary Movement* (Los Angeles and Berkeley: University of California, 1967), which covers the early stages of the movement to 1896, and Anaide Ter Minassian, *Nationalism and Socialism in the Armenian Liberation Movement, 1887-1912* (Cambridge, Mass.: Zoryan Institute, 1984).

54. "Dsrakir" [Program], *Hunchak* (London), October-November 1888; also in Gidur, pp. 32-37.

55. Unsigned editorials, "Heghapokhutian ayp pen kime" [The ABC of the revolution], *Droshak,* November 1893 and January 1984.

56. "Kordsi propagand" [Propaganda for action], *Droshak,* October 1907 and passim.

57. Gidur, *Batmutiun*, p. 323.

58. *Chorrort enthanur zhoghovi voroshumner* [Resolutions of the Fourth World Congress] (Vienna, 1907); unsigned proclamation on the occasion of the Young Turk revolution, *Droshag*, September 1908.

59. The Hunchakian Party and the Dashnaktsutiune continue to function to this day; the Ramgavar-Sahmanatragan Party joined with two smaller groups in 1921 to form what has since been the Armenian Democratic Liberal Party.

60. Mosse, *German Jews Beyond Judaism*.

61. H. Elmasian, *Eprem* (Tehran: N.p., 1964), and Andre Amourian, *Heghapokhakan Yepremi Votisagane* [The odyssey of Yeprem the Revolutionary] (Tehran: Alik, 1972).

62. Ramsaur, *Young Turks*, p. 147.

63. Ramsaur recognizes the role of the resentment of European interference in the internal affairs of the Ottoman Empire in the beginnings of Turkish nationalism, but he adds, "In their attitude toward the Armenians and other subject peoples, the Young Turks are basically imperialistic" (p. 44).

64. *Droshak*, September 1980.

65. *Droshak*, February-March 1914.

66. Gidur, *Batmutiun*, p. 328.

67. "Kaghakagan hay gusagtsutiunneru hamerashkhutiune. Haydararakir" [The harmonious cooperation of Armenian political parties. Proclamation], October 1913, Constantinople. Archives of the Dashnaktsutiune, File 53-179. The document was signed by the Hunchakian Party, the Reformed Hunchakian Party, the Ramgavar-Sahmanatragan Party, and the Dashnaktsutiune.

68. *Droshak*, January 1913.

69. Sabaheddine seems to have been impressed by Edmond Demolins, *Anglo-Saxon Superiority: To What It Is Due* (New York: R. F. Fenno & Co., 1889), in which the author argues that patriotism works when it is "founded on the independence of private life" in which the individual will defend his fatherland to protect his own freedom, when the state exists to facilitate the individual's own independence, and when the fatherland is made for man and not the other way around. See Ramsaur, *Young Turks*, p. 82-83.

70. Ramsaur, *Young Turks*, p. 70; see also Gerard J. Libaridian, "Nation and Fatherland in Nineteenth Century Western Armenian Political Thought," *Armenian Review* 3 (1983), and "A Perspective on the Armenian Liberation Movement," paper presented at a University of Michigan conference on new interpretations in Armenian history, Ann Arbor, 1983.

71. Ramsaur, *Young Turks*, p. 8.

72. Jemal Pasha, *Memoirs*, pp. 97, 276.

73. Ibid., p. 276.

74. Ibid., p. 97.

75. Johannes Lepsius, *Der Todesgang des armenisches Volkes. Bericht über das Schicksal des armenisches Volkes in der Tünkei rährend des Weltkrieges* [The deathmarch of the Armenian people. Report on the fate of the Armenian people in Turkey during the World War] (Heidelberg: N.p., 1980), p. 227.

76. *Daily Telegraph*, October 9, 1915.

77. Ramsaur, *Young Turks*, p. 7.

78. *Droshak*, February-March 1913.

79. *Droshak*, June 1913, p. 97.

80. Unsigned editorial, *Hunchak*, November 1913.

81. *Aspirations et agissements revolutionnaires des comités Arméniens avant et après la proclamation de la Constitution Ottomane* (Constantinople: N.p., 1916 and 1917).

# 12

# RELATIONS OF GENOCIDE: LAND AND LIVES IN THE COLONIZATION OF AUSTRALIA

## Tony Barta

I think of land as the history of my nation. It tells of how we came into being and what system we must live. My great ancestors who lived in the times of history planned everything that we practise now. The law of history says that we must not take land, fight over land, steal land, give land and so on. My land is mine only because I came in spirit from that land, and so did my ancestors of the same land. . . .

My land is my foundation. I stand, live and perform as long as I have something firm and hard to stand on. Without land . . . we will be the lowest people in the world, because you have broken down our backbone, took away my arts, history and foundation. You have left me with nothing. Only a black feller who doesn't care about anything in the world. My people don't want to be like you![1]

—Galarrwuy Yunupingu

The basic fact of Australian history is the conquest of the country by one people and the dispossession, with ruthless destructiveness, of another. The recorded effects of this encounter are as clear as they are terrible. Of the black people who inhabited the continent as "Aborigines," "from the beginning," and who had developed complex languages, cultures, and social organizations in more than 50,000 years of tribal life, only small minorities survived the first generations of contact with the white invaders. Driven from their lands, deprived of traditional food supplies, decimated by introduced diseases, many thousands died of causes the Europeans would list as "natural." Thousands more—perhaps 20,000—were killed in the raids and reprisals of frontier war, in massacres, in countless individual acts of violence.[2] Wherever Europeans were determined to settle, Aborigines were fated to die. Not only in Tasmania but in all the rapidly occupied south and east of Australia the processes of colonization and economic expansion involved the virtual wiping out of the Aboriginal population. Australia—not alone among the nations of the colonized world—is a nation founded on genocide.

This is not a view which many white Australians share. The majority have in any case little consciousness of the violence in their past and resent the increasingly outspoken Aboriginal references to it. They would prefer to celebrate their bicentennial in 1988 free of black counter-demonstrations and untroubled by the mounting Aboriginal claims for restoration of land. Among the historians who have shaped the Australian consciousness of the past only very few, very recently, have emphasized the destruction of the Aborigines as a central fact. If they have not spoken of genocide—the word appears very rarely[3]—it is for reasons of definition which have made the concept inadequate in a case crying out for its use. What we need, I shall argue, is a conception of genocide which embraces *relations* of destruction and removes from the word the emphasis on policy and intention which brought it into being.

That genocide must be seen as a *policy,* for which individuals could be held responsible and called to account, was the main argument behind Raphael Lemkin's conception. The new word was meant "to signify a coordinated plan of different actions aiming at the destruction of essential foundations of the life of national groups, with the aim of annihilating the groups themselves."[4] This emphasis on *intention* and scope, on purposeful annihilation, has given the word its terrible leading edge. It has succeeded in devaluing all other concepts of less planned destruction, even if the effects are the same. To be *really* terrible, an ordeal inflicted on a people now has to be "genocidal." These essays, too, are written under that shadow.

"The *deliberate* destruction of a race or nation"; "acts committed *with intent* to destroy in whole or in part a national, ethnical, racial or religious group as such": all subsequent definitions of genocide have pressed home the emphasis on planning and purpose.[5] Yet we know that the destruction of many peoples, genocidal *outcomes,* have been the result of complex and only obscurely discerned causes, and in that respect genocide should properly lose its uniqueness—the uniqueness of having intentionality as its defining characteristic. It should not be possible after more than a century of Marxism and other varieties of historiography intent on teasing out dialectics of change behind apparently singular events to accept the construing of policy as a substitute for explorations of its contexts. This is the issue Karl Marx addressed early on, when he attempted to establish the sets of relationships structuring historical reality as the proper object of historical enquiry, rather than only the intentions and actions of individuals.

In the investigation of *political* conditions one is too easily tempted to overlook the *objective nature of the relationships* and to explain everything from the *will* of the persons acting.  There are *relationships,* however, which determine the actions of private persons as well as those of individual authorities, and which are as independent as the movements in breathing.  Taking this objective standpoint from the outset, one will not presuppose an exclusively good or bad will on either side.  Rather, one will observe relationships in which only persons appear to act at first.[6]

Marx did not have genocide—or Australia—in mind; nor was he yet thinking primarily in terms of economic relationships.  Discussion of capitalism, of imperialism, of colonialism has of course embraced the kinds of violence associated with the clash of cultures and the imposition of an alien economic, social, and political order.  It is in this way that Leo Kuper (somewhat reluctantly, it seems to me) acknowledges a contribution of Marxism to our understanding of genocide.  He quotes Eric Wolf on the extermination of hunting and gathering peoples in the name of civilization, whose representatives then inherit the land: "The progress of civilization across the face of the earth is also a process of primary accumulation, of robbery in the name of reason."  And while Jean-Paul Sartre is seen as too readily equating colonization with genocide, Kuper recognizes in Sartre's reference to Americans "*living out . . . a relationship of genocide*" with the Vietnamese as a way around some of the more legalistic approaches to the problem of intent.[7]

It is this kind of "living out a relationship of genocide," one structured into the very nature of the encounter, which I wish to explore in the case of Australia.  I will not, I hope, beg the question of how relationships might be expressive of intentions; I expect to construe intentions from action (and inaction) and from words as well.  But I will assume of actions that they imply relationships, and entail consequences, which people do not always envisage clearly.  Genocide, strictly, cannot be a crime of unintended consequences; we expect it to be acknowledged in consciousness.  In real historical relationships, however, unintended consequences are legion, and it is from the consequences, as well as the often muddled consciousness, that we have to deduce the real nature of the relationship.

In Australia very few people are conscious of having any relationship at all with Aborigines.  My thesis is that all white people in Australia do have such a relationship; that in the key relation, the appropriation of the land, it is fundamental to the history of the society in which they live; and that implicitly rather than explicitly, in ways which were inevitable rather than intentional, it is a relationship of genocide.

Such a relationship is systemic, fundamental to the type of society rather than to the type of state, and has historical ramifications extending far beyond any political regime.  Irving Horowitz (misleadingly, in my view) calls Germany "a genocidal society" because during one terrible period of *political* aberration the "state bureaucratic apparatus" was used for "a structural and systematic destruction of innocent people."[8] My conception of a genocidal *society*—as distinct from a genocidal state—is one in which the whole bureaucratic apparatus might officially be directed to protect innocent people but in which a whole race is nevertheless subject to remorseless pressures of destruction inherent in the very nature of the society. It is in this sense that I would call Australia, during the whole 200 years of its existence, a genocidal society.

Nothing could have been further from the minds of its founders. Captain James Cook had taken possession of eastern Australia as "terra nullius," land not effectively belonging to anyone, so that there was never any negotiation with the Aboriginal inhabitants.[9] In this certainly were the seeds of the subsequent genocide: because the Aborigines had never mixed their labor with the soil to make it productive they had no right to it and would be cleared from it by those who did. However, when Captain Arthur Phillip arrived with the first fleet at Botany Bay in 1788 his instructions were unequivocal: he was "by every possible means to open an intercourse with the natives," to "conciliate their affections," and to enjoin everyone to "live in amity and kindness with them." He must punish all who should "wantonly destroy them, or give them any unnecessary interruption in the exercise of their several occupations."[10] The problem, of course, right from the beginning, would be in defining "wanton destruction" and "unnecessary interruption." Colonizing activity in itself—founding a settlement, planting crops, pasturing animals—could not be considered under either heading. To "wantonly destroy" the Aborigines was something very different from taking land they appeared to make no use of, and the distinction became more important in the maintenance—and modification—of colonial attitudes as the area of settlement expanded and Aboriginal resistance increased.

The impulse to expansion was economic. In 1812 it was demonstrated that Australian wool could sell profitably to the Yorkshire mills. Having displaced the peasant farmers from the British countryside by enclosures and larger-scale farming (a process of social dislocation not unrelated to the rise in urban crime and the pressure to transport convicts to Australia), the agrarian revolution in Britain now helped finance an expanding textile industry which it could not supply with raw materials from home production. In 1822 the British government dropped the duty on wool from its own colony on the other side of the world to one-sixth of that on German wool. A new wave of free settlers, often only with sufficient capital for a small starting flock, knew that enterprise and determination—with much of the frontier hardship borne by convict or ex-convict stock-keepers—might bring rich rewards. Sheep may seem unlikely instruments of genocide, but together with the cattle that trampled edible plants and fouled the water holes, they were the innocent embodiment of historical pressures which wrought massive and irremediable destruction. The tide of strange animals loosed on the Aborigines' carefully tended grazing lands displaced the Aborigines' game and the Aborigines themselves. If the kangaroo, so curious to the eyes of white men, represented the ecologically delicate economy of the hunter-gatherers, the sheep, equally odd in the eyes of the blacks, were suitable representatives of the incomprehensible concepts of individual ownership and private property. The imported animals and the appropriated land were soon shown—like Byron's stocking-frame—to have a higher value than human life. The most drastic demonstration was in Tasmania.

In 1817 the European population of Van Diemen's Land stood at 2,000, the Aboriginal population at about the same. By 1830 the Europeans' numbers had increased to 23,500, some 6,000 of whom were free settlers with capital to invest in the pastoral industry. They had been granted almost half a million hectares, which they stocked with 1 million sheep—more than in the whole of New South Wales.[11] Nobody seriously considered the effect of this on the few Aborigines encountered; the settlers were more worried about escaped convict bushrangers. But the Aborigines were shortly to make their attitude plain, and in the necessity of fighting a virtual war to protect the settlers Australia was to at least brush with that more classical mode of genocide, the direct sanctioning of violence by the state.

The imperial administrator called on to test the viability of humane principles on the frontier was Colonel George Arthur. He arrived in Hobart as Lieutenant Governor of Van Diemen's Land in 1824 with a reputation for having stood up to the slave owners of British Honduras in defense of an indigenous people, the Mosquito Indians. One of his first duties, indicative of the way things were to develop, was to approve the trial and execution of the first two black resistance leaders—one of them called Mosquito. He also issued a proclamation, in accordance with Colonial Office instructions, placing the Aborigines under the protection of British law and warning the stock-keepers that if they continued to "wantonly destroy" the Aborigines they would be prosecuted. Neither during his tenure of office, which saw the rapid escalation of frontier violence, nor in the subsequent history of the colony was any European charged, let alone committed for trial, for assaulting or killing an Aboriginal.

Arthur was no doubt sincere in his desire to protect the Aborigines. But attacks on settlers continued, and in November 1826, only two and a half years after his arrival, he gave the settlers the right to drive off any Aborigines they suspected of meaning them harm, and if their own force was insufficient they could call on assistance from the nearest detachment of troops. There followed three years of warfare during which Arthur could find no alternative to the policy being urged on him by the settlers; the Aborigines would have to go. As the clamor increased for their forcible removal to some kind of reserve—or else for a free hand to the settlers—he confessed, "I cannot divest myself of the consideration that all aggression originated with the white inhabitants," but it is not clear that he ever saw this aggression as being synonymous with the very act of settlement. Settlement, after all, was Arthur's business; whatever Colonial Office principles of fair treatment might be, they did not include the re-embarkation of the colonists and the restoration of the land to savages who had never known how to make it productive. If the blacks would not allow white expansion to proceed uncontested (and thirty white deaths in 1827 showed that they would not) their exclusion from the settled areas was the only option. Under pressure from the local press—the *Hobart Town Courier* recalled the removal of the Indians to the other side of the Mississippi forty years earlier—the final solution came to be envisaged as removal of all Aborigines from the main island of Tasmania.

Arthur was only reluctantly pushed into declaring martial law, into sponsoring the Black Line, a drive across the entire island which despite ridicule hastened success in clearing the settled areas of Aborigines, and into the removal of the remainder to special camps on outlying islands. He was persuaded that the Aborigines were ready to go for their own good, that removal was necessary for their protection, that once removed from their traditional lands they would more readily accept the blessings of white civilization—Christianity and the work ethic—as the only means to survival. He knew that they might "pine away"; he also knew that their end would be more violent if they were left among the settlers. The despair and disease which finished off the last full-blood Aborigines was not ameliorated by Arthur's hope that their passing be attended by "every act of kindness." Nor was this decline confined to the southern-most colony, with the smallest black population. In fundamental respects the pattern was repeated in the rest of Australia: pastoral invasion, resistance, violent victory of the white men, mysterious disappearance of the blacks.

When a House of Commons Select Committee in 1837 attempted to understand what was happening to the Aborigines it quoted the Bishop of Sydney:

They do not so much retire as decay; wherever Europeans meet with them they appear to wear out, and gradually to decay: they diminish in numbers; they appear actually to vanish from the face of the earth. I am led to apprehend that within a very limited period, a few years, those who are most in contact with Europeans will be utterly extinct—I will not say exterminated —but they will be extinct.[12]

The bishop had observed well. By 1850 whole tribes from the region of Sydney had disappeared. The story was the same at Newcastle, further north. In the Port Phillip area, after the settlement of Melbourne in 1835, the numbers dropped from more than 10,000 to less than 2,000 in eighteen years—a decline of over 80 percent. Around Geelong, a center of pastoral expansion, the decline was from 279 to 36. In the new colony of South Australia, the number of Aborigines in the region of Adelaide fell from 650 to 180 in the fifteen years after 1841. Relatively few of these deaths—perhaps a fifth of them—were the result of direct violence. The countless undocumented atrocities and the known killings on the advancing frontier of settlement do not account for the vast proportions of the disaster. By far the greatest number—possibly two-thirds—were killed by the previously unknown illnesses against which Aborigines had no resistance (chiefly smallpox) but also by alcohol and malnutrition. Aborigines had a low resistance to alcohol and tobacco and the respiratory complaints which were exacerbated by the European conventions of clothing (often worn when wet) and housing (now fixed, but without adequate sanitation). Malnutrition, in the almost instantaneous adaptation to a high carbohydrate European diet—flour and sugar were irresistible innovations—played a part in the dramatically lowered birthrate, as did venereal disease.[13] A greater part, too easily underestimated, was played by demoralization and despair. If the Europeans only half understood the inability of the Aborigines to withstand civilization and too readily saw them as a race doomed to extinction, Aborigines themselves had reason to be fatalistic. With many of their women bearing mixed-race children to white men, the black birthrate dramatically in decline, their social structure destroyed, and their traditional culture impossible to maintain, many Aborigines could hardly envisage a future in such a cataclysmic world. They knew the white men's ways, and they knew that the kind of statements now treated as empty rhetoric by many historians expressed the white man's view of the real relationship between the races, the genuinely historic terms of the encounter.

We cannot shut our eyes to the inevitable destiny of the Aborigines—the incontrovertible fact that the propagation of the race has ceased—and the consequence, that the present generation of Aborigines is the last that will have existence. . . . we have already expressed an opinion, which under the expectation of receiving obloquy of pseudo-philanthropists, we unhesitatingly repeat, that the perpetuation of the race of Aborigines is *not to be desired*. That they are an inferior race of human beings it is in vain to deny; (the probable extinction of the race from natural causes is a proof of this); and it is no more desirable that any inferior race should be perpetuated, than that the transmission of an hereditary disease, such as scrofula or insanity, should be encouraged. In the case of the Aborigines, the process of their extinction is the result, in a great degree, of natural causes; and even if not beyond cure, is scarcely to be regretted. . . . This may be considered a harsh, cruel view of the question, but it is founded upon clear conviction, and is not unkindly meant.[14]

The immediate context of this statement, an expression of editorial opinion by *The Geelong Advertiser* in 1846, was a discussion—intended to be realistically supportive—of missionary efforts to help the Aborigines. The larger context was Geelong's new status, within a decade of its foundation, as one of the busiest wool ports in the world, the center of pastoral expansion into that area of potential wealth called by its white discoverer "Australia Felix." In these vast grasslands individuals with sufficient capital and pioneering spirit could take up "runs" as "squatters" on Crown Land.[15] If not every squatter had to kill for the land which would now be his, he knew that the necessity to protect his flocks and stockmen from Aborigines might arise and that if the Aborigines did not threaten him it was because some of them had already been killed—"taught a lesson"—by other settlers. *The Geelong Advertiser,* which since the previous year had added "*and Squatters' Advocate*" to its masthead, was vocal in retailing the "depredations" and "outrages" of the blacks and in demanding military protection from a too philanthropic government. So the reality of land seizure by whites, and clearing or at least "pacification" of blacks, was the context of all government policy in Victoria, too, as it had been in Tasmania.

The strategies adopted by a harassed, undermanned administration were to be the same elsewhere, until every yard of the continent had been appropriated. "Protectors" would be appointed to round up the Aborigines and "civilize" them, while saving them from the settlers. Those who resisted this path to social and cultural destruction risked more immediate annihilation at the hands of a new and deadly force of black troopers formed in response to settler demands. Expert at tracking down and "dispersing" Aborigines accused of crimes against people or property, the Native Mounted Police were an effective instrument for securing the displacement of one people by another in most of Australia. Nowhere was the displacement achieved without official and unofficial killing. Everywhere the killing—whether officially sanctioned or not—was understood as necessary to the establishment of the new economic and social order.

The connection between appropriation and violence was lost on no one. From the first expansion of the zone of settlement around Sydney there had been official encouragement for the settlers to form vigilante groups, and in 1824, to protect the flocks and herds spilling out onto the plains beyond the mountains, martial law was declared for five months. No casualty figures were ever reported, but in that time the Aboriginal problem was generally considered solved: there was no more trouble in the Bathurst area. Later the missionary L. E. Threlkeld gave an account of what had been told to him. It is thick with the language of genocide.

One of the largest holders of Sheep in the Colony, maintained at a public meeting at Bathurst, that the best thing that could be done, would be to shoot all the Blacks and manure the ground with their carcases, which was all the good they were fit for! It was recommended likewise that the Women and Children should especially be shot as the most certain method of getting rid of the race. Shortly after this declaration, martial law was proclaimed, and sad was the havoc made upon the tribes at Bathurst. A large number were driven into a swamp, and mounted police rode round and round and shot them off indiscriminately until they were all destroyed! When one of the police enquired of the Officer if a return should be made of the killed, wounded there were none, all were destroyed, Men, Women and Children! the reply was;—that there was no necessity for a return. But forty-five heads were collected and boiled down for the sake of the skulls! My informant, a Magistrate, saw the skulls packed for exportation in a case at Bathurst ready for shipment to accompany the commanding Officer on his voyage shortly afterwards taken to England.[16]

Such massacres took place on every colonial frontier: in Australia the terrible story of shootings, decapitations, and poisonings continued into the twentieth century.[17] There was open discussion of atrocities in the press, many of them involving troopers supposedly upholding the law, and many more incidents than were ever reported lived on in Aboriginal memory. One of the best documented, because the Attorney General of New South Wales was determined to show that the law (unlike the land) could not be taken into private hands, was the Myall Creek Massacre of 1838. Some thirty peaceful and friendly Aborigines on Myall Creek station were kidnapped by twelve white stockmen and the entire group, men, women, and children, slaughtered. Although the bodies were burned beyond recognition, seven of the killers were tried and—at the second attempt—convicted. Amidst enormous public outrage at this victimization of men who had acted no differently (it was asserted) from government agents in the same area some weeks before, and despite a defense lobby organized by the squatters, they were hanged. Their jailer reported that right to the end all of the men maintained "that as it was done solely in defence of their masters' property . . . they were not aware that in destroying the aboriginals they were violating the law, or that it could take cognizance of their having done so, as it had (according to their belief) been so frequently done in the colony before."[18]

It is true that the colonial government, prodded by the disquiet expressed in the House of Commons, now attempted to assert its authority over the settlers and to make its protection of the Queen's black subjects more effective. But the government knew it was dealing with a larger historical encounter whose effects it could at best mitigate. It knew that its own position represented a fundamental denial of Aboriginal claims "whether as sovereigns or proprietors of the soil," and the settlers knew it, too. When they demanded that "energetic and effectual steps" be taken against the Aborigines because they were "convinced that such a course will eventually prove to be the most humane and merciful," they knew there was after all no dispute about the necessity to protect "the laudable and enterprising pursuit of a pastoral life in the interior" or their status as "pioneers of civilisation." [19] The government was able to proceed with the appointment of protectors because it was understood that their mission would be a civilizing one—rounding up Aborigines and showing them the benefits of Christianity. They would not interfere—and would in fact stop the Aborigines from interfering—with the "laudable and enterprising" incorporation of the continent into the capitalist economy.

The settlers won on the ground, and it is their history, pioneers of civilization in a harsh continent, inevitably displacing the stone age tribes, which remains the conventional view. Very few Australians are aware of the ruthlessness of the process; sympathy for Aboriginal fringe-dwellers, out of sight and out of mind, is low. Claims for land rights are often met with derision. References to the subsequent history of attitudes to the Aborigines—"smoothing the pillow of a dying race," removing children from parents, forcing assimilation of half-castes, insisting that the majority culture of white Australians *must* be embraced by Aborigines if they are to survive (this has remained the basis of policy in most areas up to the present)—are assumed to be either excusable ("that's the way they thought in those days") or, in common-sense way, inevitable. Certainly nobody now, despite occasional remarks later passed off as jokes, thinks in terms of extermination. So the idea that the consistent, indeed mounting pressure toward incorporation in the now even more internationalized Australian economy is in some way related to genocide is incomprehensible. In fact, all the subsequent pressure on the Aborigines *as a people* is a direct result of their losing the unequal war for possession of the land. It is possible that a people less weakened by disease might have resisted more successfully; it is not possible to imagine a settler class less determined to break that resistance. The killing on the frontier, then, had to be of a kind that would destroy the ability of Aborigines to survive as independent peoples, with their own social organization, ethnic separateness, and cultural value system in conflict with the world view and economic interest of the invaders. This was clearly understood at the time, by both sides. The Europeans knew that if they could not establish their right to secure property—possession of the land—they had no future; the Aborigines knew that when they lost the fight for the land, all was lost. The fatalism of the black people's "fading away" from those areas where the white man's civilization so quickly triumphed was not very mysterious. In the ten years to 1849 only twenty births were recorded amongst all the seven tribes around Melbourne. But without the land to which their whole being belonged, without the sacred sites and ceremonies which expressed the meaning and purpose of Aboriginal life, how could a future life be envisioned? Derrimut, of the Yarra people, said to a European in the 1840s:

You see . . . all this mine, all along here Derrimut's once; no matter now, me soon tumble down. . . . Why me have lubra?  Why me have picca-ninny? You have all this place, no good have children, no good have lubra, me tumble down and die very soon now.

And Billibellary, an elder of the same group, apparently explaining the increase in the traditional practice of infanticide:

The Black lubras say now no good children, Blackfellow say no country now for them, very good we kill and no more come up Pickaninny.[20]

To veil the realities of this conflict behind the cloudy rhetoric of "the fatal impact" is to deny historical responsibility by refusing historical analysis. "We Australians," a Melbourne sociologist recently assured newspaper readers, "have inherited the wreckage of one of the many cultural tragedies that litter human history. When a strong and a weak culture meet, the latter invariably dies." It was not a matter of anyone being at fault in the past, so we should not overreact in the present— notably by "rushing in dripping with guilt to give away huge sections of the country" which might (through mining) be of benefit to all Aus-tralians.[21] I am aware that the large-scale "relations of genocide" I pro-pose can imply a similar "no one is to blame" approach. The difference, I hope, is in an insistence that relations imply connections within sys-tems, and that the whole system needs to be critically explored.

What Marx said in 1843 referred to the economic and societal pres-sures on the Moselle wine growers, but it is equally apt to the situation of Australian wool growers at the same time. It was not "an exclusively good or bad will on either side" which caused the destruction of the Aborigines but "the objective nature of the relationships" between (white) capitalist wool producers and (black) hunter-gatherers. Local en-counters were always between individuals, and individual attitudes could make an immediate difference between life and death. The quality of personal relationships varied according to the whole range of individual character and circumstance, but the larger encounter and the *inescapable relationship* was between totally incompatible forms of economy and society.

At the center of this relationship—both in consciousness and in actuality—was the land. Both peoples, the Aboriginal inhabitants and the invaders, needed the land. Because of the uses for which each people needed the land, and because of the cultural gulf in under-standings about the land, coexistence was impossible. The black people belonged to the land, their being was part of it and it was part of them. Collectively and individually, it was their life. To the white people it was land to be brought into production; that production was at the center of their culture and the basis of their social order. Collectively, taking over the land was the driving force of the colonists; individually, they saw the land as potential and then actual property. Once appropriated by one man it belonged to him alone—even if normally owned by the state power which had claimed it all. Very few of the invaders had a sense of alienating the land from the Aborigines; how extreme a form of alienation it was they understood even less. The men who put their capital into land knew they had a relationship, through wage labor, with the men who helped them make the land productive, even if they would not have recognized any alienation of labor into capital through that relationship. With the Aborigines there were generally no relations of production, only relations—again by means of capital—through the land. So the key relation between white and black was one of total alienation: that was the condition of the triumph of a taken for granted economic, social, and political order in an "alien" land.

It will still be objected that taking over a continent and destroying its inhabitants are two very different things. And—as I have been at pains to agree—the determination to do one did not imply the *intention* to do the other. Only a minority "had to" kill, as they saw it, in defense of their property, or in defense of their own lives—lives on the line because of commitment to property. But the violence accompanying the appropriation of the land was of a scale and ruthlessness—largely uncurbed by official intervention—which could leave no doubt in black or white minds as to the fate of those who resisted the "inevitable" course of events, and it can be no coincidence that it was accompanied, among those with no thought of murder in their minds, by much talk of the "inevitable" dying out of the black race. I do not think it is too simplistic to see in this dominant opinion the most comfortable ideological reflection of a relationship which could not be recognized in good conscience for what it was—a relationship of genocide.

In some larger human reckoning, it has been pointed out, the economic development of Australia benefited more people than it harmed. By the end of the nineteenth century, "three million Australians and millions of people in other lands were being fed by a continent which in its tribal heyday had supported only a fraction of that number." The new sheep industry in Australia provided work in English mills and warmth to millions in Europe and North America.[22] And it was the blanket, a typical and beneficent product of the new capitalist world economy, which provided the symbol both of the production relations and the relations of dispossession which came together in the appropriation of the land. Made productive according to the original justification for its seizure, the land was never acknowledged in principle or practice as having been taken from previous owners. Therefore no payment or compensation was ever offered. But for many years the acknowledgment that a black fringe-dweller was a full-blood Aborigine, deserving at least of government charity, was the issue of a new blanket, completing its journey from the wool of the seized grasslands, through the mill of the industrial economy, to the survivors of the dispossessed.

We were hunted from our ground, shot, poisoned, and had our daughters, sisters and wives taken from us. . . . What a number were poisoned at Kilcoy. . . . They stole our ground where we used to get food, and when we got hungry and took a bit of flour or killed a bullock to eat, they shot us or poisoned us. All they give us now for our land is a blanket once a year.[23]

Times change, commodities at the center of the economy change, ways of negotiation change. Aborigines in the far north of Australia, where the climate and landscape were less congenial to European settlement, met the white onslaught later and with greater numbers. Some who still remember the massacres—the last shooting by a police party took place in 1928—finally, in the 1970s, acquired rights to significant areas of reserve land. But the pressure at the frontier of the yet more transnational economy has not let up. Bauxite, industrial diamonds, uranium—a substance whose genocidal potential for the first time threatens the white peoples of the world as well—have joined pastoral products as necessary commodities which black peoples, in the name of the greater good, should not stand in the way of. Some would have the Aborigines stand firm against uranium mining. The Aborigines know the uranium will be mined when there is a market for it and that their choices in the future are not separable from what has happened in the past. They know that the relations of power between black and white may still be modified, but that their fundamental weighting will not be changed.[24] In that sense the relations of genocide are alive, and every negotiation will continue to be witnessed by the Aboriginal dead.

## NOTES

1. Galarrwuy Yunupingu, Northern Land Council, in a letter to white people, Black News Service, 1976. Quoted by Janine Roberts, *From Massacres to Mining* (London: War on Want, 1978), p. 6.

2. The estimate of numbers of Aborigines killed in direct conflict is from Henry Reynolds, *The Other Side of the Frontier* (Townsville: James Cook University of North Queensland, 1981), p. 99. This is an indispensable account of the colonial encounter between whites and blacks.

3. Exceptions include Bernard Smith, *The Spectre of Truganini*, ABC Boyer Lectures (Sydney: The Australian Broadcasting Commission, 1980),

and Annette Hamilton, "Blacks and Whites: The Relationships of Change," *Arena,* no. 30 (1972), pp. 34-48.

4. Raphael Lemkin, *Axis Rule in Occupied Europe* (Washington, D.C.: Carnegie Endowment for International Peace, 1944), p. 79.

5. *Concise Oxford Dictionary;* 1946 U.N. Genocide Convention, re-printed as Appendix 1 in Leo Kuper, *Genocide* (New York: Penguin, 1981), pp. 210-14. Emphasis added.

6. Karl Marx, "The Defense of the Moselle Correspondent: Economic Distress and Freedom of the Press," 1843, in Loyd D. Easton and Kurt H. Guddat, eds., *Writings of the Young Marx on Philosophy and Society* (New York: Doubleday Anchor, 1967), pp. 144-45. Marx's concept of relations is usefully elucidated in Bertell Ollman, *Alienation* (New York: Cambridge University Press, 1971).

7. Kuper, *Genocide,* pp. 34, 40, quoting Eric R. Wolf, "Killing the Achés," in Richard Arens, ed., *Genocide in Paraguay* (Philadelphia: Temple University Press, 1976), and Jean-Paul Sartre, *On Genocide* (Boston: Beacon Press, 1968).

8. Irving Louis Horowitz, *Genocide: State Power and Mass Murder* (New Brunswick, N.J.: Transaction Books, 1976), p. 18.

9. Alan Frost, "New South Wales as *Terra Nullius:* The British Denial of Aboriginal Land Rights," *Historical Studies* 19, no. 77 (October 1977), pp. 513-23.

10. W.E.H. Stanner, "The History of Indifference Thus Begins," *Aboriginal History* 1 (1977), pp. 3-26.

11. Lyndall Ryan, *The Aboriginal Tasmanians* (St. Lucia: University of Queensland Press, 1981), p. 83. The account of Arthur's policy is also derived from Ryan, chaps. 5-9. See also Lloyd Robson, *A History of Tasmania,* Vol. 1 (Melbourne: Oxford University Press, 1983), Parts 1 and 2.

12. Report from the Select Committee on Aborigines, 26 June 1837 (extract), *Historical Records of Victoria,* Vol. 2A, Melbourne (1982), p. 62.

13. Richard Broome, *Aboriginal Australians* (Sydney: Allen and Unwin, 1982), p. 61. Subtitled "Black Response to White Dominance 1788-1980," this is the best overall survey. Noel Butlin, *Our Original Aggression* (Sydney: Allen and Unwin, 1983), speculates on the possibility that the Aboriginal population of southeastern Australia was already severely depleted by smallpox before most contact with settlers occurred.

14. *The Geelong Advertiser,* 22 April 1846. Italics in original. From Darren Baillieu, *Australia Felix* (Mount Maceden, Victoria: The Hawthorn Press, 1982).

15. Edward M. Curr, *Recollections of Squatting in Victoria (1841-1851)* (first published 1883), 2nd ed. (Melbourne: Melbourne University Press, 1965), is a lively and reliable account. A later history with the same qualities is Margaret Kiddle, *Men of Yesterday* (Melbourne: Melbourne University Press, 1961).

16. L. E. Threlkeld, *Australian Reminiscences and Papers,* ed. Niel Gunson (Canberra: Institute of Aboriginal Affairs, 1974), Vol. 1, p. 49.

17. See Part 1, "The Nigger Shall Disappear," in Raymond Evans, Kay Saunders, and Kathryn Cronin, *Exclusion, Exploitation and Extermination: Race Relations in Colonial Queensland* (Sydney: Australia and New Zealand Book Company, 1975).

18. Sharman Stone, ed., *Aborigines in White Australia, A Documentary History of the Attitudes Affecting Official Policy and the Australian Aborigine, 1697-1973* (Melbourne: Heinemann Educational Books, 1974), p. 58. For a fuller account of the massacre and trials see R.H.W. Reece, *Aborigines and Colonists: Aborigines and Colonial Society in New South Wales in the 1830s and 1840s* (Sydney: Sydney University Press, 1974). The incident is set in its larger context by Judith Wright, *The Cry for the Dead* (Melbourne: Oxford University Press, 1981), and C. D. Rowley, *The Destruction of Aboriginal Society* (Canberra: Australian National University Press, 1970).

19. The correspondence between Governor Gipps and "The Memorialists" is reprinted by S. G. Foster, "Aboriginal Rights and Official Morality," *Push from the Bush,* No. 11 (November 1981), pp. 68-98. He shows how the House of Commons' recognition that the land had been taken from the Aborigines "without any other title than that of superior force" was suppressed in official pronouncements.

20. Broome, *Aboriginal Australians,* p. 62.

21. John Carroll in *The Age,* 10 May 1984.

22. Geoffrey Blainey, *A Land Half Won* (Melbourne: Macmillan, 1980), p. 98.

23. Rowley, *The Destruction of Aboriginal Society,* p. 158. At Kilcoy, in 1842, perhaps more than one hundred Aborigines were poisoned; in the 1928 massacre thirty-one Aborigines were officially admitted to have been shot—justifiably, in self-defense.

24. As I write, an advertising campaign by the mining industry, estimated to have cost a million dollars, has paid off. Faced with elections, the West Australian and Federal Labor governments have announced that they will not allow Aborigines to block mining on Aboriginal land. Jan Mayman, "How White Money Feeds White Fear," *The Age* (19 September, 1984), and further reports 27-29 September. Galarrwuy Yunupingu (see note 1) has become a leading advocate of the necessity for Aboriginal communities to negotiate royalty agreements with the uranium mining companies.

# 13

# MIDDLEMAN MINORITIES AND GENOCIDE

## Walter P. Zenner

Africans have rioted against Asians in South Africa and Kenya. The Asians were expelled from Uganda. Chinese have been persecuted throughout Southeast Asia and expelled from Vietnam. Japanese Americans in the United States were interned in 1942. Armenians by the hundreds of thousands and Jews by the millions were slaughtered in this century. All of these events have given rise to the connection between middleman minorities and the victims of genocide.[1] "Middleman" or "trading" minorities are ethnic groups which are disproportionately represented in occupations related to commerce, especially in the small business sector. As minorities, they are not part of the ruling elite, although many may become quite affluent. It is this lack of power which makes them vulnerable to violence. The connection is certainly present in the last two cases, although the other cases, while reporting inter-ethnic conflict and violence, do not refer to genocide per se.

Genocide is defined legally in terms of the intentional physical annihilation of all or part of a group of people on racial, religious, or ethnic lines. This definition approximates what Helen Fein, following Vahakn Dadrian, has called "optimal genocide" and the manner in which Yehuda Bauer has distinguished the Nazi Holocaust against the Jews from most other "genocides."[2] Genocide is a species of the more general category of "massacre," which involves "the intentional killing by political actors of a significant number of relatively defenseless people." Genocide, however, differs from ordinary massacres, because of its scope and aims. In the case of genocide, the aim is to transform a social field by removing a whole group of actors, not merely to terrorize the group's survivors. It also differs from another favored form of population elimination, namely, expulsion or enforced emigration.[3]

Genocide by this definition has been directed at a wide variety of peoples. Probably the largest number of ethnic groups in recent times subject to genocide, although usually involving small numbers of individuals, have been peoples subsisting by hunting, gathering, and shifting horticulture (see Chapter 12). Other groups have also been subjected to genocide and various other forms of liquidation, such as the kulaks (or so-called wealthy peasants) in the Soviet Union under Stalin, or the Communists of Indonesia after the attempted coup of 1965, or the Muslims of Hamah (Syria) in 1982. None of these events points to a connection between middleman minorities and genocide. Still, the fact that two large-scale genocides were committed against groups generally identified as middleman minorities means that the link cannot be ignored. Indeed, the international convention against genocide was formulated in the wake of the Nazi campaign against the Jews, which can be seen as the prototype for the concept of genocide itself.

In this essay, those theories which have examined the middleman minority phenomenon will be examined in terms of what they say about the victimization of these ethnic groups in general and with regard to genocide in particular. This will be followed by a brief comparison of middleman minorities which have or have not been subjected to various forms of persecution.

## MIDDLEMANISHNESS AS A PRECONDITION FOR VICTIMIZATION[4]

Middleman minority theories in modern social science began with theories which strove to explain the special position of the Jew in medieval and modern Europe. Several of these theories, particularly those of Werner Sombart and Max Weber, debated the role of the Jew in the creation of modern capitalist economies, not in understanding the reasons for hostility toward the Jew. Indirectly, both sociologists suggest that Jewish culture is responsible for hostility against Jews. Sombart was generally hostile to the bourgeois-capitalist form of enterprise, for which the Jews as well as other ethnic groups were responsible. Weber saw traditional Jewish forms of capitalism as being quite different from the rational capitalism that arose out of Puritanism. Unlike the Puritans, according to Weber, the Jews practiced a double standard of economic ethics, treating out-group members differently from members of their own group and not viewing work and business as a sacred vocation. While Sombart and Weber differed in their views on the roles of Judaism and Puritanism and in their politics, neither dealt with the victimization of the Jews per se.[5]

Wilhelm Roscher, Georg Simmel, and Ferdinand Toennies saw the Jewish problem in terms of intergroup relations. Roscher, the earliest of these three, analyzed the Jewish role in the medieval economic European economy, although he compared Jews with other groups as well. Roscher, based on then available historical data, found that the Jews controlled commerce in the early Middle Ages, only to be displaced by Christian merchants in the latter part of that period. In the early period the Jews were dominant, because they, as strangers, introduced monetary commerce into a feudal economy. They occupied a niche in the society as traders. As the society grew, Christians aspired to the position which Jews occupied, and through use of their power they displaced the Jews.

Simmel and Toennies considered the role of the trader as an intermediary between different groups of people, as one who is simultaneously within a society and outside it, as one who is distant even when physically nearby. The marginality of the intermediary makes him more objective, thus serving his success as a trader (and in other roles), but causing ambivalence on the part of others. They suggest a dialectical relationship between the intermediary who may or may not be a member of an out-group and members of a particular community.

An important part of the "stranger-intermediary" involves credit. In borrowing, the debtor reveals much of himself to the borrower. One may prefer to borrow from a stranger, who has little power over other aspects of one's life, but the high cost of such credit also breeds resentment. The ambivalence toward credit from a "stranger," even a familiar alien, lies at the heart of commercial arrangements involving minority middlemen and their majority clients.[6] Even though the role of intermediary may be a necessary one, it may produce deep-seated hostility.

The elements of "middlemanishness" stressed by these five authors continue to be the ones which form the basis for middleman minority theory. The term "middleman minority" comes from Howard P. Becker, but the theories, which increasingly have been concerned with Asian immigrants and others rather than with Jews, have continued to make use of ideas formulated in an earlier time. The minority's ethnic specialization, in the first instance, is created by a status gap. The societies need people to do certain jobs in commerce and crafts; this is especially true of feudal and colonial societies, but such gaps may appear in modern industrial societies as well. The minority which occupies this niche is generally of foreign origin or otherwise distinguished from the rest of the population. Its success in occupying this niche is enhanced by its ethnic solidarity and by certain attributes such as frugality and a double standard of economic ethics. Hostility toward the minority is the result of the tensions between the minority as successful traders and entrepreneurs against majority group members who are their clients, employees, and competitors. As more and more majority group members compete with the minority, hostility against the minority increases. The minority is also a convenient scapegoat, because of its frequent association with the ruling classes, who were their initial patrons.[7]

Edna Bonacich's revision of middleman minority theory by applying it to immigrant groups in contemporary capitalist societies has renewed interest and debate. She has connected the middleman minorities to other ethnic groups by showing the similarities between the split-labor market and the situation of immigrant small businessmen. Both pertain to sectors of the economy which are shunned by natives because of the paltry rewards for hard labor, but, at the same time, both the immigrant laborer and the alien small businessman are seen as unfair competitors. While pointing to empty niches in the economy which minority middlemen fill, she did not see the necessity of positing a status gap in these societies.[8]

From the debates of Weber and Sombart on, those explaining the connection between ethnicity and commerce have often disagreed with each other quite sharply. Rather than thinking of a single theory of middleman minorities, it is more appropriate to see middleman minority theory as a subset of hypotheses and propositions which deal with the meeting of economics and ethnicity.

One issue in the discussion of middleman minorities and victimization is determining situations in which these minorities escape persecution. Among the factors which appear to cause such reactions are competition with the out-group (or groups), visibility as strangers, and visibility as a separate ethnic group.

The first of these involves objective features of the economic scene. In the ideal model of the Indian caste system, there is a caste division of labor into which foreign groups could be incorporated. Each group contributes to the whole, and the society is permeated by an ideology recognizing the role of each without challenge. Indeed, we find that the Parsis, a fairly typical middleman minority in western India, and the Jews of India, who served in various occupational roles, did not suffer from persecution.[9] In the ideal status gap setting, such as in early medieval Germany or even in eastern Poland during the inter-World War period, the situation is similar. Again, various authorities suggest that persecution of Jews in pre-Crusades Germany, pre-World War II Volhynia, and the Belorussian areas was not as severe as in other times and places.[10]

Another objective feature is that minority members are more likely to be seen as non-threatening in an open society with a growing economy. Then they may be seen as individuals, not group members, and their contributions are welcome. The openness to innovation may be limited to certain sectors or regions of a country or may encompass the whole society. Thus, in frontier areas minority members will be welcomed more than in old areas, while they may find opportunities in either abandoned sectors of the economy, such as urban slums, or in new lines, such as the film industry in the early 1900s. Thus, such niches will be filled by disproportionate numbers of minority members.[11] Contrariwise, a shrinking economic base with growing impoverishment is likely to result in anti-minority sentiment. This is especially true if the minority is growing and if its share of the societal wealth is growing. Perception of such growth, even if only apparent, may be sufficient to cause a rise in xenophobia.[12]

The perception of the minority by the majority is important when theorists speak about such variables as visibility and ethnic solidarity. Bonacich, who isolated ethnic solidarity as a factor in both the success of the minority and in their persecution, has also pointed to the fact that such minority communities are frequently rent by intense factionalism and other rivalries.[13] If there is much solidarity, it is most frequently found at an interpersonal familial level or in friendships formed in the community of origin. Yet, to outsiders, the minority is often *seen* as more united than it is: the famous psychological principle that all outgroupers look alike.

The effects of discrimination and persecution are twofold. On the one hand, they may induce group members to seek assimilation into the majority, especially its elite. On the other, they may react defensively and thus such action may reinforce group solidarity. These two reactions may come simultaneously, affecting different segments of a single minority. Thus we find that European Jewry during the late nineteenth century spawned assimilationists, Christian converts, and universalistic revolutionaries on the one hand, and Zionists and fervent Orthodox Jews on the other.

While most middleman minority theories see ethnic solidarity as reinforcing the xenophobia of the majority, assimilatory trends may have a similar effect. Minority members attempting to assimilate compete even more directly with majority members for places in universities, the army, the civil service, and other niches in the society. Since the majority tends to perceive all members of the minority as being part of a unified whole, it is easy to see how they may come to see all members of the minority, whether assimilationist, radical, conservative, or religious, as playing different roles in a single conspiracy against the majority.[14]

The proportion of the minority to the majority may play a role in the way it is perceived by the majority. Stanislav Andreski has argued that if the minority is 10 percent or more of the population, it has reached a critical point of conspicuousness.[15] The only exception he claims to a high proportion leading to such molestation is in New York City, where the position of the Jews has made it possible to fend off persecution. He sees the importance of numbers in that it leads to points of friction between majority and minority members. On the other hand, he does not claim that smaller numbers inevitably lead to freedom from discrimination.

Numbers and proportions, however, are tricky indeed. Germany in 1933 gave rise to the movement which caused the Holocaust par excellence. The proportion of Jews was less than one percent of the total population. Yet the total "war against the Jews" was initiated and organized by a German, not a Polish, government. Again, perception is important. The proportion of Jews in prominent social positions and in the major German-speaking cities, including Vienna, was higher than in the country as a whole. There also were Jews throughout the country, including many in rural areas. This made the Jew in early twentieth-century Germany loom larger than percentages would suggest.

An important part of a perception is whether one is seen as a "native" or as a "stranger." (Alternatively, a minority member may wish to be seen as an individual on one's own account, rather than as a representative of a collectivity.) Entrepreneurs in early nineteenth-century Britain might be primarily Scots or Dissenters, like Quakers—i.e., members of distinctive groups within the society, but natives. The businessmen of Casablanca include Berbers from the Sous region and Arabs from the city of Fes, both groups of Moroccan Muslims, albeit distinctive ones. In addition, there are Jews, who are Moroccans but not Muslims, and Frenchmen who are neither.[16] Thus there are degrees of "nativity" and "strangerhood."

Urbanization and other forms of internal migration may upset the feelings of neighborliness which may have come to mark relations in rural areas. In the older cities or in the countryside, an equilibrium based on complementarity and toleration may have been established. With massive urbanization, however, all out-groupers may be seen as hostile strangers, and competitiveness and envy of successful minority members may be the new order of the day. Large-scale international migrations would amplify such a perception. The mass emigration of Jews from Russia and the Polish provinces of the Austro-Hungarian Empire during the late nineteenth century upset relations between the small Jewish populations of Western Europe and the United States and their Gentile neighbors. The large-scale emigration of Chinese to Southeast Asia in the late nineteenth century had similar effects for the more acculturated Chinese in those countries.

Visibility of the minority is heightened by its own characteristics, such as concentration in certain occupations, a special religion or religious practices, racial signs, and speaking a separate language. This occurs most obviously when the minority consists of recent immigrants, but in multilingual or multi-religious areas, members of several ethnic groups may have shared a single region for generations, such as in much of Eastern Europe and the Middle East.

For these elements of estrangement to result in conflict, other elements must be added. Political mobilization which may utilize the minority as a target is an important one. In such a case, the members of the minority are seen as representatives of a group. Usually such a political mobilization is connected with an ideology. Two elements combine in anti-middleman ideology. One is to view commerce, especially that engaged in by stranger-middlemen, as evil and as violating the rights of natives. In its extreme form, moneymaking is seen as diabolical.[17] The second is to view the minority middlemen as foreign agents who are enemies of the nation, whether this is the Bolsheviks, the Pope, or the Japanese Empire. Both serve to dehumanize the minority middlemen; when combined they form a potent weapon to use against them, and this helps exacerbate the normal frictions between businessmen, their competitors, and their clients.

While those opposed to particular minorities follow strategies to convince the majority and the ruling classes of the minorities' estrangement, the minorities follow various strategies with an opposite intention. They may seek to lower their profile and to be less conspicuous. Thus they may refrain from open political activity as an ethnic group and may give up their language, religion, and the like. They may strive to convince their fellows that while they maintain a separate identity, they are full members of the nation. Thus they may stress their participation in the struggle for independence by the nation-state. They may try to change the ethnic group's occupational structure and otherwise reform themselves so as to answer their critics. Finally, they may stress a political ideology that gives them full rights of citizenship as individuals. In post–World War II North America, several ethnic groups once labeled middleman minorities have made considerable progress along these lines, including the Jews and the Japanese.[18]

Middleman minority status thus seems to cause victimization when the friction derived from trade relationships is compounded by ethnocentrism and by ideologies which dehumanize all alien-traders. Even if the minority, however, is in some ways victimized, the types of victimization range from mild discrimination to optimal genocide. Middleman minorities have a special vulnerability to attack because their social position is one with some wealth but with little authority or power. Even if most members of the minority are extremely poor, there are usually some who are affluent and excite envy. The minority is usually dependent on the ruling class, which sacrifices the minority as a scapegoat. The minority is generally unarmed. Because of its business connections, it must be essentially sedentary.[19]

Some of these qualities may under some circumstances be a strength. The weak, unarmed nature of the minority may make it possible for the majority to tolerate the minority. Such was indeed the position of the Jews under Islam, where for centuries they were outside the power struggle. Jewish officials might serve as scapegoats, and mobs might attack Jews as a whole when they fell, but they were also to be tolerated if they showed proper deference for the majority. The occasional attacks can be seen as a ritual to restore the proper deference.[20]

Middleman minorities as groups may have some protection through their dispersion, in that one place may be a refuge when another is perilous, although if the net used against them is wide enough this is of little avail. Since such minorities are often recent immigrants, their former homeland may offer protection and/or refuge. This, however, has often proven hazardous, especially if the homeland is the enemy of their present place of residence and makes the sense of threat seen by their hosts realistic, as in the cases of the Jews of Syria after 1948 and the Japanese Americans during World War II.

## PROBLEMS IN THE COMPARISON OF GENOCIDES

Certain problems of comparison can be found throughout the social sciences. First, no two situations, events, or other units of analysis are identical. When taken to the extreme, realization of this fact would make any comparison impossible, but it should be kept in mind. Two, studying more than one case often necessitates spending less time and effort on each case than if one were devoting all of one's attention to a single instance. While several examples will bring out crucial features which need to be compared, the presentation of each case becomes more superficial as the number of cases increases. Where a great many cases are used, as in cross-cultural or cross-national correlational studies, complex patterns must be reduced to relatively simple abstractions. Three, the definition of the units of analysis is always a difficult task. Four, studies on particular cases are often quite different in quality.

These problems are acute in the study of genocides. Uniqueness has, of course, been argued with regard to the Jewish Holocaust of 1941-1945, although in the process both Bauer and Dawidowicz have compared these events to others. Bauer comes close to admitting that the Holocaust does have some resemblance to the Armenian genocide during World War I.[21] The second problem is one endemic to comparison and not particular to this area. Problems of unit definition are, however, important. Social scientists are accustomed to dealing with nation-states as units; yet problems spill over national frontiers. This is especially true in times of armed conflict. The Jewish Holocaust and attendant genocides of other groups during World War II took place at a time when Germany rapidly spread its control over most of the European continent and then retreated. Thus the nation-state approach has had to be modified considerably.[22] The Armenian genocide was contained within the Ottoman Empire. On the other hand, in the East African cases of

Asian expulsions possible demonstration effects of the Kenyan partial expulsion on Uganda must be taken into account. In addition, the reaction of receiving countries, particularly Great Britain, depended on internal factors. This was also relevant with regard to other expulsions, as we shall see, such as the role of Malaysia and Indonesia at the time of the 1978-1979 refugee crisis involving ethnic Chinese. In defining the unit of analysis, attention must be paid to temporal dimensions as well as spatial ones. In considering European Jewry, does one begin the Holocaust in 1933 with the rise of the Nazis to power or in 1939 with the invasion of Poland? Does one consider the 1894 massacres under Abdul Hamid II as forerunners of the 1916 genocide or as part of it? When one concentrates on the preconditions, this question is less crucial than in dealing with other aspects of the genocidal events, but the question is still relevant. Scale also plays a role in our consideration since some ethnic groups discussed here are much smaller than others.

A problem faced by comparativists is that of the differing bodies of literature on each group or crisis. There is an immense and growing literature on the Holocaust and a smaller but substantial body of material on the Armenian massacres and genocide. Those dealing with Asians in East Africa and Chinese from Vietnam are much smaller, especially since these are events which occurred much closer to the present. The former two literatures are dominated by participants and historians, while the latter two are dominated by social scientists. The richness of the work on European Jewry, anti-Semitism, and the Holocaust is overwhelming, compared with the much thinner data available on the other communities.

In this essay, I will compare a number of middleman minorities, beginning with those who were not subjected to extreme harassment. They will be compared to those persecuted and expelled, as well as to those subjected to "optimal genocide." The comparison made here is suggestive and not definitive; the units used are not strictly comparable. For our cases of non-persecution or only minor harassment, the Parsis of western India and the Jews of Morocco will be used. In dealing with expulsions, recent cases from Africa and Asia are cited. One such example, that of the Chinese in Vietnam, is considered in greater detail. This particular instance was quite recent and, at the same time, suggested many parallels to one phase of Nazi persecution which preceded genocide proper, namely, the refugee crisis of 1938-1939. It is important that we understand what differentiates such forms of population elimination from the full-scale Holocaust.

There is some agreement that total or near-total murder of peoples occurred in only two cases of persecution of middleman minorities—that of the Jews by the Nazis and that of the Armenians by the Young Turk regime. The material on these two cases is better formulated than that on the others. Dadrian and Robert Melson, in particular, have analyzed the events which led up to the deportations and liquidation of Armenians in

1915 in social scientific terms, which makes comparison easier.[23] The work done on the Nazi "war against the Jews" is huge; various authorities, such as Bauer, Dawidowicz, and Fein, have addressed themselves to a number of issues of interpretation in which they have summarized the literature available. Rather than summarizing the history of the Armenian and Jewish holocausts again, I will refer to these events, assuming some knowledge on the part of the reader. In all cases, descriptions will be brief, and those interested are referred to the sources listed in the notes.[24]

All of the minorities in question are concentrated occupationally in commercial and related occupations. While the ramifications of this vary from place to place, this is not gone into here. Among the points to be compared are the following:

a. recency of foreign origin;
b. visibility of the group;
c. degree to which the minority is separated from the majority on cultural, racial, religious, and linguistic lines (nativity and strangerhood);
d. degree of impoverishment of the society at large at the time of conflict;
e. the minority's proportion of the population at large;
f. the minority's perceived share of the national wealth (separate occupational role);
g. extent of complementarity and/or competition with the majority;
h. the absence of common foes and the relationship of the internal ethnic conflict to external relations of the nation.

These points of comparison suggest that the occupational specialization of the minority is but one aspect influencing its ultimate fate.[25]

## EXAMPLES OF MIDDLEMAN MINORITIES

Just as middleman minorities are not the only victims of genocide, so they are not inevitably the subjects of persecution. One example is that of the Parsis of western India, who were neither persecuted in premodern times nor in the twentieth century when India was the scene of much inter-religious and inter-ethnic conflict. Previously, the Indian Parsi and Jewish cases were explained in terms of the complementarity implicit in the traditional caste system, but this does not explain why no persecution (apart from two minor instances of riots) took place when other conflicts and massacres engulfed India. Here structural explanations have some cogency. The Parsis are neither Hindu nor Muslim;

rather, they belong to the ancient Persian religion of Zoroastrianism. They have been in western India for a thousand years and they speak Gujerati, the local language. While the Parsis were clearly demarcated as an ethno-religious group which was concentrated in certain sectors of the economy and were more prosperous than the general populace in an impoverished nation, they were a small and declining group. In 1971, there were approximately 91,000 Parsis in India, approximately 70 percent living in Bombay. This was fewer than in 1941, in a country where the population was over 400 million and growing. Even within Bombay their proportion of the population was declining and their once great local political power had vanished. Until very recently Bombay had prided itself on its inter-religious harmony, and the Parsis benefited from that as well. Although the Parsi community as a whole had favored a conservative pro-British course, enough Parsis, including Indira Gandhi's husband, had been proponents of independence to give them a place in the national constellation. Many of the Parsis who feared the consequences of independence emigrated quietly, thus contributing to the community's decline. Intermarriage was increasing. Despite their coolness to Indian nationalism, the Parsis were not identified with either China or Pakistan, the main enemies of the Indian Republic since independence.[26]

Another case where no major persecution took place in a potentially threatening situation is that of the Jews in Morocco. Again we have the instance of a middleman minority which (although containing numerous poor people) is more prosperous in the aggregate than the majority in a Third World nation. Like the Parsis and the Jews of Europe, the Moroccan Jews had lived in the country for many centuries; they were not recent immigrants. They spoke the local Arabic dialects. Later, many adopted French as a domestic language. As in India, the Moroccan Jews occupied specific economic niches in a traditional pre-industrial economy, although there also was some competition in commerce between Jews and Muslims. Jewish occupations ranged from craftsmen and rural peddlers to international traders.

The Jews were clearly subordinated to the Muslims in traditional Islamic fashion. While this resembles the hierarchy of the Indian caste system, there is a difference. The Jewish and Christian religions are viewed as past and potential rivals of Islam. The Jews could also convert to Islam. Moroccan history contains instances of pogroms against Jews, especially when Jewish officials were deprived of office, and scholars dealing with North Africa dispute the degree to which Jewish-Muslim relations were marked by subordination and persecution or by peaceful symbiosis, based on patron-client relations.[27] There is little dispute, however, that these relations were never marked by such massive upheavals as the Rhineland massacres during the Crusades, the medieval expulsions from England, France, Portugal, and Spain, or the Cossack depredations of the seventeenth century.

Like the Parsis in British India, the Jews in both Spanish and French Morocco welcomed the protection offered by European colonialists. They were perceived as being collaborators. At the same time, they were subjected to French anti-Semitism, but when this came to a head during World War II under the Vichy regime, the Moroccan Sultan, Mohammed V, protected them as his subjects. The postwar period was marked by the Arab-Israeli conflict and the Moroccan struggle for independence. While some Moroccan Jews identified with Moroccan nationalism, others stood aside, preferring the continuation of French rule or emigration to Israel, France, or Canada. Although far to the west of the Levant, Morocco is a member of the Arab League and contributed troops to various countries fighting Israel in 1967 and 1973. The potential for large-scale violence and/or government sponsored restriction and harassment has been present, but it has not occurred.[28]  Indeed, in April 1984, Morocco was the scene of a public meeting between Moroccan and non-Moroccan Jews and the King of Morocco in Rabat. The Jewish leaders included members of the Israeli Parliament. This was an unprecedented event, especially since Morocco is a member in good standing of the Arab League.

Several structural features may explain why Morocco has not been the scene of such persecution. One is that the patron-client relationships which were marked by dyadic contracts between an individual Jew and his family on the one hand, and a powerful Muslim and his family on the other, characterized intergroup relations in many parts of the country. The patron would consider an attack on his Jewish client as an attack on himself. While such patronage was primarily found in rural areas, it could be extended to urban areas, and the present king and his father have considered the Jews as their clients.[29]  This serves as a deterrent to persecution, although such patronage has not been unknown elsewhere in countries where pogroms have occurred.

The rapid and unimpeded emigration of Jews since 1950 has made the Jews less vulnerable. Anticipating trouble, the Jewish community has declined from over 200,000 to less than 20,000 today. This is a much more rapid decline in numbers than that of the Parsis. While it has increased the perception of the Jews as a foreign and unassimilable minority, it also makes them less and less of a threat and a scapegoat.[30]  Few Jews are prominent in politics.

In post-independence Africa, Southeast Asian and various middleman minorities have been affected by legal discrimination and expulsions, involving either the whole community or particular segments of it. The groups involved have generally been of recent immigrant origin and, for the most part, bearers of foreign nationality. Victims of persecution have included civil servants and labor migrants as well as those involved in commerce. In West and East Africa, for instance, victims of forced repatriation have included both Africans from neighboring countries and Asians.[31] Many of the migrants entered these countries during the colonial period to serve in the newly expanding economy, crossing what were basically provincial boundaries between colonies of the same metropolitan power. There were some exceptions to this, such as the Chinese and Lebanese. Many Indians from British India migrated into French-controlled areas. While the expulsions of this variety which have drawn the greatest world attention have been those of Asians from Kenya and Uganda and of Chinese from Vietnam, equally large expulsions have occurred involving labor migrants from neighboring countries. For instance, Idi Amin's actions against the Indians and Pakistanis in Uganda in 1971 were preceded by the expulsion of the Kenyan migrant workers, especially members of the Luo ethnic group, by his predecessor, Milton Obote.[32] This earlier event was less publicized outside of Africa because the expellees were repatriated to a neighboring country, requiring little action on the part of European countries. The Asians, however, attracted greater world attention because many had claims as British subjects; but Britain was reluctant to accept non-white commonwealth subjects as immigrants. On the other hand, India and Pakistan, the lands of origin of these expellees, felt that those who claimed British nationality were the responsibility of Britain, which at the time of Ugandan independence had promised them protection.[33] While there have been massacres, pogroms, and other genocidal actions in Africa since independence, they have generally not been directed primarily against middleman minorities. One possible exception is that of the massacres directed at the Ibo in northern Nigeria in 1966, which led to the attempted secession of Biafra and a hard-fought civil war. These massacres, however, had been preceded by a military coup in which Ibo officers had overthrown a government dominated by northerners and in which northern officials had been assassinated. Subsequently the Ibo-dominated junta was violently overthrown and pogroms were conducted against Ibo outside of their region in Nigeria. Dadrian (1975) sees the anti-Ibo pogroms as retributive genocide.[34]

The separateness of the groups considered here varies. As recent immigrants to the various countries where they live, they are generally separated by culture and social structure. In some cases, they are racially similar, as in the case of Nigerians in Ghana or Thais in Malaysia. The degree of linguistic separation also varies, as does willingness to intermarry with the local populace. Most separated from the local populace were probably the Indians and Pakistanis in East Africa. In addition to their linguistic and racial distinctiveness, most South Asian groups also maintained rigid caste and sectarian boundaries and did not even intermarry with other Asians. This was more true for Hindus than for Muslims.

Some of the instances of expulsion from African and Asian nations have evoked images which remind many in the West of events related to the Holocaust. The massacres in northern Nigeria were very effectively used by proponents of Biafran independence. The homelessness of Asian refugees from East Africa and the "boat people" from Indochina reminded many of the refugee ships of the World War II era which went from port to port with unwanted people, sometimes sinking under the weight of their overcrowded passengers in a hostile sea. It is clear, however, that these middleman minorities have not suffered the "optimal genocide" which constituted the holocausts of the Armenians and the Jews. One instance of this variety will be examined in some detail before considering the similarities and differences between that case (as representative of such expulsions) and that of the holocausts.

## THE CHINESE OF VIETNAM AND THE SOUTHEAST ASIAN CONTEXT

The vast majority of Chinese immigrants in the world, especially prior to the revolution, came from the southeastern provinces of China. Prior to the nineteenth century, junk trade between China and Southeast Asia was carried on through these provinces. The vast labor migrations to both Southeast Asia and the Americas were primarily from this region during the nineteenth and twentieth centuries. While most of the migrants were farmers by origin, commerce and moneymaking were familiar to countryfolk there, and commerce carried greater prestige in the southeast than in other parts of China.

The initial migration as part of a traditional trade diaspora, and later migrations of single men unaccompanied by families, produced a situation in which Chinese men frequently formed liaisons with or married local women. In many places, their offspring assimilated into the local population, although in some places, such as Java, they formed a distinctive part of the local Chinese community. Through such intermarriages and unions Chinese communities had kinship links with the non-Chinese population. However, a large immigration of Chinese families during the twentieth century changed this and led to greater isolation of the Chinese from the local population. Coupled with rising Chinese and local nationalisms and fears of the "Yellow Peril," conflict between the Chinese and host populations increased. The immigration into Vietnam and other parts of French Indochina followed this pattern. In fact, the high point of Chinese immigration was reached during the civil unrest and the Sino-Japanese war of the 1930s.

Chinese participation in the economies of the various Southeast Asian countries followed two patterns. One was labor migration. During the nineteenth century and the early twentieth century, Europeans recruited many Chinese to work in mines and on plantations throughout Southeast Asia, as well as in other areas of the world. Such laborers were indentured or otherwise indebted to their employers. The vast majority were single males, often leaving spouses and children behind in China. The second pattern was for Chinese migrants to open enterprises of their own, ranging from small mining operations and truck farms to large rice mills and rubber-trading corporations. While many laborers returned home, others went into business for themselves or worked for Chinese employers.

The situation of the Chinese in Vietnam was fairly typical of such populations throughout Southeast Asia, with some special conditions stemming from Vietnam's proximity to China itself. The history of Sino-Vietnamese relations prior to the French conquest in the nineteenth century was marked by trade, tribute, and occasional warfare. Although not expansionary in the Western sense, Chinese civilization did incorporate areas south of its original heartland, some of which are seen by modern Vietnamese as part of their own homeland. In premodern times, Vietnam was seen by the Middle Kingdom as a tributary state, even when it was independent. Struggles for independence from Chinese domination are part of Vietnamese history; at the same time, Vietnam absorbed important cultural complexes from China. This history has ramifications for contemporary Sino-Vietnamese relations.

During the early Ching or Manchu period (seventeenth-eighteenth centuries), Chinese fleeing from Manchu rule were settled in Cochin China (what is now the southern part of Vietnam, including Saigon/Ho Chi Minh City). The Vietnamese rulers of the time encouraged such immigration. Under French rule (1859-1954), Chinese immigration increased. By the end of the French administration, the majority of ethnic Chinese in Vietnam were either immigrants themselves or the descendants of recent immigrants, many of the earlier migrants having been assimilated. In 1978, there were approximately 1.5 million Chinese in Vietnam, only 300,000 of whom lived north of the 17th Parallel, which divided the two Vietnamese states from 1954 until 1975. The Chinese were approximately 10 percent of South Vietnam's population and under 5 percent of Vietnam's population as a whole.[35]

The Chinese practiced a wide range of occupations, although they were, to a large extent, involved in trade. In northern Vietnam (especially Tonkin), there were Chinese factory workers, fishermen, and miners. Prior to independence, certain avenues to economic mobility were reserved by the French for themselves, including mining, forestry, and large plantations. Most Chinese business firms were small in terms of their capital and simple in their organization. The most important industry in which the Chinese were predominant was rice-milling, crucial in a rice-exporting country. At one time, this industry appears to have been monopolized by the Chinese. In 1958, 60 percent of the rice-mills

in the Saigon area were still owned by Chinese. The Chinese also in-
vested in spinning and weaving shops, generally small in size. Chinese
also owned groceries, medicine shops, rice shops, second-hand goods
stalls, export and import firms, inland and maritime transportation,
banks, and insurance companies. Some Chinese, especially those originally from the island of Hainan, specialized in the cultivation of specific
crops, such as pepper. In general, the Chinese in South Vietnam in
particular played central roles in the commercial economy.[36]

As with other minorities, the political status of the Chinese throughout
Southeast Asia and in Vietnam was problematical. This status was further complicated by the continuing struggle for international recognition
and for the sympathies and loyalties of overseas Chinese by the rival
governments of Peking and Taipei during most of the post-1949 period.
The Peking government in particular varied between policies encouraging overseas Chinese to assimilate and measures to recruit these people
for its cause and for their protection. On the one hand, the Peking government would tell overseas Chinese to be good citizens in their host
countries. On the other hand, overseas Chinese students would be encouraged to study in the homeland. When governments persecuted their
Chinese residents, Peking sometimes sent a ship to repatriate overseas
Chinese from that country.[37]

The nationality of the Chinese in Indochina was complicated by
various arrangements which the French had established for the control of
Chinese populations in their colonies. During the colonial period, the
French administration ruled the Chinese indirectly through "chiefs"
whom they appointed to maintain law and order. The chiefs ruled the
Chinese "congregations," which thus helped segregate the Chinese from
other Indochinese. This system was abolished by both the Communists
in the north and by the Diem regime in the south. The Chinese in Indochina remained Chinese nationals but were granted rights combining
those given to the natives and those granted to French nationals. They
were technically under the protection of the Chinese government. The
status of Chinese in Vietnam was thus comparable to that of Europeans
who had been granted extra-territoriality in various Asian and African
countries, although as nationals of a weak power the ability of China to
help them effectively was limited.[38]

After the partition of Vietnam the situation became more complicated,
since there were two Vietnams, each of which had diplomatic ties with a
different Chinese government. In the north, there was a partial maintenance of the status quo ante but with encouragement for the Chinese in
Vietnam to become naturalized. In 1961, the People's Republic of China
recognized North Vietnamese jurisdiction over its Chinese residents and
ceased issuing Chinese passports to such residents of Vietnam. In South
Vietnam, the Diem government followed a policy of forced naturalization

by which many Chinese residents became citizens in order to remain in business there. Their importance for the economy of the region remained intact. After the fall of Saigon, the Vietnamese government viewed the Diem measures as valid, but the Chinese government contended that they were invalid as the products of an illegitimate government.[39]

The dispute over the citizenship of the South Vietnamese Chinese was entangled with other issues. There were some unresolved territorial disputes and trouble over Cambodia, in which China sided with the Pol Pot regime.[40] In addition, Hanoi's decision to nationalize the South Vietnamese economy and to integrate South Vietnam with North Vietnam impinged on the Chinese large and small businessmen of the Saigon area. By May 1978, Hanoi had decided to clamp down on the Chinese businessmen of South Vietnam, and China reacted by announcing an intention to send two ships to Vietnam to evacuate Chinese residents. As relations between Hanoi and Peking worsened, negotiations over this and other issues broke down. By the summer of 1978, ethnic Chinese residents of both former North and South Vietnam were encouraged to leave, and refugees began flowing over the Sino-Vietnamese border and into the seas off Vietnam.

While this precipitated the refugee crisis of 1978-1979, the exodus was initially illegal. Extortion and departure taxes were demanded from potential refugees. Often Chinese businessmen acquired a boat and fares were paid in cash and gold, half of which would go to the government and for bribes to officials. In this way, it was similar to the departure of ethnic Vietnamese, who were the majority of "boat people" during the other refugee waves out of Vietnam since 1975. By July 1979, nearly 300,000 ethnic Chinese had fled from Vietnam.

What made this refugee crisis comparable to the pre-World War II crises was the attitudes engendered in other nations, especially those of Southeast Asia and the West. The People's Republic of China (PRC) and Taiwan did accept refugees who arrived by land or sea. In the case of the PRC, however, refugees in some cases had to undergo re-education, much like that which they were trying to avoid in the New Economic Zones of Vietnam. This was less of a problem for proletarian refugees from northern Vietnam than for those from Saigon.[41]

Vicissitudes of travel by sea in an open boat were many. The ships and boats were often barely seaworthy. The passengers faced storms, but also pirates. Many of the pirates were Thai fishermen who found that robbing refugees was a lucrative occupation. At the height of the refugee crisis, many ships avoided sealanes where there were refugees. If landfall was achieved, there was no certainty that one would be allowed to land. Even the predominantly Chinese "city-states" of Singapore and Hong Kong were reluctant to accept refugees. Other neighboring countries, particularly Malaysia, Indonesia, and the Philippines, were unwilling to accept ethnic Chinese refugees because each had its own "Chinese" problem.

In Indonesia and in the Philippines, the Chinese constitute a small percentage of the population (in both cases less than 5 percent). In these countries, conflict between local "native" populations and the Chinese, who are seen as controlling certain sectors of the economy, has been acute for the past century. In both, dual nationality of the Chinese has been an issue, with alternate policies of exclusion or forcible assimilation of Chinese having been followed. In both, one also finds high degrees of assimilation by certain segments of the Chinese population. "Mestizos" of partial Chinese ancestry have played an important role in Philippine life; Jose Rizal, the father of Philippine nationalism, was such a mestizo. In Indonesia, many people of mixed Chinese and Indonesian ancestry speak the local language. However unwilling they were to accept Chinese refugees, these countries played a less prominent role during this crisis than did Malaysia.[42]

The government of Malaysia was quite vocal during this period. In the summer of 1978 it threatened to tow refugee boats back into the sea if they reached land in its territorial waters, and at times it backed up its threat. The Chinese constitute 35 percent of Malaysia's total population. Thus an ethnic Chinese wave of settlers would threaten a delicate ethnic balance. Malaysia had quietly resettled Muslim refugees from Indochina in 1970. The balance between Chinese and Muslim Malays can, in fact, be seen as crucial to the formation of the present Malaysian federation. Singapore was expected to be part of this federation, but was excluded, in part because it would have made a Chinese majority in the federation possible. The Chinese had come to Malaysia as laborers to work in the mines and the plantations, and many have continued to do so. The range of Chinese occupations is broader in western Malaysia than in other Southeast Asian countries. While the Chinese in Malaysia cannot be seen exclusively as a middleman minority, they are prominent in commerce, and Singapore, with a Chinese majority, is the financial center of the region. In general, the politically dominant Malays have felt that they were weak economically relative to the Chinese and that the latter would take over their country. The present Prime Minister Mahathir bin Mohammed, expressed this fear in a controversial book published in 1970.[43]

The dramatic events of 1978 and 1979 filtered to the West with reports that the South China Sea was full of refugees who were being cynically allowed to leave Vietnam after paying extortionate taxes and bribes; robbed, raped, and killed by pirates; and refused permission to land by various governments, especially that of Malaysia. This aroused memories of the late 1930s and early 1940s, and a wave of sympathy swept over certain Western countries. An international conference was called. Pressure was put on Vietnam to control the flow of refugees and on Malaysia to allow them to stay until other arrangements could be made. Certain countries, especially France and the United States, accepted substantial numbers of these refugees. This relieved the transit camps in various Southeast Asian countries, though large numbers continue to live in such camps and continue to leave the Communist nations of Indochina through a variety of means. It is my impression that the "boat people" of 1978 and 1979 were viewed by most Americans in a manner similar to previous and subsequent groups of Southeast Asian émigrés and not as ethnic Chinese. While all of the Indochinese refugees in the United States have encountered anti-alien racist prejudices and opposition, no specifically anti-Sinic current differentiated the 1978-1979 wave from the others.

The Sino-Vietnamese case shares many features with other such instances, although it resulted in a rather brutal expulsion rather than an optimal genocide. In Vietnam proper, especially southern Vietnam, the minority was visible and conspicuous. Poverty was general and aggravated by many decades of war, both domestic and foreign. The minority was apparently more prosperous than the majority, and the occupation of the south by the north increased poverty. While the minority was probably not increasing relative to the majority, it did control more wealth than did the majority Vietnamese population. The minority's economic role was resented, and the Chinese were blamed for economic problems in South Vietnam as early as 1957. This was also the case under the Hanoi occupation.[44] Clients and competitors, as well as the officials of a nationalistic and socialistic government, all resented the role of the Chinese. After 1975, the Chinese in Vietnam were no longer related to a fraternal socialist government on the one side or to an anti-Communist ally (Taiwan) on the other, but to the enemies of Vietnam, i.e., the Chinese to the north and the Americans. They did have wealth to plunder, through taxation and extortion.

So far, the preconditions for expulsion and genocide coincide. Why, then, did the Vietnamese government carry out the former program rather than the latter? There may be several reasons. One, the Vietnamese government at this time was justifying its invasion of Cambodia on the basis of the brutality of the Pol Pot government. While governments are not particularly consistent in this regard, some form of legitimation plays a role in political actions. Two, at least some of the Chinese were accepted by China proper. Three, the Vietnamese were themselves vulnerable to attack by China and the United States, although neither was in a strong military position in 1978-1979. Still, some retaliation was possible. Four, the creation of a refugee crisis by expelling or encouraging emigration is useful in embarrassing one's neighbors and foes. This crisis did do this, although not as effectively as the Mariel refugee flow from Cuba in 1980. Five, the Vietnamese were not ideologically prepared for an optimal genocide.[45]

## COMPARISONS WITH HOLOCAUSTS

Looking at a number of examples is instructive. The two holocausts of middleman minorities were committed on groups who were long-standing residents in the regions where they were murdered, not relatively recent immigrants. In this way, the Jews of Germany and Eastern Europe and the Armenians of Anatolia, the main bodies of victims, resembled the Parsis and the Moroccan Jews more than they did the Indians in East Africa or even the Chinese in Vietnam.

In Europe, however, the Holocaust had been preceded by a period of great migrations and urbanization. The Jews, in particular, were part of these migrations, especially after the pogroms and May Laws in Russia in the early 1880s. While the anti-Semitic movement in Germany began well before that period and anti-Semitic ideas were commonly held at an earlier time, large numbers of East European Jewish immigrants in Germany and throughout Western Europe and North America certainly reinforced the view that Jews were essentially an alien people. The growing numbers of foreign Jews similarly lent credence to fears of Jewish domination.

The recentness of migration is also relevant to the degree to which the minority is visible as a separate group, although both the Jews in Eastern Europe and the Armenians in Anatolia remained loyal to a separate language for a long period of time. Such language loyalty, however, was breaking down in Eastern Europe during the interwar period, and many Armenians spoke either Turkish or a mixture of Turkish and Armenian. Genetic markers are also blurred with durable co-territoriality, since sexual relations between members of the various groups take place, whether in the form of marriage or of illicit seduction, rape, and concubinage. While linguistic, genetic, or sumptuary markers may persist as ideals or as stereotypes, their breakdown may give anxiety about assimilation and/or infiltration on the part of both groups in contact.

The fact of being old-timers in the region should also mean that a minority is viewed as "native." At the very least, one would expect them to reinvest resources in the country of their residence rather than sending them abroad. Yet in most of the cases discussed here, such an expectation was upset for both old and recent residents. The major exception was probably pre-1914 Germany. One cause of such foreign investment was the general impoverishment of the country. In most cases, this was strengthened by moves of discrimination coupled with fears of escalating persecution. To a lesser extent this was found among the Parsis of India, but it is certainly true of the other cases.

While it is hard to describe economic trends simply, most of the countries under consideration have had economic difficulties during the period preceding persecution (or expected harassment). Population growth in many developing areas, depression, and inflation all contributed to a sense of impoverishment in the countries under consideration. The other part of the economic picture is the relationship of different classes with the minority, which had characteristics of a class in itself. In India and Morocco, there were a variety of mercantile groups competing with reasonable success. In Vietnam, East Africa, and Poland, the minority was perceived as having some kind of monopoly on trade and was particularly resented. In the Ottoman Empire, the Armenians were one of several non-Muslim minorities who were perceived as controlling commercial enterprise; the degree to which Muslim Turks desired to compete is not indicated in the literature. Germany, of course, has been studied and dissected, and yet the results are inconclusive. It should also be pointed out that those who were most integrated into the society, whether in Poland or Germany, often competed most directly with members of the majority ethnic group. It was the German-speaking or Polish-speaking Jew who sought to enter the university, become a professional or civil servant, or pursue success as an artist. When positions of this kind are limited, competition is often intense. While anti-Semitism was central to the Nazi ideology, it is still unclear whether anti-Semitism itself was part of the core of its appeal to those who became Nazis or voted for the Nazi party. Andreski, when offering his economic interpretation of anti-Semitism, explicitly argued that anti-Semitism in Germany was weaker than in Poland and Hungary, roughly corresponding to the relatively small percentage of the population which was Jewish. Lately even the thesis that it was the lower middle class that was most in competition with Jews and in the forefront of German Fascism has been called into question. Istvan Deak agrees with Andreski's argument that anti-Semitism was secondary to other factors in drawing Germans to the Nazi movement and in leading them to comply with the systematic genocide which followed.[46] Still, the Nazis incorporated the stereotype of the Jew as an alien middleman into their propaganda.

Where does this leave middleman minority theory in its relationship to genocide and ethnic conflict in general? As indicated early on, middleman minority theory is primarily applicable to the preconditions for inter-ethnic conflict and genocide as a manifestation of such conflict. Like most sets of theory, it provides us with questions to ask. Unquestionably, economic conflict between competing merchants, workers and employers, and buyers and sellers takes on an ethnic dimension when those on one side tend to be members of a different ethnic group from those on the other side. There is a wide range of options for the end results of majority–middleman minority relations, including substantial assimilation, occupational integration, or the development of complementarity, all with minimal conflict, as well as the conflicts resulting in voluntary emigration, harassment, expulsion, and genocide. There is thus no necessary connection between middleman minority status and victimization.[47] In a period which has seen the mass murder of Indians in Brazil, Paraguay, and Guatemala; Communists in Indonesia; large segments of the total population in East Timor and Cambodia; landowners and others in China; the ruling Afro-Shirazis in Zanzibar; the dominant Tutsis in Rwanda; Hutu in Burundi; and dissident members of ruling groups in the Soviet Union, it is difficult to say that any group is not subject to genocide. Still, the vulnerability of middleman minorities is related to their economic position and has been demonstrated dramatically in this century. In all cases of victimization, other factors were present, but the images of minority middlemen as economic parasites and collaborators with alien enemies of the nation were intertwined and served to justify their liquidation from the body social.

As noted earlier, middleman minority theory's historical roots are shared with the ideologies used to justify anti-minority actions. The denigration of trade and moneylending and the ideal of a national economy controlled by members of the national community, excluding strangers, were important in the foundation of the social sciences as well as in the formulation of both socialist and nationalist ideology. Jacob Katz[48] in his study of modern anti-Semitism concluded that many of the observations of anti-Semites on the Jewish position in Europe were empirically based, but the conclusions which they drew were colored by extremely negative attitudes toward the Judaic heritage and the Jews themselves. This observation can be extended to attitudes toward middleman minorities elsewhere and to social scientists studying these groups. As social scientists and scholars, we must pursue the economic reasons for inter-ethnic conflict, even though our writings may be used to justify oppression and persecution. With this awareness, however, we might paraphrase Avtalyon: Beware scholars of your words, for evil may follow from your speech.[49]

## NOTES

1. This chapter is a product of a long research project in which I examined theories dealing with middleman minorities, for the purpose of comparing Jewish and non-Jewish communities globally. In that work, however, I was only partially concerned with genocide as one form of "host-hostility" and anti-minority actions.

2. Helen Fein, *Accounting for Genocide* (New York: The Free Press, 1979), pp. 7-10. Vahakn Dadrian, "A Typology of Genocide," *International Review of Modern Sociology* 5 (1975), pp. 201-12. Yehuda Bauer, *The Holocaust in Historical Perspective* (Seattle: University of Washington Press, 1978), pp. 34-37.

In recent years, the term "genocide" has been applied to a variety of events. The term "cultural genocide," for instance, has been used to describe the Soviet campaign against Jewish culture in the U.S.S.R. Raphael Lemkin, who first introduced the concept of genocide in 1944, also injected a measure of ambiguity into it. While defining genocide as "the extermination of nations and ethnic groups," he wrote that genocide is carried out through a variety of attacks on the peoples affected.

These include destroying institutions of self-government; colonization by the invaders; killing and removing national elites (e.g., the intelligentsia); disrupting social cohesion; prohibiting or destroying cultural institutions and activities; prohibiting higher education; shifting wealth to the invaders; extermination; and moral debasement (through promotion of pornography and alcohol). Lemkin introduced this concept during World War II, when the full extent of the Nazi program and the fine distinctions made by the National Socialists themselves were not fully comprehended, although the basic outlines had been revealed. See Raphael Lemkin, *Axis Rule in Occupied Europe* (Washington, D.C.: Carnegie Endowment for International Peace, 1944), pp. xi-xii.

3. Robert Melson, "A Theoretical Inquiry into the Armenian Massacres of 1894-6," *Comparative Studies in Society and History* 24 (1982), pp. 481-509.

4. For other reviews of middleman minority theory, see Edna Bonacich and J. Modell, *The Economic Basis of Ethnic Solidarity: The Case of the Japanese-Americans* (Berkeley and Los Angeles: University of California Press, 1981), pp. 13-36; and the following works by Walter P. Zenner: *Middleman Minority Theories and the Jews: A Historical Assessment* (New York: YIVO Working Papers in Yiddish and East European Jewish Studies Series, No. 31, 1978); "Theories of Middleman Minorities: A Critical Review," in *Sourcebook on the New Immigration*, ed. Roy S. Bryce-Laporte (New Brunswick, N.J.: Transaction Books, 1980), pp. 313-26; "The Jewish Diaspora and the Middleman Adaptation," in *Diaspora: Exile and the Jewish Condition*, ed. E. Levine (New York: Jason Aronson, 1983), pp. 141-56, and *Minorities in the Middle: A Cross-Cultural Analysis* (manuscript). Also see Jack Nusan Porter, "The Urban Middleman," *Comparative Social Research* 4 (1981), pp. 199-215.

5. See especially Max Weber, *Ancient Judaism* (Glencoe, Ill.: The Free Press, 1952), especially pp. 336-55, and W. Sombart, *The Jews and Modern Capitalism* (Glencoe, Ill.: The Free Press, 1951). The general work of both sociologists also reflected their views on commerce, ethnicity, and religion.

See Max Weber, *Economy and Society* (New York: Bedminster, 1968), and W. Sombart, *The Quintessence of Capitalism* (New York: E. P. Dutton, 1915). Both Weber and Sombart tended to view Jewish economic activities in a negative light. Sombart incorporated anti-Semitic racial explanations into his analysis long before he actually joined the Nazi party.

6. For an English translation of Roscher's 1875 essay, see W. Roscher, "The Status of the Jews in the Middle Ages from the Standpoint of Commercial Policy," *Historia Judaica* 6 (1944), pp. 13-26. For Toennies' views on "intermediaries," see F. Toennies, *Community and Society* (East Lansing: Michigan State University Press, 1957), and Toennies, *On Sociology: Pure, Applied and Empirical* (Chicago: University of Chicago Press, 1971), pp. 308-10. Cf. Georg Simmel, "The Stranger," in *The Sociology of Georg Simmel,* ed. K. Wolff (Glencoe, Ill.: The Free Press, 1980), pp. 402-8. For a discussion comparing Weber's "pariah" concept with the Toennies/Simmel ideas of intermediary and stranger, see W. Cahnman, "Pariahs, Strangers and Court Jews," *Sociological Analysis* 35 (1974), pp. 155-66. On the use of the stranger concept in the social sciences, see Donald N. Levine, "Simmel at a Distance: On the History and Systematics of the Sociology of the Stranger," in *Strangers in African Societies,* ed. William A. Shack and Elliott P. Skinner (Berkeley and Los Angeles: University of California Press, 1979), pp. 21-36.

7. Cf. H. P. Becker, "Constructive Typology in the Social Sciences," in *Contemporary Social Theory,* ed. H. E. Barnes, H. Becker, and F. B. Becker (New York: Appleton-Century, 1940), pp. 17-46. Also see I. Rinder, "Strangers in the Land," *Social Problems* 6 (1958), pp. 253-60; S. Stryker, "Social Structure and Prejudice," *Social Problems* 6 (1958), pp. 340-54; T. Shibutani and K. Kwan, *Ethnic Stratification* (New York: Macmillan, 1965); W. Wertheim, *East-West Parallels* (The Hague: Mouton, 1964).

8. Cf. E. Bonacich, "A Theory of Middleman Minorities," *American Sociological Review* 38 (1973), pp. 583-94, Bonacich, "Middleman Minorities and Advanced Capitalism," *Ethnic Groups* 2 (1980), pp. 211-20, and Bonacich "Class Approaches to Ethnicity and Race," *Insurgent Sociologist* 10 (1980), pp. 2, 9-23. Jonathan Turner and Edna Bonacich, "Toward a Composite Theory of Middleman Minorities," *Ethnicity* 7 (1980), pp. 144-58. Also see Bonacich and Modell, *Economic Basis.* For a critique of Bonacich's application of middleman minority theories to modern societies, see F. Bovenkerk, "Shylock of Horatio Alger: Beschouwingen over de Theorie der Handelsminderheden," in *Neveh Ya'akov: Jubilee Volume Presented to Dr. Jaap Meijer,* ed. L. Dasberg and J. N. Cohen (Assen: Van Gorcum, 1982), pp. 147-64.

9. Cf. Stryker, "Social Structure and Prejudice." Richard A. Schermerhorn, "Parsis and Jews in India: A Tentative Comparison," *Journal of Asian Studies* 1 (1976), pp. 119-22, and Schermerhorn, *Ethnic Plurality in*

*India* (Tucson: University of Arizona Press, 1978). E. Kulke, *The Parsees in India* (Munich: Weltforum Verlag, 1974).

10. Stanislav Andreski, "An Economic Interpretation of Anti-Semitism," *Jewish Journal of Sociology* 5 (1963), pp. 201-13. Bauer, *Holocaust in Historical Perspective,* pp. 55-58. As for Poland, one finds that during World War II Jews were assisted much more in these areas, especially Belorussia, than elsewhere in the former Polish Republic.

11. Cf. S. Kuznets, "Economic Life and Structure of the Jews," in *The Jews: Their History, Culture and Religion,* ed. L. Finkelstein (New York: Harper, 1960), pp. 1597-1666. Also see Ellis Rivkin, *The Shaping of Jewish History* (New York: Scribner's, 1971).

12. Andreski, "Economic Interpretation."

13. Bonacich, "A Theory," and "Middleman Minorities and Advanced Capitalism."

14. See Abraham J. Duker, "Acculturation and Integration: A Jewish Survivalist View," in *Acculturation and Integration: A Symposium,* ed. J. L. Teller (New York: American Histadrut Cultural Exchange, 1965).

15. Andreski, "Economic Interpretation."

16. John Waterbury, *North for the Trade* (Berkeley and Los Angeles: University of California Press, 1972).

17. For a discussion of the diabolic nature of moneymaking in a peasant context, see Michael Taussig, "The Genesis of Capitalism among a South American Peasantry: The Devil's Labor and the Baptism of Money," *Comparative Studies in Society and History* 19 (1977), pp. 130-55.

18. Bonacich and Modell, *Economic Basis.* Walter P. Zenner, "American Jewry in the Light of Middleman Minority Theories," *Contemporary Jewry* 5 (1980), pp. 11-30. Richard Alba and Gwen Moore, "Ethnicity in the American Elite," *American Sociological Review* 47 (1982), pp. 373-82.

19. Some of these attributes are paradoxical. In the ultimate case of optimal genocide or total expulsion, the scapegoat is permanently eliminated and can never serve that purpose again. This has been pointed out by writers who reject the scapegoat theory with regard to the Holocaust. Yet, since many leaders think in the short term, it is sufficient to make the sacrifice once. Similarly, the strangers may be sojourners or recent immigrants, but relative to true itinerants, they are sedentary.

20. Ralph Austen (personal communication) has suggested that some reports of attacks on Jews in Moroccan Muslim historiography are fabricated, because each new dynasty begins by "overthrowing the Jews," whether they actually do this or not. Of course, for such a ritual to occur, there must be Jews in the society. The situation was similar to that of the popes who saw the Jews as witnesses to Christ, even if they rejected them. See Norman Stillman, "Muslims and Jews in Morocco," *The Jerusalem Quarterly* 1 (1977), pp. 76-83, and Allan R. Meyers, "Patronage and Protection: The Status of Jews in Pre-colonial Morocco," in *Jewish Societies in the Middle*

*East,* ed. S. Deshen and W. P. Zenner (Washington, D.C.: University Press of America, 1982), pp. 85-104.

21. Cf. Bauer, *Holocaust in Historical Perspective,* pp. 30-38; Lucy Dawidowicz, *The Holocaust and the Historians* (Cambridge, Mass.: Harvard University Press, 1981), pp. 4-21.

22. Cf. Fein, *Accounting.*

23. Cf. Vahakn N. Dadrian, "A Theoretical Model of Genocide with Particular Reference to the Armenian Case," *Sociologia Internationalis* 14 (1976/1980), pp. 99-126, and "The Common Features of the Armenian and Jewish Cases of Genocide: A Comparative Victimological Perspective," in *Victimology: A New Focus* (Lexington, Mass.: Lexington Books, 1974), vol. 4, pp. 99-119. Robert Melson, "Provocation or Nationalism: A Critical Inquiry into the Armenian Genocide of 1915" (Paper delivered at the Annual Meeting of the Middle East Studies Association, Chicago, November 4-7, 1983).

24. Bauer, *Holocaust in Historical Perspective;* Dawidowicz, *Holocaust and the Historians;* Fein, *Accounting.*

The controversy over whether the Armenian massacres in Anatolia were a state-sponsored genocide or the product of an extremely bloody civil war continues. The latter viewpoint is presented in a volume using demographic data by Justin McCarthy, *Muslims and Minorities: The Population of Ottoman Anatolia and the End of the Empire* (New York: New York University Press, 1983). Nevertheless, my own reading of the historical record is that the deportations of 1915, which were ordered by the Ottoman government, were genocidal. A full-scale comparison dealing with both the differences and similarities between the Nazi "war against the Jews" and the deportation and massacres of Armenians is sorely needed. It is beyond the scope of this already lengthy chapter.

25. These points are largely based on Andreski, "Economic Interpretation."

26. Kulke, *Parsees.*

27. Stillman, "Muslims and Jews"; Lawrence Rosen, "Muslim-Jewish Relations in a Moroccan City," *International Journal of Middle Eastern Studies* 3 (1972), pp. 435-49; Meyers, "Patronage and Protection." One must be careful in generalizing from Morocco to other parts of the Middle East.

28. See Mark Tessler, "The Identity of Religious Minorities in Nonsecular States: The Jews in Tunisia and Morocco and the Arabs in Israel," *Comparative Studies in Society and History* 20 (1978), pp. 359-73, and Mark Tessler and Linda Hawkins, "The Political Culture of Jews in Tunisia and Morocco," *International Journal of Middle Eastern Studies* 11 (1980), pp. 59-86. The anticipatory exodus of Jews from Morocco is also well portrayed in the documentary film *Routes of Exile: A Moroccan Jewish Odyssey* (New York: First Run Films, 1983).

29. On patronage, see L. Rosen, "A Moroccan Jewish Community During the Middle Eastern Crisis," *American Scholar* 37 (1967), pp. 435-51, for an excellent illustration.

30. But why has anti-Semitism been so potent in postwar Poland, where the numerical decline of Jews was even more precipitous? Ideological anti-Semitism was much more of a force in Poland during the twentieth century, and Jews were more prominent in the ruling Communist elite during the early phases of post-World War II Poland than was the case with regard to anti-Semitism or Jews in the governments of post-independence Morocco.

31. See William Shack and Elliott P. Skinner, eds., *Strangers in African Societies* (Berkeley and Los Angeles: University of California Press, 1979), for descriptions of various stranger-groups in Africa, both African and non-African, which have been affected by partial and total expulsions. The best general survey of the Chinese in Southeast Asia before 1975 is Mary F.S. Heidhues, *Southeast Asia's Chinese Minorities* (Hawthorn Victoria: Longman Australia, 1974). On the less publicized expulsion of Indians from Burma, see Usha Mahajani, *The Role of Indian Minorities in Burma and Malaysia* (Westport, Conn.: Greenwood Press, 1973). A general consideration of anti-Indian and anti-Chinese violence is found in Fred R. von der Mehden, "Pariah Communities and Violence," in *Vigilante Politics,* ed. H. Jon Rosenbaum and Peter C. Sederberg (Philadelphia: University of Pennsylvania Press, 1976), pp. 218-33.

32. Ali Mazrui, "Casualties of an Underdeveloped Class Structure," in Shack and Skinner, *Strangers in African Societies,* pp. 261-78.

33. On the Asians expelled from East African countries, see Y. Tandon, *Brown Briton* (London: Runnymede Trust, 1972); Michael Twaddle, ed., *Expulsion of a Minority: Essays on Uganda Asians* (London: Athlone Press, 1975); Bert N. Adams and Mike Bristow, "The Politico-Economic Position of Ugandan Asians in the Colonial and Independent Eras," *Journal of Asian and African Studies* 13 (1978), pp. 151-66; B. N. Adams and M. Bristow, "Ugandan Asian Expulsion Experiences: Rumor and Reality," *Journal of Asian and African Studies* 14 (1979), pp. 190-203. Two works which report African attitudes toward Asians in neighboring Kenya during the period of the partial expulsion are Peter Marris and Anthony Somerset, *The African Entrepreneur* (New York: Africana, 1971), and Donald Rothchild, *Racial Bargaining in Independent Kenya* (London: Oxford University Press, 1973).

34. See Dadrian, "Typology." A problem in any typology is that various factors may contribute to a complex event such as a genocide. Officially, *Kristallnacht,* when the Nazis broke into Jewish homes, burnt synagogues, and sent large numbers of Jewish men to concentration camps in November 1938, was an act of retribution for the assassination of a German embassy official in Paris. In Nigeria in 1966, the massacres were associated with a realistically based interpretation of an open power struggle for control of the government, not with a minor "provocation" linked to a mythical conspiracy.

35. A major source on the Chinese in Vietnam is Luong Nhi Ky, *The Chinese in Vietnam: A Study of Vietnamese-Chinese Relations* (Ph.D. dissertation, University of Michigan, 1963).

On the crisis of 1978-1979, see the following: Bruce Grant and the *"Age"* Investigators, *The Boat People: An Age Investigation* (Harmondsworth: Penguin Books, 1979); Nguyen Manh Hung, "The Sino-Vietnamese Conflict: Power Play among Communist Neighbors," *Asian Survey* 19 (1979), pp. 1037-52; Gareth Porter, "Vietnam's Ethnic Chinese and the Sino-Vietnamese Conflict," *Bulletin of Concerned Asian Scholars* 12, no. 4 (1980), pp. 55-60; Charles Mohr, "A Vietnamese Refugee's Story: War Hero to Unwanted Alien," *New York Times,* September 11, 1979, p. A6; Sheldon Simon, "China, Vietnam, and A.S.E.A.N.: The Politics of Polarization," *Asian Survey* 19, no. 12 (1979), pp. 1171-88; Judith Strauch, *The Chinese Exodus from Vietnam: Implications for the Southeast Asian Chinese,* Occasional Papers, No. 1 (Cambridge, Mass.: Cultural Survival, 1980).

36. Ky, *Chinese in Vietnam,* pp. 27-60, 62-107; Tsung-to Way, "Overseas Chinese in Vietnam," *Far Eastern Economic Review,* (January 2, 1958), pp. 20-21.

37. See Stephen Fitzgerald, *China and the Overseas Chinese: A Study in Peking's Policies* (Cambridge, England: Cambridge University Press, 1972).

38. Ky, *Chinese in Vietnam,* pp. 131-41, 175-76.

39. Ibid., pp. 151-66; Hung, "Sino-Vietnamese Conflict."

40. Hung, "Sino Vietnamese-Conflict," points out that the Chinese government never protested the treatment, often extremely harsh, which the Chinese in Cambodia received from the Pol Pot government alongside other urban populations.

41. On refugees in China, see James P. Sterba, "Some Refugees Safe at Home in China Again," *New York Times,* September 5, 1979; and "Some Vietnamese Ethnic Chinese Find Life Hard in China," *New York Times,* September 11, 1979, p. A6. On the reasons for avoiding repatriation in Taiwan, see "After Nightmare of Vietnam: Valedictorian at City College," *New York Times,* May 24, 1984, pp. B1, B8.

42. For an overview of the Chinese in the area as a whole, see Heidhues, *Southeast Asia's Chinese.* A brief survey concentrating on citizenship is H. and P. C. Mabbett and C. Coppell, *The Chinese in Indonesia, the Philippines, Malaysia* (London: Minority Rights Group Report No. 10, n.d. [ca. 1971]). Also see Strauch, *Chinese Exodus.*

43. See Simon, "China, Vietnam, A.S.E.A.N." Strauch, *Chinese Exodus,* briefly deals with the implications of other overseas Chinese. The Prime Minister's analysis of Malaysia's problems, including ethnic conflict, is Mahathir bin Mohammed, *The Malay Dilemma* (Singapore: Donald Moore, 1970).

44. Tsung-to Way, "Overseas Chinese"; Hung, "Sino-Vietnamese Conflict."

45. William Shawcross, "In Vietnam Today," *New York Review of Books* 24 (September 14, 1981), pp. 62-72, reports a visit to a Chinese-run factory in Cholon. This indicates that some Chinese remain in Vietnam.

46. Cf. Istvan Deak, "How Guilty Were the Germans?," *New York Review of Books* 31 (May 31, 1984), pp. 37-41.

47. Whether such a status is the product of deliberate action on the part of the minority or the lack of success in being accepted on the part of minority members as it was in Germany and much of East Europe makes no difference.

48. Jacob Katz, *From Prejudice to Destruction: Anti-Semitism, 1700-1933* (Cambridge, Mass.: Harvard University Press, 1980), pp. 257-59, 324.

49. Abot I:11. The original is "Beware sages of your words lest you incur the penalty of exile and be exiled to a place of evil waters, and the disciples who come after you drink thereof and die and the Name (of God) be profaned." In a secular context, taking ethical consequences into account is the equivalent.

# AFTERWORD: GENOCIDE AND CIVILIZATION

## Richard L. Rubenstein

Although there have been thousands of books written about the destruction of the European Jews, few have been devoted to the more general problem of genocide per se. Indeed, a number of contributors to this volume have commented on the avoidance of the subject by political and social researchers. Kurt Jonassohn and Frank Chalk observe that until recently scholars participated in a process of pervasive, self-imposed denial concerning the importance of genocide in history. In their introductory essay, editors Isidor Wallimann and Michael Dobkowski note the relative silence of social scientists on the subject. They argue that social scientists have, e.g., been far more interested in poverty than in the "nature of social conflicts and their possible escalation into war and destruction." At the 1983 convention of the American Political Science Association, a session on genocide, which featured papers by a number of leading authorities, drew an audience of no more than ten. It is this writer's thesis that the relative silence on the subject of genocide stems from the unwillingness of both scholars and their audiences to confront the fact that, far from being a relapse into barbarism, genocide is an intrinsic expression of civilization as we know it. Put differently, the genocidal destructiveness of our era is an expression of some of its "most significant political, moral, religious and demographic tendencies."[1] If indeed genocide expresses some, though obviously not all, of the dominant trends in contemporary civilization, it would hardly be surprising that few researchers would want to spend much time on the night side of the world we have made for ourselves.

In the present volume the connection between civilization and genocide is raised most directly by Tony Barta's chapter, "Relations of Geno-

cide: Land and Lives in the Colonization of Australia." A professor at
an Australian university, Barta asserts that the basic fact of his nation's
history has been the conquest of the country by one people and the dispossession "with ruthless destructiveness" of another people, the Aborigines, those who were there *ab origine,* "from the beginning." Barta argues that, although it was by no means the initial intention of the British
government to destroy the Aborigines, Australia is nevertheless a "nation
founded on genocide." According to Barta, genocide was the inevitable,
though unintended, consequence of the European colonization of the
Australian continent. Barta's thesis puts him somewhat at odds with
those scholars, such as Walter P. Zenner, who hold that genocide is "the
*intentional* physical annihilation of all or part of a group of people on
racial, religious or ethnic lines." According to Barta, in order to comprehend genocide we need a conception of the phenomenon that embraces
*relations of destruction* and removes from the term the emphasis on
policy and intention with which it is normally associated. Barta argues
that the history of his own country amply demonstrates that genocidal
outcomes can come into being without deliberate state planning. Moreover, he fully appreciates the degree to which the destruction of Australia's Aboriginal population was not the consequence of the actions of
isolated men acting out their aggressions on a lawless frontier far from
metropolitan centers of civilization but was in fact *the outcome of economic, social, political, and religious transformations in the mother
country,* the first European nation fully to enter the economically
rationalized world of the modern era.

If we wish to comprehend the roots of genocide in the modern world,
the beginnings of the modernization process in Great Britain may
provide an excellent starting point.[2] The beginnings of English modernization are to be found in the acts of enclosure which transformed the
subsistence economy of premodern English agricultural into the money
economy of our era. In the process, the customary rights to land usage
of the economically unproductive English peasant class were abrogated
and that class was largely transformed into a congeries of individuals
whose survival was entirely dependent upon their ability to find wage
labor. Absent gainful employment, the dispossessed peasants could
only turn to a harsh and punitively administered system of poor relief,
vagabondage, or outright crime. A crucial social by-product of England's economic rationalization was the creation of a large class of people
who were superfluous to England's new economic system.

A class of more or less permanently superfluous people is a potential
source of acute social instability. Having no hope of receiving society's
normal rewards, it has little incentive, save fear of punitive retaliation, to
abide by society's customary behavioral restraints. Even if such a group
is tied to the rest of the population by common ethnicity and religion, it is
likely to be perceived and to perceive itself as having been cast outside of

society's *universe of moral obligation.* Implied in a universe of moral obligation is the expectation that, consistent with their social location, its actors will, under normal circumstances, subordinate their individual inclinations to the good of the whole. A measure of self-sacrificing altruism rather than self-regarding egoism will normally characterize the behavior of members of such a universe toward each other. At a minimum, members will not normally regard other members as potential sources of injury or even personal destruction. To the extent that trust is possible between human beings, the actors within a shared universe of moral obligation will normally trust each other, an attitude they will find impossible to extend to strangers. Such attitudes have less to do with the moral virtuosity of individuals than with the way social relations are structured. The enclosure laws had the effect of expelling England's displaced peasants from the only universe of obligation they had ever known, that of the manor and the parish. This was clearly understood by English decisionmakers as early as the enactment of the Elizabethan Poor Laws, which were as much police measures aimed at controlling England's first redundant population as they were philanthropic efforts to supply that population's irreducible needs for survival.

In the case of the modernization of England, the arable land taken from the displaced peasants was devoted to sheep raising, a cash crop, and economically rational large-scale farming. Out of the vast social dislocation engendered by the process, England was able to finance its first large-scale modern industry, textiles. However, the transformation of arable land to pasture seriously diminished England's ability to produce its own food supply. Moreover, by the beginning of the nineteenth century, that country was no longer able to produce all of the raw materials necessary for its burgeoning industry.

Australia was an ideal land for sheep raising. It was also a convenient outlet for the relatively humane elimination of a significant portion of England's redundant population. As Barta points out, the convict population exported by England to Australia was not unrelated to the dispossession of England's peasantry by the acts of enclosure. In addition, England contained large numbers of undercapitalized small holders and artisans who were faced with the prospect of downward economic mobility in an increasingly capital-intensive home economy. Many of the more enterprising small holders took their meagre assets to Australia in the knowledge that an ever-increasing demand for both sheep's wool and sheep's flesh in the mother country presented the undercapitalized free colonizers, who were willing to work and capable of prudent management, with opportunities for prosperity which could not be duplicated at home. Australia was thus an important safety valve for those segments of England's population made redundant by the progressive rationalization of its economy and society.

As we know, Australia was not an unsettled country. Its Aboriginal people had developed a viable human ecology which was altogether incomprehensible to the settlers, as indeed the ways of the settlers were incomprehensible to them. Moreover, sheep raising and the settlers' rationalized agrarian economy was incompatible with Aborigine land use. Since both sides were absolutely dependent upon the land, albeit in radically different ways, loss of the land necessarily entailed the complete destruction of the defeated way of life. As Barta writes, co-existence was impossible.

The issue was decided by the superior power and technology of the settlers. Since their survival was at stake, the Aborigines had no choice but to resist. The predictable response of the settlers was to root out the menace to their way of life. There were a number of bloody massacres. There were also government-sponsored attempts to diminish settler violence, but even without direct violence the Aborigines were destined to perish. Having lost their way of life and having been deprived of a meaningful future, most of the Aborigines who were not killed by the whites "faded away." Barta writes that between 1839 and 1849 there were only twenty births recorded among the seven Aboriginal tribes around Melbourne. He concludes that, whatever the official British intent, the encounter between the white settlers and the blacks was one of *living out a relationship of genocide, a relationship that was structured into the very nature of the encounter*. Barta distinguishes between a genocidal society and a genocidal state. National Socialist Germany was a genocidal state. Its genocidal project was deliberate and intended. Australia was a genocidal society. It had no conscious genocidal project. Nevertheless, its very existence had genocidal consequences for the original population. According to Barta, the basic pattern of the colonization of Australia was everywhere the same. It consisted of white pastoral invasion, black resistance, violent victory of the whites, and finally the mysterious disappearance of the blacks.

Although Barta confines his description to Australia, it is clear that the process he describes was repeated in other European colonial settlements. In his biography of Oliver Cromwell, the English historian Christopher Hill comments:

A great many civilized Englishmen of the propertied class in the seventeenth century spoke of Irishmen in tones not far removed from those which the Nazis used about the Slavs, or white South Africans use about the original inhabitants of their country. In each case the contempt rationalized a desire to exploit.[3]

What Hill could have added was that Cromwell was fully prepared to exterminate those Irish Catholics who resisted exploitation and to turn their lands over to Protestant colonizers. The towns of Drogheda and Wexford refused to surrender to Cromwell. They were sacked and those inhabitants unable to flee were massacred. In the case of Wexford, after all the inhabitants had been killed, Cromwell reported that the town was available for colonization by English settlers. An English clergyman commended the place for settlement: "It is a fine spot for some godly congregation where house and land wait for inhabitants and occupiers."[4] Even in the seventeenth century, it was clear to England's leaders that the more Ireland was cleared of its original Catholic inhabitants the more available it would be for Protestant English settlement.

The extremes to which England was prepared to go to empty Ireland of its original inhabitants became clear during the famine years of 1846-1848. It is estimated that within that period the population of Ireland was reduced by about 2 million out of an estimated 1845 population of 9 million. Approximately 1 million perished in the famine. About the same number were compelled to emigrate in order to survive.[5] Elsewhere, this writer has attempted to show that the relief given by the English government to the Irish, who were, technically speaking, British subjects at the time, was deliberately kept at levels guaranteed to produce the demographic result which came to pass. Moreover, the demographic outcome was welcomed by leading members of England's society and government. The deaths by famine and the removal by emigration were lauded as achieving for Ireland what the enclosures had done for England, namely, clearing the land of uneconomic subsistence producers and making it available for rationalized agricultural enterprise.[6] The candor of an 1853 editorial in *The Economist* on the benefits of Irish and Scottish emigration is instructive:

It is consequent on the breaking down of the system of society founded on small holdings and potato cultivation. . . . *The departure of the redundant part of the population of Ireland and Scotland is an indispensable preliminary to every kind of improvement.*[7]

Unfortunately, the "departure" welcomed by *The Economist* entailed mass death by famine and disease for a very significant proportion of Ireland's peasant class. In the eyes of the British decision-making class of the period, Catholic Ireland was an inferior civilization.[8] A class that was indifferent to the fate of its own peasants was hardly likely to be concerned with that of the Irish.

The basic colonizing pattern described by Barta, namely, white settlement, native resistance, violent settler victory, and, finally, the disappearance of most if not all of the natives, was played out in North and South America as well.[9] If Australian society was built upon a genocidal relationship with that of the indigenous cultures, so too was American society. There was a time not so long ago when it was taken for granted that "the only good Indian was a dead Indian."

The connecting link between genocidal settler societies of the eighteenth and nineteenth centuries and twentieth-century genocide can be discerned in Adolf Hitler's *Lebensraum* program. As a young man, Hitler saw the settlement of the New World and the concomitant elimination of North America's Indian population by white European settlers as a model to be followed by Germany on the European continent. As John Roth points out in his chapter, Hitler was keenly aware of Germany's population problems. He was determined that there would be no surplus German population even if a significant portion of Germany's Slavic neighbors were exterminated to provide "living space" for German settlers adjacent to the homeland. Put differently, Hitler proposed to repeat in Europe, albeit with infinitely intensified viciousness, the exploitative colonialism practiced by other Europeans overseas. In Hitler's eyes the Slavs were destined to become Europe's Indians. They were to be displaced, uprooted, enslaved, and, if necessary, annihilated to make way for Germany's surplus population. Unlike the earlier colonizers, Hitler had no illusions concerning the genocidal nature of such an undertaking. He had the historical precedents of earlier European efforts at colonization and imperial domination. He regarded the defeat of native cultures by white settlers and colonists as evidence for his version of Social Darwinism, the belief that history is the theater in which the races enact their life and death struggle for survival and the superior races destroy their racial inferiors. As is well known, this same Social Darwinism became an important component in the legitimating ideology for the Holocaust. In Hitler's eyes, the Jews were the most contemptible of all of the inferior races destined by fate and German strength for destruction.

As noted above, there was a fundamental difference between the behavior of the older European colonizing powers and Hitler's in that his policies were intentional and deliberately formulated. If the destruction of the Aboriginal cultures of Australia was an unintended consequence of state policy, the destruction and eventual extermination of Germany's neighbors was fully intended by Hitler and National Socialist Germany. Nevertheless, that difference should not obscure the fact that (a) both colonizing policies were intended to solve the same fundamental problem, namely, the relatively humane, non-genocidal elimination by the mother country of a redundant or potentially redundant sector of its domestic population, and that (b) both could be successfully implemented only by the merciless elimination of the indigenous population of the colonized lands. Moreover, the very success of the earlier projects invited their repetition by political leaders, such as Hitler, who believed their nation to be faced with the problem that had led to the original colonization. Such leaders could no longer pretend ignorance of the consequences of their policies. One of the differences between Hitler and his predecessors was his lack of hypocrisy and illusion concerning the extent to which his project entailed mass murder. Nevertheless, it is clear from the history of the English in Ireland and Australia as well as that of Europeans in the New World that the destruction of the indigenous population never constituted a reason for calling colonization to a halt. There is thus a historical continuum between the unintended genocides of the period of Europe's demographic projection beyond its original territorial limits and that of the period of Europe's deliberate auto-cannibalization.

If the above argument has merit, it will be possible to define genocide as *the most radical means of implementing a state or communally sponsored program of population elimination.* It should be noted that (a) the issue of intention is not raised in this definition, and that (b) genocide is grasped conceptually within the wider context of programs of population elimination. This definition allows for a comprehension of the larger historical conditions under which a population is likely to be identified as redundant and targeted for one or another form of elimination. This definition also helps to structure the connections between population redundancy, emigration, expulsion, colonization, modernization, and genocide.

According to Walter P. Zenner, the *aim of genocide* is to transform a social field by removing a whole group of political actors. Without necessarily disagreeing with Zenner, Roger Smith argues that the fundamental issue in genocide is *Who belongs, who is to have a voice in society?* It is this writer's conviction that, unless the identity of society and the political order is assumed, a highly questionable assumption, the real issue is *Who is to have a voice in the political order?*

The issue of a voice in the political order is in turn related to the universe of moral obligation. In ancient Greece, members of the polis belonged to a common universe of obligation. This was especially evident in war. Only those who shared common origins, belonged by *inherited right* to the same community, and saw themselves as partaking of a common fate could be trusted in a life-and-death struggle. Neither the slave nor the stranger could be so trusted. Hence, they were regarded as outside of the shared universe of obligation.

A very grave problem arises when, for any reason, a community regards itself as having within its midst a sub-community or a group of strangers who cannot be trusted. The problem is especially urgent in time of war. The perception of disloyalty may be mistaken, as in the case of the Armenians in Turkey during World War I and Japanese Americans during World War II. The fundamental reason for the mass incarceration of the Japanese Americans was the belief of most Americans that the majority of Japanese Americans were loyal to the Emperor rather than to their adopted country. Similarly, Rabbi Meir Kahane's extremist agitation to expel all Arabs from contemporary Israel ultimately rests upon the conviction that Israelis can only trust each other and that as long as the state contains potentially hostile elements, the safety of the community remains precarious. This author is convinced that, were Kahane's policies ever implemented, the consequences would be disastrous. Nevertheless, even those Israelis who find Kahane's "solution" abhorrent do not advocate opening the ranks of the Israeli armed services to its Arab population. The problem Kahane proposes to "solve" is the classic problem of the nature of membership in a community.

Sometimes the question of a voice in the political community takes on a class rather than an ethnic dimension. When Kampuchea fell to the Pol Pot regime in 1975, the victors had a very clear idea of the kind of agrarian Communist society they proposed to establish. Rightly or wrongly, they regarded Kampuchea's entire urban population as being *objectively hostile* to the creation of the new political order. This perception was consistent with the Marxist idea that the bourgeois class is destined to disappear with the coming of socialism. Not content to let this process take its course nonviolently, the regime determined upon the immediate elimination through genocidal measures of all those who were regarded as either incapable of fitting into the new system or of being objectively committed to its destruction.[10] In the aftermath of the Russian Revolution, a very similar logic compelled the departure from the Soviet Union of millions of "objective enemies" of the new system. Similarly, the Cuban revolution resulted in the enforced emigration of over a million Cubans who could not fit into Fidel Castro's system, primarily to the United States.

A related development is currently taking place in South Africa. Because of the overwhelming number of blacks and their indispensability to the functioning of the economic order, it is impossible for the Afrikaners to eliminate them. Indeed, save for some ultra-rightist groups, there is no evidence of any Afrikaner interest in so doing. Nevertheless, the Afrikaners have answered the question "Who shall have a voice in the political community?" by excluding non-whites. Of crucial importance is the consistent refusal of the Afrikaners to admit the blacks to any meaningful kind of suffrage. Apartheid and the denial of electoral rights are attempts to define membership in the political community without resort to outright mass murder. Nevertheless, it is important to recognize that all of the policies cited above—segregation, concentration camp incarceration, expulsion, and genocide—are attempts to cope with a common problem.

Gunter Remmling's discussion of the progressive steps taken by the Third Reich to deny legal rights to the Jews is especially helpful in acquiring an overview of the process by which Jews were stripped of membership in the German political community until finally even the right to life itself was denied them. The question "Who is to have a voice in the political community?" was absolutely decisive for National Socialism. The political emancipation of the Jews in Europe in the late eighteenth and nineteenth centuries bestowed upon the Jews a voice in the political communities in which they were domiciled. With the dour wisdom of historical hindsight, the extermination of the Jews can be seen as an unintended consequence of their emancipation. Emancipation made membership of the Jews in Europe's political communities a political issue for the first time. Emancipation was opposed by all who believed such membership should be restricted to Christians. An important reason why so little was done to assist the Jews during World War II, both in Germany and in the occupied countries, was the almost universal European acceptance of the National Socialist objective of excluding the Jews from membership in the political communities in which they were domiciled. This certainly was true of the mainstream Protestant and Catholic churches, which everywhere saw the denial of political rights to the Jews as a beneficial step toward the creation of a Europe that was culturally, intellectually, socially, and politically Christian. The fundamental difference between Hitler and the churches was that Hitler had no illusions concerning the measures necessary to carry out such a program. The churches never faced frankly the question of implementation. Nevertheless, one must ask whether the silence of the overwhelming majority of Europe's church leaders during World War II concerning the Holocaust may have been at least partly due to the fact that church leaders fully understood that extermination was the only viable means of eliminating the Jews. Having no direct responsibility for carrying out the process of elimination, they preferred to wash their hands of the question of implementation. In any event, it is now clear that the insistent calls for the elimination of the Jews from membership in the body politic of the European nations was in fact a demand for their extermination.

The question of uniqueness looms large in the discussions of the place of the Holocaust in the larger subject of genocide. Surprisingly, none of the writers discusses one aspect of the Holocaust which was absolutely unique. *In no other instance of genocide in the twentieth century was the fate of the victims so profoundly linked to the religio-mythic inheritance of the perpetrators.* In Christianity, the Jews are not simply one of the many peoples of the world. They are the people in whose midst God himself reigned to be incarnated. According to the classic Christian account, instead of being the first to recognize this supreme act of divine graciousness, the Jews both rejected God-in-the-flesh and were responsible for the violent and vicious way in which he was removed from the human scene. The Jews are depicted as the God-bearing and the God-murdering people par excellence. No other religion is as hideously defamed in the classic literature of a rival tradition as is Judaism by Christianity. Moreover, starting with the fall of Jerusalem in 70 C.E., Christianity has taken the disasters of the Jewish people to be a principal historical confirmation of its own truth. These have been interpreted in the classic sources to be God's punishment of a sinful Israel for having rejected Christ. The practical consequences of (a) the ascription of a demonic identity to Jews and (b) the interpretation of their misfortunes as just chastisements of a righteous Lord was to cast them out of any common universe of moral obligation with the Christians among whom they were domiciled. In times of acute social stress, it had the practical effect of decriminalizing any assault visited upon them, as Hitler and the leading National Socialists fully understood. The implementation of the Holocaust was greatly facilitated by the deicidal and demonic interpretation of the Jewish people in the Christian religious imagination. If the Holocaust was to some extent a unique event, its religio-mythic dimension constituted a significant component of that uniqueness.

In addition to the religious aspect of the Holocaust, there was a highly significant economic element. The European Jews were a middleman minority. The question of the proneness of middleman minorities to genocidal assault is raised by Walter P. Zenner. Zenner points out that the Armenians were also a middleman minority targeted for extermination. He also points out that a third middleman minority, the Hoa or ethnic Chinese of Vietnam, were the object of a large-scale, state-sponsored program of population elimination.[11] Zenner ends his examination of middleman minority theory with the conclusion that there is no necessary connection between middleman minority status and genocide. Nevertheless, he concedes that such a status can be a precondition for genocide if other factors are present. According to Zenner, middleman minority theory has yet to face the question of why "economically integrated non-wage labor groups" are more likely to be victimized, while wage laborers, the marginalized, and the poor are not usually targets. In actuality, middleman minorities are permitted domicile in a community in order to do work that, for some reason, is not being done by the indigenous population. Their presence as strangers is tolerated because they constitute an *economically or vocationally complementary* population. They are most likely to be targeted for elimination when their roles can be filled either by the state or by members of the indigenous population. When this development takes place, the minority members become competitors of members of the majority. Usually, they compete against one of the most dangerous and potentially unstable groups within the larger population, the majority middle class. In the case of indigenous wage workers, the marginalized, or the poor, the same bitter rivalry with a dangerous class does not arise. When political leaders perceive vocationally redundant members of the majority to be a source of social or political instability, they have encouraged emigration, as was the case in Western and Central Europe during much of the nineteenth century. Nevertheless, there is usually some residual sense that, even when they become redundant, the marginalized or the poor remain to some extent part of the community's shared universe of moral obligation. This is not the case with middleman minorities, especially when they are outside of the majority religious consensus. They are often tolerated only as long as they are needed. Moreover, in premodern societies it was not socially or economically functional for middleman minorities to share a common religion with the majority. The impersonal, objective attitudes necessary for successful commerce were less likely to develop between people who considered themselves to be kin with the same gods. Commerce rested on an in-group, out-group double standard. It was only with the rise of Protestantism that the personalized ethics of tribal brotherhood gave way to universal otherhood and a universal money economy could come into being.[12]

Elsewhere, this writer has attempted to show that the situation of Europe's Jews became progressively more hopeless as the economies of Western and Eastern Europe were modernized.[13] For example, as the agriculture of Eastern Europe was rationalized, large numbers of Polish and Russian peasants were dispossessed of their holdings and forced to seek scarce wage labor in the villages and cities. Desperate for any kind of work under conditions of massive unemployment and underemployment, members of the former peasant class began to compete with the Jews for wage labor and those middle-class slots which had previously been predominantly Jewish. In seeking to displace the Jews, the dispossessed peasants and their urbanized offspring had the support of the Tsarist government, which, after 1881, made the Jews the targets of one of the most highly successful state-sponsored programs of population elimination in all of history. From 1881 to 1917, the fundamental objective of the Tsarist government vis-à-vis the Jews differed little from that of the National Socialist regime in Germany. Both sought the elimination of the Jews as a demographic presence in the areas under their control. Most American Jews are alive today because the two regimes did not share a common method of implementation.

In addition to serving as a method of radically redefining and restructuring society, genocide has since ancient times been the most unremitting kind of warfare. According to Kurt Jonassohn and Frank Chalk, genocide began in ancient times when warring peoples realized that their victories were only temporary. Elimination of a potential future threat became a powerful reason for wars of genocide. Undoubtedly, the human cost to the perpetrator played an important role in determining when a war was carried to such an extreme. After total defeat, the cost to the victor of eliminating a future threat was minimal. Since the enemy was outside of the victor's universe of moral obligation, defeat removed the only practical impediment to genocide. As long as an enemy retained the power to injure, a would-be perpetrator had to weigh the relative costs of a precarious peace against those involved in genocide. If neither side had the power to achieve a decisive victory, there was no possibility of a "final solution." In the case of the Holocaust, the Jews were perceived as a defenseless enemy with no significant capacity to retaliate.

The problems involved in their extermination were reduced to the bureaucratic management, transport, and elimination of the target population. A principal Jewish motive for the establishment of the state of Israel was to escalate the cost of killing at least those Jews who are Israeli citizens. There is little doubt that the cost now includes nuclear retaliation.

Irving Louis Horowitz points out that genocide very frequently follows military defeat. An important element in the decision of the Young Turk regime to initiate the program of extermination against its Armenian Christian minority was Turkey's defeat by Bulgaria in 1912. Similarly, Germany's defeat in World War I created the conditions in which a radically anti-Semitic, revolutionary, revisionist National Socialist movement could come to dominate German politics. As a consequence of defeat, the fringe became the center.

Horowitz also argues that the most massive destruction of Jews during World War II began in earnest in 1942 after Stalingrad. When German defeat appeared inevitable, extermination of the Jews became a paramount goal. In a similar vein, Barbara Harff suggests that a lost war sometimes leads to genocide against defenseless minorities regarded as enemies. While Harff stresses the element of battered national pride, a related element may be that military defeat intensifies the urgency with which the question of membership in the community is posed. As noted above, a fundamental issue in genocide is the question of who can be trusted in a life-and-death struggle. All minorities suffer some discrimination and experience some degree of resentment and incomplete identification with the majority, a situation which is as obvious to the majority as to the minority. In normal times, such tensions can be held in check. In the aftermath of catastrophic military defeat, they can get out of hand. Aggressive energies can achieve cheap victories over a defenseless minority. The reality of defeat itself can be denied and responsibility for the misfortunes of war ascribed to the minority's hidden "stab in the back." The accusation of secret treachery can legitimate genocide against the minority. If such a group is perceived as bringing about national catastrophe, *while appearing to be loyal,* it can become a matter of the greatest public urgency to eliminate them from the body politic.

Almost from the moment Germany lost World War I, the Jews were accused of bringing about its defeat through treachery, an accusation that appeared ludicrous in view of the extremely high proportion of German Jews who had served as front-line soldiers and who had made the ultimate sacrifice for what they regarded as their Fatherland. Elsewhere, this writer has argued that the tradition of Judas betraying Jesus with a *token of love,* a kiss, provided an enormously powerful religio-mythic identification of the Jew with betrayal to German Christians.[14] Since the identification of the Jew with Judas takes place in earliest childhood and is constantly reinforced by religious tradition, it is more deeply rooted and less subject to rational criticism than beliefs acquired at a later stage in the life cycle. When Hitler and the German right ascribed Germany's defeat to the Jews, they had working for them this immensely powerful pre-theoretical archetype. Here too, we discern a unique religio-mythic element of enormous power that sets the Holocaust apart from other instances of genocide in our times.

Given the presence of religio-mythic elements in the Holocaust, it is not surprising that many scholars have argued that the Holocaust was irrational in its objective if not in its method. Barbara Harff has argued that though the Holocaust may have been a "rational choice of the Nazis," the utility of its implementation was thoroughly irrational. Robert G.L. Waite, a historian of preeminent rank, concludes that there is no adequate explanation for the Holocaust. By contrast, Roger Smith argues that genocide is a "rational instrument to achieve an end." In order to understand the force of Smith's argument, it is important not to confuse that which is humane with instrumental rationality. The experience of our era should leave no doubt concerning the enormous potential for inhumanity present in autonomous practical reason.

Ronald Aronson argues that the Holocaust systematically outraged the norms of the "normal world." He insists that the Holocaust was a product of madness, which he defines as a systematic derangement of perception, a seeing what is not there. The National Socialists saw the Jews as the source of Germany's problems and their riddance as a major element in the solution. Aronson argues that when rulers organize a society against false enemies and propagate the view that society is being mortally threatened by them when it is not, we may speak of madness as much as when an individual behaves in the same manner.

Aronson's arguments summarize the thesis he presents with greater force and detail in his book, *The Dialectics of Disaster*.[15] It is not surprising that Aronson and Roger Smith do not agree on the rationality of genocide. Smith sees genocide as a violent means of determining who is to have a voice in a community. Aronson stresses the patently false character of the defamation of the intended victim and of the analysis of society as mortally endangered by his presence. However, Aronson does not deal with the underlying reason why the question of "who shall have a voice in the community" is raised in the first place. A community is more than a congeries of individuals living in close proximity. As noted above, it is a group whose members may have to sacrifice their lives in a life-and-death struggle with external enemies in a crisis. When the group regards itself as secure, it can afford to take a relatively benign view of the presence of a limited number of strangers in its midst. However, in times of acute national stress, such as war, economic dislocation, or military defeat, the group is likely to view strangers with suspicion and hostility. In an extreme situation, it may decide upon the total elimination of strangers.

Aronson insists that the Nazi attempt wholly to eliminate the Jews as a demographic presence first in Germany and then in all of Europe was insane because the Jews in no way constituted the threat the National Socialists alleged them to be. The issue of the truth of National Socialist defamations is, however, irrelevant to the crucial fact that the overwhelming majority of Germans regarded even the most assimilated Jews as aliens whose elimination would be a positive benefit. The Germans were not duped by mendacious Nazi propaganda. They wanted the volkisch homogeneity Hitler promised them. When it was all over, some of them regretted the *methods employed* but not the fact that Europe was largely free of Jews.

If Aronson were right, it would be irrational to want an ethnically or religiously homogeneous community consisting of those with whom one shares a sense of kinship and trust. In reality, there is nothing irrational about the desire for such a community. One wonders whether Aronson considers the colonization of the Americas and Australia, which was largely achieved through genocide, to be instances of madness. It is not the irrationality of such communities that is the problem, but the extreme cruelty and inhumanity which all too frequently attend their creation. Neither Hitler's ends nor his methods were irrational. They were obscenely cruel and graphically demonstrate what citizens of one of the world's most advanced civilizations were willing to do to other human beings for the sake of national homogeneity.

Finally, there is the issue of genocide and national sovereignty. Roger Smith observes that the United Nations never detected a single instance of genocide by a member nation. Kurt Jonassohn and Frank Chalk argue that the sovereignty of the perpetrator is the practical problem in cases of deportation and extermination because the nation-state is both the most dangerous violator and the ultimate guardian of human rights. Elsewhere, this writer has argued that National Socialist Germany probably committed no crime at Auschwitz.[16] It was under no circumstances this author's intention to mitigate the inhumanity and the obscenity of what the Germans did, but to point to one of the most urgent moral dilemmas involved in the notion of political sovereignty in our era. Crime is a violation of behavioral norms defined by political authority. Homicide, for example, is only a crime when the victim is protected by the state's laws. Even in National Socialist Germany, there were actually a very small number of SS officers who were punished for the *unauthorized* murder of Jews during World War II. The state determined when homicide was an offense against its law and when it constituted the implementation of those same laws.

If it be argued that the National Socialist state was by its very nature a criminal state because it violated God's laws or the laws of nature, one must ask what practical difference such violations made to the perpetrators. As long as the leaders of National Socialist Germany were free to exercise sovereignty, no superordinate system of norms constituted any kind of restraint on their behavior. As is well known, neither the German churches nor the Vatican ever asserted that the genocidal program of the National Socialist state was a violation of God's law, although the program was well known. *In reality, there are no human rights there are only political rights.* That is why the question "Who is to have a voice in the political community?" is the fundamental human question. Membership in a political community is no absolute guarantee of safety. Nevertheless, to the extent that men and women have any rights whatsoever, it is as members of a political community with the power to guarantee those rights. This was clearly evident in the fate of the Armenians in Turkey during World War I and the Jews of Europe during World War II. Genocide is the ultimate expression of absolute rightlessness.

While highlighting the extreme moral limitations of contemporary civilization, genocide is nevertheless an intrinsic expression of that civilization. Genocide is most likely to occur when men and women refuse to extend the benefits and protection of their societies to strangers whom they cannot or will not trust. Obviously, that perception is highly subjective and may very well be in error. Nevertheless, one of the privileges of power is the ability to define social reality. The objective facts are of far less practical consequence than the subjective perceptions of the majority.

## NOTES

1. This thesis is a generalization of the author's fundamental thesis concerning the Holocaust as expressed in Richard L. Rubenstein, *The Cunning of History* (New York: Harper and Row, 1975), p. 6.

2. This conviction is spelled out in some detail by the author in Richard L. Rubenstein, *The Age of Triage: Fear and Hope in an Overcrowded World* (Boston: Beacon Press, 1983), pp. 34-59.

3. Christopher Hill, *God's Englishman: Oliver Cromwell and the English Revolution* (New York: Harper Torchbooks, 1972), p. 113.

4. R. P. Stearns, *Hugh Peter: The Strenuous Puritan, 1598-1660* (Champagne and Urbana: Illinois University Press, 1954), p. 356; cited by Hill, *God's Englishman*, p. 117.

5. Cecil Woodham-Smith, *The Great Hunger: Ireland, 1845-1849* (New York: E. P. Dutton, 1980), pp. 411-12.

6. See Rubenstein, *The Age of Triage*, pp. 120-27.

7. "Effects of Emigration on Production and Consumption," *The Economist* (February 12, 1853), pp. 168-69 (emphasis added). See this author's comments in Rubenstein, *The Age of Triage*, p. 122.

8. See "The Irish Priesthood and the Irish Laity," *The Economist* (June 19, 1852).

9. For a study of the fate of the Indians of North America, see Bernard W. Sheehan, *Seeds of Extinction: Jeffersonian Philanthropy and the American Indian* (Chapel Hill: University of North Carolina Press, 1973).

10. See Rubenstein, *The Age of Triage,* pp. 165-94.

11. For a discussion of the elimination of the ethnic Chinese from Vietnam, see Rubenstein, *The Age of Triage,* pp. 165-94.

12. See Benjamin Nelson, *The Idea of Usury: From Tribal Brotherhood to Universal Otherhood,* 2nd ed. (Chicago: University of Chicago Press, 1969).

13. Rubenstein, *The Age of Triage,* pp. 128-64.

14. Richard L. Rubenstein, *After Auschwitz* (Indianapolis: Bobbs-Merrill, 1966), pp. 30-64.

15. Ronald Aronson, *The Dialectics of Disaster* (London: Verso, 1983).

16. Rubenstein, *The Cunning of History,* p. 90.

# BIBLIOGRAPHICAL ESSAY

Below is a working bibliography of the most important books and articles that have informed our contributors in their reflections on genocide. Although not exhaustive, they constitute the most significant works in the field and have shaped our thinking on the problem.

For general sources on theories and typologies of genocide, see:

Antonov-Ovseyenko, Anton. *The Time of Stalin.* New York: Harper and Row, 1981.

Arendt, Hannah. *The Origins of Totalitarianism.* New York: Harcourt, Brace and World, 1966.

Arens, Richard, ed. *Genocide in Paraguay.* Philadelphia: Temple University Press, 1976.

Aronson, Ronald. *The Dialectics of Disaster.* London: Verso, 1983.

Becker, Ernest. *The Denial of Death.* New York: The Free Press, 1974.

———. *Escape from Evil.* New York: The Free Press, 1975.

Charny, Israel. *How Can We Commit the Unthinkable? Genocide: The Human Cancer.* Boulder, Colo.: Westview Press, 1982.

Conquest, Robert. *The Great Terror: Stalin's Purge of the Thirties.* New York: Macmillan, 1968.

———. *The Nation Killers.* New York: Macmillan, 1970.

Dadrian, Vahakn. "Factors of Anger and Aggression in Genocide." *Journal of Human Relations* 19, no. 3 (1971), pp. 394-417.

———. "The Structural-Functional Components of Genocide." In *Victimology: A New Focus.* Ed. Israel Drapkin and Emilio Viano. Lexington, Mass.: Lexington Books, 1974.

Davies, Nigel. *Human Sacrifice in History and Today.* New York: William Morrow, 1981.

Elliot, Gil. *Twentieth Century Book of the Dead*. New York: Charles Scribner's Sons, 1972.

Ellul, Jacques. *The Technological Society*. New York: Vintage, 1964.

Fromm, Erich. *The Anatomy of Human Destructiveness*. Greenwich, Conn.: Fawcett Publications, 1975.

Harff, Barbara. *Genocide and Human Rights: International Legal and Political Issues*. Denver, Colo.: University of Denver, 1984.

Horowitz, Irving Louis. *Genocide: State Power and Mass Murder*. New Brunswick, N.J.: Transaction Books, 1976.

———. *Taking Lives: Genocide and State Power*. New Brunswick, N.J.: Transaction Books, 1980.

Kuper, Leo. *Genocide: Its Political Use in the Twentieth Century*. New Haven: Yale University Press, 1982.

———. *The Prevention of Genocide*. New Haven: Yale University Press, 1985.

Lang, Berel. "The Concept of Genocide." *Philosophical Forum* 16, nos. 1-2 (Spring 1984).

Lasch, Christopher. *The Minimal Self: Psychic Survival in Troubled Times*. New York: W. W. Norton, 1984.

Lemkin, Raphael. "Genocide." *The American Scholar* 15, no. 2 (Spring 1946), pp. 227-30.

———. "Genocide as a Crime under International Law." *American Journal of International Law* 41 (1947), pp. 145-71.

Lenski, Gerhard E. *Power and Privilege: A Theory of Social Stratification*. New York: McGraw-Hill, 1966.

Lifton, Robert Jay. *Boundaries*. New York: Random House, 1967.

———. *Death in Life: Survivors of Hiroshima*. New York: Random House, 1967.

Lifton, Robert J., and Richard Falk. *Indefensible Weapons*. New York: Basic Books, 1982.

Lorenz, Konrad. *On Aggression*. New York: Harcourt, Brace and World, 1977.

Ludwig, Gerhard. *Massenmord im Weltgeschehen: Bilanz zweier Jahrtausende*. Stuttgart: Friedrich Vorwerk Verlag, 1951.

Manvell, Roger, and Heinrich Fraenkel. *Incomparable Crime: Mass Extermination in the Twentieth Century*. London: Heinemann, 1967.

Milgram, Stanley. *Obedience to Authority*. New York: Harper and Row, 1973.

Mizruchi, Ephraim H. *Regulating Society: Marginality and Social Control in Historical Perspective*. New York: The Free Press, 1983.

Moore, Barrington, Jr. *Injustice: The Social Bases of Obedience and Revolt*. New York: Harper and Row, 1975.

Nekrich, Aleksandr. *The Punished Peoples: The Deportation and Fate of Soviet Minorities at the End of the Second World War*. New York: Norton, 1978.

Oldenbourg, Zoé. *Massacre at Montségur: A History of the Albigensian Crusade*. New York: Pantheon Books, 1961.

Porter, Jack Nusan, ed. *Genocides and Human Rights*. Washington, D.C.: University Press of America, 1982.

Robinson, Nehemiah. *The Genocide Convention*. New York: Institute for Jewish Affairs, 1960.

Rubenstein, Richard. *The Age of Triage: Fear and Hope in an Overcrowded World*. Boston: Beacon Press, 1983.

Sartre, Jean-Paul. *On Genocide*. Boston: Beacon Press, 1968.

Saunders, J. J. *The History of the Mongol Conquests*. London: Routledge and Kegan Paul, 1971.

Sennett, Richard. *Authority*. New York: Alfred A. Knopf, 1980.

Sereny, Gitta. *Into That Darkness*. New York: Vintage Books, 1983.

Smith, Roger W., ed. *Guilt, Man and Society*. Garden City, N.Y.: Anchor Books, 1971.

Tucker, Robert W. *The Just War*. Baltimore: The Johns Hopkins University Press, 1960.

Walzer, Michael. *Just and Unjust Wars*. New York: Basic Books, 1977.

Weisbord, Robert. *Genocide? Birth Control and the Black American*. Westport, Conn.: Greenwood Press, 1975.

The relationship between racial myths, culture, and oppression is explored in Leon Poliakov, *The Aryan Myth* (New York: New American Library, 1971), and George Mosse, *Toward the Final Solution* (New York: Harper and Row, 1978). On the connection between religion and repression see Jules Isaac, *The Teaching of Contempt* (New York: Holt, Rinehart and Winston, 1964).

The connection between culture and genocide or oppression is examined in some of the following: Ernest Becker, *Escape from Evil* (New York: Free Press, 1975); Nachman Blumenthal, "On the Nazi Vocabulary," *Yad Vashem Studies 1* (Jerusalem, 1957); Mary Douglas, *Purity and Danger* (London: Routledge and Kegan Paul, 1966); Marvin Harris, *Cows, Pigs, Wars and Witches* (New York: Vintage Books, 1973); Jules Henry, *Culture Against Man* (New York: Vintage Books, 1965); Philip Rieff, "The Impossible Culture," *Salmagundi*, nos. 58-59 (1982-1983); George Steiner, *Language and Silence* (New York: Atheneum, 1967); and George Steiner, *In Bluebeard's Castle* (New Haven: Yale University Press, 1971).

For historical and theoretical works on the Nazi Holocaust, see:

Arendt, Hannah. *Eichmann in Jerusalem*. New York: Viking Press, 1965.

Bauer, Yehuda. *The Holocaust in Historical Perspective*. Seattle: University of Washington Press, 1978.

―――. *The Jewish Emergence from Powerlessness*. London: Macmillan, 1979.

Bauer, Yehuda, and Nathan Rotenstreich, eds. *The Holocaust as Historical Experience*. New York: Holmes and Meier, 1981.

Baum, Rainer C. *The Holocaust and the German Elite: Genocide and National Suicide in Germany.* Totowa, N.J.: Rowman and Littlefield, 1981.

Cohn, Norman. *Warrant for Genocide.* New York: Harper and Row, 1967.

Dawidowicz, Lucy. *The Holocaust and the Historians.* Cambridge, Mass.: Harvard University Press, 1982.

————. *The War Against the Jews: 1933-1945.* New York: Holt, Rinehart and Winston, 1975.

Des Pres, Terrence. *The Survivor: An Anatomy of Life in the Death Camps.* New York: Oxford University Press, 1976.

Dimsdale, Joel E., ed. *Survivors, Victims and Perpetrators: Essays on the Nazi Holocaust.* New York: Hemisphere Publishing Co., 1980.

Dobkowski, Michael N., and Isidor Wallimann, eds. *Towards the Holocaust: The Social and Economic Collapse of the Weimar Republic.* Westport, Conn.: Greenwood Press, 1983.

Fein, Helen. *Accounting for Genocide: National Responses and Jewish Victimization During the Holocaust.* New York: The Free Press, 1979.

Fest, Joachim C. *The Face of the Third Reich.* New York: Pantheon Books, 1970.

Friedlander, Henry, and Sybil Milton. *The Holocaust: Ideology, Bureaucracy and Genocide.* Millwood, N.Y.: Kraus, 1982.

Gordon, Sarah. *Hitler, Germans, and the "Jewish Question."* Princeton, N.J.: Princeton University Press, 1984.

Graber, G. S. *History of the SS.* New York: David McKay Co., 1978.

Hilberg, Raul. *The Destruction of the European Jews.* Chicago: Quadrangle Books, 1961.

Katz, Jacob. *From Prejudice to Destruction: Anti-Semitism, 1700-1933.* Cambridge, Mass.: Harvard University Press, 1980.

Katz, Steven T. "The 'Unique' Intentionality of the Holocaust." *Modern Judaism* 1, no. 2 (September 1981), pp. 161-83.

————. *Post-Holocaust Dialogues: Critical Studies in Modern Jewish Thought.* New York: New York University Press, 1983.

Kenrick, Donald, and Grattan Puxon. *The Destiny of European Gypsies.* New York: Basic Books, 1972.

Kren, George M., and Leon Rappoport. *The Holocaust and the Crisis of Human Behavior.* New York: Holmes and Meier, 1980.

Lemkin, Raphael. *Axis Rule in Occupied Europe.* Washington, D.C.: Carnegie Endowment for International Peace, 1944.

Lifton, Robert Jay. *The Nazi Doctors: Medical Killing and the Psychology of Genocide.* New York: Basic Books, 1986.

Mendelsohn, John, ed. *The Holocaust: Selected Documents in Eighteen Volumes.* New York: Garland, 1982.

Merkl, Peter H. *The Making of a Stormtrooper.* Princeton, N.J.: Princeton University Press, 1980.

Mosse, George. *Toward the Final Solution.* New York: Harper and Row, 1978.

Poliakov, Leon. *Harvest of Hate*. Westport, Conn.: Greenwood Press, 1971.

Prager, Dennis, and Joseph Telushkin. *Why the Jews? The Reason for Antisemitism*. New York: Simon and Schuster, 1983.

Reitlinger, Gerald. *The Final Solution*. London: Valentine, Mitchell, 1961.

Rubenstein, Richard. *The Cunning of History*. New York: Harper and Row, 1975.

Sereny, Gitta. *Into That Darkness*. New York: Vintage Press, 1974.

Sanford, Nevitt, and Craig Comstock, eds. *Sanctions for Evil*. Boston: Beacon Press, 1971.

Steiner, George. *In Bluebeard's Castle*. New Haven: Yale University Press, 1971.

————. *Language and Silence*. New York: Atheneum, 1977.

Stern, Fritz. *The Politics of Cultural Despair: A Study in the Rise of Germanic Ideology*. Berkeley: University of California Press, 1961.

Tal, Uriel. "On the Study of the Holocaust and Genocide." *Yad Vashem Studies 13* (Jerusalem, 1979), pp. 7-52.

Waite, Robert G.L. *The Psychopathic God: Adolf Hitler*. New York: Basic Books, 1977.

Weingarten, Ralph. *Die Hilfeleistung der westlichen Welt bei der Endlösung der deutschen Judenfrage: Das "Intergovernmental Committee on Political Refugees."* Berne: Peter Lang, 1981.

For reflections on the Armenian genocide, see:

Arlen, Michael J. *Passage to Ararat*. New York: Farrar, Straus and Giroux, 1975.

Boyajian, Dickran. *Armenia: The Case of the Forgotten Genocide*. Westwood, N.J.: Educational Book Crafters, 1972.

Bryce, James. *The Treatment of the Armenians in the Ottoman Empire*. London: Macmillan, 1916.

Chaliand, Gerard, and Yves Ternon. *The Armenians: From Genocide to Resistance*. London: Zed Press, 1983.

Dadrian, Vahakn. "The Common Features of the Armenian and Jewish Cases of Genocide: A Comparative Victimological Perspective." In *Victimology: A New Focus*. Ed. Israel Drapkin and Emilio Viano. Lexington, Mass.: Lexington Books, 1975.

————. "A Theoretical Model of Genocide with Particular Reference to the Armenian Case." *Sociologia Internationalis* 14 (1976/1980), pp. 99-126.

————. "A Typology of Genocide." *International Review of Modern Sociology* 5 (1975), pp. 204-7.

Fein, Helen. "A Formula for Genocide: Comparison of the Turkish Genocide (1915) and the German Holocaust (1939-1945)." *Comparative Studies in Sociology* 1 (1978), pp. 271-93.

Housepian, Marjorie. "The Unremembered Genocide." *Commentary* 42, no. 3 (September 1966).

Hovannisian, Richard G., ed. *The Armenian Genocide in Perspective.* New Brunswick, N.J.: Transaction, 1986.

————. *The Armenian Holocaust: A Bibliography.* Cambridge, Mass.: Armenian Heritage Press, 1978.

————. *Armenia on the Road to Independence.* Berkeley: University of California Press, 1967.

————. *The Republic of Armenia.* Berkeley: University of California Press, 1971.

Lewis, Bernard. *The Emergence of Modern Turkey.* Oxford: Oxford University Press, 1961.

Libaridian, Gerard, ed. *A Crime of Silence.* London: Zed Books, 1985.

Melson, Robert. "A Theoretical Inquiry into the Armenian Massacres of 1894-1896." *Comparative Studies in Society and History* 24, no. 3 (July 1982), pp. 481-509.

Nalbandian, Louise. *The Armenian Revolutionary Movement.* Berkeley: University of California Press, 1967.

Ter Minassian, Anaide. *Nationalism and Socialism in the Armenian Liberation Movement, 1887-1912.* Cambridge, Mass.: The Zoryan Institute, 1984.

Ternon, Yves. *The Armenians: History of a Genocide.* New York: Caravan Books, 1981.

Werfel, Franz. *The Forty Days of Musa Dagh.* New York: The Viking Press, 1934.


For sources on the destruction of Aboriginal society, see:

Blainey, Geoffrey. *A Land Half Won.* Melbourne: Macmillan, 1980.

Broome, Richard. *Aboriginal Australians.* Sydney: Allen and Unwin, 1982.

Butlin, Noel. *Our Original Aggression.* Sydney: Allen and Unwin, 1983.

Evans, Raymond, Kay Saunders, and Kathryn Cronin. *Exclusion, Exploitation and Extermination.* Sydney: Australia and New Zealand Book Company, 1975.

Reece, R.H.W. *Aborigines and Colonists.* Sydney: Sydney University Press, 1974.

Rowley, C. D. *The Destruction of Aboriginal Society.* Canberra: Australian National University Press, 1970.

Travers, Robert. *The Tasmanians: The Story of a Doomed Race.* Melbourne: Cassell Australia, 1968.

Wright, Judith. *The Cry for the Dead.* Melbourne: Oxford University Press, 1981.


For general works on genocides in Africa, Asia, and South America, see:

Beshir, Mohammed Omer. *The Southern Sudan: From Conflict to Peace.* London: C. Hurst and Co., 1975.

Bridgman, John. *The Revolt of the Hereros*. Berkeley: University of California Press, 1981.

Chaudhuri, Kalyan. *Genocide in Bangladesh*. Bombay: Orient Longman, 1972.

Davis, Shelton H. *The Victims of the Miracle: Development and the Indians of Brazil*. Cambridge, England: Cambridge University Press, 1977.

De St. Jorre, John. *The Nigerian Civil War*. London: Hodder and Stoughton, 1972.

Drechsler, Horst. *"Let Us Die Fighting": The Struggle of the Herero and Nama against German Imperialism (1884-1915)*. London: Zed Press, 1980.

Emprile, Cecil. *War and Peace in the Sudan 1955-1972*. London: David and Charles, 1974.

Helbig, Helga, and Ludwig Helbig. *Mythos Deutsch-Südwest: Namibia und die Deutschen*. Weinheim: Beltz Verlag, 1983.

Lemarchand, Rene. *Rwanda and Burundi*. New York: Praeger, 1970.

Madiebo, Alexander A. *The Nigerian Revolution and the Biafran War*. Enugu, Nigeria: Fourth Dimension Publishing Co., 1980.

May, Brian. *The Indonesian Tragedy*. London: Routledge and Kegan Paul, 1978.

O'Ballance, Edgar. *The Secret War in the Sudan: 1955-1972*. London: Faber and Faber Limited, 1977.

Ponchaud, François. *Cambodia Year Zero*. Harmondsworth: Penguin Books, 1978.

Schwab, Peter, ed. *Biafra*. New York: Facts on File, 1971.

Vickery, Michael. *Cambodia 1975-1982*. Boston: South End Press, 1984.

Wallenkampf, Arnold. "The Herero Rebellion in South West Africa, 1903-1907." Ph.D. dissertation, University of California, Los Angeles, 1969.

Wingert, Norman. *No Place to Stop Killing*. Chicago: Moody Press, 1974.

Wooding, Dan, and Ray Barnett. *Uganda Holocaust*. Grand Rapids, Mich.: Zondervan Publishing House, 1980.

# INDEX

Aborigines, 237-49, 284, 286
Abraham, 174-75
Absolute war (Speier), 109
Accountability, 23, 28-29, 33-34, 223, 247
Africa, 264-66, 273. *See also* names of individual countries
Aggression, 171-73
Ainsztein, Reuben, 167
Algeria, 54
Allen, Francis, 114, 116
Ambrose (Saint), 164
Amin, Idi, 30, 55, 169, 175, 265
Andreski, Stanislav, 257-58, 273
Anthropology, 66
Anti-Semitism: of Adolf Hitler, 69, 164, 165, 176-78, 185-86; in Africa, 263; history of, 72, 163-65, 273, 275; psychology of, 170-72; used by the Nazis, 51, 66-71, 86, 89, 112, 164-65, 170, 189-95. *See also* National Socialists (German), policy to oppress Jews; Nazism, and the Jewish problem
Archaeology, 13

Arendt, Hannah, 35, 36, 126, 167, 171, 172, 173
Arlen, Michael, 33
Armenian genocide, 77, 178, 203-27, 260-62, 273, 289, 292, 294, 297; compared to Jewish Holocaust, 50, 51, 62, 64, 65, 272
Arnold, Henry H., 111
Aron, Raymond, 105
Aronson, Ronald, 295-97
Arthur, George (Colonel), 241-42
Asians, in Africa, 264-65
Assimilation, 257, 259, 266
Ataturk, Mustafa Komal, 77
Augustine (Saint), 164
Australia, 54, 237-49, 284, 285-86
Austria, 185, 193
Authoritarianism, 110, 111, 113, 117, 176, 177, 210, 218, 225
Avinori, Shlomo, 86, 88

Balkan wars (1912-13), 49-50, 217-18
Bangladesh, 52, 53, 54
Barta, Tony, 283-84, 285-87

# ABOUT THE CONTRIBUTORS

RONALD ARONSON is Professor of Humanities in the University Studies/Weekend College Program at Wayne State University. He is the author of *Jean-Paul Sartre: Philosophy in the World* (1980), *The Dialectics of Disaster: A Preface to Hope* (1984), and *Sartre's Second Critique,* which is forthcoming from the University of Chicago Press. He has received fellowships from the National Endowment for the Humanities and the American Council of Learned Societies.

TONY BARTA is a lecturer in History at La Trobe University, Melbourne. His teaching and research interests include the social and political history of Bavaria (in particular the town of Dachau) in the twentieth century, relations between Europeans and Aborigines in Australia, and the role of film and television in historical understanding.

FRANK CHALK is Associate Professor of History at Concordia University in Montreal, Canada. He is chairman of the education committee of the Montreal Holocaust Memorial Center and of the research committee of the League for Human Rights of B'nai B'rith Canada, Eastern Region. His previous publications deal with American foreign policy and African history. He and Kurt Jonassohn teach a course on the history and sociology of genocide at Concordia University and they are working on a book together.

MICHAEL N. DOBKOWSKI is Associate Professor of Religious Studies at Hobart and William Smith Colleges. He is the author of *The Tarnished Dream: The Basis of American Anti-Semitism* (1979) and *The Politics of In-*

*difference: A Documentary History of Holocaust Victims in America* (1982), and editor, with Isidor Wallimann, of *Towards the Holocaust: The Social and Economic Collapse of the Weimar Republic* (1983).

BARBARA HARFF is Visiting Assistant Professor of Political Science at the University of Colorado at Boulder (1985). She holds a Ph.D. from Northwestern University (1981) and has taught at La Trobe University in Melbourne, Australia, and at Marquette University, Milwaukee. Her research interests are the philosophical and legal foundations of international responses to human rights violations. She is also concerned with the problem of genocide from a comparative and empirical perspective. Her publications include a forthcoming chapter in the *Yearbook of State Violence and State Terrorism,* edited by George Lopez and Michael Stohl, and a monograph, *Genocide and Human Rights: International Legal and Political Issues,* Monograph Series in World Affairs, Graduate School of International Studies, University of Denver.

IRVING LOUIS HOROWITZ is Hannah Arendt Distinguished Professor of Sociology and Political Science at Rutgers University. He has written widely on political sociology and international development and is also editor-in-chief of *Transaction/SOCIETY,* the publication of record in social science and public policy. Among his writings are *Taking Lives: Genocide and State Power* (1980) and *Winners and Losers: Social and Political Polarities in the United States* (1984).

KURT JONASSOHN is Professor of Sociology at Concordia University in Montreal, Canada. He has been secretary-treasurer of the Canadian Sociology and Anthropology Association and executive secretary of the International Sociological Association. He has published in a number of areas. Most recently he has, together with Frank Chalk, been teaching a course on the history and sociology of genocide for several years. They are also collaborating on a book on the same subject.

GERARD J. LIBARIDIAN is the Director of the Zoryan Institute for Contemporary Armenian Research and Documentation and editor of the *Armenian Review.* He has authored a number of articles on the Armenian genocide and is completing graduate studies in history at the University of California at Los Angeles.

ERIC MARKUSEN, M.S.W., Ph.D., is Assistant Professor of Sociology at Old Dominion University in Norfolk, Virginia. He is also a Research Affiliate with the Harvard Nuclear Psychology Program, the Cambridge Hospital, Harvard Medical School and a Research Associate with the Center for Death Education and Research, University of Minnesota. Recent publications include "The Role of Education in Preventing Nuclear War," with

John Harris, in the *Harvard Educational Review;* "The Second Death: Psychological Survival after Nuclear War," with Robert Jay Lifton and Dorothy Austin, in *The Counterfeit Ark: Crisis Relocation for Nuclear War,* edited by J. Leaning and L. Keyes; and *Nuclear Weapons and the Threat of Nuclear War: Critical Issues,* edited with John Harris.

GUNTER W. REMMLING is Professor of Sociology at the Maxwell Graduate School, Syracuse University, New York. He was educated at Worksop College, Notts, England, Bard College, New York, and Berlin's Freie Universität. He has conducted research at the Institute of Political Science, Berlin, in various South American republics, and in Spain. He has contributed articles to many scholarly journals and anthologies of essays. His books include *South American Sociologists* (University of Texas, 1966), *Road to Suspicion* (Appleton-Century-Crofts, 1967), *Wissenssoziologie und Gesellschaftsplanung* (Ruhfus, 1968), *Basic Sociology* (Littlefield, Adams, 1970), *Towards the Sociology of Knowledge* (Routledge and Kegan Paul, 1973), *Der Weg in den Zweifel* (Enke, 1975), *The Sociology of Karl Mannheim* (Routledge and Kegan Paul, 1975), *Hacia la Sociología del Conocimiento* (Fondo de Cultura Económica, 1982, and *La Sociología de Karl Mannheim* (Fondo de Cultura Económica, 1982).

ALAN ROSENBERG is a Lecturer in the Department of Philosophy at Queens College, the City University of New York. He is the author and co-author of a number of articles that appeared in a variety of journals including *Modern Judaism, Cross Currents, European Judaism,* and *SHOAH.* He is currently writing a book entitled *The Genocidal Universe: A Conceptual Framework for Understanding the Holocaust,* and is under contract with Temple University Press to do an anthology with Gerald Myers entitled *The Holocaust: Its Philosophical Impact.*

JOHN K. ROTH is the Russell K. Pitzer Professor of Philosophy at Claremont McKenna College, where he has taught since 1966. In addition to serving as a Special Advisor to the Chairman of the United States Holocaust Memorial Council, Washington, D.C., he has been Visiting Professor of Holocaust Studies at the University of Haifa, Israel. Presently the book review editor for *Holocaust and Genocide Studies,* Roth is the author of numerous articles on the Holocaust, and he has also published ten books, including *A Consuming Fire: Encounters with Elie Wiesel and the Holocaust.* Co-authored with Richard L. Rubenstein, his most recent book, *Approaches to Auschwitz: The Legacy of the Holocaust,* will appear in 1986.

RICHARD L. RUBENSTEIN is Distinguished Professor of Religion and founder and director of the Center for the Study of Southern Culture and Religion at Florida State University. He is also the author of seven books, including *After Auschwitz, The Cunning of History, The Age of Triage,* and

*The Religious Imagination,* for which he was awarded a Portico d'Ottavia
Literary Award.

ROGER W. SMITH teaches political theory at the College of William and
Mary, where he is a Professor of Government. He was born in Alabama in
1936 and educated at Harvard and the University of California at Berkeley.

ROBERT G.L. WAITE is the Brown Professor of History at Williams
College. He is the author of *Vanguard of Nazism: The Free Corps Move-
ment in Postwar Germany, 1918-1923* and *The Psychopathic God: Adolf
Hitler.* He has delivered papers on the Holocaust at meetings of the Inter-
national Scholars' Conference on the Holocaust held in Bloomington,
Indiana, and in Tel Aviv.

ISIDOR WALLIMANN studied economics and sociology and holds a
Ph.D. in sociology from Syracuse University. At present he is lecturing in
sociology at the School of Social Work in Basel, Switzerland. He is the auth-
or of *Estrangement: Marx's Conception of Human Nature and the Division of
Labor* (Greenwood Press, 1981) and editor (with Michael Dobkowski) of
*Towards the Holocaust: The Social and Economic Collapse of the Weimar Re-
public* (Greenwood Press, 1983). In addition, he is the author or co-author
of several articles that have appeared in *Zeitschrift für Soziologie, Sociology,
Australian and New Zealand Journal of Sociology, Humanity and Society,
Youth and Society, International Journal of Sociology and Social Policy,* and
in other journals and edited works.

WALTER P. ZENNER is Associate Professor of Anthropology at the
State University of New York at Albany. The comparison of inter-ethnic relations, with special regard to middleman minorities, has been a central theme
of his work. He is co-editor of *Urban Life: Readings in Urban Anthropology* (1980) and *Jewish Societies in the Middle East* (1982), as well as author of
*Minorities in the Middle,* due to be published in the near future.